THE ROUGH GUIDE TO

Unexplained Phenomena

written by
John Michell and Bob Rickard

ROUGH
GUIDES

Credits

The Rough Guide to Unexplained Phenomena

Text Edit, Layout & Design:
Peter Buckley
Proofreading: Amanda Jones
Production: Aimee Hampson

Rough Guides Reference

Series editor: Mark Ellingham
Editors: Peter Buckley, Duncan Clark,
Tracy Hopkins, Sean Mahoney, Matthew Milton,
Joe Staines, Ruth Tidball
Director: Andrew Lockett

Acknowledgements

Besides all those who contributed to the first edition, to whom we remain ever grateful, the authors would like to thank the following for help with this revised edition: Gail-Nina Anderson, Jonathan Bryant, Luis R. Gonzalez, Peter Hassall, Gordon Rutter, and George Wagner for essential references; Peter Bennett, Tuuri Heporauta (posthumously) and Susan Lung for translations; Nicholas Allen, Janet Bord, John Heymer, and Peter Mulacz for valued help in locating pictures; Merrily and Patrick Harpur, Roy Kerridge, Steve Moore, Owen Whiteoak, and Paul Sieveking for their readiness to answer calls for help with obscure matters; and again to Paul Sieveking for heroic proofing far beyond the call of duty. In addition, Bob Rickard would like to thank his family and friends for their support when it really mattered.

Publishing Information

This second edition published September 2007 by Rough Guides Ltd,
80 Strand, London WC2R 0RL
375 Hudson St, 4th Floor, New York 10014, USA
Email: mail@roughguides.com

Distributed by the Penguin Group:
Penguin Books Ltd, 80 Strand, London WC2R 0RL
Penguin Putnam, Inc., 375 Hudson Street, NY 10014, USA
Penguin Group (Australia), 250 Camberwell Road, Camberwell, Victoria 3124, Australia
Penguin Books Canada Ltd, 10 Alcorn Avenue, Toronto, Ontario, Canada M4V 1E4
Penguin Group (New Zealand), Cnr Rosedale and Airborne Roads, Albany, Auckland, New Zealand

Printed in Italy by LegoPrint S.p.A

Typeset in Georgia, Minion and Helvetica Neue to an original design by Peter Buckley

A catalogue record for this book is available from the British Library

ISBN 13: 978-1-84353-708-3
ISBN 10: 1-84353-708-7

1 3 5 7 9 8 6 4 2

‡

Contents

Wild Talents

The Madness of Crowds

The Fairy Folk

Mysterious Entities

The Haunted Planet

Signs and Portents

Simulacra and Other Images

Monsters

Living Wonders

Tail Pieces

Notes and Further Reading

⚜

Introduction

The phenomenal world

Our purpose in this book is to describe the rich variety of anomalous, unexplained, sometimes totally bizarre phenomena that people have experienced in all times and places and that are still occurring today. We ourselves have studied and written about these things for years, and one thing we have learnt is that the nature of the world and of our existence are quite different from that which we were taught at school. The reality is far more interesting, humorous and expansive than any religious or rational, scientific world-view can possibly accommodate.

It is not our intention here to dispute anyone's beliefs or theories – but we should like to point out their limitations. There are things that happen in this world – and have occurred throughout the whole of human experience – for which there has never been a lasting explanation. Explanations are temporary products, coming and going in response to fashions. Meanwhile, the happenings they are supposed to explain carry on as mysteriously as ever.

Yet mysterious phenomena are also to some extent influenced by fashion. For example, clusters of hibernating swallows and living toads encased in rocks, so regularly recorded by nineteenth-century naturalists, seem virtually to have died out; mariners today hardly ever witness sea-serpents; and rings of dancing fairies, once a commonly described part of country people's experience, are now very rare. To make up for these perhaps temporary losses, other types of weird phenomena have flourished in modern times – UFOs for example, together with alien or demonic entities; rapes and abductions by "spacemen"; obscene mutilations of horses and cattle and – on a brighter note – the beautiful phenomenon of crop circles. At the same time, the standard mysteries, those which have puzzled humanity from the beginning, continue to do so. Creatures and artefacts fall, sometimes slowly, from unknown sources; poltergeists bring floods, fires and stone-showers to tormented households; people are levitated, walk over hot coals, are invisibly attacked, encounter monsters in lakes and mountains, are subject to amazing coincidences, and so on. You hear about these things in myths, legends and folklore, and you can read about their modern continuations in scientific journals and the daily press.

We, the authors, share a common interest in the views and writings of Charles Hoy Fort (1874–1932), the remarkable thinker, dreamer, humorist and intellectual iconoclast who lived

Charles Hoy Fort (1874–1932), pictured in 1930 with one of his diversions from collecting anomalies of science and natural history, the game of "supercheckers", which he invented.

in the Bronx district of New York. Much of his life was spent in the New York Public Library, the British Museum reading room in London and other repositories of records. Sifting through back numbers of newspapers and scientific journals he collected thousands of items on strange events and phenomena which could not be reconciled with any established theory or rational doctrine. These reports and records were called "anomalous"; they were ignored or laughed at and soon forgotten. Often they were published in professional, academic journals, but the scholars and scientists who read these publications were only interested in the data that supported their own particular theories and had no time for such anomalies. Fort came to realize that all theories and systems of

belief are upheld by "exclusions". None of them are entirely true, and they are only made to seem plausible by excluding the awkward facts that do not fit them.

In the interests of justice and clear thinking, Fort used his collections of unexplained events to create his own pictures of reality – "expressions" he called them. They were utterly, outrageously different from the prevailing scientific view of things, but Fort pointed out that his expressions were based on the same types of empirical evidence as the official theories. He merely selected differently. It is not that scientific orthodoxy is totally wrong, he said, for nothing in this illusory world is ever totally anything, but he criticized it as being arbitrary. There are many different ways of perceiving and describing reality, and it seemed to Fort that much of the data that orthodox thinkers rejected gave a more complete picture of the world than any of the established theories.

Fort called the anomalous items he collected "the damned facts" – damned by exclusion from the pale of scientific consideration. His first book, published in 1919, was called *The Book of the Damned,* and in the first twenty pages of it he outlined a picture of reality in which the damned facts were given equal rights with those accepted by science. The result was a world-view similar to that of traditional mysticism, in which there are no hard-and-fast laws, merely tendencies, and in which human imagination plays a significant part. In the course of time, he foresaw, the damned facts of the present would be accepted and made orthodox; new theories would be built upon them, and these in turn would then become exclusive, disregarding all evidence that challenged them. The situation, said Fort, is that nothing in our changing, fluctuating world is actually and permanently real, so our attempts to categorize and pin down nature are doomed to failure. The nearest thing to reality that he admitted was the Universe itself. He saw it as a great, single organism, moving automatically, or perhaps even consciously, to satisfy its own desires and to direct whatever was needed to its various parts. As to the means by which this was done, Fort suggested an unknown force or mechanism which he called teleportation.

Fort was among the first to draw attention to several types of phenomena which are now widely recognized, and he was also original in noticing connections between them – between poltergeist events and the presence of a distressed or mentally disturbed young person; between unknown lights or objects in the sky and possible otherworldly intelligence; between outbreaks of hysteria or religious fervour and fires, earthquakes and other disasters. Of all his conceptions teleportation proved to be the most useful. One of his special interests was in the anomalies of animal distribution, whether it was the spontaneous appearance of life in newly dug ponds, the mys-

Some of Charles Fort's notes from the collection of over 40,000 in the Manuscript Section of the New York Public Library.

teries of bird and insect migration or the strange ability of certain pet animals to find their owners, even when they have moved far away to unknown locations. Together with these phenomena Fort collected cases of lost possessions miraculously rediscovered, modern artefacts excavated from ancient geological strata, and objects that manifest themselves at spiritualist sessions, at the behest of shamans and holy men, in response to prayer or intense desire or simply of their own accord. In connection with these and other mysteries, Fort spoke of teleportation, but not as a scientific theory to be proved or clamouring with for precise explanations, which will never be forthcoming.

This is a humorous subject, but while laughing at it we are also somewhat respectful towards Fort's damned facts, and we are wholly respectful towards his inclusive attitude and world-view.

There is nothing to be gained by worrying about or wilfully rejecting aspects of our human experience which can never be explained. The greatest of human pleasures (purer and more long-lasting than sex or any of the appetites) is to investigate the world, generally and in its various parts – and much more so if it is done honestly, without regard to prejudices, taboos, inhibitions and other people's conventions.

In this book we make all sorts of connections between the various types of mysteries and wonders described in it, but we do not ask readers to follow us, believe in us or accept any of our tentative conclusions. The most we hope for is to bring relief to those among us who have experienced strange happenings and have been told by their doctors, parents or contemporaries that this is unnatural and perhaps even a sign of madness. Our message of comfort to such readers is that you are not alone. As we carefully demonstrate in the following chapters, these things have always happened, they can happen to anyone, and at least some of them probably happen to everyone in the course of a lifetime. Our very existence in this world is an unexplained mystery, and that is something we have to accept and be happy with.

John Michell and Bob Rickard

About the authors

John Michell is the author of many books on archeology, ancient science and the mysteries of our existence, including *The Flying Saucer Vision*, *The View Over Atlantis*, *Simulacra* and *Old Stones at Land's End*.

Bob Rickard founded *Fortean Times* in 1973 as a forum for news and discussion of anomalous phenomena. In addition to editing *Fortean Times* he co-wrote, with John Michell, the earlier incarnations of this book, *Phenomena* and *Living Wonders*.

1

Teleportation

1

Teleportation

Teleportation:
its effects and uses

In his book *Lo!* (1931) Charles Fort presented some of his amazing collection of recorded phenomena which, he suggested, might be caused by teleportation. He began with the well-recorded cases of stones and liquids falling "out of the blue" – the sort of cases that are conventionally attributed to mischievous spirits or poltergeists. Psychologists have often succeeded in linking such happenings to repressed juvenile passions or mental disturbance in the people involved with them. No one, however, has been able to identify the mechanism behind the physical effects in "poltergeist" cases – the leaping pots and pans, the showers of stones and missiles and so on. If we attribute strange events to invisible spirits, we are merely personifying the agency behind the spontaneous movement of objects. We prefer the more neutral term of teleportation, and having adopted it, we find that it fits a wide range of phenomena of the type that has eluded rational explanation.

There is often something quite unusual about these falls that makes them hard to explain in terms of anything known. We agree with Fort in finding no apparent distinction between falls of living things and falls of stones and other inanimate objects, and in suggesting that the same notion of teleportation might be applied to both

types of phenomena. For instance, in reports of showers of stones from many parts of the world, observers have noted that the objects fell slowly, or even floated down, as if under the influence of some anti-gravitational force. In this connection, Fort drew attention to the curious lack of injury to most falling creatures, as if they too had had the benefit of a slow descent; an effect we see mentioned time and again in poltergeist phenomena.

If a force exists that acts to redistribute animals and objects about this Earth – a force transcending the currently known laws of physics – there is no reason why its influence should be limited to this planet. Fort's notion of teleportation derived from his view of the universe as a huge unified entity which is more like a vast organism than Newton's "great machine", and whose parts interact with each other. He compared teleportation to the automatic process in the human or animal body which balances its energies and makes it self-healing and self-regulating. A deficiency in one part of a living body evokes responses from the organism as a whole, and the same, as Fort saw it, is true of the universe.

Although teleportation sometimes seems to act efficiently, sending fish to new ponds and predators to deal with insect swarms, it also has lapses, resulting in the appearance of strange animals in incongruous places. At other times it appears to overcompensate, as in the case of droughts broken by excessive downpours. Fort noted that these incidents often followed ceremonies or prayers for rain, and he suggested that the tribal rainmakers, by adding their own desires to the desires of nature, might have caused a violent response. Another of Fort's excuses for the whimsical or mischievous aspect of teleportation was that it was past its prime, senile even. As he put it: "The crash of falling islands – the humps of piling continents – and then the cosmic humor of it all – that the force that once heaped the peaks of the Rockies now slings pebbles at a couple of farmers near Trenton, New Jersey."

Fort was no mystic. He passed over the supernatural elements of occultism and spiritualism to focus on the practical phenomena of apports. He recognized that there are certain people who, particularly during adolescence, are more susceptible than others to teleportation – probably the very same people who are prone to poltergeist attacks.

It is now well established that households which become victims of poltergeist disturbances – bombarded by stones for example – often contain a lonely or repressed teenager who seems to be related in some way to the troubles, usually as a victim or focus. Fort was one of the first to notice this. In his day, this "agent" was often a poorly educated youth or servant girl attached to the disrupted family, who was commonly blamed, on little evidence, for creating the effects by trickery. In many cases the injustice of such accusations was plain; the unhappy suspect could hardly have manifested the reported phenomena single-handed or by intent.

Fort wondered whether the suspicions might be correct in a less obvious way, that the "poltergeist" effects were produced unwittingly. "It may be that, if somebody, gifted with what we think we mean by "agency", fiercely hates somebody else, he can, out of intense visualisations, direct, by teleportation, bombardments of stones upon his enemy."

The connection between poltergeists and puberty also occurred to the psychologist Nandor Fodor, who thought they were related to "the awakening of sex-energies". As he explained it in *Hereward Carrington's Story of Psychic Science* (1930), "It would almost seem as though these energies, instead of taking their normal course, were somehow turned into another channel, at such times, and were externalized beyond the limits of the body, producing the manifestations

in question." We shall see many more examples of this elsewhere in this book.

If there are some people who can, unconsciously, set teleportation to work, it is likely that there are other people who have observed this and have studied how to manipulate the force by will. History provides many examples of a technology developed for practical use long before the processes involved were scientifically understood – gunpowder, medicines and electricity for example. In 1926, the French psychical researcher Gustave Geley proposed that "genuine" witches might simply be people with some control over their "powers", their "wild talents", as Fort called them. In a typical flight of fancy he imagined adolescent "poltergeist girls" employed in industry (to keep motors running) and, terrifyingly, in warfare: "The alarm – the enemy is advancing. Command to the poltergeist girls to concentrate – and under their chairs they stick their wads of chewing gum. A regiment bursts into flames, and the soldiers are torches. Horses snort smoke from the combustion of their entrails. Reinforcements are smashed under cliffs that are transported from the Rocky Mountains. The snatch of Niagara Falls – it pours upon the battlefield. The little poltergeist girls reach for their wads of chewing gum."

The record of involuntary teleportationists is long and varied if you accept the testimony about the saints of Christianity, Buddhism and Islam who have been prone to unexpected levitations or materializations. As numerous are the secular reports of ordinary people subjected to mysterious forces (see LEVITATION AND SPONTANEOUS FLIGHT, p.15) or puzzling abductions and time lapses (see OTHERWORLDLY ABDUCTIONS, p.166). Three traditional explanations for such things are that they are caused by fairies, spirits or poltergeists, sometimes directed by witches, and today they are commonly blamed on extraterrestrials.

Yet despite the variety of explanations, the phenomenon is essentially the same in all ages: people are unaccountably levitated, or hurled through the air, or made to disappear for a while. The experience usually has side-effects; those who experience teleportation are never quite the same afterwards. They develop sensitive or mediumistic qualities, and in modern societies their lives are often ruined thereby. John Keel's *UFOs: Operation Trojan Horse* (1970) has some sad accounts of "contactees" or "abductees" in alleged UFO cases who have been unable to reconcile themselves to

A typical "poltergeist girl" case. In March 1849, a young maid, Adolphine Benoît (seen in the background) is blamed for the objects flying around the baby's nursery in Guillonville, France.

This photograph, taken in the office of a heating company in Leeds in 1970, is said to show papers flying around the room anomalously. There were other disturbances too, all centring on a 16-year-old typist.

their experience and have ended up in disgrace or madness or worse. Yet in traditional and tribal societies, according to anthropologist Mircea Eliade's *Shamanism* (1964), people who undergo spontaneous levitation – or abduction to another world or dimension – are marked out as potential shamans. One of his examples is of a man who became a noted prophet among the Basutos after he had been suddenly lifted up into the air in the company of a multitude of spirits. (See also, AWAY WITH THE FAIRIES, p.157.)

In contrast to the "civilized" religions, which have always discouraged their levitating ecstatics from practising or investigating their involuntary powers, shamanistic societies have encouraged levitators to cultivate the art. Thus the powers of shamans and witch doctors traditionally include the ability to ascend aloft in magical flight. Nor is the deliberate practice of teleportation confined to archaic societies; the Greeks knew of Abaris the "Sky-traveller", who "traversed rivers, seas and steeps as if walking on air". In Porphyry's *Life of Pythagoras* (third century AD) it is claimed that the sage addressed meetings at Metapontum and

Tauromenium on the same day, even though these places are two hundred miles apart and separated by the sea.

Fort accepted that the wonders and miracles attributed to shamans, witches, magicians, saints and holy men could be real events brought about by the use of teleportation. He saw it, however, as an amoral, universal force, not confined to any particular religion or to religion in general, nor to the human race. If it exists, it must of necessity be an active principle throughout nature, a force which responds to desires in nature wherever located. It could procure a local rainfall for a needy tree in times of drought, just as, biblically, a people in a wilderness might receive "heaven-sent" manna in a time of need. In RAINS OF SEEDS AND ORGANIC MATTER (see p.58), we tell of showers of grain from the sky which hungry locals made into bread. Another of Fort's favourite examples was of newly made ponds unaccountably found to be full of fish. This is a phenomenon that has puzzled country people for centuries; we recently came across a statement by the writer Michovius, to the effect that the Russians take the fish-teleportation effect for granted. They "do not stock their lakes and ponds with fish, as is done in other countries, but instead, when ponds are made, fish drop into them out of the heavenly dew without human intercession or effort." Fort's idea was that intense desire on the part of humans, animals, plants, ponds or any other natural entity was liable to set in motion the distributive, compensating energies of teleportation.

He also wondered whether the ability to use teleportation was one which people were gradually developing or losing. Eventually, he favoured the idea that it was more common in earlier stages of society. In ancient times a talent for teleporting fire, water and other necessities would have been a social asset to wandering tribes, but now "with political and economic mechanisms somewhat well established, or working, after a fashion" such talents are no longer so valued. They linger on, particularly among children, who are more atavistic than their elders and "may be in rapport with forces that mostly human beings have outgrown."

On the other hand, perhaps knowledge of teleportation belongs not so much to the past as to the future. In that case, said Fort lightly, it might be commercialized. "Cargoes, without ships, and freights, without trains, may be the traffics of the future. There may be teleportative voyages from planet to planet", he wrote around 1930, long before space travel was taken seriously. In fact, one of Fort's most appealing qualities was that he did not take his own ideas any more seriously than he took anyone else's. Of the social future of teleportation he wrote: "Here is an idea that may revolutionize industry, but just now I am too busy revolutionizing everything else, and I give this idea to the world, with the generosity of someone who bestows something that isn't any good to him."

Our reason for beginning this book with a summary of the concept of teleportation is that it provides a unified theory for so many of the natural wonders and enigmas described later in these pages. We are fascinated by the way in which the parameters of science keep expanding towards the point of embracing Fort's "unthinkable" notions, including that of teleportation. Modern physics recognizes so many instances of apparent bilocations and instantaneous teleportations among particles, that phenomena, once regarded as irrational and impossible, now have good claims to be accepted as natural.

The teleportation of people

We begin with a startling proposition: that human beings can rise up off the ground, fly through the air and travel from one location to another without seeming to pass through the intervening distance ... even passing through solid objects such as walls. It sounds like fantasy, yet there are rare accounts in which witnesses believe that these things actually happened. In many of the sections of this book, we will touch on this theme of "teleportation" as it manifests in a number of different forms.

The idea behind "teleporting" is familiar to anyone who watches or reads science fiction: as demonstrated, for example, by the *Star Trek* franchise, where both people and objects can be instantaneously "beamed" to a faraway location.

Less well known is the fact that Charles Fort coined the word in 1931. Fort's hypothesis was of a mysterious force that could transport matter, objects and even living creatures between two points without seeming to travel the intervening distance; it could also manipulate them at a distance. If such a force exists, it could account for observations of such psychical phenomena as "apports" (the sudden appearance and disappearance of things in the presence of a medium), as well as provide a fundamental mechanism behind the more mysterious distributions of living creatures. By 1945, Fort's teleportation was being discussed by psychical researchers, such as Harry Price, as a reasonable hypothesis for poltergeist activity.

According to our present understanding of the laws of science, teleportation is not supposed to happen, but in later sections we quote cases where we conclude that it actually has. We are impressed by the evidence from centuries of human experience suggesting that living creatures and things are occasionally transported vast distances in the proverbial twinkling of an eye. But first let us consider the claims of human teleportation, of which we only have hints and images.

An old Spanish ghost story, suggestive of teleportation, has astonished people for four centuries and, as retold by the pioneer UFO writer M.K. Jessup, has influenced the modern generation of mystery writers. It is the tale of a soldier who was instantaneously transported from the Philippines to Mexico City (over nine thousand miles) in October 1593. The uniform that he was wearing, when he appeared in the city's main plaza, was unfamiliar to the inhabitants but later turned out to be that of a regiment stationed in the Philippines. Questioned by officers of the Inquisition, the soldier could only say that, moments before his appearance in Mexico, he had been on sentry duty at the Governor's palace in Manila – the Philippine capital. The Governor, he said, had recently been assassinated. How he came to be in Mexico he had no idea. Months later a ship from the Philippines confirmed the news of the assassination and other details of the soldier's story.

A simple experience of the teleportation effect is claimed by the respected mystic, Wellesley Tudor Pole, in his book, *The Silent Road* (1962): "On a wet and stormy night in December 1952, I found myself at a country station some mile and a half from my Sussex home. The train from London had arrived late, the bus had gone and no taxis were available. The rain was heavy and incessant. The time was 5.55pm and I was expecting an important trunk call from overseas at 6pm at home. The situation seemed desperate. To make matters worse, the station call box was out of order and some trouble on the line made access to the railway telephone impossible. In despair I sat down in the waiting-room and having nothing better to do, I compared my watch with the station clock. Allowing for the fact that this is always kept two minutes in advance, I was able to confirm the fact that the exact time was 5.57 pm. Three minutes to zero hour! What happened next I cannot say. When I came to myself I was standing in my hall at home, a good twenty minutes walk away, and the clock was striking six. My telephone call duly came through a few minutes later. Having finished my call, I awoke to the realization that something very strange had

"Transit of Venus": a satirical view of Mrs Guppy's teleportation across London.

happened. Then much to my surprise, I found that my shoes were dry and free from mud, and that my clothes showed no sign of damp or damage."

The implication here is that Major Tudor Pole was instantly transported home in response to his strong desire to be there, but without any conscious magic on his part. Yet if it could so happen spontaneously, why not at the direction of the will? We think of witches and spiritualists and particularly of the incident – much satirized at the time – of the hefty psychic Mrs Guppy. In Harry Price's memorable account, in *Poltergeist Over England* (1945), on 3 June 1871, Mrs Guppy was "instantly precipitated from her home at Highbury (London) to a house in Lamb's Conduit Street, some three miles away, where she came down bump right in the middle of a séance"

Mary of Agreda appears to the natives of New Mexico. A woodcut from Father Benavides' *Letter To The Friars* (1730 edition).

– dressed only in her underclothes.

An even more remarkable feat of teleportation, or bilocation, concerns the Venerable Mary Jesus of Agreda. Although she was never known to have left her Spanish convent, it was officially estimated that, between the years of 1620 and 1631, she made over five hundred trips to America to convert the Jumano Indians of New Mexico. This estimate was not arrived at lightly. At first, the Catholic authorities – made wary by the delusive claims of religious hysterics – put considerable pressure on Sister Mary to dissuade her from insisting on the reality of her transatlantic flights. Only the testimony of missionaries to the Mexican Indians persuaded them to authenticate her experiences. In 1622, Father Alonzo de Benavides, of the Isolita Mission in New Mexico, had written to Pope Urban VIII and to Philip IV of Spain asking who had pre-empted him in his mission to convert the Jumano Indians. The Jumanos themselves declared their knowledge of Christianity to have come from a "lady in blue", a European nun who had left with them crosses, rosaries and a chalice which they used for celebrating Mass. This chalice was believed to have come from Mary's convent at Agreda.

It was not until 1630, when Father Benavides returned to Spain, that he heard of Sister Mary and her fantastic belief that she had converted the Jumano Indians. He obtained leave to examine her and did so closely, receiving from her exact accounts of her visits to the Indians with details of their appearance and customs. She kept a diary of her experiences, but burnt it on the advice of her confessor. In it she described many details of her travels – including a vision of the planet Earth as a sphere revolving on its poles. In his *Life of the Venerable Mary of Agreda*, James A. Carrico concludes: "That Agreda really visited America many times, is attested to by the logs of the Spanish conquistadors, the French explorers, the identical accounts by different tribes of Indians a thousand miles apart. Every authentic history of the Southwest of the United States records this mystic phenomenon unparalleled in the entire history of the world."

There are unsatisfactory aspects to Father Benavides' 1631 account of the legend and his interview. It was a best-seller in its day and many people had a vested interest in the legend as a means of encouraging colonization of the New World. Benavides claims that Mary gave him many proofs of her flights to the Jumanos, carried by Saints Michael and Francis. In fact, in unpublished records, she never directly confirms her bodily transportation and later doubted it. She had narrowly escaped being condemned as a witch in her youth and was wary of official reprimands for her frequent ecstasies and levitations. She had to choose her words carefully and so, pressed to explain her undoubted visions of the faraway Indians, Mary supposed that angels had impersonated her while allowing her to witness their exploits. What further complicated the matter was that often while she was in an ecstatic state, or isolated in her cell, the nuns would tell visitors that she was "away with the Indians".

Nevertheless, Mary's dream-like impressions of travelling through the air accord with similar descriptions from mystics who levitated or bilocated. The coincidence of her clairvoyant visions of the Indians and their insistence on the physical presence of a nun cannot be dismissed completely. One of Mary's memoranda includes a detail that will delight all phenomenalists. Just as the folk traditions of all lands warn the traveller into Fairyland against taking gifts from fairies, eating fairy food, or lusting after fairy women, so Mary says she was warned by God, "that neither by thought, word nor deed must I presume to long for or touch anything, unless it were God's express will that I should do so."

That widely travelled fortean sage, Ion Alexis Will, spotted a remarkable story of a teleporting boy as he passed through Africa's Ivory Coast in 1993. The priests at the Catholic church of St Augustin, in Yamoussoukro, were agitated by the boy's apparent ability to pass into and out of locked rooms. On 18th August, the nine-year-old boy – judged homeless, like so many others that come to the mission for food and shelter – was fed and then locked in the church's storehouse for the night. When the store was opened in the morning the boy was gone; he was later found fast asleep in a priest's locked car. The priests decided to keep a close eye on the boy. The next day, they told the local paper that the boy vanished as he ate breakfast with other people and could not be found until he was spotted, slightly dazed, outside the church.

He aroused the interest of Father Emile Kouakio, the chief priest, and Kambiré Elie, a journalist from the newspaper *Ivoir'Soir*; they attempted to trace the boy's origins. He had stayed at the house of one of Yamoussoukro's officials, who had, in turn, traced the boy to the town of Duékoué, 155 miles away. At Duékoué, he had been found wandering the streets in a daze and was taken to the police station where the officers had conducted their own investigation.

N'Doua Kouame Serge was just five, in 1989, when he was taken to hospital after a sports injury in his hometown of Tiassalé. He disappeared en route (it is not said how) and found himself in San Pédro, 200 miles along the coast. His father set out to collect him (it is not said how he learned where his son was) but by the time he got to San Pédro, the boy was again found, dazed, 410 miles inland in the town of Odienné. The police inquiry established that the boy had turned up in a string of other towns – including Arrah, Dimbokro, Séguéla, and the capital Abidjan – hundreds of miles apart, spending months, even years, at these locations.

As the story of N'Doua Kouame Serge's nomadic life was pieced together, his various benefactors were in agreement that there was something very strange about the boy's vanishings and appearances. "I believe he is possessed by a demon," said Father Kouakio,

"an evil spirit that teleports him." When asked by the reporter, Kambiré Elie, to account for his travels, the boy simply said: "I don't know. I'm here and suddenly I find myself in another town." (*Fortean Times* 101, Aug 1997)

There are many more accounts of teleported children with more impressive and better corroborated testimony from highly qualified witnesses, such as the Sandfeldt case of 1722 and the poltergeist incidents in the household of Dr Ketkar (a famous Marathi historian) in Poona, India, in the late 1920s. Both included the levitations and teleportations of children. At Poona, the younger of two adopted brothers claimed that on several occasions he had felt himself lifted up and transported into a locked car in a locked shed – rather like what happened to N'Doua Kouame Serge. There were no other witnesses, but the incidents frightened him severely enough for his parents to take it seriously.

However, an incident involving the elder brother was clearly witnessed by the German-born Mrs Ketkar, herself an accredited scholar, who regularly described the happenings in letters to her sister, Miss Kohn, who taught languages at the Deccan College. According to Mrs Ketkar, early on the morning of 23 April 1928, the elder boy "suddenly materialised in front of me … like

A boy is carried through the air to an upstairs room; an English case attributed to witchcraft. Detail of frontispiece to Joseph Glanvill, *Sadducismus Triumphatus* (1666, 1681).

a rubber ball. He looked bright but amazed, and said 'I have just come from Karjat'. He didn't come through any door." Miss Kohn continued: "My sister describes the posture of the boy as having been most remarkable. When she looked up … she saw him bending forward; both his arms were hanging away from his sides … his feet were not touching the floor, as she saw a distinct space between his feet and the threshold. It was precisely the posture of a person who has been gripped around the waist and carried, and therefore makes no effort but is gently dropped at his destination." (*Journal of the American SPR*, vol.24, 1930)

These cases usually describe very complex phenomena with many aspects that forteans call "high strangeness"; for example, a poltergeist might include a frightening attack on its teleported victim – see also INVISIBLE ASSAILANTS (p.173) – or the transportation may have involved an apparent passage through solid material such as a wall or locked door, as happened to the Ivory Coast boy.

In another case, one Florence Newton was famously tried as a witch in Youghal, County Cork, in 1661, accused of bewitching a young maidservant called Mary Longdon. Mary began to see grotesque figures about her house and she would vomit pins, wool and straw, sometimes falling in fits – "so violent three or four men could not hold her". Then this sad, conventional story becomes more interesting; Mary was pelted by showers of stones inside her home – see MISSILES FROM ABOVE (p.47) – according to eyewitness testimony given in court. Joseph Glanvill wrote that the stones "would follow from place to place, and from one room to another, and would hit her on the head, shoulders and arms, and fall to the ground and vanish away." At the height of the paranormal persecution, Mary was teleported about her house. "Sometimes she should be removed out of her bed into another room," continued Glanvill, "sometimes she should be carried to the top of the house, laid on a board betwixt two [garret] beams, sometimes put into a chest…" (*Sadducismus Triumphatus*, 1666, 1681)

In another famous case that began in December 1761, the children of Richard Giles in Bristol suffered terribly at the "hands" of a violent poltergeist; they were struck, dragged, pelted, bitten, throttled, stuck with pins and slobbered over. On occasions, several men could not hold them down as they rose into the air. These events

had many adult witnesses and were recorded in a diary each day by Henry Durbin, known as a pious and conscientious man.

A significant element of "high strangeness" in many of these tales, echoed across centuries of documented narrative, is that teleported children have described in their own words being attacked by strange or frightening beings. In the case of the Giles family, Dobby, who was afflicted the worst by the invisible assailant, told Durbin that she had been carried upstairs by a witch-like woman in ragged dress. The witch had clamped a hand over the girl's mouth so she could not call out, and that she was aware of her feet not touching the ground. Yet, according to the witnesses, the girl simply vanished from view, to be found later.

There are some similarities here to St Teresa of Avila's description of the sensation of levitating, but it bears a direct comparison with Mary Longdon's "grotesque figures". Similarly, N'Doua, the Ivory Coast boy, when asked to account for how he was transported out of the storeroom of St Augustin's church, told the reporter that while he slept, an ugly "strangely shaped" person took him to a big house where a winged being came to his assistance. The two fought and the ugly entity was consumed by fire, the boy said; then the "angel" placed him inside the car.

Just as weird was the explanation of the children teleported in the village of Sandfeldt, East Germany, in 1722. Here, a poltergeist not only plagued the farmer and his large family with tricks over three months, it seemed to enjoy upending the children, dangling them in mid-air or vanishing them, returning them to the same spot some considerable time later, incidents well-witnessed by the anxious parents, lodgers and others who saw these strange events at close quarters. The case was so meticulously investigated and reported in 1722 that Alan Gauld and Tony Cornell, who summarize it in their historical review of 500 cases, *Poltergeists* (1979), call it an "impressive document".

In recent years, other remarkable cases of involuntary teleportation have been reported, mostly within the UFO context, some of which are summarized in John Keel's *Our Haunted Planet* (1971). Another example, described in detail in *The Unidentified* (1975) by Jerome Clark and Loren Coleman, is that of José Antonio da Silva who turned up on 9 May 1969 near Vitoria, Brazil, shocked and dishevelled. He had vanished from near Bebedouro, some five hundred miles away, four and a half days earlier. His story – that he had been captured by creatures about four feet tall, taken by them to another planet and then returned to Earth – sounds fantastic, but the case was thoroughly investigated and no one doubted that da Silva's account was sincerely given. The significant feature of the UFO-linked teleportation cases is that the victim reappears in a state of shock, trance or semi-amnesia, exactly as is reported of the abductees of earlier generations.

Though usually spontaneous and unbidden, in some cases teleportation seems as though it is directed and purposeful. The man who was teleported from Goa to Portugal in 1655 was judged by the Inquisition to have procured the effect by magic, and he was therefore burnt for the prohibited use of occult powers. No one then doubted the existence of such powers, and the further back into history we go – through times of witches and tribal shamans to the powerful state magicians of archaic civilizations – the more exact is the knowledge claimed of techniques of teleportation and magical flight.

The phenomenon used to be largely unrecognized outside religious hagiographies, folklore and the annals of witchcraft. Instead of the legendary feats of flying mystics – for example the aerial transport of great stone slabs by the builders of Stonehenge – we hear of out-of-the-body journeys and the malicious pranks of poltergeists, or abductions by "aliens".

The materialization and flight of objects

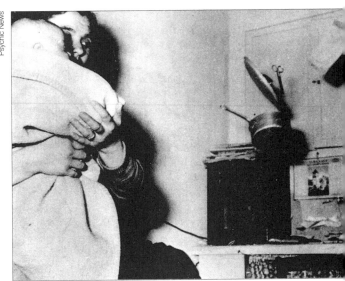

In December 1894 a house on Lord Portman's estate at Durweston, Dorset, was the scene of inexplicable events. The residents told of objects rising into the air and being propelled toward their dwelling. The gamekeeper, Newman, investigated, and inside the house saw beads and a toy whistle come up and hit a window without breaking it. He decided to wait and see what developed, and later told his story to the Society for Psychical Research:

"I sat down and was looking at the door opening into the garden; it was wide open leaving a space of fifteen inches between it and the inner walls when I saw, coming from behind the door, a quantity of little shells. They came round the door from a height of about five feet, one at a time at intervals varying from half a minute to a minute. They came very slowly and when they hit me I could hardly feel them. With the shells two thimbles came so slowly that in the ordinary way they would have dropped long before they reached me. Both thimbles struck my hat. Some missed my head and went just past and fell down slantingwise (not as if they were dropped). Those that

Mrs Teresa Costa and her baby, terrorized by flying kitchen equipment in June 1955. The Costa family had gone to stay in a 14th-century cottage in the village of St-Jean-de-Maurienne on the French–Italian border, when, almost immediately, loud knocks were heard on doors and in walls, the furniture and the stove shook and objects took flight. After several days of disturbances, they were visited by reporters and one took this photograph. He stated that he saw the objects over an extended period, "slide from their places, make a semicircle in the air and fall in different locations".

Psychic News

This photograph – taken by Leon Isaacs in February 1939 – seems to show a heavy table and books in mid-flight during a séance. The London medium Jack Webber (centre) became well-known for manifestations of physical phenomena.

struck me fell straight down."

Similar accounts – with many detailed observations from reliable witnesses with no motive to distort or lie – abound in the literature of spiritualism and psychical phenomena, where they are put down to so-called "noisy spirits" or poltergeists. In using this word we do not commit ourselves to belief in the agency of a geist or spirit; though there sometimes appears to be intelligence or purpose behind such activity, we are inclined to see such occurrences as evidence of some unrecognized universal force rather than of wilful persecution by ghosts and demons.

There are two aspects of Newman's story which particularly interest us – the materialization of objects (presumably from somewhere else), and their strange, slow flights through the air. Both present an exciting challenge to science, because they appear to suspend what we think of as established laws of how matter should behave. The trajectory and force of the missiles that hit Newman defy our understanding of the laws of motion and of gravity, and yet his testimony is so honestly given that we have to wonder what happened here to normal inertia and mass.

We have many good reports of objects that fell or flew, either faster or slower than would normally be expected, often swerving to evade grasping hands. Professor Sir William Barrett addressed the Society for Psychical Research on this subject in 1911; and the Jesuit scholar Father Herbert Thurston gives many examples in his *Ghosts and Poltergeists* (1953) after a lifetime's study of the phenomenon. For instance, Thurston cites a case from Germany in 1718, in which "a large stone seemed to be falling perpendicularly and with great velocity right on the minister's head. One of the maids who was looking on shrieked in terror, but the stone turned aside in full career, though at the cost of a pane of glass through which it passed into the court outside."

Apart from the problems of authentication, what often makes such stories unpalatable to serious scientists is a sense of mischievous, frequently malicious, intent in the actions. For example, Thurston quotes a German pamphlet about a doctor whose house was effectively demolished in 1713 by a constant bombardment of missiles that became solid and visible seconds before they hit anything. During this harassment the doctor took to swiping about him with his sword and once, upon re-sheathing it, found the scabbard stuffed full of dirt.

A lengthy disturbance in 1928–29, involving the eight-year-old adopted son of an Indian family at Poona, was reported in *Psychic Research* (May 1930) by Miss H. Kohn who, with her sister, lodged with the family. One day both sisters counted some eggs into several baskets and shut them in a cupboard. Almost immediately an egg shot past the girls from the direction of the cupboard to smash on the floor. Looking in the cupboard, they found one egg missing. As they cleaned up the mess, another egg smashed nearby, and again an egg was missing from the baskets. Three more eggs suffered the same fate, and then one basket containing forty-two eggs vanished out of the cupboard and was never seen again. Several times the girls saw coins fall: "At first we could not always see the coins in mid-air, but merely saw them fall, being startled by the contact of the coin with the floor. Soon, however, we were able to observe more closely, and actually saw the money appear in the air."

The term "apport" is applied by spiritualists to objects that move through the air or materialize at séances and hauntings. Guy Lyon Playfair gives an unusual example in *The Flying Cow* (1975). The famous Brazilian medium, Carlos Mirabelli, was asked to locate the missing remains of a woman who had died insane. A séance was held at which, according to the sworn testimony of Enrico de Goes, director of the São Paulo Municipal Library, there was a foul smell of decomposition as numerous human bones fell on the heads of those present along with a gruesome rain of hair and other remains. More pleasantly, we note many instances of the materialization of flowers and living plants, some out of season at the time. The phenomenon is, we know, a stock item in the repertoire of stage magicians as well as spiritualists but we are impressed by the record of a blue marshland flower, said to have materialized from heaven and given to the French explorer Alexandra David-Néel in mid-winter in Tibet, as recounted in *My Journey To Lhasa* (1927).

It may be that the materialization and flight of objects is a form of manipulation, another famous skill of the poltergeist, for the literature is more replete with accounts of objects moving "by themselves". Some of these manipulations take very complex forms, like the still-life tableaux made out of clothes by the Stratford, Connecticut, poltergeist in 1850 (see PROJECTED THOUGHT-FORMS, p.84). One of the most extraordinary events of this sort that we know of was a scene that might have come from a cartoon or a child's imagination. In 1682, a young lad by the splendidly appropriate name of Francis Fey, of Spreyton, Devon, was the focus of much activity of the kind we have seen attributed to mischievous poltergeists or fairies. Like other poltergeist victims, he often saw apparitions of his tormentor, sometimes in the form of an old woman, "sometimes in forms very horrid, now and then like a monstrous dog belching fire".

The strange incident to which we refer involved his shoelaces: "…one of his shoe-strings was observed (without the assistance of any hand) to come of its own accord out of its shoe and fling itself to the other side of the room; the other was crawling after it, but a maid espying that, with her hand drew it out, and it strangely clasp'd and curl'd about her hand like a living eel or serpent; this is testified by a lady of considerable quality, too great for exception, who was an eye-witness". Other witnesses cited in the account, published in 1683, were the Rector of Barnstaple as well as staff and visitors to the home of Sir Philip Furze, who employed the boy.

Universally regarded as a spirit of some kind, the "poltergeist" and its activities are commonly dealt with by exorcism. Sometimes this treatment is effective, yet the phenomenon is not always respectful of religious people and their rituals. Quite the reverse: the twelfth-century English saint, Godric, was pelted by all the moveables in his hermitage, including his Mass utensils. In *Itinerarium Cambriae*, Giraldus Cambrensis recorded a case in Pembrokeshire in 1184 in which a "foul spirit" threw excrement at the exorcising priests and ripped their vestments. Church reformer Martin Luther was tormented by "poleter geister", and so was the preacher John Wesley.

Charles Fort was inclined to replace the notion of poltergeists, angels, etc with the less anthropomorphic concept of teleportation as a universal force responsible for many of the reported aberrations in normal reality. Here are a couple of examples that did not rely on supernatural entities. In about 1200, Gervase of Tilbury wrote in his *Otia Imperialia* of a merchant from Bristol who lost his favourite knife over the side of his ship while on a far ocean. When he returned to port, his wife told him that one day, while she

During Professor Zoellner's tests, at Leipzig University in 1877–78, on the American medium Henry Slade, these solid wooden rings, threaded on a sealed string, vanished to reappear on the central pillar of a table, apparently travelling through solid material.

was sitting in her parlour, his knife fell in through the skylight and stuck in the table below. Both had kept a record of the disappearance and reappearance of the knife, and the times were found to be "simultaneous".

Harold T. Wilkins, in *Strange Mysteries of Time and Space* (1958), tells a modern knife story in which a man's need coincided with a discovery. The man was working on electric power-lines in a field at Brockworth, Gloucestershire, in February 1956. At lunchtime he found to his annoyance that he had forgotten to pack a knife in his lunchbox. Suddenly he noticed a knife at his feet. It was a brand new table-knife which was not his and which, he claimed, had not been there seconds before. The man kept the knife until his death, when it vanished forever.

Levitation and spontaneous flight

No modern historian of witchcraft has taken seriously the claims of witches that they could levitate and fly, yet there is impressive evidence that passages through the air (transvection) are not purely flights of fancy. We draw our data from several different categories, for the subject is bedevilled by exclusionism. Christians cherish their own levitating saints but with no regard for flying mystics of other persuasions. Collectors of folklore delight in stories of people who have ridden off with fairies, but show no enthusiasm for levitations by modern spirit mediums. Orthodox science has no interest in any of them.

There is no doubt in our minds that the phenomenon of human flight does, on occasion, take place. In most modern instances it is involuntary and hardly ever premeditated. Clearly, there is some natural force, unknown to our present science, by which people can achieve levitation. The further we move away in time and culture from the rationalistic world-view of modern times, the more evidence we find that this force has been recognized, studied and made use of.

Father Herbert Thurston's two chapters on levitation, in his *Physical Phenomena of Mysticism* (1952), are the most impressive we have read, containing detailed and often startling evidence, much of it given under solemn oath and the threat of eternal damnation. For example, Thurston quotes from the process of canonization of St Bernardino Realino, who died in 1616. Questioned by senior clerics, a minor noble told how he saw "a certain glow or radiance" streaming around the slightly ajar door of the saint's room in 1608. Concerned that there might be a fire in the room he peeped in and saw the saint in a kneeling posture, face turned upwards, hovering two and a half feet in the air. His feelings of awe and fear gave way to a sense that he was intruding on something intensely private and so he crept away. The ecclesiastical court admonished the man several times during his testimony to think whether or not the scene was an hallucination and the glow a reflection of sunlight; but the man stood firm,

saying: "The thing was so clear, unmistakable and real, that not only do I seem to see it still but I am as certain of it as I am speaking now." He said he had noticed the strange glow at least four times before he wondered about the danger of a fire, "and so I stood up on purpose and pushing open the door I saw with my own eyes Father Bernardino raised from the ground as unmistakably as I now see your Illustrious Lordship."

Records of levitation in a religious context are extremely common. Olivier-Gilbert Leroy's *La Lévitation* contains the legends of some 230 Catholic saints to whom this feat is attributed and a similar number are listed in *La Stigmatisation* (1894) by Dr. A. Imbert-Gourbeyre. Father Thurston provides another twenty less well-known but well-attested cases that Dr Imbert-Gourbeyre had overlooked. They include St Ignatius Loyola who was known to hover just above the ground while meditating; St Adolphus Liguori who was raised into the air in front of a whole congregation in 1777; and, in the nineteenth century, the Syrian Carmelite, Sister Mary of Jesus Crucified, who would sometimes be levitated into the treetops of the garden of her Bethlehem nunnery. Some levitators, like Passitea Crogi, a Sienese nun who died in 1615, are seen travelling a considerable distance just above the ground; others hover in an attitude of prayer; while St Joseph of Cupertino (d.1663) rose in great swoops to the ceiling of his chapel.

The public and involuntary flights of St Joseph were something of an embarrassment to him and his superiors. He would suddenly cry out and fly up in the air, and so disrupted church services that he was barred from public worship. Once, according to a witness, "he rose into space and, from the middle of the church, flew like a bird on to the high altar, where he embraced the tabernacle." On another occasion he flew into an olive tree, "and he remained kneeling for half an hour on a branch, which was seen to sway as if a bird had perched on it." Eventually the authorities moved him from one Franciscan house to another in an attempt to avoid publicity.

While the "divine" radiance is mentioned in some cases, most levitations seem to occur while the levitator is in a trance or ecstasy. Father Thurston was particularly impressed by the

The levitations of medium Colin Evans took place at packed London séances in the 1930s. He preferred to perform in darkness with luminous bands on his arms and feet, claiming that flashlights interfered with the "power of the spirits".

illuminated levitation of Father Francis Suarez, a Spanish Jesuit theologian (see also HUMAN RADIANCE, p.76) as recorded by the monk who had been sent to wake him: "I noticed that the blinding light was coming from the crucifix … and in this brightness I saw him in a kneeling position in front of the crucifix … his body lifted above the floor." The witness was, understandably, stunned: "Bewildered and as it were beside myself … I went out, my hair standing on end like the bristles of a brush."

In the fourth century, the Roman historian Palladius saw the levitation of a child with his own eyes. The child, thought to be possessed, had been brought to St Macarius, an Egyptian hermit, for exorcism. Palladius says that the boy rose and remained suspended in the air for some time while the saint prayed. The phenomenon is not, of course, exclusive to Catholic saints. Muslim levitators include the twelfth-century Iranian dervish, Haydar, noted for his sudden flights to treetops and roofs of houses. The French official and travel-writer in India, Louis Jacolliot, claims to have witnessed two levitations of a fakir called Covindasamy. As recorded in his *Occult Science in India* (1884), they were in broad daylight and one, on the terrace of his home, lasted ten minutes.

In Europe, where spontaneous levitation outside the Christian context is either unrecognized or classified in terms of diabolism and the supernatural, its occurrence is unwelcome and often painful to the person affected by it. When such things happen in traditionalist communities, they are usually taken as marking out a future shaman. Many instances are given in Mircea Eliade's *Shamanism* (1964) of the levitations of witch doctors, shamans and Eastern mystics, which cannot all be dismissed as imagination or figures of speech. Thus, in Sumatra, "he who is destined to be a prophet-priest suddenly disappears, carried off by spirits; he returns to the village three or four days later; if not, a search is made for him and he is usually found in the top of a tree, conversing with spirits. He seems to have lost his mind, and sacrifices must be offered to restore him to sanity." We shall return to this theme in our section titled AWAY WITH THE FAIRIES (p.157).

An interesting English example of this is the account of a series of violent psychical assaults on a young man, recorded in a letter from a Devon clergyman and printed in John Aubrey's *Miscellanies* (1696). Francis Fry (also see image overleaf), a servant at a farm in the parish of Spreyton, became the target of flying missiles and blows that seemingly came out of thin air; the whole house became so disturbed that a young girl living there had to be sent away for safety (see also INVISIBLE ASSAILANTS, p.173). On Easter Eve, 1682, Fey disappeared and was searched for; much later he was found half-naked in a bog, whistling and singing and quite out of his senses. His shoes were scattered one each side of the farmhouse and his wig was found at the top of a tree. "Coming to himself an hour after, he solemnly protested that the daemon carried him so high that he saw his master's house underneath him no bigger than a hay-cock, that he

was in perfect sense, and prayed God not to suffer the Devil to destroy him; that he was suddenly set down in the quagmire."

The records of the Society for Psychical Research contain similar stories of people being raised into the air, thrown across the room, and so on, by unseen forces, but they are interpreted as the action of poltergeists. Had Francis Fry experienced this involuntary levitation in tribal society, it would have distinguished him as a seer and spirit medium; at the height of the witchcraft persecu-

There are many eyewitness accounts of the ecstatic flights of St Joseph of Cupertino, including one by the High Admiral of Castile who noted the Saint's "customary shrill cry" as he took off.

In his *Sadducismus Triumphatus* (1666, 1681), the Somerset divine Joseph Glanvill (1636–80) reported the well-witnessed levitations and vanishings of a county youth named Francis Fey (as depicted here in Glanvill's frontispiece). Different authorities have blamed fairies, demons, witch-craft, or an inherent "wild talent" for the deed, according to their own beliefs. See the text (p.17) for a account by the diarist John Aubrey (1626–97) of another West Country teleporter called, similarly, Francis Fry (which may well have been the same case differently reported).

tions he might have been burnt. By Aubrey's time, he was able to record the curious phenomena he delighted in (like any true scholar) without the necessity for moralistic comment. The huge lit-erature on UFOs, likewise, has cases involving descriptions of levitation (often associated with a beam of light), sudden teleportation, and dream-like encounters with entities who appear to be engineering the incident.

In the heyday of Victorian spiritualism there were many demonstrations of levitation – the most famous being that of the celebrated medium Daniel Douglas Home. In July 1871, Lord Adare and two other nobles claimed they saw Home float out of one window of a London flat and come in through another. Regrettably, the story does

The levitation of medium D.D. Home in 1871 before a group of eminent observers is probably the most famous incident in Victorian spiritualism. In that age of science and scepticism, Home's "magical" feats challenged science and belief. He was presumed to be a fraud, yet was never discredited or caught out in any trickery.

not hold up and many critics, including Father Thurston, have shown convincingly how Home could have fooled his credulous witnesses.

One explanation of the transports of witches is that the sensation of flight was brought about by drugs, trances and the power of suggestion. While it is certain that shamans use such aids in their ecstatic journeys, this does not explain many well-documented observations of levitation. Leroy believed that the levitations of psychics – indeed of anyone who wasn't an approved saint – were tricks of the Devil to confuse the faithful. Of the pioneering psychical investigators, Sir Oliver Lodge suggested it was by the action of spirits, while Professor Charles Richet thought there might actually be an undiscovered anti-gravitational force involved.

There is another hypothesis – that reality itself is restructured by the intense imaginings of the mystics. After all, levitation is the perfect metaphor for being lifted in spirit just as the strange accompanying light is for spiritual illumination. St Teresa of Ávila (d.1582) gives a valuable first-hand account of the experience in her autobiography: "It comes as a shock, quick and sharp, before you can collect your thoughts or help yourself in any way and you see and feel it as a cloud or as a strong eagle rising upward and carrying you away on its wings." On another occasion she was calm enough to take note of what was happening: "It seemed to me … as if a great force beneath my feet lifted me up … I confess that it threw me into a great fear, for in seeing one's body thus lifted up from the Earth, though the spirit draws it upwards after itself (and that with great sweetness if unresisted) the senses are not lost; at least I … was able to see that I was being lifted up … after the rapture was over, my body seemed frequently to be buoyant, as if all weight had departed from it."

St Teresa would try to resist the levitations, wanting the ecstasy but fearing the bodily rising would give her delusions of grandeur and might distract her nuns from their proper devotions. Once, feeling it come upon her, she clutched at mats but rose into the air still holding them; on another occasion the effort made her vomit blood. She writes of being worn out "like a person who had been contending with a strong giant; at other times it was impossible to resist at all; my soul was carried away, and almost always my head with it – I had no power over it – and now and then the whole body as well, so that it was lifted up from the ground." Anyone reading her accounts cannot fail to be impressed by them: they challenge us to accept their reality however mysterious that reality may seem.

2

Strange Rains

2

Strange Rains

Falls of fishes and frogs

Rains of fishes or frogs sound biblical, but it would be wrong to dismiss the phenomenon simply because it seems as improbable as an Old Testament miracle. The hundreds of eyewitness accounts, collected by scientists and others, place the reality of such events beyond dispute. Works of early history and geography, and the memoirs of travellers, explorers and colonial administrators form the bulk of sources from antiquity until the nineteenth century; after this, accounts begin to be found in scientific journals as well as in newspapers. No one has yet tabulated all the known cases, so precise numbers and statistics must remain guesswork, even so, we suspect that the collected examples only really scratch the surface.

The quality of evidence for rains of fishes and frogs is good, with a canon of well-observed cases going back into antiquity. The *Deipnosophistae*, compiled by Athenaeus (c. AD 200), summarizes the writings of around eight hundred authors that he read at the Library of Alexandria – most of which were lost when the Library was destroyed. Under the heading "De pluvius piscium" (Rains of Fishes), he wrote: "Phaenias, for example, says, in the second book of *The Rulers Of Eresus* that in Chersonesus it rained fishes for three whole

days. And Phylarcus in his fourth book says that certain persons have in many places seen it rain fishes, and the same thing often happens with tadpoles."

Conventional science has tended to be sceptical about the phenomenon. In an 1844 issue of the *Zoologist* the editor, Edward Newman, included an item about a shower of little frogs, "about the size of a horse-bean", that occurred at Selby in Yorkshire. Those witnessing the occurrence had convinced themselves that the frogs had come down with the rain by holding out their hats into which falling frogs landed. Newman, of course, knew better. "I am continually receiving similar accounts not only of frogs, but toads, white fish and eels," he wrote, before exhorting his correspondents to check their facts more rigorously. "Methinks it would be no difficult matter to trace the presence of the animals to more natural sources than the clouds." (For a further discussion of expert reactions, see THEORIES AND EXPLANATIONS, p.27.)

A more open-minded approach emerged in the late nineteenth century, when a small number of scientists began to discuss the anomalies of their chosen field. Among them were the English meteorologist D.P. Thompson, the naturalist George Buist, the French astronomer Camille Flammarion, the German naturalist G. Hartwig, and the American ichthyologist E.W. Gudger. The first popular article on creature showers appeared in 1917, when Waldo

A chapter-heading from Olaus Magnus's *Historia de gentibus* (1555) in which he discusses many falls of fishes, frogs and animals, events which have repeated in every age up to the present.

McAtee, a distinguished biologist with the US Bureau of Biological Survey, became intrigued by his father's tale of coming in from the rain to find earthworms on the brim of his hat. McAtee went on to compile a broad survey of showers of organic matter and animals that, in turn, inspired both E.W. Gudger and Charles Fort.

E.W. Gudger confined his data to falls of fish, but Fort's researches extended wider and further than even McAtee, to include falls of organic matter, liquids, ice, stones and even artefacts. Fort's work is particularly significant because his eclectic reading brought so many different citations together for the first time and he attempted a critique of conventional explanations which exposed the weaknesses of dogmatic authorities such as Newman.

One case that Fort looked into took place in the Aberdare valley in South Wales. On the morning of Friday, 11 February 1859, a storm broke over the village of Mountain Ash bringing "thousands" of living fish, between one and four inches in length. There were two falls about ten minutes apart. The local curate sent a report to *The Times* (2 March 1859) which stated that locals, seeking to preserve some living specimens, put some in salt water and others in fresh water; those in saline died. The greatest peculiarity is that the fall occurred only in the vicinity of a lumber yard; many were found on roofs in the area. Specimens were sent to the British Museum, where Dr John Gray, Keeper of Zoology, identified them as minnows and sticklebacks.

In his discussion of this case, Fort's sarcasm was fired by the reactions of narrow-minded scientists. After identifying the fish, Dr Gray expressed the opinion that they had come from a local stream, in a bucket of water which one citizen had playfully emptied over another. Or, as Fort summarized, "someone soused someone else with a pailful of water in which were thousands of fishes, some of which covered roofs of houses."

More modern examples include the following. On the morning of 23 October 1947, A.D. Bajkov, a biologist with the US Department of Wildlife and Fisheries, was in a restaurant in Marksville,

Louisiana. He was having breakfast with his wife "when the waitress informed us that fish were falling from the sky … We went immediately to collect some of the fish." Several people had been struck by the fish, which were two to nine inches long, and some said they were icy to the touch. Bajkov later identified them as freshwater bass and shad, fish native to local waters (*Science*, vol.109, p.482).

At West Ham in London, following a heavy rainfall on the night of 27 May 1984, a builder found nearly a dozen small fish on the roof of the house of Ron Langton (pictured). When Bob Rickard visited the site, nine days later, the builder was still able to find some in the guttering – cats had got the rest. The fish were identified at the Natural History Museum as smelts and flounders. In the same night, fish also fell at three other locations in the same part of London. They were all of the kind you would expect to find in the nearby River Thames, leading to speculation that they were dropped by waterspouts or by regurgitating herons (*Fortean Times* 42, p.28).

In Fort Worth, Texas, Louis Castoreno thought someone was playing a trick on him when dozens of small fish flopped into his backyard on 8 May 1985. As he noticed a dark cloud passing above, he had to leap out of the way as "a whole bunch came down at one time. It scared me." A local spokesman for the National Weather Service confirmed that it had happened before in the past five years, usually just before a tornado or heavy storm (Fort Worth *Star Telegram*, 9 May 1985).

A storm, again, features in the account of hundreds of two-inch-long fish that fell in a small area of the Norfolk seaside town of Great Yarmouth on 6 August 2000 – a fine way to celebrate Charles Fort's birthday in the millennium year. Fred Hodgkins (pictured opposite), a retired ambulance driver, saw them covering his garden when he went to investigate what sounded like "heavy hail". The sky was dark with storm clouds and he heard several claps of thunder. "The whole of my back yard seemed to be covered in tiny slivers of silver. I looked again and saw scores of tiny silver fish." Fred thought they looked like sprats but they were never formally identified. He called out his neighbours to witness the spectacle – "because I knew no one would believe me" – and, together, they found three other gardens in a similar state. The fish were all dead but looked quite fresh. A wind had been blowing but *towards* the sea, scotching suggestions that a waterspout must have been responsible. (*Fortean Times* 139)

Many hundreds of living fish, "still wriggling" were among the "millions" that fell on fields in a drought-stricken part of southern Ethiopia at the end of May 2000. A local paper said the incident "caused panic among the religious farmers" (*Reuters*, 1 June 2000). Similarly, in June 2005, thousands of still-living tiny frogs fell from storm clouds over the north-western Serbian town of

Ron Langton and some of the small fish that fell on the roof and path of his terrace house in West Ham, in east London, during the night of 27 May 1984.

Newham Recorder

Fred Hodgkins, of Great Yarmouth, collected some of the "hundreds" of small silver fish that fell into gardens on 6 August 2000.

Writing in *English Mechanic* (1911, p.21), a witness describes how he was drenched during a violent thunderstorm in Bournemouth in 1891 and saw "small yellow frogs dashed on the ground all around me". When the rain stopped, he found hundreds around his shelter and "thousands impaled on the furze bushes on the common close by." The stench of their rotting corpses lasted for days afterwards.

Similar incidents abound in the literature, each with reliable witnesses. Mrs Sylvia Mowday, told us of her experience, on 12 June 1954, while crossing Birmingham's Sutton Park in a sudden downpour. "We tried to reach some trees. My four-year-old daughter put up her little red umbrella and we heard things thudding against it. To our amazement it was a shower of frogs, coming down from the sky, hundreds of them. We looked up and saw the frogs coming down like snowflakes. The ground was absolutely covered with them for about fifty square yards. We were afraid to tread on them, they were so tiny."

Before we move on to the scarcity of observa-

Odzaci. One witness told the Belgrade *Blic* newspaper (7 June 2005) that he "saw countless frogs fall from the sky". The paper said they looked quite different from local frogs and those that survived the fall hopped away in search of water.

When it comes to frogs, both the number of recorded incidents and the quantity of falling creatures is larger. At Carnet-Plage, France, "thousands" of frogs fell "just prior" to a heavy storm (*Journal of Meteorology*, 1977, p.300). On 23 September 1973, "tens of thousands" of small frogs fell during a storm at Brignoles France (*Times*, 24 September 1973). While, according to *Nature* (1915, p.378), "millions" of small frogs fell from the clouds during a storm over Gibraltar.

A fall of frogs in Scandinavia, illustrated in the *Prodigiorum ac ostentorum* (1557) of Conrad Lycosthenes.

One of the band of little frogs found in the Bedford garden of Mrs Vida McWilliam in June 1979, believed to have fallen with rain the previous day. Tadpoles littered her lawn, and her bushes were found draped with frogspawn, making this one of the most unusual cases in our "frog fall" records.

tions of falling spawn or tadpoles, we must briefly touch on the case of the thumbnail-sized frogs reported from several locations in Gloucestershire in October 1987 (*Fortean Times* 51, p.14). A naturalist from the Gloucestershire Trust for Nature Conservancy (GTNC) thought they might be a North African species, on account of their colouring, but was baffled as to how they could have reached the UK. Two reports helped suggest a solution: in the first, an unnamed woman told of "tiny rose-coloured frogs" coming down in torrential rain near Stroud. They were "bouncing off umbrellas and pavements and hopped off in their hundreds to nearby streams and gardens," she said (*Daily Mirror*, 24 October 1987). The *Fortean Times* (no.51, p.10) notes that parts of England – including the West Country – had experienced at least four falls of Sahara sand between May and September. At first we wondered whether the winds that lift sand into the stratosphere over the Sahara and blast it towards western Europe where it falls in "red rains" could also have transported the little frogs. However, Mark Nicholson of the GTNC later announced that the colourings fell

within the normal and albino variations of the common frog (*Fortean Times*, no.76, p.8). So, if these frogs were local, were the red rains and Stroud frog fall coincidental? As in so many other fortean cases, we are left with more questions than answers.

Tadpoles are smaller and more numerous than frogs, and should, therefore, be more likely to be lifted up from ponds by waterspouts. Fort, however, could find no records of tadpole showers and in all our own researches, far and wide, we have had little more success. Only four reports have come to our notice, one more a matter of folklore than record. *FATE* magazine (January 1958) tells of the Pueblo Indians of Acorna, New Mexico, whose explanation for the millions of tadpoles found in isolated pools of rainwater in the desert, is that they fall with the rain.

The second reference to tadpole showers is more specific, but still not very satisfactory as evidence. In *A Naturalist's Sojourn in Jamaica* (1851), Philip Gosse tells how he visited San Domingo on the island of Haiti in the West Indies. There, he learnt from his colleague, Richard Hill, of the local belief that a certain species of frog had first appeared on the island following a shower of tadpoles many years ago. Hill's words, as recorded by Gosse, were: "I was told that some frogs I used to hear croaking at night in the boggy ground about Port au Prince, in Haiti, were not known there till a shower of rain brought them to the island. The precise period of this occurrence was mentioned to me, and I have a note of it somewhere. If I could be satisfied that what the historian Moreau de St-Méry likened to "tetards" (bull-heads) were tadpoles, I should say it was the same shower as the one he commemorates in May 1786." Têtard is the French word for tadpole.

Our third instance is the recollection of eighty-year-old Leonard Burrough, the accuracy of whose memory we have no way of judging. In the Maidenhead *Advertiser* (4 December 1981), he tells of the day, in 1910, when his family relocated to the Berkshire town. It was shortly before a violent storm, "the worst in memory", when the sky became "darker than the darkest night" and the thunder and lightning terrified him. When young Leonard later went out onto the High Street, he was astonished to find it alive with thousands of tiny frogs and tadpoles.

In Moreau de St-Méry's *Description de St Domingue* (1796) there is an account of what may be one of the few showers of frogspawn on record. It fell during a drought over the whole of San Domingo (now Haiti and the Dominican Republic) on 5 May 1786. De St-Méry wrote: "There fell, during a strong east wind, in several parts of the city of Port an Prince … a great quantity of black eggs, which hatched the following day … They shed their skins several times [and] resembled tadpoles."

Theories and explanations

By the end of the eighteenth century – when the first efforts were being made to fit Natural History into the straitjacket of scientific rationalism – the notion that frogs or any other creatures could fall from the sky had been officially banished. Gilbert White, in 1789, called it a "foolish opinion", and academics of the day dismissed it as "popular error". A striking example concerns the interpretation that pious locals gave to the shower of snails which fell on a farm near Bristol in July 1821. They believed that it was a divine punishment of the farmer, who had been guilty of "disrespect to the virtues of our late Queen". We feel that this explanation is in a class of its own, but there are a number of serious and historical explanations of how creatures can rain from the skies which we review and assess below.

Under the date 23 May 1661, Samuel Pepys notes in his *Diary* his attendance at a dinner hosted by the Lord Mayor of London, where: "At table I had very good discourse with Mr Ashmole, where he did assure me that frogs and many other insects do often fall from the sky ready formed." Elias Ashmole was one of the most renowned alchemists and astrologers of the day, a distinguished member of the Royal Society who gave his name to the Ashmolean Museum at Oxford. He was in town because, the previous day, the Royal Society had held a special debate on the subject of the spontaneous generation of insects.

The idea that desiccated frogspawn may be drawn or blown up into the clouds, where it hatches, causing showers of little frogs to fall to Earth, is an ancient and well-debated one. Robert Plot in his *Natural History of Staffordshire* (1686) credits "spontaneous generation" theory to the Italian polymath, Jerome Cardan, whose encyclopedia, *De subtilitate*, appeared in 1550. Plot gave two illustrations in support of the theory. The first one featured little frogs, all of the same size, which had sometimes been found on the roof of a "stately gate-house", to which they had no ordinary means of access. The second was of someone who, while walking through low marsh ground on a foggy morning "had his hat almost covered with little frogs that fell on it as he walked." If that story is true, says Plot, then Cardan's theory must also be true – in some cases at least. To combat the objection that frogs from the clouds would probably be killed or damaged by the fall, Plot advocated a rival notion, that frogs found on house-tops had been generated from a special kind of dust blown there by the wind which "fermented" under the action of Sun and

On *Wednefday* before *Eafter*, *Anno* 1666. a Pafture Field at *Cranftead* near *Wrotham* in *Kent*, about Two Acres, which is far from any part of the Sea or Branch of it, and a Place where are no Fifh Ponds, but a Scarcity of Water, was all overfpread with little Fifhes, conceived to be rained down, there having been at that time a great Tempeft of Thunder and Rain ; the Fifhes were about the Length of a Man's little Finger, and judged by all that faw them to be young Whitings, many of them were taken up and fhewed to feveral Perfons; the Field belonged to one *Ware* a Yeoman, who was at that *Eafter-Seffions* one of the Grand Inqueft, and carried fome of them to the Seffions at *Maidftone* in *Kent*, and he fhowed them, among others, to Mr. *Lake*, a Bencher of the *Middle-Temple*, who had One of them and brought it to *London*, the Truth of it was averr'd by many that faw the Fifhes lye fcattered all over that Field, and none in other the Fields thereto adjoining : The Quantity of them was eftimated to be about a Bufhel, being all together. Mr. *Lake* gave the Charge at thofe Seffions.

A letter from Dr Robert Conny to Dr Robert Plot, a fellow of the Royal Society, as recorded in the *Philosophical Transactions* (1698).

rain to produce the creatures. He was not dogmatic about this latter theory and thought it only applied in some cases.

Pliny, in his *Natural History* of AD 77, mentions the falls of a number of organic and inorganic substances, including fishes. Although he alludes to the spontaneous generation of some animals from dormant dust or slime which contains their "seeds", we find no discussion there of falling frogs. It was the natural philosopher Giovanni Battista Porta who first formally associated the idea of spontaneous generation with falling frogs. In *Natural Magick* (1678) he stated that: "Frogs are wonderfully generated of rotten dust and rain; for a summer shower, lighting upon the putrefied sands of the shore, and dust of the highways, engenders frogs … The generation of them is so easy, and sudden, that some write it hath rained frogs, as if they were gendered in the air."

The idea of spontaneous generation continued to be put forward, in all seriousness, as recently as 1915, with the publication of *The Ages of Ice and Creation* by George Prentiss. Prentiss was more radical than today's Scientific Creationists because he believed that Creation did not stop at a certain time, but is continuing at this very moment all around us. His most dramatic evidence was a number of tales from the southern United States of the sudden appearance of fish, found in fresh puddles of rainwater, between rows of cotton, just after storms. To Prentiss the fish had obviously just come into being; he did not even consider that they might have fallen with the rain.

The most favoured official explanation for the phenomenon is summarized in the magazine *Science* (7 June 1946) by the naturalist Dr E.W. Gudger. "The explanation is to be found in the action of whirlwinds and waterspouts and possibly of strong typhoon and monsoon winds. A "twister" or whirlwind starts in front of an approaching storm and as it gains in size the "snout" elongates and approaches the water. This, caught by the whirling wind, rises up in a cone. The two unite, and the swirling column moves along, picking up water, fishes and any other fairly light objects at or near the surface of the water … Everything moveable would be sucked up in the whirling vortex. Furthermore, whirlwinds, originating inland, will not only progress over land, picking up various objects, but over ponds and lakes, becoming waterspouts. As such they will there pick up frogs, fresh-water fishes, snails, etc. and carry them away over the land. Sometimes the fishes are found in a long narrow, fairly straight row over some distance, evidently having been dropped as the waterspout progressed over the country with lessening speed and carrying power. When the waterspout or whirlwind, with its load of fishes breaks, water and fishes will fall as a rain of fishes."

Dr E.W. Gudger of the North American Museum of Natural History had a special interest in nature's enigmas and wrote scientific articles on many of the subjects covered in this book. He was the great authority on fish rains, which he concluded were caused by waterspouts or whirlwinds.

Charles Fort cited a case that demonstrated exactly what happens when a waterspout travels over a pond; things are not so much sucked up as violently raised and scattered about. There are also cases – to which Gudger alludes – in which fish have been found deposited in a straight line, but we venture to suggest that nothing so neat has ever been clearly witnessed by observers of whirlwinds. Fort protests: "It is so easy to say that small frogs that have fallen from the sky had been scooped up by a whirlwind … In the exclusionist imagination there is no regard for mud, debris from the bottom of a pond, floating vegetation, loose things from the shores [only] a precise picking out of frogs … A pond going up would be quite as interesting as frogs coming down. Whirlwinds we read of over and over – but where and what whirlwind? It seems to me that anybody who had lost a pond would be heard from."

A waterspout – the aquatic equivalent of a tornado – is created when the whirling column of air touches down on water and sucks up huge quantities of it. Any fish near the surface would be included. In Dr Gudger's third collection of accounts, in *Annals and Magazine of Natural History* (January 1929), he mentions a waterspout deluging an open boat in the Gulf of Mexico in 1921. The witness saw it form and then break, showering the boat with fish along with dangerous amounts of water. This was the only clear incident involving a whirlwind or waterspout in Gudger's total of seventy-one records.

In January 1975, a correspondence in the pages of the *East Anglian Magazine* yielded a number of recollections of earlier instances, including one from an old farmhand who experienced a rain of frogs in direct association with a waterspout. Frogs from a waterspout, though, must be considered a rarer occurrence than frogs from clear skies or with light rain, to judge by the recorded observations. Fort said of his own data: "Of all the instances I have that attribute the fall of small frogs or toads to whirlwinds, only one definitely identifies or places the whirlwind."

With some reservations, whirling winds provide the most logical explanation for many falls, but there are many other cases – reported throughout this book – in which they are simply not relevant. For example, when he was a boy in Montreal, Canada, in 1841, Sir George Gibb came across myriads of frogs on an isolated road. The road was wet in that part and, as he wrote in his booklet *Odd Showers* (1870), "We took it for granted there had been a shower of frogs." Rationalizing the event (which had happened to him 29 years earlier), Sir George opted for the waterspout theory, although his account reveals nothing more violent than "a smart rain just before we came up … on a beautiful summer's day."

One anomalous aspect of the evidence is voiced by Minnesota fortean Robert Schadewald, who wonders why there are "so many fish falls from Great Britain but none whatsoever from Minnesota, the "Land of Ten Thousand Lakes" which averages seventeen tornado touchdowns a year."

In 1771, the meteorologist, Raphael Eglini, was in the rare position of having friends who reported to him directly that they had observed fish falling when they were caught in a thunderstorm. They even provided him with specimens, which Eglini passed on for identification. Unmoved, he published a note of the event in the German scientific journal, *Wittenbergisches Wochenblatt*, with the comment that if they should turn out to be a local fish the explanation lay in an overflow from a neighbouring stream, or a waterspout. Later in the same journal it was stated that the fish were a species of "trout not found locally". Eglini's only comment was: "Incredible!"

Eglini favoured the theory that frogs and toads are flushed out of their hiding places by rainwater. The same opinion was put forward by the nature writer E.A. Ellis, in his column for the *Eastern Daily Press* (11 July 1975): "It is tempting to assume that these young creatures had arrived in a shower from the sky, but the explanation, at least in most cases of sudden swarming after rain, is that young amphibians, having migrated from the water where they developed as tadpoles, tend to remain under the cover of grass and other herbiage by day and move only at night, but are tempted out of cover at any time by a shower." Ellis doesn't use this to explain all fish and frog falls and indeed he expresses some faith in the whirlwind theory, adding: "I think it very unlikely that the alleged phenomenon occurs at all frequently but having myself seen a variety of objects sucked up in waterspouts and whirlwinds on several occasions and having also been at the receiving end of the material showered down afterwards, I can see no reason to discredit every tale of objects descending from the air."

Some fish, it seems, have organized their lives around periodic rains. In *Fortean Times* (106, p.1) Tony Healy and Paul Cropper describe several sudden appearances of numbers of "grunters" at Wellbourne Hills in the northern desert of South Australia coinciding with drought-breaking rains. There are other species of fish known to migrate across tracts of land, usually using pools of water made by recent rain or floods. This theory clearly does not apply to cases involving dead fish, species not known for migrating, or fish found in high inaccessible places.

We have referred above to the archaic theory of "spontaneous generation", but there is a natural phenomenon which, to an untutored observer, would appear to be similar. This is aestivation, the ability of some fish, amphibians and molluscs to survive periods of drought by hibernating in soft mud before a pond or stream dries up. It usually involves living eggs and young forms which are revived again, often with surprising rapidity, when rains or floods bring fresh water. When offered as an explanation for fish falls, it is assumed that the young fish are flushed out of their hiding places to appear suddenly, in great numbers, on the wet ground and in puddles. It fails to account for eyewitness accounts of fish falling, those found in high inaccessible places, or the fact that many "falls" involve fish that are not known to aestivate.

Large fish-eating birds, like herons, swallow fish whole or carry them off in their beaks or claws. Sometimes, when attacked in flight, they drop or vomit their recent catch. While this could be a reasonable explanation of falls of single fishes (of which there are a significant number) it fails to explain falls involving great numbers of fish. Some authorities have sought to explain the fall of thousands of fish by supposing that a whole flock of birds must have disgorged simultaneously.

In our first chapter we describe teleportation, the concept introduced by Charles Fort in connection with mysterious comings and goings of creatures and objects. This unknown, hypothetical force, he suggested, has been active from the beginning of the world, piling up mountains, populating remote islands and bringing fish to isolated lakes. Regarding the universe as a single organism, a hermaphrodite satisfying its own wants, Fort identified teleportation as its means of self-regulation.

It is an old idea that nature has nerves or imagination that communicate the needs of each part to every other, producing compensatory reactions. It is inherent in the mystical view of the world and in the operations of ritual magic. There are more rational ways of explaining fish falls than by teleportation and the imagination of nature; but none of them is entirely satisfactory and in many cases the mystical view seems more adequate than any of its rivals.

Fort frequently noted the tendency of authority figures to trot out explanations that sounded reasonable yet actually accounted for

A waterspout at Hurst Spit, Milford-on-Sea, Hampshire, on 6 July 1966.

very little of the observed phenomenon. A prime example occurred on 30 May 1881, when great quantities of periwinkles and crabs fell on the English city of Worcester. The "official" response was to suggest that a mad fishmonger or practical joker must have travelled the byways of the city, unseen, shovelling thousands of periwinkles off the back of his cart.

Anomalies and questions

In the *Sourcebook Project*, an ongoing encyclopedia of natural anomalies compiled by William Corliss, the phenomenon of fish falls is not rated as a "serious anomaly", meaning that there are many examples which can adequately be explained. While this is undoubtedly true generally, there are other well-observed aspects of the phenomenon that cannot be easily accounted for and which are consistently overlooked by those seeking to explain it away.

Among the most troublesome of these are the observations of some kind of selection process at work; not only are falling frogs and fish often separated from the mud, water, vegetation and debris of their normal environment, but there is a peculiar selectivity at work among the creatures themselves. Mixed showers do occur, but in nearly all cases only one species is involved. Also, the falling creatures are usually of about the same size and age, and frequently young or immature. The most strikingly "unreasonable" feature about such happenings, however, is that we rarely hear of falling creatures being crushed or damaged. One of the few cases we can recall occurred at Newcastle in the South African province of Natal, on the morning of 14 April 1909, when hundreds of fish of the species *Barbus gurneyi* were found on wet ground "some alive and unhurt, some dead, and some smashed to a pulp".

It is worth dwelling further on this point, but we must first mention the mixed fortunes of the fish that fell on Calcutta in 1839, as cited in Charles Tomlinson's *Raincloud and Snowstorm* (1864). Observers noted that the fish that landed on hard ground were killed, while those falling on grass survived. A curious feature of this case was that the fish fell in a straight line, indicating – according to some – the operation of a waterspout. Yet it was an upholder of the waterspout theory, W.H. Carey, who, in describing other Indian fish

These panels (below and opposite), from Erasmus Francisci's book *Der wunder-reiche Überzug unserer Nider-Welt* (1680), depict various recorded showers of wheat, fish, frogs and worms.

falls in *Good Old Days of the Honourable John Company* (1907), wrote: "The fish are … swept up by whirlwinds from ponds and held suspended in the rain cloud until they are thrown down in showers. The curious part is, that the fishes are found on the ground alive and uninjured."

The idea that grass or other soft surfaces saved falling fish from smashing on impact was popular for a time. Fort commented: "The devotees of St Isaac [Newton] explain that they fall upon thick grass and so survive; but Sir James Tennant, in his *History of Ceylon*, tells of a fall of fishes upon gravel, by which they were seemingly uninjured." Fort's reference is to Tennant's *Natural History of Ceylon* (1861), in which the author describes seeing a short, torrential rainstorm and of finding at the spot "a multitude of small silvery fish … leaping on the gravel of the high road, numbers of which I collected and brought away."

Another anomaly is the falls of dead fish, in some cases dead so long that they are decomposing. A baffling fish fall occurred on 19 February 1830 at Jelalpur in India, detailed by James Prinsep with the affidavits of nine witnesses in the *Journal of the Asiatic Society of Bengal* (1833), in which thousands of dead fish fell on a factory; "some were fresh, others rotten and mutilated". Many of the fish were stinking and headless, which is difficult to attribute to the action of a

whirlwind. Nine witnesses testified to being hit by them or finding them on roofs. Yet there was no storm. One said they were seen up in the sky "like a flock of birds descending rapidly to the ground." In contrast, in another Indian case, recorded by Major J. Harriett in his *Struggles Through Life* (1808), marching troops experienced a shower of fish so light and gentle, that the fish found in the soldiers' hats were shaken out and made into a curry for their general.

Robert Schadewald has calculated, from experiments, the terminal velocity of a small falling fish to be very nearly 32 miles per hour, yet Fort noted the singular lack of any account of fish being seriously damaged or killed by their fall. Summing up his notes in *Lo!* (1931) Fort wrote: "In all the hosts of stories that I have gathered … of showers of living things, the rarest of all statements is of injury to the falling creatures." With his theory of teleportation in mind, Fort suggested "the creatures may not have fallen all the way from the sky, but may have fallen from appearing-points not high above the ground – or may have fallen a considerable distance under a counter-gravitational influence."

A splendid example occurred on 17 May 1996 at Hatfield, Hertfordshire. Mrs Ruth Harnett and her husband David were unloading the weekly shopping from their van. It was not raining but

the air became suddenly chilly. Ruth heard a metallic thump and noticed a fish on the van's roof. She looked up and saw a second fish fall on the bonnet. Her immediate thought was that someone was throwing them at her, but there was no sign of any culprit. "Then three more fish dropped on my garden and I realised they were falling from the sky." She called her husband and looked up again only to be hit in the face as a few more fell. As some passing children stopped to stare, laughing in wonder, they all saw about 20 more fall around them (*Fortean Times* 87, August 1996). Again, Schadewald's experiments would have predicted that Ruth should have been seriously injured by being hit by fish falling from cloud height, but she was not, nor were so many others hit by falling fish. Either the fish did not fall from a great height or some unknown process absorbed their momentum.

Ruth's experience also presents us with another damned anomaly: her fish were all dead but seemed warm to the touch, as though they had been heated in their aerial travels.

In cases where the fish are not decaying we can suppose that the shock of aerial transition killed them. In the case of fish found dried and stiff, we must ask how this could be accomplished in damp winds or the wet interiors of clouds? In the Natal case (discussed above), the mix of unhurt, intact but dead and "smashed" fish challenges every explanation.

Many fallen fish are reported to be unusually cold to the touch and some have been found frozen or mixed with hail. This is quite consistent with being held within a storm cloud, whose interior temperatures drop well below freezing. For example, the lifeless, icy cold fish that rained on the seafront pier at Ocean Springs, Mississippi, on 13 July 2004, were frozen stiff and "coated in ice". The fall, which followed a hailstorm from dark clouds over the ocean, was witnessed by Melissa Perez, a Gulf Islands National Seashore Ranger, and volunteer Adam Wilson, who said it was confined to a small area of about 6 metres in diameter. (Biloxi, Mississippi, *Sun Herald*, 15 July 2005). Severe cold of this sort may also allow fish to be transported great distances by keeping them in a state of suspended animation. We keep a special place by the fire of curiosity for those completely frozen into the ice. During a fall of frogs and fish at Derby, in 1841, lumps of half-melted ice fell with the creatures (*Atheneum*, 17

July 1841), while at Dubuque, Iowa, on 16 June 1882, small frogs were found inside hailstones, some still alive (*Monthly Weather Review*, 1882). The most extreme note we have is of a six-by-eight-inch gopher turtle that came down with a hailstorm, entirely encased in ice, at Bovington, Mississippi – an event respectably recorded in the *Monthly Weather Review* for May 1894.

Also noticeable, in a number of cases, is the good marksmanship in the placing of falls. Instead of being scattered widely, as one would expect from a powerful, chaotic, whirling wind, the fall is frequently almost poured, or dropped, onto a location from a seemingly stable point above it. There are cases in which several falls have taken place over a few days. It seems highly unlikely that whirlwinds would follow the same track with such precision although, in the Aberdare case (see FALLS OF FISHES AND FROGS, p.22) the principal witnesses noted "two showers, with an interval of ten minutes and each shower lasted about two minutes." George Buist gives a case from near Calcutta, in 1839, in which a witness says: "The most strange thing which ever struck me … was that the fish did not fall helter-skelter … but in a straight line not more than a cubit in breadth."

Fort noticed a correlation between some falls and seismic phenomena. For example, the Count de Castelnau witnessed a fall in Singapore during a three-day rainstorm that immediately followed an earthquake. In Ecuador, in 1691, Baron Humboldt observed a shower of cooked fish, ejected from a steaming vent near a volcano. A possible explanation, according to the Canadian psychologists Michael Persinger and Gyslaine Lafreniere, is that subterranean stress may generate strange electromagnetic fields which, in turn, trigger events like fish falls.

Many historical instances of "jelly falls" (see RAINS OF SEEDS AND ORGANIC MATTER, p.58) occur in association with unexplained aerial lights. The German physicist Ernst Chladni (1756–1827) tells of a viscous mass that fell with a "luminous meteorite" in Italy in 1652, and of a "gelatinous matter" that fell with a globe of fire on Lethy Island, India, in 1718.

It is hard to avoid the conclusion that, in a great many falls, some sort of selection seems to have taken place; the creatures are typically all of one species, or at the same stage of development. Schadewald's experiments allowed him to predict that fish in the updraft of a waterspout would rise

Waterspouts are the commonest scientific explanation for the mysterious transportation of marine creatures from sea to dry land.

at different speeds, according to their weight and aerodynamic qualities. Further segregations could be performed by cross winds ... so some form of "selection" seems logical at first glance. However, if this were the case, one might reasonably expect all manner of pond or aquatic debris of similar weight or shape to accompany fish falls and this is generally absent from witness' descriptions.

We now have a great many more cases than those McAtee considered and we can say that, for the most part, falling animals are living, young specimens which are undamaged by the fall and quickly disperse after landing. Just two years after McAtee, Fort wrote: "If living things have landed alive on this Earth, in spite of all we think we know of the accelerative velocity of falling bodies, and have propagated ... the exotic becomes the indigenous." Or to put it another way: "If hosts of living frogs have come from somewhere else, every living thing upon this Earth may, ances-

trally, have come from somewhere else."

We close this section by mentioning two other puzzling anomalies observed in some showers of fishes and frogs; but we will meet them again in other sections of this book. The first is what forteans call a "point fall", an example of paranormal marksmanship, as occurred in the Aberdare case (see p.23), where two separate falls of thousands of sticklebacks and minnows fell into the confines of a lumberyard. What whirlwind could repeat such a feat of accuracy?

A more recent example of a very localised "point fall" occurred in a suburb of Medicine Hat, Alberta, on 16 July 2001. One of the witnesses, Richard Bates, heard a "swishing sound" in the trees outside his bedroom window, followed by a dull thump. Going outside to investigate, he found the bonnet of his car, a nearby tree and the pavement between them wet; all of the surrounding area was dry. To add to the strangeness, in the centre of the wet area was a large, dead frog, later identified as a leopard frog and quite rare in the area. (*Medicine Hat News*, 18 July 2001)

Australian forteans Paul Cropper and Tony Healy have patiently researched the nation's fish falls and have amassed more than 70 incidents occurring between 1879 and 1997, including the following feat of temporal marksmanship. Their records show that at the crossroads in the tiny hamlet of Dunmarra, 600km south of Darwin, fish fell on four separate occasions over five years, between 1989 and 1994. Two of the showers occurred in the same week of February 1994, the first of which dumped "thousands of little fish" in the Dunmarra Road House car park.

The second and most mysterious of anomalies is that now and again we hear of a "repeater" – someone to whom an extremely rare phenomenon has occurred more than once. It is similar to the hypothesis of "agency" in poltergeist cases – someone who seems to trigger the phenomenon in some way. After *Phenomena* was first published in 1977, Bob Rickard took part in a radio phone-in in which a caller to the radio station said that he had twice experienced rains of frogs while in a boat on a lake at Rickmansworth, outside London.

A variation of that was told to *Fortean Times* by Ruth Harnett. This was not the first time this had happened in her family, she said: "I remember my father telling me that his father was caught in a shower of fishes and frogs near Welwyn Garden City, just seven miles away, about 60 years ago."

Fort himself never insisted that teleportation was the true or only answer to the problem of falls of creatures. Some – perhaps all – the theories we have mentioned (whirlwinds, waterspouts, fish-vomiting birds, practical jokers, etc) might adequately explain some aspects of certain cases, but, from our own investigations, we have found that they are useless in many others. The existence of this variety of explanations is an indication that nothing has really been fully explained over the centuries. Certainly, in cases of frog and fish falls, as we have seen, there are features of some reports that no scientific or "rational" theory has yet accounted for satisfactorily. You'll find this is true generally, as we extend our discussion into some of the other varieties of falls.

Insect showers

One of England's earliest newspapers, the *Exeter Flying Post*, reported on 27 August 1789 that "London and its environs were, on Thursday, covered with a black insect in an astonishing manner. They seem to have been engendered in the atmosphere at a considerable distance from the Earth." Countless numbers of this insect fell into the streets barely alive.

This unexpected arrival of a cloud of insects may well have something to do with migration or swarming but, at this remove, it is difficult to determine precisely what happened. While it seems reasonable to suppose that a swarm of insects encountering a region of cold air might fall to ground numbed and lethargic, we are struck by the attempt to explain their *sudden* appearance. Like the falls of toads that baffled Pliny, Plot and Ashmole (see THEORIES AND EXPLANATIONS, p.27) is is suggested that they are spontaneously generated in the upper atmosphere. It is also possible to consider them in the light of Fort's notion of teleportation.

In the annals of falling creatures, records of insect falls are as numerous as those of frogs and fishes but in recent years less frequent than they were. The most recent report in our files – a cloud of unidentified insects that littered the French town of Luçon, in Vendée, on 24 April 1977 (*Le Progrès*, 27 April 1977) – hardly does justice to the exotic accounts of earlier times in which great numbers of insects are found in circumstances which suggest that they fell recently from the sky.

Entomologists who study the dispersal of insects tend to scorn the notion of falls. Canadian forestry naturalist W.R. Henson and his colleagues often discussed, in the pages of entomology journals, the theory that insects could be carried into the upper atmosphere by strong winds and carried great distances before plummeting to Earth with rain or snow. Then in 1951, while in the Banff National Park, Alberta, Henson experienced a shower of ice crystals, one of which

The case of the coach travelling from Gournay to Gisors in France, turned back by an inpenetrable cloud of cockchafer beetles in May 1832, was treated by Flammarion as an insect fall. It is now believed to have been a mass migration.

contained the body of a midge. The crystal was perfectly developed and completely enclosed the insect, suggesting it had been suspended for a while in a high, ice-forming air layer (*Nature*, 5 January 1952). We shall come across other ice-encrusted falls in later sections.

Other entomologists and meteorologists hold the opinion that was summarized by Waldo McAtee in one of the first collections of data on anomalous falls of living creatures and organic matter. McAtee declared: "The rains of insect larvae that have been investigated have proved to be merely the appearance in large numbers on the surface of the ground, or upon snow, of the larvae of soldier beetles, or sometimes caterpillars, which have been driven from their hibernating quarters by the saturation of the soil by heavy rains or melting snow" (*Monthly Weather Review*, May 1917). We need not be too impressed with this appearance of certainty, since a few pages further on McAtee himself presents cases of witnessed falls of insects. Somewhat taken aback, he admits "but there have been apparently a few real rains of insects."

Certainly not every discovery of masses of insects lying on the snow can be explained by the "forced-out-of-hibernation" theory. In December 1855, a "strange rainstorm", which turned to snow, fell on Alexandria, Virginia. The next morning residents found that the snow for several miles "resembled a vast field of dark velvet". The cause was an unimaginable number of tiny black bugs, "each slightly larger than a grain of gunpowder". The unidentified "bugs" were stiffened by the cold and in no condition to have burrowed upwards. When thawed out by firesides they were quite lively, but of a kind unfamiliar to the locals. Henry Splitter, who cites this incident in his collection of curious North American falls (*Fate*, October 1953) also mentions a shower of angleworms on Virginia City, Nevada, in April 1879. There had been a rainstorm during the night and in the morning the whole town lay under a blanket of wriggling worms. They were not indigenous and could not have come out of hibernation, since they were found on the streets, sidewalks and on roofs.

In 1946 the butler of the Cope family, in Philadelphia, took advantage of a lull in a torrential rainstorm to take out some refuse and, to his great surprise, found "thousands of tiny worms, none larger than one third of an inch, blanketing the yard, the fence and the highway". As reported the next year in *Doubt* (the journal of the original Fortean Society) this was in July, so snow could hardly be blamed. The creatures eluded identification. Unlike more familiar worms, these had "almost microscopic legs and walked like caterpillars".

According to the London *Evening Standard* (3 January 1924) red worms snowed at Halmstad, in Sweden. They ranged from one to four inches long and were seen coming down with snowflakes. At Pakroff, in Russia, immense numbers of an unidentified black insect fell during a snowstorm in 1827 (*Scientific American*, vol. 30). Also in Russia, in December 1830, a snowstorm was peppered with multitudes of gnat-like insects (*American Journal of Science*, vol.1, p.22). At Bramford Speke, in Devon, large numbers of three-quarter-inch worms came down with snow (*Times*, 14 April 1837). In May 1955, the residents of Kinomacki,

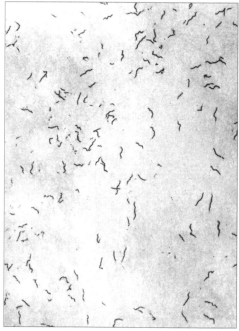

Snow-worms on a small patch of snow, some of the vast number "thickly strewn" over more than a quarter of a mile in a pass on Mount Olympus, Washington State. They were photographed on 1 June 1907.

in Finland, were horrified by a torrent of worms from the sky, with no accompanying rain or snow. A Reuter's report at the time blamed the event on "a violent wind whipping them up from a wet meadow". From Charles Fort's data, we note: Silesia, Germany, 1806, "snowing larvae"; Eifel, Germany, 1847, snow and larvae "fell together"; Switzerland, 1890, falls of "incalculable numbers" of two distinct kinds of insect larvae.

Further records reveal more detailed observations. In 1869, French naturalist Rey de Morande reported two remarkable cases to the Association Scientifique de France. The first, occurring near Turin in November 1854, involved a Monsieur Tissot who witnessed several thousand living insects "thrown down by a violent wind ... some were larvae and some adult ... of a species of hemiptera that had never before been collected [outside] Sardinia".

Rey de Morande himself investigated a combined shower of a great quantity of insect larvae and spiders at Arache, in the French Alps (and we can't help noting that "Arachne" is the Greek word for a spider). It happened in the early hours of 30 January 1869 – the same year that saw the remarkable insect appearances in England. For days the temperature had been very cold, so there was little possibility they had hatched out there. The spiders were of a species more commonly found on old trees in the forests of southern France than on Italian mountains and, although Rey de Morande favours the "violent wind" mode of transport, he does not venture a guess as to how so many insects could have been collected together by a wind in such a way that only creatures of two species were selected and, furthermore, distinguished from woodland debris of the same size or weight.

The well-known characteristic of some spiders of spinning a web and sailing off on a breeze can hardly apply to insect larvae; besides, these particular spiders do not have that characteristic. We mention many unusual gatherings of animals in this book; perhaps some creatures occasionally congregate in the open in expectation of windy transport, as was suggested in the case of the Finnish worms.

Another example of mixed rain of insects, this time in Switzerland in March 1922, was summarized by Charles Fort from reports in the international press. One bulletin read: "During a heavy snowstorm in the Alps recently thousands of exotic insects resembling spiders, caterpillars and huge ants fell on the slopes and quickly died. Local naturalists are unable to explain the phenomenon, but one theory is that the insects were blown in on the wind from a warmer climate." The use of the word "resembling" probably implies they were unfamiliar species. In commenting upon this case, Fort suggested that the important thing was not the fall of unknown insects during a snowstorm (of which he had found many examples) but the segregational powers of a wind capable of lifting small objects from a faraway place, keeping them in the air together over great distances, and yet ensuring that a variety of different insects of different specific gravities could fall together in the same place. We shall encounter this mysterious selecting process with other phenomena in this book.

Strange and ominous clouds have been associated with some well-observed falls. On 25 July 1872, Bucharest, Romania, was threatened by a small dark cloud that approached from the horizon on a generally cloudless and stiflingly hot day. At 9.15pm, the lurking cloud discharged its contents on the city below. According to *Nature* (1872) the townsfolk were filled with horror as, not rain, but small, fat, black worms or grubs covered most of the streets. In a similar case the *Meteorolgische Zeitschrift* (1901) describes a deep, black cloud that appeared in the evening sky over Szentes, in Hungary, on 14 August 1901. A heavy downpour began, "not of rain, but of winged insects, which in a few minutes covered the ground a foot deep". The insects are not identified, but only a few days before, another Hungarian village suffered similar rains, composed partly of winged ants and partly of four-winged *Neuroptera*.

At Bath, in Somerset, on 22 April 1871, there occurred what was described as "a storm of insects". During a heavy thunderstorm, a large number of glutinous drops fell near the city's railway station, where a boy first noticed them falling on his coat. Soon the whole platform was covered with jelly. According to Symons' *Meteorological Magazine* (1871), the egg masses hatched quickly into annelid-like worms. The event was investigated by the Reverend L. Jenyns, who sent his conclusion to the *Zoologist* and the Ento-

In July 1903, during a voyage between islands off Normandy, a fishing vessel steamed through a blizzard of white butterflies which lasted for the best part of two days.

Walter and Val Jervis examine the handiwork of millions of tiny spiders covering a fence on the Robson Valley farm.

mological Society of London. The culprit, said Jenyns, was a whirlwind "acting in a gyratory manner" that had scooped up a shallow pond, or one that was almost dried up, in which the eggs were concentrated into a small area. This explanation satisfied the savants because it exorcised the numerous difficult questions.

Curiously, another helping of jelly fell on Bath a few years later, in August 1894. It was described in *Notes and Queries* (8 September 1894) as consisting of thousands of shilling-sized jellyfish. Fort wondered if this was not misidentified frogspawn because, he notes, on the same day many small frogs fell at Wigan in Lancashire.

More recently it was the turn of Eton, Buckinghamshire, to be pelted with masses of jelly on 24 June 1911. They were insect eggs in clusters the size of peas and found covering the ground after a heavy rainfall. Once again we read of a rapid development, as if according to some cosmic restocking schedule, they had arrived just in time to hatch. It was reported in *Nature* (6 July 1911) that they yielded larvae of a species of midge.

Holinshed, in his *Chronicles* (1577) mentions a rain of blood-like matter in England, "during the rule of Rinall, which began fifteen years before the building of Rome". The foul rain lasted three days, "after which raine ensued such an exceeding number and multitude of flies, so noisome and contagious that much people died by reason thereof." Although this was long before microscopes could be used to identify micro-organisms, it was clear in Holinshed's mind, and those of his

sources, that the plague, the flies and the evil rain were all connected. So many of the more famous "red rains" or "blood rains" (see RAINS OF SEEDS AND ORGANIC MATTER, p.58) have been found to consist of "insect excreta", infusoria and other organisms such as algae, that we wonder how many of the red rains mentioned frequently in historical chronicles might not be falls of insect eggs.

A phenomenon related to showers of insects concerns the curious occasions when millions of hatchling spiders take to the air on strands of web. It is known as "ballooning", by which young spiders use a light wind to disperse over a larger territory. When this is successful, the air can fill with a vast quantity of ropes and sheets of webbing, swarming with spiders, which are carried for miles. Our illustration (above) shows some of the webbing that covered sixty acres of clover fields in the Robson Valley, in British Columbia, at the end of October 2002.

An early account is given by Gilbert White in his *Natural History of Selbourne* (1789). He records that he went out into his fields at dawn on 21 September 1741 and found the grass thickly covered with cobweb. Later that morning, he saw: "a shower of cobwebs falling from very elevated regions and continued without interruption until the end of the day". They were not the expected "filmy threads" but "perfect flakes or rags, between an inch and five or six long, which fell with a degree of velocity that they were considerably heavier than the atmosphere. On every side the observer looked might he behold a continual succession of fresh flakes falling into his sight, twinkling like stars as they turned their sides towards the Sun." He estimated they covered a triangular area about eight miles on each side.

Strands coloured blue and black have been reported and even short brittle fibres, which may account for some instances of the phenomenon known to ufologists as "Angel Hair".

Rats, mice and lemmings

Captain J. Ben Jones, of Pwllheli, was fishing off the north coast of Wales, when a live rat dropped into his boat from a clear sky. Recounting the story in the *Liverpool Echo* (6 July 1954), Captain Jones says he chased it around the boat until he killed it and tossed it overboard. As he watched, a gull swooped on the rat's carcass. Pressed to explain the event, Captain Jones supposed the gull must have dropped the rat in the first place. Perhaps – or it fell from an appearing point above his boat. That was a single rat and so the gull explanation seems perfectly likely, but huge flocks of rat-carrying birds seem quite improbable in the following stories.

From the Indonesian island of Lombok comes a story of rats from the sky which threatened the islanders' precarious rice crop. It was told in the sober *Wall Street Journal* (25 August 1969). The reporter writes: "On the outskirts of Batudjai, a half dozen farmers are squatting in a ricefield … 'The rats came six months ago, before the rains stopped,' says [a] farmer. How did they come? 'They fell from the sky.' From the sky? 'Yes, in bunches of seven, and then they spread out across the land,' the farmer adds matter-of-factly. 'They are led by a great white rat as large as a cat,' says [another] farmer. 'The white rat is very smart. It knows when we plan to harvest. If we plan to harvest a field the day after tomorrow the rats will eat the field tomorrow night. If we plan, in secret, to harvest the field tomorrow then the rats will eat it tonight.' A visit to the village chief, the only fat man to be seen in Batudjai ('He is of a higher caste,' explains a villager) repeats the farmers' story. Led by a white 'king of rats as large as a dog,' the rats appeared last December, falling from the sky in bunches of seven, he says. As they landed the rats separated and spread in seven different directions, he says. Some farmers saw

In his great history of the northern nations, Olaus Magnus illustrated the occasional falls of lemmings in parts of Norway. Many of these animals were devoured by ermines, whose especially luxurious fur was attributed directly to this unusual diet and caused them to be much sought after by trappers.

In his compendium of wonders, published in 1680, Erasmus Francisci elaborated on Olaus Magnus's brief mention of showers of rodents and included this illustration of falling shrew-mice.

directly contrary to the normal behaviour of rats which pop out of the ground."

Beyond that, we are impressed with the mythical quality of the story, which seems of a kind more likely to be collected by a folklorist or cultural anthropologist than by a naturalist, meteorologist or agricultural scientist. These mythic elements include: the mystic number seven (prevalent in East Indies folklore); the geomantic connotation of the seven directions as a terrestrial mandala; the magical mode of transportation; an abnormal happening in nature preceding some disaster; and the vanishing crops (see also RAINS OF SEEDS AND ORGANIC MATTER, p.58). They also include the distinctive leader or "king", larger and more cunning than the other animals, who in true fairytale tradition grows larger with each retelling of the story. If there had indeed been a disastrous fall of rats on an illiterate community, this is how the account of it might have been preserved.

A plague of mice in Inverness-shire in May 1832 has features in common with the Lombok story, even though no one claimed to have seen mice falling from the sky. The mice appeared suddenly and in such huge numbers that the foxes reformed, giving up chickens for easier meat (in the same way the wolves of Alaska ignore their usual prey, caribou, when the lemming population explodes). In its account of the Inverness mouse plague, the *Magazine of Natural History* (vol. 7) said that the mice were quite unlike any local species known to naturalists. They had brown bodies with white in a band around the neck and on the tip of the tail. Even if a few foreign mice had escaped from somewhere, they could hardly have multiplied into such vast numbers without their appearance and increase being noticed earlier. The sudden arrival of this alien horde of mice has the hallmark of an animal shower or teleportation.

this happen, says the chief, and several farmers nearby nod."

The sceptical will interpret this story as the superstition of country yokels, but in his discussion of it (*Pursuit*, October 1969), the late Ivan Sanderson thought that a pest which could plunge already poor farmers into famine would not be made light of. Besides, he said, "The farmers of Lombok are not nearly as superstitious as one might suppose, and they know their local animal life very well indeed. The "falling from the sky" is

Most people have heard of the periodic suicidal dash of lemmings (a kind of vole) in Norway, attributed to a frenzy engendered by overpopulation. A few lemmings, we are told, resist the death-urge and survive to rebuild their tribe.

Regional traditions, from the earliest times, however, suggest that their numbers may be restocked by more periodic aerial drop-shipments.

In a book about the wonders of this Earth's atmosphere (*Der wunder-reiche Überzug unserer Nider-welt*, 1680), Erasmus Francisci has a long, learned discussion about falls of rodents, frogs, snakes, fish, grain, stones and other things, mostly in the northern countries of Europe. He cites contemporary reports and also gives the views of many ancient and medieval writers on the subject. Chief among them was the geographer Olaus Magnus (1490–1557), who believed that falls of rodents were most common in the far north, particularly in Norway and the districts of Helsing and Uppsala, where rains of lemmings were said to occur during storms.

Lemmings on the run. People in many Arctic countries believe that they fall to Earth from a distant star, thus accounting for their sudden proliferation.

Two popular theories were current in the sixteenth century about where the creatures came from: some believed that they had been carried by winds from distant islands, others that they dropped out of thick mists and clouds. Olaus favoured the latter theory and so did Francisci, who argued reasonably that "If showers of stones can fall from the atmosphere why should it also not rain rats and mice?"

Francisci presents some interesting details about falling rodents, from people who had dissected them: that fresh, undigested grass is found in their stomachs; that every green thing they gnaw or touch withers, producing famines; and that they eventually die in great heaps, poisoning both land and people. Francisci was particularly convinced by the observation that, following rain or dense fog, hordes of lemmings had been discovered on the tops of mountains, even when the mountains were covered by deep snow. It could not be said that they had been driven by the weather out of their holes, because these were frozen up and blocked by the snow.

A similar phenomenon was noted in Alaska by the remarkable explorer-naturalist, Sally Carrighar. While staying in Nome in the hope of catching a few lemmings to take back to California, she was told by Eskimos that the creatures often drifted down slowly from the skies. Proof of this was that their tracks began abruptly in the snow. She did not take the stories seriously until, one day in April 1952, the Eskimo postmaster at Unalakleet informed her that a few of the little creatures had that day touched down, appropriately, at the end of the town's airstrip. What happened next is worth citing in full, from Carrighar's *Wild Voice of the North* (1959): "The blacktop was covered with less than an inch of new, light, soft snow too shallow for any lemming to tunnel under it without thrusting up a ridge on the surface. And there, indeed, were the mysterious little trails, just as the Eskimos had described them. In fifteen places a track began rather faintly for a couple of inches, as if an animal had come down and gently coasted onto the snow. The tracks then continued more deeply, the individual footprints showing clearly, and also the slight brush marks between the footprints where the hairs on the lemmings' feet dragged. They were not mouse tracks, for then there would have been a tail mark between the footprints … In each case the tracks led off the blacktop to a clump of grass, where the lemmings evidently had burrowed down among the roots.

"And how could those tracks just begin suddenly, out there on the smooth white surface? I have no idea. Lemmings cannot jump even a fraction as far. They have no membranes between their forelegs and hind legs, as bats have, and therefore they cannot fly. They do have long, soft, thick fur, and briefly I wondered if the wind could have picked up the fluffy little creatures and set them down on the airstrip. That possibility would have been reasonable, perhaps, if the wind had been strong enough on that day to have drifted the snow. It wasn't; the snow was as light as eiderdown and it lay as level as it had fallen. That owls did not pick up the lemmings as they were venturing out on the surface is obvious because the tracks led to the clumps of grass, not away from them. An owl … might have dropped one squirming lemming – but hardly fifteen in a space about twenty yards square."

No scientist has yet given a convincing explanation of the migrations of lemmings, not even of whether their "mass suicides" by drowning are a side-effect or the purpose of the migrations. In fact, we should like zoologists to explain how it is that this supposedly genetically-based instinct has not been bred out of the stock that resisted or survived it. Of course, the traditional belief that new breeding stock drops from the sky from time to time partly answers that objection, but no orthodox zoologist would express it openly. Sally Carrighar asserts that all the native peoples living near or within the Arctic Circle call the lemmings "mice from the sky". She continues:

"The Eskimo word is *kay-loong-meu-tuk*. Several serious-minded Eskimos told me of seeing the lemmings come down, 'falling in bigger and bigger circles that turned same way as Sun' or, as we would say, clockwise. Eskimos who had not seen the lemmings descend, could all describe lemming tracks that 'start where the lemmings landed, without any footprints going out to that place'. The late Reggie Joule, an Eskimo bush pilot and son of native teachers, said that the familiar spurs of lemming tracks are often found on the roofs of the Eskimo cabins at Point Hope, where he grew up, 'and there weren't any tracks outside the cabins.' He concluded, 'I think lemmings fly.'" The more commonly held Eskimo explanation is that lemmings float down to the Earth from some distant star.

Falls of other animals

In the Pacific, a Soviet ship spots a capsized boat. Its only survivor tells his rescuers an astounding story: "A cow fell into our boat!" The poor man is packed off to a mental institution but one official investigates further. He finds that a supply plane was smuggling a cow when the beast broke free in the cargo bay. After attempts to restrain it failed, the crew unceremoniously dumped the cow out of the hatch and into the sea … or so they thought.

When we first heard this story, we were suspicious about the absence of corroborating detail. Since then, we have noted a number of repetitions of the same story, each with its own appropriate details of location, date and people. The evidence of falls of larger animals is widespread but always circumstantial. Here are just a few items from our collections of news clippings, beginning with humble crustaceans and working up to something very strange indeed.

The German city of Paderborn was afflicted with a shower of living pond mussels on 9 August 1892, as reported in *Das Wetter* (December 1892). This was witnessed by a meteorological observer who sent an account to the Berlin Museum. A strange yellowish cloud had attracted the attention of onlookers "because of its colour and the rapidity of its motion; when it suddenly burst, a torrential rain fell with a rattling sound, and immediately afterwards the pavement was found to be covered with hundreds of the mussels". Dozens more living mussels fell within the walled confines of the Pittsburgh Gaol on 9 August 1834. The inmates were quick to seize the opportunity and most of the mussels were soon opened, salted and swallowed. *The Times* (30 September 1834) reported that the remaining mussels, some frogs and a number of largish stones (which all fell with the mussels during a storm) were put on exhibition.

On 24 April 1985, the Minneapolis *Star Tribune* reported that starfish – another rarity in the annals of falling creatures – had fallen on parts of St Cloud, Minnesota, three days earlier. It was supposed that students from the nearby State University had thrown them off a high building, a mile away, into the wind, but they turned out to be a type found only hundreds of miles to the south, off Florida.

From Fort's collection we select the following examples of snake falls. The *Scientific American* in 1860 tells of a man walking in the rain down a street in South Granville, New York, who, hearing a sound at his feet, looks down and sees a stunned snake which quickly revives and wriggles off. *Pearson's Weekly* (June 1900) reports a shower of "poisonous young rattlesnakes" dropping from the sky onto a party of Irish immigrants in Arizona, some thirty-five years previously. Conventionalists argued that they were there hidden on the ground in the first place, and were woken by the rain. Rather harder to explain are the "many thousands" of dark brown snakes found squirming on sidewalks, in backyards and along streets after a violent storm in Memphis, Tennessee, on 15 January 1877. Conventionalists again offered an explanation – this time a whirlwind. But there is a difficulty, that even *Scientific American* acknowledged: "In what locality snakes exist in such abundance is yet a mystery." It seems the snakes were so numerous that some were in tangled clumps.

The *San Francisco Chronicle* (27 October 1956) tells of the mystery of the Philippine monkey in the backyard of Mrs Faye Swanson of San Mateo, California. On the morning of 26 October, Mrs Swanson stepped into her yard to find the dead monkey in a position that suggested it had fallen from above, striking her clothes-line, splintering its solid post. Assuming it had fallen from a plane,

In an inspirational tract of 1489, the religious scholar Franciscus de Reza illustrated a case reported by Albertus Magnus of a calf raised into the sky by the drawing power of the Sun's rays.

the police and Civil Aviation Authority made an investigation but failed to find a culprit. There had been no planes over the area that day, leaving the official spokesman at a loss to account for a falling monkey.

Frank Edwards reports a very similar occurrence, also involving a backyard in California. In his *Strange World* (1964) he tells how the Trucker family heard a heavy thump outside their Long Beach home, one day in the autumn of 1960. The noise was followed by a loud, pained grunt and, stepping into the yard to investigate, they found a surly five-foot alligator. The Truckers were convinced the saurian had just dropped in.

Perhaps a similar fall accounts for the alligator found frozen to death, in 1892, in Wisconsin, hundreds of miles north of its usual habitat in the south-eastern US. Among other cases we could mention, we note a fall of young alligators in South Carolina reported in *The New York Times* (26 December 1877) with no mention of a storm or a whirlwind: "Dr J.L. Smith, of Silverton

Western Mail

After a violent hailstorm one September night in 1981, Cliff Davies of Killay, Swansea, found dozens of crabs on his lawn.

Township, while opening up a new turpentine farm, noticed something fall to the ground and commence to crawl toward the tent where he was sitting. On examining the object he found it to be an alligator. In the course of a few moments a second one made its appearance. This so excited the curiosity of the Doctor that he looked around to see if he could discover any more, and found six others within a space of two hundred yards. The animals were all quite lively and about twelve inches in length. The place whereon they fell is situated on high sandy ground about six miles north of the Savannah River."

The most astounding record of a falling – or teleporting – alligator we know of occurs in John Toland's sober history of dirigibles, *Ships in the Sky* (1957). In 1934, the US Navy airship *Macon* was on its way westwards after successfully participating in Caribbean manoeuvres as an experimental lookout under the command of Leading Chief Robert "Shaky" Davis. "The return trip was a quiet, uneventful one," writes Toland, "and throughout Shaky Davis wandered about the ship in contented unease. Just as the ship was crossing into California, late in the afternoon of May 17, he heard a loud splashing over his head from one of the ballast bags. Suspecting a major casualty, he climbed into the rigging. The splashing was louder. He opened the ballast bag and looked in. Swimming around excitedly was a two-foot alligator."

According to Toland, the presence of the interloper was never explained. The incident occurred several days into the flight and it seems inconceivable that the restless captain could not have detected its noisy presence before. The circumstances are strongly suggestive of teleportation and it is acceptable to us that if the ballast bag of water, or the airship, had not surrounded the errant alligator's appearing point at the right moment, it would have been a case of "Look out, below!"

Our prize exhibit is the following account of a completely unknown type of animal. In his *Brontologia theologico-historia* (1721), Rhyzelius, Bishop of Linkoping in Sweden reports that a strange creature "like a beaver" dropped into a street in Norrkoping during a thunderstorm in August 1708. Its startling appearance terrified the townsfolk, who took it for a troll.

After the publication of an earlier version of this book, we were contacted by Swedish fortean Sven Rosén who had traced the story to an even earlier source – Gustaf Otto Bilberg's *Almanackia* (1709). Bilberg wrote: "On the night between August 8 and 9, a great thunderstorm with continuous lightning raged over the country and set many villages on fire, causing much damage. Then, according to testimonies by trustworthy men, it so happened that in Norrkoping, just as the lightning flashed and the thunder and rain seemed heaviest, a strange animal fell from the sky into a street not far away from the chemist's shop. It somewhat resembled a beaver, but its body was a little smaller than that of a full grown beaver, although its head was a bit larger, and its lower jaw a little longer than its upper jaw. It had rather small eyes, short hind legs and a tail, and rough brownish fur."

According to Rosén, the astronomer and mathematician Bilberg (who was in Norrkoping at the time but didn't see the creature) scorned as ridiculous the rumour that the thing was a troll. It was spread, he said, by the gossip of people who had not seen the carcass. Bishop Rhyzelius refers to the view of a local scholar, that a leather worker had poured into the street a barrel of seal lard that had gone bad. This is far from being a valid conclusion as the bishop and his informants assume that the barrel contained the body of a flayed or bald young seal, revealed by the heavy rain; and the description given by Bilberg is not very seal-like. All Bilberg could suggest was that the animal had been transported by a whirlwind, but what it was and where it came from he was unable to say.

Missiles from above

Pierre Gassendi (1592–1655) and Antoine Lavoisier (1743–94) are just two of the pioneering scientists who investigated reports of stones dropping out of the sky. Having touched them, probed them, and cross-examined witnesses, neither could face the implications of the evidence they had unearthed. "There are no stones in the sky," Lavoisier, infamously, told the Academy of Sciences in Paris, "therefore stones cannot fall from the sky." On 13 September 1768, a meteorite weighing seven and a half pounds dropped, with a loud explosion, near Luce, in Maine, France. Lavoisier made his investigations once more, but concluded the stone must be of terrestrial origin, probably unearthed by being struck by lightning. "In spite of the belief of the ancients," he wrote, "true physicists have always been doubtful about the existence of these stones."

The existence of meteorites is so obvious to us now that it seems incredible that intelligent minds could so stubbornly hold onto opinions in the face of overwhelming data to the contrary. Both believers and sceptics use this stick to beat each other with. Non-scientists can often be forgiven their ignorance, but Lavoisier's obstinate stand against meteorites – like Voltaire's against fossils and Sir Richard Owen's against Darwinism – shows how the narrow-mindedness of scientists can actually hinder the development of science. The existence of meteorites was finally accepted in 1803, but falls of a non-meteoric character, which often occur in odd circumstances or in connection with other phenomena, still raise some interesting questions. For instance, it is a little known fact that the famous Dharmsala meteorite, which fell in India on 28 July 1860, was not only covered with ice but preceded several unusual occurrences.

Dharmsala's Deputy Commissioner reported, in the *Canadian Institute Proceedings* (vol.2, no.7, p.98) that within months of its descent there was a fall of fishes at Benares, a fall of red matter at Furruckabad, an earthquake, a dark spot on the Sun's disc, an "unnatural darkness of some duration" and peculiar auroral displays. The evening after the event, he himself saw many lights in the sky that, today, would probably be called UFOs. The first great catalogue of meteorites, compiled by R.P. Greg, describes the Dharmsala object as "so intensely cold as to benumb the fingers and hands" (*Report of the British Association*, 1860). In any conventional sense, the Dharmsala phenomenon does not seem to have been meteoric in origin.

The most interesting and unusual falls of stones are those that fall slowly; those associated with a particular person; and those which seem to have some kind of portentous significance. We pick a few stories at random. *The Times* (1 May 1821) reports showers of stones falling upon a house in Truro, Cornwall, during many days of guarding and investigation by the mayor, soldiers and others.

In Charleston, South Carolina, on 4 September 1886, stones bounced off the pavement outside the offices of the *Charleston News and Courier*. It was 2.30am, and no one could see any likely perpetrator, but the stones were found to be warm. Two days later the edition of the paper carried the testimony of the editor, who had

Harrow Observer

stones continued to fall around the girl. Weeks of fruitless investigation followed and, all the while, the girl was persecuted by showers of large stones, even as the police watched.

A disturbing case of a personalized stone fall was reported in the *Journal* of the International Fortean Organization (INFO). On the evening of 27 October 1973, two men fishing in a lake at Skaneatles, New York, were disturbed by a large stone splashing into the water near them. It was followed by a second and third stone, each progressively larger. They searched the area with their torches but saw nothing. Then a rain of small pebbles around them forced them to pack up. The pebble shower seemed to follow them as they ran to their car. They drove off in a hurry but, later, when they stopped to change their clothes, stones fell on them again. They stopped for a drink and were bombarded once more as they emerged from the bar; and again when they parted company outside one of their homes. The only comment from orthodoxy was the analysis on samples (grabbed by the men) by the Geology Department of Syracuse University; they identified the pebbles as local rock-types (*INFO Journal*, n.14).

A stone-throwing poltergeist had first manifested itself at a farm at Mayanup in 1955. Cyril Penny, a young Aborigine farm worker, went to see the phenomenon with many others. Two years later stones began raining around Cyril at Pumphrey in Western Australia. Conventionalists explained it away as due to "freak winds", but there seems to have been a lot more to it than that. Two witnesses swore that, while they were in a closed tent with the young man, stones fell at their feet. There had been no trickery, they said, and no holes in the tent material from either stones or freak winds (*The Daily Express*, 22 March 1957). Fed up with the persecution at Pumphrey, Penny relocated to a new camp 16km away, but stones fell on him there too, so he was advised by tribal elders to move out of the district entirely. That worked, but as the phenomenon died away at Pumphrey, it started up on the Dickson farm fourteen kilometres away.

A car had its bonnet smashed by a massive ice-block in Pinner, Middlesex, on 25 March 1974. This is just one fragment of the ice-block.

himself witnessed two further showers of warm stones at 7.30am and 1.30pm on the same day. He noticed that the missiles seemed to come from a point overhead and were, strangely, confined to an area of about 75 square feet.

The *Rand Daily Mail* (29 May 1922) carries an even stranger story. For several months a chemist's shop in Johannesburg, South Africa, was bombarded with stones. The phenomenon was thought to centre on a Hottentot girl employed there, so the police staked out the garden and the girl was sent into the shop. Stones were seen to fall in quantities vertically all around her. The police noted this verticality because they were hoping to trace an accomplice by the trajectory. They searched the vicinity, nevertheless, while the

Like Cyril Penny, Mr Dickson had made the trip to Mayanup to gawp at the phantom stone-thrower and it seemed to have followed him home. The phenomenon seemed to concentrate on Dickson's son Harvey – just eleven years old at the time – but never hurt him. On one occasion a storm of stones raged around Harvey as he sat in his father's car with the windows up. According to Healy and Cropper, the phenomenon was not confined to stones. "Stones fell indoors and outdoors or rose from the ground to the roof. Shovels jumped and a four-gallon drum soared into the air, circling three times before landing. Visitors saw half-bricks, potatoes, bottles, stones, a spade and a broom fall out of thin air." The Haunted Farm, as it is called, has ever since been visited by such disturbances.

Healy and Cropper go on to detail two other older cases, at Cooyal in 1887 and Guyra in 1921, both of which mixed stone falls with classic poltergeist phenomena. Blows would be felt on the sides of houses, strong enough to shake the buildings, yet little damage was done. Stones that should have hurt people, by virtue of their size or speed, struck them gently and harmlessly. Finally Healy and Cropper tell of their personal investigation of the "haunting" at Humpty Doo, near Darwin in the Northern Territory. Once more they found a baffled community, a variety of flying and falling objects, and (despite close vigils) no detectable culprit or method.

One detail – possibly unique in the annals of falls – occurred in February, when residents noticed long, shallow troughs in the gravel driveway, shortly after being showered with gravel. One evening, a visitor said he saw a small, black, spherical object, flying from the driveway, through the porch and away at high speed. It was trailing a long stream of gravel behind it. "He may have caught a glimpse of a polt reloading," remarked Healy and Cropper.

Something similar happened to Miyi Shiongi, a South African woman. Her stone-thrower followed her about and terrified neighbours to such an extent that she was driven out of Lombani village in July 2004. She went to live with rela-

A Turkish painting showing an incident in which a rain of stones, dropped by birds, saved Mecca from the attacking Yemenite army.

tives in Nhombelani village and, within two days, stones rained on her again. She believes she has been cursed by a Zimbabwean trader for welshing on the credit he gave her. When it first started, the family called the police, saying: "We were up nearly the whole night and saw stones falling from the sky like rain." They searched roofs and the environs for stone-throwers but found nothing that could account for the strange rain. Her mother told of a hissing sound when the stones hit their roof, some seeming to pass through the roof and fall inside the house. Those that fell inside Miyi's own room had her family screaming in terror (News24, 2 August 2004). Untraceable stone-throwers and falls inside rooms are a familiar feature of many poltergeist accounts and stories of haunted houses.

These stories seems to us to have more in common with the poltergeist cases given elsewhere in this book – see THE MATERIALISATION AND FLIGHT OF OBJECTS (p.11) – than with a natural phenomenon, especially when the rains of stones occur inside. We return to this theme in HAUNTED PEOPLE AND PLACES (p.196).

By far the largest category of falls in our files is that of ice, in particular large jagged chunks of ice. Various theories have been put forward to account for them: that they are fragments of ice comets; that they were created in storm clouds by strong winds or by super-lightning in the upper atmosphere; that they formed from leakage from aircraft toilets. None of these explain every occurrence and we must warn against excessive reliance on the apparently rational explanation that they drop off aircraft, by pointing to the abundance of cases from before the advent of powered flight.

The astronomer Camille Flammarion refers to a huge mass – 4.5m long, 2m wide and over 3m thick – falling at the time of Charlemagne (L'Atmosphere, 1888). The Times (14 August 1849) reported that the previous evening an irregular shaped mass of ice had fallen at Ord, Ross-shire, after an extraordinary peal of thunder. It was about six metres in circumference and must have weighed nearly half a ton. According to Dr George Buist, a number of massive "hailstones" have fallen in India, including one at Khandesh in 1826, which was apparently 1m wide, and at Seringapatam, around the year 1800, which was said to have been "the size of an elephant. It took three days to melt."

Every so often the planet's weather conditions inflict a devastating storm of giant hail on some of its long-suffering inhabitants. According to The Guinness Book of World Records, one of the worst in modern times occurred in Bangladesh in 1986. Individual hailstones weighed in at a kilogram each and killed 92 people. The legends of Nepal and Tibet are replete with gods, saints and magicians who can bring down a terrifying rain of these lethal missiles upon their enemies.

Perhaps the most dramatic event of this nature came to light in 1942 when the well-preserved remains of more than two hundred people were revealed near the Roopkund glacier in the remote Himalayan region of Gahrwal, 16,500ft above sea level. It is estimated that as many as six hundred bodies may still lie under the ice. Those

Dorset Evening Echo

Steve Clark and some of the dozens of red and blue stones that fell outside his house in Kings Road, Radpole in Dorset, over a weekend in December 1994. He was alerted by a man who saw them fall as he sat in his car. "There are too many of them to have been thrown by children," he said, adding that he didn't recognize them as anything local.

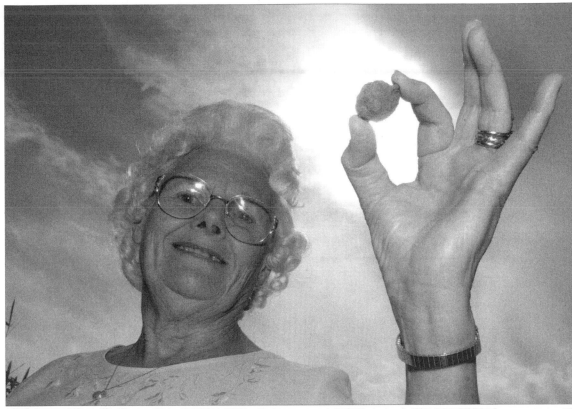

Pauline Aguss of Lowesoft, Suffolk, was hanging out her washing when she felt something hit her arm. Looking down she was horrified to see a large gash, bleeding profusely. Later, her husband Jack found a brown, metallic-looking, walnut-sized pebble where she had been standing and it was sent to the British Astronomical Association for identification. It is possible it was connected to the Perseid meteor shower, which occurs annually about this time.

recovered had died from massive blows to their skulls 1,154 years ago. Recent work by teams from Delhi University and the Deccan College, sponsored by National Geographic, studied the head-wounds and the DNA of the bodies; their results suggested that they were a mixed group of high-caste Hindu pilgrims from central India, trapped by bad weather near Roopkund Lake. "Our view is that they were killed by giant hailstones," said Dr Subash Walimbe, who described the hail as "blunt objects the size of cricket balls" travelling at 160km/h (100mph).

The ice fall phenomenon came to world attention in 2000 when a swarm of large chunks fell across Spain in the week up to 20 January, fortunately not as fatal as those of the Himalayas. Accounts vary according to source, but 10 blocks were said to have fallen in the week up to the 17th, including one seen to fall in the centre of Cadiz; forty on the 18th (the majority of which were later found to be misidentifications or hoaxes); and six on the 19th (said to have fallen in a straight line from Valencia in the north to La Union in the south). One woman claimed to have been hit on the 20th; and before that, on the 10th, a two-kilogram block smashed into a car at Tocina. There were other reports, too, from Italy, Austria, Argentina, the Netherlands, Colombia, and Canada.

Such was the prominence given to the stories that a number of scientific studies were under-taken, including one by the Consejo Superior de Investigaciones Científicas (CSIC), an elite research committee created formed by leading members of Spanish academia. The CSIC study found that the authentic chunks were not frozen

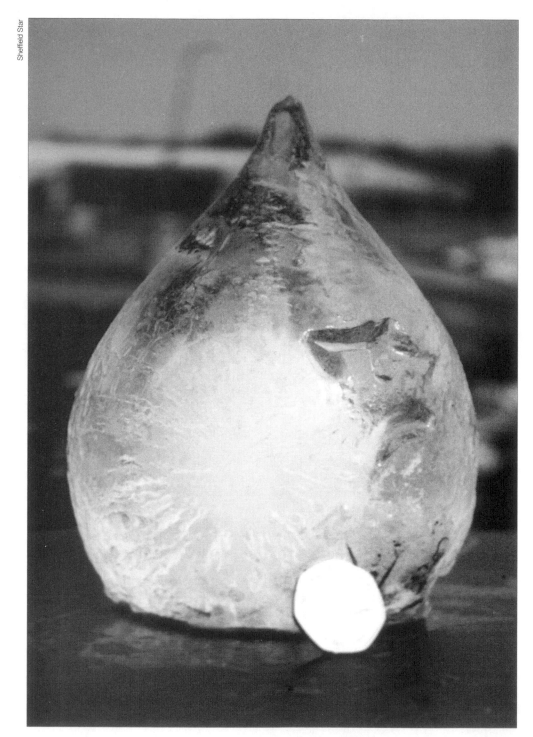

This magnificent teardrop of ice is nearly *double* the weight of the largest recorded hailstones.
It fell out of the sky over Ecclesfield, near Sheffield and landed on a grass verge. In March 1996
it was rescued and photographed by firemen from the Tankersley station. It weighed about 1.8kg.

waste from aircraft and, in any case, had fallen well away from commercial flight paths. Their spokesman said that as the sky was clear in most cases, "there was no obvious meteorological condition to explain them". Even though the break-up of a hypothetical ice-comet would account for the distribution and number of missiles, he added, they would have been large enough to show up on radar and a search of records found no trace of them.

The most damning problem for conventional explanations is that the largest known hailstones – known as hydrometeors – rarely exceed one kilogram by much, such as in the case of the lethal hail at Roopkund Lake. The Spanish hail of 2000 was generally twice that size and it was suggested that some blocks could have been up to 100 times larger before melting or shattering on impact. As size depends upon how long they can be suspended in freezing updrafts, meteorologists are stumped as to how something so massive could have formed in the stratosphere, a region known to be short on moisture.

This particular problem fascinated Jesus Martínez-Frías, a planetary geologist with the Centrefor Astrobiology in Madrid (who also works for the CSIC) as soon as he began his own study of the 2000 Spanish swarm. He confirmed that the ice they were able to analyse matched the isotopic and chemical composition of frozen rainwater. In addition, the presence of some air bubbles and evidence of layering convinced him they were a species of hailstone and not fragments of an ice comet.

Martínez-Frías coined the term megacryometeors in a statement in 2002 and it seems to have "taken". Early in August 2005, a huge lump of clear ice crashed through the roof of John Worthy's home in Fontana, California, as he was doing the dishes. The news media reported it as a megacryometeor. (NBC4.tv, 14 August 2005)

Once again, we observe that a classic fortean phenomenon can be absorbed smoothly into the scientific pale as soon it is given pseudo-scientific credibility with an impressive new name.

Cases continue to be reported to this day and there have been some spectacular incidents. In November 1950, a farm on Exmoor, in Devon, was found littered with lumps of ice the "size of dinner-plates". Among them was a dead sheep, its neck cleanly slashed by the 14lb chunk embedded in the ground by its shoulder (London *Evening News*, 9 November 1950). But this hardly compares with the thousands of sheep killed by ice bombardment in Texas, as reported in *Monthly Weather Review* (May 1877); nor with the bizarre death of a carpenter on the roof of his house near Düsseldorf, Germany, on 10 January 1951, skewered by a spear of ice 15cm in diameter and 2m long.

Falls of artefacts

The largest category of artefact falls are stones that have apparently been worked. Ancient flints and shaped stones – called variously "thunder-stones", "thunderbolts", "sky-axes" and "lightning arrows" – are universally prized as talismans against lightning. C. Blinkenberg's *Thunder Weapons* (1911) states that the natives of Burma, China and Japan believed these objects to be manufactured in the sky. Tallius, writing in 1649, alluded to the belief that thunder-stones "are generated in the sky by fulgurous exhalation conglobed in a cloud by the circumfused humour". An impressive explanation for those who understood it, and certainly ahead of its time. Several centuries were to pass before scientific orthodoxy was ready to accept that stones could fall from the sky.

Fort was particularly interested in the number of accounts in which "axe-shaped" stones were found near lightning strikes or were embedded in trees struck by lightning. Blinkenberg says that, as far and wide as Jamaica, Norway, Malaya and the British Isles, it is popularly believed that these "axes" come down with the lightning. To these Fort adds the similar beliefs of the Indians of North America and South America.

When we see the term "sky weapons", we immediately think of the numerous cultural traditions of gods or spirits with supernatural weapons – Jove with his thunderbolts or Thor and his thunder-hammer. The Anglo-Saxons believed that fairies manufactured and threw tiny, enchanted missiles they called "elf-shot" or "fairy arrows" (see THE PHYSICAL FRAGMENTS

OF FAIRYLAND, p.142). These were regarded as particularly terrifying, since to be struck by one meant being knocked senseless and was followed by bad luck, disaster and illness. (Some etymologists think this may be the origin of the usage of the word "stroke" to mean a paralytic seizure following brain haemorrhage; others say it refers to a stroke or touch of God's hand.)

A fine, modern account of "elf-shot" is related in A.A. MacGregor's book, *The Haunted Isles* (1933): "A specimen of these fairy arrows was picked up at Loch Maddy some years ago by a young girl, who on going out into the darkness for an armful of peats, heard something whizz through the air and drop at her feet." When we come upon data repeating in different countries and times, we think of folk-memories that may once have been founded on real incidents and vice versa; what was once a fiction has a way of becoming fact.

One of the strangest Christian traditions holds that the "Pillar of Saragossa" was carried to that place by angels in the company of the Virgin Mary (during her lifetime), and that from the top of it she gave instruction to the Apostle St James. The traditions of cultures all over the world include artefacts, like the Pillar, that are alleged to have fallen from the sky. They used to be held sacred, preserved in temples or put to magical use; nowadays they languish in museum basements, or in some forgotten display, labelled "Stone Age Ritual Object" or something similar. We note with interest that R.P. Greg's great meteorite catalogue in the *Report of the British Association* (1860) lists a pillar-like worked stone that fell from the sky in Constantinople in about AD 416.

A disc of worked stone, "très régulier", fell at Tarbes, France, in June 1887. The *Comptes rendus* (1887) suggested a whirlwind was responsible, but the stone came down without attendant debris and was covered in ice. Data like this directly challenges the orthodox definition of "meteorite" as merely fragments of nickel-iron asteroids. Another challenge is posed by the 1910 controversy, which raged in the pages of *Scientific American*, when Charles F. Holder announced that he had deciphered a deeply incised inscription on "a strange stone resembling a meteorite"

A rain of crosses in 1503 as recorded by Lycosthenes in *Prodigiorum ac ostentorum* (1557).

A red-hot chain fell on a bulldozer at Rockhill, Missouri, on 14 May 1959.

which had fallen into the Yaqui Valley, Mexico. Holder's assertion that the signs were Mayan was easy to discredit, and the matter was conveniently dropped, leaving uninvestigated the original claim that a stone bearing inscriptions had descended to the Earth.

All kinds of balls – big and small, metal and plastic – have dropped since the early nineteenth century. At Bijori, India, beads of many colours, holed ready to string, have apparently fallen regularly for nearly a hundred years. At times they are so plentiful that you can scoop them up by the handful. According to *FATE* (January 1955) all efforts to trace the source have failed. Similarly, a police investigation failed to account for the rain of golf balls that occurred during a storm at Punta Gorda, Florida, on 3 September 1969.

Police were similarly baffled by a "small, egg-shaped canister" that fell from the sky onto a farm near Muchea, Western Australia. The canister disintegrated, but the farmer collected a sample of the liquid oozing from it. He described it as "green bubbling fluid". This reminds us of the Chinese folk tale about Lei Kung, the Duke of Thunder, in which the god drops a bottle of healing lotion

down from heaven to help a woman who had been struck by lightning (see E.T.C. Werner's *Myths and Legends of China*, 1922). Parallels could be found in modern accounts of the sky-gods, the extraterrestrials (see OTHERWORLDLY ABDUCTION, p.166).

In October 1975, Lynn Connolly was in her garden in Hull, hanging washing, when she felt a light tap on her head. She reached up to find a small silver notecase tangled in her hair. If it fell from the clear sky, it cannot have fallen a great distance or she would surely have been harmed. Perhaps it "materialized" close to her head? It was engraved with initials and the word "Klaipeda", an old Lithuanian seaport, had a clip-on pencil and, inside, a half-used notepad. When *Fortean Times* correspondent Anthony J. Bell went to see Mrs Connolly, she confessed that she had experienced much odd phenomena since childhood, reminding us of the poltergeist targets in earlier chapters.

Fortean archives contain a huge catalogue of artefact falls. Four times during 1968 a mix of mud, wood-chunks, stones, broken glass and pottery fell during storms on the Cuban town of

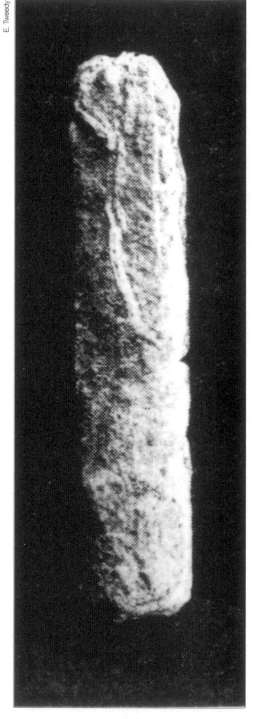

An unusual "meteorite", thought to be a 12-inch cylinder of marble that fell in Ohio in August 1910.

Piñar del Rio (*Beyond* magazine, October 1969). On the night of 12 October 1888, a great quantity of nails dropped out of the night sky onto the wife of the lighthouse keeper at Point Isabel, Texas. The *St Louis Globe-Democrat* (16 October 1888) said the nail-shower was repeated the next night but, this time, accompanied by clods of earth and oyster shells. The report attracted crowds of sightseers, many of whom later testified to seeing nails plummeting down near the lighthouse.

The periodic rains of airplane parts tend to have a reasonable explanation, but we collect them nonetheless. For example, in 1969, a wheel dropped out of the sky and badly damaged the roof of a car travelling along a road in Palm Springs, California. According to *The New York Times* (17 April 1969), investigating authorities could find no report of any plane with a missing wheel.

A particular favourite with us are falls inside rooms, for they seem doubly damned. A rain of buckshot fell at intervals over several days inside an office at Newton, New Jersey. *The San Francisco Chronicle* (3 March 1929), called it the greatest mystery in the history of the town; and there was no apparent means by which the shot could have entered the building. After a similar case was reported in the *Religio-Philosophical Journal*, its issue for 24 April 1880 carried a correspondent's description of bullets that fell at intervals in broad daylight in every room of his house in 1867. The falls of "large birdshot" increased to last an hour or more and yet, whenever he went to gather them up, he could never find more than half a dozen. The rest had vanished as mysteriously as they came.

Particularly well observed, among indoor falls, were the pieces of furnace-made brick that kept up a regular rain inside various rooms of the Sri Aurobindo Ashram at Pondicherry, India, in December 1921. The *Bulletin of the Sri Aurobindo International Centre of Education* (February 1974) has a lengthy recollection by an eyewitness to continuous falls in the courtyard, kitchen and stairwell, although searches revealed no culprit or cause. Observers reported that the bricks were visible only a little distance below the level of the roof, as though they simply came into being at that height, falling as soon as they materialized. Some of the residents noticed that the phenomenon seemed associated with a young boy, assistant to the cook. They locked

The garage in Athron Street, Doncaster, in South Yorkshire, had a reputation for being haunted by ghosts of people killed in World War II. In March 2003, the apparitions gave way to typical poltergeist activity; tyres were moved around overnight and things were thrown around and once, garage manager Nigel Lee was pelted with stones as he worked alone outside. But the real curiosity was the continuous lobbing of small denomination coins, witnessed on many occasions by customers and visitors. Nigel said he had collected about £7.

him in a room with no apertures, and bricks still fell around him, wounding him. Forty-one years earlier, in a schoolroom near Government House in Madras, bricks had also fallen, and had continued to fall in the presence of thirty investigators for at least five days. *The Madras Mail* (5 March 1888), says that the clergy advised marking a brick with a white cross and placing it in the centre of the room. To their utter astonishment, "a brick of a corresponding size, but bearing a black cross, dropped out of the air onto the top of the first brick", so precisely that it stayed balanced there.

In the section on RAINS OF SEEDS AND ORGANIC MATTER (see p.58), we cite an eighth-century Irish record of a rain of silver. To many modern minds, a rain of money would be the equivalent of a rain of manna in the concrete wilderness. Most of these seem to occur during "poltergeist" hauntings: eg pennies fell with pieces of soda and lumps of coal during the famous 1927–28 disturbance at Battersea, London, investigated and recorded by Harry Price in *Poltergeist Over England* (1945). One of the most devastating poltergeists of all time is that which completely

demolished a house near the Sorbonne, Paris, in 1849. The continuous bombardment of building materials every night for three weeks is recorded in the official French police magazine, the *Gazette des tribunaux* (2 February 1849). The account includes an undated allusion to similar excitement in Paris, when "a rain of pieces of small money drew together the loungers of Paris every evening in the Rue de Montesquieu".

From a Finnish collection of strange tales by Aikki Perttola-Flink – *Ihmistiedon rajamailla* (1972, "On the fringe of human knowledge") translated for us by Tuuri Heporauta – comes a story of a group of young Finns whose ghost story-telling session in 1917 was interrupted by coins that fell intermittently over several hours. They would hear the metallic "clink" on the wooden parquet floor of both the dining room and the living room, then rolling in a circle before coming to rest. Becoming fearful, they called first a neighbour, then some planning officers from a nearby office, then a professor who turned up with some of his students. Also among the witnesses was a religious man who attempted to exorcise the phenomenon by reading from his Bible. When a coin fell into his open book he fled the house.

Another of the witnesses, Mrs Ester Hallio, said: "The coins continued to come down". They had amassed more than ten marks when the friends decided to spend the night at the planning office instead. When they returned in the morning the coins were still there, with another falling while one of the witnesses made a phone call. They took the coins to the Bank of Finland, who authenticated them; they then decided to spend them on a slap-up meal. It's easy to dismiss such a tale but its homely honesty comes with assurances that the witnesses were sober and truthful, that Professor Arvi Grotenfeldt's account is on record, and that the sum was "a considerable amount at that time".

Closer to home, we can report that pennies and halfpennies dropped around children going home from school in Hanham, Bristol, according to the *London People* (30 September 1956). At Meshehera, Russia, silver coins fell "all over the district" during a storm (*Daily Express*, 5 August 1940). *The People* (17 February 1957) reported that a woman at Gateshead in County Durham was in her yard when "two objects whizzed past her head" which turned out to be halfpennies. About forty to fifty pennies came down in short bursts over fifteen minutes at Ramsgate, Kent. According to the *Daily Mirror* (10 December 1968), "You could not see them falling. All you heard was the sound of them bouncing off the pavement." Curiously, they were all bent.

Rains of seeds and organic matter

Rains of blood are among the oldest prodigies known to man yet, despite many modern recurrences and ancient allusions (eg Homer and Plutarch), the phenomenon is still regarded as mythical. On 15 May 1890, a blood-like substance fell at Messignadi, Calabria. *Science News* (vol.35, p.104), reported that the Italian Meteorological Bureau identified it as bird blood. They suggested that a flock of birds had been torn apart by a violent wind – but their own records contained no mention of such a wind, nor could they explain why no carcases fell with the blood.

On 17 August 1841, workers in a tobacco field in Tennessee were startled by the rattle of large drops on the leaves. Looking closer they saw that the drops looked like blood, and that they fell perpendicularly from a peculiar red cloud overhead. They fetched the owner and a certain Professor Troost who, on arrival, saw the field strewn with foul-smelling bits of matter. The *American Journal of Science* (October 1841) carried a report from Professor Troost in which he declared that the stuff was animal fat and muscle tissue, though he would venture no opinion on the "blood". No one bothered to take statements from the workers; instead, the learned journal seemed to accuse them of perpetrating a hoax and, for reasons never explained, scattering a decayed hog over the field. In contrast, an account of flakes of meat drifting down from a clear sky into a field in Kentucky had many credible witnesses. According to the *Scientific American* (March 1876), the fall was strangely confined to the oblong field, occurring nowhere outside it. One investigator found that the meat-flakes (one was 3–4 inches square) were "perfectly fresh" and ate some. He said they tasted like "mutton or venison".

The phenomenon seems to happen far less frequently now; the most recent occurrence in our files comes from the *Flying Saucer Review* (November 1968, quoting from Brazilian papers). For more than five minutes on 27 August in that year, meat and blood fell on an area, one kilometre square, between Cocpava and São José dos Campos.

Rain can be coloured red for a number of reasons. For example, *La Nature* (28 September 1880) relates that Professor Brun of Geneva investigated reports of a blood-rain in Morocco, and found rocks and vegetation covered in dried red scales, which he identified as the remains of colonies of the minute organism *Protococcus fluvialis*. He believed that they had been deposited there by a whirlwind, but confessed he was puzzled by the extraordinary selection involved. The colonies were uniformly made up of young organisms. Other rains – red, black, yellow, etc – have been found to be coloured by varieties of dust (eg sand

A rain of blood at Lisbon in 1551, pictured by Lycosthenes in *Prodigiorum ac ostentorum* (1557).

from the Sahara), or colonies of blue-green algae, or infusoria, or pollen, or the exudations or eggs of insects.

Other falls of organic matter are more enigmatic, such as the jelly-like substance believed by rural folk to have fallen from the stars in association with a light. According to the *Scientific American* (vol.2, p.79), a bright object, four feet in diameter, was seen to fall, at Loweville, New York, on 11 November 1846, and subsequently became – or left behind – a mass of "foetid jelly". More recently, the Dublin *Evening Herald*, 7 February 1958, reported a strange light passing over West Meath and landing in a field. It was thought to be a UFO, but investigators rushing to the spot found only a mass of what they called "bog butter".

The continuity of this phenomenon is well documented. For example, the Bishop of Cloyne, writing in 1696 (quoted in *Philosophical Transactions*, vol.19, p.224) spoke of many such falls in his lifetime in Ireland, and said that this "bog butter", whatever it is, was highly prized by the local people as a treatment for scalds. Professor McKenny Hughes, in *Nature* (23 June 1910), wrote that the notion of falling stars turning into jelly was very common; he claimed he had seen "the rot of the stars" for himself and that the Welsh called it *Pwdre Ser*. Attempts to explain it as the gelatinous fungus *Tremella mesenterica* are inconclusive.

Fort advanced the idea that, just as nourishment is supplied to the developing parts of

an egg, perhaps these organic and vegetable falls are attempts by our existence to nourish itself, or a vestige of the processes that originally prepared our environment for our arrival. Eccentric though this sounds, it is quite in accordance with the evidence: for, as we hope we have shown, things do fall from the heavens, and many of them are alive and edible. There was, after all, a positive response to the Israelites' prayers for quails and manna, and, as far as we know, showers of edible lichen still occur in Asia Minor to this day.

The seeds that rained into the streets of Kirkmanshaws, Persia, in 1913, were thought to be manna, but they were later identified (London *Daily Mail*, 13 August 1913) as "like Indian corn". *INFO Journal* (no.8, 1972), tells of a rain of West African beans on a farm in northwest Brazil in the summer of 1971. In these cases and others, we note how predictable it is that the whirlwind explanation is brought in, often without regard for the circumstances. Consider the torrent of an incalculable number of strange seeds upon several towns in the Italian province of Macerata in 1897. In *Notes and Queries* (18 September 1897) they are identified as fruit of the Judas tree, a native of Central Africa, and most were in the first stage of germination. What kind of whirlwind can pick up *only* these seeds in such quantity (no twigs, leaves, etc) and transport them to Italy, keeping them together in the air without dropping any in between?

Records of seed falls in medieval chronicles are more numerous than those of frog falls. A good example is in the *Annals of Clonmacnoise*, which exists only as a sixteenth-century English translation of the lost Irish original. Niall Frosach began his reign as a king in Ireland, in AD 759, while a severe famine gripped the land. He made a public appeal to God, praying, in the company of "seven godly bishops", on a hill at Ard-Uilline. Three strange rains followed; first silver, then honey and finally wheat. The record says it was "pure wheat, which covered all the fields over that the like was never seen before, soe that there was such plenty & aboundance of wheat that it was thought that it was able to maintaine many kingdoms". Even if the first two rains seem fanciful, the account of the third comes across as one of honest astonishment.

In 1749, Dr Thomas Short of Sheffield published his *General Chronological History of the Air*, which compiled meteorological data from old histories. Although modern historians regard his methodology as unreliable and often unreferenced, it is worth noting some of his entries on this topic. In Campania, in 722, there was a fall of wheat and barley; in Saxony, in 987, something like wheat came down; and near Oxford, in 1656, a further fall of wheat occurred.

Fortunately, the phenomenon has continued and reliable reports can be found; for example, the *Philosophical Transactions* (vol.16, p.281) states that grains of wheat fell in Wiltshire in 1686 but contained in hailstones. In our own time it rained rice on Mandalay, Burma, where, according to the *Daily Telegraph* (10 January 1952), people in the streets gathered handfuls. In 1950 men working high on New York's Empire State Building were stung by an odd-looking hail that turned out to be grains of barley (*FATE*, April 1951).

Nuts have rained, too. On the night of 9 May 1867 a number of streets in Dublin were peppered with hardened berries, "like a very small orange … and when cut across seem as if made of some hard, aromatic dark brown wood". Further accounts of them were published in Symons' *Meteorological Magazine* (June 1867): one said they had fallen "in great quantities and with great force", driving even policemen with protective helmets to take shelter; another declared them to be hazelnuts which had been "preserved in a bog for centuries". The author of that last opinion never revealed how he arrived at this conclusion or suggested how they might have been plucked from the bog by a whirlwind.

According to Charles Fort's notes, the following year (1868) saw nearly simultaneous rains of small black stones in Italy, Hungary, Switzerland and Birmingham, England. What if they were not stones but shrivelled hazelnuts? We raise the question because Birmingham had seen a number of frog and stone falls. In 1868 hazelnut husks came down with stones in a prodigious shower (Birmingham *Daily Post*, 1 June 1868).

On 13 March 1977 hazelnuts dropped into a Bristol street beside Alfred Wilson Osborne and his

Roland Moody with some of the broad beans and other seeds that deluged his home in Southampton in 1979.

A shower of wheat, one of a number of "strange signs" in the year 1680, which the writer and illustrator of a contemporary broadside hoped would make the sinful repent.

wife, making clicking sounds on the pavement. Mr Osborne, a chess correspondent for a local newspaper, thought at first that buttons had come off his coat, but quickly realized something had fallen from the clear sky. Suddenly, hundreds more nuts fell around them. Another person experienced a nut shower on the same spot a few minutes later. Mr Osborne bit into one and said it was "fresh and sweet" but not only were there no nut trees in the vicinity, the hazelnut season is much later in the year. "I have thought that a vortex [might have] sucked them up, but I don't know where you suck up hazelnuts in March," he said.

The experience of Roland Moody (pictured opposite), in 1979, is even stranger. The conservatory at the back of his Southampton house was the target for many kinds of falling seed. On the morning of 12 February he heard a "whoosh" on the glass roof. It was snowing so he took no notice until, nearly an hour later, the sound came again. He found the entire roof covered with many thousands of tiny mustard and cress seeds. "The cress seeds were coated in jelly," he said. There were five or six more batches through the day covering Mr Moody's entire garden.

The next day, he consulted his neighbours. One, Mrs Stockley, had some in her garden and then made a startling confession to Mr Moody. The previous year, she said, the same seeds had fallen to cover her front garden and it had taken all year to get rid of them. The phenomenon did not end there. The following day down came peas, maize and haricot beans, while his neighbours on both sides were pelted with bean and pea seeds. Mrs Stockley, interviewed for Arthur C. Clarke's TV series *Mysterious World* in 1980, said "I got masses of broad beans every time I opened my front door. They travelled right up the hall into the kitchen, which is some ten yards." Police were called but no obvious source could be found.

Eventually the phenomenon, which targeted only these three houses in the road, faded away, but not before 10lb of beans had been collected from at least twenty-five showers. Mr Moody gathered eight bucketfuls of cress seeds from his garden alone. The victims were baffled but appreciative: when we spoke to him, Mr Moody said all the seeds they collected grew healthily and the crops were "excellent".

Erasmus Francisci, in *Der wunder-reich* (1680) has a discussion on whether seeds that fall from the sky should be eaten. He answers by citing a rain of grain in Carinthia, in 1558, that fell for two hours over an area of two square miles and yielded good bread when baked. He also referred to rains of wheat in Alsace, that occurred when the harvest failed, as evidence of God's Providence. We could add the fall of oranges near Naples in July 1833, or the young peaches at Shreveport, Louisiana, in July 1961.

Within a few years of the mighty eruption of the Indonesian volcano Krakatoa (on 28 August 1883) its remaining terrain had been recolonized by plant and even insect life. Of course we are not suggesting that they arrived by teleportation – the distributive powers of winds, ocean currents and birds are well known and sufficient – but we do wonder if falls of seeds play some part in such recoveries.

Mysterious flows and oozings

Before leaving behind this summary look at the voluminous records of strange falls, we want to mention another category of teleportation in which liquids appear from "nowhere" and ooze or flow from objects or drop down from mid-air. It was only when Charles Fort collated his notes on falls that he spotted such localized repetitions as the remarkable series at Geneva. The *Comptes rendus* (vol.5, p.549) carried a report that large, well-separated drops of warm water fell on Geneva from a clear zenith at 9am on 9 August 1837. This was repeated on 31 May the following year and twice on 11 May 1842 (*Comptes rendus*, vol.15, p.290). During a series of quakes at Inverness in June

1817 hot water fell on the 30th of that month (*Report of the British Association*, 1854, p.112).

Intense localized rain is called "point rainfall" by meteorologists. As an example, *Symons' Meteorological Magazine* (vol.47, p.140) records a "cascade" of water and hail upon an area of London of no more than 200 acres on 9 June 1809. The *Toronto Globe* (3 June 1889) described the townsfolk of Coburg, Ontario, looking up to see a vast bag-like body of water crossing the town and flopping down two miles away. It was explained away as a "waterspout".

As well as such cloudbursts, there also exist more steady flows. According to the *Comptes rendus* (vol.14, p.664) a steady stream of water fell from a stationary point in the sky over Noirfon-

A whirlwind lifts straw at Beckhampton Down, Wiltshire, in July 1989.

taine, France, for at least two days in April 1842. The *New York Sun* (24 October 1886) reported that water had been falling steadily for fourteen days out of a cloudless sky onto the same piece of ground in Chesterfield County, South Carolina. About the same time a similar fall at Aitken was confined to an area of ten square feet. The following month a fall at Dawson, Georgia, concentrated on a spot 25 feet wide. In each case it was as if an invisible, stationary tap had been left running in the sky.

In North Carolina the *Charlotte Chronicle* (21 October 1886) reported: "Citizens in the southeastern portion of the city have witnessed for three weeks or more a very strange phenomenon. Every afternoon at 3 o'clock there is a rainfall in one particular spot, which lasts for half an hour. Between two trees at the hour named there falls a gentle rain while the Sun is shining, and this has been witnessed every day during the past three weeks." A Signal Service observer later sent a report on this to the *Monthly Weather Review* (October 1887), saying he had seen it himself over several days. The trees were red oaks and "sometimes the precipitation falls over an area of half an acre, but always appears to centre at these two trees, and when lightest, there only".

At Brownsville, Pennsylvania, it was a peach tree that received this watery manna. According to the *St Louis Globe-Democrat* (19 November 1892), witnesses saw the water falling from a little way above the tree and covering an area round it of about fourteen feet square. Could these trees, Fort wondered, act like mediums and attract rain to themselves?

Other mysterious manifestations of liquids are called, conventionally, "poltergeist flows". In early February 1873, the Bank House at Eccleston, Lancashire, was the scene of an extraordinary series of events. Torrents of water rained down inside the rooms, soaking the elderly inhabitants and ruining their furniture. There was no question of imposture; everyone who investigated the case was impressed by the genuine misery the phenomenon caused. The water did not appear to come from leaking domestic pipes; a report in the *Chorley Standard* (15 February) noted that "the most singular feature of the affair is that the ceilings themselves were quite dry". Again, on 9 September 1880, a reporter from the *Toronto Globe* described his investigations of improbable occurrences at a farm near Wellesley, Ontario,

where windows were broken by unlocatable missiles and furniture moved about of its own volition. He told of such volumes of water falling inside the house – often while the rooms were full of sightseers – that the family's effects were ruined. Yet neither walls nor ceilings bore any trace of the water's passage.

A liquid poltergeist that plagued the (appropriately named) Waterman family of Windsor, Vermont, is recorded by Frank Edwards in *Strange World* (1964). It began one morning in September 1955, when beads of moisture appeared on their furniture as though a heavy mist had settled on it. They sponged off the strange dew, but it repeatedly returned, sometimes copiously. Checks made by service engineers found all the pipes tight and dry but the water appeared relentlessly. One day, says Edwards, as Dr Waterman "transferred a shallow dish of grapes from one room to another, it filled with water during the transit".

An article on mysterious flows of all kinds in the American paper *Grit* (26 July 1970), mentioned a watery persecution that drove the Martin family from their house in Methuen, Massachusetts, in 1963, and resumed its harassments in their new home in another city. Water was described as "spurting" from different points throughout the house, as well as seeping from the walls and ceilings. We know from studies of poltergeist cases that the activity can transfer to the new home, but we also know of cases where the disturbances have remained with the house to plague the next occupants.

The case of nine-year-old Eugenio Rossi is reminiscent of other "persecution" cases. Eugenio was in hospital in Nuoro, Sardinia, for a liver complaint, when, according to *The Sun* (30 November 1972) large quantities of water began to seep through the floorboards around his bed. He was moved five times, each time for the same reason – water came through, or appeared on, the floor around his bed. Again we read of baffled officials and service engineers failing, despite a thorough search, to find any acceptable cause. People who, even unwillingly, possess this natural affinity with water must surely have been the water-finders and rainmakers of ancient societies.

Possibly the classic case of a "liquid poltergeist" occurred at the Rectory at Swanton Novers, Norfolk, and was chronicled in most of the leading English papers of the day. On 30 August 1919, an oily substance was noticed seeping through the

The ceilings at Swanton Novers Rectory, from the *Daily Mail*, 3 September 1919. The rector, the Reverend Hugh Guy, said to a reporter who noticed drops of paraffin, "Next time it will be methylated spirit, or just water. I'm sorry you can't see it gushing … gallons of water came from that ceiling … the queer part is that the ceiling, the paper, and the laths are quite dry."

ceilings of some rooms, or rather collecting in patches on the ceilings. Over the next few days these seepings became constant flows, sometimes, as witnesses described, spurting from the walls. It was suggested the house was built over an oil well, but it was not crude oil that was flowing, but paraffin (kerosene) and petrol (gasoline). It arrived at the rate of a quart every ten minutes, and a report dated 2 September said that about fifty gallons had been caught in receptacles. Of the thirteen indoor showers on 1 September, two were of water while the others consisted of methylated spirits (alcohol) and sandalwood oil.

Everything in the house was ruined and the vapours became so dangerous that evacuation became necessary. Walls were torn open and the ceilings probed and exposed, but no clue to the flows' origin was ever found. The rector, the Reverend Hugh Guy, employed a young housemaid, and attempts were made to implicate her. The *Times* (9 September) reported that an "illusionist", Oswald Williams, while investigating the

mystery had witnessed the girl throwing water on the ceiling. On 12 September *The Times* printed an interview with the girl; she had gone into the house with Williams, and when water appeared on the ceiling Williams accused her. He gave her one minute to admit it or he would see she was sent to prison. Later she brought a charge against Williams and his wife, claiming that they had beaten her. The case was dismissed. It was never explained why the girl should spend her low wages on exotic liquids, where she could have obtained them, or how she could transport fifty gallons of oils onto a ceiling in the midst of investigations without being detected.

Liquid poltergeists remain fairly rare occurrences, but a recent example, which occurred in Rochdale, Lancashire, attracted the attention of investigator Peter Hough. Water dripping inside a house, occupied by the Gardner family, was investigated by the local council without the cause being identified. As chairman of the Northern Anomalies Research Organisation (NARO),

At the village of Arles-sur-Tech, in the Valley of Vallespir, France, close to the border with Spain, lies the abbey of Ste Marie, founded by Charlemagne in AD 778. In it is a mysterious sarcophagus bearing the Christian Chi-Rho cipher but no other identification. According to local tradition, for the last thousand years, the ancient stone container has issued a pure, fresh water credited with healing properties. It is estimated that 80–150 gallons are siphoned off each year and bottled for pilgrims. In 1794, the lid was prised off and the interior cleaned out but within a month it was full of clear water. The sarcophagus was drained and lifted and searched for pipes or, as had been supposed, a hidden mountain spring, but there was no findable source. Careful watches have been kept and no one is refilling the tomb. Analysis of the water found that it is of a different composition to local spring water and cannot be accounted for by condensation. The practical abbey and town officials decided to make the most of their good luck and tend it continuously as an historical attraction.

Hough, with a small team of fellow investigators, visited the Gardners' house on 31 August 1995; it was a hot day during a near-drought and a hose-pipe ban was in force.

The Gardners told the NARO team that the drip of water from walls and ceilings had completely disrupted their lives for the last ten months. The flow would move from room to room. "It would start dripping in one place then shoot from corner to corner", said Mrs Vera Gardner. Supposing that condensation was to blame, the council installed extraction fans, but dripping ceilings and sodden bedding continued to plague the family. Besides, as Jim Gardner pointed out, "You don't get condensation in summer."

Hough found the attic side of the ceiling, adjacent to a seeping patch in the room below, to be "bone dry". Alicia Leigh, one of the team, saw the kitchen door become wet: "I noticed the bottom of the door was wet and was about to alert the others when thousands of tiny droplets instantaneously covered the entire door. It happened right before my eyes." Stephen Mera, another NARO member, saw water flash across a bedroom ceiling as the Gardners were being questioned in another room. "It was as if the ceiling was a floor and someone had thrown a cupful of water across it." Hough said: "It had defied gravity!"

These phenomena were accompanied by the usual poltergeistery: household objects hovered and flew around, sometimes hitting the family; objects would appear and disappear; there were strange sounds and smells, and a mark appeared on Stephen's back where he felt sure a "phantom" had "flicked" him. The investigation was concluded with no one any the wiser. No source for the indoor rain could be found, and neither the NARO team's cameras nor analysis of water samples yielded anything useful. The council fobbed off the Gardners with a facile explanation; the best that Hough was able to come up with was a "poltergeist".

The most disquietening form of the appearances of liquid have occurred in several violent poltergeists cases, in which a slimy saliva-like substance is found on the young victims, often in the vicinity of "bite" marks. In 1926, the Romanian girl Eleonore Zugun was brought to London and then Berlin for study; her period of torment was coming to an end but she was still plagued by mysterious scratches and bites, now accompanied by large amounts of what looked like saliva. Samples were taken and compared to samples of Eleonore's own saliva and they were found to be quite different; Eleonore's being low in micro-organisms, and the "poltergeist dribble" high. Saliva from dribbling phantom attackers also plagued the Giles children in Bristol, during the winter of 1761–62, where they were tormented by slaps, needle pricks and savage bites – see INVISIBLE ASSAILANTS (see p.173).

All these phenomena, in different combinations, echo through this book; they indicate to us that teleportation, or something very like it, must be considered as a connecting link between them.

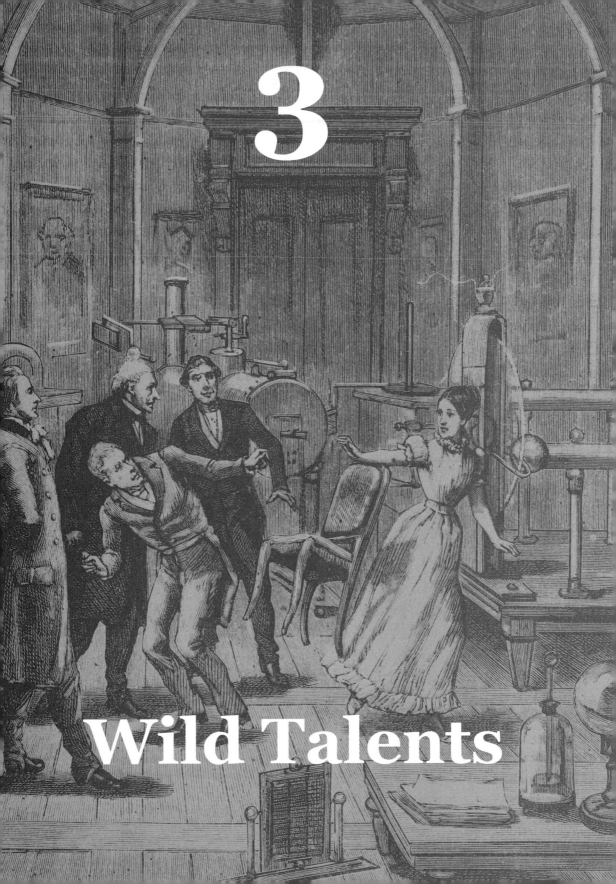

3

Wild Talents

3

Wild Talents

Fire-walking and fire-immunity

No reasonable person would attempt to walk barefoot across a pit of fiery coals or hot stones, so we can only suppose that those who do so are not in their right minds but in some other state. How is it possible for people to so delude themselves as to the nature of physical reality that they voluntarily undertake such a feat? And yet the fact is that they do – universally and with impunity. Fire-walking is one of the last remaining tokens of the power over nature attributed to the ancient magicians; and, according to Professor Mircea Eliade, modern shamans especially value it for that reason.

In *The Miracle Hunters* (1959), George Sandwith gives several detailed accounts of the Hindu fire-walks that he witnessed while a government surveyor on the island of Suva, Fiji. After one dramatic ceremony he returned to his hotel with another spectator, a banker, who was obviously deeply disturbed by the experience. "Very grudgingly he admitted the fire-walking was genuine, for he had thrown something on the pit and it caught fire at once, but he was strongly of the opinion that the Government ought to stop it! When asked why, he became very annoyed

replying that it does not conform with modern scientific discoveries. When I suggested that something of value might be learned from the fire-walkers, he was so furious he turned on his heel and left me." This turning on the heel and leaving is a not uncommon reaction among people confronted with the types of phenomena described in this book.

One of the first "scientifically controlled" fire-walks was held at Carshalton, Surrey, in September 1935 under the auspices of the University of London. The walker was a young Indian Muslim, Kuda Bux, who strode across the twenty-foot trench four times without signs of burning. It was described in *Fifty Years of Psychical Research* (1939) by Harry Price who rationalized that the secret lay in brief contact and the low thermal conductivity of the burning wood. We recently saw some unpublished notes on the incident, made at the time by Harold S.W. Chibbett, which include many of the rationalizations that he overheard that day. One doctor loudly pronounced that anyone could do it, as, despite appearances, the temperature was only that of a cup of tea (it was over 800°F). He was invited to try it if he was so sure of his theory, but declined, saying he was not suitably dressed for the occasion.

Andrew Lang, the great folklorist, was one of the first to point out the ubiquity of the fire-walking ritual. He collected many modern instances from widely separated countries but the practice was already old when it was recorded by Plato, Virgil and Strabo. Eliade pushes its antiquity back to the very origins of shamanism, and in *The Forge and the Crucible* (1979) he has much to say on fire-immunity rituals. These are practised in different forms by many people, from the fire-dancing Navajo Indians of North America to the Hindus, and even occur within a nominally Christian tradition in Europe. To this day, on the feasts of St Constantine and his mother St Helen, the villagers of Langadas in Greece dance on glowing coals, clutching icons of these saints.

Many earlier examples of fire-immunity among devout Christians are given in Father Thurston's *The Physical Phenomena of Mysticism* (1952). Olivier Leroy's key work on the subject, *Les Hommes salamandres* (1931), gives even more cases; for example it is reliably recorded that when St Polycarp of Smyrna was put to the stake in about AD 155, the flames formed an arch over him, and he was unscathed until a soldier stabbed him with a spear. The Protestants are also reported to have had their fire heroes. Vincent Gaddis in *Mysterious Fires and Lights* says that during the Huguenot revolts in seventeenth-century France, Claris, a Camisard leader, was condemned to be burnt yet continued unsinged and still talking in the midst of the flames. When the fire died down, "not only was he unhurt, but there was no mark of fire on his clothes". The Camisard general, Jean Cavalier, and other witnesses confirmed the story when they were later exiled to England.

Behind the universal demonstrations of the fact of fire-immunity lies a bewildering variety of methods by which it is achieved. Trance and religious ecstasy seem to be a vital prerequisite in the Hindu rituals (whether in India, Sri Lanka or Fiji), yet Kuda Bux and many others have reproduced the effect without trance. Sometimes there are elaborate preliminaries involving chanting, dancing and sexual abstinence, yet there are many other cases in which the walking has been performed without preparation or after a merely perfunctory ritual. E.G. Stephenson, a professor of English Literature, attended a Shinto ceremony in Tokyo and was seized by the urge to cross the ninety-foot charcoal trench himself. An officiating priest insisted that he must be "prepared" and took him to the nearby temple where the priest sprinkled salt over his head. Professor Stephenson later described, in the *Journal of Bor-*

Chief Terrii Pao. a Hawaiian Kahuna (shaman), clutching sacred leaves, walks calmly across white-hot stones.

derland Research (vols. 2 and 5), how he walked, in quite a leisurely way, over the fire and felt only a tingling in his feet. He mentions one interesting detail, that during his crossing he felt a pain in one foot and later found a small cut, evidently made by a sharp stone. Dr Harry B. Wright wrote in *True* (March 1950) of a fire-walk he witnessed on Viti Levu, Fiji, over a twenty-five-foot pit of heated stones. He imagined the walkers to be in a pain-suppressing state of ecstasy, but when he examined their feet before and immediately afterwards, he found them ordinarily sensitive to prodding with a pin or his lighted cigarette.

Saints Cosmas and Damien, two early martyrs, were brother doctors whose ministrations to the poor were unpopular with the authorities. Legend says that they were, unsuccessfully, drowned, crucified, stoned and burnt (as in this painting by Fra Angelico).

The majority of fire-walks are over beds of coals – though Dr Brigham, whose adventures in Hawaii are described later, walked on lava; and Mircea Eliade refers to the Lolo shamans of China whose speciality was a walk over glowing ploughshares, recalling the medieval Christian "trial by ordeal". Dr B. Glanvill Corney, chief medical officer of the Fiji Islands, wrote in *Notes and Queries* (21 February 1914) that he had seen five mass walks over red-hot stones and had found no burnt feet among the walkers.

Now we come to two of the central mysteries of fire-immunity: the apparent selectivity of the fire in the matter of what it will or will not burn; and the ability of certain people to bring this selectivity under their own control.

Leroy's "Human Salamander" was the sobriquet of Marie Sonet, one of the *convulsionnaires de Saint-Médard* in Paris in the 1750s (of whom a good account is given by Dr E.J. Dingwall in *Some Human Oddities*, 1947). She would lie rigid over a roaring fire for long periods of time, supported at head and feet by stools and wrapped in a sheet. She would thrust her shod and stockinged feet into a brazier of coals and withdraw them only when the hosiery was completely burnt away. Just why the shoes and stockings should

burn when the sheet did not remains a mystery, but we do know that something similar happens in a fire-walk. Max Freedom Long, in *The Secret Science Behind Miracles* (1948) quotes the account by Dr John G. Hill of a walk over red-hot stones on a Tahitian island, in which a white man took part. The pit was so hot that his face peeled, yet the glowing rocks made no impression on his leather boots.

Leroy's *Les Hommes salamandres* is also the source for what is probably the classic fire-walk, which took place near Madras in 1921 in the presence of the Catholic Bishop of Mysore (who sent the account to Leroy) and the local Maharajah. The proceedings were conducted by a Muslim, who never went into the fire himself, but conferred immunity on those who did. Many went through voluntarily; others were literally pushed into the fire by the Muslim, and the bishop tells how their looks of terror gave way to astonished smiles as they completed the walk. The Maharajah's brass band (all Christians) were induced to march through the flames, and they were so thrilled at their success that they went through a second time, trumpets blowing, cymbals clashing, etc – a performance we would have gone far to attend. According to the bishop, the flames rose up, licking their instruments and faces, yet their boots, uniforms and even sheet-music were all unscathed.

Max Freedom Long also recounts how his mentor, Dr W.T. Brigham of the British Museum, was taken onto fresh boiling lava near a volcano on Kona island by three Kahunas – local magicians. They instructed him to take his boots off as they would not be covered by the Kahuna protection, but he refused. As he watched one of the three walk calmly onto the lava flow, the other two suddenly pushed him and finding himself on the hot lava, he had no choice but to keep on running to the other side. In the course of the 150-foot dash, his boots and socks were burned off. The three Kahunas, still strolling barefoot on the lava, burst into laughter as they pointed out the trail of bits of burning leather.

What does go on in a fire-walk? Dr White expresses the widely held view that the walkers are in an exalted state of mind which suppresses pain. Yet there are fire-walks without trance or ecstasy. Neither is there any evidence to suggest that damaged tissues heal up so rapidly that they are not noticed (a process sometimes observed among Dervish, Hindu, Balinese and other body-piercing devotees). In *The Crack in the Cosmic Egg* (1973) by J.C. Pearce, the author suggests that the fire-walk is a classic illustration of the creation of a new reality (albeit temporary and local) in which fire does not burn in the familiar way. As long as this reality is maintained all is well, but the history of the fire-walk contains many accounts of gruesome fatalities and shocking damage to those whose faith snapped so that they were plunged back into the world where fire burns. The magical state of affairs in which flesh, and sometimes other material, is immune to fire is created, it seems, by the person who officiates at fire-walking ceremonies. Leroy's Muslim writhed on the ground in agony as soon as the Maharajah announced the end of the proceedings. It was explained to the bishop that the man had taken the burning upon himself. In *Women Called Wild*, Mrs Rosita Forbes describes a fire-dance ceremony in Surinam, presided over by a virgin priestess, among descendants of African slaves who had intermarried with the local Indians. The priestess was in a trance for the duration of the fire-dance, and if she had emerged from it unex-

Danny Pharr

Wings of Fire is a US organization which uses fire-walking as a transformational tool for personal growth. Here instructor Ariel Frager undergoes a fire-walk near Sonora in California. The temperature of the red-hot embers can be anything between 900°F and 1200°F.

pectedly, the dancers would no longer have been immune to the flames. We have to agree with Dr Corney that psychical and psychological theories alone do not account for what happens, and that some physical phenomenon takes place which has not been understood or explained.

Pearce's theory of fire-immunity as a product of a state of temporary reality invoked by a magician explains why the fire-walk has so shocked and offended those who depend on using the reality they have grown accustomed to as a bulwark against the apparition which Freud called "the black tide of occult mud". In recent years, however, fire-walking has been used in the West as a motivational tool in the more extreme types of leadership training as well as in courses for personal growth and development. The successful fire-walker achieves a "natural high" through the conquest of his or her rational fear, a triumph of "mind over matter" that sets them apart as a kind of shaman and enables them to believe that they are capable of achieving anything.

Fire-affinity and fire starters

From *Time* magazine (7 April 1947) comes this brief story: "In Woodstock, Vermont, a fire broke out in the basement of the Walker home on Sunday; the staircase caught fire on Monday; an upstairs partition blazed on Tuesday; the jittery Walkers moved out on Wednesday; the house burned down on Thursday." We know a few briefer ones. Twenty-eight fires of unknown origin in one day forced the Hackler family to flee their Oclon, Indiana, farm (*Collier's*, April 1941); and about forty fires in a few hours drove the Hoyt family from their home in Woodstock (another Woodstock), New Brunswick.

Every so often we hear of prolonged series of fires which defy the efforts of local firemen. One of many examples occurred in the West Virginian town of Wharncliffe. Throughout the summer of 1983, homes there and in nearby Beech Creek were afflicted with outbreaks of fire. Some homes suffered more than ten fires in a single day, others could not be saved as they burned to the ground. Fire chiefs blamed arsonists; locals blamed microwave radiation. Kendall Simpson, chief at the Gilbert Fire Department, said: "I've never seen anything like it in my twelve years here." (Columbus, Ohio, *Dispatch*, 24 July 1983)

We have noticed there are sometimes interesting details, overlooked in the more sober reports. In 2000, for example, a series of seven fires broke out in less than a week in a building owned by the Wackenhut security company in Iquique, Chile. The company specializes in providing services to high security prisons and at secret sites, so this is not a case of someone wandering in and setting fires. Locals said the site had been well-known for ghostly noises, flying objects and moving furniture; apparently, an infamous magician called Gait had once lived there, who liked to summon spirits. Firefighters tackling one of the blazes spoke of plates, pictures and clocks flying off the walls and down the length of the main hall. Several crews struggled to quell the main inferno, saying the flames appeared to come from no identifiable source. (*El Mercurio*, 8 October 2000)

Also in 1983, six "spontaneous fires" broke out in five days in the home of the late Khotso Sethunsa, a millionaire witch doctor, in Kokstad, Transkei, South Africa. A report in the *South African Star* (13 August 1983) stated that the house was occupied by 39 people who rented it from one of Khotso's 26 wives. (You might think that provides a lot of suspects, but it also provides a lot of witnesses.) Everything from mattresses and boxes to floorboards, clothing on a line, a plastic bucket, and shoes were said to have flamed of their own accord, some in front of investigating fire officials. The residents all agreed on one thing – the spirit of the late owner was tormenting them – and they all camped on the lawn until there were no more outbursts.

In the small Georgian hamlet of Lesken, in North Ossetia, the home of pensioner Kazbek Yekanov was plagued for two days by poltergeist-type phenomena, including unexplained fires. It began in January 2003 when his bed shook and the headboard burst into flame, followed by fires in the carpet at different locations around the house. As soon as one was put out, another started; mattresses, curtains, clothes, furniture – nothing was safe. Firemen and neighbours who rushed to help were mystified until they saw objects igniting in front of them. (*Pravda*, 22 Jan 2003)

What could cause such destructive series? Could there be a connection with the fires that invariably accompany poltergeist outbreaks? And what of those unfortunate people, like Carole Compton, in whose presence fires seem to flourish? (British nanny Carole was tried for arson in Italy, in 1983, where she was accused of being a witch – see FIERY PERSECUTIONS, P.181.)

What interests us here is the notion that some people are fireprone, or somehow act as catalysts for a process that causes outbreaks of fire in their vicinity. Charles Fort called such a person a fire genius: "By genius I mean one who can't avoid knowledge of fire, because he can't avoid setting things afire." These genii, he thought, might have been very useful in the days before men knew how to make fire artificially. In this section we examine some of the evidence which suggests that human

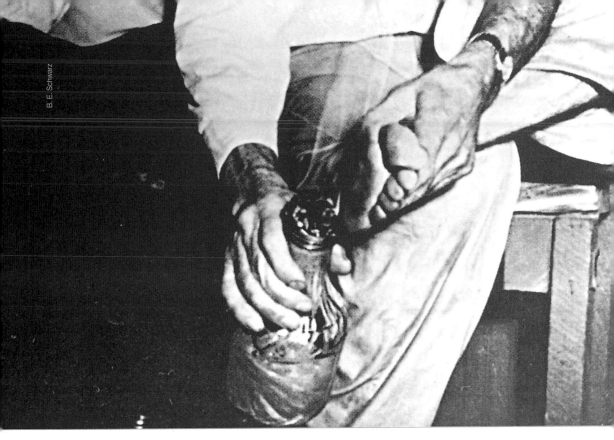

Bradley Shell, one of the "Saints" of the Pentecostal Holiness Church of Kentucky who demonstrate their faith by drinking strychnine, handling snakes and placing their limbs in fire, holds a flaming torch to his feet.

beings possess both a capacity to project fiery heat and also something called – for lack of any better description – fire-immunity, one aspect of which we have illustrated in connection with the fire-walk.

As an example of fire-immunity the case of Nathan Coker, a blacksmith of Easton, Maryland, is of great interest because, unlike some other famous fire-handlers, he needed no trance or preparation to demonstrate his powers. Three authorities, Vincent Gaddis, Dr Nandor Fodor and Father Herbert Thurston, accepted the validity of the account, in the *New York Herald* (7 September 1871) of Coker being tested before many prominent local officials. A shovel was heated to a white glow, and when all was ready, Coker "pulled off his boots and placed the hot shovel on the soles of his feet, and kept it there until the shovel became black". Coker also swilled molten leadshot around in his mouth until it solidified; held glowing coals in his hands; and took a red-hot iron out of the fire with his hands.

He told them: "It don't burn. Since I was a little boy, I've never been afraid to handle fire." This talent may be more common than we think. In *Mysterious Fires and Lights* (1967) Gaddis mentions the report of a New York physician, Dr K.R. Wissen, who met a shy backwoods boy while on a hunting trip in the Tennessee mountains in 1927, and found that he could pick up and hold firebrands without injury. The boy told him that he had discovered the ability by accidentally picking up a red-hot horseshoe in his uncle's smithy.

In *The Physical Phenomena of Mysticism* (1952) Father Thurston tells the story of a Canon charged with investigating reports of the immunity to fire of St Francis of Paola, who died in 1507. The Canon witnessed St Francis's performance but made light of it, saying that it was easy for him to bear the heat because he was not of "gentle blood" but a peasant "used to hardship". St Francis replied that that was quite true. "He bent down to the fire, which was a big one and burning fiercely. Filling his hands with the brands and live

Josephine Giraldelli, billed around 1819 as "The Original Salamander", holds her arm in flames while standing on a red-hot shovel.

coals, he held them there while he turned to the Canon and remarked: 'You see, I could not do this if I were not a peasant.'"

Whatever the explanation, the phenomenon of fire-immunity is ancient and universal. Mircea Eliade in *Shamanism* (1972) says that it is a common practice for the smiths of the Dogon tribe to handle red-hot metal "to re-enact the practices of the first smiths". Nor do we doubt that there are some genuine performances among professional entertainers, such as that recorded by Max Freedom Long in *The Secret Science Behind Miracles* (1948). Long was so astonished by the fiery conjurings of a magician that he obtained a private performance and brought along with him a dentist to examine the man's mouth, for as part of his fire-handling repertoire, the magician would play the hottest flame of a welding torch over the inside of his mouth, keeping his jaws wide open to allow close inspection. He also heated an iron bar to red heat and, gripping the glowing part with his hands and teeth, bent the bar up and down.

We think that the historical evidence demands reconsideration, not only the many tales of the fire exploits of holy men, but also the sort of incident recorded by John Evelyn in his *Diary* on 8 October 1672. Evelyn, who had a scholarly interest in the curious, had been invited to dine with Lady Sunderland. Afterwards she sent for the entertainer Richardson, well known throughout Europe. According to Evelyn, Richardson "devoured brimstone on glowing coales before us, chewing and swallowing them, he melted a beareglasse and eate it quite up; then taking a live coale on his tongue, he put upon it a raw oyster, the coale was blown on with bellows till it flamed and sparkled in his mouth, and so remained until the oyster gaped and was quite boiled; then he melted pitch and wax with sulphur, which he drank down as it flamed; I saw it flaming in his mouth a good while; he also took up a thick piece of yron, such as laundresses use in their smoothing boxes, when it was fiery hot, held it between his teeth, then in his hand … with divers other prodigious feates."

Further testimony to Richardson's abilities is quoted in Olivier Leroy's *Les Hommes salamandres* (1931) from the *Journal des savants* of 1677. During a test he held "a red-hot iron in his hands for a long time without any mark being left upon it afterwards".

In the nineteenth century Daniel Dunglas Home performed similar feats on demand and in clear light under scientific scrutiny. Sir William Crookes wrote in the *Quarterly Journal of Science* (1 July 1871) of seeing about thirteen different types of phenomena, including some astonishing displays of fire-handling, which proved to him the existence of an unknown "Psychic Force". When his full "Notes on Seances with D.D. Home" finally appeared in the *Proceedings of the Society for Psychical Research* in 1889, he had "nothing to retract or alter", despite eighteen years of merciless ridicule from his colleagues. Lord Adare in his *Experiences with D.D. Home* (1924) bears witness to many of these events and says that Home would allow other people to hold coals without injury, after making "passes" over their hands.

At the opposite pole to people who are immune to fire are those who, willingly or not, attract it or project it. In reviewing some of these cases we are reminded of the old belief that combustion depends on the presence of latent "seeds of fire", and that there is a magic by which they can be made to blossom. There is the celebrated case of A.W. Underwood, of Paw Paw, Michigan, about whom Dr L.C. Woodman wrote in the *New York Sun* (1 December 1882): "He will take anybody's handkerchief, hold it to his mouth, rub it vigorously, while breathing on it, and immediately it bursts into flames and burns until consumed." Underwood would strip, rinse his mouth out and set any cloth or paper alight by his breath. It was most useful, he said, when he was out hunting; he could have his camp fire going in seconds.

If that sounds far-fetched, consider the fate of a young West Indian woman, Lily White, of Liberta, Antigua, whose clothes would suddenly burst into flames. Fire attacked her garments when she was at home and also in the streets, leaving her naked. *The New York Times* (25 August 1929) reported that she had become dependent on neighbours for things to wear, and that even as she slept her sheets burnt up and yet she herself was never harmed by the fires that consumed all around her. Consider also the strange story in the *Daily Mail* (13 December 1921) of the boy who, with his mother, was driven from their home in Budapest by "alarmed" neighbours who claimed that some of them had seen flames flicker over him as he slept, singeing his pillow. It was said that since the boy's thirteenth birthday furniture had moved and fires had repeatedly broken out in his presence.

The Soviet parapsychologist Dr Genady Sergeyev referred, in an interview in the *Sunday People* (14 March 1976), to the powerful telekinetic medium Nina Kulagina: "She can draw energy somehow from all around her, electrical instruments can prove it. On several occasions, the force rushing into her body left four-inch-long burnmarks on her arms and hands ... I was with her once when her clothing caught fire from this

R. Lannoy

In *Man, Myth and Magic* (1970) Kenneth Grant tells how a disciple of Anandamayi Ma asked her to show her power and burn him to ashes. As she joined him under a sunshade he felt a fierce heat beat down upon his head. It grew so intense that he begged her to stop. Grant says the sunshade was quite burnt in parts.

energy flow, it literally flamed up. I helped put out the flames and saved some of the burned clothing as an exhibit." (For more on Mrs Kulagina and others manifesting strange paraelectrical forces, see ELECTRIC PEOPLE, p.79.)

There is also evidence to suggest that the tendency to attract or be immune to fire can be brought under human control. Max Freedom Long's exotic magician (see p.74) said that, although he was of white parentage, he was orphaned in India and adopted by local firewalkers, who trained him from an early age. He was taught to meditate on a burning lamp, to "sense the God behind the flame" and thus enjoy his protection. The power to confer fire-immunity is attributed to many gods. The Hindu invokes the protection of Agni, the Kahuna calls on Pele, and the Greek villagers dance on fires clutching icons of St Constantine and St Helen. All their different invocations are effective, but so also were those of Home and Richardson who asked no favours of any god.

In the art of most cultures holiness or sacred power has been represented by bodily light known as an aura or halo. In this manuscript illustration from *The Apostle's Biography* (c.1368), the Prophet Mohammed is shown wrapped in a golden flame during his vision of the angel Gabriel.

Human radiance

Our subject here is light emanating from human bodies. As with many of our phenomena, examples can be given from antiquity to the present day. The data comes mostly from three types of source: from medicine, religion and folklore. The effect, however, is the same throughout – people are lit up.

In May 1934, the "Luminous Woman of Pirano" was a sensation that spilled out from the squabbles of the Italian medical press into news-papers across the world. Signora Anna Monaro was an asthma patient, and over a period of several weeks she would emit a blue glow from her breasts as she slept. Many doctors came to witness the phenomenon, which was visible for several seconds at a time. One psychiatrist said it was caused by "electrical and magnetic organisms in the woman's body developed in eminent degree", which is one way of saying you don't know. Another doctor suggested "electromagnetic radiation from certain compounds in her skin". This was a reference to theories, then current, of bioluminescence, as found, for example, in E.N. Harvey's *The Nature of Animal Light* (1920). Dr Protti, who made a long statement on his observa-tions of Signora Monaro, postulated that her weak condition, together with her fasting and religious zeal, increased the amount of sulphides in her blood, and that since the normal radiant power of human blood is in the ultraviolet range, and that sulphides can be stimulated into luminescence by ultraviolet radiation, here was a reasonable expla-nation (see *The Times*, 5 May 1934).

Clearly this did not explain the strange perio-dicity or localization of the blue flashes, and the embarrassed investigators fell silent. Harvey himself talks of luminous bacteria that feed on nutrients in sweat, but by Protti's own testimony Anna Monaro would break into a heavy sweat only *after* the light emissions, during which her heart rate doubled. Numerous toxicology text-books discuss "luminous wounds", some in terms of bacteria, and others in terms of the modern view that the secretions contain the biochemicals luciferin and luciferase, and a substance called

St Francis of Paola (d.1507) is one of many saints whose bodily radiance has been well-documented. He is also credited with possessing the power of fire-immunity.

ATP (adenosine triphosphate), which are normally kept apart, but when brought together give off a faint luminescence. The identical process lights up the glow-worm and firefly. Yet, if this theory were applicable the Signora should have glowed all over.

In *Death: Its Causes and Phenomena* (1911) Hereward Carrington tells of a child who died of acute indigestion. As neighbours prepared the shroud they noticed the body surrounded by a blue glow and radiating heat. The body appeared to be on fire; efforts to extinguish the luminescence failed, but eventually it faded away. Medical records of the human glow-worm effect are almost always in reference to pathological cases. For instance, Gould and Pyle in their monumental *Anomalies and Curiosities of Medicine* (1896) tell of a woman with cancer of the breast: the light from the sore could illuminate the hands of a watch several feet away.

The only occurrence of light emission from an otherwise healthy person that we have on file (apart from saints) is in a letter to the *English Mechanic* (24 September 1869): "An American lady, on going to bed, found that a light was issuing from the upper side of the fourth toe on her right foot. Rubbing increased the phosphorescent glow and it spread up her foot. Fumes were also given off, making the room disagreeable; and both light and fumes continued when the foot was held in a basin of water. Even washing with soap could not dim the toe. It lasted for three quarters of an hour before fading away, and was witnessed by her husband."

Rare as these physiological conditions are, they still occur, if unexpectedly, as in the case of a 56-year-old Vietnamese woman in Hué. In an account approved by the commune elders, Mrs Nguyen Thi Suong emitted a soft yellow glow for four hours on the night of 4 February 2003. Her

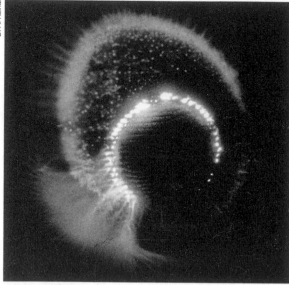

D. A. Keintz

Modern photographic techniques have revived interest in the aura: a fingertip seen with the Kirlian high-voltage method.

husband, a commune doctor, confirmed that this continued every night for the next five days, but thought it might have something to do with a build-up of static electricity. All Mrs Suong would say was: "My life is being disturbed by curious visitors." (*Melbourne Age*, 21 February 2003)

Sometimes human radiance seems to be connected with inexplicable electromagnetic phenomena, and in ELECTRIC PEOPLE (see, p.79) we give several accounts of luminous infants. But no amount of disease-based cases can match the show of luminosity put on by the mystics. The halo or shining aura is everywhere the attribute of the spiritual man; and we can only suppose that this universal symbol is derived from a universal phenomenon of common experience. Holy men glow, sometimes blazingly. Even in everyday speech we refer to faces "shining" or "beaming" with happiness. That this is not always simply a figure of speech is warily accepted by the Church. Prosper Lambertini (1675–1758) – later Pope Benedict XIV – was responsible for formulating the process of beatification. In *De beatificatione* he wrote: "It seems to be a fact that there are natural flames which at times visibly encircle the human head, and that also from a man's whole person fire may on occasion radiate naturally, not however like a flame which streams upwards, but rather in

the form of sparks which are given off all around."

As one of many examples, we can quote the biography of St Lidwina by Thomas à Kempis (1379–1471). "And although she always lay in darkness, and material light was unbearable to her eyes, nevertheless the divine light was very agreeable to her, whereby her cell was often so wondrously flooded by night that to the beholders the cell itself appeared full of material lamps or fires. Nor is it strange if she overflowed even in the body with divine brightness."

Father Herbert Thurston admitted: "There are so many stories of holy priests who lit up a dark cell or whole chapel by the light which streamed from them or upon them, that I am strongly inclined to adhere to the more literal interpretation … It is unquestionably true that there are hundreds of such examples to be found in our hagiographical records, and although a great number of these rest upon quite insufficient testimony, there are others which cannot lightly be set aside … There can, therefore, be no adequate reason for refusing credence to the report of similar phenomena when they are recorded of those whose eminent holiness and marvellous gifts of grace are universally recognized."(*Physical Phenomena of Mysticism*, 1952)

Perhaps the most interesting thing in Father Thurston's statement is the reference to light streaming "from them or upon them". Both kinds of light are clearly implied in the passage about St Lidwina. Thurston goes on to relate the following story about the Spanish theologian, Father Francis Suarez, at the Jesuit College at Coimbra in Portugal. An elderly lay-brother, Jerome da Silva, came to tell the Father of the arrival of a distinguished visitor. The outer room of his quarters was in darkness, shuttered against the afternoon heat. Suarez's biographer Father R. de Scorraille records da Silva's account of the incident:

"I called the Father but he made no answer. As the curtain which shut off his working room was drawn, I saw, through the space between the jambs of the door and the curtain, a very great brightness. I pushed aside the curtain and entered the inner apartment. Then I noticed that the blinding light was coming from the crucifix, so intense that it was like the reflexion of the Sun from glass windows, and I felt that I could not have remained looking at it without being completely dazzled. This light streamed from the crucifix upon the face and breast of Father Suarez, and in this brightness I saw him in a kneeling position in front of the crucifix, his head uncovered, his hands joined, and his body in the air five palms [about three feet] above the floor on a level with the table on which the crucifix stood. On seeing this I withdrew … as it were beside myself … my hair standing on end like the bristles on a brush, and I waited, hardly knowing what I did."

About a quarter of an hour later, the Father came out, surprised to see the Brother waiting. "When the Father heard that I had entered the inner room, he seized me by the arm … then, clasping his hands and with eyes full of tears, he implored me to say nothing of what I had seen, at any rate, as long as he lived." They shared the same confessor, who suggested da Silva write his account and seal it with the endorsement that it should not be opened and read until after the death of Father Suarez. All three parties were well-known for their piety – they had nothing to gain by deception – and the account has a ring of honesty.

In the same manner, St Francis of Assisi was lifted (see LEVITATION AND SPONTANEOUS FLIGHT, p.15) and illuminated, and the radiance of Saints Philip Neri, Catherine de Ricci, Francis of Paola, Alphonsus Liguori, and many others who were holy but never beatified, shines out of their biographies. Some legends might not, then, be as mythical as it is comfortable to suppose. When Moses came down from Sinai, it is written (Exodus 34, 29–35) that "the skin of his face shone" so brightly that all who beheld it were afraid to go near him. For some time after, in the presence of others, he had to wear a veil.

The idea of the aura as a physical manifestation of the energy field which surrounds each living thing gained wider currency with the advent of Theosophy at the end of the nineteenth century. Though the Theosophists believed that human auras were only visible to clairvoyants, this did not prevent several enterprising photographers from attempting to capture the phenomena on film (see Thelma Moss: *The Probability of the Impossible*, 1974). The most successful of these attempts was made by the Russian Semyon Kirlian and his wife who, in 1939, experimented with film exposed to the electrical discharges from selected objects or people placed on a special apparatus. Kirlian photographs of human auras, with their rich and varied colours, have subsequently been used as a diagnostic tool – mainly by alternative therapists – although critics remain unconvinced that they show anything other than colourful discharges of static electricity.

Electric people

One of the earliest scientifically investigated cases of an "electric person" was that of Angélique Cottin of La Perrière, France, whose strange condition began on 15 January 1846 (when she was fourteen) and lasted ten weeks. Whenever she went near objects they retreated from her. The slightest touch of her hand or dress was enough to send heavy furniture spinning away or jumping up and down; and no one could hold an object she also was holding without it writhing from their grasp. A study group was appointed by the Academy of Sciences, and a famous physicist, François Arago, published a report in the *Journal des débats* (February 1846). He noted that her power seemed to be like electromagnetism – compasses went wild in her proximity – that it was stronger in the evening, and seemed to emanate from her left side, particularly her left wrist and elbow. Poor Angélique would often convulse while the phenomenon was active, her heartbeat rising to 120 a minute, and she was so frightened by it that she repeatedly fled from the scene.

We have no way of knowing just how many historical poltergeist cases were in fact instances of the high-voltage syndrome. Dr E.J. Dingwall presents a collection of accounts of compass deflection and movements in furniture, etc in his four-volume history of *Abnormal Hypnotic Phenomena* (1967), the earliest case referred to occurring in 1786.

Cases are reported throughout the nineteenth century. Seventeen-year-old Caroline Clare of London, Ontario, became ill in 1877.

Angélique Cottin causing furniture to move, in Paris in 1847.

subject of a study in 1889. When he felt charged he had to keep moving, because if he stopped his feet became glued to the spot and he had to ask passers-by to lift his feet and release the charge. Similarly, sixteen-year-old Louis Hamburger was studied by the Maryland College of Pharmacy in 1890. He too was a "human magnet" and could make metal objects dangle from his skin. With the tips of three fingers he could lift a glass jar full of iron-filings weighing about 5lb. These cases and those of a few other electric people have been briefly chronicled by Frank Edwards, Vincent Gaddis and others. Drs Gould and Pyle in their monumental *Anomalies and Curiosities of Medicine* (1896) also deal with electric humans.

In 1938 the Universal Council for Psychic Research met in New York to offer a prize of $10,000 for demonstrations of psychic phenomena not reproducible by trickery. An elderly lady, Mrs Antoine Timmer, showed how cutlery stuck to her hands as if her skin were magnetized – but her case was dismissed because the chairman, the illusionist Joseph Dunninger, said he could do the same himself with a concealed thread. Thus another opportunity for research was lost for ever.

Perhaps the most famous case from that astonishing period was that of Lulu Hurst, who, between 1883 and 1885, made a stage career as "The Georgia Wonder" before quitting to marry her manager. The phenomena began, as in a classic "poltergeist" case, shortly after she was fourteen. China would smash in her presence, and at night there would be knocking sounds and frighteningly heavy thumps in the bedroom she shared with a younger sister. Soon it was discovered that questions spoken in the room were answered by raps for "yes" and "no". The day after the noises started, Lulu handed a relative a chair. As the chair twisted in Lulu's grasp four men tried to hold it, but the forces were too great, the chair broke into pieces and they were flung violently backwards. Lulu, like Angélique, ran screaming from the house.

Within two weeks her parents had persuaded Lulu to turn her affliction into an act. In it she

Her weight dropped to 90lb and she would suffer dramatic fits, describing faraway places she had never seen. When she recovered about a year and a half later, her life was made a misery by strong discharges of electricity. Objects in contact with her became magnetized. Cutlery would stick to her skin and had to be pulled off by another person. She was the subject of an investigation and report by the Ontario Medical Association in the summer of 1879. In the 1890s, another teenager, Jennie Morgan of Sedalia, Missouri, became similarly highly charged; sparks would fly from her to nearby objects, animals would avoid her, and those people forgetful enough to shake her hand or touch her were often knocked unconscious.

Frank McKinstry of Joplin, Missouri, was the

presented variations on the theme of a little girl thwarting several grown men. She would hold one end of a billiard cue while two men struggled and failed to force the other end to the ground. She could also lift three men sitting on each other's laps on the same chair, merely resting her open palms on its back. She would then lightly touch the chair while five men tried in vain to budge it from the spot. Frank Edwards in *Strange People* (1961) quotes from many contemporary accounts. Investigators, who were allowed to get as close as they wished, consistently found no evidence of strain or trickery in the girl. Fort mentions two other "immovables" from that period: Mrs Annie Abbott demonstrated her powers in London, November 1891, and Mrs Mary Richardson in Liverpool, September 1921. Holms investigated both cases for his *Facts of Psychic Science* and concluded that the ladies did not resist pressure, but that in some inexplicable way pressure against them did not reach or touch them.

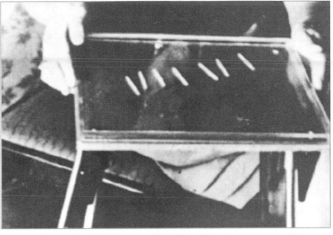

A row of matchsticks is moved by Nina Kulagina, apparently without touching them. From a Russian film made in 1967.

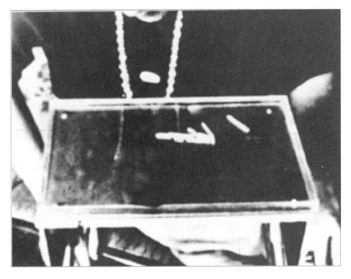

Forces without reaction seem to crop up in most "poltergeist" cases, yet we urge caution in explaining away these effects as products of unusual bioelectrical fields. In many cases of poltergeist activity there is no known human agency. Every attempt to establish a constant factor in our phenomena can be countered by contrary cases, as though the phenomena delighted in teasing us. It is astonishing that little serious research, if any, has been done on the pathological causes of para-electrical effects. Scientists seem to have been scared off by the "occult" or "poltergeist" element in the phenomenon. The only analogies for the appearance and discharge of such high voltages are in the bio-electric processes of animals like eels. Each cell in our body can generate a small charge. Dr Mayne R. Coe (*FATE*, July 1959) believed that a cubic inch of human muscle cells could (in theory) generate 400,000 volts of very low amperage, but it would need a high amperage to cause the effects that we have mentioned, and they are still unexplained.

The phenomenon of electric people is not only associated with adolescents. As early as the 1930s, the new field of bioelectrics was attracting the likes of Harold Saxton-Burr, a professor of anatomy at Yale University, who discovered that probably all living creatures generate their own electromagnetic fields, usually fairly weak ones. One extraordinary experiment with a colleague, Dr Leonard J. Ravitz,

Some people are so highly charged with static that they can light up some kinds of bulbs merely by holding them. For example, 12-year-old Vyvyan Jones of Henbury, Bristol, became unaccountably electric after breaking his arm in February 1976. For two days his hair was permanently on end and he shocked people with powerful discharges whenever touched: TV and lights flickered in his presence and watches stopped. A doctor treating him at Southmead Hospital, Bristol, said it was not unusual and that he had seen people with magnetic fields strong enough to lift iron bars.

suggested that bioelectricity may sometimes be affected psychosomatically. In his *Blueprint for Immortality* (1972), he records that "an emotion of grief recalled under hypnotic regression caused a 14-millivolt rise for two and a half minutes".

In the 1980s, the adventurous Oxford don Dr Michael Shallis made a four-year study of 600 people whose minds or bodies were somehow affected by electricity. In his *Electric Shock Book* (1988), he describes Mrs Jacqueline Priestman, 22, of Sale, Manchester, who registered charges of static electricity more than ten times the "normal" level. "She was able to transmit miniature bolts of lightning," he said, that caused 30 vacuum cleaners and many other domestic appliances to short out or malfunction, either in her presence or when she touched them.

Gould and Pyle mention a six-year-old Zulu boy who gave off intense shocks and was exhibited in Edinburgh in 1882. Fodor, in his *Encyclopaedia of Psychic Science* tells of a baby born at Saint-Urbain, France, in 1869, who badly shocked all who touched him. Luminous rays would shoot from his fingers, and when he died, just nine months old, a radiance was observed around his body for several minutes. Douglas Hunt, writing in *Prediction*, (January 1953) gives two other cases of high-voltage infants: one was able to charge up a Leyden jar, and the other caused "vibrations" in objects held near him, and was also seen to be surrounded by a soft, white radiance.

Another curious piece of the jigsaw appeared in the *Electrical Experimenter* (June 1920) in which Dr J.B. Ransom, chief physician at Clinton

In 1990, Nikolai Suvurov, 55, a militia patrolman in a village in the Kirov region of Russia, claimed to be able to generate a "magnetic" attraction at will, that allowed objects, even heavy ones, to stick to his skin. Similar abilities were claimed by the 300 contestants of a "human magnet" competition held in Bulgaria. Three generations of the Tenkaev family, also from Russia, were tested by the physics department of Saratov State University, where the father, Leonid, was able to "glue" objects to the weight of 52lb to himself. He likened the process to imagining heat building up inside his body. Further tests in Japan seemed to authenticate the Tenkaevs family's ability. In a similar case, it is claimed that a 12-year-old girl from Byelorussia, Inga Gaidochenko, allegedly, can lift a 4kg sledgehammer with the flat palms of her hands. None of the original news reports say whether the attractive force is magnetism – even though this could be easily determined. If true, these are both strange forms of magnetism indeed. Both glass and plastic are reported to stick equally well to Suvorov; while Inga can attract wood and plastic but not glass.

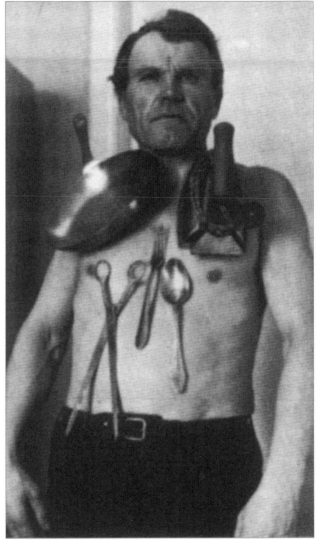

Prison, New York, reported on thirty-four convicts suffering from botulinus poisoning. One had tried to throw away a piece of paper and found it stuck to his hand. Soon all the afflicted were in the same highly charged condition, varying in intensity with the severity of the poisoning. Compasses went wild in their vicinity and metal objects were deflected from their grasp; but the effects faded as they recovered.

The history of the poltergeist shows many electromagnetic interferences, from dimming lights to gadgets running without power, as seen in a famous case at Rosenheim, Bavaria, in 1967. Translations of the investigation by Professor

H. Bender, Dr Andreas Resch and others can be found in *The Journal of Paraphysics* (vols. 3 and 4). Interferences with telephones, electric power and lights were centred on a girl, Annemarie Schneider, and the phenomena stimulated by her presence included many of the "normal" mechanical tricks of the poltergeist repertoire, like bulbs unscrewing themselves from sockets, drawers opening, pictures rotating on the wall, etc. From this case alone, with its mass of documentary and even filmed evidence, it is clear that the "electric people" phenomenon exists, whatever the explanation.

Projected thought-forms

The idea of a reciprocal relationship between the subjective world of thoughts and the "real" world of objective events and objects is as old as philosophy itself. It can be seen operating in all forms of magic and ritual, and is the basis of many artistic and literary metaphors. Throughout history the belief that events and objects may be as ephemeral as thoughts, while thoughts can occasionally become concrete and objective realities.

With the rise of modern science such a notion became heresy, yet it has always persisted, and the latest findings from both paraphysics and subatomic physics have given it some degree of respectability. Previously forbidden but now generally recognized are such concepts as the transmutation of matter and the relativity of the so-called "laws" of space, time, matter and energy. We are told that an electron can travel between two points in space without physically traversing the distance between them, just as objects in our own mundane world have been observed to disappear and reappear elsewhere. When solid objects spontaneously change their

Eusapia Palladino, at the height of her powers in the 1890s, could impress her features into putty in sealed containers, supposedly by an effort of will.

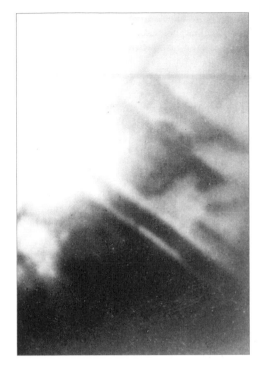

In the 1960s, Dr Jule Eisenbud studied the claims of Ted Serios to project mental images onto sealed film. Eisenbud found no evidence of trickery during his long investigation. The clearer picture of Westminster Abbey is the "target" image, while the blurred image is Serios's projection.

structure, colour or motion, these effects might be logical consequences of the inexplicable randomness that Heisenberg showed to exist in the motions of the subatomic particles. In the world of particle physics, anything conceivable can happen, and our evidence suggests that the same is true in the world of physical objects.

The discovery of telekinetic forces was the main motivation behind the experiments of Dr J.B. Rhine at Duke University, who began research into what is now called psychokinesis in the 1930s. Psychokinesis, or PK, is the enigmatic process more popularly described as "mind over matter", and in 1945 Dr Rhine announced that he had conclusive evidence of PK effects in influencing the way in which dice fall. Rhine divides the subject into PK influences on "moving targets", like the dice; "living targets" which might imply anything from levitation and spontaneous flight to influencing the growth of plants; and "static targets" which include the "thoughtography" associated with Ted Serios (see picture above).

The projection of an image onto sealed film, apparently by PK or some other mysterious means, gives results that are more accessible to analysis. It is interesting to note that with Serios and the small number of others who can repeat this effect, their "hits" are far outnumbered by "wild" images or complete disruption of normal optical processes, "overexposing" the film. The ability to affect, consciously or unconsciously, unexposed film may be more widespread than most people realize, judging from the number of accounts we can find of "wild images" turning up on photographs taken by ordinary people.

We are particularly interested in cases where a desired effect has been achieved purely through the exercise of imagination. In 1935, Mrs Gertrude Smith of York, Pennsylvania, discovered she could mentally coax her hens to lay eggs bearing images. The *York Gazette and Daily* (4 April 1940) quoted her as saying: "I would stand near the hen yard and visualize sunflower petals along with my initials. In a few days my father came into the house all excited and said: "Here is the sunflower egg". The pattern of a sunflower was incised into the shell on the flattened part." Soon Mrs Smith obtained more patterned eggs, one of them marked with the reversed letters of her initials: "When I broke one open, the design appeared raised on the inner surface of the shell." A later edition of the *Gazette and Daily* testified to the genuineness of the patterned eggs and referred to a sworn deposition by other witnesses.

Mrs Smith said she tried visualizing an egg with a triangular cross-section, and when one arrived she became so frightened by her power that she never tried again.

In several of our sections we tell of objects or images that appeared in response to conscious or unconscious demand, and observe their synchronous nature (see COINCIDENCES, p.241). Catherine Crowe gives an example in *The Night Side of Nature* (1848) of a girl who dreamt she was offered two roses, one red and one white, and chose the red one. She woke with a pain in her arm, on which by degrees "there arose the perfect figure of a rose, perfect in form and colour. It was rather raised above the skin". It took a fortnight to fade away. The case of Mrs L. Forbes, of Thornton Heath, near London, was often quoted by Dr Nandor Fodor to support his opinion that poltergeists are genuine psychological phenomena, or as he put it, "bundles of projected repressions" (*On the Trail of the Poltergeist*, 1958). One night in 1938 Mrs Forbes dreamt of being pulled in two directions by her dead father and her husband. Her father then drew a cross on her left breast with a finger. In the morning Mrs Forbes discovered on that spot an inflamed mark. An examination by a doctor disclosed a previously unsuspected cancer in that position, necessitating an operation.

There are many other examples of "skin writing" in response to unspoken thoughts as well as to hypnotic suggestion. In his study, *Stigmata* (1998), Ted Harrison says the phenomenon has been widely discussed in medical literature. He refers to the cases of Domenica Lo Bianco (see STIGMATA, p.88) and an unnamed man brought to a London teaching hospital in the 1950s. He was in a terrible state, reliving a traumatic episode in his past in which he had been tied up with ropes. Under the gaze of doctors the unmistakeable marks of tightly bound rope would appear on his arms.

To this we would add the remarkable story of the Romanian peasant girl Eleonore Zugun (pictured opposite). In 1923, when she was about eleven, she became the focus of poltergeist activity. Small objects around her would move, seemingly on their own account, and bite-like marks would appear on the skin of her face and arms; many impeccable accounts of these well-observed phenomena exist in the literature. Harry Price, who brought Eleonore to England for study in 1926,

witnessed "time and time again" marks appearing on her arms as indentations which puffed up into weals which lasted "a few minutes and rapidly disappeared". When asked, the girl said the Devil ("Dracu") was attacking her. Price never found any sign that the girl might be biting or scratching herself.

An independent report on Eleonore was commissioned by Price from a Captain Seton-Karr, FRGS, which gives the following account of how it all began. "When the so-called poltergeist phenomena became first apparent, the simple peasants so threatened her with Dracu and what he would do to her that her subconscious mind became obsessed with the idea of whippings, bitings, etc, which the ignorant peasants said would be her lot." Seton-Karr concluded, "Remove the Dracu complex and the girl would probably be troubled no further with stigmatic markings." (*Proceedings of the National Laboratory of Psychical Research*, January 1927). In fact Eleonore's phenomena ceased about this time anyway, coincident with her fourteenth birthday and the onset of menstruation.

In the entry on "Dermography" in the second edition of *The Encyclopedia of Occultism and Parapsychology* (1984), editor Leslie Shepard refers to the hypersensitivity of the skin in some hysterical patients, such that the slightest brush against it would raise a mark. Even he admits that this theory fails to account for the remarkable pictographic power of a girl in the service of a Lewis Burtis of New England in the 1860s. She seems to have been a living sketchpad with all sorts of images and words appearing on her skin as she went about her daily work. In a well-witnessed account, reported in Emma Hardinge's *Modern American Spiritualism* (1870), red lines on one arm formed "a distinct and beautifully represented picture of a kneeling man, with a woolly head and African cast of features, a chain around his waist terminating in two balls which were ingeniously fitted into the veins ... above was written in fine character the words 'A poor old slave'." Even more remarkable is that the girl was acknowledged to be "nearly illiterate". It seems likely then that she had, by means unknown, reproduced something she had once seen.

The whimsical and sometimes sinister character of PK projection is indicated by a series of disturbances that occurred in the house of Dr E.E. Phelps, a Presbyterian minister of Stratford,

In 1927, the Romanian "poltergeist girl", Eleonore Zugun, then aged 14, was brought to London and Germany to be studied by various groups of parapsychologists. These stills are from a film made in Munich for one of the pre-eminent parapsychologists of the day, Baron Schrenck-Notzing, in the presence of her mentor Countess Wassilko. Eleonore is examined and then shows the distinctive marks appearing on her arms, chest, neck and cheeks. Eleonore herself said they were made by a tormenting spirit she called "Dracu" (Romanian for devil). She was even induced to make a drawing of "Dracu" (below).

Connecticut, in March 1850. The *New Haven Journal and Courier* (19 April 1850) quotes a witness to the disturbances, Dr Webster. "When the Phelps family returned from church, they found the furniture strewn about the rooms, and curious figures constructed of clothing arranged in one of them, constituting a sort of tableau, depicting a scene of worship. There were eleven figures, arranged in life-like attitudes. All but one were female figures; all were in postures of extreme devotion, some with their foreheads nearly touching the floor; others kneeling about the room with open Bibles before them, which indicated different passages sanctioning the phenomena then going on. In the centre of the group there was a figure suspended as though flying through the air." Other figures were later

found. The clothing they were made from came from all parts of the house. A close watch was kept, but no one ever saw the images being formed. One figure, made from Mrs Phelps's dress, looked so convincing that her young son was moved to say, "Be still, Ma is saying prayers". A good account of this, drawn from Dr Phelps's own records, can be found in E.W. Capron's *Modern Spiritualism: its Facts and Fanaticisms* (1855). Weird though this episode is, it is not unique. In *Poltergeists Over England* (1945) Harry Price quotes from a pamphlet of 1695 a story of similar clothing-figures during a haunting at Ringcroft, Galloway.

The many reports of "mind over matter" in both mythology and daily experience, suggest that the only limit may be human imagination itself. Dr W.Y. Evans-Wentz and the remarkable Alexandra David-Néel, both highly credible scholars and explorers of Tibet, spoke of the power of the *dubthab* rite by which Tibetan adepts materialize a human apparition called a *tulpa*. This power is claimed by many kinds of occultists and magicians. David-Néel attempted to manifest a *tulpa* of her own, using the prescribed meditation and visualizing exercises. How she succeeded is told in chapter eight of her *Magic and Mystery in Tibet* (1931). This was no subjective fancy, for the little monk-like figure she dreamt up was seen on many occasions by others. She tells how the *tulpa* slipped away from her control, acting independently and becoming more and more tiresome. Reflecting her fears, the *tulpa*'s placid features turned sly, mocking and malignant. In the end, she had to dematerialize it by an exhausting reversal of the whole process.

As with many of the phenomena in this book, the spontaneous occurrences outshine the feeble performances of exceptional human beings, and both of them pale before the controlled displays of power put on by the great mystics. In his life of Milarepa (*Tibet's Great Yogi*, 1928) Evans-Wentz says that the sage, while dying at the Red Rock, projected numerous *tulpas* of himself. Similar tales are told of Jesus after his Resurrection, of Pythagoras and of many saintly people, such as Padre Pio – that they were seen in several places at the same time. One example, the transatlantic bilocation of Mary of Agreda, is outlined in the section on THE TELEPORTATION OF PEOPLE (see p.8).

Humans have the collective "wild talent" of seeing what they want or need to see – or rather, interpreting a visual experience in terms of a shared iconography (see SHARED VISIONS AND VISUAL RUMOURS, see p.110). Can processes like these, that seem to project perceptible images, account for such phenomena as ghosts, fairies and UFOs? We simply don't know. We are conditioned to think it rational to divide the world into subjective and objective phenomena. Living experience tells us this is arbitrary, as the basis of perception itself is to bridge both realms. And in such transitional processes, as Fort reminds us, where does one end and the other begin?

Stigmata

Strange marks and rashes can appear on any person's body, but when that person is an intensely religious Catholic and the marks seem to reproduce the nail and spear wounds believed to have been inflicted on Jesus at his Crucifixion, they are called stigmata and the person who displays them is generally considered a saint. The earliest recorded stigmatic was St Francis of Assisi, who received his marks during an ecstatic vision in September 1224, two years before his death, although the notion of stigmata seems implicit in St Paul's words: "I bear in my body the marks of the Lord Jesus." (Galatians 6:17).

The arguments about stigmata are voluminous and complex, but there is no doubt that the phenomenon exists. A.R.G. Owen's summary article for the encyclopedia *Man, Myth and Magic* (1970) suggested there have been at least three hundred cases. Father Herbert Thurston, the soundest authority, isolates about fifty cases as having adequate documentation and presents them in his *Physical Phenomena of Mysticism* (1952). Ted Harrison, former religious affairs correspondent for the BBC, states in *Stigmata* (1998) that in the eight hundred or so years since the death of St Francis of Assisi there are records of around 406 stigmatics: of these 276 were members of established religious orders; 352 were female; and 25

VVLNERA QVAE PROPTER CRISTVM FRANCSE TVLISTI
ILLA ROGO NOSTRIS SINT MEDCINA MALIS :~

The first major stigmatic was St Francis of Assisi, who received the marks of Christ's crucifixion in 1224 during a vision of a seraph. This woodcut depicting the event is by Albrecht Dürer.

unrivalled in the annals of hagiography. They were described in the *Tractatus de miraculis* (ascribed to Thomas de Celano, and written not later than four years after St Francis died) as having the appearance of black nails which protruded considerably, as though a real nail pierced the hand with its point and head projecting on either side. Celano says that they were visible long after death, and he gives a bizarre description of pilgrims filing past the radiant and still pliant body of the saint (see also THE INCORRUPTIBLES, p.95).

Celano then describes an extraordinary detail: the marks were not just "the prints of the nails, but the nails themselves formed out of his flesh and retaining the blackness of iron … marvellously wrought by the power of God, indeed implanted in the flesh itself, in such wise that if they were pressed in on either side they straightway, as if they were one piece of sinew, projected on the other". St Bonaventure's *Legenda minor* (pre 1274) gives further details of the projecting points, saying that they were clinched over, and projected so far that the soles of the feet could hardly be placed on the ground. We would be inclined to doubt this phenomenon if we did not also know of Domenica Lazzari's hard, black, nail-like formations – though these did not project as far.

This might involve psychogenic processes similar to the less well-known phenomenon of the "Divine token of espousal", a "wedding ring" around the appropriate finger. The effect here obviously relates to the status of the devout man or woman as a "bride of Christ" and manifests variously as a vivid red line circling the finger, a thick ridge on the skin or a depression completely around as if made by an invisible ring. This is only one of many bizarre phenomena associated with stigmata.

In 1837 the *Annali universali di medicina* (vol. 84) published a study by Dr Dei Cloche of a girl, Domenica Lazzari, who had developed an astonishing degree of hyperaesthesia after a traumatic shock. All her senses were heightened so that she was in constant pain, dazzled by lights, and deafened by sound. For the rest of her life she took no nourishment at all and remained bedridden till her death in 1848. In the year his paper appeared, Dr Cloche revisited Domenica and discovered that she had developed stigmata.

He saw wounds in her hands, feet and side, and a row of punctures across her forehead. Her hands were tightly clasped all the time, and on

Padre Pio Forgione (1887–1968) is probably the most famous modern stigmatic, having born the marks since he had an intense experience of Christ in September 1918. He is credited with bilocation, levitation and healing miracles and was beatified by Pope John Paul II on 2 May 1999.

were alive in the last twenty years.

While St Francis's experience created the stereotype for all subsequent manifestations, the wounds in his hands were extreme and largely their backs he saw, between the middle and fourth fingers, a black, domed lump, perfectly circular, like a blackened nail about an inch across. The palms had deep incisions in the corresponding places, from which blood flowed copiously. Lord Shrewsbury stated in his *Letters* (1842) that he had no doubt that the wounds perforated her hands. Overcoming Domenica's reluctance to reveal the sources of her constant pain, he "distinctly saw the wounds and the blood and serum, quite fresh and flowing down over the wrist". Examining her feet he noticed something equally remarkable. "Instead of taking its normal course, the blood flowed upwards over the toes, as it would do were she suspended on a cross". This curious, gravity-defying effect was corroborated many times. T.W. Allies's *Journey into France and Italy* (1849) records the author's visit to Domenica with two friends. One of them, J.H. Wynne, wrote: "The Doctor has seen her feet a hundred times which are marked like the hands, but the blood runs up towards the toes, as it does up [to the tip of] the nose, as we saw."

Like many other stigmatics, Domenica bled every Friday – the day Christ was believed to have been executed – and in the eleven years during which she bore her stigmata there was never any suggestion of trickery. On the contrary, all who visited her took away impressions of great suffering. Her hypersensitivity continued, and Lord Shrewsbury once saw her face covered in blood that flowed from the punctures in her forehead, as though from an invisible crown of thorns. He wrote that her face was never washed because she could not bear the sensations of water and wiping, and that the blood seemed to disappear "of itself".

The records of many famous stigmatics disagree with the opinion of D.H. Rawcliffe (*Psychology of the Occult*, 1952) that the only "true" stigmata are what he calls "topoalgic hallucinations" (ie localized pain without visible injury), and that all else is a mixture of imposture, gullibility and delusion or "purposive self-mutilation during hystero-epileptic attacks followed by amnesia". The impeccable accounts of the sufferings of St Teresa of Avila (1515–82), the recently canonized Padre Pio (1887–1968), and other stigmatics show no overt symptoms of hysteria yet plainly illustrate that so-called suggestion neuroses are not incompatible with lives of the deepest sanctity. Furthermore, Father Thurston has shown that, as

with Domenica and Palma Matarrelli (1825–88), stigmata are not always the product of excessive devotion or morbid brooding on the sufferings of Christ. For modern examples, we could point to the ten-year-old Californian Cloretta Robertson and the case of Eleonore Zugun (see PROJECTED THOUGHT-FORMS, p.84).

Father Thurston is cautious of using the term "hysteria" in connection with stigmata, suggesting that its connotations of violent and uncontrolled emotional outbursts are misleading. In a clinical sense hysterical disorders are not confined to the overtly neurotic, the unbalanced, the weak-minded, or pathological liars. Ted Harrison, who studied six modern stigmatics over a seventeen-year period, found that they had lived "difficult lives", sometimes involving sexual or physical abuse (both as a victim and self-administered), Münchausen's Syndrome and "extremely low self-esteem bordering on self-hatred" (*Fortean Times*, 96, p.37). It is a neurotic profile that is repeated among many of those who claim they were experimented upon by aliens (see OTHERWORLDLY ABDUCTION, p.166).

Even so, every theory of stigmatization that we know of breaks down when tested against the wide variation of the actual cases. There is strong evidence that some kind of psychogenic process is involved and this has led to experimental attempts to reproduce stigmata by hypnosis. For example, in 1933, Dr Alfred Lechler published *Das Rätsel von Konnersreuth,* in which he ventured to explain the stigmata of Theresa Neumann (1898–1962) with reference to his own experiments on a young Austrian girl. Dr Lechler induced all the classic stigmata on her by suggestion during hypnosis, including sweating blood, tears of blood, the "crown of thorns", and an inflamed shoulder caused by her imaginary carrying of the cross. But despite this result and numerous other less dramatic experiments, induced stigmata cannot compare in intensity, persistence and strange detail with the genuine, spontaneous cases.

Stigmatization seems to involve a degree of selection in its imagery that suggests some subjective involvement in the process. The wounds themselves range from small red patches that never bleed to deep and completely penetrating holes. Straight cuts, square, oval and oblong shapes have also been recorded. In some cases the "nail-heads" are said to be in the palms; in others they appear on the back of the hand or on a foot.

physician and psychotherapist Dr Marco Margnelli hypnotized her, and convinced her that it was the appointed time for her stigmata to appear. Harrison reported: "Under laboratory conditions … and over a period of an hour, during which time she was closely monitored and videoed, the religious images on her arm re-appeared" (*Fortean Times*, 96, p.37).

We suggest that this mysterious process is related to other phenomena in this book and may simply be a different manifestation of the same force. One correlation, noticed by Fort, is with records of liquids oozing from invisible sources (see MYSTERIOUS FLOWS AND OOZINGS, p.62); he suggested that wounds might be teleported on to both bodies and statues (see IMAGES THAT WEEP AND BLEED, p.287).

Whether such a theory is acceptable, some process analogous to Fort's teleportation is suggested by the effects. Gemma Galgani's stigmata began as red marks; then a fissure would open slowly, visible beneath the skin, until finally the skin tore, revealing the cavity filled with congealed and flowing blood. This happened every Friday, and the hole would be healed by the Sunday. Could a similar process explain the scare in Japan, in 1890, in which inch-long slashes appeared on people's necks in broad daylight (*The Religio-Philosophical Journal*, 17 May 1890).

Another variation of the stigmata effect has wounds appearing *inside* the body. In 1659 Caterina Savelli was stigmatized during communion by, she told her confessor, five rays that shot from the host. After her death in 1691, two surgeons performed an autopsy before many clergy, and found a deep wound "of old date" on her heart. Similarly, the heart of the Blessed Charles of Sezze (d. 1670), examined post-mortem under papal orders, was found to be completely pierced by a wound and bore a facsimile of a crucifix on its surface, and of a nail, four or five inches long, buried within it. These cases are given by Thurston and in Dr Imbert-Gourbeyre's *La Stig-*

Nineteen days before before Easter 1972, Cloretta Robertson, of Oakland, California, was the first black, and the first non-Catholic stigmatic. Doctors found that the blood appeared through her skin for a few minutes several times a day. It ceased that Good Friday and never reappeared.

"Lance-wounds" have been found on right sides and left, and also assume different shapes, from deep slashes and holes to the cross-shaped scar that bled at its edges on Padre Pio's left side.

The role of suggestion is clear in some cases, even if the mechanism remains mysterious. St Francis was stigmatized on the feast day called Exaltation of the Holy Cross as he passed into an ecstasy in which he begged God to let him share the burden of Christ's suffering on the Cross. The unique Y-shaped cross on the breast of Catherine Emmerich (1744–1824) resembled the unusual cross in the church at Coesfeld where she meditated as a child. Gemma Galgani (1878–1903) manifested bleeding "scourge-marks" identical to those depicted on a large crucifix before which she often prayed.

Ted Harrison actually filmed this process of imprinting, or something very like it, for a TV documentary. It involved the modern Italian stigmatic, Domenica Lo Bianco, on whose arms would appear, every Good Friday, raised red marks in the shape of a rosary and a cross. As

A photograph of Theresa Neumann (d.1962) "weeping blood". She lost nearly a pint of blood from hands, feet, side and forehead, and 8lb in weight, every Friday in a re-enactment of Christ's suffering. Her stigmata conformed to the description of St Francis's wounds.

matisation (1894) which quotes from affidavits signed by the doctors and surgeons involved.

The "purity" of such older cases has been replaced in more recent instances by a kind of cross-pollination with phenomenologically similar categories of mystical experience. Nowhere is this more dramatic than in the case of Giorgio Bongiovanni who was stigmatized during a pilgrimage to Fátima in 1989 with deep cross-shaped wounds on his hands, feet, side and forehead. A small but significant number of modern stigmatics now share with Bongiovanni the highly visible cross-shaped wounds on their foreheads, including the Spanish Palmarian heretic Clemente Domínguez (pictured opposite), who proclaimed himself Pope Gregory XVII in 1978 and who died in March 2002; a Puerto Rican woman Ana Luz Hernández (stigmatized in her sleep on 21 July 1990 while

Emiliano Aden was stigmatized at the age of 19, on 21 February 1996, as he returned home from his job in a supermarket in Buenos Aires. He felt as though his forehead was being pierced but his girlfriend could see nothing there. At the Pirovano hospital an X-ray and tests on blood and urine seemed normal so he was told it was just a migraine and sent home. He felt hot, and the touch of water seemed to make his sensations unbearable, "as if my head was opening". He started bleeding from a point in the centre of his forehead. "It was not ordinary blood. It was cold ... very cold," he told *Fortean Times* correspondent Enzo Daedro. Back home, he fainted and efforts to stop the bleeding failed. His mother called several priests to come but none would; they jumped to the conclusion that he had made the wound himself, which they regarded as blasphemy. Since then, he has bled regularly from his wrists, the now cross-shaped forehead wound, and an undisclosed "deep" wound. Otherwise, he spends his days in prayer and ecstasies.

George Wingfield

The Italian stigmatic and UFO contactee Giorgio Bongiovanni.

waiting for cancer surgery); and Argentina's Emiliano Aden (pictured above). Giorgio Bongiovanni had, for eleven years, been a protégé of Eugene Siragusa, Italy's most famous UFO contactee. Siragusa claimed contact with space beings lasting nearly twenty years and taught that angels and aliens were synonymous. Bongiovanni is often to be found at UFO conventions describing his visions of Jesus and Mary arriving in and descending from UFOs accompanied by "luminous beings" (who, he says, are responsible for some crop circles).

According to George Wingfield, who interviewed him for the *Cerealogist* in 1995, Bongiovanni also claims to be the reincarnation of

The Spanish heretic Clemente Domínguez who proclaimed himself Pope Gregory XVII in 1978.

Francisco Marta, one of the original child visionaries of Fátima (see RELIGIOUS VISIONS, p.124). But perhaps of greater relevance to this chapter is the independent testimony of doctors who have examined his stigmatic wounds. Wingfield records their astonishment at the rapidity with which the fresh blood coagulates (ten seconds), the absence of infection (to be expected in any large wound open for some time), and Bongiovanni's lack of anaemia (to be expected in anyone who bleeds as regularly and as copiously as he does).

Surprisingly, for such a curious phenomenon whose history goes back centuries, there is no let up in the supply of stigmatics to the present day. Among the many known to us are Canadian Lilian Bernaz, who now lives in England and has suffered the pain of crucifixion every day since 1992; the late Heather Woods, a very devout lady who lived quietly in Lincoln and only displayed her wounds to others with great reluctance; and Audrey Santo, a 14-year-old in Massachussetts, who is blind and brain-damaged from nearly drowning in 1994.

But what would the Inquisition have made of the German girl Anneliese Michel (see p.100). Not only did she die during an exorcism, her body was said to be incorrupt and bearing stigmata.

The incorruptibles

A French historian once commented that the true religion of the Middle Ages was the worship of relics. We now examine a subject that extends beyond the usual definition of a relic as a preserved piece – usually a body part – of a saint, to examples of the "miraculous" preservation of entire bodies. Although much of the documentation of such cases comes from religious sources, not every example of the phenomenon is confined to the ecclesiastical or the "holy".

One of the earliest cases with a convincing narrative is the story of the early Roman saints Gervase and Protase who were martyred in AD 64, during the reign of Nero. Over three hundred years later, Ambrose, Bishop of Milan, had a "presentiment" (his student St Augustine later called it a dream) in which St Paul revealed the location of their long-missing bodies. "I then called together the bishops of the cities thereabouts ... and we went together to the place indicated", wrote Ambrose in his *Epistle 22*. "I was the first to ply the mattock and throw up the earth, but the rest helped me, and at length we came upon a stone chest (twelve feet underground) in which was found the bodies of the two martyrs whole and perfectly sound, as if they had been laid there only that very day."

The assembled clergymen were intrigued and examined the bodies closely. After performing various tests, Ambrose and his colleagues discovered that the limbs of the two saints were "entire, their blood fresh, and the bodies emitted a sweet odour which spread through the city." Ambrose was in no doubt about the identity of the bodies: the spot had been revealed to him in a dream by an authority he would not dare question and, as also foretold in the dream, at their heads was a book containing an account of their lives and martyrdom. Ambrose built a church on the spot, located as many early churches were by similar dream revelation or divination.

While modern historians are unconvinced by the identification of the two bodies, we are left with the simple narrative of the finding of remains that had defied corruption for over three hundred years. It is a story that is consistently repeated and so often well-observed by many authoritative witnesses. The usual processes of mummification – drying out, using preservatives, petrification or saponification (literally, turning to soap) – seem hardly to apply in such well-documented circumstances. Also, in many instances, the incorruptible corpses are surrounded by other unremarkable bodies or graves.

A good example of this is the fate of the Blessed Margaret of Citta-di-Castello, a blind and crippled dwarf who devoted her life to helping the poor in Metola, in Italy's Apennine Mountains, before dying in 1330. In 1558, she was transferred to a new coffin because the old one had rotted away, as had her clothing. She was never preserved in any way and yet, after 228 years, her arms were flexible and her eyelashes and nails were intact. Today, perhaps a bit more dried out and darker, and dressed in a Dominican habit, she lies under the high altar of the Church of St Domenico in her home town.

Among many other examples we could mention are St Teresa of Ávila (d.1582) whose body did not decay after lying for years in wet mud; and the bodies of St Francis Xavier (d.1552) and St John of the Cross (d.1591) which remained "fresh" after being covered for months by sacks of quicklime.

Also, consider the fate of St Isidore, who died in Madrid in 1130. A farm labourer, Isidore was buried directly in the earth, without the benefit of a tomb or coffin. Forty years later, prompted by a parishioner's dream, the local church dug up his body for a more worthy resting place. A historian of the day recorded: "It was found to be perfect as if it had but just died although it had been lying in the earth for forty years. Not only was no sign of decay perceptible but a sweet ravishing odour proceeded from it, an odour which all extolled."

In 1622, Isidore was canonized and his body exhumed for a second time, before many witnesses, for removal to a splendid new tomb. The history of his canonization, printed by order of King Philip III of Castile, says: "Not only was the body sound and fresh but there issued from it a heavenly odour." The document was signed by Philip's minister, de Groote, on 18 June 1625. In May 1969, St Isidore's body was transferred to Madrid's cathedral, where it was exposed for ten days. Many thousands filed past the "darkened, rigid, but perfect" 800-year-old body.

Other cases abound in Christian archives and hagiographies. *The Incorruptibles* (1977), by Joan Carroll Cruz, details 102 cases and refers to a great many more little-known and unpublicized reports. One of the most impressive cases Cruz cites is of "the perfectly preserved and bleeding body" of the Lebanese saint Charbel Makhlouf. This Maronite monk died on 24 December 1898, eight days after having a seizure while conducting Mass. During his life he practised a severe corporeal discipline: he wore a hair shirt, slept on the ground and ate only one meal a day. According to the custom of his monastery in Annaya, Lebanon, St Charbel was buried in his daily robes, unembalmed and without a coffin. It is acknowledged that he would probably have been forgotten but for an extraordinary phenomenon: for forty-five nights following the interment (reckoned to be the usual period of decomposition) a bright light surrounded his grave. The monastery officials requested permission from the superiors of their Order to exhume the body and this was done, three months later, in their presence with a crowd of villagers in attendance.

Because of the regular, heavy rains which had inundated the cemetery, St Charbel was found almost floating in a grave full of muddy water. After the body was washed and reclothed a curious fluid seeped from its pores. Described as a mixture of perspiration and blood, it had the smell of blood and was regarded as such by the faithful. The flow increased, necessitating a change of clothing twice a week; portions of the soaked clothing were distributed as relics and were credited with cures. This continued until July 1927, when the body was placed in a wooden coffin lined with zinc, along with a sealed zinc tube containing notarized testimonies of the phenomena from some very senior Catholic officials. For the next twenty-three years the coffin was sealed in a special crypt in the oratory wall, raised on stones to protect it from moisture.

The piety of St Charbel attracted a huge following, causing a flow of pilgrims to Annaya which continues on an even greater scale today. In February 1950, pilgrims noticed liquid seeping through the oratory wall onto the floor. Fearing damage to St Charbel's tomb, it was opened up in April and his body was again found to be "flexible and lifelike" and free of any corruption. As Cruz reports: "The sweat of liquid and blood continued to exude from the body, and the garments were found stained with blood, the white content of the fluid having collected on the body in an almost solidified condition." Following this news, the flow of pilgrims reached five thousand a day. His body is examined each year (on which occasion around three inches of "blood" are found) but has

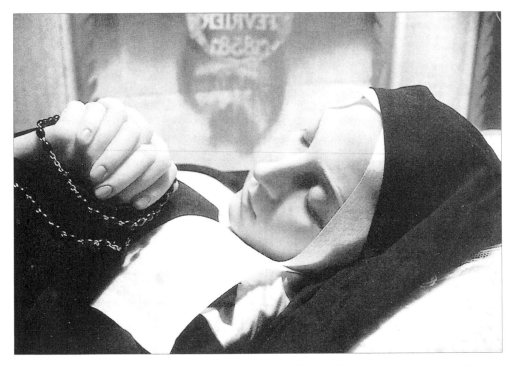

The body of St Bernadette of Lourdes, preserved in the Saint Gildard convent at Nevers. She died in April 1879 and was exhumed thirty years later before a small crowd of church officials, all of whom attested to the lack of decay, even though her clothes were damp. She was washed, reclothed and reburied in a sealed, double casket. A second exhumation took place ten years later and the body, although intact, was slightly discoloured. A thin coating of wax was applied to the face before the body was placed in a glass coffin for viewing, and a comparison of this new face with her "old" one does suggest a degree of re-modelling was involved. Of course critics have used this cosmetic change to discredit the idea the body beneath the wax was incorrupt, but sound testimony supported the claim for incorruption long before the beauticians began their work.

When Reverend Father Paul of Moll, in Belgium, was exhumed on 24 July 1899, three years after his death, his preservation was said to be "perfect".

not been on public display since 1950.

While people generally take such phenomena as levitation, stigmata, visions and incorruption as miracles and tokens of sanctity, the Church's Congregation of Rites (which decides on canonization and beatification) itself warns that "alleged charismata and supernatural favours are common to good and bad alike". In our researches, we have had many occasions to admire the Congregation of Rites' discerning, and at times quite scientific, attitude towards the evidence for miracles. Contrary to what is claimed by sceptics, miracles alone do not make a saint. On the other hand, the more simple among the faithful frequently take "miraculous" phenomena – including incorruption – to be tangible signs of sainthood. They are the first to be shocked when the remains of people who were definitely not saints during their lives, are found to be incorrupt.

When the body of Cardinal Schuster of Milan was discovered to be incorrupt in 1985, nearly thirty-one years after his death, the mood of the Roman clergy was one of dismay. Schuster was remembered as a friend of Mussolini and

an open supporter of fascism and of Italy's war in Abyssinia. One religious writer called it "the most embarrassing discovery since Eve noticed her nakedness". Nevertheless, supporters of Schuster began a campaign for his beatification which was instantly countered with allegations that "injection marks" had been found where he had been injected with preservatives.

An interesting non-Christian case involved the famous yogi Paramahansa Yogananda (1893–1952), who settled in Los Angeles in 1920, where he taught classical yoga techniques and philosophy and founded the Self-Realization Fellowship. Part of his teaching included the idea that an advanced yogi could induce a state of suspended animation in which the vital functions were undetectable and which enabled the body's ageing processes to be controlled. In other words he could simulate death for long periods and extend his lifetime.

The biographies of Yogananda record that he predicted that his death would occur on 7 March 1952, and that his body would reveal a sign that he was a true yogi. Although seeming in perfect health, he died on the appointed day of a heart attack. According to his instructions, his body was not to be embalmed but placed in a glass-topped coffin for twenty days. When it was finally buried, the body was said to be without any sign of decay and exuding a pleasant fragrance. This "perfect preservation" was confirmed by Harry T. Rowen of the Forest Lawn Memorial Park in Glendale, California, in a notarized statement. It was, he said, "unparalleled in mortuary annals" (*Grit*, 2 July 1972).

However useful it may be to assume that highly developed yogic control over biological processes may be a factor in the mystery of incorruptible corpses, it clearly played no part in the case of two-year-old Nadja Mattei, who died in Rome in 1965. Her mother told reporters that for the following twelve years her daughter's voice would come to her in dreams, asking to be brought out of her coffin. When the girl's body was exhumed in 1977 it was found to be quite undecayed (*News of the World*, 8 May 1977).

We still hear reports of "incorruption", too many to give here, but included among the most recent cases are the Romanian Orthodox priest Ilie Lacatusu, who died in Bucharest in December 1983. Father Lacatusu was exhumed in September 1999, 16 years after his death, and found to be dry, brown and to have a "pleasant smell". As yet another example of incorruption outside a religious context, there is also the 1992 case of an unnamed woman in the Hubei province of China. It was said that three and a half years

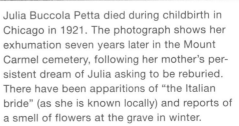

Julia Buccola Petta died during childbirth in Chicago in 1921. The photograph shows her exhumation seven years later in the Mount Carmel cemetery, following her mother's persistent dream of Julia asking to be reburied. There have been apparitions of "the Italian bride" (as she is known locally) and reports of a smell of flowers at the grave in winter.

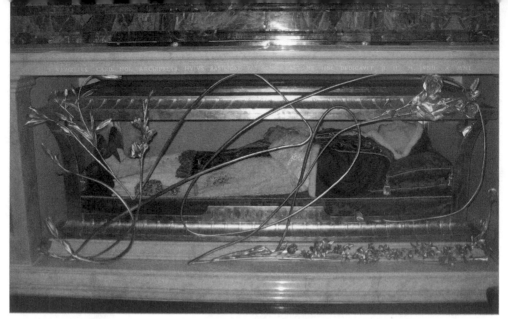

As we come into the present, "incorrupt" bodies are more likely to have benefited from subtle and technologically improved preservation methods that stop short of full embalming. Pope John XXIII, for example, was exhumed in March 2001, 37 years after his death. His body showed little sign of decay, was put on view at the Vatican and drew huge crowds before it was re-interred. It is interesting to note that, in contrast to the popular belief that the state of his body was "a miracle", the Vatican's own Information Service announced simply that it was "remarkably well preserved". It is a matter of record that formaldehyde was injected into his tissues and that he was placed in a triple-sealed marble crypt. A spokesman from the University of Rome said: "The body of the Holy Father was well protected. Oxygen couldn't get into the coffin and any in there would have been used up [by normal decomposition] very quickly." The inner caskets, he added, "used materials like lead and zinc which oxidise and slow the decomposition process".

after her death from heart failure the woman's face was "radiant" and her joints still supple. Two days after she died, rigor mortis still had not set in, said her son, so the family decided to keep her corpse unburied. At the time of the report, just over three years later, there was no sign of decomposition despite fluctuating temperatures from freezing to 34°C (93°F). (*Reuters*, 18 April 1996)

The most recent case known to us is that of Maria Regina Tobon Restrepo of Medein, Colombia, whose body was exhumed four years after she died in a diabetic coma, aged 33. Martha Valencia, a mortician with eighteen years' experience, said Maria Regina's eyes were intact, there was no sign of fungus, nor any smell of decay. Even her dress was preserved. "She looked like a precious doll," said Valencia (*El Tiempo*, 8 October 1998). It has been suggested that Maria may have been preserved by the doses of insulin she needed. Instead of creating an object of veneration, the family decided the body should go to the University of Antioquia for research purposes.

There is a strong tradition of prescient dreams (containing messages from the deceased) associated with this topic but our last story shows that this is not always a reliable indicator. In 1976 a 33-year-old German girl, Anneliese Michel, died during an exorcism ordered by the Bishop of Wurzburg. The circumstances of her death were shocking: believing her to be possessed by demons (including the spirit of Hitler), the exorcists starved her during their protracted rites and were subsequently tried for criminal neglect.

After her death a feeling grew that a great injustice had been done to the girl. In 1977 a nun told the girl's parents that Anneliese had visited her repeatedly in dreams, saying: "Let my coffin be opened for all to see. They will find my body untouched by mortal decay, as you see me now, with the nail wounds of Christ on my hands and feet." Subjected to mounting pressure from the family, priests and the public, the local authorities agreed to exhume the body. On 26 February 1978 a crowd of many thousands gathered and overflowed the cemetery near Klingenberg in expectation of seeing a double miracle – the stigmatized and uncorrupted body of a saint.

The police tried in vain to control the crowds as they scaled walls and stood on graves and monuments for a better view. In the *News of the World* (12 March 1978), reporter George Edwards gives a first-hand account of the scene. As the earth-covered coffin was lifted and taken to the mortuary to be opened, the crowd spontaneously (and prematurely) shouted, "It's a miracle! She looks as if she's alive!" In the mortuary it was a different story. The coffin was opened before the Bavarian State prosecutor and the Mayor of Klingenberg to reveal the body in an advanced state of decomposition. According to Edwards, the crowd was stunned with dismay and dispersed "feeling they had been cheated".

Miraculous provisions

In his article, "Miracles", in the encyclopedia *Man, Myth and Magic* (1970) A.R.G. Owen writes that Christ's miraculous feeding of the five thousand tends to be interpreted today as a parable of "spiritual feeding" rather than as a factual record of a multitude of people dining off five loaves and two fishes divided between the lot of them. The story may seem more rational that way, but St Mark in the sixth chapter of his Gospel, described it as a contemporary, eye-witnessed event. If Jesus actually performed such a miracle, he is by no means the only holy man to have done so. The feeding of very many on very little is called theologically a "miracle of abundance" and merits a whole chapter in Pope Benedict XIV's definitive guide to mystical phenomena, *De servorum Dei beatificatione et canonizatione*. Father Herbert Thurston re-examines a number of these in *The Physical Phenomena of Mysticism* (1952) and concludes that the phenomenon of multiplication cannot be lightly dismissed as belonging solely to the domain of legend.

It is claimed that such miracles of abundance are performed today by the Indian holy man Sai Baba. In *Sai Baba: Man of Miracles* (1971) Howard Murphet gives an account of a party after a religious ceremony at the house of Mr and Mrs Ramachandran, near Poona. A hundred guests had been catered for, but about a thousand turned up. Sai Baba was present and saved the day by miraculously multiplying the food tenfold during its serving so that all were fully satisfied. At other times, Murphet writes, the saint could instantly

Mosaic of loaves and fishes on the altar of the Church of the Multiplication which stands on the site where Jesus worked the miracle of the feeding of the five thousand.

Among the well-documented recipients of a materialized Communion Host is St Catherine of Siena (d.1380). In Christian art, this miraculous transportation is usually attributed to an angel – here shown, middle right, bringing the Communion wafer to St Catherine, middle bottom.

radishes for a salad, a tart, and a basket of strawberries for dessert, all of which were very scarce because of drought.

One of the most authoritative cases of multiplication procured the beatification of St Andrew Fournet (d.1834), founder of Les Filles de la Croix, a house for educating the poor at La Puye, in Poitou. One year, about 1824, the sisters at La Puye were in despair because they had very little corn in their granary and no money to buy more. After admonishing their lack of faith in a sermon about Christ's multiplication miracle, St Andrew bade them gather what corn they could find into two heaps, around which he walked in prayer. Subsequently, the sister in charge of the granary drew enough to feed some two hundred sisters daily, and for the next two and a half months the heaps did not diminish at all. According to the *Summarium* for his beatification, St Andrew performed this miracle on several occasions and kept the house in cornflour from July to December.

Auffray's *Life of the Blessed John Bosco* also quotes from beatification documents in evidence of this saint's power to perform the miracle of abundance. One day in 1860 Don Bosco was informed there was nothing for breakfast in the Salesian house in Turin in which he was staying. The eyes of three hundred hungry boys were on him as he asked for all the scraps of bread of any size to be brought to him. Everybody there could see there were only fifteen or twenty small pieces of bread in the basket he held as he walked among them yet each person received a piece.

In some of these accounts the miracle takes

produce sweets still hot from cooking. These and other miracles are still witnessed by pilgrims to Sai Baba's sanctuary in India.

Prolific feats of edible magic were attributed to St Angiolo Paoli (d.1720), who delighted in multiplying small quantities of food to distribute to the poor of Rome and rarely refused any genuine request. According to his biographer, he was often sent on picnics arranged by the sponsors of some of the Carmelite missions. On one hot June day the saint took a group to a garden party where he provided lettuces and place in the dough while the bread is still being made. For example, in the hard winter of 1845 the Bon Pasteur convent at Bourges was faced with supplying the daily needs of 116 people from a depleted granary. Blessed Mother Pelletier instructed the nuns to pray for the intercession of St Germaine Cousin, confident that the small supply would be replenished. The cooking sisters were urged to use about a third of the customary amount of flour; and, sure enough, within minutes the dough had swollen to overflow the kneading trough with enough for twice the usual number of loaves. This was repeated many times between November 1845 and February 1846, during which time the nuns did not have to buy any more flour. The documentation of these wonders was thorough enough to be cited for the canonization of St Germaine in 1854, and the beatification of Mother Pelletier.

It is interesting to note that traditional folklore stories of Christ's and St Peter's wanderings on Earth include variants of this phenomenon. One story, in G.W. Dasent's *Popular Tales from the Norse* (1903), tells of how the two came to a baker's house and begged some bread from his wife. Believing them to be mere ordinary beggars, she took a small piece of dough which then expanded to cover the whole griddle. Not wanting to give away so much, she broke off another small piece but this also expanded and she decided not to give it away at all. Christ angrily turned her into a woodpecker.

Accounts of miracles of abundance go back to well before Christian times. They can be found all over the world, in legends of magic cauldrons and fairy cups that can never be drained and which provide everybody they serve with whatever they wish to eat or drink. Legends of the ever-full cups of the fairies are continuous with stories of miraculous draughts of wine in the lives of the saints. It is said that St Dominic, who died in 1221, blessed a cup of wine from which 26 people drank. It was then carried to a convent, where 104 nuns each swallowed a mouthful. It was returned to the saint still full. At the risk of being thought literal minded, we imagine that there may be some truth in these tales, but we also believe that such miraculous provisions must have come from somewhere. Being aware of the teleportation effect, and suspecting that it may sometimes be used by saints and magicians, we look around for corresponding stories of missing provisions and, indeed, could fill this book with accounts of food and other objects which vanish from one place and appear in another.

The supply of provisions to people who desperately need them sometimes takes place without the intervention of a holy man. In *Fortean Times* (48, p.16), Bob Skinner quotes an example of answered prayers from Increase Mather's *Remarkable Providences* (1684). Twelve people in a small boat were adrift for five weeks in the North Atlantic after their ship sank off New England. "God sent relief to them by causing some flying fish to fall into the boat which they ate raw and were well pleased therewith." Even better is the account of three fishermen from the islands of Kiribati in the Pacific. In April 1986 the engine of their boat failed and they were adrift for 119 days before being rescued. They had survived by catching sharks with their bare hands, drinking their blood and eating their raw flesh. When sick of this diet, they prayed for a change, and while they were praying something fell into the boat. It was a rare blackfish. Police sergeant Paul Aingilia of Naurui, the island off which the men were rescued, was amazed by this. The blackfish, he said, never comes to the surface. "It lives about 620 feet down and cannot be caught by trawling."

In RAINS OF SEEDS AND ORGANIC MATTER (see p.58) we mention cases of seeds, all of one kind, falling from the sky onto a specific area of land. These falls were seen and recorded. Imagine a fallow field that lies waiting for seed, like the empty ponds that yearn for fish (see FALLS OF FISHES AND FROGS, p.22), and an unobserved fall of seed which later sprouts. In 1919 there were two recorded instances of the mysterious appearance of wheatfields: the *Cardiff Evening News* (1 July 1919), said that in a field in Lincolnshire, which had been fallow since its last crop of barley ten years before, there appeared a crop of wheat said to be finer than that in surrounding fields; and the London *Sunday Express* (24 August 1920) tells that after a drought had killed off a field of wheat near Ormskirk, Lancashire, the previous year, "one of the best crops of vigorous young wheat" the farmer had ever seen appeared without his re-seeding the field. A more modern tale of wheat appearing unexpectedly took place near Milan where a farmer noticed a fine crop in a 21-acre field. According to the *Daily Mirror* (29 April 1968) this had happened several times in preceding years, but as soon as the crop ripened it

vanished overnight despite careful observation. We wonder if the grain ever materialized in some destitute convent's granary.

Records of vanishing seeds are less common, since this is a subject that is hardly likely to excite the interest of newspaper reporters, and few cases have been recorded. One that we have discovered took place in 1974 when farmers in Worcestershire and Shropshire were faced with a bill for £2,000 when their sugar-beet seeds inexplicably vanished from the fields. Blaming a plague of mice, they took elaborate preventative measures – flattening the furrows and laying poison – but the seeds continued to vanish. According to the *Sunday Mercury* (26 May 1974) experts tried all that they could think of but remained baffled as to a possible explanation.

In Malory's *Morte d'Arthur* (1485), the materialization of the Holy Grail brought each of the knights of the Round Table generous helpings of their favourite food and drink. Similar beliefs were held about the magical cups and cauldrons of fairies and witches.

Near-death experiences and the Life Review

What happens to us – to our mind and personality – after our body dies? This remains one of the great questions facing modern science. Writing in 1935 of his interest in this subject, the respected Jesuit hagiographer Herbert Thurston (1856–1939) noted that: "…none of us know what mysteries may underlie the last moments of human existence". He was aware of many popular sources for such accounts, but being a scholar and critic of spiritualism, dismissed as "quite unreliable" stories told via mediums or attributed to "ghosts". What interested him, particularly, was "the degree to which the conscious exercise of the mental powers may remain and possibly even be intensified during proximity to death".

Thurston's interest had been sparked by an incident involving his father, when he was young and they were living on Guernsey. He recollected this in the Catholic periodical *The Month*

(1935): "One day, I remember very clearly that my father came in looking different from his usual self and, as even I could tell, apparently a good deal shaken. My mother asked him what was the matter …There was a public bathing place, which I knew well, with a sort of stone jetty running out into deep water. My father had accidentally slipped off the end of this, and being unable to swim or to clamber up the smooth stone surface, he had sunk twice and been rescued with difficulty … 'Everything', he said, 'that I had ever done in my life passed before me in a flash.'"

This particular experience has come to be called "the Life Review" and another good example was provided by Thurston's colleague John Gerard, then editor of the *The Month*. Writing in February 1913, he drew on an entry in his diary for 15 December 1859. He was with two other students at Stonyhurst College, the Catholic seminary in Lancashire, when one fell through a hole in the ice. The young Gerard lay flat to reach his friend and he too was pulled into the icy water below. He could not swim and struggled towards the small grey patch of light above.

The very moment he plunged into the freezing

water, he recalled, "…there flashed across me, along with the realisation that death was, apparently, immediately inevitable, a perfect picture of my past life in every minutest detail. It was not a chronicle of successive events but a picture, or rather a map, which thought instead of sight perceived – everything was seen simultaneously and everything with equal clearness, yet without any confusion, as an insect may be supposed to see through its compound eyes".

"Everything seemed to be included, however trivial," wrote Gerard, "but it was only my own part I saw; nobody else appeared. Conscience appeared to play no part in the matter. I can remember nothing in the way of recognition of good and evil in my past actions – but, on the other hand, there was an overwhelming sense of responsibility."

Returning to the first example, Thurston said that his father "was not an imaginative man", which is why his apparent reference to an old folk belief – that a drowning man's life will flash before his eyes – "more than anything, impressed my childish imagination". In the years that followed, Thurston collected a number of similar accounts, learning that they were not confined solely to the experience of drowning, but were told by those who had returned from the brink of death. Today, we call them near-death experiences (NDEs).

In 1871, the Swiss geologist, Professor Albert Heim, fell while mountaineering. Later, he wrote: "I saw my whole past take place in many images, as though on a stage at some distance from me. I saw myself as the chief character in the performance. Everything was transfigured as though by a heavenly light and everything was beautiful without grief or anxiety, and without pain. The memory of very tragic experiences I had had was clear but not saddening. I felt no conflict or strife … and like a magnificent music, a divine calm swept through my soul."

He, too, was turned into a collector of similar "near-death" stories by his experience and he published his data in *Notes on Deaths from Falls* (1891). As he collated his material, he found that most of the stories shared some elements in common: the absence of fear; a "speeding up" of subjective time; and the whole experienced with a sense of detachment that was generally described as a "divine love" that seemed to transcend the mundane.

S.W. Cozzens spoke of these aspects of the

The writer Thomas de Quincey (1785–1859), recorded the experience of a near relative who "having in her childhood fallen into a river, and being on the very verge of death, but for the assistance which reached her at the last critical moment … saw in an instant her whole life, clothed in its forgotten incidents, arrayed before her as in a mirror, not successively, but simultaneously".

phenomenon after he stumbled and fell while climbing a mountain in Arizona. "Convinced that death was inevitable, I became perfectly reconciled to the thought. My mind comprehended in a moment the acts of a lifetime. Transactions of the most trivial character … the remembrance of which had been buried deep in memory's vault for years, stood before me in bold relief; my mind recalled with the rapidity of lightning and yet retained a distinct impression of every thought. I seemed to be gliding swiftly and surely out of the world, but felt no fear, experienced no regret at the prospect." (*The Marvellous Country*, 1875)

Among many similar accounts of identical experiences of a personal "Judgement Day" – picked at random from the impressive collections of modern cases referenced here – include statements that show a remarkable consistency. "I could not believe that this is where my life would end … Scenes from my life began to pass before my eyes at super-high speeds. It seemed as if I was a passive observer in the process … I was looking at my life objectively for the first time ever … I saw the good as well as the bad."

Today, the Life Review is subsumed into the general study of "Out-of-the-Body Experiences" (OBEs) – a less emotive term than "near-death experiences". There is also considerable anecdotal evidence that OBEs can occur naturally and spontaneously in circumstances that are not always near-fatal; it is regarded by some researchers as a special or "altered" state of consciousness. And, as the archives of survivor narratives have swelled, more and more medical men have turned their attention to the prospect of a more productive analysis.

David Lorimer's excellent overview of OBEs, *Whole In One* (1990) cites a study by two psychiatrists – Russell Noyes and Ray Kletti – who interviewed 57 survivors of falls, 48 survivors of drownings, 54 of car accidents, 29 of serious illnesses and 27 of miscellaneous near-fatal accidents. The highest percentage of those reporting "Life Reviews" were the nearly drowned (47 percent), while those surviving falls were the lowest (16 percent). They also refer to a range of studies by medical men that show considerable variation in the incidence of the OBE. Lorimer seems confident it is somewhere between 2 and 47 percent of those brought back from the brink of death. Another great student of the phenomenon, Dr Kenneth Ring (d.1994), thought that the triggering factor is the suddenness of the life-threatening situation.

Modern writers on OBEs owe a huge debt of thanks to two pioneers who began their systematic study. The first authority on the subject was the American writer-experimenter Sylvan Muldoon (1903–71). Muldoon claimed to be able to have been able to "project" voluntarily since the age of twelve. Putting his wealth of experience at the disposal of Hereward Carrington (1880–1958), a physicist and SPR pioneer, resulted in several published studies of experimental methods of inducing such experiences voluntarily.

They were followed by Dr Robert Crookall (1890–1981) who, while a confirmed Spiritualist, made a heroic attempt to systematize the known phenomena. In a stream of books, he collected many hundreds of personal accounts of Astral Projection, as it was then known to Spiritualists and Theosophists, identifying the Life Review as a critical stage in the individual's spiritual evolution – a view later adopted by Dr Kenneth Ring.

Dr Crookall categorized his own database of 160 cases according to circumstances – so we had the "natural" experiences of those who were dying but recovered (namely the seriously ill), the physically exhausted and the completely well; as distinct from the "enforced" experiences of those under anaesthetic, or from potentially fatal accidents (drowning, falling, etc), and those experiences induced by hypnosis.

He also realized that the structure of OBEs tended to follow a pattern, although not all the elements in his list occur in every case. So, as well as the Life Review, which is one of the most common or constant elements, the experiencer might also report a sensation of floating; a travelling, "externalized" viewpoint that can look back and see their physical body; travelling through a tunnel and emerging into some beautiful environment; a pervading sense of wellbeing and calm; and, sometimes, meeting with entities who may be departed friends, family or spiritual figures.

Dr Crookall is also credited with being the first to notice that the details each percipient encounters are often interpreted differently, according to disposition, culture or education. Thus, the transition between in-body and out-of-body environments is not always described as travelling through a tunnel towards light; other metaphors include crossing a river by boat, going down a corridor or path, through a doorway or up a flight of stairs.

Given the nature of this material, its origins and emotional baggage, and its far-reaching implications for ethics and morality, it is not surprising

"Projectionist" extraodinaire, Sylvan Muldoon.

that many scientists regard it with hostility and distaste. It may be that diehard sceptics will never be convinced of the reality of the phenomenon, even if it provides all the proofs they require. What *is* heartening is the growing number of serious scientists and medics who are taking the trouble to examine the huge volume of firsthand narratives, analyses and objective studies.

The extraordinary consistency of the phenomenon strongly suggests its reality, and this echoes the arguments of folklorists and psychologists for the persistence of archetypes or motifs found in the religious and mythological canons of other cultures and times. It is not enough to say, as some critics do, that there is no guarantee of the veracity of these narratives. Considerable effort has been made by modern, medically trained investigators to address that important question, to consider only material whose circumstances can be verified, so that, even if all the doubtful accounts were eliminated, there would still be a body of serious data.

Nevertheless, the scientists and doctors who have studied the topic are quite divided, on both the matter of evidence and the ideology. On the one hand, you have the materialists, and, on the other, the more spiritually inclined. In between are the agnostics, who recognize that there seems to be a genuine phenomenon here and who are not distracted by the spiritualist and religious terminology and explanations.

The OBE presents difficulties in terms of providing objective "scientific" proof. It is purely personal, and cannot be studied "on demand". This difficulty is discussed in chapter two of Dr Kenneth Ring's *Lessons From The Light* (1998), but his writings are optimistic: "Fortunately, as a result of nearly twenty years of research on NDEs, such examples are not difficult to come by." These include observations of people and things from viewpoints the experiencers could not have had while unconscious; and clear visual descriptions of people and things by the blind. One of Ring's impressive cases concerned a patient who, after being under anaesthetic for an operation, gave a description of a shoe on the hospital roof. It was subsequently proved correct and no one involved had prior knowledge of it.

However, those basing their objections entirely in materialism may never be convinced. Dr Susan Blackmore, for instance, argues that such experiences can be happily accounted for

Dr Kenneth Ring, who, while conducting his research, worked with over one hundred individuals who had lived through near-death experiences.

as being entirely generated in the dying brain. In her book *Dying To Live* (1993), she attributes the feelings of wellbeing to a flood of endorphins in the temporal lobe, and the tunnel and light experiences to oxygen-starvation and perhaps a neural hallucination from the optic nerve. In response, we might reasonably ask how a dying brain – in which the neural integrity is disintegrating, and in which we might expect increasingly random processes – experiences order, purpose, clarity, certainty, direction and detailed recall.

The Life Review does seem to have purpose (however one explains it) to judge from its life-changing consequences. This impressed Professor Ring, who went beyond the phenomenology of OBEs to explore its moral and spiritual implications. Narrators are, again, nearly unanimous in implying that the Life Review somehow transcends orthodox religious teaching to reach a higher level of pure ethics. In Ring's view, it is an ethical function that does more than simply eliminate negative attachments and emotions; the Life Review appears to be structured as a learning experience.

"[OBEs] teach us, unmistakably in my judgement, how we are to live ... No one who undergoes one of these encounters can avoid

Stainton Moses, (1839–92, pictured standing) told of what happened to him while boating on the Isis at Oxford. "I was run down and, as I could not swim a stroke, I soon sank ... I floundered about until, I suppose, I became unconscious. At any rate, a strange peacefulness took the place of my previous feeling. I recognised fully that I was drowning, but no sort of fear was present to my mind. I did not even regret the fact. By degrees, as it seemed – though the process must have been instantaneous – I recollected my life ... The next thing I remember was the interruption of this peaceful state by a series of most unpleasant sensations which were attendant on resuscitation." Moses went on to become famous as a medium and as the first editor of the spiritualist periodical *Light*. In this photograph a ghostly apparition is seen invading an otherwise normal portrait.

becoming aware of these teachings ... because they are shown to be self-evident," writes Ring. This experience, while absolutely personal, seems to be universally applicable; the narratives agree on this to an astonishing degree. In addition, while all your actions – whether doing good or harming others – are reviewed for their consequences, the process is, apparently, detached from any kind of conventional moral judgement.

We are repeatedly told that the experience was neither an escapist fantasy nor an evasion of responsibility, but a gritty "inescapable self-knowledge" obliging one to recognize one's personal responsibility. Statistically, the majority of survivors return changed to some degree, losing their fear of death and intent on living a more fulfilling and moral life.

Other aspects of the Life Review are equally, if not more, remarkable. Ring noted that those who undergo it: "...stress that their experience does not take place in time but in a state of virtual simultaneity – all at once. When they recall the experience, however, they are forced to do so under the artificial but compelling constraints of clock time ... It is important not to confuse the experience itself with its description." This seemingly absurd paradox recalls accounts of mystical illumination or of time spent in "Fairyland" in which, similarly, a subjective sense of time is expanded or contracted independently of time in the everyday world.

Some experiencers, according to Ring, "...are, at the same time, in these scenes and are living through them as if they are actually experiencing them again". A woman recovering from a serious illness told Crookall: "Before my inner sight there flashed a complete series of pictures embodying my life ... It seemed that I became both actor and witness in these pictures." Another, cited by Ring, said: "I was the very people that I hurt, and I was the very people I helped to feel good." For the writer P.M.H. Atwater, the experience "...was hell itself ... a total reliving of every thought I had ever thought, every word I had ever spoken, and every deed I had ever done."

Many stated that the direct experience of the consequences of this "Do unto others" rule felt like a powerful form of natural justice. This is the profound realization to which we are guided, argued Ring, taking it to the inevitable, mystical, conclusion: "Psychologically and spiritually there is really only one person in the universe – and that person is yourself." It seems to be an unequivocal demonstration of the interconnectedness of all things; something that forteans are – intellectually, at least – inclined to appreciate.

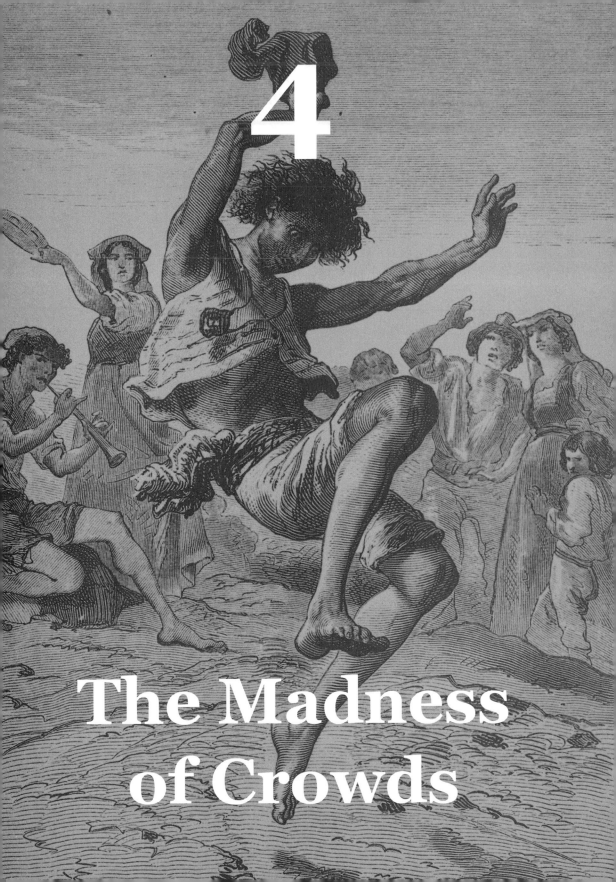

4

The Madness
of Crowds

4

The Madness of Crowds

Shared visions and visual rumours

People see visions. It is a recurring feature of human experience, both private and collective, and one on which rationalism has made little impact. In fact visionary experiences of all kinds seem to be on the increase, as almost weekly we learn of some new sighting of a phantom animal, an unidentified flying object (UFO), or the Virgin Mary. A wide range of explanations is available, from psychology and pathology to the occult. Our interest here is in those visions which are perceived by more than one person.

Edmund Parrish in *Hallucinations and Illusions* (1897) discusses an incident which began with the death of a lame ship's cook. Several days later the form of the cook was clearly seen and identified by all on board the ship, limping across the waters towards them. As the vision drew nearer it suddenly resolved itself into a piece of floating wreckage. Parrish suggests that initially one person, brooding on the loss of a friend, thought he saw the cook and in telling the others planted the suggestion in their minds. This, he says, may be the genesis of all ghosts. Perhaps, but we have some doubts; things are not always so conveniently explicable.

A vision was shared by the Abbé Caucanas and thirty of his congregation in the Languedoc village of Castelnau-de-Guers, at Easter 1974 and reported in many papers. The Abbé was rising from kneeling at the altar when he saw "the face of Our Lord" on the white napkin covering the ciborium containing the Eucharistic bread. He cried out and when the congregation surged forward to help him, they too saw the face. The Abbé said he saw "the right eye closed, the left open. The nose was bruised and swollen and bore an expression of pain." Others saw tears flowing, and some a crown of thorns. After fifteen minutes the Abbé lifted the napkin to continue the service and the image disappeared. (See also VERONICA AND THE SHROUD, p.281.)

The Eucharist has been the setting for many extraordinary incidents – some of which are mentioned elsewhere in this book – so "set and setting" (as Dr Timothy Leary used to say about LSD trips) must play an important part. A faithful priest and his flock would certainly be aware of the lore surrounding one of the most magical rituals of Christianity. Was the priest's gasp enough to influence the congregation?

Professor E.R. Jaensch (*Eidetic Imagery*, 1930) explained away, in a brief footnote, hundreds of accounts by people who saw statues and paintings come to life. They were "eidetic images", he said – persistent images generated in the eye and

FATE magazine

In December 1929 two crewmen died on board the SS *Watertown* and were buried at sea. The next day their likenesses were seen in the waves, always from the same position on deck. The vision recurred on the following two voyages and then disappeared.

superimposed onto normal vision. But taking a panoramic view of strange phenomena, we can point to many accounts of groups of people who see previously inanimate objects move or speak, shed tears or bleed. The consistency of these accounts demands our respect and we have given them their own sections – IMAGES THAT WEEP AND BLEED (p.287) and STATUES THAT COME TO LIFE (p.291).

To account for mass visions which occur without any apparent element of suggestion, modern writers have proposed some kind of telepathic exchange. An earlier version of this theory – given by Catherine Crowe in *The Night-Side of Nature* (1848) – is that a seer, by touching or otherwise spellbinding other members of a group, can induce them to share his or her vision. In FIRE-WALKING AND FIRE-IMMUNITY (p.68) we have noticed the similar role of an officiating magician, who creates temporarily the spell of a different order of reality.

Another classic example is the "Indian Rope Trick" (pictured overleaf). In its full form, a small boy goes up the rope, the magician (also known as a *fakir*) follows with a knife, and both seem to vanish at the top. Screams are heard, followed by a grisly rain of dismembered parts. The magician comes down with a bloody knife, collects and places the bloody remains in a box, makes some magical flourish and soon the boy emerges whole and smiling. In some performances witnesses may

see a dog run off with an arm or leg – a moment of comedy, perhaps – which has to be recovered before the assistant can be resurrected.

In *This Baffling World* (1968), John Godwin states his belief that the Indian rope trick is just that, a trick; and he suggests how it could be worked as a conjuring illusion. Against this is the experience of two investigating psychologists, described in Andrija Puharich's *Beyond Telepathy* (1962), who saw the act with hundreds of other witnesses.

Puharich's psychologists saw the magician collect the parts of the boy in a basket, go back up the rope and return with the boy whole. When they developed their film, they saw to their astonishment the *fakir* and boy simply standing impassively by the rope, which was all the time coiled on the floor. The entire sequence had been imagined and conducted in silence. Puharich concludes that "the hallucination originated with the *fakir* ... was telepathically inspired and extended to the several hundred people present". In 1934 the trick was performed twice in London, and on the second occasion the organizers concealed cameras. When developed, the film revealed the rope on the ground and the boy scuttling for the bushes. Those present were witnessing an event that did not take place in normal reality.

In an increasingly materialistic world, the growing list of religious apparition sites is a reminder of deep psychological and spiritual

needs, unfulfilled by society, often expressed in new and surprising ways. We'll reserve the overtly religious phenomena for its own section (see p.124), but point out here the significance of events that merge at their periphery into other categories of phenomena. Underlying all is the continuity of phenomenal existence and experience. We'll see visions of the Virgin Mary couched in terms that could describe a UFO, apparitions of saints that resemble holograms, holy symbols that may be patterns in seeds and clouds or the reflections of street lamps.

For example, towards the end of 1995, the Baptist Church at Copper Ridge, Tennessee, attracted great interest when some of its congregation reported seeing huge crosses of light in its windows. Rejecting any suggestion that they were created by street lighting or a product of the glass, Pastor Joe Bullard encouraged investigation believing the phenomenon to be a portent for a global revival of Christianity. Over several years, the phenomenon grew: crosses were seen during daylight and seemed to glow. What lifts this out of the ordinary is that enigmatic, seemingly non-religious apparitions were also seen.

Writing in *Fortean Times*, Xan Phillips reports how Rev Bullard and a number of others "...were sitting on one side of the church when we saw a fully formed man wearing a turban appear on the opposite side of the church and walk slowly forward. Two other people with a cloudy appearance materialized and followed him. Every couple of steps the last person in line turned slightly towards us and waved in a friendly manner." When this curious procession reached the far wall it retraced its route again with the turbaned man in the lead. They marched thus, back and forth, three times before disappearing. "Even the normally voluble Bullard was at a loss to say what this might signify." (Xan Phillips, "Do you see the light,

The popular image of the Indian Rope Trick as performed by an English illusionist and assistant. In India itself, the illusion is created by *fakir*s who brilliantly manipulate the imaginations of their audience.

brother?", *Fortean Times* 95, February 1997)

Over the last three decades, *Fortean Times* has collected hundreds of reports of people seeing what we might call "a different reality" in the hope that they will shed some light on the strange processes involved. To illustrate the rich variety involved, we select a few examples from its pages: an "alien" washed up on a beach turns out to be a dead shark; hunters shoot a "bear" only to find it was one of their party; mountain rocks perceived to be climbers in trouble; a yoga-class mistaken for a robbery in progress; a floating log thought to be a Japanese submarine; a poster for a Willie Nelson concert on the wall of a church was whitewashed over and mis-taken for an image of Christ's face; and a huge crowd gathered all night to watch police and vets try to rescue a bear up a tree only to find, in the morning light, that it was a black bin-liner.

Collective visions and hal-lucinations range from the rela-tively harmless (such as the many hundreds who "saw" the canals of Mars through their telescopes in the decade either side of 1900) or the sudden obsession with the value of tulips that gripped the normally prudent Dutch around 1600 (when many bankrupted themselves to obtain a few bulbs of the newly introduced flower). Others related to non-specific collective anxiety (such as the dancing manias of the 14th and 15th centuries) or the more lethal persecutions of "witches" that lasted hundreds of years throughout Europe. Some relate to quite specific fears of invasion or conquest (for example, as inspired by the infamous radio broadcast of a Martian invasion, see WARS OF THE WORLDS, p.120); and still others seemingly inspired by spiritual devotions and expectations (such as the rumour that swept through Ireland in 1985 that statues of the Virgin Mary were moving, see STATUES THAT COME TO LIFE, p.291).

As we mentioned earlier, individual incidents often, in true fortean fashion, defy categorization. In early November 2003, about 50 people were arrested in Iran's Holy City of Qom, as police broke up a crowd that had gathered to see the hanging of a person said to be half-woman, half-tiger. As reported in the *Jomhuri-Eslami* newspaper, a rumour spread rapidly through the city that a woman had blasphemed during the Ramadan period and suffered the divine pun-ishment of having her head turned into that of a tiger. Drawings of the tiger-headed woman were circulating, especially among young people in

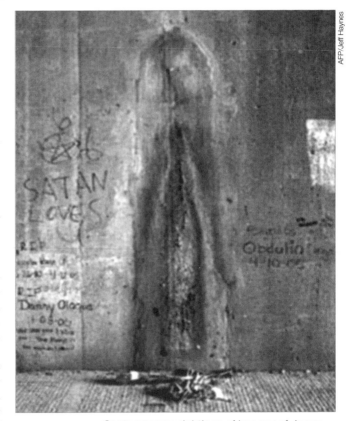

AFP/Jeff Haynes

Contemporary sightings of images of Jesus, the Virgin Mary and numerous saints are increasingly reported in recent years. In the imagination a spontaneous simulacrum – in reflected light on a refrigerator, in patterns of seeds or wood grain or, as here, in the stain on an underpass wall, can become a holy image. After thousands in the Catholic com-munity in Chicago worshipped the Virgin Mary at this spot near Fullerton Avenue, in April 2005, the icon-like stain was defaced with the words "Big Lie" and whitewashed over by a city road maintenance crew.

schools, with the news that she was to be hanged after prayers in a public square. The crowd became unruly when the police tried to convince them the rumour was unfounded. (*Associated Press*, 10 November 2003)

But where, in any precise way, does folklore end and delusion, or even religious faith, begin? In May 2003, the *News Agency of Nigeria* reported that the economy of the Zamfara region was being "crippled" by rumours that a fearful creature, said to be half-man half-horse, was "terrorising" local women. A similar, but more gentle, rumour spread through Hong Kong in 1993 – that a fisherman was heading into harbour with two blond, beak-faced, limbless mermaids that had been caught in his nets near Hainan Island. By the evening, a crowd of over 2,000 gathered on the jetties eager to see this amazing catch. When the boat eventually pulled in the next morning, Captain Hien To and his crew were amazed at the fuss; he said they had caught nothing except several large sun-fishes in their three-day trip. The whole sensation had escalated from a phone-call he made to a friend in which he described sun-fish. (*South China Morning Post*, 14 October 1993)

Mass delusions of this sort undoubtedly provide a means by which the chimeras of mythology and imagination step into our world – a process that also has important implications for some of the more problematic creatures of cryptozoology. We have often wondered how much of the strange phenomena reported by our sources is down to misperception and misinterpretation.

This question has certainly come up in UFO research, where various studies have concluded that more than 90 percent of reports of odd objects seen in the sky are probably the result of misperception. This is not grounds to dismiss any aspect of the matter; on the contrary, it makes it all the more interesting. Not only do we have the intriguing prospect of a small number of authentic unidentified cases which lend their mystery to the mundane majority; we also have to understand the mechanisms of this ostension, for it seems to be driven by need, expectation and imagination in ways which shape the lives of individuals and whole cultures.

The perceptual mechanism at the heart of this phenomenon seems to be predictive; ie reading meanings into preliminary data and jumping ahead to a conclusion that is not borne out later. No doubt the evolutionists would say it has had its uses, but we are reminded by Charles Fort that the mechanism is double-edged. "Why, sometimes, do they see when there is nothing to see?" he asked. "The answer is the same as the answer to another question. Why don't they see, when sometimes magnificently, there is something to see?"

Plagues, poisons and panics

What makes a person ill? Today, doctors know a lot about the actions of organisms but there are times when that knowledge seems of little use. In 1906 members of several families in New York were stricken with typhoid. Investigations revealed that a girl named Mary had worked in all these households as a cook, and the authorities branded her a carrier of typhoid germs even though she herself was immune. After three years in hospital, she was finally certified "free of germs", but was banned from food-handling jobs and required to report for regular check-ups. Instead, she absconded.

About five years later, 25 cases of typhoid occurred at a New York maternity home. Once the health authorities learned that "Typhoid Mary" was working in the kitchens they looked no further, and she was detained again. What is less obvious is where, if she was free of germs, did she get re-infected? And why were no cases traceable to her either during the five years she used aliases to get kitchen-work, or before 1906?

We have an idea that mysterious outbreaks of disease overlap with some of our other sections. In Stigmata (p.88) and Invisible assailants (p.173) we mention cases where marks and wounds have appeared on bodies, producing effects that are "medically impossible". But if wounds can be teleported, why not germs? We suspect that "Typhoid Mary" was one of those unfortunates, mentioned in some of our other sec-

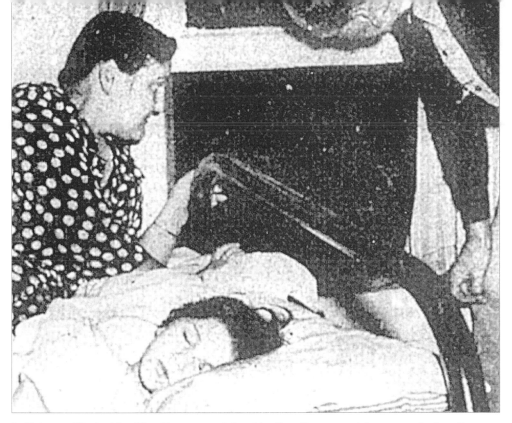

In Mattoon, Illinois, Mrs Aline Kearney and daughter Dorothy re-enact the moment when they were overcome by a mysterious gas attack through the open window.

tions, who are somehow the focus of unexplained fires, accidents, lightning strikes, bombardments of stones, etc.

But if some people seem to be the focal point of contagious diseases, others appear to have a level of immunity that defies medical science. The germ theory that damned "Typhoid Mary" should have killed John Peck, but brought medical theory near to farce. In 1916, in New York, Peck was the target of a murderous plot by his son-in-law, Dr Arthur Waite. Waite fed the old man diphtheria germs and doctored his nasal spray with tuberculosis. When Peck survived this, Waite weakened him with calomel, loosed typhoid on him and then influenza. In the end he gave up and poisoned him with arsenic.

We can only speculate on what Waite, a professional bacteriologist, must have thought about germ theory. He had plenty of time to brood on it in prison. But even poison does not always work. Peck eventually died, but the Russian priest Rasputin, confidante of the Tsarina Alexandra at the beginning of the twentieth century, lived on after eating enough poisoned cake to kill a regiment.

His assassins had to finish him off by shooting him twice, beating him with an iron bar and pushing him through a hole in the ice into a freezing river. He was found to have drowned.

If some people fail to die when they ought to, others have died when there seemed no reason why they should. Marjory Quick, daughter of the Bishop of Sheffield, drank what she believed to be medicinal paraffin, vomited and died immediately. The report in *The Daily Express* (3 October 1911) says that no trace of paraffin could be found in the cup, her throat or her mouth. To the authorities it seemed obvious that she was in a suicidal state – whatever that may mean. An Associated Press report, which appeared in most American newspapers in January 1968, said that the wife of army Sergeant Robert Rush woke him up at 6am, screamed out and died instantly. The inquest disclosed that her sister had expired in a similar fashion five years earlier, having climbed out of a swimming pool, looked around her with a horrified expression, screamed and dropped dead. Autopsies on both sisters failed to find the cause of death. Referred to today as SUNDS

This bizarre drawing, dated 1564 and once ascribed to Pieter Brueghel the Elder, is entitled *The Epileptic Women of Meulebeek*. The explanatory text along the bottom states that "These are the pilgrims who on St John's day had to dance outside Meulebeek and when they leapt over a bridge then they are cured for a whole year of St John's disease." The women may have been suffering from convulsive ergotism.

(sudden unexplained death syndrome), instances continue to be reported in the papers. Some of these may have a relationship with the disturbing phenomenon of "cot deaths" and are, even now, largely unexplained.

When the Massachusetts State Commissioner of Health, Dr G.H. Bigelow, spoke after a supper at the Harvard Medical School, Boston, thirty students and doctors fell ill. Food poisoning was suspected but no cause could be discovered. The experts declared it was paratyphoid; then another twenty people were struck down. The circumstances were strange yet no evidence of any communication of the disease could be found. We note with some amusement that the subject of Dr Bigelow's speech was "Food-poisoning", a fact which did not go unnoticed by the headline writers of the *New York Herald Tribune* (30 January 1932). While real mass poisonings occur and are quickly identified, there are also growing numbers of cases (eg swimmers breaking out in rashes, field workers having trouble breathing, cinema audiences feeling nauseous) in which all obvious causes have been eliminated leaving only mystery.

Unidentified fumes are a particularly common complaint. The magazine *Human Behaviour* (January 1975) admits that "accounts of victims gassed by undetectable vapours dot the annals of psychology", and details one case in March 1972 when 39 women at a data-processing centre in Kansas became dizzy, swooned and vomited. Analyses of air, blood and urine failed to find any trace of the "gas" they said made them "feel hot", their eyes sting and their heads reel. The next day they again dropped like flies. On the third day the management, under advice from psychologists, announced that the cause had been located; it was only "atmospheric inversion". The trick worked and the trouble ceased; or the trouble ceased despite the trick, for our records show that these attacks may repeat but rarely last more than a few days. The psychologists concluded that these cases were "examples of mass hysteria" which they defined as "a sort of psychic contagion".

The classic case of this sort occurred in the Illinois town of Mattoon in September 1944. It began when a woman complained to police that someone had opened her bedroom window and sprayed her with "a sickish sweet-smelling gas". She felt ill and her legs were paralysed for a while. The headline in the local paper the next day shouted: "ANAESTHETIC PROWLER ON THE LOOSE". As others came forward to say they too had been attacked by this maniac, many residents armed themselves and lay in wait for any suspicious prowler. Despite further "attacks" and immediate police responses, no "phantom anaesthetist" was ever caught.

A strong parallel with Mattoon is Halifax, West Yorkshire. Ten years before the panic at Mattoon, in November 1938, the town was brought to a standstill by its collective fear of a supposed razor-wielding maniac who stepped out of shadows at night to slash at solitary pedestrians. As folklorist Michael Goss points out, the wounds on the Slasher's first victims were all too real but a corporeal culprit was never caught (*The Halifax Slasher*, 1987). As at Mattoon, the longer the case went unsolved the more the press capitalized upon it, publicizing further claims. As at Mattoon, intense police and vigilante activity failed to stem the claims of further attacks. In the end the Halifax police, faced with an uncatchable perpetrator and increasingly dubious testimony from self-confessed "victims", were forced to put much of it down to "imagination". In time, the "Halifax Slasher" became just another example of mass hysteria.

Perhaps there is something to the notion of "psychic contagion", not as those glib psychologists used it but as some human equivalent of, for example, the great sheep panic of 3 November 1888. On this morning, according to accounts in British papers shortly after the event, thousands of sheep throughout an area measuring 25 by 8 miles near Reading, Berkshire, were found scattered far and wide, panting with terror. What spooked them during the night was never ascertained.

Psychic contagion works like an imitation of pathological contagion; it doesn't matter how absurd the circumstances, it spreads through panic and anxiety – or, sometimes, through excitement and expectation – wherever large numbers of like-minded people interact. In America in June 1899, doctors across America were alarmed by thousands of new patients seeking medical attention for their lips, swollen and with tiny punctures. A fruitless search for the "kissing bug" drew criticism from senior medical authorities. Writing at the height of the scare, in *Popular Science Monthly*, Dr L.O. Howard noted that only six species of insect in the country could give such bites, and since this was the work of none of them, he dismissed the whole affair as "a senseless scare" and likened it to the tarantula bite scares that gripped southern Europe in medieval times.

The phenomenon of mass hysteria was

In Southern Italy there was a tradition that the bite of the tarantula spider could only be cured by wild dancing. The dance, the Tarantella, later became formalized by Neapolitan composers.

certainly known of old; we refer readers to the curious records of many such scares in Charles Mackay's famous *Extraordinary Popular Delusions and the Madness of Crowds* (1852). For example, he details the almost incredible extent of the "poison manias" that swept Italy and France in the sixteenth and seventeenth centuries, in which hundreds of people believed themselves victims of a colourless, tasteless, odourless poison. In response to this panic, the authorities carried out a vigorous campaign of executing alleged poisoners. It's highly likely – in the light of what we now know about such epidemics – that many, if not all, of the condemned were quite innocent.

Similarly, dancing manias raged like forest fires throughout Europe between the fourteenth and fifteenth centuries. It seems as if almost anything could set one off – the sound of music, the sight of pointed shoes, or a fiery preacher

A painting illustrating the Salem witch trials showing an "afflicted" girl collapsed on the floor before the judge.

– and once the dancers hove into view, many found themselves compelled to join the line. They pranced or convulsed until exhaustion or restraining friends finally stopped them (in much the same way as was said about dancing in a fairy ring). An early example of compulsive dancing comes from the German town of Aachen in July 1374; within a short time the mania had spread to Liège in Belgium and Utrecht in Holland.

Some of these dance manias may have had an underlying medical cause. The condition now called Sydenham's chorea in which the victim is prone to making involuntary jerky and spasmodic movements was known in the Middle Ages as St Vitus's Dance. A not dissimilar condition was the, now uncommon, disease known as convulsive ergotism. Ergot is a fungal growth that sometimes appears on cereal crops, in particular rye. If accidentally harvested with the grain and consumed, ergot can produce two serious and unpleasant diseases: gangrenous ergotism (known as St Anthony's Fire) in which the limbs shrivel up, and convulsive ergotism in which the limbs twitch and shake in a violent and uncontrollable fashion. There were many recorded epidemics of ergotism from the end of the sixteenth century to the beginning of the eighteenth. Ergot also has medicinal qualities and was prescribed from the Middle Ages as a means of quickening childbirth.

The "tarantism" referred to by Dr Howard persisted from the fourteenth to the eighteenth centuries and was popularly believed to be caused by the bite of the southern European wolf spider or tarantula (named after the Italian city of Taranto). In reality the bite was only slightly toxic but, such was the power of communal belief that victims were made to dance frenetically in order to rouse them from the lethargy and inertia which the bite was thought to cause. The melodies which they danced to were called "tarantellas" and the cure was achieved when the patient collapsed in a convulsive crisis or exhaustion. Athanasius Kircher included several songs for curing the tarantula bite in his *Magnes sive de arte magnetica* (1641).

The element of compulsive behaviour here recalls the automatisms of the hypnotic state and this can be very significant in collective religious experiences. Gerald de Barry (Giraldus Cambrensis) describes a dancing mania he witnessed in Wales in 1188. An annual feast at the beginning of August at the church of St Eluned in Breconshire became famous for its procession of penitents; males and females would dance, sing or, "on a sudden falling on the ground as in a trance", would act out "in a frenzy with their hands and feet whatever work they have unlawfully done on feast days". Helpers take them into the church where, after prayers, "you will see them suddenly awakened and coming to themselves" (*Itinierarium Cambriae*, 1191). Similar phenomena are commonplace in Pentecostal and

Charismatic Christian services today, especially those involving the so-called "Toronto blessing" in which rapt members of the congregation collapse laughing, crying or barking.

Historically, episodes of "mass hysteria" or "socially shared psychopathology" – however it may be defined – have been triggered in small, psychologically isolated communities, often appearing first among close-knit groups of young people; illuminating comparisons can be made with the children at the heart of the "witch" persecutions (eg at Salem, Massachusetts, in 1692, pictured opposite), or those that initiated major Marian vision series (see RELIGIOUS VISIONS, p.124). Even the birth of the modern Spiritualism may be seen in this context, generally credited to the three teenage Fox sisters of Hydesville, New York, in 1848, who claimed to be able to communicate with "spirits" who answered with raps and knocks. We have no comparable figures of the young people centrally involved in poltergeist and UFO cases, but we believe the numbers would be significant.

On the more mundane level, outbreaks of contagious "social panic" involving illnesses of one sort or another can be found in many different cultures up to the present day. They tend to take the form of mass fainting, suffering nausea and breathing problems from a "mystery bug" or a repulsive smell; usually attempts by authorities to trace the source of the problem find nothing conclusive. A typical example is the 84 people, mainly teenagers, that collapsed while watching the film *Paper Moon* in a theatre in Gillespie, Illinois, in December 1973. A few complained of feeling ill and left the theatre for fresh air and the numbers soon escalated until the pavement outside was lined with groaning and unconscious youths. No cause was ever found. (Champaign-Urbana, Illinois, *Courier*, 30 December 1973)

Cases in the UK are rare, the most dramatic taking place at a junior brass band parade at Hollinwell, Nottinghamshire, on 13 July 1980. Some 200 children collapsed, complaining of sore throats, watering eyes, dizziness and nausea. According to a recent BBC review of the case, more than twenty years after the event, checks on available food and water found no possible agents, nor had there been any field spraying by local farmers. A full analysis of the news reports on the Hollinwell incident appears in *Fortean Times* 33, Autumn 1980.

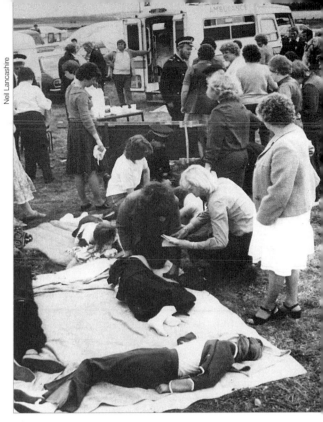

Neil Lancashire

At Hollinwell, Notts, in 1980, around 200 children parading in a brass band competition on a hot July day, collapsed "like nine pins", according to one witness. "It looked like a battlefield," said another.

One scholar of "mass sociogenic illnesses" is Dr Robert Bartholomew - who has examined the phenomenon in forms as varied as the "convent fever" prevalent in the Middle Ages to modern "panics" in factories, theatres and schools – has taken to calling the illness "protean" in that it can take on or mimic the symptoms of other illnesses appropriate to the cultural milieu. In particular, Bartholomew has studied the numerous cases of "hysteria" that afflicted many of the "socially isolated all-female religious boarding schools" in Muslim countries. He describes one modern episode in the Malaysian state of Kedah which "affected 36 girls over a period of 5 years. Native healers (bomohs) were summoned intermittently to exorcise demons. Symptoms included crying fits, screaming, abnormal movements, possession states and histrionics." It seems that the heavily restrictive regime in the school made the girls increasingly desperate and seemingly without any remedy. It climaxed in 1987 when, during an outbreak, the girls took hostages at knife point and demanded changes. The phenomenon ended when an ex-Prime Minister agreed to meet the girls and oversee their transfer to a more liberal school. (Robert Bartholomew, *Exotic Deviance: Medicalizing Cultural Idioms – From Strangeness to Illness,* 2000)

On the global stage, the phenomenon is increasing with ever more dramatic cases. Over a period of 15 days, in the Spring of 1983, more than 900 residents of the Jordan West Bank complained of fainting, headache, abdominal pain and dizziness. This was at a time when rumours were circulating among Palestinian communities that they were being targeted with poison gas. At least one episode involving 64 residents in Jenin was triggered by a passing car, belching thick smoke from a faulty exhaust system. "A similar episode occurred in Soviet Georgia during political unrest in 1989," writes Bartholomew and his colleague Dr Simon Wessely. "Symptoms spread among 400 adolescent females at several nearby schools. The incident transpired after rumours that students were exposed to poison gas by Russian authorities who had recently used the chemical agent chloropicrin to disperse an opposition rally." The authors also point to a similar panic of "mimicked symptoms" in Japan, in 1995, after the Aum Shinrikyo sect used sarin nerve gas on the Tokyo subway system.

However, just to show how complicated the whole issue of "mass hysteria" is, we refer to the case of tens of thousands of Japanese youngsters who tuned in to watch an episode of the cartoon adventure *Pokémon* on the 16th December 1997. According to medical spokesmen, around 12,000 children went into trance-like states, or suffered vomiting, convulsions and blackouts. As the next day's TV news and papers reported the astonishing extent of the affected children, mothers' and children's advisory groups expressed their outrage. Some doctors and psychologists blamed one segment of the programme which contained flashing lights and images; but Fort's law holds up, that for every expert there is an equal and opposite expert. A study of the offending episode found it was little different from any other episode and the graphic technique of alternating light and dark colours (called paka-paka) is fairly common in Japanese animation. Toshio Tamauchi, an expert on epilepsy at Saitama University of Medicine, said: "There have been many similar cartoons … I don't understand why the programme this time caused so many attacks."

While the usual ingredients of "mass hysteria" appear in that last case, it is difficult to see how the "contagion" was spread among the children, each watching television at home … unless it was, in some way, suggested and triggered instantaneously. Ben Radford, who investigated the case for *Fortean Times*, concluded that the event was a form of "mass hysteria" and serves to remind us that many cases might not be recognized as such at first.

Wars of the worlds

Few illustrations of a large-scale "social panic" can be more instructive than the Orson Welles radio version of *The War of the Worlds*, which terrified millions of listeners when it was first aired on the evening of 30 October 1938. Welles and his script writer, Howard Koch, updated the H.G. Wells novel of 1898, transplanting the action from Surrey to New Jersey and presenting part of the narrative as a live news event.

It began with an observation of explosions on the surface of Mars, followed by the landing on the US of huge Martian machines that strode over the landscape destroying people and property with their heat rays. The play ended with an announcer on the roof of the New York radio station, describing the advance of the Martian tripods towards Manhattan. The final silence was as powerful as the mounting panic in the voice-overs delivering news of the casualties and the mobilization of military battalions.

Reactions to the play were most intense in New Jersey and New York. Joseph Bulgatz devotes a chapter to the incident in his analysis of panics and mass hysteria, *Ponzi Schemes, Invaders from Mars and More* (1992), providing a comprehensive account of what happened that night. People rang friends and family, the police, radio stations, hospitals, newspapers, bus stations, etc, asking for more information, volunteering their help, or simply to warn others. The congestion of the phone system only added to the general anxiety, as did the fact that no one was sure in which direction safety lay.

All of this was reinforced by newspaper headlines the following day; wire messages spread around the world stories of "weeping, hysterical women", people "gathering in groups and praying", and chaos in the streets. "Probably never before have so many people in all walks of life and in all parts of the country become so suddenly and so intensely disturbed as they did on this night," wrote Hadley Cantril, a psychologist at Princeton.

Ironically, most of Welles's colleagues, including CBS executives, had thought the play "too fantastic" and "just not believable" before it was broadcast. So what made it so effective? Welles and his Mercury Theater Company had been engaged by CBS for a series of one-hour plays. Eager to experiment, Welles realized the dramatic potential of the "front line" news reports from Europe which was then on the verge of war with Germany. As Bulgatz notes, people "had become accustomed to news bulletins that interrupted the regular programming."

When the broadcast was condemned as "irresponsible" many writers and celebrities sprang to Welles's defence. Influential columnist Dorothy Thompson praised him for exposing the failure of popular education. Where Hitler used armies to terrify Europe, she added, Welles had demoralized a nation with a single microphone. That, at least, is the legend, but was the reaction really that extreme? Recent studies suggest the influence of the broadcast has been greatly exaggerated but the incident provides a remarkable perspective into the psychology of collective imagination and "mass hysteria".

This was the heyday of Flash Gordon, massive popular interest in Mars and its "canals" and growing political tensions in Europe and the Far East which, within a few months, dragged Britain and America into World War II. The grave tones of Welles's fake announcers and reporters – however fantastic their words – seemed utterly convincing in the general context. The records show that several public notices were given before and during the play, broadcast at Halloween. At one point Welles declares that the play is "the Mercury Theater's own radio version of dressing up in a sheet and jumping out of a bush and saying

Bettman / Corbis

Orson Welles in the CBS studios at the time of his historic broadcast.

boo". Many other signs of the fictional nature of the broadcast were present – eg compression of the action of days, even months, into less than an hour. The least-fooled were young people who recognized Welles's distinctive voice as that of the hero of another drama series, *The Shadow*.

Almost immediately after the broadcast, Hadley Cantril had the brilliant idea of collecting stories of the panic for a study that was eventually published in 1940 as *The Invasion from Mars*. His material was widely cited as an academic endorsement of almost all the extreme claims of what happened that night. Since then, several scholars of epidemic hysteria have criticized Cantril's sweeping generalizations from what was, in reality, a very small and localized sample (135 people from New Jersey). Dr Robert Bartholomew of Queensland's James Cook University, writing in *Skeptical Inquirer* (November 1998), suggests that panic had been the exception and not the rule. "There is little doubt that many Americans were genuinely frightened and some did try to flee the Martians," Bartholomew notes, "[Nevertheless] there is a growing consensus among sociologists that the extent of the panic, as described by Cantril, was greatly exaggerated."

When British ufologists John and Anne Spencer looked for evidence of the scale of the panic in the files of civil authorities in New Jersey and New York, they found very little. They confirm the picture of a minority of panicked individuals who, they argue in their *Encyclopedia of the World's Greatest Unsolved Mysteries* (1995), would surely have encountered, sooner or later, someone who knew the broadcast had been just a play.

The evidence, then, is that more people enjoyed or ignored Welles's broadcast than were alarmed by it. The real scare mongering followed later when newspapers blew it out of all proportion creating, in the collective imagination, the stereotype of the full-out, chaotic urban panic beloved by Hollywood movies. As Bartholomew said in a BBC interview on the sixtieth anniversary (October 1998) of the Welles broadcast: "The supposed panic was put down to the power of the media. The fact that many believe a panic took place when it did not is also testimony to the power of the media."

The result of the gradual mythologizing of the incident has been far-reaching. The potential for mass panic was the main reason the US government kept their knowledge about UFOs from the public – evidently envisaging a level of civil catastrophe based on the misreported reactions to Welles's broadcast. By 1947 the growth of interest in "flying saucers" was a major concern to senior echelons of the US military and here was the perfect, plausible excuse for secrecy.

In January 1948 – just six months after the Kenneth Arnold sighting of flying discs skipping along like "flying saucers" – the US Air Force initiated Project Sign to study reported sightings. By August 1948, their infamous "top secret" report – *Estimate of the Situation* – was delivered to the Chief of Staff, General Hoyt Vandenberg. It presented the conclusion of many Sign consultants that "UFOs are interplanetary devices systematically observing the Earth". Many officers were opposed to the continuing policy of cover-up and denial, arguing that it was politically dangerous.

Some of them urged Vandenberg to publicly acknowledge the presence of UFOs in US airspace. Vandenberg refused.

A further significant influence on military thinking was the report commissioned in 1960 by NASA from the Brookings Institution, a Washington think-tank, on the possible social consequences of public confirmation of a genuine extraterrestrial (ET) artefact or contact. Citing many historical examples of cultures that "have disintegrated when confronted by a [technologically] superior society," they concluded, gravely, that any contact with ETs could cause "the downfall of civilization on Earth". Richard Hoagland of the Enterprise Mission has argued that the Brookings Report, coming as it did at the height of Cold War paranoia, set the seal on military secrecy and assured that many discoveries concerning the Moon, Mars and deep space are reserved for military eyes only.

And so the cover-up continued for decades. In a memo dated 24 September 1952, H. Marshall Chadwell, Assistant Director for Scientific Intelligence, wrote to his CIA boss, Walter Smith, that: "A fair proportion of our population is mentally conditioned to the acceptance of the incredible. In this fact lies the potential for the touching-off of mass hysteria and panic." Even the notorious Condon Report (*Scientific Study of Unidentified Flying Objects*, 1968) – which described the Welles broadcast as "a coast-to-coast state of panic" – expressed the high-level opinion that there was more danger from a stampeding public than from the UFOs themselves. Worse, in the words of the Robertson Panel report (1953), the public was now vulnerable to "enemy psychological warfare".

Hadley Cantril has often been asked whether modern society has become too sophisticated for a panic, of the type precipitated by Welles's broadcast, to happen again. "Unfortunately, I have always had to reply that of course it could happen again and on a much more extensive scale," he wrote in the 1966 edition of *Invasion from Mars*. To some extent he is right. Many radio stations around the world have tried to re-create the hysteria of the original broadcast – usually on its anniversary. *Fortean Times* (120, p.42) lists nine of them; the most famous taking place in Quito, Ecuador, on 12 February 1949, was followed by widespread, genuine panic when listeners believed the country was being attacked by Peru or the Russians. The station's director deliberately

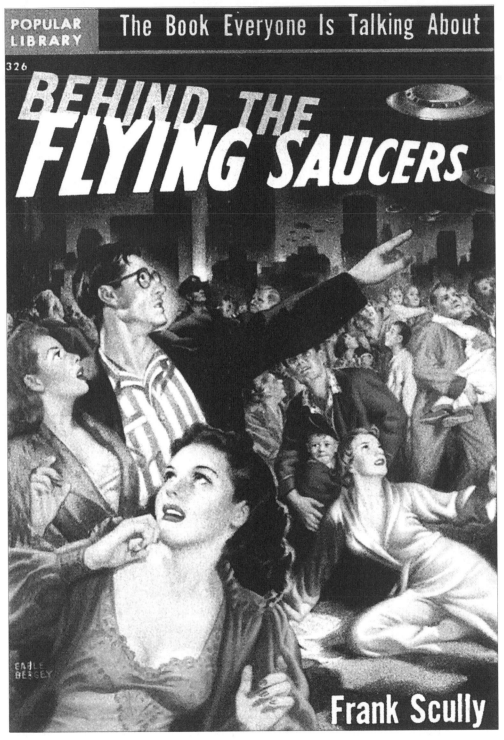

POPULAR
LIBRARY

326

The Book Everyone Is Talking About

BEHIND THE
FLYING SAUCERS

EARLE
BERGEY

Frank Scully

The cover of Frank Scully's *Behind the Flying Saucers* (1951), the first explicit, if credulous, discussion of crashed UFOs, recovered bodies, government conspiracy and mass panic.

did not announce the play was fictional. By the time he apologized it was too late; an angry mob besieged the station building and torched it. In the ensuing battle with troops six people were killed, fifteen were injured, some actors were arrested and the director fled the country. More recently, on 30 October 1998, when Radio Antena 3, a subsidiary of Portuguese National Radio (RDP), ended their re-enactment by planting a story in a later news bulletin, saying Martians were heading for the capital, Lisbon, hundreds panicked.

But, while academics argue over the scale of the *War of the Worlds* panics, the concern of the military has been exonerated. There can be no doubt about the power of collective imagination – which we examine further in the next two sections – to create predicaments which are damaging personally or socially. We are brought up to trust authority and we do not expect governments, priests, scientists or newsreaders to mislead us. We know how to react, it seems, when real newsreaders are used in spoof newscasts on comedy shows, but calamity can follow if the usual signals of "authority" are confused, misread or deliberately exploited. The military complex fears that malicious foreign agents could use a nation's credulity and anxiety against itself but, historically, the only signs of social manipulation on this scale are the lies many governments, dictators and tyrants have told their own peoples.

In 1959, Carl Jung devoted some time to such collective experiential phenomena in a remarkable book, *Flying Saucers: A Modern Myth of Things Seen in the Sky*. It seemed to him that the widespread reports of UFOs were "symptoms of psychic change" in a society – a collective equivalent of the visionary phenomena that sometimes marks changes in the psyche of an individual. He suggested that the "flying disc" was a profound symbol of wholeness "…best suited to compensate the split-mindedness of our age". Others – notably Jacques Vallée, a decade later – thought this ufological form of collective anxiety might stem from the growth in scientific knowledge about our place in the universe, especially the lack of certain evidence of other civilizations in our solar system and among the detectable stars. When faced with this persistent "loneliness", suggested Vallée, society has repeated what was done during "the great miseries of times past" and recreated Fairyland, with its surreal lands and unimaginable treasures, but relocated to the stars and peopled with entities every bit as enchanting and dangerous as the ancient fairy races.

Religious visions

Do a quick search on the Internet and you'll find a number of sites that provide lists of apparition events. They include the experiences of single visionaries as well as those that occur to groups collectively. Of course we cannot guarantee the accuracy of that data, but as a rough method of assessing the scale of the phenomenon we can see that there are, on average, about six reported visions a year.

The best-known examples of mass visions of the Virgin Mary are those that took place at Lourdes, France, in 1858, at Pontmain, France, in 1871, and at Fátima, Portugal, in 1917. Each of them had a far-reaching influence on the conventional Catholic veneration of the Virgin Mary; on the popular following of miracles, prophecy and conspiracy; and even on today's contactee ufology.

Perhaps the most dramatic – and certainly best documented – are the series of visions by three young peasant children at Fátima, which culminated in the famous incident of the "dancing Sun" observed by tens of thousands. Surely this must be one of the largest "mass hallucinations" on record, if that is what it was, and it deserves a bit more detail.

On May 13th, 1917, Lúcia dos Santos, and her cousins Jacinta and Francisco Marto, were looking after sheep on a hillside called Cova de Iria, when they saw a flash of light over an oak tree. Fearing the onset of a storm, they began gathering the sheep and became aware of a lady by the tree. She was "shining white, brighter than the Sun". It is worth noting that the children thought she was an angel "who descended from the sky", rather than the Virgin Mary. According to Lúcia's later account, just before she ascended, light streamed from the apparition's hands, piercing the children's chests. The "shining lady" announced that she was

Large communities can be gripped suddenly by irrational fears about real and imaginary illnesses, alien invasion or invisible wizards and assassins. We suspect the same process also creates or governs the expectations of large crowds. For example, thousands of the faithful gathered on a hillside at Pescara, on Italy's Adriatic coast, on 28 February 1988, to see an apparition of the Virgin Mary, prophesied by a local Catholic visionary. When the apparition failed to materialize, people were disappointed yet their faith was not dented in the slightest.

from heaven and would appear to them by the tree on the same day for the next five months.

At first, their family was horrified at the children's blasphemous presumption; Lúcia was scolded and threatened with a beating unless she confessed it was a lie. Just before the August apparition, the children were kidnapped by the regional administrator who interviewed them separately. When he could not break their conviction he threatened to boil them in oil, and when that failed to sway them, he locked them in the local jail overnight. Through these and other pressures, the children's serenity and humility impressed all who met them and won over many doubters. Word spread, and on the 13th of each month increasing numbers of pilgrims gathered around the oak at Cova de Iria, to watch the three entranced children who seemed to see and hear things that no one else present could.

According to the children, the "shining lady" made many predictions, including the early deaths of Jacinta and Francisco. She also promised to reveal her identity and a final miracle on the 13th of October. On that day – the last of the promised apparitions – a crowd of 50,000 or more waited

in the rain. Lúcia pointed and shouted: "Look at the Sun!" What followed was extraordinary by any standard and much of it was attested by credible witnesses on the day or immediately after. Through the haze, the Sun's disc seemed to change colour and to move – some fainted as it seemed to fall towards them – after which many said their clothes had dried out and ills were cured.

Writing a few days later of his experience at the scene, the editor of the Lisbon newspaper, *O Seculo* – who made no secret of his scepticism about the apparitions – noted: "From the road, where the vehicles were parked and where hundreds of people who had not dared to brave the mud were congregated, one could see the immense multitude turn toward the Sun ... at that moment a great shout went up ... Before the astonished eyes of the crowd, whose aspect was Biblical as they stood bareheaded, eagerly searching the sky, the Sun trembled, made sudden incredible movements outside any cosmic laws – the Sun 'danced' according to the typical expression of the people."

Another Lisbon paper, *O Dia*, published on the 17th a long editorial, including a description

On 13 May, 1917, three children from the Portuguese village of Fátima were attracted by a flash of light and saw a "shining lady" above a small oak tree…

of the strange light effect. "At one o'clock in the afternoon … the rain stopped. The sky, pearly grey in colour, illuminated the vast arid landscape with a strange light. The Sun had a transparent gauzy veil so that eyes could easily be fixed upon it. The grey mother-of-pearl tone turned into a sheet of silver which broke up as the clouds were torn apart and the silver Sun … was seen to whirl and turn in the circle of broken clouds. A cry went up from every mouth and people fell on their knees on the muddy ground. The light turned a beautiful blue as if it had come through the stained-glass windows of a cathedral and spread itself over the people who knelt with outstretched hands. The blue faded slowly and then the light seemed to pass through yellow glass. Yellow stains fell against white handkerchiefs, against the dark skirts of women. They were reported on the trees, on the stones and on the serra. People wept and prayed with uncovered heads in the presence of the miracle they had awaited."

Another educated observer was Joseph Garrett, a natural sciences professor at Coimbra University, who later wrote: "This was not the sparkling of a heavenly body, for it spun round on itself in a mad whirl, when suddenly a clamour was heard from all the people. The Sun, whirling, seemed to loosen itself from the firmament and advance threateningly upon the Earth as if to crush us with its huge fiery weight. The sensation during these moments was terrible."

Monsignor John Quareman, who was there,

recalled the moment Lúcia, the main visionary, reached the oak tree in which she saw the Virgin. "To my surprise, I saw clearly and distinctly a globe of light advancing from East to West, gliding slowly and majestically through the air." As the Bords put it, if we didn't know the context, the Monsignor might well have been describing a UFO. Another writer, D. Scott Rogo, points out, in his book *Miracles* (1982), that "Most writers on Fatima claim that the disc was the Sun. But judging by the descriptions we have … the disc was at the wrong elevation and azimuth to have actually been the Sun." He concludes: "[It] seems to have been an immense UFO-like silver disc."

The physics of an oscillating solar body approaching the Earth are not of our everyday reality, so what did the expectant crowd see? Janet and Colin Bord, who have a special interest in visionary phenomena, suggest that it might have been more than a simple delusion: "One person can hallucinate, two together might share a hallucination, but it is beyond all possibility that 70,000 people could share a hallucination." (*Modern Mysteries of the World*, 1989). In addition, other witnesses reported a shower of what they believed to be white flower petals that disintegrated before they touched the ground just before the "dance of the Sun"; still others felt the "Sun" dry their clothes or saw prismatic auras and shadows around them.

Attempts to rationalize the phenomenon as an eclipse also founder for lack of any astronomical verification and in the vacuum of data some have preferred to believe the whole event made more sense when interpreted as a UFO encounter. This interpretation appealed to two Portuguese historians who also had an interest in ufology. Dr Joaquim Fernandes and Fina D'Armada spent six years studying the original depositions and interviews with the principal seers and witnesses. They are certainly well-placed to compare the complex worlds of Catholic visions and modern ufology in the context of religious anthropology.

In their highly recommended study, *Heavenly Lights* (2005), Dr Fernandes and Ms D'Armada discovered that a whole range of strange phenomena was clearly observed during the apparition series and described by credible witnesses, including: the peculiar lightning; strange lights seen inside clouds or emerging from the Sun; odd buzzing sounds when the children were seeing the Virgin; "thunder" that announced the arrival and

accounts of encounters with fairies and poltergeists. Just what this means is one of the great questions which we are all seeking an answer.

The events at Cova de Iria quickly assumed legendary status and on its thirteenth anniversary (13 Oct 1930), the Bishop of Leiria announced the formation of a special commission; it eventually sanctioned the creation of a new cult, that of Our Lady of the Rosary Fátima. By then Francisco and Jacinta had died; they were beatified on 13 May 2000 (the 83rd anniversary of the first vision) by Pope John Paul II on his third visit to Fátima.

Lúcia herself continued to experience visions, although most were private. She revealed that at the ages of eight and nine, she had similar experiences; the first was of "an angel ... wrapped in a sheet", and the latter resembled "a boy of great beauty ... whiter than snow, transparent as crystal" who called himself "the Angel of Peace" (more recently referred to as "the Angel of Portugal"). On three occasions, Lúcia, Francisco and Jacina saw this angel, who taught them special prayers and showed them a vision of the Eucharist dripping blood into a chalice. Later, through the 1920s, Lúcia had more visions of Mary and the child Jesus.

departure of the apparition; incomparably marvellous odours; "ramps of light"; unusual breezes; a "rain of flowers"; and the way animals behaved during the visions. On the day of the "solar miracle", besides the phenomena reported above, the clouds were seen to behave oddly; figures were seen in the Sun by the children; and a strange "suction" (the opposite of a wind) was observed to effect the trees. The authors also discovered an almost-ignored account by a "fourth seer" of a small being that communicated telepathically.

In conclusion, say Dr Fernandes and Ms D'Armada, each of these elements has a direct parallel with almost identical phenomena found in classic UFO cases. As we hope to show in this book, these elements also have parallels in

Lúcia lived out her days in seclusion in the Carmelite convent at Coimbra, in central Portugal, moving there in 1948 after her previous abode was besieged by visitors. Over the years, she wrote four separate accounts of the 1917 visions, at the request of spiritual directors, the last in 1941. Most recently, she tried to answer the constant stream of questions from the public in a book, *Appeals of the Fatima Message* (2000). Among her last visitors, in July 2004, was Mel Gibson, who presented her with a DVD of his film *The Passion of the Christ* – which she was spared from watching, having been deaf and blind since 2003. Lúcia died in February 2005 at Coimbra, aged 97, and will almost certainly follow her cousins into sainthood.

An equally spectacular and astonishing event took place in the small French village of Pontmain on the evening of 17 January 1871. Two young brothers became aware of a beautiful lady in the sky smiling at them. She was stationary in the air about 25 feet above a neighbour's house. Their parents and a neighbour could see nothing; but twice more the boys described the same vision in the sky, unchanged for an hour or so. We take our details from a contemporary account by Abbé Richard, *What Happened at Pontmain*, reprinted in 1971: "After supper, their excited cries soon attracted a crowd of neighbours, none of whom could see anything. The boys pointed out an equilateral triangle of three bright stars, one above the Lady's head, the others by her elbows. The crowd saw these and nothing else and, curiously, these stars were never seen again."

The adults then took measures to rule out confabulation. "As more children arrived they were asked to describe what they saw but were not allowed to confer with the others. Three confirmed exactly the vision of the boys. Then the vision began to change, and the children, now separated by the adults, spontaneously and together shouted out a joyful commentary. A white banner had unfurled at the Lady's feet and letters successively winked into existence."

While some began singing hymns, other children, in unison, called out the letters as they appeared. "The first sentence went: 'But pray, my children. God will answer your prayers in a short time'. There were interruptions as the children exclaimed on the beauty of the apparition. The second line began: *Mon fils se laisse ...* (My son lets himself...) to which a nun commented, 'That doesn't make sense,' and urged the children to look carefully. 'It should be *Mon fils se lasse ...*(My son is wearied).' Several times the children spelled out what they saw, with no mistake: 'No, sister, there is an I.' Then the sentence completed itself: *Mon fils se laisse toucher* (My son lets himself be moved to compassion)."

Finally a white vapour obscured the figure from the feet upwards, and slowly the blue oval and stars disappeared. The entire sequence had lasted from 5.30pm to 8.45pm, in the bitter cold of the evening.

Many of these apparitions seem to have been portentous – another element that can be found in

The fourth stage of the Pontmain vision. Many people gathered but only five children actually witnessed the phenomenon.

encounters with fairies and UFOs. The very same evening as the Pontmain vision, the advancing Prussian army stopped at nearby Laval, and a few days later the armistice was signed ending the Franco-Prussian War. At Fátima, three secrets were revealed to one of the children, Lúcia, by the Virgin Mary. The first was a message of peace (this was during World War I) and a vision of Hell. The second was more prophetic and controversial: "If you pay heed to my request," the vision declared, "Russia will be converted and there will be peace. If not, Russia will spread her errors through the world, causing wars and persecution against the Church."

The third secret, read by successive popes on their accession but supposedly too horrible to be revealed, was finally divulged to the world on 13 May 2000, in a text prepared by (the then) Cardinal Ratzinger (now Pope Bennedict XVI). This occurred at the end of a Mass at Fátima in which Pope John Paul II beatified Jacinta and Francisco Marto. Speaking at the Mass, Cardinal Sodano revealed that the children had spoken of a "bishop clothed in white" who "falls to the ground, apparently dead, under a burst of gunfire". It is now widely believed that this referred to the attempted assassination of Pope John Paul II which took place on 13 May 1981 – sixty-five years to the day after the original vision. Although the Pope always attributed his survival to the direct intervention of the Virgin that day, and later donated the assassin's bullet to the shrine, this is the first official statement that directly links the attempt on his life to the prophecy.

As we have seen in previous chapters, many categories of strange phenomena seem to involve or be initiated by groups of young people. It is especially true in the case of religious visions; for example, of over 300 vision series between 1900 and 1999 – listed on the Internet by the Marian Research Institute, Dayton, Ohio – more than a third involved young children. Besides Fátima and Pontmain, these include La Salette (1846); Beauriang, Belgium (1932); Garabandal, Spain (1961); and Medjugorje, in Bosnia-Herzegovina (part of former Yugoslavia) and Kibeho, in Rwanda (both 1981).

In his account of his own investigation of Medjugorje, *The Miracle Detective* (2004), Randall Sullivan makes an interesting comparison between the Medjugorje visions and those at Kibeho. Both began in the same year, 1981; both in regions on the brink of terrible "ethnic cleansing"; both featured a "shining woman" appearing to a group of youngsters to plead for repentance before it was too late; and the visionaries in both seemed insensible to bright lights and needle-pricks during their ecstasies. Among the differences, Sullivan mentions that Medjugorians experienced their visions together, collectively, in a serene and contemplative manner; where the Rwandans often experienced them singly, eyes bulging and arms flailing, before collapsing unconscious for some time afterwards. Both groups said the Virgin took them on "mystical voyages" to Hell, Heaven and Purgatory, but the Rwandans' trances were much longer than the Bosnians and their bodies became so rigid that several men could not lift them or separate their hands (see also ELECTRIC PEOPLE, p.79). Both spoke of the Virgin more as an "incomparable beauty" than as a physical presence.

The visions at Medjugorje are particularly interesting as they caused a rift between the Catholic bishops (who have not recognized the claims) and the tens of millions of believers from all over the world who throng there on organized pilgrimages. A report in the *Catholic Transcript* (10 September 1993) by clinical psychologist Michael W. Petrides reported that two separate medical teams, from Italy and France, closely examined the six visionaries during the period they claimed to be seeing and hearing the Virgin Mary. It is the first time such behaviour has been studied scientifically – in situ, so to speak - and it has confirmed some of their curious synchronized behaviour. It seems that in one fifth of a second all the seers knelt together, looked to the same location (where there was no reference point visible to the non-seers present), slowed or ceased any further eye movements including blinking, and were measurably insensible to loud noises. In one test, a 1,000-watt light bulb was brought near their eyes; not only did they not blink, but their measurable brain activity was a regular alpha rhythm (associated with relaxation) instead of the expected beta rhythm normally associated with visual stimulus. Their pupils responded – which implied that the brain registered the painful intensity of the light – but there was no measurable cortical activity. "This is scientifically inexplicable," says Dr Petrides.

All the signs point to some kind of altered state of consciousness in which the young visionaries seem to share a collective experience of seeing and hearing the Virgin Mary. Yet, to the dismay of the visionaries, their huge circle of helpers, devout followers and millions of avid pilgrims, none of this has convinced two successive Bishops of the Mostar-Duvno diocese that any of the "spectacle" of Medjugorje has a divine origin.

The current bishop, Dr Ratko Peric, has gone so far as to issue a pretty definitive statement justifying his opinion that far from bringing unity and peace, the Medjugorje visions have been false and divisive. Dated February 2004, he lists his principal objections. Firstly, the unfeasible number of individual and collective visions, totalling over 33,000 between 1981 and 2004 – compared with, say Lourdes (1858) – pictured overleaf – and Fátima (1917). Secondly, not one of the six visionaries has taken up a religious vocation. They tried in various ways but it was either too demanding or they would not obey orders from superiors to

A painting by Hoffbauer of the gatherings outside the grotto at Lourdes, on 25 March 1858, as the young Bernadette Soubirous saw and heard the "Immaculate Conception".

cease their public vigils or promoting their "messages" and "secrets" – compared to visionaries at Lourdes and Fátima who promptly took up virtuous lives, some spending the rest of their days in holy orders. Thirdly, that the visions occur even when the visionaries travel abroad. Fourthly, prophecies have been put into the Virgin's mouth which never transpired, as well as some of the visionaries making statements which were untrue, defiant and even theologically dubious. Fifthly, the Medjugorean community actively fosters numbers of expelled priests and "false bishops" who carry out unauthorized holy sacraments and services. Finally – even though there is a lot more – the seers have displayed shocking hubris on occasions; eg one of the seers, Jakov, claimed at the height of the recent civil war that he was told by the Virgin that he could stop the war if he prayed for peace every day. The exasperated bishop is moved to write angrily: "Then why didn't he go pray and bring it to an end? During the war over 2 million people were displaced, over 200,000 were killed, thousands of religious sites and tens of thousands of homes were destroyed."

There are still so many interesting questions to be answered about these visions. Could the visions of the Medjugorje youths be mimicking the approved classical apparitions? The Catholic Church has published guidelines for its bishops to distinguish between the two but, being largely based on doctrinal matters, these are of little help to scientific inquiry. More questions arise from the nature of the visionaries and the phenomenology of their experiences. There are undoubted correspondences between religious visions and historical encounters with fairies, poltergeists, UFOs and for that matter, other forms of ecstatic mysticism. Are the seers natural shamans?

One final concern: consider the locale of Fátima; historians have discovered earlier accounts of encounters between local children and apparition type phenomena. In 1100, a girl from a nearby hamlet met a woman on a mountain who foretold where the girl would find fresh bread; and around 1380, a disembodied voice told a woman where to dig to uncover a spring for her village. About the same period, it was said a Portuguese army, passing through Fátima to battle the Castilians, saw angels, which caused even their horses to kneel. Is Fátima what we would call a phenomena "window area"? We will consider "haunted places" in a later section.

Social anxiety attacks

In times of great social stress it is understandable that large numbers of people are united by the strength of a shared emotion, as happened, for instance, during the London blitz, or in the wake of the tragic death of Diana, Princess of Wales. These cases and the sense of expectation felt by crowds at religious apparition sites (see SHARED VISIONS AND VISUAL RUMOURS, p.110) are some of the more positive aspects of collective imagination.

However, it is the destructive aspect of collectively shared emotions that seem more common. Under the heading "Panic" in the indexes to 28 years of reportage in *Fortean Times*, evidence of mankind's capacity to over-react to the slightest (and strangest) provocation is endlessly recorded. The 1990s alone saw major social scares over body organ thieves; child-sacrificing Satanic cults; the preposterous blood-sucking beast of Hispanic America (called Chupacabras); sinister clowns or bogus social workers kidnapping children; and knife-wielding maniacs who hide under cars at shopping malls. The list of contemporary fears of this sort grows weekly – outstripping even cultish anxieties about the end of the world – and is chronicled by folklorists such as Jan Harold Brunvand as well by as forteans.

The common thread seems to be a sense of vulnerability and helplessness before an overwhelming threat to personal and social stability. It is not surprising, therefore, that huge numbers of people today are prepared to believe that they are the "prey" of insidious conspiracies run by impersonal, complex and secretive government agencies.

Many of these panics involve either a fear about supernatural assault or, less specifically,

In the mid-1800s, North America seethed with anti-Catholic propaganda. Popular lectures by Maria Monk and Edith O'Gorman convinced a credulous public that monasteries and convents were hotbeds of vice and corruption and that many captive nuns met horrible deaths under the pretext of exorcism or were walled-up with their unwanted babies. It was the forerunner of the scare in the early 1990s in the USA and Britain about babies bred for sacrifice by all-powerful Satanic covens. Exorcisms often provide a sanctioned opportunity for collective hysteria among the exorcists at the expense of the unfortunate victim. Illustration from O'Gorman's *Convent Life Unveiled* (1871).

the threat from forces beyond our control. At the end of the first millennium, a shift in the perception of evil meant that theologians felt increasingly under direct attack from the agents of Satan. The Devil was no longer content with mere famines and diseases, but began mounting personal assaults on the pious and the faithful. The proof was apparently self-evident; wherever the Church authorities looked, they managed to find it. By the fourteenth century the accusation of devil-worship – imagined or real – had proved so useful in the suppression of heresy, and as a means of social control, that it was extended to attack Jews, who were accused of sacrificing Christian children and stealing Eucharist wafers, and then to witches (see Norman Cohn's *Europe's Inner Demons*, 1976). Demonic possession became an explanation not just for obsessional and deviant characteristics but also for behaviour that was simply eccentric or unusual. Cases of "demonic assaults" abound in the literature, like the famous case of the Ursuline nuns of Loudon whose mass hysteria culminated with the execution of their priest, Urbain Grandier, in 1633.

The catastrophic notion of "Satanic child abuse" that obsessed some Fundamentalist groups and social workers in Britain in the 1980s led to the break-up of many families. Convinced that Satanic "covens" were kidnapping or breeding unbaptized children for sacrifice in Cleveland, Rochdale, Nottingham, Orkney and Wales, well-meaning childcare workers conducted dawn raids to "rescue" children thought to be at risk. Unorthodox examinations for "tell-tale" marks and relentless questioning of children failed to secure any convictions in court (and made still harder the work of social workers investigating genuine cases of child abuse).

The parallels with the "questioning" of those accused of witchcraft in earlier times was not lost on Jean La Fontaine, commissioned to report on the issue to the Department of Health in 1994. In her unofficial account, *Speak of the Devil* (1998), she describes a modern version of the "witch-finder". In one case – which would be funny if the consequences were not so tragic – a sinister Latin-like chant taken as evidence of a Satanic ritual turned out to be based on a child's description of the "Doh, Re, Mi" song from *The Sound of Music*. A similar series of high-profile cases in the US led at first to extraordinary miscarriages of justice, as recorded by Mark Pendergrast in *Victims of*

Memory (1997). Many of these were overturned in court as judges condemned the use of hypnosis and related methods by psychotherapists to "recover" alleged suppressed memories.

Psychosexual anxiety is a particularly fertile area of investigation as Sigmund Freud was quick to realize. Freud's idea of a castration complex applies not just to the case studies of individuals. In *Sex and the Paranormal* (1999), Dr Paul Chambers examines the widespread social panics involving anxiety about penile loss or disfigurement. In the fear known throughout the Far East as "koro" – from the Malay word for turtle – the sufferer imagines his penis is withdrawing into his body; in females this applies to breasts and labia. Koro is not a trivial phenomenon; the outbreak in Singapore in 1967 resulted in the hospitalization of 446 men and 23 women in a single day. Medical studies of the phenomenon are full of tales of victims' bizarre attempts to prevent their genitals being seized by "fox spirits" or vanishing forever, including the application of special clamps. The novelist Anthony Burgess, in his autobiography *Little Wilson and Big God* (1987), describes the desperate behaviour of a terrified Chinese koro victim in Kuala Lumpur: "He stole a superfine jeweller's knife and rammed it in [his penis], screaming on the sunlit street."

Koro panics, observes Chambers, tend to be short-lived as they spread in precisely the same way as rumours. Their subjective nature is evident, as thoughtful doctors have successfully ended epidemics by treating victims with placebos. One panic was sparked by a boy frightened by an insect bite on his penis, while another, in Thailand, was blamed on duck eggs sold by immigrant Chinese farmers.

In the African variant, chronicled in *Fortean Times* (56, p.33), black magic is blamed. It seems to have begun in 1990, in Nigeria, with rumours that magicians seeking penises to sell as magical amulets could steal them with a simple touch. In the town of Enugu, a man getting off a bus suddenly screamed that his penis had been stolen. The passenger in front of him was grabbed on suspicion of being a magician and a riot ensued in which the bus driver was accidentally shot dead by police. Similar incidents occurred across West Africa. In August 1996, a mob in Cameroon hung three men for penis thefts and others were badly beaten. One eighteen-year-old said that, after shaking hands with a Nigerian friend of his, he

Episodes of "convent fever" have been recorded in the literature of witchcraft and demonic possession since at least the 14th century. The best known being the collective hysteria that, in 1632, afflicted the young nuns (and their Mother Superior) at the convent of St Ursule in Loudon, France. They were seized with violent (often overtly sexual) convulsions and cataleptic trances, screaming blasphemies and obscenities. Working at the Salpêtrière hospital in Paris in the late 19th century, Dr J.M. Charcot (pictured here) pioneered the new field of psychopathology by demonstrating the connection between suggestible personalities, hysteria and the convulsions typical of possession cases.

"felt an electric-like current run through him, and a feeling that his manhood had retreated into his stomach".

In January 1997, the panics spread west along the Gold Coast to Ghana, where at least twelve people accused of being sorcerers died at the hands of mobs. In Abidjan, the capital of neighbouring Ivory Coast, a suspected penis-snatcher was burnt to death by a mob, triggering three days of rioting in which a further two people died. In an attempt to calm the situation the Ivory Coast government issued a statement denying the penis-snatching rumours. Other, minor, incidents were reported from Gabon, Cameroon and Togo until, in August 1997, over forty "suspects" were lynched during serious rioting in Senegal. Chambers points out that most of these locations lie along the same international highway and speculates that "the rumours were spread along it, possibly by truck-drivers".

In 1985 Enugu was once again the location of a strange panic when a rumour circulated that a female spirit, called "the mermaid", was due to visit schools in the town to avenge the killing of her daughter. When several children at a school near the Idaw River screamed that they saw the mermaid entering their classroom, the others fled

in terror and nine were killed in a crush on the staircase (see *New York Post*, 1 November 1985).

In 1993, an extraordinary rumour spread rapidly through the south-western Chinese city of Chongqing. For reasons that were never explained, children had convinced each other that a huge American robot was out of control and heading their way. They believed it would destroy the city and devour any child dressed in red. Soon most of the city's children were refusing to go to school unless they were protected by garlic and crucifixes made from chopsticks (see *South China Morning Post*, 22 March 1993).

A very similar panic had occurred ten years earlier in Houston, Texas, where, in January 1983, a story flashed through several junior-high schools that an army of Smurfs – the blue cartoon characters – carrying guns and knives, had invaded several other schools, killing their headmasters. According to the rumour, anyone wearing blue clothing would also be killed. To add to the confusion the opposite rumour – that anyone wearing blue was safe – also circulated. Many children refused to go to school. The panic took a few days to wind down, helped by teachers claiming other cartoon characters were being drafted in to fight the Smurfs and by the appearance of the

This remarkable 13th century mural was found recently during restoration of a house in Massa Marittima in Tuscany. According to George Ferzoco, director of the Centre for Tuscan Studies at the University of Leicester, it is a propaganda painting and "by far, the earliest depiction in art of women acting as witches", but it could also refer to the ancient belief that witches could directly attack or control male virility. Below the tree – in which 25 phalluses are sprouting – two women are fighting over a phallus in a basket. "In Tuscan folklore," says Ferzoco, "there was a well-known story about witches removing men's penises and placing them in bird nests in trees, where they would then multiply and take on a life of their own." Something of the sort is alluded to in the *Malleus Malificarum* (1486) in which witches are blamed for stealing men's genitals. "[Witches] sometimes collect male organs in great numbers … and put them in a bird's nest, or shut them in a box, where they move themselves like living members…" This led Reginald Scot, who spoke out against the anti-witch madness in his *The Discoverie of Witchcraft* (1548), to satirize the belief with the ribald tale of a youth who goes to a witch to recover his penis which vanished after a bit of illicit sex. She took him to a tree where her imps kept the members they harvested in a nest. "[She] bade him climb up and take [his penis]. And, being in the top of the tree, he took out a mighty big one, asking her if he might not have the same. 'Nay,' quoth she, 'that is our parish priest's tool, but take any other which thou wilt'." What makes this even more interesting is that these historical obscurities are currently undergoing a form of ostension in several African and Far Eastern countries, where hundreds of frightened victims fear they are losing their penises and blame sorcerers and ghosts (see p.132).

supposedly dead headmaster. It seems the story was sparked by a garbled version of an innocuous local TV report of the arrests of forty members of an adolescent gang called The Smurfs, for petty crimes (*Newsweek*, 4 April 1983).

Children figure prominently in many of these social anxiety attacks. The famous Salem witchcraft persecutions of 1692 began with the careless talk of children, as did the awful pogrom at Mora in Sweden in 1669 which ended with 85 people burned alive accused of taking 300 children to a witches' sabbath. What interests us here is the role of the imagination – which children possess in unfettered abundance – in creating anomalous experiences. When communicated to other children who participate enthusiastically, a kind of collective "possession" takes place. This applies to adults too; in fact the capacity to "play" imaginatively, by the so-called "high fantasizers", seems to be a key ingredient in many accounts of strange phenomena. Some UFO investigators automatically assess the fantasizing ability of those who have claimed abduction by aliens. In many of the phenomena we discuss in this book the question of whether an event "really" happened takes second place to the fact that the witness *believes* that it did. And their tales, told with conviction, go on to convince others. This might not be scientific in approach or content, but these matters are a core part of human experience. Dreams and beliefs can change "reality" just as much as anything factual or physical can.

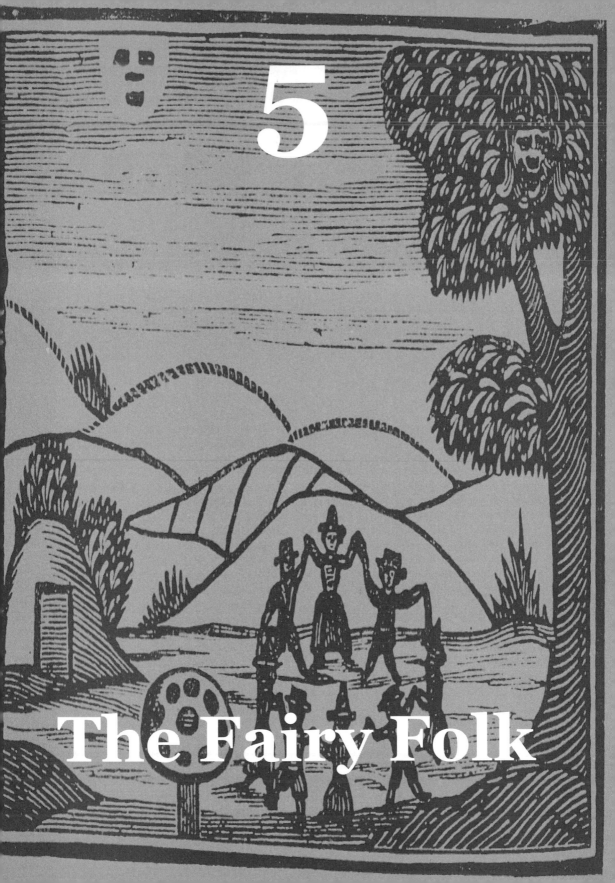

5

The Fairy Folk

5

The Fairy Folk

Fairies: ancient and modern

These times are so busy that we are no longer in a condition to see fairies. That was said about a hundred years ago by an old blacksmith in the Isle of Man. He was one of the last speakers of the old Manx language, and his remarks on fairies were quoted at an exhibition in 1998 at the Manx Museum in the island's capital, Douglas. In the old days, he said, fairies were quite common, but they seemed to have died out with the language. It was thirty years since he had last seen any.

Stories of old country life tell of frequent encounters with a mysterious race of beings, similar to us but smaller and "less solid". At one time they played an active part in daily existence and it was important to keep on good terms with them. In archaic societies and wherever the modern world has not intruded, the existence of fairies and spirits is considered an obvious fact, constantly confirmed by experience.

Late in the nineteenth century – when the Manx blacksmith saw his last fairies – these little folk were supposedly extinct. But like other creatures that were thought to have died out (see RETURN OF THE LIVING DEAD, p.362) they have

reappeared in modern times. Today, in the 21st century, sightings of traditional fairies are regularly reported.

On 25 August 2005, for example, Guy and Vivienne Reid-Brown reported their clear though brief sighting of a fairy. That evening they were driving home after dining out and suddenly, in the headlights of their jeep, they both saw a fairy, "…about seven inches tall, coming out of mid-air … a gleaming silver-white with flowing robes and gossamer wings … simply beautiful". They immediately compared notes and both had observed the same details. Vivienne, who was driving, had the more direct view. She is a teacher, the Head of Department at a Middlesex comprehensive school. The fairy was seen on a small road with hedges either side between West Peckham and Plaxtol, near Sevenoaks, Kent. It was, said Guy, "…just like a Victorian fairy painting".

The systematic persecution of fairies began in early Christian times. The early saints of the Celtic Church in Britain lived as hermits in the loneliest, most haunted corners of the country, conducting rituals for the "spiritual cleansing" of the district. The campaign reached a climax in the Middle Ages when zealous young priests, instructed in arts of exorcizing demons, were sent out to cleanse every part of the kingdom. Services were held in remote fairy glens, by woods, streams, springs and rustic dwellings. "That maketh that there be no fairies", explained Chaucer in the fourteenth century. Previously, he said, "All this land was full of fairies". He was rather sceptical about the result of their expulsion. On the plus side, women could now walk about the country without fear of being molested by elves and incubi. The drawback, however, was that these menaces had been replaced by the young priests, who treated women in much the same way as the rude spirits they had been trying to expel.

The pogrom for the elimination of fairies was carried out ruthlessly, with the executions of witches and persecution of anyone suspected of dealings with unauthorized spirits. A late campaigner was John Wesley. Throughout most of the 18th and 19th centuries he and his Methodist followers were fervent in the struggle against the fairy lore and pre-Christian practices of the Celtic lands where their sect prevailed. Even children were forbidden to talk about fairies, and no one who saw such things dared to tell.

The actual date when fairies finally died out is recorded in several districts. 1879 is remembered in the Shetland Islands as the year in which Dr Jamie Ingram, a locally renowned preacher, died at the age of 103, having finally completed his life's work of driving out the last of the dwarfish, coarse-featured race of Shetland fairies known as "trows", who had at one time occupied the whole country and the minds of its people. That is apparent from the vast number of trow, or "troll", place-names and similar terms in the old *Norn* language of Shetland. The story of their expulsion was told to John Nicholson, author of *Some Folktales and Legends of Shetland* (1920) by a native Shetlander who had heard it directly from an aged "trow-woman" not long after the event. She and her clan had been driven to distraction by Dr Ingram's prayers and preachings, and they decided to emigrate to the Faroe Islands. But she felt too feeble to travel and stayed behind.

Yet within living memory trows were still being observed in the northern islands. An account from the 1940s is given in *The Folklore of Orkney and Shetland* (1975) by E.W. Marwick. In response to something he had written about trows in a magazine, Marwick received a letter from Mr W.E. Thorner of Luton, Bedfordshire, who had spent two years on the Orkney island of Hoy during World War II. He described a "never-to-be-forgotten experience" that proved to him that trows still existed.

"One stormy day in winter I was walking or struggling along the cliff top at Torness. The wind was high and howled about, low-lying, swirling clouds part-enveloped the land in misty rain. At times the pressure was so great that I was forced to bend and clutch at the heather to retain a footing. On one such occasion, on looking up, I was amazed to see that I had the company of what appeared to be a dozen or more 'wild men' dancing about, to and fro … These creatures were small in stature, but they did not have long noses nor did they appear kindly in demeanour. They possessed round faces, sallow in complexion, with long, dark, bedraggled hair. As they danced about, seeming to throw themselves over the cliff edge, I felt that I was witness to some ritual dance of a tribe of primitive men. It is difficult to describe in a few words my feelings at this juncture or my bewilderment. The whole sequence could have lasted about three minutes until I was able to leave the cliff edge."

Mr Thorner, no doubt, had the experience he claimed, but his view of the trows as primitive little savages seems to have been influenced by a popular theory of his time. In *The Testimony of Tradition* (1890) and subsequent writings, David MacRitchie concluded that fairies, trows and their kin were folk-memories of an ancient, aboriginal race, small and secretive, who had only recently died out. They had retired to wild, lonely districts where they dwelt underground, in the prehistoric mounds and burial chambers that are traditionally haunted by fairies. This idea fitted the rationalizing spirit of the time, and there was an added thrill to it, that perhaps the little people still lived on and might one day be rediscovered.

In many accounts of fairy sightings, and visions generally, the episode begins with the appearance of some kind of strange light. One example is the story quoted by W.Y. Evans-Wentz, the Tibetan scholar and initiate in the Celtic mysteries, in *The Fairy-Faith in Celtic Countries* (1911). It was told him by the witness himself, Mr T.C. Kermode, a member of the Isle of Man parliament. As a young man, Kermode was walking across country one autumn night when a companion he was walking with suddenly exclaimed: "Oh look, there are the fairies. Did you ever see them?" Kemode looked where the man was pointing and saw "…a circle of supernatural light which I have now come to regard as the 'astral light' or the Light of Nature, as it is called by the

A classic fairytale scenario; children stumble upon fairies cavorting in a circular dance.

mystics and in which spirits become visible". Into the circle of light he saw, arriving in twos and threes, "... a great crowd of little beings dressed in red ... They moved back and forth amid the circle of light". When Kermode's friend shouted and waved his stick the fairies vanished.

A connection between fairy sightings and sunlight was made by the Rev Sabine Baring-Gould, the prolific nineteenth-century author and collector of strange lore. As a small boy he was on an outside seat of his father's carriage on a hot summer day. In front of him, over the backs of the horses, fairies were running and playing. He told his father who took him inside the carriage, out of the Sun, whereupon the vision faded. He accepted that it was brought on by the sunlight, but why was it in the form of fairies? And what is the origin of those creatures? Later in life Baring-Gould came to realize that fairies are adaptable and appear in the conventional forms that people expect at the time. When children see them, they look like fairies in the stories and illustrations they are familiar with. But artists and story-tellers did not invent these beings; their original source was

people who had actually seen them.

Modern reports of luminous apparitions and mysterious little beings tend to support Baring-Gould's suggestion that fairies are seen in the form that is conventional at the time. The convention today, in the age of space fantasy, is to identify them as alien intruders rather than spirits of the Earth. C.G. Jung, author of the bold and controversial book *Flying Saucers* (1959), was the first major writer to examine the UFO phenomenon in the context of mythology and folklore. He compared these modern "things seen in the sky" with the signs and wonders that traditionally appear in times of great changes. We are now, he pointed out, in a period of transition as the Age of Pisces gives way to Aquarius, and he identified UFOs as portents of a revolution in our way of thinking that should be expected at these times. Many writers since then have drawn attention to the continuity of folklore themes in the stories produced by the UFO saga.

An obvious connecting link between fairies and UFO occupants is their common habit of abducting people – removing them from Earth and, after a lapse of time, bringing them back again. The striking effect in each case is that those who undergo the experience are somehow changed by it, becoming more sensitive or spiritually minded and sometimes developing the psychic qualities of a shaman or spirit medium. See AWAY WITH THE FAIRIES, p.157.

The modern appearances of little people in association with UFOs was well documented back in 1967 by C. and J. Lorenzen in their book, *Flying Saucer Occupants*, describing about fifty encounters of this kind. For example, at noon on 20 August 1965

A 17th-century woodcut of fairies dancing. Other interesting ingredients include the face of the Green Man in the tree and the door to the Otherworld in the hill shaped like a classic UFO.

an engineer, Alberto Ugarte, his wife and another man were visiting Incan ruins near Cuzco, Peru, when they saw a shiny disc, only about five feet in diameter, land on an ancient stone terrace. Several little creatures of dazzling brightness stepped out of the craft, but on seeing people they climbed back in and departed.

A more recent collection of modern fairy sightings is Janet Bord's *Fairies: Real Encounters With Little People* (1997). Some of them are highly bizarre, such as the account by two sisters in Cornwall in 1940 who looked out of their bedroom window and saw a white-bearded little man in a red, pointed hat, driving a tiny car in circles around their lawn. Also recorded is the fairy aircraft seen by some children in Hertford. A miniature biplane, with a wingspan of about a foot, swooped over their garden fence. It landed briefly, almost hitting a dustbin, and then took off again, its leather-helmeted pilot waving a cheerful goodbye as he flew off.

In many of these modern cases the apparitions have clearly been shaped by current TV or cartoon imagery. The influence of Enid Blyton's character Noddy was detected in 1979, when a

group of children, playing in Nottingham's Wollaton Park, reported seeing a cavalcade of thirty brightly coloured little cars, each with two gnome-like occupants. The children were not frightened but noisily excited, claiming that the cars had chased them. The cars reportedly had no steering wheels and flew over obstacles in their path.

Reviewing these and other "high strangeness" narratives in his book *Borderlands* (1997), historian Dr Mike Dash comments: "If the fairies who used to get around on foot or on horseback can now drive cars and fly aeroplanes, there is no reason why they could not pilot UFOs."

Janet Bord cites a modern fairy encounter from a Theosophical source of 1945, although it took place some years previously. The narrator spoke of afternoon walks on Oxford Hill, Dorset, in the company of a friend. They were walking at some distance from the main party "...when, to my astonishment I saw a number of what I thought to be very small children, about a score in number, and all dressed in little gaily-coloured short skirts, their legs being bare. Their hands were joined, and all held up, as they merrily danced round in a perfect circle. We stood watching them, when

vertical text: plantclinic.cornell.edu

Two views of "fairy rings". The shot above shows the discoloration and visible changes in the quality of grass caused by fungal growth taking place beneath the surface of the soil. The image below shows the more traditional aspect with the fruiting bodies (mushrooms) clearly visible. Rings grow by expanding outwards on the leading edge and dying off on the trailing edge, leaving the centre more deficient in nutrients.

in an instant they all vanished from our sight." The companion told him, as a matter of fact, that they were fairies and often came to that locale for their revels. The association with dancing – and circular dances in particular – is a significantly constant element in encounter stories, and one that, according to Katherine Briggs' *Dictionary Of Fairies* (1976), has been described since the 16th century.

Fairies continue to be seen, albeit unexpectedly, to the present day. A letter to *Country Quest* (November 1973) told of a botanist in an area near Brecon who had spotted "… hordes of tiny people playing". A few years later, Police constable David Swift bravely reported that on inves-

tigating an odd "bank of fog" in a field in East Hull, he saw three oddly dressed figures dancing as around an imaginary maypole. Thinking they might be drunks, he approached them but they vanished. (*Hull Daily Mail*, 10 August 1977)

In another incident, a correspondent to *The Ley Hunter* magazine in 1973, out walking near Alderwasley, in Derbyshire, went to doze in the sunshine on a small, grassy mound. He woke to find a strange little man beside him, "a dumpy little chap" whose clothes were all "the same colour as the grass". They spoke, or rather "exchanged thoughts" and the writer learned that the little man had the important job of "breaking down decaying materials into food for plants".

One place where modern fairies have some civic influence is Akureyri, in northern Iceland, one of the most fertile of the island's farming districts and one of the very few with a wood. In 1984, when a run of bad luck and mishaps delayed the building of a new road, residents had no hesitation in attributing it to fairy disapproval of the disruption. They had seen it happen before, twenty years earlier, during the construction of the town's harbour. Blasting of certain rocks failed inexplicably and accidents to workmen were unusually high. At that time, in 1962, a young man, Olafur Baldursson, came forward saying he could mediate between the council and the fairies that inhabited the harbour rock. Some residents said they could clearly see a whole fairy town in the bay and the coming and going of fairy ships. The magistrates accepted the offer and the harbour was completed without further problems, as the officials themselves were happy to confirm to news reporters.

A recent poll showed that just over half of Icelanders accept the existence of the "Hidden People", who look indistinguishable from us but wear old-fashioned clothing. One of these believers was Tryggvi Emilsson, a founder of Iceland's Communist Party, who was fond of relating an incident that happened to him at the age of fourteen. He became stuck in a mountain crevice while rescuing one of the family's lambs. Reconciled to spending an uncomfortable night, he was surprised when he found a young girl looking at him. She said she came from a farm nearby, pointing to it. Now the boy was even more astonished, as he had walked these mountains all his life and had never known of another farm in the area. The girl laughed, saying: "You wouldn't have.

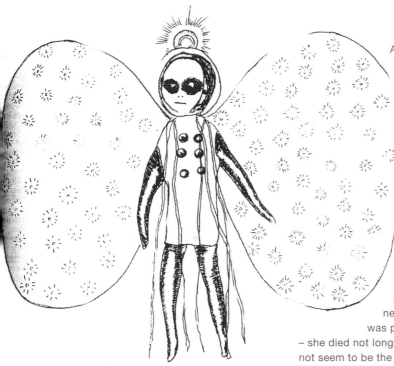

A sketch of one of the three tiny fairy-like aliens that took tea and mince pies with pensioner Jean Hingley in January 1979, in the Midlands town of Rowley Regis. It is rated as one of the strangest and most absurd of British close-encounter cases, and yet includes some important evidence in the form of marks in the snow where the "craft" landed, as well as physiological and electromagnetic effects. The experience was painful to Mrs Hingley – she died not long afterwards – and she did not seem to be the sort of person who would make up such a strange and complex story.

We come from a world parallel to yours." At that moment, the girl said her father was calling her back and she ran off. Writing in *Fortean Times* 201, Claire Smith said that Emilsson continued to visit those hills for the rest of his life, "…until his death in 1986, [but] never saw the girl or the farm again".

Since 1982, Magnus Skarphedinsson has been collecting first-hand accounts of such encounters and to date has spoken to over 700 witnesses; of these, according to Claire Smith, around 200 have had conversations with elves and "Hidden People" and around forty have had continuing friendships. The popular belief has been so strong and active that Vegagerdin, the national road building company, now has a protocol that takes this into account in new projects. Viktor Ingólfsson of the Public Roads Administration says, "If oral tradition, passed on from one generation to the other, tells us that a certain location is cursed, or that supernatural beings inhabit a certain rock, then it must be considered a national treasure … This is simply good public relations." At least one town, Hafnarfjördur, has embraced the elves to the extent of having an appointed "elf-finder"; and both Rekjavik and Hafnarfjördur publish handy maps of local fairy locations.

In many of these stories, both ancient and modern, the little creatures are said to have developed from a sort of misty light. That is also the case in many UFO reports. It happens repeatedly that, say, a couple are driving home one evening when they see a strange light hovering in the sky above them. They stop for a closer look, and then everything gets weird. The birds stop singing, there is total silence and it seems as if time stands still. The light pulsates and changes colour, with hypnotic effect. Then it fades out or moves away, and the spell is broken. Afterwards, the couple talk about what they have seen but can find no explanation for it. But the experience has somehow changed their attitude to life. Often they say, "It made us realize that we are not alone."

These repeated happenings – and there must be thousands of the same type – tend to justify Jung's insight, that UFOs are agents of radical changes in our understanding of the world. Again we emphasize that the first stage in these and other visions is the appearance of a weird luminosity – the astral light, as Evans-Wentz's witness Kermode called it – in which fairies are seen. From it also come will-o'-the-wisps, visions of saints and goddesses, unearthly creatures, space aliens and much of the phantasmagoria recorded in this book. What is the nature of this light and where is it from? For more on this subject, see MYSTICAL LIGHTS, p.148.

Physical fragments of Fairyland

"But where's your evidence?" The question is often, and not unreasonably, put to people who have seen fairies. There is hardly ever a satisfactory answer to it, for the evidence of all strange phenomena is notoriously elusive or ambiguous. At crucial moments witnesses forget their cameras, or they fail to work, and in the rare cases where apparitions are photographed the resulting prints are too blurred or inadequate to prove anything. The hard evidence for these phenomena is always, as Patrick Harpur writes, "...just enough to convince those people who want to believe in their physical reality, but just too little to win over the unbeliever".

The hardest evidence for fairies that Harpur illustrates in his masterwork *Daimonic Reality* (1994) are two items of fairy clothing which he describes from an article in *Country Life* (Irish edition), 24 May 1973. One is a tiny, well-worn shoe (pictured). "It was found by a labourer on the Beara Peninsula, south-west Ireland, in 1835. It is black, worn at the heel and styled like the shoe of an eighteenth-century gentleman. But it is only two and seven-eighths inches long, and seven eighths of an inch at its widest – too long and narrow even for a doll's shoe. If it were an apprentice-piece, say, how did it come to be found on a remote sheep track? Why is it such an odd shape? How did it come to be worn? Who would possess tools fine enough to make such a curiosity?

The man who found the shoe assumed it belonged to the "little people" and gave it to the local doctor, from whom it passed to the Somerville family of Castletownshend, Co Cork. On a lecture tour of America, the author Dr Edith Somerville gave the shoe to Harvard University scientists, who examined it minutely. The shoe had tiny hand-stitches and well-crafted eyelets (but no laces), and was thought to be of mouse skin.

Other shoes, equally odd, have been found in Ireland, not to mention other items of clothing, such as the coat found in a fairy ring by John Abraham Ffolliott in 1868. It was only six-and-

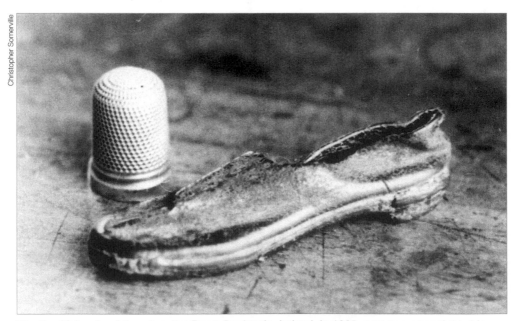

Christopher Somerville

The tiny "fairy shoe" found on the Beara Peninsula, Ireland, in 1835, next to a normal thimble.

This cache of delicately made "fairy coffins" containing dressed wooden effigies was discovered in a cleft below Arthur's Seat, in Edinburgh, in 1836. Some had rotted away, from which it was thought that a series of burials had been made over many years.

a-half inches long and one and three quarter inches across the shoulder. Fully lined and with cloth-covered buttons, its high, velvet-trimmed collar was greased and shiny from, presumably, long wear, while other parts were frayed and "…the pockets holed and scorched as if from a tiny pipe."

The reference above to an "apprentice-piece" brings in the conventional explanation for all such items: that they were made by craft apprentices to demonstrate their skill and to serve as easily carried trade samples. This, of course, does not account for the fairy shoe and coat both being so well used, as if they had been discarded by wearers no more than a foot or so tall.

Another form of fairy artefacts are "fairy arrows", the thought of which terrorized country-dwellers in earlier times (see also INVISIBLE ASSAILANTS, p.173). They were tiny flints shaped like arrow heads, sometimes known as "elf bolts", and "flung like a dart" according to Robert Kirk (*Secret Commonwealth*, 1692).

Nelly Dean, in Emily Bronte's *Wuthering Heights*, was accused by Cathy Linton, in her delirium, of "gathering elf bolts" on Penistone Crag with which to harm Cathy and her live-stock. But, like holed stones and "fairy crosses", elf bolts were also regarded as prophylactic magic. Holed stones were used to fend off lightning and fairy thieves. In some archaic societies, some illnesses were explained as being caused by elf bolts embedded in the victim; for example, in Asia, normal arrows would be used in curing

appendicitis by creating a sympathetic bond with the elf missile. Shamans would heal victims by "removing" the fairy missiles; in a similar fashion, so-called "psychic surgeons" enact an operation to remove offending matter. We must also mention the similarity between elf bolts and "alien implants", both unwanted intrusions by supernatural entities.

Other objects from Fairyland are the goblets, glasses and drinking horns whose legends are

A "fairy stone" from County Antrim, Northern Ireland. Holed stones like these were tied to cows' horns to stop the Little People stealing the milk. In some places they were used to ward off lightning. Image courtesy of Warrington Borough Council Libraries, Heritage and Learning Division.

Peter Vangslev-Nielsen, the sexton of Agerup Church in Holbek, Denmark, shows the silver chalice that is kept there. It was said to have been part of a fabulous fairy hoard and to have been stolen from the fairies several hundred years ago.

that they were stolen from the fairy folk. Goblets are related, etymologically, to the goblins who drank from them at their feasts. In 1891, when Edwin Hartland wrote a chapter on them in *The Science Of Fairy Tales*, these relics were fairly common in parts of Britain, Scandinavia and north Germany. But even then they were disappearing from the churches and old family houses where they had been kept for centuries, and now only a few survive in their original settings. The story of the stolen goblet is told by several of the old writers on "popular antiquities", beginning in the twelfth century with the chroniclers William of Newborough and Gervase of Tilbury. William's story is located at Willie Howe, a large barrow in Yorkshire (now Humberside). A man riding home at night heard music and revelry within the barrow, went into it and was made welcome at a magnificent fairy feast. One of the attendants offered him a cup of wine, but he spilt the drink and rode off with the cup. This curious relic was afterwards sold for a large sum to King Henry I who presented it to his brother-in-law, King David of Scotland. For many years it was kept in the Scottish treasury until a later king, William, passed it on to Henry II. Gervase's tale is similar, except that the fairy chalice was stolen from a barrow in Gloucestershire.

In the Isle of Man – an area with a rich history of fairy lore and relics – the sacramental chalices in several churches were said to have been taken from fairies. One of them was kept in the church of the Malew parish. An early account appeared in 1731 in George Waldron's *Description of the Isle of Man*. The story is that a farmer, walking home one night, heard sweet music coming from Fairy Hill, a barrow in Orrisdale. He peeped through the entrance and beheld a host of merry little people eating, drinking and dancing. One of them offered him a beautiful silver beaker brimming with wine. But the farmer knew his fairy lore and that you should never eat or drink with fairies or they would never let you go again. So he threw the wine over his little hosts who instantly disappeared. Then he ran full speed for home. The fairies pursued him and almost caught him, but he reached his front door just in time to slam it against them. The silver beaker was still in his hand, and next day he asked the minister of his parish what he should do with it. He, "with the instincts of his profession", as Hartland puts it, advised him to devote the cup to the service of the Church. But as a sacramental vessel the fairy chalice proved a failure. It was noticed that people who drank from it went mad, so its use was discontinued.

An expanded version of the same story is given by Sophia Morrison in her *Manx Fairy Tales* of 1911. In her account the cup stolen from fairies was not the Malew chalice but another, of finely worked silver, which became the communion vessel on the church at Rushen. It was, she says, "sent to London" some time in the nineteenth century and was never seen again.

Best known of all the cups and vessels that were snatched from fairies is the Luck of Eden Hall, which is now exhibited in London's Victoria & Albert Museum. It is an ancient glass vessel, about six inches in height, of greenish hue, ornamented with a geometric pattern in white and blue enamel with touches of gold and crimson. A leather case was made to hold it in the fifteenth century, but the Luck itself may be much older. Experts say that it is probably Saracen work. For many generations it belonged to the Musgrave family of Eden Hall in Cumberland, and before that it was supposedly used by local fairies. The Musgraves say that the butler to one of their ancestors went to a spring to draw water, and saw there a drinking party of little people. He rudely grabbed their glass cup and ran off with it. The fairies could not catch up with him, but one of them shouted out a warning "If this glass do break or fall, Farewell the luck of Eden Hall". That is how the Luck was named.

The Musgraves treated their Luck with reverence, each successive heir being sworn to preserve it. Eventually, according to one of their stories, a dissolute youth became head of the family and, while drinking with boisterous

friends, demanded that the Luck be brought to him. The butler of the time handed it to him and stood attentively behind his chair. As he had anticipated, young Musgrave dropped the Luck as he was drinking from it, but the butler, with the agility of a slip fielder, caught it inches from the floor.

One of the many fairy drinking horns that Hartland located in Scandinavian countries is the Oldenburg Horn at the palace of Rosenborg in Copenhagen. It is of silver gilt, engraved with the Danish royal arms, and is dated to the fifteenth century. It must be a replica of that time, for its legend was known much earlier. It goes back to 20 June 990, when the Count of Oldenburg went hunting on a hot day and felt thirsty. A beautiful fairy woman appeared with a drinking horn and offered it to him. But he too was forewarned about fairy liquids and refused. She urged him to drink, promising him fortune and happiness if he did so and ruin if he did not. Oldenburg mistrusted her and poured away the drink. Some of it splashed his horse, removing its hair. Then he galloped off with the horn and, sad to say, got away unpunished.

Hartland believed that these fairy cups were in a tradition that went back to pagan, Druid times. With the prevalence of Christianity and its disapproval of all things pagan, these vessels were retained by certain families who, for years to

This illustration by Phiz, from Keighley's *Fairy Mythology* (1828), shows the similar theft of a chalice from fairies.

come, privately upheld the rituals that kept them on good terms with the fairy world. In that sense they are indeed fairy cups. Later they were given up to, or confiscated by, the Church and adapted to the service of Christ.

These stories of fairy cups leave us puzzled. How is it that the same fantastic legend is attached to so many ancient, sacred cups and horns throughout the whole of northwestern Europe?

Not covered by the "sacred chalice" theory are the secular, utilitarian vessels whose traditional origin is "Fairyland". An example is the "extraordinary great kettle or caldron" in Trensham church, Surrey, that John Aubrey described in his 17th century *Natural History & Antiquities of Surrey, vol. 3*. The locals called it a porridge pot and told how it had been borrowed from the fairies at a stone on nearby Borough hill. At one time, they said, the fairies would lend whatever anyone wanted, but only for a year and a day. They were strict about that, and when the porridge pot was returned late they refused to receive it, and from that day there was no more borrowing.

The fairies of Iceland present gifts to those who treat them with respect and kindness. According to a fairly modern account, the wife of the district police superintendent and public prosecutor who lived in Vopnafjördur, a village on the eastern edge of the island, received a "bolt" of cloth (forty yards) from a fairy woman to whom she acted as midwife. This cloth is now in the National Museum in Reykjavik.

Another artefact can be found at Dunvegan Castle of the Scottish isle of Skye. Here the lordly MacLeods proudly exhibit their possession: the Fairy Flag. There are several stories, all of them supernatural, of how it came into their possession.

The most complete is that it came from a fairy woman. It is difficult to establish the date when it appeared; like many such legends it is set in "time beyond memory". On one of those distant days a nurse was sitting by the cradle of a new-born MacLeod heir. She looked up and saw that a fairy woman had wrapped the baby in the famous flag and was "crooning" over him, praising him in the Gaelic tongue and prophesying his brilliant future. Then she slipped quietly away. The nurse remembered every word and note of the croon and it proved so effective as a baby's lullaby that the MacLeods insisted that every nurse they employed should learn it. The flag was useful to them over many generations. It was never to be unfurled except in times of great danger. On one occasion it halted a cattle plague that threatened their livelihood, and it routed a raiding party of the MacDonalds by creating the illusion that the MacLeods who waved it were many times their actual number.

This is not the only relic that the MacLeods acquired from Fairyland. One of their ancestors, according to the family legend, was invited to a fairy feast at Dun Osdale, one of the "fairy fortlets" of Skye. When invited to drink wine, he refused and, like everyone else who ever seems to have been in this predicament, ran off with their goblet.

And we have not forgotten that dancing and making music are a staple of the many recorded glimpses of fairy folk. Many storytellers maintain that their music is the most valuable gift that fairies have given to humans. We leave this subject to our later section: PHANTOM MUSIC AND STRANGE VOICES, p.152.

Fairy photography

The physical evidence for Fairyland – the little shoes and coats, the horns and goblets, the fairy flag – is as Patrick Harpur says, good enough for those who believe in fairies anyway, but making no impression on those who refuse to believe. Perhaps it is a mistake to expect fairies to provide hard-and-fast evidence of themselves, because they are not hard-and-fast by nature. Many photographers have claimed to have taken pictures of fairies, often inadvertently; unfortunately, all the documented examples have either been proved fake or require the eye of faith to see coherent figures in them.

The most remarkable fairy photographs, causing many sceptics to waver in their unbelief, were published in the Christmas 1920 edition of *The Strand Magazine*. They showed two young girls in the company of elves and fairies. The photographs illustrated an exciting article by

One of the "fairy photographs" taken by two young Yorkshire girls which so fascinated Sir Arthur Conan Doyle.

Sir Arthur Conan Doyle (who spent the large royalties he received from his Sherlock Holmes stories on promoting psychical research). He proclaimed an event "...so sensational as to mark an epoch in human thought". Two innocent country girls, playing in a Yorkshire dale, had attracted the company of fairies and had photographed each other with them. On these photographs Conan Doyle built his fundamental faith in the reality of fairies. In *The Coming of the Fairies* (1922) he called them good evidence for "...the existence on the surface of this planet of a population which may be as numerous as the human race, which

pursues its own strange life in its own strange way, and which is only separated from ourselves by some difference of vibration".

The two girls who photographed the fairies (not named at the time to preserve their privacy) were sixteen-year-old Elsie Wright of Cottingley near Bingley, Yorks, and her little cousin Frances Griffiths, aged ten. In 1917, after they had made friends with the fairies in the glen behind their home, Frances borrowed her father's camera to photograph them. The father, a Theosophist, showed the prints to Edward Gardner, a friend of Conan Doyle, and that is how they became

Elsie Wright in the 1980s with one of the Cottingley fairy photographs taken by herself and Frances Griffiths sixty-five years earlier. They maintained to the end that they had not set out to trick anyone and their images were an attempt to replicate what they had actually seen.

famous. They passed the scrutiny of experts, and Conan Doyle was joined by other distinguished people in believing them genuine. It was not until 1982 that science judged otherwise.

The case of the Cottingley photographs is well summarized by folklore professor Paul Smith, in his contribution to Peter Narvaez's collection of modern fairy studies, *The Good People* (1991). The images themselves received a detailed forensic examination by Geoffrey Crawley, editor of *The British Journal of Photography*. In a series of ten articles in that journal, beginning in December 1982, Crawley showed that the girls had used cut-out illustrations of fairies, retouching them to create fakes. Elsie and Frances were still alive, 65 years older than at the time of their escapade, and they readily admitted that they had fabricated the fairy images, much as Crawley had deduced. But it had been a "pious fraud" (a deception practised for a good purpose). To their dying day both the ladies insisted that they really had seen fairies in the Cottingley glen and had merely imitated them in their rigged photographs.

Mystical lights

Lights in the sky, under the sea and in caverns deep beneath the Earth. Mysterious lights that flit across marshes, hover over ancient burial mounds and haunt the paths to cemeteries. Lights that enter houses and explode. Lights that seem to follow people. We hear of fairy lights, spook lights, aerial lights and others that cannot be categorized – playful or menacing, gaseous or animate, casual or purposeful.

The phenomenon has many names and identifications – UFOs, fireballs, spirits of the dead, fairies, will-o'-the-wisps, jack-o-lanterns, Earth lights, sky dragons. Ball lightning is a comfortable name for floating balls of light, but no one quite knows what it means. As recently as 1943 W.J. Humphries in *Ways of the Weather* still upheld the traditional opinion that light balls were "a humbug" or optical illusions. Here are the conflicting views of two other "authorities": "Floating ball lightning is not dangerous to human beings, even when it appears in the middle of a group of persons; it appears to avoid them [as] it avoids good conductors." (Professor B.L. Goodlet, *Journal of the Institute of Electrical Engineers*, July 1937.) "It is very dangerous to touch a fireball. An inquisitive child once kicked one and thereby caused an explosion which killed eleven cattle and threw the child and a companion to the ground." (Frank Lane, *The Elements Rage*, 1945)

Lane illustrates the "ball lightning" phenomenon with the following incident: "A young girl was seated at a table when she noticed a large ball of fire moving slowly across the floor of the room in her direction. As the fireball neared her it rose and commenced to spiral round her. It then darted towards a hole in the chimney and climbed up it. On reaching the open air it exploded just above the roof with a crash that shook the entire house."

Tradition associates the appearance of floating lights with death, and many incidents are recorded to support this belief. Several examples were collected from witnesses by the former US Consul in Wales, Wirt Sikes, author of *British Goblins* (1880). He heard about the pale, moving lights

called "corpse candles"; their appearance on a path leading to a burial ground was taken as a warning that a funeral party would soon pass that way. On one occasion three corpse candles were seen by all the passengers on the coach from Llandeilo to Carmarthen as they crossed the river bridge by Golden Grove. A few days later three men were drowned at the spot when their coracle capsized.

The number of lights is supposed to foretell the number of coming deaths. John Aubrey's *Miscellanies* (1696) contains the story of a woman who saw five lights in the room occupied by five maids in the house where she worked. When the room was then plastered a fire was lit to dry it, and the fumes stifled the girls in their beds.

Baron von Reichenbach, famous for his earnest inquiries into the nature of the "magnetic" lights which some people see as auras, was curious about the lights, wraiths, spectres or whatever, often seen in graveyards. One of his colleagues, Miss Leopoldina Reichel, had

Explanations for the will-o'-the-wisp vary from ignited marsh gas to spirits of the dead. Often it is said to display intelligence or purpose, sometimes malevolent in intent but sometimes revealing treasure.

A "ghost light" photographed in Basle Zoological Gardens in 1907.

Book of Folklore (1913) also invoked "phosphuretted hydrogen" as the explanation of graveyard lights. On one occasion his brother's overcoat, thrown over a grave, became impregnated with the stuff, causing him to faint. Baring-Gould quotes several instances of lights which have appeared to give warning of death by travelling along a coffin route or entering the house of a doomed person; but though he is prepared to accept the reality of stationary lights above graves, he rejects the moving variety: "That these flames should travel down roads and seek houses where there is one dying is, of course, an exaggeration and untenable."

The moving lights which are called ball lightning when they occur indoors become wildfire or will-o'-the-wisps in the open air. They are variously explained as combusted methane (marsh gas), fairies or spirits, but there is no proof for any theory. According to the 1970 *Encyclopædia Britannica*, "no entirely satisfactory explanation has been put forward" for the phenomenon. It may be significant that as the fairies disappeared from their once familiar haunts, so did the will-o'-the-wisp. In 1855 a correspondent in *Notes and Queries* asked whether in fact such a thing existed outside poetic tradition and was answered by several people claiming direct experience and providing descriptions.

Dermot MacManus in *The Middle Kingdom* (1959) tells of personal encounters with "fairy lights", which he says are different from the will-o'-the-wisp because they are of many colours and "as bright and stable as electric lights". One procession of such lights was seen to fly in formation from their usual haunt, a "fairy fort" named Crillaun near Castlebar in the west of Ireland, to another such earthwork on the opposite side of a lake. About the nature of the will-o'-the-wisp MacManus is undecided. Sometimes it seems to be inanimate and may be kicked or whisked about like Leopoldina's kobolds; yet there was a girl he

the gift of seeing such things. They appeared to her as dancing lights, some as big as men, others small, "like dwarfish kobolds". She was able to move among them and whisk them about with her skirt. Reichenbach, who believed himself to be the discoverer of an essence he called "odic force", applied his theory to the evidence and produced this impressive-sounding explanation of graveyard luminescence. "It is a carbonate of ammonium, phosphuretted hydrogen and other products of putrefaction, known and unknown, which liberate odic light in the course of evaporation. When the putrefaction comes to an end, the lights are quenched, the dead have atoned." (*Letters on Od and Magnetism*, 1926)

The Reverend Sabine Baring-Gould in *A*

knew, "very intelligent and well balanced", who was followed by a moving light, coming for her at running speed and changing direction to pursue her home. "To this day she is convinced that it was directed by real intelligence."

A terrifying moving light chased and caught Terry Pell of Spalding, Lincolnshire, as he drove his vegetable lorry towards Warminster in Wiltshire in the early morning of 10 August 1965. Warminster at the time was undergoing one of its periodic plagues of weird aerial visitations, details of which are faithfully chronicled by local journalist and author Arthur Shuttlewood in his book *The Warminster Mystery* (1967). Forty-five minutes before Mr Pell had his adventure, at 3.45am, Mrs Rachel Atwill a few miles away, saw what many others in the district have reported seeing, a bright light in the sky. She was awakened by a loud droning noise, looked through the window of her bungalow and saw the light, dome-shaped on top, hovering over the range of hills opposite. It stayed there for twenty-five minutes, humming and flickering, then vanished. Mrs Atwill suffered a headache and had to drink brandy. She recognized the shape in a photograph taken nineteen days later by Gordon Faulkner of Warminster and published in *The Warminster Journal* and *The Daily Mirror*. When Mr Pell saw the light it was floating fifty yards in front of his lorry, having flashed into view from over

the hills to his left. It was red and looked like a giant headlight or a human eye. It advanced on Mr Pell's lorry and fastened itself to the windscreen, vibrating. The lorry stopped. Its sleeping passengers, Mrs Pell and daughter Wendy, woke up to see the light ball soar aloft and away. They were frightened but unhurt.

This incident is far from unique. UFO literature abounds in modern events of the sort, and many older cases are to be found in collections of folklore. Here is a report from Brad Steiger's *Flying Saucers are Hostile* (1967), given without reference to its original source. Mr William Howell of Texas was driving home at 11.15pm in the summer of 1965. Like Mr Pell he had two sleeping passengers, his brother's children, and he was also near a prominent local landmark, Foggy Hill. A light appeared overhead: "It seemed to head directly for my car. It gave off a bluish light that became so bright the entire car seemed bathed in a blue haze. If that thing would have been a meteor, it would have landed with a big crash. It didn't. It made a sharp turn to the southwest and shot off in a burst of speed."

When religious people see visions, they may identify them as saints or archangels, but their accounts usually begin with the appearance of a glowing light. Modern encounters with "extraterrestrials" often begin the same way. Strange lights feature in many sections of this book, associated

A fireball seen during a storm in Salagnac, France, in September 1845.

Ball lightning startles Louis Otto and friends in Gorges du Loup, near Nice, in France.

with many different kinds of phenomena. Some of them have an otherworldly quality, as if they are the lights of Fairyland, the underground kingdom or some other world which we can never deeply explore. Reichenbach and other scientists have tried to find explanations, but nothing has ever been established, and it may be in the nature of things that nothing ever will be.

Phantom music and strange voices

In every treatise on hallucinations there are references to phantom music and disembodied voices, discussed in terms of mental and nervous aberrations. Psychiatrists are suspicious of this phenomenon, and a patient who admits to hearing voices is usually a candidate for the madhouse. The following example of "fallacious perception" by a patient is quoted by Edmund Parrish in *Hallucinations and Illusions* (1897): "Every tree which I approach, even in windless weather, seems to whisper and utter words and sentences ... the carts and carriages rattle and sound in a mysterious way and creak out anecdotes ... the swine grunt names and stories, and hens seem to scold and reproach me, and even the geese cackle quotations." In the sounds of nature, however produced, men have always heard the music and poetry of other worlds. To reduce the phenomenon to clinical terms is to damn at a swipe all that is intuitive and mystical in human nature.

Voices seem to manifest both internally and externally, though we are aware that this dis-tinction may be an illusion. This question was raised by C.G. Jung in his *Alchemical Studies*. He tells of an African soldier who was spoken to by a tree. Modern psychology assumes that the voice was imagined or "projected" by the soldier. But between that and the traditional belief that the tree actually spoke, Jung suggests a third attitude that accepts the reality of a spiritual or daimonic existence, often mingling with our own. Patrick Harpur's *Daimonic Reality* (1994) demonstrates the advantages of this overview of irrational phenomena.

Among examples of voices heard internally are the famous cases of Martin Luther, St Ignatius Loyola, Benvenuto Cellini and Sigmund Freud. Socrates had a *daemon*, a voice that warned him of actions likely to offend the gods. Some voices torment the listener, and others urge on to action, as in the cases of St Joan (who heard the Archangel Michael and Saints Catherine and Margaret), St Francis of Assisi (who heard a voice from a crucifix bidding him to "rebuild my church"), or George Fox (who founded the Quaker movement at a similar prompting). The phenomenon continues today and is interpreted by many UFO "contactees" as telepathic contact with beings from other worlds or dimensions.

In 1765 the violin virtuoso and composer Giuseppe Tartini had a dream in which he gave the devil his violin who then played "on a level I had never before conceived was possible". Tartini awoke and tried to transcribe what he had heard but the resulting "Devil's Trill" Sonata, though better than anything he had written before, was apparently a pale reflection of the original.

Of the "externalized" voices, there can be no greater claims than those of the gods who thunder down laws, messages and warnings from above. Before this materialist age people were more sensitive to communications from nature; objects and animals could speak like men if the spirit moved them. The classical historian Herodotus was told by the priestesses of the Dodonian oracle of Zeus that the sacred grove containing the famous whispering oak was revealed by a talking bird that alighted in its branches. Wood from this tree was said to have been set into the keel of the Argo by Athena, giving the ship the vocal power to warn Jason of danger ahead. Disembodied voices are still associated with portents, especially warnings of the death of a friend or relative, and are so astonishingly common that even Camille Flammarion's great three-volume compilation, *Death And Its Mystery* (1922) could not exhaust the fund of anecdotes. Newly bereaved widows – including Anna, the wife of Charles Fort – often tell of hearing their late husband's voice.

We are interested in the sounds and voices that often accompany "poltergeist" activity. They have a very strange quality; sometimes faint, sometimes so abnormally loud that they are more like shock-waves of great force. Consider the fantastic story of Calvados Castle in France, which suffered an astonishing range of phenomena from October 1867. They were still continuing when reports were published in the *Annales des sciences psychiques* in 1893. They told of furniture levitating and moving about, the vanishing of Lourdes medals and other holy charms used in a continuous exorcism, doors and windows opening by themselves, and the pulling-off of bedclothes. With these effects came a variety of sounds. They ranged from creaks, groans and footsteps to organ music being heard for hours after one of the occupants had ceased playing. The castle constantly shook under heavy blows "so strong that objects suspended on the wall rattled in their places… To acquire some idea of their violence, one must imagine a wall collapsing, or a horse, or cannon-balls thrown against a door." At times the whole building shook violently "from top to bottom", yet there was little damage, and the noises could only be heard inside the castle.

These effects are typical of poltergeist sounds, the characteristics of which are exaggeration and imitation. Alfred Monin's biography of the Curé of Ars, St John Vianney, says he was particularly persecuted by this kind of phenomenon. At times his courtyard would ring with the noise of a great army, camping, marching or charging. In the winter of 1824–25, the Curé could not sleep for the noise of a large flock of sheep passing over his head, and whenever he entered a lower room of his house, everyone could hear sounds, as though "a large, escaped horse" was prancing round him invisibly. The Curé was a noted ascetic, but a demon voice used to mock him and accuse him of indulging in luxury, crying, "Vianney, Vianney, you truffle-eater, you! Are you still alive; haven't you died yet? I'll get you!" A similar vocal persecution is described by Evelyn Waugh in *The Ordeal of Gilbert Pinfold* (1957).

One of the strangest of the loquacious entities in our records took up temporary lodgings with the Dagg family of Clarendon, Quebec, in 1889. According to *Light*, December 1889, an investigator, Percy Woodcock, visited the family on 15 November, and was taken by the adopted daughter of the house, Dinah, to a shed where previously she had seen a strange man. Nervously she called out, "Are you there, Mister?" To Woodcock's astonishment, from the middle of the empty shed, about four feet away, came the clearly audible voice of an old man. It cursed them both in deep, gruff tones, using language that Woodcock would not record and which *Light* would hardly have printed. It said, "I am the devil. I'll have you in my clutches. I'll break your neck."

Woodcock and Mr Dagg talked to the voice for several hours, during which it admitted causing the mysterious fires (see FIERY PERSECUTIONS, p.181) and teleportation of household objects. It apologized for the inconvenience it had caused. During the conversation the foul and obscene language abated, and the voice promised to leave the following Sunday night.

When the news spread, people came from miles around. On the Sunday the voice was on good behaviour, though at times rather tactless. It answered questions and seemed to display an intimate knowledge of anyone who entered the house, often proclaiming aloud embarrassing details of their lives that they would rather have kept private. On being congratulated about his change of character the voice said: "I am not the person who used the filthy language. I am an angel from heaven sent to chase him away." The transformation was not yet complete, for the entity occasionally lost its temper in a volley of blasphemy, but by Sunday evening it was joining the crowds in singing hymns in such a "beautiful

An engraving illustrating Robert Burns's poem *Tam O'Shanter*. As he passes by Kirk Alloway, the inebriated Tam witnesses "Warlocks and witches in a dance" presided over by "Auld Nick in shape o' beast".

flute-like voice" that it was now implored to stay. The next day the Dagg children announced that it had finally left them. They described how a "beautiful man", resplendently dressed in shining clothes, had hugged them and bid them goodbye. They sang a final hymn together (the "angel" playing a small harp-like instrument) and as the children watched they saw a light, "...red like a fire", blaze at his feet, rising to surround him as he ascended, singing sweetly, into Heaven. Fort adds a typically laconic footnote to his account of the story: "It sang a hymn and departed."

Some of these voice phenomena must have been quite impressive. A poltergeist case recorded by Dr Reid Clanny, *A Faithful Record ... of Mary Jobson* (1841), features "exquisite music", heard by many witnesses independently, followed by a voice of "angelic sweetness" quoting from the scriptures. Another person who attracted disembodied voices was Clement Hofbauer, who later became a saint. In 1801 his sermon to a crowded church in Warsaw was frequently interrupted by the cries of a phantom baby. When he continued, voices broke out in the air all over the church, crying that it was on fire. Flames and smoke were seen everywhere, even from the street. Some minutes later, after panic subsided, these were found to be as ethereal as the voices. In the process of St Clement's canonization, the Church accepted the evidence of demonic intervention in his mission.

Forteans also collect accounts of anomalous sounds heard in the countryside, from regular thuds and rolling thunder to the strange mix of hum, drone and buzz that has come to be called the "hummadruz". According to John Billingsley, who began researching the subject in 1978 after an experience of his own, the term seems to have been coined in the last century: "In 1878, R.E. Bibby, a local musician and composer, recalled from his 1820s childhood, a low drone or humming noise heard in suburbs to the south and east of Manchester, especially Gorton, Rusholme and Longsight. It was heard on calm, clear days, usually in the early morning or at dusk." Despite vigils and studies at locations throughout the British Isles where the phenomenon has been reported, no cause has been identified satisfactorily.

It reminds us very much of the "buzzing" heard at Fátima (see SHARED VISIONS AND VISUAL RUMOURS, p.110) and the "humming" that many witnesses of fairies report. John Aubrey, typically records that during the time he attended a Latin school near Chippenham, Wiltshire, between 1633 and 1634, Mr Hart, the school curate "...was annoy'd one night by these elves, or fayeries". Coming home over the downs in the dark, Mr Hart had strayed into a fairy ring: "He all at once saw an innumerable quantitie of pigmies, or very small people, dancing rounde and rounde and singing and making all manner of small odd noyses." Unable to flee, seemingly immobilized by fear and amazement, Mr Hart collapsed, whereupon "...these little creatures pinch'd him all over and made a quick humming noyse all the time". When he awoke he found himself sore all over. Aubrey heard the story from Mr Hart himself a day or so later, and went out to the circle with a schoolfriend but "...sawe none of the elves or fairies".

Phantom music is a favourite ingredient in ghost and fairy stories; here are two modern accounts. An empty office in Peter Street, Manchester, was haunted by thin piping tunes heard by many people in the building. A letter to *The Manchester Evening News* (24 October 1968) suggests it was the same phantom flautist heard in the same office block two years previously. A weird strumming from a piano gave over a hundred impromptu concerts in a house in Humber Avenue, Coventry, Warwickshire. According to Bill Duncan, the occupier, quoted in the *News of the World* (13 January 1974): "It sounds as though someone is plucking the strings ... It doesn't sound anything like modern music."

So far, we have emphasized the strange, demonic side of phantom voices and music, but these phenomena have their positive aspects. Many people have been inspired to sainthood or great deeds by voices from the far blue yonder. And many favourite tunes in Celtic and other traditions of folk music owe their origin to someone who heard the music played by fairies.

The fairy lullaby of the MacLeods (see p.146) is an example of this most valuable gift of fairies, while all over the British Isles there are numerous hills and ancient mounds, traditional abodes of fairies, where their music is said to be audible on certain days. Many of them are listed, county by county, in Leslie Grinsell's *Folklore of Prehistoric Sites in Britain* (1976). Each site has its own special songs, and some of these have been remembered and recorded by people who heard them. In Celtic, Scandinavian and other traditions of folk

The phantom drummer of Tedworth, Wiltshire, as represented in Joseph Glanvill's *Sadducismus triumphatus* (1666, 1681). The Tedworth case, in which a noisy and violent haunting made life a misery for the Mompesson family, is probably the first major poltergeist case in British annals. The disturbances were blamed on the spirit of a drummer boy but, over the course of a year from January 1662, the drumming noise gave way to heavy blows which shook walls, moving furniture, and foul smells, leading to physical assaults and levitations of Mompesson's children.

music, the accepted origin of many old tunes is the music of fairies. It is, they say, the purest, most enchanting sound imaginable. Those who hear it are often inspired and become great musicians by reproducing the melodies.

One of the last places in Britain where local songs and tunes were regularly derived from fairy music was Fetlar – one of the smaller Shetland islands at only about six miles across. Though once highly populated, the island is now sparsely inhabited, but holds many ancient relics, including great walls that were traditionally built by the mysterious Finn folk of prehistory. The music of trows and fairies was frequently heard there and in many cases it was adapted by local fiddlers into popular dance tunes. A well-known Shetland air, "Trowie Spring", was learnt from a fairy festival at Haltadans, an ancient ring of stones at the centre of the island. Nearby, a Fetlar watermill, Winya-depla, gave its name to a tune that was reportedly first heard there in 1803. Its story is that an old

man, Gibbie Laurenson, was tired after grinding corn at the mill and took a rest on the grass outside. In a drowsy state he heard some lively music and saw a group of trows dancing to a strange kind of fiddle. Gibbie was no musician, but he remembered the tune, and his son, who played the fiddle, recorded the song as his father whistled it.

In some cases music was passed on in the other direction, from humans to fairies. The little folk would kidnap an accomplished piper or fiddler, take him to their underground feast and make him play for them. They would then let him go with some tricky form of payment. It happened, says Ernest Marwick (*The Folklore of Orkney and Shetland*) to John Scott, a famous fiddler in the Shetland Islands. After playing all night while the trows danced and revelled, he received no tangible reward but was promised that every time he put his hand into his pocket he would find money in it. This served him well for a time, but one evening Scott boasted about it to his drinking companions, and from that moment he never had another penny.

The county of Dorset is particularly rich in sites where fairy music has been heard, including two named "Music Barrow". Another Hillock of Music, on the Hebridean isle of Gigha, was locally famous as the place where fairy songs could be heard. It was so popular that in 1923 the religious authorities took it over by building the parish church on top of the hillock, and the fairy music was silenced.

A specific case of fairy music passing into human culture (another example from the Isle of Man) is in Evans-Wentz's *Fairy Faith in Celtic Countries*. "William Cain, of Glen Helen, was going home in the evening across the mountains near Brook's Park, when he heard music down below in the glen, and saw there a great glass house, like a palace, all lit up. He stopped to listen, and when he had the new tune he went home to practise it on his fiddle; and recently he played the same fairy tune at Miss Sophia Morrison's Manx entertainment at Peel."

This is the same Sophia Morrison who described the theft of the fairy goblet at Rushen (see p.144). She was a fluent Manx speaker, one of the last to live on into the twentieth century, and she learnt many tales which would otherwise have died out. She was an active campaigner for the revival of Manx culture; it is largely due to her that the Isle of Man has retained so much fairy lore.

In Ireland, where interchange of fairy and human music is still occasionally practised, music itself is regarded as a gift of the fairies, a product of the country itself, an expression of the native spirit. The only musicians who are called truly great are those who have received the gift at birth or have been initiated through an encounter with fairy music. First hand accounts of these experiences are still being recorded. In an article, "Music learned from the fairies", folklore writer Ríonach Uí Ógáin reviews the phenomenon academically and against the background of similar gifts of musical inspiration in the Hebrides, Shetland, Norway and further afield. One thing he points out is that the fairies' gift is not always a pure blessing. It brings quality to a person's music, but is sometimes a cause of melancholy, sickness, madness and death.

Finally, in another account from Wales, we have the remarkable adventure of David Williams of Penrhyndeudraeth in Gwynedd, as told by Elias Owen in his *Welsh Folk-lore* (1888). One evening, Williams, a servant, was walking home behind his mistress; he thought she was a few minutes ahead of him but, when he arrived at the door, he was amazed when told she had arrived three hours earlier. He reported seeing a brilliant meteoric light "…followed by a ring or hoop of fire, and within this hoop stood a man and woman of small size, handsomely dressed … When the hoop reached the Earth these two beings jumped out of it and immediately proceeded to make a circle on the ground [in which] a large number of men and women instantly appeared and to the sweetest music that was ever heard commenced dancing round and round the circle".

The sight was so entrancing that Williams stopped a few minutes, or so he thought, to observe the legendary dance of the fairies. "The ground all around was lit up by a kind of subdued light," and he could see every movement with clarity. "By and by, the meteor … appeared again and then the fiery hoop came to view and when it reached the spot where the dancing was, the lady and the gentleman who had arrived in it jumped into the hoop and disappeared in the same manner in which they had reached the place." Immediately, the other Little People "vanished from sight" and Williams was left alone in the darkness to continue his journey.

There are peculiar details in this account, reinforcing our view that fairylore has much in common with ufology and the association takes place in our psyches as well as in our culture. Apart from the strange light, the luminous transport, repetitive movements and the celestial beings, this case embodies the motif of "missing time" that so strongly features in modern UFO encounter cases, preceding its famous exemplar (the Betty and Barney Hill incident) by nearly a century (see OTHERWORLDLY ABDUCTION, p.166).

Away with the fairies

People are always vanishing. Some do it once and for all, either of their own volition or somebody else's; others turn up again. Not surprisingly, those who return from a mysterious absence feel the need to explain, but some of these explanations, far from enlightening, only make us wonder more about the people who did not return. Whatever explanation is on offer – "murdered by colleagues"; "went out for a pack of cigarettes and wandered off"; "abducted by fairies" or "extraterrestrials" – the phenomenon is essentially the same: a person inexplicably vanishing and unaccountably returning. Any hypothetical explanation, as we keep pointing out, varies with fashion.

We have many records of people disappearing, suddenly, mysteriously and finally, but from the storyteller's point of view there is something wrong with all of them. They are too short, without proper endings. For example, the London *Daily Chronicle* (30 July 1889) said that on the thirteenth of that month Mr Macmillan of the famous publishing firm had climbed to the top of Mount Olympus. He was seen waving from the summit but, despite careful searches and rewards offered, no trace of him was ever afterwards found. That is all. Again, on 25 November 1809, Benjamin Bathurst went to enter his carriage outside a German inn. Then, says the Reverend Sabine Baring-Gould in *Historical Oddities* (1889), "he stepped round to the heads of the horses – and

Dragged from the fairy ring. Illustration from Wirt Sikes's *British Goblins* (1880).

was never seen again".

As Dr Mike Dash explains, in his study of the disappearance, Bathurst was a British intelligence agent on active service in Prussia during the Napoleonic Wars and his disappearance took place in a busy courtyard at night, so perhaps we should not make too much of it. Of course famous and notorious cases are often explained in time or by diligent research, but many others have no satisfactory conclusions.

Hoaxes and false cases clutter this field and obscure the material of value. For example, through poor scholarship, early ufologists have enthusiastically promoted a clutch of stories that seemed to suggest people could be abducted into another dimension through a vortex in full view of witnesses. These stories generally concern a young man – variously called David Lang, Oliver Lerch or Charles Ashmore – who is last seen crossing a field. Search parties find nothing. Sometimes there are a trail of footprints which end suddenly, or a faint voice calling for help is heard on the anniversary of their disappearance at the very spot the person vanished. We confess that we too were taken in by some of these stories but excellent work has gone into investigating many of them. No fewer than seven stories of this type have been found to be variants of some of the supernatural stories of Ambrose Bierce, an American writer

whose own disappearance in war-torn Mexico in 1914 is still unsolved.

But genuinely mysterious disappearances do happen. Sometimes they lead to dreadful miscarriages of justice. The seventeenth-century legal writer Sir Edward Coke refers, in his *Institutes*, to a case in Warwickshire in which a little girl of eight or nine went missing. She was an orphan, looked after by her uncle, and due to inherit the family estate at the age of sixteen. The uncle was required to produce her, could not do so, and in panic dressed up another little girl and presented her as his niece. He was exposed, charged with the niece's murder, convicted and hanged. Years later the girl, having reached the age of sixteen, turned up and claimed her estate. She had run away, she said, and had been living with some kind people in the next county.

In earlier times, similar incidents probably gave rise to the kind of stories recorded by nineteenth-century folklorists such as T. Crofton Croker. In his *Fairy Legends* (1825), Croker repeats a first-hand account he heard in the Vale of Neath, South Wales, of the disappearance of a certain Mr Rhys. One evening Rhys and another man, Llewellyn, were driving some horses to the farm where they worked. On the way Rhys fancied he heard music and told Llewellyn to go on ahead with the horses as he wanted to stay behind for a while and have a dance. By morning his friend still had not returned and when searches failed to discover him, Llewellyn, was suspected of Rhys's murder. Fortunately a local farmer persuaded all parties, including Llewellyn and the narrator, to revisit the scene of the disappearance. There Llewellyn heard the music. His foot was on the edge of a fairy ring. "Put your foot on mine, David," said Llewellyn to Croker's informant. The man did so, and the others likewise. Then all heard the music and saw a crowd of little figures dancing in the ring with Rhys among them. Llewellyn dragged him out of the ring and it seemed to Rhys that he had only been dancing for five minutes or so. The experience left him so melancholy that he soon died.

A record of an abduction by fairies, reprinted in J.O. Halliwell's *Illustrations Of The Fairy Mythology* (1845), from a pamphlet of 1678 in the British Museum, is the most interesting we know of. Its details are remarkable – not least because it illustrates how many of our phenomenal sections overlap – and it is attested to both by the man who was taken away and by the witnesses to his disappearance and return. Three weeks before the pamphlet was written, a Dr Moore with two companions was travelling in Wicklow, Ireland, and staying at an inn in Dromgreagh, near Baltinglass. He began to speak of fairies, saying that as a child in that country he had several times been taken off by them, on which occasions his mother would call in a local wise woman who was effective in retrieving him. As he spoke it seemed to him, as he said later, that a troop of men entered the room (see SPECTRAL ARMIES, p.255) took hold of him and dragged him off.

All that his companions saw was that Dr Moore was being drawn out of the room by an unseen force (see INVISIBLE ASSAILANTS, p.173). They tried to hold on to him, but he vanished and they raised the alarm. The innkeeper, who was apparently used to such happenings, sent for the old woman. She declared that Dr Moore was in a wood about a mile away with the fairies and that, if by her magic she could prevent him from eating or drinking during his absence, he would be restored unharmed. Early the next morning Dr Moore re-entered the inn, hungry and thirsty from a night spent in rapid travel between places of fairy feasts and revelry. Every time his abductors had offered him food, he

said, it had been unaccountably struck out of his hand – presumably through the woman's magic – and at daybreak he had found himself alone within sight of the inn.

Local histories everywhere are full of such incidents, and the theme continues in the many similar reports of our own time. We can even find them shorn of any association with fairies or spirits, except that these are often replaced by appeals to a "fourth" dimension, or aliens. Consider the tale of a terrified elderly couple, in December 1873, who were discovered dazed and in their nightclothes at a Bristol railway station. As reported by *The Times* (11 December 1873), Mr and Mrs Cumpston were asleep in a Bristol hotel when they were wakened by noises. Mr Cumpston stepped out of bed onto the floor, which seemed to open, he said. He felt he was falling into a black void and was saved only when his wife seized him and pulled him back. Panic-stricken, they climbed out of the room by a window and went in search of a reassuring policeman.

A phenomenon which was once very active, but seems scarcely to have been reported in recent

Fairies abducting a human baby. Illustration from Wirt Sikes's *British Goblins* (1880).

years, is that of the changeling – the substitution, by the fairies, of a sickly alien child for a healthy human one. An old history of the Isle of Man, quoted in Halliwell's *Illustrations Of The Fairy Mythology* (1845), provides the story of a Manx woman whose babies strangely disappeared shortly after their births. On the first two occasions, the disappearances were attended by various noises and disturbances in her house, which brought the neighbours running. The babies were each found some distance from the bed … dropped by the fairies, as they explained it. Soon after her third baby was born, the woman saw it being levitated out of the room by an invisible force. She cried out and her husband came in and pointed to the baby by her side; but it was a sallow, wrinkled child, not like her own, and it lay naked with the original baby's clothes tied in a bundle beside it. It lived on for a few years, never speaking, walking or defecating, and eating nothing but a few herbs.

Wirt Sikes, in *British Goblins* (1880), has an anecdote about Jennet Francis of Ebwy Fawr valley in Wales. One night she awoke to feel her infant son being pulled from her arms. Screaming out and praying, she succeeded in pulling him back. An interesting detail, in view of the spiritual powers which many cultures attribute to people who have been teleported (see AVIAN ABDUCTIONS, p.384), is that the son grew up to become a famous preacher.

In earlier times, when the existence of an abducting or teleporting force was recognized in the terminology of the fairy faith, local witches or magicians were at hand with the appropriate spells to remedy the "sudden disappearance" effect. In the case of changelings, the folklore record is full of various procedures by which parents can regain their abducted baby. Other traditions hint at forgotten methods of recapturing older people whom the fairies had taken. Robert Kirk, minister of Aberfoyle in Scotland and the author of *The Secret Commonwealth of Elves, Fauns, and Fairies* (1691), is said to have died on the Fairy Hill near his home in 1692. One legend about him is that on the anniversary of his death (or, variously, the christening of his posthumous child) he appeared again with the fairy host and could have been liberated if the right spell had been enacted.

In our section THE TELEPORTATION OF PEOPLE (p.6), we mentioned the young African boy, N'Doua Kouame Serge, who many believed vanished from one place and reappeared in another many times. However circumspect the case may appear, it fits in with popular universal beliefs about magical flight and transportation. Take, for example, the boy's account of what happened to him when he was mysteriously transported out of the storeroom of St Augustin's church. N'Doua told the reporter that while he slept, an ugly "strangely shaped" person took him to a big house where a winged being came to his assistance. The two fought and the ugly entity was consumed by fire, the boy said, then the "angel" placed him inside a locked car in which he was found the next morning.

His claim of being whisked away by supernatural figures seems very like the "grotesque figures" that servant girl, Mary Longdon – in the 1661 witchcraft case against

A statue of a *yamabushi tengu* (a tengu in the disguise of a mountain monk) – with a characteristic long nose and hawk wings – at the Hansobo shrine in the ancient Japanese capital, Kamakura. The tengu were a kind of trickster figure in Japanese lore; feared for kidnapping children but also revered as teachers of swordsmanship and magic.

Florence Newton (see THE TELEPORTATION OF PEOPLE, p.6) – said transported her from one place to another in her house, leaving her in a stupor in some inaccessible place. It also accords with the statements of the children subjected to dramatic teleportations in the village of Sandfeldt, East Germany, in 1722. According to Alan Gauld and Tony Cornell, the children "...returned with great tales of having been transported under the Earth, where they met a race of little crooked people". When the children refused to stay with them they were returned. (See the case of the "Green children of Woolpit" in WILD PEOPLE, p.344).

What are we to make of these children's stories of abduction by mysterious beings; stories which lift an already extraordinary phenomenon into the realm of the fantastic? It occurs to Gauld and Cornell that there is a similarity between the "little people" encountered by the Sandfelt children and stories of kidnap by fairies, to which we will add their modern counterpart, encounters with aliens.

The great hagiographer Father Herbert Thurston, who made a life-long study of poltergeist cases, did not think that the unfortunate children at the centre of many of these cases were lying or manipulating the credulity of adults. Rather, he proposed that in "the susceptible mental faculties of children … fancy and reality lie nearer together [just as] they commingle strangely in our dreams". He is right, of course, but the underlying process and meaning may lie deeper in the core of our humanity, for the magical abduction seems to be a fundamental archetype.

In her study of Japanese shamanism, *The Catalpa Bow* (1975), Carmen Blacker writes about supernatural spirits called tengu (pictured opposite) – half-man and half-hawk, with a long beak and wings on a human body – which had a penchant for kidnapping children. She says the antiquarian Hirata Atsutane collected examples of this for his *Kokon Yōmikō* in which tengu in the guise of golden eagles take boys and rear them in hollow trees. They eventually return, "...either as halfwits or as miraculous persons". In fact there is a whole genre of such tales of "supernatural kidnap" with the young victim disappearing from their home unaccountably, only to be found later "...deathly pale, in some oddly inaccessible spot such as the eaves of the local temple, or the cramped space between the ceiling and the roof of his own house". Recall that this is precisely what

is said to have happened to the servant girl Mary Longdon.

One of the best known English accounts of fairy abduction is that of Anne Jeffries (1626–96), a servant girl who lived in the Cornish parish of St Teath, who had a keen interest in the fairies. Janet Bord summaries her story: "One day they showed themselves to her in her master's garden and carried her away through the air to a beautiful land with palaces of gold and silver, and trees full of fruit, where she joined in with the dancing. [..] Eventually they took her home, and she was found lying on the ground, seemingly having suffered a fit." (*Fairies: Real Encounters with Little People*, 1997)

The boys in the Japanese stories usually lie in a stupor for several days before regaining consciousness, whereupon they either become shamans or remain disturbed. Dr Blacker regards the tales they tell on recovery – of travelling up in the sky and down to subterranean caverns, to distant and wondrous lands where they meet Immortals and frightening creatures, and of enduring terrible austerities or being given magical gifts – as essentially formulaic tales of shamanic initiation and transformative vision.

Mircea Eliade tells of an almost identical form of shamanic abduction, believed among some tribes of Sumatra: "He who is destined to become a prophet-priest suddenly disappears, carried off by the spirits (probably the youth is taken into the sky); he returns to the village three or four days later; if not, a search is made for him and he is usually found in the top of a tree, conversing with spirits." The youth is judged to have lost his mind and rituals are enacted to restore him to sanity. (*Shamanism*, 1951, 1972)

This could almost be a script for the disappearance and return of Travis Walton, except for the last part. Shortly after sunset, on 5 November 1975, Walton and six fellow forestry workers in Arizona's Apache-Sitgreaves National Forest began driving back to Snowflake when they saw a light among the trees. They stopped and attempted a closer look; some later said they saw "a large, glowing object hovering in the air below the treetops about 100 feet away". As Walton approached on foot, a dazzling light, seemingly emanating from the hovering object, struck him. His workmates spoke of seeing him flung backwards through the air. When they recovered enough to check on him, he was gone. Over the

Illustration of Travis Walton's abduction by UFO in November 1975, from *Official UFO* (July 1976). Walton, of Snowflake, Arizona, said he was hit by a bolt of light and awoke on an alien craft, managing to escape a few days later.

next few days, searches with helicopters and dogs failed to find him, and fears for his welfare grew as overnight temperatures plummeted.

Five days later, Walton was found in a distressed state a few miles from Snowflake –thin, unshaven and in the same clothes. Initially, his memories of what happened to him were fleeting and "confused". He thought he might have been gone a few hours and was said to be stunned when he found out it was days. As media attention mounted, his friends closed around him and, in a clumsy attempt to protect him, made deals with a UFO organization and a popular national periodical; inevitably, this dismayed the sceptics. Eventually, all seven men took polygraph tests – their terror had been genuine – which generally confirmed their account of the experience.

Walton failed one; to be fair, his metal condition was described as "emotionally unstable" at the time, but prominent UFO sceptics used this to brand the case as a hoax. More recent re-examinations assert that there is far more substance to the mystery of the incident than the sceptics would have us believe.

Attempts to explain away the "magical" abduction experience as due to actual extraterrestrials on the one hand, or some sort of mental illness on the other, are simply not borne out by the wealth of data, narrative or objective. We have seen no unequivocal example of either. Experiments to induce similar experiences by hypnosis can produce only pale comparisons; although experiments using the drug DMT found it induced similar experiences in one in four users. Seeking confirmation that modern abduction claims are patterned on elements in fairy tales, folklorist Dr Thomas Bullard, of Indiana University, found after a lengthy analysis that they were two different species; the encounter tales did not share the storytelling structure of folkloric material. This suggests that abduction accounts cannot simply be dismissed as the products of fertile imaginations.

The arch-sceptic and astronomer Carl Sagan found himself reaching for a more meaningful answer too. In *The Demon-Haunted World* (1996) he compared modern tales of alien abduction to historical narratives about encounters with demons. "Most of the central elements of the alien abduction account are present, including sexually obsessive non-humans who … communicate telepathically, and perform breeding experiments on the human species. Unless we believe that demons really exist, how can we understand so strange a belief system … reinforced by personal experience in every generation, and taught by Church and State? Is there any real alternative besides a shared delusion based on common brain wiring and chemistry?"

The short answer would be, yes! It would seem to be a close relative of the mystical encounters with "spirit" entities experienced by shamanic types the world over. This is a conclusion also reached by Prof John Mack in his studies of the psychology of the modern UFO abductee, by Dr Kenneth Ring in his studies of near-death experiences, and by Dr Bullard and a number of ufologists of the so-called "psycho-social" school.

The case of Betty Andreasson-Luca – a devout Christian and mother of seven children – seems to demonstrate the proximity of the UFO abduction to states of mystical ecstasy. This kind of case has been hard for the so-called "nuts-and-bolts" ufologists to accommodate. As Jerome Clark summarises their position: "[Her account] is among the most complex of abduction stories, and so fantastic that even those who believe UFO abductions are possible have had a hard time crediting some aspects of it. Yet the sincerity of the participants seems beyond dispute." (*UFO Encyclopedia*, 1998)

Betty's experiences began on the evening of 25 January 1967, in the kitchen of her South Ashburnham, Massachusetts, home. The family, including her parents, noticed a reddish light shining through the kitchen window at the same time the house lights failed. Betty's father saw a group of diminutive humanoids "hopping" towards the house; five of them entered, appearing to walk right through the door. They seemed to "freeze" everyone (except Betty) and their leader – who had, said Betty, a "...giant bee head with big eyes" – established telepathic communication with her, escorting her to a small saucer-shaped craft not far from the house. She was returned to the house about four hours later to find her family still in a state of suspended animation. Under the aliens' control, they were all sent to bed before the aliens left. The family began remembering these events some days afterwards.

The full story was recovered through hypnosis (a questionable business at best) in 1977. It makes for a fascinating story, recorded by Raymond Fowler in a book titled *The Andreasson Affair* (1972) and its sequel. Betty was subjected to an "examination" by the aliens, in which objects were removed from her body, painfully, with needle-like probes – much the same way the shaman elect is dismembered and rebuilt by the tutelary spirits in his initiatory vision. The alien ship seemed bigger on the inside, with many rooms and corridors like subways. After a journey they seemed, paradoxically, to be underground, for they exited the alien ship through what looked like a tunnel in a coal mine that came out, eventually, in a "beautiful" place, where were fish-like birds flew in the bright misty air.

Betty Andreasson-Luca continues to have mystical experiences couched in the imagery of UFO-type abductions. Here, one of her drawings shows her accompanied by a tall "Elder" figure and a fairly conventional "Gray" "...standing before the Great Door leading to the Light".

Among many wondrous sights, Betty was confronted by a 4.5m high eagle-like apparition. She watched in horror as the bird caught fire, emitting flecks of gold and rays of light as it burned to ashes. Shocked by the dying phoenix, Betty heard a powerful but unseen speaker who told her, telepathically, that she had been chosen to experience this and to help the beings both heal humanity of its "self-destructive impulses" and to bring them spiritual knowledge. Betty kept asserting that she was a Christian, and the fairly authoritative but ambiguous answers she was given led her to believe the beings were angels and the invisible speaker (called "The One") was both God and Jesus. She was left sobbing with strong emotions before being taken home in an almost identical but reverse journey.

Subsequently, Betty married again – to one of her UFO investigators – and their home was, for a time, haunted by apparitions and strange sounds. Betty herself, had further abductions – sometimes taken from her bed while her husband slept – as well as sleep-paralysis, out-of-the-body experiences and periods of "missing time". During hypnosis, when recalling the messages of the invisible entities that she called "the caretakers of nature", she would speak in a language unknown to the investigators. Her childhood, too, was probed, and further incidents came to light, including hearing voices in her head speaking of future events and being struck on the head by a "luminous bee" that made her pass out.

Betty continues to have her experiences, strengthened in her belief that they are from "God and his messengers", but few now know what to make of them.

As for Walton, instead of being restored to society like the young shamans of the East, Walton was both idolized and vilified, plunged into the modern media circus and an acrimonious debate about whether he had made it all up. In terms of phenomenal experience, it didn't matter either way. Whether Walton was actually abducted by aliens or concocted the story with his friends – or perhaps a bit of both – the result conformed to an ancient stereotype of abduction by supernatural entities from a world that is alongside ours. In an archaic society that followed the old ways, we have no doubt, Walton, Mrs Andreasson-Luca and the poltergeist girls would have been welcomed back to honoured and socially useful places as mediators between this world and the Otherworld.

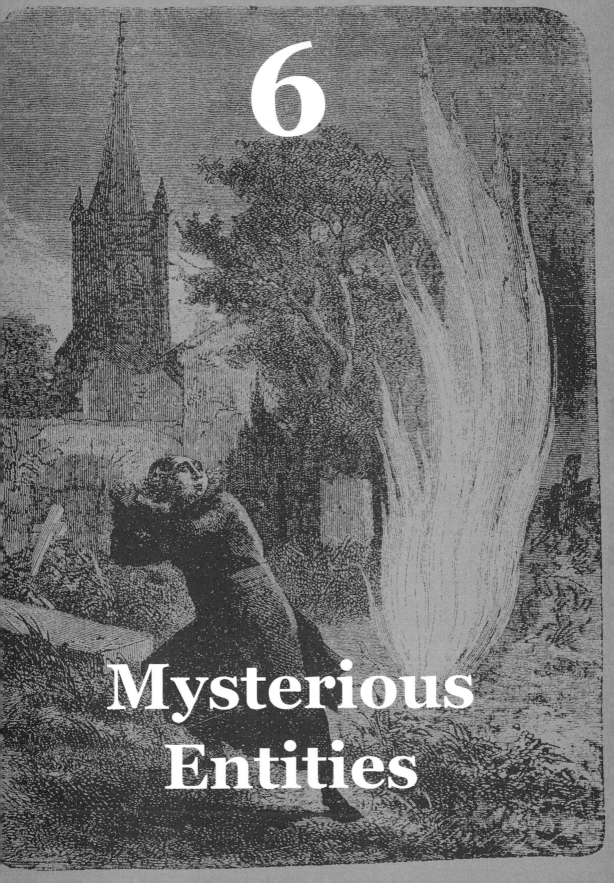

6

Mysterious
Entities

6

Mysterious Entities

Otherworldly abduction

Perhaps the single largest subject dominating the spectrum of strange phenomena today concerns extraterrestrials, a lively topic which has seen a succession of bloody skirmishes between many different schools of interpretation. Are aliens really in control of Earth space and, as some claim, abducting humans with ease and impunity for their nefarious experiments?

The first attempt at communicating with ETs that we know of was early in the 19th century, when the mathematician Karl Friedrich Gauss tried to persuade the Russian government to send a signal to Mars. He proposed marking out huge geometrical figures across the snowy plains of Siberia. Scientists, however, gave the subject little consideration prior to 1959, when physicists of Cornell University decided that the only practical means of making contact with intelligent life elsewhere in the universe was through radio waves. Their monitoring programme has intensified in the 21st century. In 2005 the giant Allen Telescope Array at the Hat Creek Observatory, north of San Francisco, came into operation, its 350 radio dishes catching every whisper from the cosmos. Millions of people are now engaged in the quest through the seti@home programme, conducted by the Arecibo radio telescope in Puerto Rico. Those who sign up download a screen saver that analyses the data received from Arecibo for the benefit of scientists at Berkeley's University of California. For details of a previous initiative from Arecibo, the transmission of a coded message into outer space, see ANCIENT SITES AND THE ET CONNECTION, p.226.

The results so far have been negative (unless you count the crop circle message, see p.229). Either there are no such things as intelligent, technologically advanced ETs or, if there are, they are not interested in talking to us. Or perhaps they are too far away to be reached, or to reach us. For these and other reasons, critics of the SETI programme are casting doubt on the value of the whole enterprise. It is "…a waste of time and money", declared science-writer John Gribbin in the *Daily Telegraph* (5 October 2005). Our solar system, he pointed out, could well be unique in its ability to support and shelter life. Similar arguments are used by the Intelligent Design (ID) advocates who believe that there are too many finely tuned components in our world for it to have evolved by chance. The IDs are scientific in their approach and carefully sidestep naming or worshipping the "Intelligence", hoping to avoid contamination by the Bible fun-

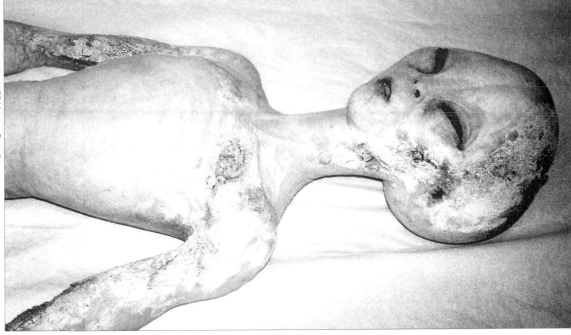

From time to time, this picture of a dead alien surfaces on the Internet or in news media as evidence of the recovery of alien bodies from the legendary UFO crash at Roswell, New Mexico. It is, in fact, a model made for the 1994 TV movie *Roswell* and was donated to the International UFO Museum in Roswell by producer Paul Davids.

damentalists. The ET researchers, of course, lump them together as cranks and reactionaries.

It is only a matter of time before scientists discover for certain whether the origin of life on Earth was a unique event – an idea that Bible Fundamentalists share with some conservative scientists. Through the 1990s, biologists discovered several different kinds of terrestrial nanobacteria capable of living in hostile or toxic environments without light, heat or oxygen. Their tiny size and toughness are perfectly suited to travel through space in meteoric or cometary debris. If nanobacteria are discovered on Mars, by the armada of probes that will be sent there in the coming years, the ubiquity of life will be confirmed.

Perhaps the ancient historians were right in accepting the stories of alien beings in the past. It is not unreasonable to speculate that other civilizations may somehow have travelled across space in our distant past, intervening in our biological and cultural development, as the ancient gods were said to have done. This is the view of the "ancient astronaut" theorists, who interpret suggestive myths and anomalous archeological data as evidence of alien intervention.

Modern ufology, meanwhile, revolves around whether this intervention has continued to the present day and accounts for UFO sightings and abductions – this is the "extraterrestrial hypothesis" (ETH). Opposing it are the cultural and behavioural interpretations of UFO abduction phenomena, which maintain that they are the product of folkloric and psychological processes.

To unravel this important mystery we have to make a small detour to understand how sightings of "lights in the sky" could become so intimately associated with alien spaceships. The sighting which kick-started the "UFO era" was made by pilot Kenneth Arnold while flying a plane over the Cascade Mountains, Washington state, on 24 June 1947; he described the motion of several shining bat-winged craft as like "saucers skipping over water". Fascinated, first the US press and then the rest of the world's media adopted the term "flying saucers" and reports of mysterious lights in the sky became commonplace in daily papers.

These reports and the people who made them might have remained figures of fun if not for a significant development that occurred about a fortnight later. On 8 July 1947, an unspecified accident occurred at the Roswell Army airfield in New Mexico (the precise details of which have always remained unclear). The USAF spokesman of the day made a lighthearted reference to a crashed flying saucer and produced debris. At the height of the Cold War, this was a clumsy attempt to distract media attention from several top secret projects. The base was home to the first nuclear bombers; high-altitude radar balloons and parachutes were being tested, the latter using crash-test dummies (which may account for the later rumours of alien bodies). When it was apparent that the ploy had backfired – it was headline news across the world – the military commanders again mishandled the story by denying the initial flying saucer story for one involving one of their balloons. The farce provided the stereotype for most cases of official denial of UFOs and the now-common accusation of "cover-up".

British sociologist and ufologist Hilary Evans called the popular imagination in 1947 "prepared ground". Recognizing the influence of ancient myth and legends about inhabited other worlds, Evans and others sought specific origins for the key motifs of ufology and found them in the pulp science fiction of the 1930s and 1940s. In the anthology *The UFO Mystery* (1998), he wrote: "It is no exaggeration to say that virtually every feature of the flying saucer myth – paralyzing rays, levitating beams, telepathic communication and alien abduction – was anticipated by the ingenious authors."

Between 1898 (when H.G. Wells's *The War Of The Worlds* was published) and the mid-1940s, popular science fiction had become increasingly interested in secret and exotic civilizations (both terrestrial and extraterrestrial). By the time of Arnold's sighting, the idea of encounters with aliens was well-known to avid readers and it seemed a logical step to suppose the many reports of strange lights in the sky might be the craft of alien visitors. The very first edition of *FATE* magazine, launched about six months later, featured Arnold's sighting on the cover (pictured opposite). It mimicked the appearance of a science fiction magazine but its monthly "factual" servings of fortean and paranormal mysteries, mixed with increasingly lurid tales of strange encounters and cover-ups by government agents, laid the foundations of modern ufology and the complex mythology of alien abductions.

A sketch of a huge mystery airship which appeared over Oakland, California, on 20 November 1896. A wave of similar sightings across the USA in 1896–97 led to panic and curiosity in equal measure and talk of a "mysterious inventor". The craft's speed and powerful lights were in advance of anything known at the time.

By 1950, the UFO phenomenon was rampant and firmly entrenched in the popular imagination worldwide, through pulp magazines and the burgeoning genre of "B" feature films such as *The Flying Saucer* (1949) – thought to be the first representation of a UFO in a movie. This film and the Roswell incident inspired two hoaxers to convince a well-known journalist of the day, Frank Scully, to write *Behind the Flying Saucers* (1951), a book notorious for introducing the idea that the military had recovered dead aliens from a crashed UFO and puzzled out some of their technology.

Historically, the 1950s were the

"golden age" of ufology; the overall tone was optimistic, with prophets, like George Adamski, Howard Menger and George King, among others, claiming contact with "space brothers" either telepathically or in person. The channelled messages warned of impending doom if mankind did not mend its ways but also offered salvation in the form of an airlift by flying saucers.

The encounters with aliens described in this period are thoroughly romantic. For example, South African Elizabeth Klarer claimed, in 1956, an interstellar affair with Akon of the planet Meton. "I found the true meaning of love in mating with a man from another planet," she wrote later. The honeymoon between aliens and earthlings was gradually soured by more frightening experiences, such as science fiction author Whitley Strieber's claim to have been sodomized by aliens who burst into his bedroom in December 1985.

But the first big case of abduction and medical examination was that of Betty and Barney Hill in September 1961, driving on a lonely New Hampshire road late at night. Puzzled by a short journey that somehow took seven hours, unusual nightmares and strange, painful marks that had suddenly appeared on their bodies, the Hills eventually sought medical and psychiatric help. In 1963, they began sessions of hypnotism with Dr Benjamin Simon, to reconstruct their memories of that night of "missing time". To their collective astonishment Betty and Barney told of being dragged from their car by little beings and subjected to a curious fertility examination. Betty had samples of skin and hair taken, a fingernail cut off and a needle inserted into her navel. Barney suffered the indignity of a device attached to his groin to remove sperm. Betty continues to believe in the reality of her experience, long after Barney's death in 1969. Dr Simon – cited in John G. Fuller's *Interrupted Journey* (1966) – later concluded that the episode was a fantasy, a type of *folie à deux*, based on Betty's unsettling dreams which she had discussed with Barney.

Other abductions, following a more or less similar formula, were reported all through the 1970s, their publicity establishing the now familiar description of large-headed, large-eyed, slit-mouthed beings, pallid and impassive

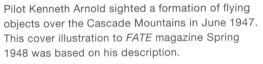

Pilot Kenneth Arnold sighted a formation of flying objects over the Cascade Mountains in June 1947. This cover illustration to *FATE* magazine Spring 1948 was based on his description.

(dubbed "Grays"). This was only one type in an increasingly surreal line-up that included reptilians, avians, insectoids, hairy dwarves, tall blond "Nordics", metal slabs and shapeless fleshy blobs (see Patrick Huyghe's *Field Guide to Extraterrestrials*, 1997).

If the variety of aliens visiting Earth doesn't strike you as absurd then consider the "...most unsettling development to date", as Huyghe calls the 1991 publication of the results of a poll by the Roper Organization on the extent of belief in alien abduction. The figures caused consternation and laughter in equal measure; extrapolating from their sampling figures, it was estimated that two percent of the American population had been abducted at some time in their lives – that is around five million per year, or 22 million per year if you extend it globally. Even Betty Hill was moved to comment, sarcastically: "With 4000 people being abducted every night, I don't know how the planes would get through!"

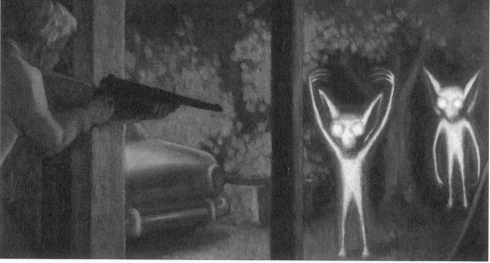

One of the most frightening forms of alien encounter is the so-called "night seige" of which the incident at Kelly, near Hopkinsville, Kentucky, in 1955 is probably the best known. On the evening of 21 August, the Sutton farm contained eight adults and three children, when a neighbour told them he saw a "flying saucer" land nearby. In the night that followed, the family believed they were under attack by waves of small, goblin-like aliens that glowed and moved on curiously stiff legs but were agile enough to scamper over the roof and peer in the windows. Shots fired at them seemed to have no effect – one simply floated to the ground, flipped back and scuttled away. Towards midnight, with high anxiety and hysterical children in tow, the family piled into two cars and headed for the police station in Hopkinsville. Impressed by the family's obvious distress, an eleven-man police posse escorted them back but left after a search found no sign of alien invaders. The glowing goblins returned but seemed to lose interest and left before dawn. Investigators seem divided over whether this was a case of collective hallucination or whether the family were the victim of a cruel and rather pointless prank. See also PLAGUES, POISONS AND PANICS, p.114.

This highlights one of the biggest problems facing those seeking to explain the abduction mystery – the dream-like character of so many narratives. A good example is the disturbing experience of Jean Hingley, of Rowley Regis in the Midlands, who was visited by fairy-like aliens on 4 January 1979 (see FAIRIES: ANCIENT AND MODERN, p.136). Investigating an orange glow in her garden, Mrs Hingley saw a hovering orange sphere. She felt its heat and noticed her dog frozen as if time had stood still. Three child-sized winged beings shot indoors past her, and began shaking the Christmas tree. They had "dead faces" and flew without using their wings. She was aware of them jumping on her sofa "like naughty children" and talking with them about Jesus, the Queen and the place of women in the home. From time to time, they would paralyse her by shooting a dazzling beam of light from their helmets.

Thinking they wanted something to drink, Mrs Hingley went to the kitchen and returned with glasses of water and some mince pies on a tray. Their motions were jerky and often concealed by the blinding ray but she thinks that they ate and drank her offerings. When she tried to show them how to smoke a cigarette they recoiled from the flame of the lighter. Deafening noises heralded the end of the visit and they glided back to their glowing sphere. Immediately upon their departure into the sky, Mrs Hingley felt pain in her arms and legs; feeling weak she crept slowly over to the sofa and lay there for a long time, numb and confused. She later had a nervous breakdown and reported trouble with her eyes and ears. Albert Budden, who investigated the case, at first suggested that Mrs Hingley experienced some kind of altered state of consciousness that had facilitated poltergeist-like and stigmata-like phenomena but later suggested that she had hallucinated due to "pollution" from power-lines and other sources of electromagnetic fields and radiation. (*Psychic Close Encounters*, 1995)

Beyond the simple apocalyptic mission attributed to the ufonauts of the 1940s and 1950s, modern abductions are not without a mystical dimension of their own. Jean Hingley was a deeply religious woman who saw continuity, not difference, between her faith, the psychic experiences she had experienced since childhood and her alien encounter. Likewise, George King believed he was contacted in May 1954 by a telepathic "voice" from a 3500-year-old divine "Master" on Venus. The Aetherius Society, founded by King in 1956, mixes yoga, Theosophy and a science fiction version of spiritualism involving trance channelling of alien entities.

Betty Andreasson-Luca, whose experiences began in 1967, also believed her abductors were sent by God. Her experiences, recalled with the aid of hypnosis, began in childhood (1944) and were still happening in the 1990s. They include the sublime (a heavily symbolic vision of a giant phoenix, described more fully on p.164) and the ridiculous (a vision of hundreds of headless "monkeys" with eyes on stalks crawling all over a building). Like Dante, Betty was granted a tour of the Otherworld, accompanied by a classic Gray called Quazgaa. (Raymond Fowler, *The Andreasson Affair, Phase Two*, 1982)

Jacques Vallee's 1969 book *Passport to Magonia* first presented the view that UFO abductions are simply continuations, in space-age imagery, of the traditional kidnappings by fairies. Today, this theory is seen as rather simplistic and a new generation of writers, led by Patrick Harpur, the author of *Daimonic Reality* (1994), have extended the idea by arguing that the fairy mythos and the alien mythos are not contiguous but both spring from the same core of subjective experience. Regardless of the different cultural imagery that colours such experiences, nearly all of them share the characteristics of shamanic visions. Folklorist Thomas E. Bullard, who analysed over thirty years of abduction cases, noted how many of them seemed to "...hark back to primitive initiatory rituals and shamanic journeys, suggesting arche-

According to an early account of her own words – in Robert Hunt's *Popular Romances Of The West Of England* (1865) – a young Cornish maid from St Teath, Anne Jeffries, was working for the Pitt family when she saw, in the garden, six tiny male fairies. They enticed her with kisses and caresses until, suddenly, she was their size and in an exquisite landscape. Eventually the fairies fell out over her and she found herself back in the Pitt's garden, lying on the ground. This was 1645 and she was 19 years old. Anne saw and heard her fairy lovers frequently, even when she became an avid Christian. She is credited with prophecy and a number of "miraculous" cures, including one injury caused by the fairies to a woman they thought had been unkind to her. However, an account written much later by Moses Pitt (who would have been quite young when Anne had her first encounter) for the Bishop of Gloucester, omits Anne's visit to Fairyland and simply says they found her collapsed in the garden after she saw "...a small sort of Airy People call'd Fairies". In a 1993 essay, the astronomer Carl Sagan wrote: "If Anne Jeffries had known about aliens rather than fairies ... would her story have been distinguishable from the one 'abductees' tell?" From our point of view, Anne's story displays all the ingredients of the shaman-contactee, who, to some extent, cures her own elective illness. Such stories, whether of fairies, angels or aliens, will always polarize those who value subjective narrative or objective fact. In fact, the alternative to both views is that stories, like Anne's, actually form a bridge between those two seemingly incompatible cultures and therein lies their true psychological and spiritual value.

Mary Evans Picture Library

typal patterning behind human experience with otherworldly beings". Such experiences seem to mark out the experiencer from the rest of society, changing their lives in some profound way and giving them a sense of mission (see AWAY WITH THE FAIRIES, p.157).

The physical and mystical phenomena of shamanism, as described in Mircea Eliade's *Shamanism* (1964), include an initiating sickness, a descent or ascent to the "Otherworld", negotiation with elemental spirits or gods and magical flight – all elements paralleled in close encounters. The initiatory trance of shamans, from Australia to the Arctic, includes variations of symbolic dismemberment and resurrection – surely the prototype of the operations of the alien doctors. Eliade describes this dismemberment as an "…initiatory death … an ecstatic experience that can be brought on by the suffering of a sickness". We think it is significant that many abductees were physically ill or under great stress mentally, emotionally or socially, at the onset of their visionary experience; the characteristic of many shamans is that they incorporate their "sickness" into their mythologizing, just as abductees do.

In our Western industrialized, computerized world there is little place for shamans and, denied a function, these individuals do not fare well. Some are resilient enough to find a niche for themselves – as teachers or alternative healers – but the rest, without a personal or social use for their visions, become disturbed and even self-destructive. It is in this negative state of mind that the "contact" experience or vision takes on a terrible malevolence.

Against this "psychological" explanation of abductions stands the influential school of ufology led by Dr David Jacobs, a historian at Philadelphia's Temple University, and Budd Hopkins, a New York artist. In their various writings, they urge us to believe in the literal reality of an ongoing alien invasion. Many confused people have come to them for help, only to be told that aliens have "prepared" selected humans for a long-term "career", using sophisticated mind-control techniques to cover their tracks (clearly with little success). The "chosen" ones are repeatedly abducted for their ova and sperm, and the women used as surrogate mothers for implanted alien-human hybrid foetuses which are removed before full-term.

The widest, most far-reaching investigation of the abduction phenomenon was by a Harvard professor of psychiatry, John Mack. He first heard about it through his patients and went on to make a professional study of the subject. This caused another investigation, of Mack himself, by a committee of other Harvard professors. They accused him of discrediting science and betraying his colleagues. Instead of trying to cure abductees of their "delusions", he was listening to their stories and assuring them that they were not the only people to have had the abduction experience. These people, insisted Mack, were ordinary, average citizens and no more insane than the rest of us. Something traumatic had happened to them, obscene and frightening in many cases, but sometimes enlightening and always with a similar effect. Those who had the experience were deeply marked by it. Their perceptions were altered, they became aware of the spiritual side of life and often they reported developing psychic powers.

A phenomenon which, however inexplicably, affects minds and personalities is a proper subject for psychological research. That was Mack's defence against his Harvard inquisitors. And at the time he got away with it. But the more he studied the abduction phenomenon, the further he was led into territory far beyond the academic pale: into UFOs, monsters, apparitions, telepathy, psychic healing, crop circles and the range of phenomena covered in this book. Patrick Harpur's *Daimonic Reality* influenced his thinking and persuaded him that all these mysteries are parts of the one great mystery and belong to an aspect of existence which we no longer choose to recognize. At the Glastonbury crop circle "cornference" in the summer of 2004, John Mack spoke on the abduction phenomenon in its wider, "daimonic" context; a few days later he was killed in a road accident, aged 74.

Our conclusion is that "abduction" is a species of visionary or spontaneous shamanic experience rooted in the human psyche, and that the potential for it is widespread in the population. So-called "rationalists" will, no doubt, be shocked to realize that after several centuries of fighting the forces of supernaturalism and superstition, modern man is just as vulnerable as he ever was to attacks by invisible and malevolent entities: but as long as the experiences of alien abductees are taken literally and their visionary elements isolated and ignored, we suspect there will be little progress in understanding them.

Invisible assailants

In May 1876 there was panic in the streets of Nanking, China. Invisible demons were on the loose, snipping off people's pigtails. The citizens took to walking about with their hair clutched in their hands for safety. The terror spread to Shanghai and other towns, and then another panic developed. This time it was the "crushing mania", a fear of being crushed while sleeping. The rampage of these demons lasted for nearly three years. Other outbreaks have occurred since, and the phenomenon has a long history. According to De Groot's *Religious Systems of China* (1892), the first recorded outbreaks of the hair-snipping panic were under the Wei dynasty in AD 477 and AD 517.

Newspaper reports of these panics in China raised many a smile at English breakfast tables, but these were wiped away when in December 1922 a similar scare broke out in London. Young ladies were being seized by a man who hacked off their hair and then disappeared "as if by magic", eluding the bands of would-be gallants who came rushing to the rescue. We have heard psychological explanations for this and respect them on their own terms, but they do not account for the physical fact that people have suddenly and mysteriously been deprived of their hair in a public street in broad daylight.

Thefts of hair seem to feature in attacks of all kinds, from poltergeists to UFOs. During the haunting of the Dagg family in Canada, as reported by *The Brockville Daily Times* (13 November 1899), one of the little girls "felt her long braid suddenly pulled; she cried out, and the family found it almost cut off, simply hanging by a few hairs. The same day the little boy said that something pulled his hair all over. Immediately it was seen by his mother that chunks of his hair, also, had been cut off."

In *The Other Side* (1969) Bishop James Pike tells of the strange disturbances that followed his son's suicide. In one incident, a female assistant awoke one morning to find some of her hair singed off in a perfectly straight line. This was repeated again the next morning, and three weeks later one of the burned-off locks mysteriously appeared on a bedside table. An even stranger case can be found in the *Religio-Philosophical Journal* (4 October 1873). During a succession of poltergeist-type happenings at Menomonie, Wisconsin, a girl was standing by her mother with no one else present when her hair was sheared off in chunks close to her scalp, vanishing as it was cut.

A recent case, demonstrating how difficult and problematic such classifications are, is the series of panics in India in which an invisible creature bit and scratched folk with long metal claws as they slept. From the 1st of April 2001 to the end of May, and from the backstreets of New Delhi to villages in the surrounding regions, there was a steady flow of reports of a shadowy figure that few could see until it was too late. It was said to have a monkey-like face and to creep up on pedestrians, break into houses and escape with prodigious leaps or simply fade away.

Like the social panics involving Spring-heeled Jack, the Chupacabras and China's "hair-clipping

A 17th-century account of an unseen attacker from John Aubrey's *Miscellanies* (1696).

BLOWS INVISIBLE.

MR. Brograve, of Hamel, near Puckridge in Hertfordſhire, when he was a young man, riding in a lane in that county, had a blow given him on his cheek: (or head) he looked back and ſaw that no body was near behind him; anon he had ſuch another blow, I have forgot if a third. He turned back, and fell to the ſtudy of the law; and was afterwards a Judge. This account I had from Sir John Penruddocke of Compton-Chamberlain, (our neighbour) whoſe Lady was Judge Brograve's niece.

ABHIMANYU

A drawing from the *Hindustan Times* (mid-May 2001) depicting the menacing, uncatchable "Monkey Man", who frightened thousands in India. One of the more fanciful descriptions claimed he had three magic buttons on his suit; one giving a boost to his strength, one toggling him between man and monkey forms, and the third to render him invisible.

demon", India's "Monkey Man" soon took on fantastic elements: red-glowing eyes, a tight-fitting jump-suit, or wrapped in bandages like a mummy. Theories were equally rich, ranging from a scientist whose experiment on himself went seriously wrong, some kind of half-man half-robot, psychological warfare by Pakistani agents, and even an alien from a secret UFO. While local police units were generally exasperated by the inconsistency in reports, some settled for looking for a man wearing a mask.

Many thousands of people were caught up in the panic as more reports of sudden and frightening encounters filled the media and thousands of children were sent away to stay with relatives. The panics were made worse by power outages and some unfortunates, mistaken for the menace, were beaten up or arrested by vigilante groups. On the 19 May, Delhi police reported that of over 300

calls, more than two-thirds were hoaxes or false alarms; and of the 60 reported injuries, 55 were down to normal rat and monkey bites. Within days, Delhi's Monkey Man mania subsided, but, perhaps primed by the recent fears, similar reports began to come from parts of Assam and Rajasthan of "bear-men" and "wolf-men" who could enter locked houses, scratch people and then become invisible in the light. (See also THE MADNESS OF CROWDS, see p.110.)

We now turn to a more shocking sort of violation, the symptom of which is the appearance of wounds, as if the victims had been stabbed or shot with invisible weapons. *The New York Times* (8 December 1931) printed a story by the captain of the German steamer *Brechsee*, which had put in at Horsens, Jutland, the day before. The captain had seen a man unaccountably wounded during a storm. Before his eyes a four-inch-long wound appeared on the man's head and he fell unconscious to the deck. On 16 April 1922 a man was brought to Charing Cross Hospital in London with a stab wound in his neck. All he could say was that he had strolled into a turning off Coventry Street, received a wound and fallen to the ground. A few hours later another man was brought to the hospital with the same wound and the same story; and later that day a third man was unaccountably wounded in that same turning off Coventry Street. The story was reported in *The People* (23 April 1922).

Charles Mackay in *Extraordinary Popular Delusions And The Madness Of Crowds* (1841) relates in detail the alarm in Paris in March 1623 at the rumoured powers and antics of the Rosicrucians, a clandestine, esoteric and mystical brotherhood. The Marais du Temple quarter soon acquired a bad name, for "...no man thought himself secure of his goods, no maiden of her virginity, or wife of her chastity ... and people were afraid to take houses in it, lest they should be turned out by the six invisibles of the Rose-Cross". Similarly, on 26 September 1923, the *Daily Mail* facetiously reported that Indian coolies in Lahore believed that a *mumiai* was abroad, an invisible thing that grabbed people in broad daylight. In 1890 the *Religio-Philosophical Journal* reported a scare from Japan, in which an "invisible" was blamed for slashes about an inch long that appeared on people's necks. This reminds us of the tale told in the second branch of the *Mabinogion* (a collection of medieval Welsh myths and folktales) in which Caswallawn, son of Beli, donned the "Veil of Illusion" to slay some rival chieftains, who could see nothing of the assassin, only the sword as it materialized seconds before cutting them down.

Frank Edwards, in *Strangest Of All* (1962), details the case of Jimmy de Bruin, who worked at Farm Datoen, South Africa, and who seemed to be the centre of poltergeist disturbances in August 1960. During an investigation, Police Chief John Wessels and three constables heard twenty-year-old Jimmy scream with pain. He was wearing shorts and they could see cuts appearing on his legs even as they watched. The next day, in the presence of two officers, a deep gash appeared on his chest, although nothing had penetrated his shirt. These cuts continued for several days. They were clean, as though made with a razor or scalpel – and all who saw them agreed that the young man could not have inflicted them on himself. Fort advanced the idea that if other things could be teleported, then perhaps wounds could be projected to appear on people. It is a common detail in cases of invisible assailants that the wounds appear on flesh beneath clothes which show no signs of penetration – a phenomenon that also occurs in cases of STIGMATA (see p.88).

The poltergeist connection was more clearly demonstrated in the celebrated Phelps case in Stratford, Connecticut, in 1850. The disturbances centred on Dr Phelps's twelve-year-old son, Harry. From the description of them in Father Herbert Thurston's *Ghosts And Poltergeists* (1953) it seems as if the boy was under constant attack. Stones were pitched at him, and a violent force would lift him off the ground to strike his head on the ceiling. Once he was thrown into a water-tank; and before the eyes of shocked visitors he was caught up and suspended in the branches of a tree while his clothes were methodically torn to ribbons by something invisible.

In another case, the mysterious assailant of the Giles children, who were staying at the Lamb Inn, in Bristol, during the winter of 1761–62, was only visible to the children. They were dragged out of bed and transported about the house, and tormented by slaps and savage bites surrounded by what looked like saliva. Bent pins would be found stuck in their skin and, once, a witness described the horrific sight of one of the girls being throttled by an invisible hand, the sides of her throat visibly pushed inwards.

The coat of Kaspar Hauser. After mysteriously appearing in 1828, Hauser was fatally stabbed on 14 December 1833 by a "black-cloaked man" of whom only the snowy footprints were found.

At the time, the girls' torment was blamed on a malicious witch, but similar persecutions in a Christian context have been attributed to jealous demons. The earliest account of this type known to us comes from the contemporary letters which record the attacks on the German nun, the Blessed Christina of Stommeln, which lasted for 28 years from 1260. Christina and her visitors were often bombarded by stones and excrement. But, besides the usual repertoire of poltergeist activity, Christina, too, was beaten, scratched and bitten. Sometimes nails were found in her flesh and sometimes they were hot, like the stones found pressing into her under her clothes. At night, bedclothes would be torn off as something dragged her from her bed. Once she was observed to have been dragged, roughly, a considerable distance.

What makes her case even more interesting is that from 1268, Christina bore the stigmata on her hands and feet, forehead and side (see also STIGMATA, p.88). Alan Gould and Tony Cornell (*Poltergeists*, 1979) have argued that Christina was probably hypersensitive and that her stigmata might "simply" be a more developed form of the bites and scratches that could have been psychosomatic, generated unknowingly by herself. Christina certainly suffered from grotesque hal-

This still from the 1989 movie *Communion*, depicts the moment, on 26 December 1985, that author Whitley Strieber woke up to find diminutive aliens around his bed. His written account – *Communion* (1987) – of his abduction and rape by the entities developed over several books into a complex tale of almost mystical love for his abductress (depicted on the cover of the original book) and despair for the pain their relationship necessitates. These "bedroom invaders" seem to be able to manipulate space and time, like space-age fairies, to get what they want ... or is it just our memories they play with?

lucinations of both divine and diabolic imagery, but no one has doubted her piety, which was said to be the direct cause of the Devil's vehemence.

The young Romanian girl, Eleonore Zugun – see PROJECTED THOUGHT-FORMS, p.84 – might also have had hypersensitive skin, welts rising in ridges where she scratched herself. However, she had another explanation: she was under attack by a demon, named "Dracu", only she could see.

In December 1965, an 11-year-old Brazilian girl was the target of similar indignities and injuries. Maria José Ferreira lodged with a family in Jabuticabal, several hundred miles from São Paulo, when so many pieces of brick fell inside the house that the family requested an exorcism. It only made matters worse. A neighbour with an interest in psychical research arranged for the girl to stay with him and, before long, large numbers of stones – the largest weighing 3.7kg

– appeared around his house too. According to Guy Lyon Playfair's account – in *The Indefinite Boundary* (1976) – a particularly large stone was observed to descend from the ceiling of a room, breaking into two pieces close to the floor. When one of the witnesses brought the pieces together, they "snapped together" as though they were magnets. On another occasion, a stone was seen to "bounce" from one person to another, lightly tapping on three heads before falling gently to the floor – see also MATERIALIZATION AND FLIGHT OF OBJECTS (p.11).

As with some other prominent poltergeist cases we have cited in these pages, the poltergeist responded to requests made by the child at the centre of the phenomenon; in this case, when Maria asked for a flower, a sweet or even a brooch, it would suddenly appear at her feet, even while the girl was under observation. The poltergeist turned nasty, however, smashing crockery, hurling vases and framed pictures, and destroying furniture. Maria herself was covered in bruises where something unseen had bitten and slapped her, and forcefully moved furniture against her. Like the Giles girls, she would be woken from sleep by a feeling of being suffocated and needles would be found in her flesh (even deep in her heel under her sock and shoe). Once, more than fifty needles had been stabbed into her, and the bandages were torn off as fast as they were applied. Mysterious fires would break out in Maria's clothes or in the rooms of her host.

In time, the torment gradually abated but never really ceased, and the girl went back to live with her mother until, in 1970, when she was about sixteen, Maria committed suicide by swallowing insecticide. Some commentators have wondered whether the poltergeist was to blame directly, by materializing the poison in her drink. Playfair points out the curious similarity with the talkative but vengeful phantom that plagued the family of John Bell of Tennessee between 1817 and 1821 – see PHANTOM MUSIC AND STRANGE VOICES (p.152). Particularly affected was Bell's youngest daughter, Betsy, who, like the other children mentioned here, was slapped and bitten by the poltergeist to the extent of being severely bruised for much of the time.

We have many other reports of "phantom snipers" whose "bullets" leave no other trace of themselves than a wound. In Chapter twelve of *Wild Talents* (1932), Fort mentions three murders in which the police could only suspect that the murderers had changed the clothes of the victims, for they had bullet wounds with no penetration of their clothes. The oldest similar account we can find is of a man pushing a cart near Berigen, Germany, on 2 October 1875. According to *Popular Science* (15, p.566), he heard a whirring sound, inaudible to his two companions, and found that his right arm had been shot through as if by a musket ball.

Here is the most disturbing account of assault by "invisibles" that we know of. In 1761 five women were returning from collecting sticks near Ventimiglia, in northern Italy. Suddenly one of them cried out and dropped dead. Her companions were shocked by what they saw. Her clothes and shoes were torn into fine shreds and scattered up to six feet around her. There were wounds on her head that exposed the skull; the muscles on her right side had given way exposing her intestines; her sacrum was broken and most internal organs were ruptured or livid; her abdominal region bore many deep and parallel incisions, and the flesh of one hip and thigh was almost carried away, exposing the pubic bone and the broken head of the femur which had been forced from its socket. This horrific event was reported to the French Academy of Sciences by M. Morand, and the *Annual Register* for that year quotes him as noting that these grievous effects took place with no sign of penetration of the woman's clothes, nor was there any blood on the scene, nor any sign of her missing flesh. It was as though she had been the focal point for an instantaneous, silent and deadly explosion.

Mystery mutilators

In 1973 panic and strange rumours spread across the American Midwest. Rustlers were using unmarked, cargo-type helicopters to spot vulnerable herds of cattle from the air and radioing information to hidden ground teams. There were hundreds of reports that these objects had been seen hovering over herds and rising from cow-pastures. A strange thing about them was that they were completely silent, as if without engines. Farmers were warned to bring their livestock in at night and some even began taking potshots at anything that flew over their property.

Stories of these phantom rustlers lasted into 1974 when they were overtaken by an even more extraordinary development: UFOs were reported to be landing and mutilating cattle. One of the first accounts was in the Florida *Miami Herald* (16 October 1973). Police at Dayton, Ohio, had received about eighty reports of flashing UFOs in the area, one of them from a woman who claimed "hysterically" that a UFO had landed, killing a couple of cows. By 1974, reports of strange lights and unidentifiable helicopters had become inextricably tied up with the ever-growing number of stories about mutilated cattle from Colorado,

Utah, North Dakota, Minnesota, Mississippi, Pennsylvania, Iowa, Missouri, Arkansas, Illinois and Nebraska.

Many of these cases are detailed in *INFO Journal* (14) and by Ed Sanders in the magazine *Oui* (August 1976). The most striking feature of the outbreak was the nature of the mutilations. Ears, eyes, lips, udders and tails were carefully removed and internal organs were surgically extracted in a purposeful, even ritualistic manner. Some carcasses were found entirely drained of blood. In one case the intestines had been drawn out through a hole in the cow's side and piled neatly by its head (recalling a similar gesture by Jack the Ripper). A sinister aspect of these mutilations was the absence of footprints or bloody trails – an encouragement to the UFO and other conspiracy theorists. Evidently gangs of mad, airborne butchers or surgeons were abroad; many believed that a rich, well-organized occult fraternity was responsible. The press had a field day, revelling in gory descriptions and stoking up the paranoia, even hinting at secret human sacrifices. Several investigators of the mystery claimed they were being threatened by "Satanists".

Tom Davies, writing in the *Minneapolis Tribune* (20 April 1975) attempted to scotch the occult and UFO theories. About 400 cases, he claimed, could be explained by a peculiar combination of blood disease (accounting supposedly for the complete absence of blood in most cases) and predators, which naturally go for the soft flesh first. But this does not cover all the observed facts. Witnesses and investigators have confirmed the surgical precision of these mutilations. The draining of blood is a feature still unexplained, and so is the lack of tracks or footprints around the carcasses, which have often been found on snowy or muddy ground. Besides, the authorities have never explained why, if disease was a factor, it was not more widespread, and attacks by predators cannot account for all the bizarre details of the mutilations.

This is a revolting subject, but it is neither new nor localized. Outbreaks of mysterious animal mutilations and killings were known to the ancient Romans, who blamed them on "demons". For lack of anything more concrete, this type of explanation has remained popular, even in modern times. The demons could be in human form, but if so they are remarkably elusive. In all the many, worldwide epidemics of animal muti-lations, human culprits have scarcely ever been detected. A rare prosecution took place in 1903 when, following a spate of sheep, cattle and horse rippings across Staffordshire, a young Anglican clergyman, George Edalji, whose father was a Hindu, was arrested. He was tried and found guilty of attacking horses. The evidence was weak, the police were suspected of prejudice and, when Sir Arthur Conan Doyle intervened on his behalf, Edalji was exonerated. Conan Doyle believed that the atrocities were caused by demons.

Typical of our data is a series of obscene attacks on horses and cattle in western Sweden during 1991 and 1992. Police were looking for a gang of perverts and sadists, but none was ever found and the horrors gradually ceased. They began again in England. In 1992, particularly in the southern counties, horse-owners were shocked to find that their animals had been tortured and sexually violated overnight, slashed with sharp knives, with broomsticks shoved into them and barbed wire attached to their genitals. Once again, sadists and cultists were sought in vain. A detail that puzzled the owners was that their horses seemed not to have resisted or kicked out against interference with their hindquarters. A suggestion was that they had been drugged or anaesthetized. This passivity on the part of the victim has also been noticed in American cattle-mutilation cases, and some veterinarians believe that, before being assaulted, the creatures were made placid by the drug Ketaset.

As in many other strange subjects, Charles Fort was an early investigator. In chapters 13 and 14 of *Lo!* (1931) are his notes on the winter of 1904–05, during which time there occurred wave after wave of dreadful attacks on animals. At Hexham, Northumberland, something was killing sheep nearly every night, sometimes on both sides of the River Tyne on the same night. That winter there was more slaughter at Gravesend in Kent and Badminton in Gloucestershire, involving "terrible losses for poor people".

In May 1910 something began killing six or seven sheep a night, biting into their necks and sucking their blood, but leaving the bodies untouched. In 1874, sheep were killed in a vampiric manner around Cavan, Ireland; as many as thirty a night had their throats cut and blood sucked, but none of their flesh was eaten. Wolves were blamed (the last wolf in Ireland was killed in 1712), and finally a dog was shot. But the killings continued in the same region. In 1906 something killed over sixty sheep in two nights at Guildford and Windsor. At Llanelly in 1919 hutches were entered by "something" that broke the backs of rabbits. In 1925 a strange black animal "of enormous size" tore sheep apart, terrifying the Edale region of Derbyshire into fears of werewolves.

In 1995 a similar phenomenon initiated a panic that swept through many Hispanic American communities. It was feared that a strange beast, characterized as a "demonic, alien, kangaroo vampire", was killing small livestock and domestic animals by sucking their blood through small puncture marks – hence its name Chupacabras (or Goatsucker). The scare began among rural farmers in Puerto Rico in March and spread to Miami, largely as a result of excited reports on Hispanic radio and TV. Despite many frightened witnesses, widespread searches found nothing and when deaths of goats and other small animals were investigated in Miami in March 1996, they were found by police and city veterinarians to be "classic canine puncture marks" and "contrary to popular belief, all the animals were full of blood".

While sociologists and folklorists were classifying this as "a social panic driven by misidentification", dozens of Chupacabras incidents were reported from as far afield as Mexico and San Salvador and in several states of the US. These did not trail off until June 1996. In Arizona, a family called police saying their home was under siege, but nothing was found. In Mexico a girl said she had been attacked by the creature but her "wounds" were shown to be love-bites. Attacks in Salvador were traced to starving bats forced to forage further than usual. The panic was so great in certain parts of Mexico that important ecosystems came under threat as farmers lit fires to ward off or kill "vampires". In each outbreak, hundreds of animals were reported killed by an uncatchable monster that was said

The mysterious death of a horse called Snippy during the 1966–67 UFO flap. No explanation was ever found for Snippy's bizarre wounds, the missing brain and vital organs, and the skin stripped cleanly from head and neck.

As the co-ordinator of interstate investigation into the spate of mysteriously mutilated cattle in the 1970s, Gabe Valdez, a state police officer in New Mexico, attended many scenes like this one in Rio Arriba County.

John Sibbick

Artist's interpretation of El Chupacabras, Goatsucker, by John Sibbick based on eye-witness descriptions for *Fortean Times* 89.

to have come from outer space, been created by witches, or even by the US military (see SOCIAL ANXIETY ATTACKS, p.131).

Sometimes there are features in these mutilations (e.g. backbreaking, the siphoning of blood, removal of specific organs) that bring to mind elements of shamanistic or Mithraic sacrifice; but, as in the classic pattern of UFO paradox, the matter is devastatingly elusive. In their *Devil Worship in Britain* (1964) Peter Haining and A.V. Sellwood confessed that they did not get far investigating the discovery of a pile of six heads of cows and horses in a wood near Luton, Bedfordshire. The eyes had been extracted, the jaws wrenched open and two jawbones removed. Nearby were two rings of trampled grass round a gnarled tree. There were no other tracks, no blood and no sign of the bodies. The heads were heavy enough to have needed two people to carry them down the two-mile bridle path to the spot, suggesting to the police a conspiracy. No farmer for miles around admitted to losing any animals, and the case remains unsolved.

The trampled rings recall similar patches reported from the sites of many of the Midwest mutilations and also the ground markings associated with UFOs. *The Sunday Mirror* (9 November 1975) tells of a black sheep, at Bray, Berkshire, found stripped of skin and meat from the neck down in a manner that suggested skill at flaying. There had been two other mutilations at Bray the week before. Phantom helicopters too are familiar objects in the UFO repertoire; and indeed their *modus operandi,* with silent night manoeuvrings and powerful spotlights, is reminiscent of the great airship flaps of the late nineteenth century (see PHANTOM SHIPS, p.260).

Other cases link animal mutilation to another of our sections, BIGFOOT, THE AMERICAN MONSTER (see p.339), with its foul-smelling mystery anthropoids. In *The Unidentified* (1975), Jerome Clark reports on his investigation into a series of bizarre animal killings around Rochdale, Indiana, during which about fifty people claimed to have seen a "gorilla-like" thing in the area. On 22 August 1972 two members of the Burdine family returned to their farm to discover about sixty chickens ripped apart but not eaten. After a close encounter with the "thing", they saw it again, by the lights of their car, framed in the door of the chicken coop. They shot at it as it lumbered off. Inside the coop all but thirty of two hundred chickens were "ripped open and drained of blood".

Now, as if to confound the UFO-link argument, we bring in the weirdest correlation of all. Fort had an inkling of what he called an "occult criminology" – that all these attacks on animals were part of one mysterious phenomenon, including "attacks, some of them mischievous, some ordinarily deadly, and some of the Jack the Ripper kind, upon human beings". Perhaps, like all great fictions, the terrifying destructive "monster from the Id", as in the 1956 film *Forbidden Planet,* is a mirroring of a repressed fact. In our INVISIBLE ASSAILANTS section (see p.173) we review some cases where wounds appear mysteriously on human bodies. Nandor Fodor, echoing Fort, suggested that childish passions of anger, hate, jealousy and frustration could be "exteriorized" and vented on objects or people in the vicinity, causing the smashing, burning and spoiling pranks of poltergeists. For example, in FIERY PER-SECUTIONS (see p.184) we tell the story of the girl in the kitchen at Binbrook Farm, who was severely burned on her back although quite unaware of the fire consuming her. In reporting the incident, *The Louth and North Lincolnshire News* (28 January 1905) mentioned incidentally the bizarre killing of 225 chickens on the property. Despite a constant watch on the henhouse, "whenever examined, four or five birds would be found dead". They were all killed in the same way: "The skin around the neck, from the head to the breast, had been pulled off, and the windpipe drawn from its place and snapped."

This sounds like a malevolent kind of poltergeist effect. And the more widely we examine this whole nasty business of mysterious mutilations, torture and killings, the more we are drawn towards the traditional acceptance of demonic powers or energies behind them. We should like to go further and be able to say whether such powers are inherent in nature or whether they are located in and projected by ourselves, but that is one of the many questions to which we have no firm answer.

Fiery persecutions

If researcher Larry Arnold is correct, there are many instances of spontaneous human combustion (see p.185) which are not fatal or stop just short of being fatal. Some of these look like attacks by poltergeists; others appear to be cases of people who attract fire (or runs of bad luck involving fire); while in others victims seem to be the object of persistent fiery assaults.

Spontaneous outbreaks of fire are a familiar feature of "poltergeist" disturbances. In the dramatic case of the Dagg household in 1889 (see INVISIBLE ASSAILANTS, p.173), the investigator, Woodcock, made a public statement citing no less than seventeen witnesses to the effect that "fires have broken out spontaneously throughout the house, as many as eight occurring in one day, six being in the house and two outside; that the window curtains were burned whilst on the windows, this happening in broad daylight, whilst the family and neighbours were in the house". The statement is quoted in full in Father Thurston's *Ghosts and Poltergeists* (1953).

The New York World (8 August 1887) says that as many as forty fires had been found in two hours in the Hoyt residence in Woodstock, New

In 1713, the Abbé Girolamo Leoni de Ceneda was terrified by a flame which suddenly burst with a roar from the ground in a village near Venice. It hovered over the spot for a while and then vanished. There are several records of the same phenomenon elsewhere. Illustration from W. de Fonvielle, *Thunder And Lightning* (1894).

Brunswick, and that they had burnt themselves out or had been inexplicably confined to very small areas. They began on 6 August, and no origin could be found for them: "Now a curtain, high up and out of reach, would burst into flames, then a bed quilt in another room: a basket of clothes on a shed, a child's dress hanging on a hook." Fort mentions a case in which fires broke out in the presence of a girl adopted into the Mac-

Donald household, of Antigonish, Nova Scotia, until in March 1922 their house finally burned to the ground.

This brings us to a significant aspect of many "poltergeist" cases and outbreaks of inexplicable fires. They generally seem to involve the agency of young girls, often lonely girls who had been adopted or worked as maids in the afflicted households. In many cases, as we shall observe, these involuntary fire-agents are bullied by authorities into "confessing" their responsibility for mysterious fires, because this suits the authorities. In April 1908, Margaret Dewar, a retired schoolteacher of Whitley, Northumberland, was bullied by the coroner, the police and the gossip of neighbours into changing her story that on 22 March she had found her sister burned to death in a bed untouched by signs of fire. Her terror was taken to be the incoherence of intoxication, and when she told the story again under oath in court, it was again suggested that she was drunk. She

persisted and the coroner adjourned the inquest until she came to her senses (see *Blyth News and Wansbeck Telegraph* for 23 and 24 March and 3 April, 1908).

The *New York Herald* (6 January 1895) tells of twenty fires the previous day in the home of Adam Colwell in Brooklyn. Policemen investigated and saw furniture burst into flames; one oficer even stated that he had seen wallpaper near Colwell's son, Willy, suddenly begin to burn. It was thought that the family's adopted girl, Rhoda, was responsible, but there was simply no way in which she could have started so many fires in full view of the firemen. A man came forward the next day to say that during the period Rhoda had been employed as a maid in his house in Flushing, New York, there had been fires, and that they ceased after he expelled her. The same paper on the next day records how the girl "sobbed her confession" when faced with the "facts" during a long interrogation. We wonder how many other confessions have been imposed on bewildered children by authorities in need of a tidy solution to an untidy mystery.

The agency behind mysterious outbreaks of fire is sometimes blatantly apparent. Fourteen-year-old Jennie Bramwell was an English girl adopted by Robert Dawson of Thorah, Canada. According to *The St Louis Globe-Democrat* (19 December 1891) the girl went into a trance after an illness. "Look at that!" she would exclaim, and the spot on the ceiling at which she pointed would start to blaze. As Mrs Dawson and the girl sat facing a wall, flames burst out of the wallpaper. In the week that followed, there were many fires in the girl's vicinity, burning her dress, the furniture, and even a kitten's fur. *The New York Sun* (2 February 1932) reported many fires of undetectable origin in the house of C.H. Williamson, of Bladenboro, North Carolina. His daughter seemed to be the centre of the disturbance, and

When St Martin of Tours (d. AD 400), celebrated Mass in Tours Cathedral, a "globe of fire" was seen to hover over his head. His successor, St Gregory, recorded this and other incidents, including one at St Martin's death and another during a parade of his relics.

once, as she stood in the middle of a room with no fire near her, her dress suddenly ignited. And again, it was told of twelve-year-old Willie Brough, in *The San Francisco Bulletin* (October 1886) that he set things on fire "by his glance". His parents thought he was afflicted by the devil and threw him out. A local farmer took him in and sent him to school: "On the first day, there were five fires in the school: one in the centre of the ceiling, one in the teacher's desk, one in her wardrobe, and two on the wall. The boy discovered them all, and cried from fright. The trustees met and expelled him that night." We have on file corroborating stories of fireprone people. Consider, for example, the case of Barbara Booley, who was involved in seven different fires in Devon, Gloucestershire and Somerset within four years (*The News of the World*, 19 October 1975).

In December 1983 an astonishing spectacle occurred in Livorno, Italy – a Scottish girl was led through a crowd as they chanted "Strega!" (Witch!) The girl, twenty-year-old Carole Compton, had been working as a nanny for the Cecchini family, was accused of arson and the attempted murder of her three-year-old charge. The previous year there had been several inexplicable fires in the house and one night, while the child slept, its cot burst into flames. The Cecchinis believed Carole was responsible for the fires, while the grandmother went even further and accused the girl of casting the evil eye on the child. There is some evidence that Carole was the focus of some poltergeist activity which – according to one theory – could have been triggered by a failed affair, her loneliness and her strained relations with other employees and with the Cecchini family. The maid of her previous employer spoke of madonnas falling off walls and things spinning in Carole's presence and that her charge at the time used to cry out at Carole's touch. The crowd around the Livorno court were apparently from the more superstitious south (where the Cecchinis lived) and were whipped up by Ciara Lobina, a healer and clairvoyant whom reporters called "the Black Nun". Lobina was frequently ejected from the court, wailing and waving her large black crucifix, claiming the Devil had revealed to her in a dream that Carole and her mother were possessed. Carole was convicted, sentenced to two and a half years, but released immediately as she had already spent sixteen months in prison awaiting trial. She later published an account of her ordeal under the

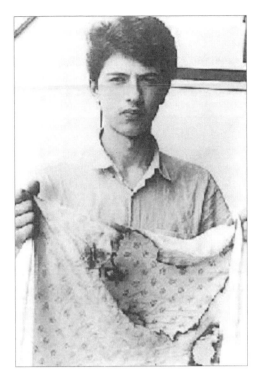

While Carole Compton was on trial in Italy, another strange case was enjoying media attention. It concerned an Italian lad, Benedetto Supino, pictured here, holding one of his chared sheets. He was said to be upset, both by the phenomenon and by his notoriety.

title *Superstition* (1990).

An interesting contrast of reaction to fire-proneness is the case of Benedetto Supino, a sixteen-year-old boy from Formia, near Rome, of whom mention was made during Carole's trial. Things would catch fire when he gazed at them, machinery would stop in his presence and someone claimed to have seen his hands glow on such occasions. But in the reportage – from November 1983 – there is none of the hysteria that coloured Carole's case, perhaps because his story lacked a superstitious grandmother and an eccentric lay-nun. After conducting some tests, Dr Giovanni Ballesio, Dean of Physical Medicine at Rome University, concluded that Benedetto was not an "electric boy". Even an archbishop stepped up to say the boy was "not malign" or "miraculous". (*Fortean Times* 42, p.21)

Let us now look at a few cases of a more sinister nature, in which the outbreaks of fire actually seem to be directed at some poor individual. In *Poltergeist Over England* (1945) Harry Price tells of a case that happened near his home. On the night of 18 November 1943, Mrs Madge Knight's screams awoke the other occupants of her house. They found her in bed, bare but covered by the bedclothes; the skin had peeled off her back, but otherwise there was no smell or evidence of burning. A doctor identified the injury as a severe burn and administered morphine. According to *The West Sussex Gazette* (23 December 1943) Mrs Knight died from toxaemia on 2 December. At the inquest, forensic experts testified that, despite a thorough examination, no evidence of fire or corrosive compounds or liquids could be found on her clothes or the bed linen. The jury gave an open verdict.

This recalls a more horrifying incident in Marylebone, London, more than a hundred years earlier. On 5 January 1820, and thereafter, fires broke out in the Wright household, where a ten-year-old girl, Elizabeth Barnes, was employed as a servant. Twice Mrs Wright found her clothes on fire while sitting in the kitchen with the girl. Once Mr Wright, hearing his wife's screams, found her in flames when the girl was not present. The Wrights' daughter moved in to guard her mother, who still caught fire by "some unknown means" and "…was so dreadfully burned she was put to bed". Wright had accused Elizabeth of causing the fires, but Mrs Wright had defended the girl. They put Mrs Wright to bed, and upon leaving the room, Wright and his daughter were immediately brought back by her screams, and found her in bed surrounded by flames. The Wrights had Elizabeth arrested. *The Annual Register* (1830–31) ends its account of this remarkable case with the magistrate saying that he had no doubt the ungrateful girl was responsible in some way, but would adjourn the matter until Mrs Wright, who had always believed the girl innocent, was well enough to testify.

At Binbrook Farm, near Market Rasen, Lincolnshire, for nearly two months objects were thrown about rooms or moved on their own, and fires broke out in unexpected places. This time the girl in the case, whom the farmer had taken from the workhouse to be a servant, was in no condition to be dragged to the police station. The farmer himself told *The Louth and North Lincolnshire News* (28 January 1905) that he saw the girl sweeping the kitchen, at the opposite end

of which there was a well-guarded small fire. "I suddenly came into the kitchen, and there she was, sweeping away, while the back of her dress was afire. She looked around as I shouted, and, seeing the flames, rushed through the door. She tripped, and I smothered the fire out with wet sacks. But she was terribly burned, and she is at the Louth Hospital, now, in terrible pain." The extent of her injuries meant that her back must have been on fire for some time, but the girl was certain that she was nowhere near the fireplace when she ignited.

During the same case something was killing the farmer's chickens (see MYSTERIOUS MUTILATORS, p.177). The girl's trance-like ignorance of the fire seems remarkably like the strange lulling in fatal cases of spontaneous human combustion (see p.185). Curiously, earlier that same month, something burned a woman, Elizabeth Clark, in the Trinity Almshouse, Hull, not many miles from Market Rasen. *The Hull Daily Mail* (6 January 1905) reported that on hearing groans from behind a partition in the dormitory at 6am the woman's fellow-inmates found her covered in burns. "Not a shred of her nightdress remained." The bed was undamaged and during the actual burning she had uttered no cry. Elizabeth Clark could give "…no articulate account" of what happened and died shortly after.

Finally we mention the fiery persecution of Paul Hayes, a nineteen-year-old computer programmer in London. On the night of 25 May 1985, he was walking in Stepney Green when, suddenly and inexplicably, he was engulfed in flames. He thought he had been doused with petrol and set alight. "It was like being plunged into the heat of a furnace … from my shoulders to my wrists my arms felt like they were being prodded by red hot pokers … my chest felt like boiling water had been poured on it. I thought I could hear my brains bubbling." Screaming, he fell to the ground and curled up thinking he was dying but, as suddenly as it began it was over. "I opened my eyes. There was no flame, no smoke … then I began to shiver with shock." He stumbled to the nearby London Hospital and received treatment for burns on his hands, forearms, face, neck and ears. The report in *The National Enquirer* (23 July 1985) says that police and medical investigators were left with a mystery. If the attack had not stopped, we might have had to tell Paul Hayes's story in the following section …

Spontaneous human combustion

The phenomenon of a living human body suddenly bursting into flames and rapidly becoming ashes has a long history; yet no one has discovered precisely how and why it takes place or the reasons behind its selection of victims. For a body to take fire in this way from no readily apparent outside source is the opposite phenomenon to the one we describe in the section FIRE AFFINITY AND FIRE STARTERS (p.72).

A popular nineteenth-century theory was that spontaneous fire victims were drunkards who had somehow saturated their bodies with inflammable spirits. Another old explanation was that of divine retribution, which parallels the view of victims of lightning as sinners or blasphemers. There was, however, at least one dissenting voice in antiquity, that of Lucretius. "Why," he wondered, "do the gods not ensure that those who have perpetrated some abominable outrage are struck by lightning? Why, instead, is some man with a conscience free of sin ... trapped and entangled without warning in the flame from heaven?"

It is a strange fire that consumes only living flesh – normally the most incombustible of materials due to the circulation of blood and the great percentage of water in its cells – leaving almost untouched the victim's clothes and other surroundings. Since the development of the theory of combustion (in the eighteenth century) the notion of such a fire has been scientifically regarded as preposterous. However, in defiance of the scientific view, cases still occur where people are suddenly attacked by fire as if from "nowhere".

One of the earliest scientific explanations of spontaneous human combustion sought to link it with those spheres of lambent light that floated over stagnant marshes. These will-o'-the-wisps, as they were known in folklore (see MYSTICAL LIGHTS, p.148), were known to be largely methane (CH_4) bubbling up from decaying vegetable matter; the real mystery was how it could ignite, something methane does not do on its own. Similarly, bacterial action in the guts of animals and humans produces methane and also hydrogen (H_2) and phosphane (PH_3, also known as "phosphoretted hydrogen"), all inflammable once they have been ignited by an external source.

Related to phosphane is diphosphane (P_2H_4), which really does spontaneously ignite on contact with oxygen; but chemists have long maintained that conditions in the human gut make the production of diphosphane unlikely. However, John Emsley, in *The Shocking History of Phosphorus* (2000), cites German research that has detected both phosphane and diphosphane in human faeces. The amounts are tiny – billionths of a gram – but according to Emsley, it is possible that on rare occasions sufficient diphosphane could build up and ignite on a chance encounter with some oxygen and set alight a pocket of methane and phosphane. This would satisfy John Heymer's observation that, in so many cases, the seat of the destruction has been the abdomen.

Emsley refers to a curious example from *Spontaneous Human Combustion* (1992) by Jenny Randles and Peter Hough. During World War II, an army patrol, crossing a field in Dorset, were "absolutely astonished" when a sheep burst into flames not far from them. They believed it was already dead but "in no way decomposed"; as it lay on its side "from its stomach issued blue flames". Why spontaneous combustion in animals (especially cows which produce huge volumes of methane) is not more frequently observed has yet to be worked out.

One modern case – the death of a young cookery student from Widnes, Cheshire – illustrates the sudden nature of the fiery attack, the helplessness of those nearby and the difficulties such cases present to the various authorities. On the morning of 28 January 1984, 17-year-old Jaqueline Fitzsimmons was leaving a class with friends, when she joked that she felt hot and smelled burning. Then, shockingly, "she suddenly became a human torch". According to one of those present, in seconds she "looked like a stuntman on television". Although the burns, mainly on her back, were judged "minor", she collapsed two weeks later and died, possibly from an infection of the damage to her lungs.

Peter Hough and Jenny Randles, ufologists with an interest in "spontaneous human combustion" (SHC) cases, were invited by the local police to attend the inquest held just over a year later. They hoped to see an official acknowledgement of this mysterious phenomenon and reasons why Jacqueline caught fire in the first place and why she suffered a delayed death, given the number of close witnesses and extended medical supervision.

As they reported to *Fortean Times*, their hopes were dashed. Witnesses were inadequately questioned and the key testimony of a special report – commissioned by the Cheshire Fire Brigade from Manchester's prestigious Shirley Institute (which established the unlikelihood of the girl's clothing catching light from a cooker) – was not ruled into evidence on instructions from the coroner. Peter Hough wrote: "The jury could have returned an open verdict, yet after ten minutes they returned with a verdict of misadventure, which endorsed the discredited cooker theory." Later, one of Jacqueline's friends, who was present at the tragedy, dismissed the verdict as "rubbish". "When we walked past [her] there was nothing; seconds later her back was a mass of flames."

One of the best documented cases of spontaneous human combustion is that of Mrs Mary Reeser, of St Petersburg, Florida, who departed this life by fire on the night of 1 July 1951. The following morning, her landlady, on taking her a telegram, found the doorknob to Mrs Reeser's apartment too hot to touch. Two painters working nearby managed to open the door and were met by a blast of hot air. They could see no sign of the plump, sixty-seven-year-old lady. Her bed was empty, and though the room bore signs of a fire, there was only a little smoke and a feeble flame on the beam of a partition that divided the single room from a kitchenette. Firemen easily put out the flame and tore away the burnt partition. Behind it, instead of Mrs Reeser and her armchair, they found a blackened circle on the floor, a few coiled springs, a charred liver, a fragment of backbone, a skull shrunk to the size of a fist, and just on the edge of the scorched patch, a black satin slipper enclosing a left foot burnt off at the ankle.

The case was investigated in detail by firemen, arson experts, pathologists and insurance men. Appliances and wiring were checked but no cause for the fire could be found. Strangely, there was no sign of fire except in the vicinity of the chair, but there it had been unnaturally intense. A mirror on a wall had cracked with the heat, plastic switch-plates had melted, and in the bathroom more plastic items were damaged. At the inquest it was said that crematoria normally use a temperature of 2500°F, sustained for hours, to incinerate a body, and even then they have to resort to grinders to

In 1888, Dr J. Mackenzie of Aberdeen attended the case of an old soldier burnt to death in a hayloft. He was resting on a beam and surrounded by unscathed bales of hay. No fire had been seen, no cries heard, and, from the preserved features of the face, no pain felt.

pulverize the remains to the state in which Mrs Reeser's body was found. Assuming that a heat of this intensity was somehow generated, why, it was asked, was the wall not scorched behind the chair and why was a pile of newspapers less than a foot away not burnt? The FBI released a statement on 8 August, suggesting that Mrs Reeser had taken her usual sleeping pills and fallen asleep in the chair while smoking – their report is quoted in full in Vincent Gaddis's *Mysterious Fires and Lights* (1967). But experts testified that even if her clothes had caught alight they could only have burned her superficially, and that neither they nor the smouldering armchair stuffing could have generated and sustained anything like enough heat to ignite a human body.

By coincidence, one of America's foremost pathologists specializing in deaths by fire, Dr Wilton Krogman, was on holiday nearby and joined the investigations. He publicly expressed his bafflement at the event, regarding it as the most amazing thing he had ever seen. Never, in all his experience, had he seen a human skull shrunk by intense heat; normally the opposite effect occurs. In an interview with fortean researcher Larry E. Arnold – for his detailed study *Ablaze!* (1995) – Dr Krogman seemed to revise his opinion of a half a century earlier; it was a hoax, he seemed to suggest, a "set-up", largely because the facts were so anomalous and the critical evidence (Mrs Reeser's ashes) "vanished" en route to the FBI for examination. "I think the case was closed with undue haste," he told Arnold. "That's all I can say."

There are many references to spontaneous human combustion (or SHC) by eighteenth- and nineteenth-century writers, including de Quincey, Dickens, Melville and Zola. These were often based on famous cases like that of Countess Bandi of Casena, of whom only a head, three fingers and both legs were found in a heap of ashes, four feet from her bed, sometime before June 1731. (The earliest account of the Countess being in the *Gentleman's Magazine* of that date.) Many similar accounts can be found in the early textbooks on medical jurisprudence, as such fires have often given rise to suspicions of criminality. For example, the *Enzyklopädisches Wörterbuch* (Berlin, 1843) mentions the pile of ashes that were the remains of the wife of a Frenchman called Millet, of Rheims, in 1725. Millet was accused of an affair with his pretty servant girl and charged

Illustration, by Phiz, of the famous scene in Dickens's novel *Bleak House* when the smoking remains of Mr Krook are discovered. "Here is a small burnt patch of flooring; here is the tinder from a little bundle of burnt paper, but not so light as usual, seeming to be steeped in something; and here is – is it the cinder of a small charred and broken log of wood sprinkled with white ashes, or is it coal? O Horror, he is here! and this from which we run away, striking out the light and over-turning one another into the street, is all that represents him."

with murdering his wife and using fire to conceal the evidence. At the inquiry, however, it was acknowledged as a "genuine" case of spontaneous combustion and Millet was acquitted.

Dr E.S. Reynolds, addressing the Manchester Pathological Society on the topic of spontaneous combustion in 1891, resorted to the current theory that most victims are inebriates. Today it is often said that they fall asleep while smoking, ignoring the cases where the victim neither smoked nor drank. But even sceptics like Reynolds tell of cases that defy their own criteria; he writes of a woman's legs carbonized *inside* her unscathed stockings – see *British Medical Journal* (21 March 1891). In the London *Daily News* (17 December 1904) is an item on the case of Mrs Thomas Cochrane of Rosehall, Falkirk, who burned to death in her chair, surrounded by unburned pillows and cushions and without uttering a cry. Clearly there is a mystery about such cases, with hints of occultism that inhibit serious investigation by doctors and scientists.

The *Madras Mail* (13 May 1907) tells of two constables carrying a woman's body, still smoking, to the District Magistrate near Dinapore, India, after it had burst into flames. Her room was untouched by fire and the clothes she was wearing were unscorched on her burnt body. What sort of fire can consume a body and leave clothing and surroundings unnaturally intact? This astonishing feature is met with time after time. Maxwell Cade and Delphine Davis in their *Taming of the Thunderbolts* (1969) suggest some kind of subatomic transaction may be involved – an idea that could be given currency by the new field of energy research called Cold Fusion – but as far as we know, no one has taken a Geiger counter to a suspected SHC scene. In another example of this strange localization of the combustion, the *New York Sun* (24 January 1930) reported an inquest on Mrs Stanley Lake, at Kingston, New York, at which the coroner said: "Although her body was severely burned, her clothing was not even scorched." In our other sections on strange fires we notice this same selectivity at work.

Several scholars of SHC have identified another recurring aspect: the victims often seem to be in a kind of trance. In *Cosmos* (ser.3, vol.6,

A typical scene of "spontaneous human combustion". The fire, in Pennsylvania, in November 1964, seems to have been intense, rapid and localized, leaving only Helen Conway's legs.

p.240) is an account by a Dr Bertholle, presented to the Société Médico-Chirurgicale, of his investigation of the case of a woman found burned to death in an almost unscorched room in Paris on 1 August 1869. He said that it was as if the body had been in an intense furnace, yet only the floor under the body had been scorched. He could not understand why the woman had made no outcry to be heard by the other occupants of the house. Another case: the charred bodies of five men were found sitting in casual positions in a car in a back road near Pikeville, Kentucky. The account in the *Syracuse Herald-Journal* (21 November 1960), does not describe the condition of the car, but quotes the coroner as being baffled at the absence of any sign of a struggle to escape.

One of the strangest cases was summarized by Fort from an English paper, the *Dartford Chronicle* (7 April 1919). At 2.30am a well-known author, J. Temple Thurston, was found dead, scorched from the waist down. There was no trace of fire on his clothes nor in his room; but outside the door of that room, firemen found a blaze and could not understand how it started or why it should have been confined to that spot. Thurston was fully clothed and alone in the house. He still had money in his pockets, and there was no sign of the fire being used to mask a robbery. The inquest produced a verdict of death by heart failure brought on by inhaling smoke, and once again surprise was expressed that, if Thurston had been up and about when he discovered the fire, he had not escaped or called for help from his neighbours.

A number of TV documentaries have tried to explain SHC, often with very suspect demonstrations of the "candle effect" (in which body fat is the fuel and the victim's clothing the wick). In August 1998, BBC TV's science series *QED* conducted a careful and impressive demonstration; Dr John de Haan, a forensic specialist at the California Criminalistics Institute, wrapped a dead pig in a blanket and placed it in a replica living room. A small amount of petrol was poured on one shoulder and set alight. Five hours later, the "body" was still burning and would have continued had it not been doused.

Proponents of SHC have tended to think in terms of an intense, localized inferno, but de Haan showed that once started, a prolonged low-intensity blaze could convincingly reproduce many of the characteristics of SHC: the pig's extremities were intact and bones were friable,

Robert C. Meslin/Larry E. Arnold/Fortean Picture Library

The remains of "Bailey the Tramp" showing the unusually localized nature of the blaze in the region of his abdomen, from which blue flames were seen to jet. His agony was so intense his teeth were embedded in the stair post.

crumbling when poked. Effects in the room were localized: a plastic radio partly melted and a nearby wooden table was lightly scorched. However, this still leaves many questions about reported SHC cases unanswered (despite the claim of the *QED* publicity). We note that an "accelerant" was used to get the fire going in the first place when, in many cases, there is no indication of a source of ignition at all or when there is clear evidence of the rapidity of the combustion.

Larry E. Arnold researched the topic for 23 years, his painstaking historical research complemented by many hours talking to fire investigators. His book is crammed with new cases and sensible discussion of theories and the first-hand observations of police and fire officers. "Contrary to what was once believed," he says, "SHC is not always fatal and the existence of survivors poses a profound challenge to the debunker."

To Arnold the chief characteristic of "true" SHC cases is the indication that the fire originates within the body and burns outwards; with conventional fire deaths it is the other way around and this is why most authorities regard SHC as scientific heresy or mere superstition based on poor observation. John Heymer – a retired Scenes of Crime Officer for Gwent CID – agrees with Arnold. Heymer's experience with SHC began with his investigation of the charred remains of 73-year-old Henry Thomas in Ebbw Vale on 6 January 1980. What he saw was contrary to his experience of "normal" fire deaths: the extremities protruded from a heap of ashes; domestic objects nearby were singed or partly melted but only the vicinity of the body was charred; smooth surfaces

(like the windows and lightbulb) were coated with yellow grease and the room was dripping with condensation of water originating in the body.

Heymer's research is detailed in his book *The Entrancing Flame* (1996), including other British cases that he learned of during his investigation. One concerned the death of a tramp (known as Bailey) on stairs in a deserted building in Lambeth, London, 13 September 1967. The fire crew was led by Jack Stacey who, in 1986, told Heymer of the most bizarre sight that he had ever witnessed in his entire career. "There was a four-inch slit in his abdomen from which was issuing, at force, a blue flame which was beginning to burn the stairs. We extinguished the flames by playing a hose into the abdominal cavity. Bailey was alive when he started burning and must have been in terrible pain. His teeth were sunk into the mahogany newel post of the staircase." The importance of this case cannot be overemphasized as a highly experienced Fire Officer is emphatic that "the fire was coming from within the abdomen".

In *Fortean Times*, archivist Peter Christie describes his search for original documentation of the oft-cited case of Grace Pett of Ipswich, who combusted on 9 April 1744. Her case was popularized by a devoted chapter in Sir David Brewster's *Letters on Natural Magic* (1868). Grace was found by her daughter on a wooden floor "like a block of wood burning with a glowing fire without flames". Her abdomen had burned to ashes. Brewster dutifully mentions that Grace had been drinking and that clothes and a paper screen nearby were "untouched". Christie found an account of the inquest on Grace Pett which

Fortean Picture Library

generally confirmed that, apart from her extremities, she had been "so far reduced to ashes as to be put in ye coffin with a shovel". An additional source (given by Christie) reveals the previously unknown local opinion that Grace was suspected of being a witch. Apparently, a neighbour who farmed sheep consulted a conjuror over why some were dying and was advised to burn one (presumably in the belief that this would summon whoever bewitched them). Coincidentally, on the night the farmer burned a sheep, Grace also died; her unburned feet were said to correspond to the tied legs of the sheep.

Firemen clean up after the discovery of the remains of Mrs M.H. Reeser at St Petersburg, Florida, 2 July 1951.

Otherworldly guardians and helpers

On 16th May, 1986, David Young – described locally as a disaffected "genius" – took 150 children and their teachers hostage at the Elementary School in Cokeville, Wyoming. He had constructed a huge bomb and gathered the children around it, threatening to detonate it if he was not paid $300 million. From his detailed diaries (found later), Young's ransom was a bluff; he planned to kill them all anyway, including himself and his accomplice wife. At the height of the siege the bomb went off accidentally; Young and his wife died but all the children survived (a few with minor injuries).

By any standard, the escape of the Cokeville children was amazing. Later, when they were interviewed separately, a number of the children spoke of shining figures that calmed their panic and instructed them to get the other children to stand over by the windows (which were open because of the noxious fumes coming from Young's home-made explosives). One of the first to see the luminous visitors was six-year-old Nathan Hartley, who looked up from the toy bricks he was playing with to see them floating down through the ceiling to stand by each person. They seemed to include both young and old and "everybody had one" … except the highly agitated Young.

Nathan said a smiling old woman came over to him and said she was his great-grandmother (who had died three years earlier). She warned him the bomb was about to go off and not to be afraid. Similarly, Katie Walker, aged seven, observed a glowing "family" group (including a baby and young girl) descend and float a couple of feet above the floor. One of them, she said, told her she was a maternal relative who had died 13 years previously. Katie's brother, Travis, said he heard a voice tell him to lead the children over to the open windows.

The children's accounts of their otherworldly rescuers only emerged later during counselling sessions and, we are assured, the children themselves had not spoken of it to their families or to each other, yet their accounts accord with the classic notion of "guardian angels". The Bible, of course, contains many accounts of angels intervening in the fates of mortals. For example, one led Lot to safety during the destruction of Sodom; and another protected Daniel in the lion's den. The greatest modern influence on this belief was the Swedish scientist and mystic, Emanuel Swedenborg (1688–1772), who declared that his book *Heaven And Hell* (1758) was based upon 27 years of personal experience of angels "…in the spirit".

It is interesting to note that the onset of Swedenborg's own career as an interpreter of visions came in 1745, during a Christmas dinner party in London, when a shadowy figure told him not to eat so much. Later that night, the same figure revealed itself to be Jesus, who "opened Heaven and Hell" to him, permitting him almost daily conversations with angels and spirits during "waking visions". However, the experience of angelic intervention is not confined to Christian theology, but can be found in nearly every culture with a rich and ancient body of lore. What interests us are the anecdotes about the appearance of divine or supernatural beings to ordinary people, outside the religious context. It suggests to us that shamanic-type visions are innately universal and spontaneous, awaiting only a suitable trigger.

What are the secular equivalents of guardian angels? The story of a phantom helmsman told by the great seaman Joshua Slocum provides a clue. Captain Slocum is celebrated as the first person to have sailed single-handedly around the world, a three-year journey that begun in 1895. In late July he left the Azores in his ship, *Spray,* heading out into the Atlantic. Having taken on fresh supplies, he "ate without stint" many plums and a Pico white cheese. "Alas! by night-time I was doubled up with cramps," he recorded. A squall loomed but he felt too ill to complete his work on the sails and went below, collapsing on the cabin floor in great pain. We abbreviate what happened next from his detailed account in *Sailing Alone Around The World* (1900).

"How long I lay there I could not tell, for I became delirious. When I came to, as I thought, from my swoon, I realized that the sloop was plunging into a heavy sea, and looking out of the companionway, to my amazement I saw a tall man at the helm ... He would have been taken for a pirate in any part of the world. While I gazed upon his threatening aspect I forgot the storm, and wondered if he had come to cut my throat. This he seemed to divine. 'Señor,' said he, doffing his cap, 'I have come to do you no harm.' And a smile, the faintest in the world, but still a smile, played on his face, which seemed not unkind when he spoke ... 'I am one of Columbus's crew, ... the pilot of the *Pinta* come to aid you. Lie quiet, señor captain,' he added, 'and I will guide your ship to-night. You have a *calenture* [a fever], but you will be all right to-morrow.'"

The phantom pilot told Slocum the source of his sudden illness. "'You did wrong, captain, to mix cheese with plums.'" He came to, eventually, and was astonished to find "the *Spray* was still heading as I had left her, and was going like

Emanuel Swedenbord at the age of 75, holding the manuscript of *Apocalypsis Revelata* (1766).

a race-horse. Columbus himself could not have held her more exactly on her course."

That night, Slocum noted, the phantom who claimed to have been Columbus's pilot came to him in a dream, much as Jesus did to Swedenborg, giving him some encouragement for future success. "'You did well last night to take my advice,' said he, 'and if you would, I should like to be with you often on the voyage, for the love of adventure alone.' ... he again doffed his cap and disappeared as mysteriously as he came, returning, I suppose, to the phantom *Pinta*."

There is something analogous here to the near-death experience (NDE). These experiences – occurring to people under conditions of extreme stress, during accidents, illnesses or surgical operations that bring them close to death – are remembered on recovery. To onlookers, the person may appear unconscious or even dead, but somehow their consciousness is active and perceptions heightened. The many collections of near-death accounts testify to patients recalling the sights and sounds that occurred during their operation or other medical procedures when they were unconscious or anaesthetized. Consistently, the narratives tell of "splitting off" from their physical body and seeing it from a viewpoint outside the body before the teller is whisked off down a tunnel of light.

NDEs and their morphological cousins, out-of-the-body experiences (OBEs), are well-documented in a solid range of sources. Read carefully, they are not a flight *from* the reality of the percipient's predicament but often feature a calm *acceptance* of it (see NEAR-DEATH EXPERIENCES AND THE LIFE REVIEW, p.104). A typical example would be the boy recovered from drowning in icy water and declared clinically dead. After resuscitation, he says that, although unconscious, he was aware of the frantic attempts to revive him as if observing it from above or from a distance, yet felt strangely objective about it. Sometimes the presence of a benign, caring entity is mentioned, such as the claim that "someone" led lost mountaineers to safety when the evidence shows no physical person in the vicinity.

In his account of the Fourth British Expedition to climb Mount Everest in 1933, Frank Smythe recorded that he had such a strong sense of an invisible companion that he broke off a piece of mint chocolate and offered it to him (*Camp 6*, 1937). It is interesting in this context to note that Smythe, on his solo climb (without oxygen) saw two curious UFOs: "floating in the sky … one possessed what appeared to be squat underdeveloped wings, and the other a protuberance suggestive of a beak. They hovered motionless but seemed slowly to pulsate." The German Reinhold Messner was the first to reach the top solo, in 1980, and he too declared he imagined an invisible companion climbing beside him, while Wilfrid Noyce, who climbed Everest in 1953, wrote of the sensation of hovering high in the air above himself (*South Col*, 1954). Commenting on the phenomenon in his *Natural History Of The Mind* (1979), the social scientist Gordon Rattray Taylor said he knew of similar stories told by explorers of the Arctic and Antarctic, high-altitude balloonists and test pilots.

In April 1936, two mine owners and a lawyer were inspecting the Moose River gold mine, in Nova Scotia, when it collapsed, trapping them, alone, underground for ten days. The lawyer died of pneumonia on the seventh day, but one of the survivors – Alfred Scadding – said that just moments before the disaster, the party crossed a side tunnel and he saw in the distance "a small light … about two feet from the ground, swinging, as if in someone's hand". Sometime later, in the darkness, Scadding and his colleague, Dr David E.

Robertson, both heard sounds, likened to children playing in the distance. "There was shouting and laughter as of little people having fun," Scadding told *Toronto Daily Star* reporter George Bryant later. "We both heard it so clearly we thought there was a vent to the surface. It went on for 24 hours." Robertson and Scadding both gave evidence to separate commissioners, but their eerie experience is not recorded in any of the official accounts or reports. Bryant recalled that miners have always feared unusual sights and sounds in the depths of the mines, regarding them as portents of disaster; rightly so, in this case. (*FATE* magazine, Sept 1956)

In another tale, an explosion in the Belva mine, near Pineville, Kentucky, on Boxing Day 1945, entombed 31 men for 53 hours. Nine men survived due to the heroism and sacrifice of Bud Towns, a black miner. When he noticed some men hallucinating, Towns, who had been in a similar mine disaster some years before, kept the men focused with sermons and prayers. After their rescue, the survivors were interviewed about their experience. Some told of a "door" opening in one of the walls and a man dressed like a "lumberjack" stepped through from a "well lit room". The visitor assured the trapped miners that they would be rescued and left the same way he arrived, closing the door behind him. These details – like those of the Moose River disaster – do not appear in any of the official reports, but emerged in later interviews with survivors appearing in local newspapers and follow-up investigations.

One of the most extraordinary stories of this type that we know of concerns two miners at Sheppton, Pennsylvania, who were trapped underground for two weeks in 1963 and when eventually rescued told of strikingly vivid experiences. As one of them summed it up later: "Pope John and the cross was there all the time, but these others things kept jumping across. They would come like a movie. First there was these men with lights and after a while the steps would come. It was real. Both of us were seeing it and we knew they was live people."

On the morning of 3 August 1963, three miners descended 390 feet into a small, privately owned old anthracite mine at Sheppton, and began loading coal into mine carts. When his winches did not respond, the operator at the top of the mineshaft knew there had been a cave-in and began the emergency help procedures. At the bottom of the shaft, Dave Fellin (58), Henry "Hank" Throne (28) and Louis Bova heard the support timbers snapping and barely had time to jump out of the way. Bova leapt to one side and was lost in the fall of rock and dust; his body was never recovered. Fellin and Throne found themselves uninjured but trapped in a small cavern with only the equipment they had on them. On the fifth day the rescuers made contact via the first of a series of bore holes drilled from the surface. Fourteen days later the two men were finally winched to safety. The two were rushed to hospital where Fellin, fearing for his own sanity, requested a psychiatric examination.

Miners have been known to suffer from decompression psychosis which can include hallucinations – the so-called "rapture of the deep", usually associated with deep-sea diving. Fellin and Throne were both interrogated by US Navy psychiatrists, eager to learn about the effects of such a long period of sensory deprivation under stressful and near-fatal conditions. They were both declared well and mentally competent by two psychiatrists.

After the initial press releases, stories began to circulate about the visions and hallucinations they had experienced. Both men were horrified and angry at the glib way they were portrayed as stupid or mad and they refused to answer any more inquiries. However, just after the first anniversary of the disaster, the two survivors agreed to speak to Bill Schmeer of Radio WAZL in nearby Hazelton, who wrote up the interviews for *FATE* magazine (March 1964), providing us with first-hand details of a remarkable view into alternative or parallel realities.

The first apparitions appeared within the first 24 hours. Dave Fellin was aware of a figure and a shining gold cross on the cavern wall, keeping quiet for fear he was imagining things. Hank Throne was the first to mention seeing the figure, asking Fellin who this happy, smiling man was. Being a Catholic he identified the figure as that of Pope John XXIII, but dared not look at the figure's face. They took some comfort from the fact that both of them could see the same thing (although later, there were slight differences in the form of the cross that they drew for Schmeer when he interviewed them separately). Both men also agreed that the Pope stayed with them until they were rescued. (Pope John died eight weeks

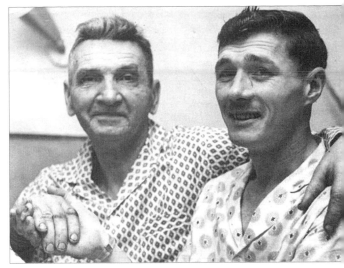

David Fellin (58) and Henry "Hank" Throne (28) in Hazelton State General Hospital immediately after their medical examination. They were rescued on 27 August 1963 after being trapped underground for 14 days, during which they experienced a variety of extraordinary hallucinations.

earlier, in Rome, on 3 June 1963.)

What was to unfold over the following days was more spectacular. First, Fellin told Schmeer, came "the linemen" (as Throne had dubbed them) – reminiscent of the "lumberjack" seen in the Belva disaster. They arrived in "a chariot-like vehicle" (without horses) and on their foreheads were funnel-shaped lights; the narrow end of the funnel emitted pulsing waves of light rather than a steady beam. To Hank Throne they looked like "ordinary guys" wearing miner's lamps and utility belts but Dave Fellin could only see them in profile and even then, only their top halves. Hank Throne said he first noticed them as they were unreeling wire from a big spool. Thinking they were part of the rescue crew, Throne asked them to bring some lights into the cavern, at which point they vanished for a while.

Both men agreed that they did indeed seem to have some kind of light after that. It would begin as a tiny point and swell until it filled the cavern. "It was bluish … soft, sort of like steam," said Fellin. "The whole area was filled up with steam and you could see shadows."

The two, however, disagree on some details: Fellin said the light was intermittent but Throne thought it was present all the time and seemed to

Sœur Thérèse de l'Enfant-Jésus, durant la guerre, entraîne un séminariste-brancardier pour ramasser les blessés sous la mitraille. (Dessin de Giroux).

An apparition of St Therese of Liseaux guides French stretcher bearers to a wounded soldier during World War I.

have no source. In answer to the critics who say there could not have been any source of light in the chamber, Fellin points to the extensive work that he and Throne did in propping up the ceiling with timbers, asking: "How could we have done that if the light was a product of our imaginations?" We have met this numinous glow before in other encounters with paranormal entities.

They only really felt fearful on one occasion and it had to do with a huge, white marble staircase that appeared one day. The steps were about 12 feet wide and went up steeply "...until they disappeared out of sight". They saw people occasionally going up the stairs where a pair of large double doors opened to admit some but remained closed for others. Hank Throne wanted to climb up the stairs, but Dave Fellin held him back, afraid that it might mean their deaths. Hank said he was going to break down the doors and as he began to hammer on them the structure disappeared, his hand hitting the rocky wall (this was

their only serious injury in 14 days). They were left in the dark for nearly an hour before the soft blue glow and otherworldly scenes resumed.

Sometime before the fifth day – when the first rescue hole broke through – an incident occurred which led them to believe they would be rescued. Fellin remembers having doubts when, suddenly, three men came to them with a plaque which seemed to show them that they would, indeed, survive. The men were tall, handsome and tanned, with "slightly pointed ears" and wore green-grey kimonos. To Throne, the large, "almost heart-shaped" plaque was blue in colour, bearing rows of holes, all but one plugged with pegs. Fellin described the plaque as orange and small and thought he saw names on it. He asked the men if he could see whether his and Throne's names were present and was overjoyed to find they weren't. The names had vanished. "So I knew me and Hank was gonna come out."

Though now in contact with the rescue team, and receiving torches and food through the freshly drilled communication shaft, the men continued to share their cavern with visitors. From the fifth to the eighth day, each time food was sent down, the miners saw "small, child-like creatures" dance around the hole, these figures visible in the full light of the men's torches.

Other groups of mysterious figures followed – "who seemed to glow with an aura of beauty" as Schmeer put it – in idyllic scenes. Only once did they see any menacing figures; these, in groups of two, would walk towards them, becoming more grotesque as they neared, "their arms and legs dropped away". While Throne did not speak of these "confrontations" to Schmeer, Fellin described how he turned aside from them and "walked … into a beautiful garden". He saw figures move into view and then take seats at tables in groups of two or three. These figures were discribed as being "...like ordinary mortals but beauty seemed to flow from their bodies". Before they sat down, they looked over towards the two miners, "like they were judging," Fellin added. Among the seated, radiant beings, he said, he recognized some as living friends and at least twelve others he knew had died.

What seems remarkable is that two relatively ordinary, down-to-earth miners both glimpsed another reality and both saw pretty much the same things. Neither man could be said to be especially religious; when Schmeer met them a year after their ordeal, he described them as "ordinary" churchgoers who had become neither more nor less religious. Some of their experiences have mystical qualities but they are not couched in the language of the religious. Regarding the soft, omnipresent blue light – reminiscent of the "astral" light associated with fairies (see Mystical lights, p.148) – Fellin said it seemed to lift them out of their tomb "…to a place where they could see for miles". Later, remembering the idyllic garden, Fellin said it seemed to stretch as far as the eye could see. He described feeling "…as though he could leave his body and look back to see himself sitting on the mine floor". The strange quality of light, far-sight (or clairvoyance), and recognition of dead friends or relatives are among the elements that can also be found in accounts of shamanic "journeys", encounters with fairies and out-of-the-body experiences.

The mining lore of the whole Appalachian region was heavily influenced by successive waves of immigration of miners from Germany and Cornwall with their tales of wights, knockers, goblins, kobolds, spriggans and gnomes – diminutive beings, seemingly a different species from the surface-dwelling fairy kind. Similar stories of "crisis encounters" can be found in the narratives of sailors and mountaineers and many other dangerous professions, but mining seems a particularly symbolic activity, carried out in the dark depths of an earthy underworld, peopled by capricious entities. In the bowels of the Earth, miners learned to pay attention to strange knocking sounds, melodious singing, unexpected voices, mimicking echoes, dreadful groans and powerful organ notes, not least because they might be portents of disaster that could save lives. Miners in earlier times would have recognized many elements of the stories told by the survivors of the disasters at Moose River, Belva and Sheppton mines, especially the sounds, lights and little figures.

Such experiences of unearthly entities might be more common than is generally supposed, and definitely not confined to the insane or unbalanced. Some processes of visualization are as little understood now as when they were studied by Sir Francis Galton and Edmund Parrish in the late 1800s, and E.R. Jaensch in the 1930s. It may be that prolonged exposure to darkness (sensory deprivation) actually enhances those synaesthetic or eidetic mechanisms that fascinated Galton, such as perceiving numbers as colours or shapes. In a paper for the *Proceedings of the Royal Institute of Great Britain* (13 May 1881), Galton spoke of "eminently sane people" experiencing very persistent and complex "phantasmogorias" that were not always under their control (ie they could not easily summon or dismiss them). Today we call them "hypnopompic" or "hypnagogic" imagery for, as Galton realized, they tend to occur "…at the instant of putting out a candle". This "twilight" consciousness features strongly in most accounts of bedroom invaders, be they abducting aliens, silent shapes that stand at the foot of the bed, or the "night hags" that suffocate paralysed sleepers.

Galton, who had surveyed friends, relatives and colleagues, said he knew three eminent scientists who often experienced "…a crowd of phantoms, sometimes hurrying past". A healthy female relative, he said, saw an endless stream of faces, "always pleasant" and it amused her to sit quietly and watch their expressions. No two were alike, she said, and when she was ill they came nearer, "almost suffocatingly close". (Fellin experienced something similar in the Sheppton mine.) Another confidant, an authoress, assured him she once saw the doll-sized principal character of one of her novels "…glide through the door straight up to her," then vanish.

From William James's pioneering study, *The Varieties Of Religious Experience* (1902), to Sir Alister Hardy's *The Spiritual Nature Of Man* (1979), nearly every authority who has studied the matter has emphasized that this sort of spiritual experience occurs widely among every section of humanity. David Hay and Anne Morisy, who worked out of Hardy's Religious Experience Research Unit (RERU) at Oxford, estimated that in as many as 64 percent of such cases, the experience had a direct influence on the personality and perceptions of the witness and was remembered often in later years.

Hardy's own research was drawn from thousands of first-hand accounts gathered from literature, media appeals and direct surveys. He was surprised to find that "elements of superstition, wishful thinking, and contradictory theological theories [were] little in evidence". In other words, the majority of people have moments in which they sense a "transcendental reality" in which institutional religion plays little or no part. Hardy's analysis included a detailed list of the ways in which the transcendental experience can manifest; these perceptions range from non-specific sights, sounds and feelings, to very specific visions, voices and feelings of joy, harmony, wonder, hope and illumination. Telepathy and precognition feature in many accounts – as when the miners "knew" they would be rescued – as do out-of-the-body experiences, apparitions, a pervading light which seems to have no source, an unearthly landscape, and sensing the presence of some "being" that was greater or different from a living human (one in five reported this).

Hardy's list of the key elements in a transcendental experience overlaps the now familiar lists of key elements of NDEs supplied by Dr Raymond Moody and others; in OBEs by Dr Robert Crookall and others; and in Dr David Hufford's account of the "night hag". The phenomena may include paralysis, travelling through a tunnel of light, a pervasive luminosity, seeing dead relatives, a sense of peace, autoscopy (an external view of oneself), some sort of judgement of one's life (see NEAR-DEATH EXPERIENCES AND THE LIFE REVIEW, p.104), and an encounter with a divine presence. Not all of these elements occur in every case, but, as we have seen, combinations of them also feature in encounters with fairies and aliens, and of course, in visionary and shamanic experiences of all kinds, especially those shared by two or more people.

While many "close encounters" and "night hags" tend to be chaotic and disturbing, the message of nearly every NDE and OBE is consistent and positive. They point to some other reality – adjacent to the one we know – the experience of which actually changes a person, bringing calm and a sense of purpose, and removes the fear of death.

Haunted people and places

When it came to ghosts, the Roman philosopher Pliny (the Younger, AD 23–79) thought the testimony of friends and those he respected more than outweighed the improbability of the subject. He was particularly swayed by the story of a Greek colleague, Athenodorus, a former keeper of the great library at Pergamon, who hired a house in Rome, cheaply, because it was allegedly haunted. Curious, he sat up all night to see the ghost and was rewarded by the apparition of a man in chains that clanked as it walked. The form beckoned and Atheondorus followed outside, to where the figure pointed at the ground. The next day, acting on Athenodorus's information, the magistrates had the spot dug up and found the skeleton of a man in chains. It is from these historians that we get the familiar, stereotypical ghost in chains.

Pliny's Greek counterpart, Plutarch (AD 46–127) concurred, and with reasons that are still valid today: "It has been claimed that no man in his senses ever saw a ghost, that these are the delusive visions of women and children or of men whose intellects are impaired by some physical infirmity, and who believe that their distressed imaginations are of divine origin. But, if ... men of strong and philosophic minds, whose understandings were not affected by any constitutional infirmity ... could place so much faith in the appearance of spectres as to give an account of them to their friends, I see no reason why we should depart from the opinion of the ancients." (*Life of Dion*)

If we admit the subject of hauntings, under Pliny's conditions, we soon find it is complicated by several fundamental questions. Firstly, what is it that "haunts"? Is it, as is traditionally believed, the spirit, or influence, of a deceased person? In which case, how are we to account for the perceived clothes – or, indeed, chains – which, as far as we know, do not have souls? We will have to leave this enigma – and the riddle of phantoms of living people – to another time.

Some modern psychical researchers contend that the poltergeist is a projection of violent inner conflicts in the person or persons on whom the phenomena seem to centre. This might be important when considering the way some poltergeists are centred on people rather than places. This leads us to the observation that the huge archive of investigated cases divides, largely, into two types of hauntings: *locus* (those that seem to be rooted in a location) and *focus* (those that seem to follow certain people, even when they move home).

If the majority of the collected accounts of simple ghost encounters are to be believed, they take the form of a rather inert figure, seen unexpectedly, usually in a bedroom. Sometimes, the phantoms are of living friends or relatives who were in some danger or dying at the time. The "bedroom invader" motif also figures in stories of alien abduction.

In the case of the latter, our interest is the relatively small number of people who claim to see ghosts regularly, bidden and unbidden, or to be the *focus* of ghostly attentions. As we have seen over the course of this book, different cultures treat such people differently. The Romanian girl, Eleonore Zugun – who manifested scratches from being attacked by her invisible "devil" and in whose presence objects moved, see p.86 – was called a "poltergeist girl". Many like her, before and since, were blamed for unexplained deaths, fires and other damaging or frightening phenomena and called witches. At times, the more violent people-focused poltergeists seem indistinguishable from cases of so-called demonic possession.

There are always exceptions. For example, in 1661, in Youghal, County Cork, Ireland, a rain of stones would follow a young maidservant from room to room, striking her, then falling to the floor and vanishing. For this devilry, someone else was tried for witchcraft. In 1761, the Giles children (see p.10) were the victims of a violent "phantom" that no one else could see, during the months they stayed in the Lamb Inn, Bristol. Yet the children were not blamed or outed as witches; nor was the inn said to be haunted, no one else

being so plagued before or after the incident. (See INVISIBLE ASSAILANTS, p.173, for other cases of this type.) Others, who have endured assaults by invisibles or who were mysteriously transported from place to place – see AWAY WITH THE FAIRIES, p.157 – have given different explanations for the appearance of their wounds or their mode of travel, and been accepted as shamans or saints. The stigmatic German nun, Christina of Stommeln (1242–1312), would be beaten, scratched and pierced with hot nails in the midst of prolonged poltergeist activity, but this was no hindrance to her beatification.

Still others, who seem to communicate with the unseen entities, find a role as mediums or prophets, as in the case of the troubled Fox sisters, in 1848, who developed a system of raps to talk with a spirit who claimed to be buried in the basement of their home in Hydesville, New York. As in the Athenodorus case, bones were actually discovered there during excavation; so their fame spread, leading to the founding of the Spiritualist movement. Tiring of the nightly disturbances – raps that would shake the house, the noises and movements of furniture – and the growing numbers of sightseers, their parents decided to move the girls to their sister's house in Rochester

A rare view of the notoriously haunted Borley Rectory, photographed the morning after much of the house was destroyed by fire in February 1939.

with the hope of breaking their contact with the spirit. In this instance, the poltergeist, or whatever it was, followed the girls and, if anything, the rappings became more frequent.

In these cases, it was not so much a ghost of the traditional sort that manifested regularly, but a poltergeist. It was Harry Price's opinion that "... poltergeists are invisible, intangible and inarticulate". It is certainly true that rarely are ghosts seen during poltergeist activity (although, during the Phelps case, the poltergeist constructed figures out of household objects and linen – see PROJECTED THOUGHT-FORMS, p.84). But it is characteristic of the poltergeist that *something* is responsible for observable and often tangible phenomena.

All we can conclude is that there seems to be a class of people – called "agents" or "repeaters" by researchers – to whom unusual events happen more often than the normal expectation, and this "agency" is not restricted to being the focus of a poltergeist's attentions. Good examples might be famous mediums who hold regular séances; seers such as Anne Jeffries, who had regular contact with the Little People; the Fátima visionaries, who experienced regular revelations from the Virgin Mary; or alien abductees such as Betty Andreasson or Whitley Strieber, both of whom claim to have been taken regularly since childhood.

The old Romans and Greeks believed in a "spirit of place" – a *genius loci* – which was the protector of sacred places. The lore of ancient sacred groves – with its references to talking or bleeding trees, apparitions of gods and ghosts,

and divine retributions – can sometimes read like poltergeist phenomena. Much the same can be said of places inhabited or used by the fairies and the prohibitions put upon them (see p.208). Any digging, demolition or building at these locations might bring retribution in some form. It is certainly common to hear, in tales of hauntings, that they were triggered when work began to disturb the site.

This occurred, famously, on Scrapfaggot Green, in the Essex village of Great Leighs, early in October 1944. The story goes that when bulldozers from the nearby American airbase worked on widening the road past the green, they moved a two-ton stone, unaware of the local tradition that it had been placed to seal the grave of a witch, buried there in the 17th century. (Scratch-faggot is said to be an old Suffolk word for a witch.) In the following days, locals reported a bewildering list of strange events, including the church bells ringing oddly, the church clock losing time, corn stooks and livestock vanishing and reappearing in neighbouring fields, hens that stopped laying and so on – complaints that, in former times, might well have led to allegations of witchcraft. The final straw was discovery by the landlord of the inn on the green, who woke up to find a huge boulder outside his door where there was none the night before. On 11 October, a ceremony was held to replace the stone in its original orientation, at which point the troubling series of events ceased.

Since the earliest times, societies have also

associated ghosts with special locations. It's not surprising that inns and houses figure prominently in lists of haunted sites, and in recent decades we have seen an increase in the number of ordinary homes, including council houses, populated with ghosts. The generally accepted reason for the hauntings is that something tragic or memorable must have happened there; but if this was the only criterion, every home in the land – where, at some time or another, something tragic or memorable has happened, or someone has died – would successfully claim to be haunted.

However, ask people to name a haunted house and it is likely that Borley Rectory will be nominated for the UK and the Amityville house for the US. The hauntings at the house in Amityville, on New York's Long Island, scene of the murder of six members of the DeFeo family in November 1974, have long since come under a cloud of suspicion and several investigations point to much of its legend being created by credulous writers, abetted by sensationalist media. Similarly, the reputation of Borley Rectory, first popularized by Harry Price as "…the most haunted house in England", has likewise come in for serious criticism. The rectory was built in 1863, in the Essex village of Borley (not far from Great Leighs), by the Reverend Henry Bull. In 1930, the Reverend Lionel Foyster moved in with his family; most of the more famous incidents date from this time. After it was destroyed by fire in 1939, it was believed by some that the "ghosts" moved to Borley Church. The village has been plagued by sightseers ever since.

Fortunately, the annals of psychical research are blessed with many more authentic cases of haunted houses, investigated and documented in impressive detail by serious scholars of the subject. Some of these have been mentioned in other chapters in this book: such as the homes of the Phelps family in Stratford, Connecticut, in 1850; and the invisible witch that persecuted several generations of the Bell family in Tennessee, between 1817 and 1821. To these we must add the hauntings at Tedworth, Ringcroft, and Epworth.

The disturbances at a large manor at North Tidworth, Wiltshire, between March 1662 and April 1663, form what is probably the first and largely unsurpassed example of an English haunted house. Then called Tedworth, it was owned by the family of John Mompesson, a respected Wiltshire magistrate; the haunting itself seems to have been triggered by the confiscation of an itinerant drummer's drum (for an illustration, see p.156). For nights on end, the house was filled with vibrations, knockings and thumps, on doors, the roof, the outside walls and on the beds of the sleeping children. Gradually the phenomena gained in intensity, warping floorboards, shoving people, making "offensive smells", pulling off bedclothes, hurling objects about and causing the furniture to "perambulate". Voices were heard, doors were opened and shut repeatedly, and noses were tweaked among many other "apish tricks". In fact, all the classic poltergeist phenomena are present, including witnesses' questions answered by patterns of loud knocks, which prefigures the Fox sisters by nearly 190 years.

Rev Joseph Glanvill and other notables (some sent by King Charles II) investigated and experienced the phenomena for themselves but despite their vigilance, they could not solve the mystery. In fact, it took a more sinister turn: when a pistol was fired at a moving pile of wood, bloodstains were found; a dark shape appeared in a servant's bedroom "…with two red and glaring eyes"; something black jumped on one of the younger children, leaving her terrified for hours; six men were lifted up when the bed they were trying to hold down levitated; a horse was overturned in the stable and a hind hoof jammed into its mouth; and a group of shadowy figures, "…seven or eight in the shape of Men", were seen about the house.

At his trial in Salisbury, the drummer claimed responsibility for the disturbances and said they would continue until his drum was returned. The court took this for a curse and the man was tried as a witch, of which charge he was acquitted but sent for deportation. The "Demon Drummer of Tedworth" was made famous by Glanvill's widely circulated collection of ghost and witch tales, *Sadducismus Triumphatus*, first published in 1666, the year after he died. He was not the first to write about the "Drummer"; Samuel Pepys mentioned it (*Diary*, June 1663) and, almost as soon as the haunting ended, it was taken up by a few ballads and broadsheets.

At Ringcroft, Galloway, Scotland, in 1695, the family of Andrew Mackie suffered terribly through March and April; heaps of burning peat would appear in the house during the night, their arms gripped by an invisible hand so hard it bruised them, and they would be pushed and pulled and beaten by staves and pelted by stones sufficiently to drive them out of the house several times. All the while things would disappear, strange lights and fires would be seen, and voices heard. On the 26th April, it predicted the day it would cease its torment, and held true to its word. The account is remarkable for its time, being carefully drawn up and signed by the chief witnesses, including two lairds and five church ministers.

To these we can add a few more famous cases, one of which being that of the Wesley family, in their parsonage at Epworth, Lincolnshire, in 1716–17. The great Protestant preacher John Wesley was a youth at the time and most of the accounts were gathered by his elder brother Samuel Wesley from letters from their parents. They detail almost constant noises – groans, rappings, thumps and smashing glass – from unfindable sources, sometimes in the floor under their feet, followed by sightings of shadowy forms, vaguely human and animal.

In the end, we find that cases can be selected to support either position – hauntings that follow people or that persist at a particular location. Our closing examples are modern illustrations of each leading to a series that combine both aspects.

In 1964, in the Philippine town of Marilao, constant rains of stones fell in the presence of a 14-year-old boy, even while he was watched by suspicious locals, according to the account in the *Daily Mirror* (26 October 1964). When the family had had enough, the boy went to live with a civic leader, whose house now suffered the bombardments. The official said she could not blame the boy as he could be seen to be asleep during these attacks. Eventually the boy was transferred to a convent, which was pelted the day the boy moved in. The report ends with the priest saying the boy will be transferred to a special home.

Conversely, in a case investigated by psychical researcher Raymond Bayless at the California resort of Big Bear in late 1962, the poltergeist stayed put. At times, as many as thirty police officers patrolled the house and its environs, without a single clue as to the origin of the stones that came down around them. The phenomenon began that autumn when the Lowe family moved in and, within a short time, they were complaining to the sheriff about the peltings in which their children were bruised. Officers, neighbours and visitors spoke of stones "floating" down, yet on other occasions they dented the police cars. At times the intermittent missiles seemed to "follow" particular people. One witness told Bayless of watching closely as a stone fell, slowly, at an angle of 30° to the ground. When he picked up some stones, they felt hot. Around Halloween time, the Lowes fled and it was not long before the new residents were watching in amazement as rocks fell and floated down.

We close with a remarkable investigation by two Australian forteans – Tony Healy and Paul Cropper – into a series of connected cases which involve *both* haunted locations and haunted people. It raises the intriguing possibility that the chance meeting of the two potentialities – a troubled *focus* and a receptive *locus* – may trigger the phenomenon in one or the other, or in both.

In 1955, a stone-throwing poltergeist manifested itself at a farm at Mayanup. Cyril Penny, a young Aborigine farm worker, was one of many who went to see the phenomenon. Two years later, stones began raining around Cyril at Pumphrey in Western Australia. Conventionalists explained it away as due to "freak winds", but there seems to have been a lot more to it than that. Two witnesses swore that, while they were in a closed tent with the young man, stones fell at their feet. There had been no trickery, they said, and no holes in the tent (*Daily Express*, 22 March 1957). Fed up with the persecution at Pumphrey, Penny relocated to a new camp sixteen kilometres away, but stones fell on him there too, so he was advised by tribal elders to move out of the district entirely. That worked but, as the phenomenon died away at Pumphrey, it started up on the Dickson farm fourteen kilometres away.

Like Cyril Penny, Mr Dickson made the trip to Mayanup to gawp at the phantom stone-thrower and it seemed to have followed him home. The phenomenon concentrated on Dickson's son Harvey – just eleven at the time – but never hurt him. On one occasion a storm of stones raged around Harvey as he sat in his father's car with the windows up. According to Healy and Cropper, the phenomenon was not confined to stones: "Stones fell indoors and outdoors or rose from the ground to the roof. Shovels jumped and a four-gallon drum soared into the air, circling three times before landing. Visitors saw half-bricks, potatoes, bottles, stones, a spade and a broom fall out of thin air." The "Haunted Farm", as it is called, has ever since been visited by such disturbances.

7

The Haunted
Planet

7

The Haunted Planet

The Hollow Earth

The regions of the North and South Poles were unknown until modern times. They were regarded as inaccessible and mysterious. The traditional view of the Earth is that it revolves upon a polar axis, resulting in perforations at its northern and southern extremities. The waters of the planet circulate through these holes which provide entrances to an inner world, inhabited by monstrous creatures that from time to time appear on the Earth's surface. The Hollow Earth is also thought of as the location of paradise. Behind the ice of the North Pole lies a beautiful, warm country of gods and mythical heroes. It is the original Eden, the generation centre of the human race and the source of all culture. At certain spots on Earth, remote and well hidden, known only to shamans and initiates, natural rifts and tunnels give access to this underground realm. These beliefs, in one form or another, have lived on through history and still flourish among a variety of cults and UFO groups. Nazi revivalists and sinister occult types lurk among them, but the notion of another dimension to this planet, a world below the surface of everyday reality, is not confined to the dark side of the imagination. The Hollow Earth is a constant theme in romantic literature and an inspiration to famous writers, from George Sand, Edgar Allen Poe, Alexandre Dumas and Jules Verne, to Edgar Rice Burroughs and Philip K. Dick.

An early picture of the Hollow Earth is given in *Phaedo*, where Plato records the last words of Socrates at his execution in 399 BC. Before drinking the hemlock he spoke confidentially to his closest friends, telling them about the afterlife and the real nature of this Earth. It is, he said, a perfect and many-coloured sphere, perforated throughout by caves and channels and with a great chasm running through it. By these passages the rivers, winds and spirits of the Earth pass in constant circulation. We do not live upon the surface as we suppose, but on one of the upper levels where we do not see the full glory of the world.

Medieval geographers gave similar accounts, and so did the great Jesuit scholar Athanasius Kircher in the seventeenth century. Kircher's Earth foreshadowed the modern Gaia hypothesis, functioning like a living creature with its own digestive and other vital systems. It was riddled with caverns and deep tunnels and pierced by an axial passage between its Poles. The waters and oceans of the Earth gravitated towards the North Pole where they joined an immense whirlpool and were sucked into the hole. Inside the Earth they were heated and purified and helped in the process of generating metals, and then together with waste material they were expelled at the Earth's rear end through the hole at the South Pole. Without this constant circulation, reasoned Kircher, the oceans would become stagnant and poison everything on

Earth. He cited as analogy a newly discovered process, the circulation of the blood. Yet even Kircher, with his scientific mentality, could not give up the old belief that in the chasms and tunnels below the Earth lived giants, demons and monsters.

Creatures of the inner Earth, offspring of the Earth goddess, are recognized in myths and folklore everywhere. Typically they are gigantic and mis-shapen, like the primitive Greek gods, the Titans. Among them are dragons and other creatures that guard buried treasures; these are also guardians of the Earth's wisdom and are encountered by initiates into the Mysteries. Lesser sprites, gnomes, elves, kobolds and such, live in caves and tunnels nearer the surface, and they are the kind most often seen and heard. This is the underworld of elemental spirits and souls of the dead. It is a dread world, a source of madness and nightmares, but it is also a source of benefits – of healing, oracles and inspiration. By all accounts there was once considerable traffic between the lower world and the upper. The old Irish histories tell of a battle between the invading Milesians and a magically skilled native race, the Tuatha De Danaan, for possession of the country. Finally it was split between them, the victorious Milesians taking the upper half and banishing the older race to the country below the surface. There they merged with the fairies, and in that guise have been familiar apparitions to every Irish generation.

A suppressed archeological secret is the existence of vast, inexplicable tunnel systems beneath the surface of a great part of the Earth. All over Britain and Ireland are records, legends and relics of underground routes between the ancient and sacred places. Sabine Baring-Gould's *Cliff Castles and Cave Dwellings of Europe* (1911) has amazing records of the extensive cave and tunnel

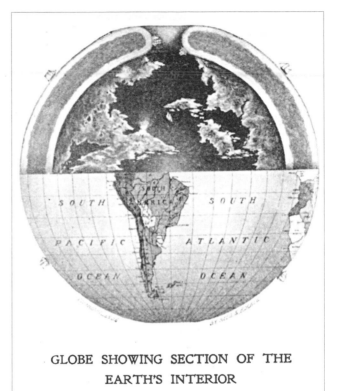

GLOBE SHOWING SECTION OF THE EARTH'S INTERIOR

The earth is hollow. The poles so long sought are but phantoms. There are openings at the northern and southern extremities. In the interior are vast continents, oceans, mountains and rivers. Vegetable and animal life are evident in this new world, and it is probably peopled by races yet unknown to the dwellers upon the earth's exterior.

THE AUTHOR.

A page from William Reed's *Phantom of the Poles* (1906).

structures beneath France and other countries. Like the tunnels much used during the Vietnam War, those of Europe were resorted to as refuges by the local people in troubled times. They also contained shrines where the underworld deities were invoked. In Harold Bayley's *Archaic England* (1919) there are reports from early travellers of great tunnels stretching under much of Africa, including one beneath a river called Kaoma, "so lengthy that it took the caravan from sunrise to noon to pass through". Other writers tell of a vast, "technologically impossible" network of mysterious tunnels in South America, running throughout the entire Andes range between ancient, forgotten stone cities.

In 1906 William Reed wrote *The Phantom of the Poles* in the hope of re-establishing the ancient theory of the Hollow Earth. "I claim", he began, "that the Earth is not only hollow, but that all, or nearly all, of the explorers have spent much of their time past the turning-point, and have had a look into the interior of the Earth." At each of the Poles, so Reed sought to prove, there is a large, round-lipped hole, into which all polar explorers inadvertently sail. Many of these, including Peary, Franklin, Nansen and Hall, penetrated quite deeply into the world of the interior, and Reed found much evidence in their writings to support his theory. Accounts of the atmosphere growing warmer as the Poles are approached, of

This satellite photograph of the North Pole seems to show a large, round entrance to the "inner Earth" – oft posited by UFO literature as evidence of the Hollow Earth. The official explanation is that the dark circle is an effect of the planet's tilt combined with the photomosaic technique used to create the image over a 24-hour period.

fertile Arctic territories abounding with animals, of floating timber and vegetation far from any known source; these he combined with noted instances of compass irregularities and displays of the Northern Lights (which he thought were reflections of light from within the Earth) to prove the existence of the inner world. Later writers have lent their enthusiasm to his cause. Much has been made of the strange aerial expedition made by US Admiral Richard E. Byrd to the Antarctic in 1956, during which it was announced on the radio (3 January 1956) that the party had penetrated to a land 2300 miles *beyond* the South Pole. Before his previous flight, in 1947, the Admiral told reporters: "I'd like to see that land beyond the Pole. That area beyond the Pole is the Centre of the Great Unknown." Speculative writers on the Hollow Earth have misinterpreted this remark by claiming that Byrd was referring to the North Pole. In fact, as made plain by the journalist Walter Sullivan, who accompanied Byrd in both his expeditions and described them in *Quest for a Continent* (1957), the Admiral's 1947 flights were in Antarctica.

The modern pioneer of the Hollow Earth theory was John Cleves Symmes (1779–1838) of New Jersey. His studious life was devoted to proving that the Earth and all heavenly bodies were made up of concentric shells with entrances at top and bottom. The doughnut-holes in the Earth were so large – 4000 miles across at the North Pole and 6000 miles at the south – that ships sailed into and out of them without noticing. Symmes was an energetic promoter of his own theory and attracted a popular following. Politicians were also persuaded that his ideas should be investigated. In a circular to rally support he summarized the matter:

"TO ALL THE WORLD! I declare the Earth is hollow, and habitable within; containing a number of solid concentrick spheres, one within the other, and that it is open at the poles 12 or 16 degrees; I pledge my life in support of this truth, and am ready to explore the hollow, if the world will support and aid me in the undertaking."

A full account of Symmes is in *Subterranean Worlds* (1989) by Walter Kafton-Minkel, a valuable compendium of Hollow Earth lore. Also valuable – uniquely so in much of its subject-matter – is Joscelyn Godwin's *Arktos: the Polar*

Subterranean kobolds excavating a fossil *Ichthyosaurus*. Engraving from Pouchet's *The Universe* (1870).

Myth in Science, Symbolism, and Nazi Survival (1992). Part of it describes the Pole-centred, Hollow Earth cosmologies that were popular in Nazi Germany and have since been developed by fantasists of the far right. Evolutionary orthodoxy has it that humankind first arose in Africa and spread northwards. Against that is the Nordic myth, that humanity and culture were generated at the centre of the Earth, in a land of paradise that lay (and perhaps still lies) behind the ice-barriers around the North Pole. From there it is but a short step to supposing that the first people on the Earth's surface came from inside it.

That step was taken by several of the writers mentioned in *Arktos*, and some of them have gone further by locating the last stronghold of "Nordic superiority" within the hollow at the South Pole. A much repeated story is that Hitler and certain henchmen escaped from Berlin in 1945 and were conveyed, either by a Nazi flying-saucer craft or by the U-boat that surrendered in South America long after the war was over, to a subterranean base in Antarctica. The most active promoter of this myth is a Canadian citizen of German extraction, Ernst Zündel, whose books, including *UFOs: Last Secrets of the Third Reich* and *Secret Nazi Polar Expeditions* (1979), serve the principal purpose of sensationalizing his neo-Nazi opinions.

Ray Palmer, editor of the American magazine *Flying Saucers*, was a keen promoter of the Hollow Earth theory, claiming that the interior is a more likely source of mysterious lights and UFOs than outer space. The idea also occurred to the pioneer ufologist Brinsley Le Poer Trench. In *Secret of the Ages: UFOs from Inside the Earth* (1974) he suggested that many of our phenomena come from within the Earth, and hinted at evidence that the intraterrestrials may already be plotting a military operation against our world of the surface.

There is much to enjoy in the Hollow Earth theory, but in this modern age of satellites etc it is difficult to take entirely seriously. Yet we do not underestimate the power of military secrecy, and there is no doubt that much was suppressed in the official reports of Admiral Byrd's strange flights. More seriously, there is an established connection between faults and rifts in the Earth's crust and apparitions of monsters, phantoms and mysterious lights. It is as if the underworld seeps out through the cracks. Loch Ness is on the geological crack across Scotland; and the Monster of Bolinas Swamp in California inhabits the fault line running north from San Francisco – the territory also of the hairy Bigfoot. Paul Devereux and others have pointed out the connection between UFO sightings and areas of geological faults. We find significance in this clustering of phantoms round clefts and caverns, traditional gates to the underworld. Perhaps they are indeed passing in and out. If we suppose, as many have before us, that there is life in a subterranean world which occasionally interpenetrates with our own, many of the strange phenomena in this book begin to seem more reasonable.

Phenomenal highways

We have written in this book of phantoms and fireballs, of mystery animals, strange lights, Black Dogs and fairies, all of them participants in the intermediate state of reality we call phenomenal. In terms of the hard reality recognized by science, their existence cannot be proved. It is evident only in its symptoms, and by analysing these symptoms we detect patterns. Haunted tracks for example; why are so many phenomena associated with certain spots and certain routes. Do the alternative realities of our records have an alternative highway system?

Reports of an elemental force that passes regularly on particular routes through the country, sometimes with destructive or ominous results, are universal. One version of it, widely known throughout Europe, is called the "Wild Hunt", the "Wild Troop" or the "Furious Army". It is rarely seen, and those who stand in its way are in danger of being killed or abducted to another world. Most terrifying is its noise, described as a rushing roar in which can be heard the neighing and pounding hooves of horses, human cries and hunting horns. The appearance of this ghostly troop is generally upon a certain day – often around Christmas or the New Year – and it follows the same lines across country, not always straight but often between ancient monuments and landmarks.

In some cases its passage is marked by bent or broken trees, and houses built in its path are destroyed. A well-recorded example is the Wild Troop of Rodenstein in Germany. This disagreeable force steers a straight course between the castles of Rodenstein and Schnellert, blasting all in its path. Up to the middle of the eighteenth century the local authorities recorded the dates of this phenomenon. Catherine Crowe's *The Night Side of Nature* (1848) states that, in about 1840, a traveller named Wirth inspected the local court records and found its last reported occurrence was in June 1764. However, it apparently went on long after the authorities had lost interest, for Wirth was shown recently ruined houses as evidence of the passage of the Wild Troop.

Sabine Baring-Gould described the Nordic Wild Hunt in *Iceland: Its Scenes and Sagas* (1863), and again in his *Book of Folk-Lore*. On the lonely wastes of Dartmoor, the sound of galloping horses, baying hounds and voices in the air were supposed to signify the Wild Huntsman, urging on his hounds in their hunt for human souls. The hunt is said to follow the prehistoric Abbot's Way and other ancient paths across the moor. The chronicler Gervase of Tilbury wrote that in the thirteenth century the Wild Hunt was frequently seen in the hills and forest lands of England. It was called the Harle-thing and its leader was King Herla, the German Erl-king. In Teutonic legends the leader of the Wild Hunt is the ancient pagan god Woden.

A rational explanation for this destructive

PAUL DEVEREUX/FORTEAN PICTURE LIBRARY

The alignments of churches, roads and other landscape features are known as leys. This ley runs for 3 miles NNW–SSE in the Cotswolds at Saintbury, Gloucestershire.

The Four Stones at Old Radnor, like many ancient stones, were said to be mobile, travelling to Hindwell Pool to drink. Several "leys" and legendary tracks converge on them.

and roaring force would be something meteorological like a whirlwind or electrical storm. But this does not explain its regular appearances on the same routes, and the strange stories that arise from it could hardly refer to a known, natural weather effect. Baring-Gould had another idea: that the mysterious noises from the sky are the cries of geese migrating southward by night at the approach of winter. This might explain the noise of the Wild Hunt, but not the damage and havoc it is said to cause.

Another kind of otherworldly force which is known to proceed along traditional paths between ancient sites is the fairy troop. W.Y. Evans-Wentz in *The Fairy Faith in Celtic Countries* (1911) writes about the haunted paths of Ireland and Brittany, which run in straight lines between the ancient hilltop forts inhabited by the "Little People" (see p.136). On certain days of the year people avoid these paths for fear of interrupting a fairy procession and, for the same reason, it is considered unwise to build houses on them. An Irish seer told Evans-Wentz that fairy paths are seasonal channels of terrestrial "magnetic" energy. No explanation is given for the visible part of the phenomenon, the fairies themselves.

Some incidents connected with fairy paths

are related by Dermot MacManus in his book of modern Irish fairy lore, *The Middle Kingdom* (1972). They warn against building houses on the traditional routes of fairy processions. Anyone who does so is likely to suffer regular disturbances, poltergeist effects, constant bad luck and, in extreme cases, the destruction of their property. In 1935, Michael O'Hagan inadvertently blocked a fairy path through building a westward extension to his house into an open field which lay in direct line between two ancient hillforts. O'Hagan's five children all fell ill and one almost died, to the bafflement of the local doctor. When a visit to a wise woman, versed in local mystical topography, revealed the problem, the new building was pulled down and the children straightaway recovered. MacManus gives other quite recent examples of Irish people being influenced in their choice of a building site by considerations of the fairies and their ways.

A similar elemental force, active at certain seasons and best avoided, is conventionalized in England in terms of BLACK DOGS (see p.322). Most books of local folklore refer to Black Dog tracks, which have the same mystical properties as our other examples. One of the best collections of Black Dog legends, Patricia Dale-Green's *Dog*

(1966), gives an account of a phantom creature rushing at midnight through a Devonshire village, along a road from the church, and demolishing a corner of the schoolhouse. Or rather, it seems to demolish it because, though falling masonry is heard, no actual damage is discovered. We have another reference to the phantom dog's habit of destroying buildings in its path, near Lyme Regis, Dorset, where it is said to have knocked down the corner of an inn called the Black Dog. This makes us wonder whether the inn was called after an existing phantom or the phantom was attracted by the name.

In Scotland, according to A.A. MacGregor's *Ghost Book* (1955), the phantom Black Dog is called *cu sith* and travels in straight lines along customary routes. The sight of it is ominous and often followed by death. A modern case illustrating this connection between phantoms, their tracks and hidden dangers is given by Ruth Tongue and Katherine Briggs in *Somerset Folklore* (1964). A straight track on the north Somerset coast is referred to as Death Mile because it is haunted by a Black Dog that is fatal to whoever sees it. In 1960, a man to whom it appeared died within a year, as did a young girl who saw it – though her companion, who did not, was unaffected.

Another reference to the dangers of spirit paths appears in the magazine *FATE* (October 1972) which quotes a first-hand account, originally published in Honolulu, by a native author, Napua Poire. One evening, as a little girl, she found herself alone on a spirit path in a forbidden part of the island. Standing rigid with terror, she heard the marching footsteps of an invisible procession drawing nearer and nearer. It was almost upon her when she felt a hand push her out of the way. Her parents later explained that she had been on a path reserved for the wandering spirits called the "night marchers", and it was the kindly shove of an ancestor spirit that had saved her from death.

A similar story is told by Sir Arthur Grimble in his book, *A Pattern of Islands* (1952). It also tells of spirit path in the Pacific, on one of the Gilbert Islands where Grimble was a colonial administrator. The ghosts of the dead, he was told, took this path on their way to a spot on the northernmost tip of the island, whence they proceeded to

the otherworld. Grimble investigated and, as he walked back to his village along the path, he met an old man who ignored him and did not even return his greeting. Back in the village when he described this person and asked who he was, he learnt that it was the spirit of a man who had died there that afternoon.

A modern writer who has made a special study of mystical pathways is Paul Devereux, one-time editor of *The Ley Hunter* magazine. In two of his books, *Symbolic Landscapes* (1992) and *Shamanism and the Mystery Lines* (1992), he summarizes the evidence of this phenomenon all over the world. In Germany they are called *Geisterwege* (spirit ways); in Holland *Doodwegen* or roads of the dead; while in England the name "Dod" or "Dodman" (dead man), attached to certain ancient paths, has a similar meaning. The formerly straight path, Dod Lane at Glastonbury,

Photograph from MacManus's *The Middle Kingdom* showing the cut-off corner of an Irish cottage which had been obstructing a "fairy path". With the corner's removal, the disturbances plaguing the cottage dwellers ceased.

lies on the extended axis of the old Abbey and was evidently regarded as a way by which the spirits of the dead entered the sanctuary. Strange events of many different kinds are associated with these lines – phantom animals, moving lights, ghosts, wild hunts, fairy processions and the flights of witches. In some cases these mysterious, haunted paths have an underground dimension, coinciding with actual or legendary tunnels. Devereux's suggestion is that the networks of straight lines, discovered across landscapes in all continents, are relics of tribal shamanism, laid out in connection with magical and out-of-the-body flight.

Leys – or "leylines" as they are now generally called – were first recognized in the British Isles by Alfred Watkins, a local businessman of Hereford. He observed that prehistoric monuments, traditional landmarks and churches built on sites of ancient sanctity were often arranged in a series of straight lines. Upon these lines or leys he found lesser, unrecorded relics of the past, such as mounds, markstones and stretches of local tracks, which in many cases ran between hilltop earthworks and "fairy forts". In his controversial classic *The Old Straight Track* (1925), Watkins suggested that leys were forgotten traders' routes, but he was also aware of their mystical character, their association with witches, phantoms and ancient religious practices. Later researchers have established that prehistoric sites were indeed laid out in straight lines, probably in connection with a ritualized form of astronomy which was itself connected with necromancy and the spirits of the dead.

There is something ominous about these lines and the natural or supernatural forces that use them. The *feng-shui* masters who designed the sacred landscape of old China were suspicious of unbroken lines of straight tracks and avenues, seeing them as pathways of a disruptive force called *sha*, which brought death or bad luck to anyone exposed to it. Similar misfortunes occur to people who see the Wild Hunt, obstruct fairy paths or interact with the forces that move along the mystical highway system. This is an area of experienced reality that modern science has hardly begun to recognize and investigate. This is not surprising, since everything known about the subject indicates that the phenomena behind it are spiritual forces, unbound by the laws of physics and therefore beyond the reach of the science that prevails today.

Invisible barriers

This section is about a phenomenon that is surprisingly common yet little studied – the occurrence of invisible barriers that unaccountably inhibit people, animals and even machines.

In the Old Testament story about Balaam and his ass, Balaam's instructions from God forbade him to take a certain way, which he immediately did. His ass shied away from the path but Balaam beat it back again. It repeated this behaviour and, finally, it lay down in the road and no amount of blows could persuade it to continue. The biblical explanation, put into the mouth of the ass, was that its refusal to move was caused by a vision of the Angel of the Lord standing in its path.

Frequently we read in accounts of fairy sightings that horses – with or without carriages – are unable to pass beyond a point in the road adjacent to where fairy music is heard or where fairies are seen at their revels. It is said that St Thomas Aquinas, who learned the art of making magical models from Albertus Magnus, was so disturbed in his studies by the clatter of horses outside his house that he made a brass horse and buried it in the street. Thereafter no horse could be made to travel that way, even when whipped.

Similar legends can also be found in a modern context. UFO reports often feature car engines that stall in the presence of a UFO or when a UFO directs a beam of light at the car. Witnesses also speak of radios failing and watches stopping.

A ghostly variation on this theme appears in *Weekend* (21 October 1970); several witnesses spoke of a phantom army which had been seen in November 1960 on a road near Otterburn, Northumberland, the site of a fourteenth-century battle. One of the witnesses, Mrs Dorothy Strong, was in a taxi. She said: "Suddenly the engine died, the fare-meter went haywire and the taxi felt as if it was being forced against an invisible wall. The soldiers seemed to close in on us then fade into thin air." Several people said it had happened around that location before.

Some believe that the interference is caused by mysterious "rays" and energy fields, similar to those beloved by early science fiction stories and movies. The subject of "secret rays" which could stop machines or cause "mysterious" accidents was enthusiastically discussed in the popular press of 1923–24 and Oliver Grindell-Matthews, the eccentric British genius, even claimed to have invented such a "projector" (*Daily Mail*, 5 April 1924). Another, long forgotten, manifestation was the incident in 1930 in which about forty cars stalled simultaneously on a road in Saxony. None of them was able to restart for about an hour (*The New York Times*, 25 October 1930). Later on, the idea of "death rays" and machine-stopping rays was revived in the classic rumours of World War II.

Today, we know that powerful magnetic pulses can be directed in such a way as to stop machines, even car engines, at some distance and these have been developed as military and police devices. But still there is a kind of fascination in recognizing that the "tractor beams" of *Star Trek* have their counterparts, if not roots, in the older traditions of fairy and ghost lore.

A similar effect to an "invisible ray" is the inhibiting magical spell which can be lifted only by the person who placed it – a power attributed to George Pickingill, said to be one of the last of the old "cunning men" of Essex who died in 1909. In Katherine Wiltshire's collection of tales from the living memory of her English county (*Ghosts and Legends of the Wiltshire Countryside*, 1973), a ninety-year-old shepherd tells of a carter who worked on the same farm as himself at Newton Tony. One day the man was driving a wagonload of wood and encountered a woman, known locally as a witch, who asked if he would carry her small bundle on his cart. He refused and tried to drive on, but the horses were unable to pull the wagon beyond that point, and he had no choice but to unhitch them and lead them home. The farmer returned with him the next morning, and again the wagon would not budge; it remained stuck until they consented to carry the woman's small bundle of wood.

In the 1820s, General Andrew Jackson (a future President of the USA) heard stories about the "Bell witch" – an active poltergeist at the Tennessee farm of John Bell – and went out of his

A lubin bewitches a Norman ploughboy. Lubins, like the English boggarts and fairies, could stop animals and carts.

way to investigate the matter. Approaching the farm, his horses halted as the wheels of his coach suddenly "froze". Jackson examined them himself and could see no reason why the pushing and pulling could not budge them. The exasperated members of his party were startled by a metallic voice ringing out in the air: "All right, General, let the wagon move."

Charles Bailey Bell, a descendant, wrote a history of the four-year "infestation", *The Bell Witch of Tennessee* (1934), which included another pertinent story. A family friend, William Porter, was sleeping in the Bell home when the "unmistakable" voice of the entity informed him it would sleep with him to keep him warm. Porter, a man not given to fear lightly, said the chilly sensation of something snake-like was "simply awful". The covers were pulled from him, forming into a roll on the other side of the bed. Porter seized the roll and carried it, struggling, towards the fireplace with the intention of throwing the "witch" into the fire. With every step the bundle seemed to get heavier and "smelled awful", he wrote later. "I had not got halfway across the room before the baggage got so heavy and became so offensive that I was compelled to drop it on the floor and rush outside."

Other accounts of invisible barriers come from fairy-lore, in particular the tradition of the "stray sod", a patch of soil on which fairies have placed a spell. Anyone who steps on this enchanted ground has great difficulty finding his way off it. Dermot MacManus devotes a chapter to it in his *The Middle Kingdom* (1973). In 1935, his aunt in Mayo hired a girl from a neighbouring village and sent her on an errand which meant passing Lis Ard, a beechwood-capped hill ringed by a famous fairy fort. As she was homesick and had time to spare, she climbed up the hill into the enclosed wood to gaze at her village from its summit. Then she walked back down the slope towards a gap in the bank. "She had just got to the opening when she felt a queer kind of jerk, a muscular jerk inside her rather than from outside, and before she realized what had happened she found herself walking quickly in exactly the opposite direction towards the centre of the wood again." The same thing happened when she tried the gap a second time. She then made for the point at which she had entered, "but now she received her greatest shock, for she felt an invisible wall which she could not pass". She was

George Pickingill (d.1909), the last witch of Canewdon, Essex, was said to be able to stop farm machinery with a glance, and was feared throughout the Rochford Hundred.

trapped for hours behind this magic wall, which felt so solid that she could follow it round with her hands. Meanwhile her absence had been a matter of concern; evening passed into night, and four search parties set out. The girl later said that one party had passed within twenty yards of her, but they could neither see her nor hear her frantic yells for help, although she could see and hear them well enough. Some time later she became aware that the barrier had gone and was able to set off home, frightened and exhausted.

There are many "haunted" locations, popularly believed to be the centre of strange forces or gateways to other worlds. Typical are those where gravity is said to be out of kilter, making cars or other objects roll backwards "uphill". Often they are not geomagnetic anomalies at all but odd optical illusions created by the lack of familiar indicators of the horizontal or vertical. Of this type is the famous "mystery vortex" near Gold Hill in Oregon. Now developed as a tourist attraction, its claimed characteristics include plumb bobs being "pulled" towards the centre where cigarette smoke forms strange eddies and the light is oddly dimmer. (A sceptical account is in Jim Brandon's *Weird America*, 1978.)

There are indeed places with geomagnetic anomalies which can affect the navigation of ships and planes as well as that on dry land. Remember the "Bermuda Triangle" – which, as Janet and Colin Bord point out "is neither a triangle nor centred on Bermuda" – where some tragic losses have been attributed to strange interference with navigation and radio equipment. Although Lawrence Kusche, in *The Bermuda Triangle Mystery, Solved* (1975), makes a diligent attempt to attribute fifty-one disappearances to misreporting (some ships never did "vanish"), lies, mistakes and natural disasters (hurricanes, etc), there are occasions when things go wrong with instruments inexplicably, such as during Sun spot activity. The Bords tell of a flight over the English Channel in 1978 that experienced a sudden and sustained change of 100° in the direction indicator and compass, twenty-five miles south of Bournemouth. On the return journey, the deviation over the same location was 20°. In both cases the new course would have taken them over Portland, Dorset. "Was something secret being tested at Portland Navy Base," the Bords ask, "some sort of weapon which might affect the magnetic field?"

We have heard of local legends of cars being forced to turn dangerously or being unable to turn as though ghostly hands had seized the steering wheel. A series of "attacks on automobiles" of this sort was noted by Fort in April–May 1927, in which cars were forced off roads into ditches, rivers and lakes. In one incident the driver described how he tried to keep the car to the right as it was being forced mysteriously to the left. Could something similar have happened to Mrs Celina Legris in Sunbury, Ontario, who was found guilty of driving negligently and causing a death when her car hit another? According to the *Recorder and Times* (24 January 1969) her defence was that "some unseen force seemed to pick my car up and violently throw it into the wrong lane just before the head-on collision". Whatever the truth of her claim, the court did not believe her.

Again, an invisible force in a car park at Durham, England, frustrated Mrs Dilys Cant's repeated attempts to back her car into a vacant space. In the *Newcastle Journal* (8 December 1975), she said that it felt as if she were always coming up against a kerb, though no obstacle was visible. Her daughter was also prevented from entering the space by "an invisible force field". Two other motorists tried to drive and then to push their cars into the space, but were unable to do so. Typically, by the time officials of the council investigated, the "haunted" bay had reverted to normality.

Our final account returns the subject once more to the realm of poltergeists, whatever they are. According to the *Daily Mail* (1 May 1907), an elderly woman in Paris complained to a magistrate that "something" compelled her to walk on her hands every time she went through the door of her apartment. The magistrate detained her, thinking she was mad, and sent an officer to investigate. He returned with the woman's son, who told the court: "I do not pretend to explain it. I only know that when my mother, my uncle and myself enter the flat, we are immediately impelled to walk on our hands." The uncle was sent for, and he too confirmed the story. Finally the magistrate summoned the concierge of the building, who said: "All you have heard is true. I thought my tenants had gone mad, but as soon as I entered the rooms occupied by them, I found myself on all fours, endeavouring to throw my feet in the air." The magistrate ordered the rooms to be disinfected!

Anomalous fossils

The geological record, as Charles Fort pointed out, is a prime example of circular reasoning in science; fossils being dated from their surrounding strata, and the strata from the fossils found in them. The matter is not helped by the bitter controversies of recent years over the anomalies and errors in such scientifically respected dating techniques as the carbon-14 and thermoluminescence tests. This lack of precision in archeological dating is emphasized by science-writer Richard Milton in his book *The Facts of Life: Shattering the Myth of Darwinism* (1992).

Yet despite the impossibility of any really positive proof, academic orthodoxy firmly upholds the cosmogonic myth that we have ascended to our present enlightened, civilized state through uninterrupted development from savage, superstitious beasts, our ancestors. This view is in opposition to the older and universal theory of human history as a decline from the primeval "Golden Age" and discounts the Platonic belief that civilizations rise and fall in cycles with intervening cataclysms.

What interests us here is the evidence of a human presence and technology on this Earth long before the evolutionists would have us believe it was possible. Some items of this evidence have been actively suppressed and deliberately ignored; some have quietly and mysteriously disappeared from museum stores and records; some are probably on display somewhere dismissively labelled as a "Ritual Objects".

We are referring to, among other things, apparently human footprints in sandstone laid down in the Carboniferous period, between 225 and 280 million years ago. That is about 200 to 250 million years before our ape ancestors split from the mainstream of monkey evolution. The *American Journal of Science* (vol.3, p.139) details the discovery of a series of human footprints found in sandstone near Carson, Nevada, in 1882. Three years later, tracks, easily identified as human, were found in sandstone near Berea, Kentucky, according to the *American Antiquarian*

(vol.7, p.9). There are other discoveries, any one of which, if accepted, could collapse the geological order of the ages overnight, bringing with it the whole Darwinian edifice.

In recent years there has been an explosion of books that exploit heretical ideas about evolution and anomalous fossils. Significantly, some of these are vehicles for the "Creationist" view that the world was created relatively recently – anywhere between 10,000–4000 years BC. As this does not leave much time for geological and evolutionary processes, Creationists argue that the current scientific interpretations are simply wrong.

The main opposing strand of active anomaly research states that the Earth is immeasurably more ancient than geologists or Creationists will credit. In *Forbidden Archeology* (1993) Michael Cremo and Richard Thompson sifted through much of the evidence for anomalous and "out-of-date" fossils.

Since the 1980s, hundreds of enigmatic metal spheres have been found in mines in western Transvaal, South Africa, extracted from Precambrian strata dating back 2.8 million years – a time when mankind's ape-like ancestors were barely mastering fire. Looking like modern cricket balls complete with "seams" (three parallel encircling grooves) they are exceedingly hard and do not seem to be natural formations.

Most academics regard such material with undisguised hostility, and in some instances the authors were actively hindered from gaining access to museum specimens and reports. This reaction was fuelled by the fact that, in casting about for a view of human origins that would accommodate artefacts apparently a million years old or older, Cremo and Thompson had to turn to the Hindu-Vedic cosmology. It was here that they found the suggestion that technological and other civilizations have risen and destroyed themselves or been destroyed many times over.

Yet another strand of interpretation holds that fossil footprints and artefacts derive from visits to this planet by aliens far in the formative past. The popular writings of Graham Hancock have developed the thesis that we were visited in this way in 10,500 BC, a magic date when, it is argued, most of the formative early civilizations appeared to gain major advances in architecture, astronomy, agriculture and mathematics.

Many of these fossil tracks, while distinctly human in appearance, are giant in size. According to a US Department of the Interior booklet, *The Story of the Great White Sands*, a government trapper, in 1932, found a line of thirteen prints in the gypsum rock of White Sands, New Mexico. They were about twenty-two inches long by eight to ten inches wide. In 1896, the *American Anthropologist* described some fourteen-inch human prints found in West Virginia. Brad Steiger gives other examples in his *Mysteries of Time and Space* (1974), including what appears to be a fossil imprint of a shoe, showing a well-cut and double-stitched leather sole, found in 1927 at Fisher Canyon, Nevada. The rock was identified by a geologist as Triassic limestone (laid down 160 to 195 million years ago). This sort of data has been eagerly collected by "Bible scientists", and two groups, the Films for Christ Association and the *Bible Science Newsletter*, have attempted to retrieve a set of prints from the bed of the Paluxy River in Texas. They are in Palaeozoic strata and show the tracks of a human being and a three-toed dinosaur crossing each other, one of the human prints squashing the edge of a dinosaur print. Indeed the large size of some of the fossil tracks, and their shape, seem very similar to the prints associated with our modern mystery anthropoid monsters (see IN SEARCH OF APE-MEN, p.334).

While critics try to dismiss these anomalies as "artefacts of erosion and weathering", it is

A photograph of a coin, dated to 1397, found embedded in Carboniferous coal, from the *Strand Magazine* (1901).

rather more difficult to explain away objects. *The Times* (24 December 1851) tells of a miner returning from California with a block of auriferous quartz which he accidentally dropped. It split open to reveal a straight-cut iron nail, firmly embedded near its centre. According to a note in the *Report of the British Association* (1845), Sir David Brewster once announced to a meeting the finding of a two-inch nail half-embedded in a lump of solid limestone from a Scottish quarry. A report of a gold thread found in a stone in Berwickshire appeared in *The Times* (22 June 1844). A lady cracking lumps of coal to fill her scuttle, says the *Morrisonville Times*, of Illinois, 11 June 1891, was surprised to find two halves of one lump linked by a small chain, the ends of which were still embedded solidly in the coal which bore a clear imprint of chain. The *Scientific American* (5 June 1852) contained a plea for help in solving a puzzle. Quarrymen blasting out fifteen feet of puddingstone on Meeting House Hill, Dorchester, Massachusetts, had found in the rubble the two halves of a metallic bell-shaped vessel. It is described as about four and a half inches high, made of some alloy and inlaid with silver in an intricate floral design. The quarrymen were in no doubt that it had come from deep within the rock. The best the editor of *Scientific American* could come up with was to suggest that it might have been made by "Tubal Cain, the first

In February 1961, gem-hunters in the mountains near Olancha, California, found an odd-looking "geode" encrusted with shells. When cut open it appeared that the saw had sliced across a solid cylinder of porcelain with a thick metal "wire" down its centre. It also seemed to have other magnetic and non-magnetic metal parts and what looked like a sheath of decomposed copper around the porcelain cylinder. They also found the impression of a hexagonal "nut" in the material that encased the object – material that seemed to date back 500,000 years. The mystery object soon attracted the attention of Creationists, one of whom brought it to the attention of the brothers Paul and Ron Willis,

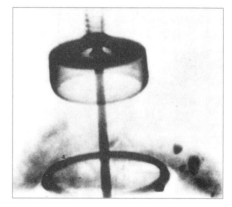

founders of the International Fortean Organization. After studying these X-ray images, Paul Willis speculated – in *INFO Journal* 4 (1969) – that the dark parts looked remarkably like an old, heavily corroded spark plug. To the Creationists, this was proof of their belief that the sedimentary layers of rock were laid down relatively recently. More recent research has established that the "Coso object" (as it has come to be known) was indeed the remains of a heavily corroded 1920s spark plug ... but how it came to be encased in rocky material in which shells were embedded, and found several thousand feet above sea level, remains a mystery.

inhabitant of Dorchester". In his *Secret Treasure* (1931) A. Hyatt Verrill gives two incidents where coins have been found inside masses of flint, one in Chute Forest near Stonehenge, and the other in a gravel pit at Westerham in Kent.

Between 1786 and 1788, coins, tools, stumps of columns and other worked stones were found in a quarry in Aix-en-Provence, France, fifty feet down and below eleven beds of compact limestone. An anonymous writer in the *American Journal of Science* (vol.1, p.144) quotes from the *Mineralogy* of Count Bourbon the details of this astonishing find. Among these artefacts from another age was a wooden board, one inch thick and about eight feet long, now turned into a "very fine and agreeably coloured agate". The Count noticed with astonishment that the utensils, board and stoneworkings followed the same pattern used by his men (even the board was worn in the same manner, being rounded and wavy at the edges). An ancient and a modern technology had duplicated each other on the same site; predictable,

perhaps, and yet, as the Count remarks, one of them "preceded the formation of this stone".

There are several different theories to account for artefacts which have been found out of their proper time or place. Quite possibly there have been civilizations in the remote, unknown past, but to postulate technological civilizations hundreds of millions of years back in time on the basis of a single nail, thread or pot is as irrational as, say, Sir Richard Owen inventing the absurdly crosslegged *Labyrinthodon* to explain fossil tracks which had "thumbs" pointing outwards! We would need much more evidence – even if we widened our acceptances to imagine the hypothetical civilization to be non-human (eg reptilian). Another idea arises out of Fort's speculations on falls and missiles from above, and on the mysterious force of teleportation, which transports objects through solid matter. Perhaps the same forces might transport occasional objects back in time to when the sedimentary strata were laid down.

We have another idea, equally preposterous

This photograph, from September 1993, shows Turkish workers uncovering the remains of a German U-boat – identified as UB-46 – that was discovered entombed in a mine, near the village of Akpinar, on the Black Sea coast. The idea of ships being found in mines seems the very opposite of the Ark story (see ARKEOLOGY, overleaf) that we had to include it here. In this case, the submarine had to be excavated from a solid dry-sand wall between the open-cast mine and the sea. It had been scuppered by exploding its torpedoes and there was no clue as to how it got there. It is not the first time such a story has surfaced. There is an often-cited case from 1460, where metal miners in the region of Berne, Switzerland, came across the remains of a ship, complete with complement of fossilised sailors. Diligent research by German fortean Ulrich Magin unearthed as much as could be found about it, but it faded away into vagaries of medieval natural philosophy, which interpreted almost anything as evidence of Noah's Flood and its survivors, conflating it with other stories of glacier-like preserved miners or mountaineers, and the remains of even earlier attempts at mining. It is possible that somewhere in there, too, are confused recollections of ancient ship burials and even the long-lost Ark itself.

and therefore no less worthy of consideration – the spontaneous generation of these anomalous buried objects *in situ*, within the womb of the Earth. Consider our section TOAD IN THE HOLE (see p.395), in which we examine the phenomenon of living animals found inside rocks. Can one seriously imagine that these animals appeared on Earth before their due time to become encased in mud and compressed into rock and to survive across millions of years against all biological reason? Is this any less incredible than spontaneous creation or teleportation? The medieval naturalists often debated whether there was a "shaping force" (*vis plastica*) that formed fossils in the earth. Some thought it a divine trick to test men's faith. But the basic nature of fossils has been well known since the Greek philosophers, so that Michael Valentini's belief that stones copulated and bore young in the earth was to his eighteenth-century colleagues deplorable backsliding. Nevertheless the *vis plastica* theory has had strong adherents including Kepler, Avicenna and Aris-

totle, and though regularly refuted it persists in dreams and popular traditions, as in the dream-theme of finding coins or other "lucky" objects in unexpected, hidden places.

In the book that he wrote with physicist Wolfgang Pauli, *Synchronicity* (1955), Carl Jung suggested that Kepler's notion of an Earth-soul, an *anima telluris*, was the forerunner of his own theory of synchronicity. The forces which harmonize the myriad independent yet interrelated systems of life and matter on the living planet are essentially the same as those which order the contents of the mind. The mind and the Earth are wombs in which things are brought into being. Among the dreams, which Jung uses to illustrate how these two great spheres of existence interpenetrate, is one in which the dreamer finds human heads in low relief on slabs lodged in Triassic rock. In another dream, an earth-coloured gnome leads the dreamer into a deep cave where he finds columns of hard "lignite", shaped into life-like human busts. They extend far back into the living rock "and must therefore have come into existence without the aid of man". If some synchronistic process can so unite mind and matter as to impress visible images onto a film or body

(see PROJECTED THOUGHT-FORMS, p.84), perhaps there is an analogous force which projects forms into the Earth.

Arkeology

We would not like to say that anything is impossible, but few things seem to us less likely than that Noah's Ark should still be where the Flood left it on Mount Ararat. We were taught at school that the Old Testament story was a myth or allegory, and at the time we believed it. After all, the legend of a great flood that destroyed all but one family is a universal one – from Mexico to Mesopotamia – and Ararat is not the only mountain reputed to be the Ark's last resting place. Mount Nisir in Mesopotamia is named in the early Babylonian account, and Al Cudi (also known as Mount Judi) two hundred miles to the south of Ararat is mentioned in the Koran and favoured by the Syrians and other Muslims. There could of course have been many floods and many arks.

In 1829 Dr Johann Jacob Parrot, professor of natural history at the University of Dorpat, was the first European to climb Mount Ararat. Though not looking for the Ark, he was shown alleged relics of it in a monastery that was destroyed by seismic activity just eleven years later. Parrot has his place in the history of arkeology for breaking an ancient taboo that prevented the local inhabitants taking foreigners up the mountain.

In 1876, Viscount Bryce discovered on a rocky ledge some 13,000 feet up the slopes of Ararat a piece of shaped wood about four feet long, possibly gopher wood. Supposing it might be a spar from the Ark, Bryce cut off a small piece as a souvenir.

Archdeacon Nouri, a dignitary of the Chaldaean Church, conducted three searches for the Ark between 1887 and 1892. On 25 April 1892, he approached the summit of Ararat and there it was! *The English Mechanic* (14 October 1892) described his feelings, as with five or six companions he contemplated from various angles the great wooden vessel. He wrote: "I was almost overcome. The sight of the ark, thus verifying the truth of the Scriptures, in which I had before had

no doubt, but which, for the sake of those who do not believe, I was glad, filled me with gratitude". The Turkish government refused him permission to ship the Ark to the World's Fair in Chicago (if he found it). Nouri was later incarcerated in a mental institution.

Sightings of the Ark had been made centuries before the claims of Bryce and Nouri. As early as 275 BC, a Babylonian historian called Berosus, whose record was preserved by later Greek writers, stated that an ark was still to be seen in the Kurdish mountains of Armenia, and "the people scrape off the bitumen, and carry it away, and make use of it". The Jewish historian Josephus also refers to pilgrimages to Ararat around 50 BC.

In the cathedral of the monastery at Echmiadzin, near the foot of Ararat, is a small fragment of wood, the relic of an earlier archeological expedition by a monk of the time of St Gregory the Enlightener (credited with bringing Christianity to Armenia in the fourth century). He is said to have made several attempts to climb the mountain but each time, after ascending a little way, he fell into a deep sleep and found himself teleported back to the monastery. Finally he was told in a vision that the summit of Ararat, where the Ark lay, was forbidden territory, but that as a reward for his persistence he would be given a piece of its timbers. The piece, duly received, became the monastery's greatest treasure. At the time of the monk's expedition the survival of the Ark was a well-established tradition. These could have been the relics shown to Parrot in 1829.

Since the invention of the airplane the number of Ark sightings and explorations of Greater Ararat has increased. In 1916, a Russian pilot, V. Roskovitsky, reported a large vessel lying on the upper slopes of Ararat. Tzar Nicholas II dispatched an expedition, and the object was found and identified as the Ark. Unfortunately the report was lost during the Russian Revolution the following year. These things tend to happen in arkeology. An article in the US magazine *Christian Herald*

(August 1975), tells of an Armenian immigrant and a lost newspaper cutting. The Armenian, who died in America in 1920, told people that in 1856, when he was a young man living near Ararat, "three foreign atheists" had hired him and his father to guide them up the mountain on an anti-arkeological expedition to disprove the Ark's existence. To their fury they found it. They tried in vain to destroy it but it was too large, so they made their guides join them in an oath to say no more of the matter. The lost newspaper item (which several people claim to have seen but no one has yet produced) reported the death-bed confession of a British scientist confirming the Armenian's story.

Another unlucky piece of evidence was the

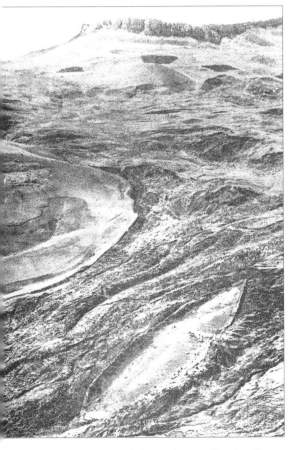

A photograph of Mount Ararat, showing the "outline of the Ark", was printed in the *Daily Telegraph*, 13 September 1965. The shape was later thought to be a natural occurrence, possibly a fossilized mudflow.

six large, clear photographs taken in the summer of 1953 from a helicopter less than a hundred feet above Mount Ararat by an American oil worker, George Jefferson Greene. They showed the apparent outline of the Ark half buried in rocks and ice on the edge of a cliff. Greene tried without success to raise an expedition and, since his death in 1962, the photographs have vanished.

For the last half century the Ararat region (where Armenia joins Turkey, Iran and Azerbaijan) has been under strict military control, and both expeditions and overflights have been extremely difficult. Nevertheless, the period between the end of World War II and 1974 was the great age of arkeology. In the summer of 1949 two parties set off to find the Ark. One led by Dr A.J. Smith, a retired missionary of North Carolina, who raised funds by convincing investors that he had had a divine revelation of its location (*Le Monde*, 24 September 1949). Smith failed in the shadow of a rival Turkish expedition, whose colourful account appeared in *France-Soir* (31 August 1949). "We have seen Noah's Ark," they cabled, "but not on Mount Ararat." The find had been made on Mount Judi in southern Armenia, which is believed by the Kurds and others to be the true resting place of the Ark. It was described as an impressive craft – 500 feet long, 80 feet wide and 50 feet high – together with some bones of marine animals and, not far away, Noah's burial place. The explorers, two Turkish journalists, also mentioned the local legend that the Ark sometimes appears like a ghost ship beneath a covering of mud. It is not clear from the account whether it was the actual Ark that was spotted or its phantom apparition.

Many arkeological expeditions have used the Kurdish border town of Dogubayazit, beneath Ararat, as a base. Farhettin Kolan, proprietor of the hotel in the town, acted as a mountain guide for the great Riquer expedition of 1952, the successful Navarra attempt of 1955 and the seven unsuccessful ones by John Libi up to 1969. Libi, a San Franciscan who claimed to have seen the exact site of the Ark in a dream, retired frustrated at the age of seventy-three after an adventurous archeological career which included the experience of being chased by a stone-throwing bear – a phenomenon unique in our records. Another familiar face on the Ararat scene was Eryl Cummings, "the grand old man of arkeology", who made thirty-one ascents, beginning in 1961.

Noah's ark perched on Mount Ararat as imagined by Hieronymous Bosch (c.1485).

samples becoming contaminated with extraneous carbon-14 and produced the more biblical date of about 3000 BC.

Such breakthroughs have now become regular events in arkeology, each new discovery upstaging the last. Mr George Vandeman, a director of the Archeological Research Foundation of New York, was reported, in *Antiquity* (1965), as stating that worked wood recovered by an Anglo-American expedition to Ararat was part of a large boat and hundreds more tons of the same timber still lay buried under the ice. Apparently, it was so hard that electric saws had been broken trying to cut it. Mr Vandeman estimated the size of the boat to be about two-thirds that of the *Queen Mary*, similar to the size of Noah's Ark as given in the Bible. In the summer of 1974, just before the Turks closed the area, there were no less than eight Ark-hunting expeditions in the field.

Then we have the excellent satellite photographs, one of which prompted Senator Frank Moss of the US Senate Space Committee to comment: "It's about the right size and shape for the Ark." However, it is not on Ararat but near Tendurik, fifteen miles to the south and closer to Mount Judi and the Iranian border. David Fassold, one of the last Americans granted an excavation permit for the vicinity of Ararat, made nine trips to the Tendurik site between 1960 and 1994, and in the end was forced to accept that it was a petrified mudflow.

In the last decade, we have seen the application of satellite imaging and digital enhancement techniques to photography of the Ahora Gorge, one of the locations favoured by Californian film-maker Robin Simmons. Simmons, who grew up in the company of Ark-hunters, joined several expeditions and has spoken with many people who claim to have seen the Ark. One of his informants was Ed Davis, who was taken by a guide on a secret route up the mountain in July 1943, stopping on the way to see relics preserved in a cave by locals. After several days more climbing, the guide pointed into a crevasse, partly obscured by mist. "Then I saw it," says Davis. "A huge rectangular, man-made structure, partly covered by ice and rock,

The most successful arkeologist of his time was Fernand Navarra, whose record was published in French in 1956 and in English in 1974 under the title, *Noah's Ark: I Touched It!* From beneath a glacier and a frozen lake high on Ararat, Navarra excavated a number of planks and a hewn L-shaped beam. In 1969 he guided a party mounted by an American organization, Search, which discovered more such timbers and brought back samples. Experts using radiocarbon dating declared them to be some 1400 years old, though other experts at laboratories in Bordeaux and Madrid thought this result was due to the lying on its side. At least one hundred feet were clearly visible. I could even see inside it, into the end where its broken off timbers stuck out." His guides told Davis that the Ark had broken into three or four pieces, and that in it were forty-eight rooms and animal cages both large and small. They planned to climb down to it the next day but had to cancel because of bad weather.

Inspired by such stories, Simmons attempted his own search in the mid-1990s. One of his guides, climbing alone, radioed back excitedly that he had photographed an object about a quarter of a mile away, "a dark area in the ice, like a barn". Simmons had the film enhanced using specialized satellite imaging software and studied by an aerial reconnaissance expert. Months later, on another visit, flying close to the Ahora Gorge, Simmons believed he saw dark shapes resembling Ed Davis's description of the Ark broken into several parts on the sheer glacier.

Over many years of collecting accounts and stories about the Ark on Ararat, Simmons is convinced that not all has been revealed and that the "truth" is considerably stranger than imagined. Much of his research contains elements that would not be out of place in a typical crashed UFO scenario, complete with recovered bodies and suggestions of high-level conspiracy. For example, he was told by a "protected" source that an espionage team, returning across Ararat in secret in 1974, fell into a structure they took to be an ancient Byzantine shrine. When it was realized what this might be, a classified report went "all the way to the White House".

This strange twist to the story has seemingly been corroborated by other accounts. A pilot, flying secret missions that took him over Ararat many times in the first half of 1960, said that he regularly saw and photographed a huge rectangular object protruding from the ice at an altitude of around fifteen thousand feet. Stranger still is the tale of David Duckworth, a young volunteer worker at the Smithsonian Institution in Washington DC, who stumbled upon a secret shipment of artefacts from Turkey including a sarcophagus containing a body. There the curtain of silence falls as Duckworth was apparently ordered to keep quiet by two FBI agents.

Why the secrecy and conspiracy? Simmons's theory is that the US military, in a case of classic Cold War paranoia, believes that public confirmation of the Ark's existence would incite Islamic Fundamentalism on a global scale. He was told by an Islamic scholar at the University of Erzurum that "the Ark is a bomb in the world", referring to a belief that its reappearance would herald the return of Mohammed to purge the Earth of heretics and unbelievers.

Judging by its post-diluvian history, Noah's Ark has an existence like that of the Loch Ness Monster or the Abominable Snowman – phenomenal rather than physical. As is usual with such things, there are legends, sightings and ambiguous relics and photographs, all of which fall short of scientific proof. Yet people continue to dream of Noah's Ark and some go in search of it, and it responds with dreamlike evidence of itself, which never quite achieves hard reality.

Crop circles

From the early years of the post-World War II UFO phenomenon, there were occasional reports of alleged landing sites – areas of crushed vegetation, sometimes in association with unidentified lights or objects. The most famous of these sites, called "saucer nests", were in Australia, and ufologists saw a continuation of these when, in about 1980, an apparently similar phenomenon began to be noticed by farmers in southern England. Circles were appearing in their fields of wheat and barley. These were not disorderly messes, as might be caused by something landing, but regular, neatly swirled circles of laid-down crops, still growing and virtually undamaged.

The ufologists were not alone in their investigations. Among the first in the field were a pair of Hampshire technologists, Pat Delgado and Colin Andrews, forming the nub of a circle-spotting group which included veteran ufologist Don Tuersley and a local pilot, "Busty" Taylor. Also in this group, though following his own line of research, was Dr Terence Meaden, a Wiltshire meteorologist. Together and separately they visited and recorded hundreds of crop circles during the following summers.

Sometimes, instead of simple circles, they would discover square formations or rings and other features. Delgado and Andrews were conscious of a spooky effect and saw the circles as the workings of an "unknown intelligence". But Meaden stuck with science. "Stationary whirlwinds" was his first explanation and this was elaborated into a theory of "electrically-active plasma vortices", unrecognized by modern science. These vortices, thought Meaden, had been known in the past; the ancient British had venerated them and temples, such as Stonehenge, were built on the sites of prehistoric crop circles.

By the end of the 1980s, crop circles had become a full-blown mystery, sensationalized by newspapers and television and provoking all kinds of ingenious theories. Supporters of whirlwinds argued with extraterrestrialists, and cases were made for fungi, fertilizer, rutting deer, hedgehogs, hippies, helicopters and hoaxers. Decoders joined in, identifying the crop markings as symbols in ancient scripts – Sumerian, Phoenician, Tifinag and the Hopi Indian language were among those claimed – producing messages of hope or doom. In 1990, the Koestler Foundation, promoters of paranormal research, offered £5000 for a definitive solution to the circle mystery and the *Sunday Mirror* made its own headlines by adding a further £10,000 to the prize.

1990 was a golden year for crop circles. There had been a spate of books on the subject, one of which – the beautifully illustrated *Circular Evidence* by Pat Delgado and Colin Andrews – became a bestseller. Mystery-seekers from all over the world headed for Wiltshire, the acknowledged centre of the phenomenon. Among the visitors was a well-equipped team of Japanese scientists, invited by Meaden to record the circle-making effect in action and to discover the nature of the energy behind it. Expectations were high and the circles phenomenon lived up to them.

The season began with a series of new crop formations, quite different from any in previous years. Researchers called them pictograms. They were elaborate compositions, up to 150 yards long, featuring not just circles but rings, rectangles and strange shapes that looked like protruding claws. The sensation of the year came on 12 July, when a huge pictogram appeared overnight in a field at Alton Barnes, near Pewsey, a place now famous for circles and a rallying-point for their investigators. Other formations followed, not only in Wiltshire and neighbouring counties but in the north of England, East Anglia, Kent, Sussex, Cornwall and elsewhere. Circles were also recorded appearing in America and Canada, on the Continent, in eastern Europe, Japan and Australia. It was an epidemic and a very exciting one.

Yet, behind the euphoria, some of the older researchers felt twinges of unease. Near the end of the 1990 season, there was a nasty incident in which prominent circle experts were publicly humiliated by an unknown team of hoaxers. "Operation Blackbird", sponsored by British and

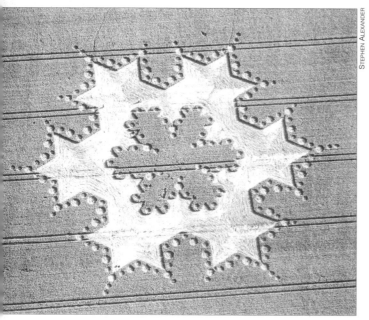

STEPHEN ALEXANDER

A masterpiece of the 1997 season appeared on 8 August in a wheat field near Alton Barnes, Wiltshire – a well-known centre of crop circle activity. Measuring 234 feet across, its "fractal snowflake" outline was fringed with 192 small circles, 150 outside and 42 within. The central area of wheat was untrodden, raising the problem of how this geometric design could have been constructed. In this and a neighbouring formation, the crop had been laid down in a way that suggested wave action rather than physical labour.

Geometric spirals featured in many crop formations during the 1990s. A particularly subtle design from 1999 was this 100m wide example in a wheat field not far from Avebury in Wiltshire.

Japanese television, assisted by the Army and staffed by leading researchers including Andrews and Delgado, was mounted on a Wiltshire hillside with surveillance equipment, hoping to record the formation of a crop circle. Six circles duly appeared in a field below and BBC listeners were told to stand by for sensational news. But when the researchers entered the circles they were dismayed to find objects in the centre of each circle, deliberately left there to prove trickery. George Wingfield, describing the event in the *Cerealogist*, the independent journal and forum for crop circle studies, edited at the time by John Michell, claimed that the hoax was a disinformation exercise by a government agency aimed at discrediting the circles phenomenon. The incident was particularly disturbing because the experts and authors of crop circle books had always insisted that the circles could not possibly be manmade.

The least popular explanation for crop circles was that they had been hoaxes. According to the experts, the plants in circles were not trampled but laid down organically by some unknown natural force. Sometimes the stalks were woven together in a skilful way that seemed beyond human art. Delgado, Meaden and most of the leading researchers had taken up dowsing and the movements of their rods told them that powerful energy fields were active within the circles. These were thought responsible for the strange experiences of circle visitors, including luminous visions and incidents of healing. Yet as the circle forms grew more elaborate, it became ever more obvious that they were not just chance products of natural forces but intelligently designed. Solly Zuckerman, former British government adviser on science, argued that, since we are the only known intelligent beings, the circles must be human artefacts. The phenomenon, he added, is still a mystery. Who is making the circles, how are they doing it and what is their motive?

The crop circles of 1991 were hailed as even better than those of the previous year. Among them was a huge, faultless "Mandlebrot Set", a fractal design discovered in a Cambridgeshire wheat field. Other designs followed and, at the

This woodcut of a "Mowing Devil" is from a pamphlet, published in 1678, describing a remarkable event that took place in Herefordshire that summer. A farmer employed a labourer to cut his field of oats but they quarrelled over payment. The farmer declared that he would rather the Devil himself mow the field than pay what the man asked. That night a fiery light was seen in the field and the following morning revealed the crop cut, with supernatural exactness, into "round circles". When rediscovered in 1989, the story was claimed as an early record of the crop circle phenomenon. But in this case the crop was cut rather than laid down. However, like all good stories, there seems to be more to it when considered in the context of rural folk culture. There are folklore associations between crop circles and everything from the agrarian spirits of corn to the Underworld, the widespread European tradition of "goat spirits" (Swedish: korn-bocks) and witches. Hence, the farmer's fearful reaction to the Mowing Devil's unnatural harvest makes sense if he believed that fairies, or "field spirits", were in some way punishing him for his disrespect.

Cerealogist's end-of-season "Cornference" in Glastonbury, speaker after speaker talked excitedly about millenarian revelations to come. The magazine had already published an article by a sceptic, Peter Williams, claiming that the circles were all manmade but this was widely ignored.

It came as a bombshell then, when, in September 1991, *Today* newspaper published a sensational account of how two men in their sixties, Doug Bower and Dave Chorley, had fooled the world by making circles themselves. Delgado, Meaden and Taylor were among those who had been caught out by identifying "Doug 'n' Dave" circles as the genuine article. Crop circle followers who had invested high hopes in the phenomenon were disillusioned and many of them abandoned the subject.

The following year, prompted by the biologist and author Rupert Sheldrake and organized by the *Cerealogist*, a circle-making contest, with a prize of £3000 for the winner, was held in a Bucking-hamshire wheat field. Eleven teams entered, some with many hands and much equipment, but the third prize was won by a young American, Jim Schnabel, working alone. The result was to prove how much easier it was to reproduce the subtle features of crop circles than the experts had proclaimed.

For many people the phenomenon was over. It was all a hoax. Schnabel's book, *Round in Circles*, made it plain that he and others had created some of the acclaimed circle designs. The press lost interest in the subject and only the die-hard enthusiasts continued to make the annual pilgrimage to Wiltshire. Yet, against all reasonable expectations, the phenomenon did not die. Every year up to the present (2007) a great many further designs, as beautiful and mysterious as before, have appeared in the usual fields and districts. Like the masterpieces of earlier years, these are still of unknown origin. Even the known circlemakers, who like to take credit for their work, are baffled by these superior designs. They attribute them to a hypothetical "A team". Despite heavy surveillance, no team of circle-makers has ever been caught in the act.

If crop circles have a meaning, it is probably indicated by the effect they have on people. Many researchers say that their minds and lives have been changed by the phenomenon. New friends have been made, new interests developed and the mystery in the cornfields has drawn attention to other mysteries, in archeology for example. Crop circles are often to be found near ancient sites, appearing alongside the old temples of Stonehenge and Avebury and other Wessex monuments. There is much speculation on the geometry of their designs, some of which are hard to construct, even on paper. To create them on a large scale, illegally, flawlessly, in the short hours of summer darkness, often in full sight of main roads, is an impressive feat.

Far from dwindling away, the mystery has actually deepened. Like most of the phenomena recorded in this book, it has been explained often and in many different ways, but never finally. Veteran researchers recall the early days when circles on remote farms were unvisited, unpublicized, sometimes peppered with little swirls of "grapeshot" and with features that convinced them that no ordinary people could possibly have made them.

The crop-circle-makers, whoever they are, seem not particularly concerned whether their constructions are seen by us or not. In many cases circles have been discovered by pure chance, by someone who happened to notice a formation just before harvest. A spectacular example was the "basketwork" circle that appeared on the morning of 6 August 1999 in a Wiltshire wheat field. It had seven spokes made up of smaller, swirled circles, and in the area between them the wheat stalks were beautifully woven or plaited. That morning the farmer was planning to reap the field, and he had just begun to do so when a young German researcher and aviator, Ulrich Kox, who got up earlier than most of his English colleagues, flew over the site and obtained a photograph. It is the only record of this unique formation.

The same thing happened with the Crooked Soley circle of 2002 (see ANCIENT SITES AND THE ET CONNECTION, p.226). It appeared at the very end of the season when many researchers had gone home, and it attracted little attention

Crop circles cause little damage to farmers' fields. Laid down in regular, sometimes elaborately woven patterns, the plants continue to grow and ripen.

at the time. No one ever went into it, and it was only recorded because a pilot happened to notice it from the air. He informed Steve Alexander, the famous crop-circle photographer, who, that morning, took the only pictures of it. He was just in time – later that day the field was harvested.

Perhaps one day the crop circle phenomenon, like many waves and outbreaks of mysterious happenings, will dwindle away and future generations will remember it as one of the quaint stories that have come down to them from the 21st century. There will be theories and explanations, and some authorities will decide that it was all a hoax. Yet, whatever explanation is eventually agreed upon, it will never account for every aspect of the crop-circle outbreak. One thing that can never be denied is the artistic beauty of crop circles. Every year brings new, original designs in the loveliest of all media, the rippling, golden cornfields of southern England. London art critic John McEwen has described crop circles as the finest examples of landscape art in modern times. We are lucky to be living through these times, when each summer a magnificent array of artworks, anonymous and spontaneously produced, is freely exhibited in the open air.

Ancient sites and the ET connection

For those who despair of trying to discover who or what is making the crop circles, there are more crucial questions. What is the point of these things? Do they have any meaning? If they are communications intended for us, what is their message?

One thing that crop circles are certainly doing is drawing attention to the prehistoric sacred sites in southern England and elsewhere. Regularly, since the beginning of the phenomenon at the beginning of the 1980s, formations have appeared in cornfields adjacent to Stonehenge. One of them, in 1992, was placed among a group of Bronze Age barrows on the south side of the monument, so artfully that four of its six ribbon-like arms lightly touched one of the surrounding mounds or the track leading to it – a marvellous feat of surveying. Many others have been beside "dolmens", long barrows and sometimes the former sites of monuments that have been destroyed. A special target is Avebury (pictured opposite), the ancient ritual centre of southern England. The whole area is studded with religious relics of 2000 BC and earlier and is thought to have been sacred land, cultivated by priests to cater for the pilgrims and festival-goers who attended ceremonies at Avebury throughout the year.

In the summer of 2005 Avebury was besieged by crop circles in every direction, just outside the village and the ramparts of its sanctuary. In turn, this stimulated interest in the forgotten science behind the placement of prehistoric sites, the straight alignments that link them and the units of measure used by the old surveyors. The basis of this science was a code of numbers, the key to which was given in the remarkable Crooked Soley circle of 2002. Also provided by the circles is the information that everyone wants – on the nature of the intelligence that is responsible for them. This was provided in no uncertain terms by the astonishing formations at the Chilbolton Observatory in Hampshire in 2001, which yielded a thorough analysis by Allan Brown and John Michell.

One of the two components in the Chilbolton crop markings was a communication, ostensibly from outer space, spelt out in binary code. The other was a large, enigmatic face, made up of dots or pixels. It was a unique event; never before has there been such a clear, seriously composed, mysteriously delivered message that, regardless of its true origins, was representing itself as the work of an alien intelligence. Nothing of this quality has previously been noted either in folklore or in the annals of ufology. Here are the facts in the case.

The formations were first seen on the morning of 20 August and Lucy Pringle, crop circle writer and researcher, flew over to photograph them. One of the two patterns, measuring 27m by 80m, reminded her of a computer chip; the other was the huge face in a rectangular frame of 44m by 57m. The face is still a mystery. People have seen all kinds of likenesses in it, one suggestion being that it is a composite portrait of the human race. The other figure, the message, was quickly decoded by Paul Vigay, a computer expert. It appeared to be a communication from space, a reply to radio signals transmitted from Earth twenty-seven years earlier.

On 16 November 1974 a government-backed group, SETI (Search for Extra-Terrestrial Intelligence), used the giant telescope at the Arecibo Observatory in Puerto Rico to beam out a coded message. The target was the globular star cluster M13 in the constellation of Hercules. The message gave technical data about ourselves and our Solar System. The reply, expressed in the symbols of the crop formation, gave corresponding data about another inhabited area of the Universe. As if to emphasize their extraterrestrial origin, the crop

One of the most beautiful crop patterns of its time, this "spider's web" of 1994 was significantly placed just outside the great circular earthwork of Avebury in Wiltshire, the main prehistoric temple of southern England. From the beginning of the phenomenon there has been a marked connection between crop circles and ancient sacred sites.

formations were in a wheat field adjacent to the Chilbolton radio telescope. Built in 1965, this installation is used for receiving and analysing radio waves from space, and it played a part in the original SETI transmission.

The SETI message was designed by Frank Drake, among others. They were men of their time, space enthusiasts working within a culture of ufology and science fiction. They believed that outer space is teeming with intelligent life and that we should contact our neighbours. Not everyone agreed. Some scientists warned against the dangers in alien communication. Any civilization in space, they reasoned, is bound to be more advanced than us, because we are newcomers to the universal community. If we let them discover us, what is to stop them treating us in the same way that Western civilization has mistreated and destroyed more traditional societies? Let us keep quiet, they said, and not alert these superior beings to our humble existence. This was considered seriously by the SETI people, but curiosity prevailed over

caution and they decided to go ahead.

The radio message from Arecibo was sent out in binary code. Every pulse represented either "1" or "0" and there were 1679 of them. That was because 1679 has only two factors, 73 and 23, both of which are primes. The only rectangle that can be made of 1679 digits is 73 by 23. The radio pulses only made sense when set out in that rectangle. Several human professors were baffled by this procedure, but SETI presumed that extraterrestrials would readily understand the message.

Shown here (overleaf) are the shape and meaning of the SETI transmission. The top row shows the binary symbols for the numbers 1 to 10, the basis of our counting system. Below it are grouped the binary symbols for 1, 6, 7, 8 and 15, the atomic numbers for the basic elements of life on Earth – hydrogen, carbon, nitrogen, oxygen and phosphorus. The next lines, down to the central, vertical bar, give the chemical formulae for the components of the DNA molecule. The vertical bar down the middle signifies the number

One of the two formations that appeared in August 2001 near the Chilbolton Observatory in Hampshire.

of nucleotides in DNA. On either side of it are diagrams of the double helix formed by our DNA.

Directly below the bar is a stylized figure of a human being. To its left is the binary symbol for 4.29 billion, the Earth's population in 1974, and to its right is the average human height (about 176cm). It is shown as 14 times the unit of 12.6cm, the wavelength on which the message was transmitted. The line below the human figure shows the Sun and nine planets of the Solar System in their approximate relative sizes. The third dot from the Sun, our planet, is raised above the others to indicate its significance. Finally, the curved line over the M shape is a diagram of the Arecibo telescope from which the message emanated. On the last line is encoded its diameter of 305m.

This is the message sent from Earth to which the rectangle in the Hampshire wheat field was a direct response, answering it line for line in the same terms. Paul Vigay, its interpreter, found nine points of difference in the reply (detailed opposite).

When the SETI scientists were informed of this miraculous answer to the message they had beamed into outer space, they showed no interest at all! It was a perfect reply from their point of view, responding carefully to the points they themselves had raised. But instead of being grateful, they reacted with scorn. Questioned by the media, a SETI spokesman said he had no time for crop circles or anything connected with them. Extraterrestrials, he said, are far too advanced to communicate through such a trivial, childish medium. If they had wanted to answer the Arecibo message they would surely have approached the scientists directly. He regarded the crop formation as a malicious hoax, aimed at discrediting the work of his organization.

At the risk of attracting "scientific" disapproval, we choose to take this phenomenon seriously. No one has claimed to have made it, nor has it been shown how it could have been done by normal methods, overnight and under the eyes

The supposed response to the original SETI message. The most obvious difference is between the human figure and the large-headed creature in the corresponding position. It looks like one of the sinister "grays" of UFO-abduction lore. Its average height is given in the symbols on its right as just over 1m. To the left of it is the number of its population, 21.3 billion, spread out over three planets. A significant difference is in the second line of the "reply" panel where, added to the atomic numbers of the elements of life on Earth, is the number fourteen, meaning silicon, the main component in computer software – perhaps implying that the circle-makers are computerized robots! The greatest surprise is the bottom feature of the panel where, in the SETI message, is the diagram of the Arecibo telescope from which it was transmitted. The corresponding feature in the crop formation is an elaborate design that puzzled researchers – until someone recognized it as a stylized version of a formation that was found the year before, in 2000, in precisely the same position in the same field as the message panel of 2001. The implication is that the new design originated, not from outer space, but from the place where it appeared, beside the Chilbolton Observatory.

of the Chilbolton astronomers. Both panels, the face and the message were faultless masterpieces. The face was a perfect optical illusion, made up of 412 little squares, each one graded in size to create the image. What appears in the photograph is largely the effect of shadows, cast by the isolated clumps of wheat, so that the laid-down areas appear to be standing out and vice versa. As the Sun goes round in the course of a day, the shadows would have moved with it, producing different aspects of a human face – an artist who made this would rightly be called a creative genius.

Apart from the quality of the work itself and the mysterious circumstances of its appearance, we have good reasons to celebrate these examples of the crop circle phenomenon. It is not every day that images of extraterrestrials, together with information on them and their native habitat, are made available to researchers. In fact, nothing like this has been seen before. There is wit and sophistication in these designs that indicate a highly developed culture behind them.

And we are intrigued by the information given. Most significant is the hint, by the final symbol in the message, that the formations were not transmitted from elsewhere but came from where they were found. This means that the beings who made them are now among us.

The following year, 2002, produced an even more blatant sign of extraterrestrial involvement with crop circles. On 15 August, at Sparsholt near Winchester, Hampshire, a huge, 120m-long rectangle appeared in a field below a radio mast installation. It framed the features of a giant ET, depicted in the popular, modern convention as a hairless and grim-looking head with bright, bulging eyes. Three little UFO shapes went with it, and the whole image was depicted using parallel lines cut through the wheat crop, each line subtly varying in width. Across the frame was a large, circular disc with 14 concentric rings of dotted symbols.

Many researchers were dismayed or frightened by this apparition. The ET face had the sinister look of the UFO entities know as "Grays". Other cerealogists (crop circle enthusiasts) stood up for the image. One should not be prejudiced, they said, by its (to us) unpleasant features. If that is how ETs happen to look, it is rude, even racist, to hold it against them.

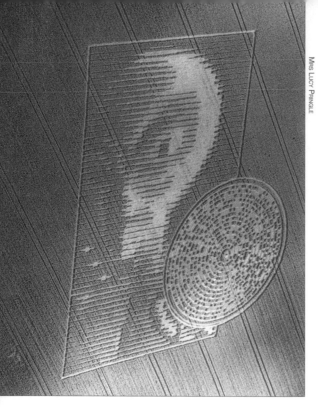

The rectangular image that appeared at Sparsholt, Hampshire, in 2002.

The disc that went with the figure was deciphered by experts in binary notation, but what it said proved to be something of a disappointment. Unlike the Chilbolton message it contained no hard information but waffled enigmatically about truth, reality and deception. It ended strangely with reference to the ringing of a bell.

We have described these two crop formations, at Chilbolton and Sparsholt, in the way they are presented to us, as products of extraterrestrial beings who are now with us upon Earth. That is what the circle-makers want us to think, and maybe it is the simple truth. Yet in the world of weird or psychic phenomena nothing is ever straightforward. In former times, when this "other world" was universally recognized, crop circle manifestations would have been attributed to spirits that can take on any form they choose. So we would not be surprised if spirits or fairies are reinventing themselves as ETs in response to modern space imagery. Nor would we be shocked if it were ever proved that inspired human beings had created all the circles.

But in that case there would have to be much explaining: Who is thinking up these beautiful, original designs? Who are the teams that, year after year, create elaborate, flawless crop formations in a short summer's night, often in full view of roads and houses, and are, apparently, never caught in the act? How is it done, and why? The patterns are far more ambitious and wonderful than would be needed to create an effect; in the early days we were content with simple, swirled circles. Even then, and even after two elderly tricksters hit the headlines with their boast, unsupported by evidence, that they were the real circle-makers, this phenomenon has had an aura of mystery that has attracted people from around the world. That is why, for lack of any contrary evidence, we accept the crop circle phenomenon for what it appears to be – the creation of an unknown intelligence for a purpose we do not yet understand.

We are confirmed in our attitude of acceptance by the most significant and informative crop circle we have ever heard of. The Crooked Soley circle (pictured opposite) is mentioned at the end of the previous chapter as an example of a circle that was discovered by chance on the day when the farmer was cutting it down. It only existed for a few hours and no one ever entered it. Its name comes from the farm hamlet where it was situated, on the Wiltshire-Berkshire border, in the parish of Chilton Foliat near Hungerford. A short distance from Crooked Soley is Straight Soley, and cerealogist Allan Brown noticed that the crop circle was placed at the same distance from the two hamlets, forming the apex of an equilateral triangle.

He also noticed a numerical pattern in the crop circle. The pattern is an interlacing of two ribbons, taken to represent a DNA strand. It occupies a band, 23m wide, which encloses a circle of undisturbed wheat 46m across. The point being that no one could have stood at the creation's centre to swing a rope – which is how circles are often explained. Outside the circle, the patterned ring was divided by 144 arcs into 1296 little sections, of which 504 were clumps of standing wheat, and in 792 of them the stalks had been laid down.

These numbers and their ratios are recognized by students of ancient science and cosmology as the chief symbols of a long-lost code of knowledge on which all previous civilizations were based. According to the old histories, this knowledge was first revealed to humanity by the gods. It is written that long ago they came down among us and ruled directly. They were said to be perfectly just, and under their guidance we enjoyed great happiness and perfect order. When it was due time for the gods to leave Earth, they instructed certain people in the code of science and wisdom by which they had governed.

Supposedly, for a time after the gods had left, their instructions were carefully followed, but human nature prevailed and decadence set in. Tyrants and great empires arose, greed and aggression flourished – and then came the great Fall. An event that correlates with Plato's allegory of *Atlantis* and *The Fall of Babylon* in *Revelation*.

It is easy to interpret ancient histories, telling of regular interventions by the gods, as records of space missionaries. And it is impossible to ignore the modern implications. The UFO saga throughout the last half of the twentieth century had the effect of opening minds to the possibilities of extraterrestrial life and contact with it. With the coming of crop circles, it has been suggested that the pressure to accept the existence of ETs has intensified. In

The Crooked Soley circle.

the circle at Crooked Soley, as in others we have described, are hints of a very high intelligence at work. Perhaps Carl Jung was right when he identified UFOs as "…portents of great changes which would shock those unprepared for them". By that he meant the reappearance of old gods.

Discs of ice

Ice-discs are circular plates of ice many metres across, circumscribed by a narrow, usually ice-free, ring or "ditch" in which the disc slowly revolves. Like crop circles, they have an immediate and striking visual appeal, but the phenomenon is relatively unfamiliar, even to scientists, and remained largely uninvestigated until the 1980s. References to the phenomenon in standard texts on meteorology, geology or hydrology are scarce.

The geometric perfection and size of the ice-discs, like that of their cereal cousins (see CROP CIRCLES, p.221), have been taken by the credulous as a sign of alien intervention. Most attempts at scientific explanation, as with crop circles, have involved discussion of vortices – only this time in the form of whirlpools rather than whirlwinds.

Many have wondered, if this was indeed a natural phenomenon, why they had never heard of ice-discs before. Thus were sown the seeds of doubt that flowered into suggestions of hoaxing. But the question of motive was even more charged than it was with crop circles: why would anyone go to the trouble of making something so difficult in places so remote that it was unlikely ever to be seen?

As in so many cases of strange phenomena, ufologists were among the first to draw public attention to this mysterious and entrancing occurrence. In January 1987 Clas Svahn, head of UFO-Sweden and editor of its journal *UFO-Aktuellt*, published an account of his visit to two rivers in northern Sweden earlier that month. The first ice-disc that he found (50m in diameter) was located a few kilometres south of the town of lvsbyn, at a bend in the Piteälven ("the River of Pite"). The entire formation of the ice-disc had been observed by a local man in mid-December 1986. "At first, all that could be seen was a large central area of ice

This early record of a slowly revolving disc of ice appeared in the *Scientific American*, February 1895. The 8m diameter disc was seen on the Mianus River, near Bedford, New York.

surrounded by many smaller chunks, all moving in a circle", wrote Svahn. By 22 December, this rotating system of ice planets was frozen together, and in early January (when Svahn visited) the huge circle was complete. The ice was 50cm thick, deep enough to support the adventurous ufologist who completed a revolution in eight minutes. "It was great fun!" said Svahn.

According to Svahn, the rate at which the Piteälven ice-disc revolved slowed from about two minutes in its early stages to about ten minutes weeks later. This was presumably due either to variations in the flow beneath it or, more likely, to the slush freezing in its ditch – or possibly both. A few weeks later, Svahn was called to Kalixälven where he saw a similar but smaller ice-disc. It was unable to revolve because its ditch had frozen, fastening the disc to the rest of the ice sheet. Clas also told us that in January 1992, a pair of discs, both frozen *in situ*, had been found on Hotagssjön, a lake near Östersund.

Inquiring at Sweden's Meteorological and Hydrological Institute (SMHI), Svahn was referred to Mrs Birgitta Raab, who took more than a passing interest in the phenomenon. She told him: "I know of three or four rivers in Sweden and Norway in which rotating discs of ice have formed, but as far as I know this phenomenon doesn't yet have a name." Mrs Raab said that a particularly massive disc formed every spring

in the River Ljusnan in central Sweden. (It has been known to measure an astonishing 200m in diameter.) In her opinion the critical factor is the way a river current flows through a bend or narrow part to form a suitable back eddy. It was possible, she said, that the shape of the shoreline in some lakes could also influence the currents to form ice-discs.

In fact an earlier ice-disc formation was reported in the *Illustrated London News* (15 February 1930), under the heading "Jack Frost Describes a Circle": it was located "in the Valley of the River Don, within a few miles of Toronto, Ontario, at a sharp turn in the stream where there is a slow-turning whirlpool, or eddy." The anonymous account went on to describe how when "this part of the river froze over, a sheet of ice in the shape of a perfect circle was formed in the centre of the whirlpool. This disc floated on a round patch of water, which was surrounded by ice on all sides, and turned slowly around with the water beneath it."

The UFO connection surfaced in October 1991 when the *UFO Journal* of the Mutual UFO Network (MUFON) carried an account of a circular formation of ice on the River Mzha in the Ukraine. It had been sent to editor Dennis Stacy by MUFON's Russian correspondent Vladimir Rubtsov. The circle was found on 7 January 1990 by Mr A.E. Vorontsov, a resident of Merefa (about 30km south of Kharkov), who had cycled to the river to check his baited fishing lines. Vorontsov claims he saw a huge, top-shaped object resting on the ice or hovering just above it. After ten minutes the luminous object, "as glorious as a sunset", sped eastward leaving the large disc of ice to sink into the water and rise again.

By chance, the story came to the attention of Dr Pyotr I. Kutnyuk of the Kharkov regional UFO group the very next day, and he promptly went to the location to see for himself. Kutnyuk noted that the ice layer was thin – it could not support a man, never mind a UFO seventy-five metres across. When Rubtsov himself visited the site five days later, on 13 January, the ice had thickened enough to support a man, and both researchers believed this ruled out a hoax. Rubtsov was intrigued by the 1m-wide ring, which comprised a number of "concentric ridges, as if it had been made by a giant milling machine cutter". The rings were still visible at the end of January, but it was a relatively warm winter and thereafter the ice soon melted.

Whatever Mr Vorontsov saw may have had nothing (or everything) to do with the ice rings, and the comparison has been made with the rare description of glowing masses in association with formation of crop circles. Nevertheless, it is clear that the Mzha River ice rings are related to ice-discs, and probably represent a variation in the process of formation.

An early theory about the ring of ridges is that they might be frozen ripples. This was proposed by another MUFON investigator, Paul Rosenfield, in connection with a set of clearly defined concentric rings, 6m in diameter, in the ice over a stretch of the Charles River that runs through the Mount Feake Cemetery in Waltham, Massachusetts. He had spotted the formation while jogging on 15 January 1991 and submitted his report to the *MUFON UFO Journal* (April 1992). Rosenfield, who was fascinated by reports of crop circles, made the visual connection immediately and ran home for his camera. As he judged the ice was not safe and there were no footprints or tracks near the circle, it did not appear likely that anyone could have faked it.

Paul Rosenfield tried unsuccessfully to get a few scientists to look at his photos; then he met Dr Jerome Carr, who had an interest in geophysics, geology and limnology. Dr Carr's considered opinion was that the circle effect had been created by the near-perpendicular strike of a meteorite through the ice and the resulting wave patterns overlapped to produce refrozen rings of broken ice. Just how the pattern of breaking and re-freezing would create perfectly circular rings is not explained. Rosenfield also managed to test the theory; in March 1991, a police diving team were salvaging a small sunken boat not far from the ring site, and he managed to convince them to search the river bottom for any unusual rocks. There was no sign of anything seemingly meteoric.

As knowledge of ice-discs became more widespread, British sceptic Peter Williams launched an explanation of his own. Ice-discs, he asserted, were made by hoaxers using an ice saw (an adapted chain saw used in ice manufacture since the 1920s). Williams envisaged one man standing at the centre holding a rope that acts as the radius. Thus guided, his partner would carve the inner edge of the "ditch", then the outer, and then both smash up the ring to set the disc free (*The Crop Watcher*, September 1993). This theory would be fine, were it not for the fact that some of our accounts involve ice too thin for any anchorman and chainsaw artist. Moreover, the Piteälven disc was observed throughout its formation, and the Ukrainian ring at different stages in its growth.

The phenomenon was thrust on the scientific community in February 1993 when a strange constellation of concentric ice-rings began to form on the surface of the Charles River where it flows through the Massachusetts Institute of Technology (MIT) campus at Cambridge, Massachusetts.

Under the supervision of Professor John Marshall of MIT's Earth, Atmospheric and Planetary Science Department, various supposed causes (such as effluent from submerged pipes, the down-draughts of helicopters, wind action, activity by aliens, bubblings of natural gas from decomposing matter, and underwater springs) were systematically eliminated. The mystery was finally solved when David Ricks, an Ocean Engineering graduate, confirmed the theory of two colleagues through first-hand observation. Crossing over the Harvard Bridge each day he observed the circles forming over several weeks. "First, a smooth sheet of ice formed over most of the river. Then large holes were formed by ice shearing and moving around." The driving force behind the ice formations were eddies from the piers of the Harvard Bridge itself. "Areas of open water froze over again … in circular patterns, even though they had irregular shapes when they were created. I saw that the ice *grew* into the holes, from

A perfect disc of ice revolving clockwise on the River Don near Toronto, Ontario, in January 1930. Around the slow-turning whirlpool, areas of thin, slushy ice can be seen, especially on the outer edges of the ditch in which the plate of ice is revolving.

Conrad Serfass surveys the ice-disc that formed in Cranberry Creek, behind his home in Tannersville, Pennsylvania, in January 1993. The 8.5m-diameter disc, a good simulacrum of the Moon, was discovered by his wife while walking the dog.

the outside edge in. Evidently this made the holes more circular," said Ricks. (*MIT Tech Talk*, 24 February 1993). We find it amazing and amusing that this high-powered think tank was completely unaware of the more perfect concentric ice rings observed by Paul Rosenfield further up the same Charles River just two years earlier (see p.233).

Over the past few years a consensus has begun to emerge about how ice-discs are formed. A slow-moving river current creates a slow-turning eddy in which a rotating disc of ice can grind out its edges, and those of the ditch, to perfection. According to Paul Fuller, writing in the *Crop Watcher* (November 1991), "this is further proof that nature can and does produce precisely-defined geometrical traces without the need for alien intervention."

Could the phenomenon be related to, or explain, the rash of holes found in ice-covered lakes in Sweden in March 1968 (*Fortean Times* 24, p.41) and in Finland in 1983–84 (*Fortean Times* 45, p.47). In the Swedish case locals believed a large object had crashed into the lake at Upprämen, in southern Dalarna, through ice 35 inches thick. The curiously triangular hole, measuring 60 feet by 90 feet, was surrounded by a wall of large ice boulders several yards high. Military divers claimed to have found nothing below it, but local people remained convinced that perhaps it was a bomb dropped by mistake or a crashed spy satellite. Two similar ice-holes were found in April 1968, some 93 miles further north in the river Dalälven at Hedfjorden and again searching divers found nothing. Upprämen lake was searched again by divers in the summer of 1998; thirty years after the first incident it still worried the locals. There was some evidence that the huge wall of ice round the hole had been thrown up by an impact or explosion. (*UFO-Aktuellt*, issues 3 and 5, 1998).

Sweden seems to be a favourite target for celestial marksmen, because the phenomenon occurred again in mid-August 1999, this time in the lake at Backsjön in the province of Värmland, where people staying in summer cottages said they saw a mysterious flying object with fins falling into the lake. For a whole month, Swedish military forces searched in and around the lake for the UFO, but no trace of the object was found.

We believe that it is perfectly possible all these related phenomena have been in the open all the time, unnoticed because (like many topics in this book) they were quite familiar to country people and regarded as too commonplace by them to warrant any comment. There again, it may be – as is the case of many other things that were "there all the time"– that the evidence for them in historical records has, simply, never been noticed.

Since the first edition of this book we have learned of more types of natural circles as landscape features. Besides impact craters and "fairy rings", we were particularly struck by these "almost perfect" circles in the snow-drift covering an iced-over Welland canal at St Catherines, Ontario, photographed in January 2005.

8

Signs and Portents

8

Signs and Portents

Lost and found

This section is about things that have been lost and have then turned up again in amazing circumstances. In particular it is about lost rings and other precious objects that have been returned to their owners in the guts of a fish.

On 23 June 1626, a Mr Mead of Christ's College, Cambridge, was walking through the city's market when exclamations from a rustic group around a fish stall attracted his attention. On the stall lay a battered book, its sailcloth binding slimy with fish gut. The fishwife had just pulled it out from the inside of a plump codfish. In a letter to Sir M. Stuteville, Mead wrote excitedly: "I saw all with mine own eyes – the fish, the maw, the piece of sail-cloth, the book – and observed all I have written; only I did not see the opening of the fish, which not many did, being on the fish-woman's stall in the market, who first cut off its head, to which the maw hanging, and seeming much stuffed with somewhat, it was searched, and all found as aforesaid. He that had had his nose as near as I yester morning would have been persuaded there was no imposture here without witness. The fish came from Lynne."

In the name of scholarship, Mead took possession of the fishy volume. It turned out to be

a theological work by John Frith, written while the author was in prison at Oxford. We do not wish to be provocative, and merely for the sake of inclusiveness we record the fact that the place of his confinement had been a fish storage cellar where the smell was so overpowering that several of Frith's fellow prisoners had died of it. His book, thus miraculously restored to circulation, was reprinted by the Cambridge authorities under the title *Vox piscis* and illustrated with a woodcut showing the book, the fish stall and the knife which had cut open the fish.

This is not the only case on record of a book found in a fish. In Rees's *Lives of the Cambro-British Saints* is the story of St Cadoc in the sixth century. He lost his favourite book, the poems of Virgil, when a gust of wind blew it into the sea. Next morning a fisherman came to his house and presented him with a large salmon. While the fish was being prepared for the saint's dinner, a book was found inside it – the precious Virgil.

In E. Cobham Brewer's *Dictionary of Miracles* is a collection of anecdotes about miraculous coincidences where a fish has restored some valued object to the person who lost it. Most of his stories are about saints, but there are many other cases, reaching up to modern times, where the incident has no religious connections. We reproduce overleaf a clipping from *The Times* (unfortunately not dated, but before 1900) about

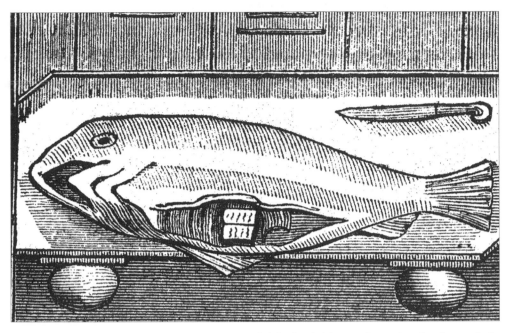

Illustration from the lost book found within a codfish in Cambridge market – showing the market stall, knife, fish and book.

a Scottish fisherman who lost his keys overboard in Loch Broom. Six weeks later, while fishing off the island of Rassay, a hundred miles away, a codfish that he had just caught vomited up his keys. The report adds a moral to the miracle. "It is a remarkable circumstance that this fish, in its migratory course, should arrive at the same spot where the sloop was ... and with its last breath discharge an act of honesty that would have honoured a higher grade or species of animal."

In most versions of this event, the object restored to its owner is a ring. An early record is in the *Histories* of Herodotus (iii, 40) from the sixth century BC. A contemporary of Herodotus was Polycrates, ruler of Samos, and it was his personal account that the historian quoted.

Polycrates was so rich and happy that he was advised to sacrifice something precious to make up for his good luck. So he rowed out to sea and threw in his emerald signet ring. A week later he was given a large, locally caught fish, and inside it was the ring. He called it "...a memorable instance of divine interposition".

Even more ancient is the "Shinto" myth of Japanese sacred history. It is about two brothers, corresponding to Cain and Abel, who divided the country between them, the elder living by the sea

as a fisherman, the younger becoming a hunter in the mountains. One day they thought they would try changing roles, but it turned out that neither was any good at the other's occupation. They would simply have reverted to their old ways, but the trouble was that the younger brother had lost the elder's precious fish-hook, and nothing could be done until he had found it again. He offered thousands of different hooks in recompense, but only the original would do. So the brother who had lost the hook set off in quest of it to the palace of the fish king. After many adventures he married the king's daughter and persuaded his father-in-law to summon all the fishes of the ocean and to ask whichever one had the fish-hook to return it. A mullet which had swallowed the hook obligingly threw it up again, it was returned to the elder brother and normality was restored.

The long list of Christian holy men who have found or conjured up some lost or needed object within a fish begins with Jesus himself. When the disciple Peter needed money to pay his taxes, Jesus told him to go down to the sea, catch a fish and look inside its mouth. Peter did so and found a valuable coin (Matthew xvii, 27).

Jesus's miracle is often supposed to be the original inspiration for the fish-and-ring legends that are attached to so many saints. But as Herodotus and the Japanese legend show, the story is older than Christianity and universal. There is evidence of it in the symbol of a fish and a ring that occurs frequently in the Pictish iconography of ancient Scotland (see illustration). This same symbol, a salmon with a ring in its mouth, is displayed on the coat of arms of the city of Glasgow, whose patron saint and early bishop, Kentigern, is also depicted with the fish-and-ring emblem. He was a prince of the Pictish royal family and a fervent Christian. The ring-and-fish badge illustrates an old story that became part of his legend. It tells of the miracle by which he saved a lady in distress.

She was the wife of Roderick, King of the North Britons in the sixth century, and the cause of her distress was a ring which her husband had given her as a love token. She in turn had given it to her young lover, a knight at the royal court. He and the King were out hunting one day by the river Clyde and stopped for a rest. The young man fell asleep, and in his hand Roderick saw his wife's ring. He took it and in silent rage threw it into the river. Then he rode home and confronted the lady,

Pictish inscribed stone from early Christian Scotland, bearing symbols of the worm bait, fish and mirror ring, reminiscent of the archetypal theme reviewed in this section.

demanding to see the ring he had given her. She made excuses and tried to calm him, but he swore that if she could not produce the ring within three days, she would be beheaded for treason. That was why she went to St Kentigern. He was a friend and adviser of her husband and she hoped he would use his influence in her favour. Kentigern did better than that; he prayed, and soon afterwards a man brought him a salmon he had caught in the Clyde. Sure enough, it had the ring in it. The lady was saved and Kentigern gained a rich and grateful follower.

Heraldry is the most conservative of arts, retaining symbols from ancient times; the ring and fish appears on another coat of arms, that of the Berry family, and with it goes another

version of the legend. A family ancestor was a young man gifted with second sight. While walking by a peasant's cottage he heard a baby crying and knew at once that she was the girl he was destined to marry. Not wanting such a low-born bride, he hatched a cruel plan, and when she was of marriageable age he took her to the seaside, meaning to drown her. When it came to the moment he had not the heart to kill her, but he was still unwilling to marry her. So he warned her never to see him again on pain of death. Then, not wishing to deny his fate unconditionally, he threw his signet ring into the sea and told the girl that if ever she found it she should come to him. She took work as a cook, and while preparing a codfish for her employer's dinner she found the

AN HONEST CODFISH.—A sloop, belonging to Rothesay, was recently lying in Lochbroom, the skipper of which, when fishing over the side, lost the keys of his lockers, &c., from his pocket into 10 fathoms of water. Attached to the bunch was a small piece of parchment, on which his name and that of the vessel were written. He, of course, gave up all hopes of ever seeing the keys again, and gazed on their rapid descent into the watery depository with deep regret. Six weeks afterwards the skipper cast anchor off the island of Rassay, about 100 miles from Lochbroom, and again resumed his piscatory employment. Among the results of his labours was a large codfish, which was speedily unhooked and thrown upon the deck; and, to the utter amazement of the skipper, the poor cod, when in the last agonies of death, vomited up his bunch of keys. The parchment, being partly preserved, proved his property beyond a doubt. At the same time, as if conscience-stricken, it disgorged a penknife belonging to a brother skipper, on which his initials were engraved. It is a remarkable circumstance that this fish, in its migratory course, should arrive at the same spot where the sloop was, sacrificing its life, and with its last breath discharging an act of honesty that would have honoured a higher grade or species of animals.—*Greenock Advertiser*.

An undated (but pre-1900) account of a particularly honest codfish as recounted in *The Greenock Advertiser*.

ring in it. She took it to Sir John Berry who duly married her.

In that case, it seems, the fish that delivered the ring was an agent of fate. So it was, even more clearly, in the case of Moses Carlton, a shipping magnate in Wiscassett, Maine, early in the nineteenth century. He was so proud and confident in his wealth that he challenged the gods to take it from him. While walking by the Sheepscot River, he took a gold ring off his finger and threw it into the water, saying, "…there is as much chance of me dying a poor man as there is of that ring ever being seen again". Not many people would dare to do such a thing, and for a good reason. There are many records of retribution following such a defiance of fate. A few days later Carlton's ring was returned to him inside a fish that was served up at dinner. Soon afterwards there was a change in Government policy that brought ruin to ship

owners along the American east coast. Carlton was made bankrupt and died in poverty.

Here are just a few more versions of the old story, beginning with a holy relic. In the cathedral at Leon in Brittany is an ancient saint's bell, quadrangular, wrought of copper and silver and nine inches in height. It was installed there by a sixth-century bishop, St Paul. Before that, it belonged to a Breton king. St Paul had always wanted this relic but could not persuade the owner to part with it. One day, while visiting rich friends, he was given the head of a large fish that had just been caught. In its mouth was the bell he had so coveted.

Another sainted bishop of the early Church, Gerbold of Bayeux, was driven from his palace when the townspeople turned against him. As he left, meaning to wander off and find a remote hermitage, he threw his episcopal ring into the sea. It soon turned up again inside a fish that someone had caught. The citizens of Bayeux were impressed by this miracle and took it as a sign of Gerbold's honesty and holiness. They sent messengers to summon him back, then reinstated him in his palace.

In William of Malmesbury's *Gesta pontifical* (repeating a slightly different version in *The Chronicle of Evesham Abbey*) is a record of the Abbey's founder in the eighth century, St Egwin, who became Bishop of Winchester. He was involved in a scandal and, hoping to clear his name, set off on a voyage to Rome. Before he embarked he locked fetters to his ankles and threw the key into the water at the mouth of the river Avon. As the ship was on its way to Italy, a fish leapt out of the sea and onto the deck. Inside it was found the key to Egwin's fetters. The Pope accepted the event, which must have been well witnessed, as a divine verdict of "not guilty", and Egwin returned to England completely vindicated.

They saw things differently in those days. But even now, in this more prosaic age, the story of something lost and miraculously found again reccurs repeatedly. An Associated Press item of 10 September 1983 reported that Ricky Shipman of Sunset Beach, California, got back the driving licence that he lost at sea eleven years earlier. It was discovered inside a mackerel.

Another good story of this kind was found in *The Halfpenny Journal*, 11 November 1861. The details are vague, with no information on dates, places or the names of the people involved. It is about a young man, the servant of a lady near a certain English town. He was sent by his mistress to take her ring to the jeweller's, but dallied on a bridge over a stream where he drew the ring out of his pocket to have a look at it. To his horror it slipped from his hand and fell into the water. He searched for it all day until nightfall, realizing that he could not return without it – the lady would accuse him of stealing her ring or losing it at gambling. So he fled the town and went off to the colonies, where over some years he accumulated a large fortune. But the lost ring was always in his mind and on his conscience, and he decided to return home, explain to his old employer what had happened and make amends to her.

He arrived by carriage in his old town and set off on foot to complete the last stage of the journey. Another man was going in the same direction and they walked together. He told his companion the story of the lost ring and when they reached the bridge he stopped to point out the details. "There," he said, "it was just here that I dropped the ring, and there is the very bit of old tree into the hole of which it fell ... Just there!"

As he spoke he thrust the tip of his umbrella into the cavity, and when he drew it out, to the amazement of both men, there was the lost ring jammed on the point.

There is something ancient and mystical about the fish-and-ring occurrence. It echoes several themes of mythology and brings to mind other mysterious "lost-and-found" episodes – where something lost or urgently wanted turns up unexpectedly, just where it always should have been, or at the opportune moment. If it has been prayed or wished for, its appearance may be claimed as an answer from the gods and spirits, but often the revelation is spontaneous, a gift of fortune. Many writers have described the luck they have had with "library angels" who guide them to the right page of the very book they need at the time (see COINCIDENCES, p.241). There is no good explanation for these effects. Sceptics may dispute the authenticity of any given case, but the phenomenon itself exists through its constant repetition and the impression it makes. Charles Fort conceived of "teleportation", an unrecognized power in nature which moves things and people about the world, haphazardly perhaps, or for its own inscrutable purposes, or in response to a conscious will or desire. This power, as Patrick Harpur sees it, is an attribute of Mercurius, the ancient, everlasting god who is both a hoaxer and a revealer of lost truths and treasures. Our own suspicion is that stories which regularly repeat themselves in human experience are inherently part of our minds, and they are also implanted in the "programming" of nature, which re-enacts them from time to time.

In the twentieth century the archetypal nature of the ring-and-fish legend attracted the attention of psychologists and anthropologists. The salmon in the Celtic tradition is a royal fish and a bearer of wisdom. Certain holy wells were inhabited by oracular fish, sometimes with golden circlets around them, which played a part in Druidic ritual and divination. The fish symbolized a stage in the initiation process, the experience of being swallowed up by the Earth, as in the stories of Christ's descent into hell and Jonah's entombment in the belly of a whale. The universal accounts of being swallowed by a fish or going down into a cavern or dark hermetic vessel are allegories of the psychological process in which the soul, in its quest for maturity, sinks into the perilous depths of the mental underworld, emerging tempered and purified.

In *Psychology and Alchemy* (1964) Carl Jung describes an episode from a patient's dream that contains many of the elements of the fish-and-ring story. "The dreamer is wandering about in a dark cave, where a battle is going on between good and evil. But there is also a prince who knows everything. He gives the dreamer a ring set with a diamond…"

Jung's purpose was to show the enduring, archetypal nature of certain themes and images, expressed in universal mythology, poetry, magical symbolism and also spontaneously in people's dreams, and to construct from them a model of human psychological reality. Our aim is to take the matter a stage further by spotting these same archetypes as they emerge from the world of dreams into the world of actual experience.

Coincidences

"When it comes to coincidences," wrote Charles Fort, "dark cynicisms arise. What if some of them were not coincidences?" In Fort's mind was his idea of "Continuity": that there is an underlying "Oneness" in which all things merge with all other things. Apparently separate phenomena, as he saw it, were like a chain of islands, outcrops from the same invisibly submerged bedrock.

One of Fort's speculations was that things happen in their own natural time, as if in accordance with some script, pattern or ideal by which we are all controlled, like iron filings in a magnetic field. The rattling of kettle lids blabbed the secret of steam power for centuries, until finally "came steam engine time", as he put it. There are several cases of unconnected people simultaneously filing similar patents on their inventions, as happened in the case of bakelite. Fort would have been pleased to know that, at the same time he was writing about "Continuity", Paul Kammerer was developing his own theory about "meaningful coincidences" which he called "Seriality".

For phenomenalists, single events cannot be isolated from the continuum that embraces all reality and ensures that anything that happens, on any level, anywhere, influences and is influenced by everything else. Nineteenth-century science attempted to study objects and events as detached entities, whereas physicists now accept that the very act of observation affects the thing observed, and that perception is a powerful act of creativity. One illustration of this is the phenomenon of coincidences, where two or more events echo each other so neatly and unexpectedly that they seem to indicate a meaning or pattern. Yet in most ordinary cases no particular meaning is apparent.

There is an endless supply of such anecdotes. Typical of its kind is one told to us by an American friend. As a little girl she was taken by her father to a soda bar. A man walked in through the door and the father recognized him as an old friend he had served with in the War and had not seen since. He rose to greet him, but then saw that he had made a mistake and it was not the man he thought. A few minutes later another man came in, and this time it really was the father's old comrade. In another example, Brighton taxi driver Barry Bagshaw was, in August 2001, called to a motel in Peacehaven, East Sussex, where he picked up a man and his girlfriend. As they conversed, the girl noticed from the displayed licence that Barry had the same surname as her companion. The man turned out to be his son Colin, whom he had not seen for 34 years. Colin, in turn, had thought his father dead all these years. Barry had joined the Army in 1967 and after serving in Hong Kong, married again, and moved to Peacehaven. Colin had grown up in South Africa but had come to Peacehaven to work as a chef. He was on the point of leaving for London, having stopped by the motel to pick up his things. Coincidences like this tend to stretch our understanding of the nature of "chance". A similar, common experience is thinking about someone, the phone ringing, and knowing before you have answered it that the caller is the person you were thinking about.

SOUTH SHROPSHIRE JOURNAL

When Mrs Margaret Bell, a well-known bee-keeper of Ludlow, Shropshire, died in June 1994, this swarm settled on the corner of Bell Lane for an hour during her funeral. According to country lore, bees should always be told of a death so they can pay their respects.

A bizarre coincidence that befell his friend, the poet Emile Deschamps, is recounted by Camille Flammarion in *The Unknown* (1902). While at a school in Orleans, Deschamps shared a table with a certain M. de Fortgibu, who on a trip to England had acquired a taste for plum-puddings, then unknown in France. He insisted that Deschamps try one. Ten years later Deschamps passed a restaurant, and saw a plum-pudding being prepared inside. His early taste, long forgotten, urged him to enter and ask for a slice; but the pudding was reserved for another, and Deschamps was obliged to beg the favour from this stranger. It turned out to be M. de Fortgibu, and both were astonished at meeting again for the second time

over the same dish. Many years passed again and Deschamps was invited to a dinner party which featured an English plum-pudding. At dinner he delighted his hosts with the tale of his extraordinary encounter with Fortgibu. They all joked about the possibility of the old man turning up, which he duly did, having been invited to dinner at another apartment in the same building and having lost his way. "Three times in my life have I eaten plum-pudding, and three times have I seen M. de Fortgibu!" said Deschamps. "My hair stood up on my head. A fourth time I should feel capable of anything ... or nothing!"

In his book *Synchronicity* (1955), Carl Jung proposes an unknown process which cuts across space-time to order events in the same manner as the archetypes order the preconscious contents of the psyche, so that events in both physical and psychological reality take on parallel meanings. Flammarion's interest was parapsychological, developing from his interest in phantoms as portents of a death. He pointed out that even if such visions are merely hallucinations, there is the problem of their synchronization with unknown events far away. Had Flammarion not turned away from his brief excursions into coincidences, he would have anticipated the work of Paul Kammerer, the ill-fated biologist, who published his work on the "Law of Series" in 1919. For twenty years he kept a detailed notebook on coincidences, meticulously analysed into categories, and was confirmed in his belief that "Seriality is ubiquitous and continuous in life, nature and cosmos".

Buried in Kammerer's work is the old alchemical notion of affinity, of like attracting like. Kammerer also noticed a periodicity of events, a theme picked up and amplified into a new area of study by Edward R. Dewey in his *Cycles: The Mysterious Forces that Trigger Events* (1971). A baby fell fourteen stories in Detroit and landed on Joseph Figlock passing below. A year later Joseph Figlock was hit by another falling baby (*Weekend*, 19 May 1976). He and both babies survived. A similar coincidence, which occurred in Bermuda and was reported in *The Liverpool Echo* (21 July 1975), ended in tragedy. Two brothers were killed by the same taxi and driver, carrying the same passenger. They were riding the same moped in the same street – but each accident happened exactly one year apart.

Fort said that he was not so much interested in things as in the relations between things, and saw all phenomena as a vastly complex continuity whose peaks occasionally project into the field of our notice: "Not a bottle of catsup can fall from a tenement-house fire-escape in Harlem, without … affecting the price of pajamas in Jersey City; the temperature of somebody's mother-in-law in Greenland; or the demand in China for rhinoceros horns."

Not only are coincidences a common factor in everyday life, but according to Ira Progoff, in *Jung, Synchronicity and Human Destiny* (1973), they can to some extent be induced, by keeping a daily record of coincidences, as Kammerer did. That effect was also observed by Alan Vaughan

Notice of the capture of "a loyal fish" appeared in *The Daily News*, 19 October 1926. The synchronicity of its distinctive markings – in the form of the Union Jack – at a time of an intense debate in South Africa about the design of their new flag, did not go unnoticed. W. Thompson of Durban, who claimed that an Indian caught the fish locally, sent this photograph to several Natal papers.

in his book, *Incredible Coincidence* (1979): "The more I focused on synchronicity," he wrote, "the more it began happening." John Keel in his UFO classic *Operation Trojan Horse* (1970) found the same thing, that as soon as he began investigating the subject of UFOs the phenomenon "zeroed in" on him and he was "plagued by impossible coincidences". Many writers tell of helpful coincidences, the type that Koestler attributed to "library angels", whereby some much-needed book or reference turns up in an apparently miraculous way. In his introduction to *The Occult* (1971) Colin Wilson wrote: "On one occasion, when I was searching for a piece of information, a book actually fell off the shelf and fell open at the right page." Flammarion recalls, in *The Unknown*, that when he was writing a chapter on the force of the wind for his *L'Atmosphere*, a gust of wind carried his papers off "…in a miniature whirlwind beyond hope of recovery". A few days later he received the proof of that chapter from his publisher, complete with the missing pages. The whirlwind had carried them down a street and deposited them at the feet of a man who worked in the publisher's office. He gathered them up under the impression that he must have dropped them.

In the "library angel" type of coincidence we see evidence of intense desire spontaneously attracting its object – or, in religious terms, acting as an answer to prayer. Solzhenitsyn gives a wonderful example in his *The Gulag Archipelago* (1976). When he was in the state prison in Len-

ingrad, a new prisoner – a famous physicist – was brought in. This man was obsessed with a certain technical problem which required mathematical tables. He seemed to have no chance of obtaining the book of tables, because the only books in the prison library were works of Party propaganda. A library worker came round each week, distributing the books to each prisoner at random. The physicist prayed for a miracle, and received one. Among the library books allotted to him was the very book of tables he had been praying for. Quickly he began memorizing the relevant tables, and managed it just in time, before a prison warder noticed the book and confiscated it.

The most commonly recognized form of coincidences – apart from the "talk-of-the-devil" effect that so fascinated Flammarion – involves words and numbers. Fort quotes a classic example ("a savage pun mixed with murder") from the *New York Herald* (26 November 1911). Three men had been hanged in London for the murder of Sir Edmundbury Godfrey at Greenberry Hill: the names of the murderers were Green, Berry and Hill. There is a punning sense of humour abroad in the world, childish at times, ominous at others. *The Scunthorpe Evening Telegraph* (26 April 1975) tells of golfer Jim Tollan, who teed off toward the fourteenth hole at the local golf club. His ball soared up and struck a mallard duck flying overhead, bringing it down on the green in front of the Mallard Inn. A striking example of the portentous coincidence occurred with *The*

Vic Burnside was attending a meditation course at the Manjushri Institute, Conishead Priory, at Ulverston, in Cumbria, in 1986, and appears in the second of two personal photos without a head. In his pocket at the time was the book *On Having No Head* by D.E. Harding.

Daily Telegraph crosswords that preceded the Normandy landing on 6 June 1944, and included many of the top-secret code names for the operations: "Omaha", "Utah", "Mulberry", "Neptune" and the blanket code for D-day itself, "Overlord". The innocent compiler of the crosswords, a schoolmaster, found himself under interrogation by Military Intelligence.

There is a category of coincidences in which nature appears to follow art, and fact fiction. As phenomenalists, we see little point in arguing out chicken-and-egg-type paradoxes, accepting that in continuity there is a little of everything in everything else, so that it is difficult to tell where "hard" and "soft" realities merge except in an arbitrary and local way. This is a realm of intermediary reality that is virtually unexplored. For example: Noel McCabe of Derby was listening to a record, "Cry of the Wild Goose" by Frankie Lane, when a Canadian goose crashed through his bedroom window (*The Sun*, 19 November 1974). The Melkis family of Dunstable, Bedfordshire, were watching a TV film when, just as the doomed Titanic was about to collide with the iceberg, their house shook under an impact of a large block of ice that had "chosen" that moment to fall from the sky and smash through their roof (*Daily Mail*, 8 July 1975). In a *Sunday Times* article Arthur Koestler notes that the *Titanic* incident itself was preceded fourteen years earlier by Morgan Robertson's 1898 novel, *Futility*, in which a giant ship, the *Titan*, collides with an iceberg on her maiden voyage in about the same place in the Atlantic. Koestler also publishes a letter from a man who was at the helm of a ship in 1939, at the exact position of the *Titanic* disaster, when he stopped the ship on a premonition. And just in time, for a giant iceberg loomed up, striking and damaging the vessel, this time with no loss of life. The ship's name was *Titanian*.

Finally, we have noted a form of coincidence that would have amused Fort, where an expert scientist witnesses something strange in his own field, as though it were a show put on for him alone. *Science* (22 April 1949) reports that Dr A.D. Bajkov, an ichthyologist, was bombarded with fish from the sky "shortly after breakfast" in Biloxi, Mississippi. Dr W.M. Krogman, a pathologist who specialized in fire-deaths, happened to be on holiday nearby on the night Mrs Reeser spontaneously combusted (see SPONTANEOUS HUMAN COMBUSTION, p.185). And on 2 April 1973, a meteorologist out strolling in Manchester was nearly brained by a falling block of ice that shattered at his feet. According to the *Meteorological Magazine* (September 1975) it was one of the best documented falls of ice on record.

Accidents to iconoclasts

Some archeologists proceed to a cheerful old age. Yet, on the evidence of history, their profession would seem a dangerous one. That so many old stones and buried treasures have survived the centuries intact is certainly due to the popular belief that no good will come to him who disturbs them. Records of the misfortunes of grave-robbers, vandals and iconoclasts are universal; and their ill luck is often inherited by later owners of relics sacrilegiously obtained.

It was widely reported in the press (15 September 1997) that a British tourist, who stole a lump of stone from the base of the Great Pyramid five years earlier, returned it to the Cairo Museum with a letter saying that "it had brought him bad luck ever since". The Museum authorities were not surprised; several such items had been returned by people who felt cursed after stealing them. A good reason for caution is the largely bogus story of an Egyptian coffin lid – or fragment of a coffin lid. It was told to Arthur Weigall, author of *Tutankhamen* (1923) by its one-time owner, Mr Douglas Murray, who purchased the coffin some time in the 1860s: "No sooner had he done so than he lost his arm, owing to the explosion of his gun. The ship in which the coffin was sent home was wrecked, and so was the cab in which it was driven from the docks; the house in which it was deposited was burnt down; and the photographer who made a picture of it shot himself. A lady who had some connection with it suffered great family losses, and was wrecked at sea shortly afterwards … The list of accidents and misfortunes charged to the spirit which is connected with this coffin

A report in *The Times* of 15 December 1967 tells of the discovery, the previous night, of the body of Evalyn McLean (above) of Dallas, Texas, with no obvious cause of death. Evalyn inherited the infamous Hope Diamond from her grandmother (also Evalyn) but was never allowed to touch it. The elder McLean acquired the diamond in 1907 after which she lost a son in a car accident, a daughter to suicide and a husband to mental illness. The diamond is named after its first known owner, Henry Thomas Hope, an English banker, who bought it in 1830 and whose family suffered a catalogue of disasters. Before Hope, the diamond was owned by two ill-fated kings of France; and between Hope and the elder McLean its string of owners committed suicide, were dethroned or assassinated. Others had tragic accidents, like Simon Montharides, whose carriage was dragged over a cliff by a shying horse, killing him, his wife and their child. The legend of the diamond is the stereotype of the cursed gem, said to have been stolen from the forehead of an ancient Hindu idol.

is now of enormous length."

The presence of an Egyptian mummy on board is sometimes blamed for the loss of the *Titanic*. It was said to have been shipped to New York on the supposedly unsinkable liner. Its coffin,

no. 22542 in the British Museum, is associated with the curse, and Museum authorities caution people who propose to photograph it.

There is an extensive record of accidents to those who vandalize tombs and ancient monuments. Some quite recent examples are given in the last chapter of *The Secret Country* (1976) by Colin and Janet Bord. Many others have been recorded in S. Menefee's articles in *Folklore* (1975 and 1976) and in L.V. Grinsell's *Folklore of Prehistoric Monuments* (1976).

People who disturb megalithic sites, even to the extent of measuring them or counting their stones, are liable to be themselves disturbed by meteorological or other portents. On 12 August 1740, John Wood, architect of Bath, proposed to take a plan of Stanton Drew stone circles in Somerset, whose stones are said to be wedding guests petrified by the devil. As he later recalled, in *A Description of Bath*, his researches were resisted: "No one, say the country people about Stanton Drew, was ever able to reckon the number of these metamorphosised [sic] stones or to take a draft of them, though several have attempted to do so, and proceeded until they were either struck dead upon the spot, or with such illness as soon carried them off." Nevertheless Wood persisted, "and as a great storm accidentally arose just after, and blew down part of a great tree near the body of the work, the people were then thoroughly satisfied that I had disturbed the guardian spirits of the metamorphosised stones, and from thence great pains were taken to convince me of the impiety of what I was about." Wood repeated his "impiety" by taking a plan of Stonehenge with the same results – a violent storm which drove him to shelter in a nearby hut.

Some years later, Dr William Borlase excavated a "giant's grave" in the Scilly Isles. That night a hurricane destroyed the islanders' crops of corn and potatoes – a direct consequence, so they claimed, of the Doctor's archeology. The incident is described in Halliwell's *Rambles in Western Cornwall* (1861).

It is well known that no one in Ireland will, or would, take timber from a rath, which is a sacred enclosure or fairy grove. The railway companies in their early days found many such impediments on their chosen lines, and the same inconvenience is still occasionally suffered by road-making contractors. At the other end of the world the Japanese refrain from cutting trees on Mount Miwa or at any other rural sanctuary. The innumerable instances of disasters visited on people who destroy sacred timber begin with that of the Empress Saimei, who, in AD 661, felled a sacred grove to build a palace. The building was immediately destroyed by the elements, killing its Grand Treasurer and many members of the court. A young Samurai, seeing good timber lying waste, took the logs to build his own palace – with the same results.

To the delight of local wiseacres at the time – and of wiseacres generally ever since – the Puritan who, in the time of Cromwell, chopped down one of the two stems of the sacred Glastonbury thorn (the tree which sprang from St Joseph of Arimathaea's staff and blossoms every Christmas morning) received a splinter in his eye which prevented him from continuing work on the second stem.

Dr Robert Plot, the old historian of Oxfordshire, records with relish the misfortunes of Cromwell's commissioners who took up quarters in the King's apartments at Woodstock Palace on 13 October 1649 and warmed themselves by burning the locally revered King's Oak. They seem thus to have invoked some of the most unpleasant classes of phenomena described in these sections. A Black Dog rushed through the rooms upsetting chairs, phantom footsteps were heard, papers were torn and scattered and ink spilt. The logs of the King's Oak were hurled around. On 20 October the commissioners were attacked in their beds, and from then on were continually buffeted by "invisible assailants". Other poltergeist effects followed. Windows were broken by volleys of stones and – something we have never heard of before in this connection – horses' bones. For all this Dr Plot blamed "immaterial beings". The last straw was when the commissioners, having planned to set aside some of the estate for themselves, and drawn up an agreement to that effect and hidden it in a pot beneath the roots of an orange tree,

ROGER WOOD

Tutankhamen's death mask is said to have a blemish corresponding to the mark of Lord Carnarvon's fatal mosquito bite.

found the earth in the pot burning with a blue, sulphurous flame; at which point they fled.

Of all such curses, coincidences, strokes of ill luck or whatever they may be, the most famous is the "Curse of the Pharaohs", which started its career of entertaining the public and infuriating the Egyptologists in 19th century fiction. On 6 April 1923 Lord Carnarvon died shortly after his expedition had forced open the funerary chamber in the tomb of Tutankhamen. The frivolous atmosphere of that occasion was described by Arthur Weigall, who was present at the opening. On Carnarvon boasting that he would give a concert down in the tomb, Weigall was inspired to remark, "If he goes down in that spirit, I give him six weeks to live." That was on 16 February. Carnarvon's death, attributed to a mosquito bite, was soon followed by that of Mr A.C. Mace, one of

> **P**ROFESSOR Walter
> Emery, the British
> Egyptologist has died in
> Cairo from a stroke suffered
> after discovering a statue of
> the ancient Egyptian god of
> death.
>   Prof. Emery, who was 67,
> was digging in his final quest-
> seeking the tomb of the ancient
> god Imhotep (god of medi-
> cine) — at Sakkara, near the
> Pyramids, when he collapsed.
>   The Middle East News
> Agency said the Professor dis-
> covered a statue of the Egyp-
> tian god of death (Osiris) and
> was handling it when he col-
> lapsed with cerebral throm-
> bosis.
>   Prof. Emery followed in a
> distinguished line of British
> Egyptologists, including the
> discoverers of Tutankhamen's
> tomb, in Upper Egypt, in 1922.
>   A curse was supposed to rest
> with anyone desecrating the
> Tutankhamen tomb, and about
> 20 people connected with the
> tomb were said to have met
> sudden or mysteriou sdeaths.

An example, from the *Birmingham Evening Mail*, 12 March 1971, of the apparent link between tomb-defilement and sudden death.

the leading excavators; and then, to the delighted applause of the press ("ninth victim … tenth … twentieth victim", etc.), the other members of the Tutankhamen party began to die off, several in mysterious or tragic circumstances. Weigall (unknown fever) was claimed as the twenty-first victim, following Carnarvon's half-brother (suicide during temporary insanity), and old Lady Carnarvon (insect bite again), until by 1930 only one of the original tomb invaders was left alive – their director, Howard Carter.

The belief that the "Curse of the Pharaohs" accounted for Lord Carnarvon is naturally unpopular with archeologists, yet it is a fact that before he opened Tutankhamen's tomb Carnarvon received clear warning that if he did so he would soon die. The warning came in a letter from Count Hamon, the famous mystic, better known as Cheiro. With the letter, written on 30 November 1922, was a message Cheiro had received by automatic writing. It read:

"Lord Carnarvon not to enter tomb. disobey at peril. if ignored would suffer sickness; not recover; death would claim him in Egypt."

This message worried Carnarvon and he sought advice from another noted seer of the time, Velma. She inspected his palm and saw the probability of his early death in circumstances connected with the occult. A few weeks later he visited her again and she declared that his hand looked even more ominous than before. Lord Carnarvon considered withdrawing from the Egyptian enterprise, but things had gone too far, and he bravely decided to "challenge the psychic powers of the ages" – his own phrase. His death and those of his colleagues is now attributed by some Egyptologists to infectious microbes, possibly left in the tomb to deter grave robbers.

With his usual significant inconsequentiality, Charles Fort's only comment on the Carnarvon affair was to draw attention to reports from British newspapers of the time: "Upon Lord Carnarvon's estate near Newbury, Hampshire, a naked man was running wild, often seen, but never caught. He was first seen upon March 17th. Upon March 17th Lord Carnarvon fell ill, and he died upon April 5th. About April 5th, the wild man of Newbury ceased to be reported."

Another of the "wild people", this time an atavistic Orcadian, was the portent of tragedy in the household of an Orkney farmer, whose son-in-law guaranteed the truth of every detail in his account published in *Old Lore Miscellany of Orkney, Shetland, Caithness and Sutherland* (July 1911). The farmer was in the process of excavating a large old mound on his land when he was approached by a wild man, its spiritual guardian, old and grey-whiskered, "dressed in an old, grey, tattered suit of clothes, patched in every conceivable manner, with an old bonnet in his hand, and old shoes of horse or cowhide tied on with strips of skin on his feet". This apparition warned the farmer that, should he persist in his attack on the mound, he would lose six cattle and there would be six funerals from his house. The six cattle actually died as predicted, and six deaths followed in the farmer's household. The writer of the account was present at the fourth death, when he was told the story.

Family familiars

Viscount Gormanston is a very charming and handsome man, but even his best friends admit that he looks a little like a fox. Foxes run in his family. There is one running on the Gormanston crest, and another, erect, supports the coat of arms. It is also a matter of repeated record that when the Viscount Gormanston of the day is on his death bed, foxes gather round the castle to honour the passing of one whom they evidently regard as of their own kind.

Viscount Gormanston and his family crest.

In the *New Ireland Review* for April 1908 is an account of events at Gormanston Castle on the night of 8 October the previous year, when Jenico, the fourteenth Viscount, was dying in Dublin. At 8pm the gardener and coachman saw about a dozen foxes lurking about the castle and its chapel. They were barking and "crying". Two days later, at three in the morning, Jenico's son, Richard Preston, was in the chapel watching over his father's body. Outside he heard stealthy footsteps, whimperings and scratchings. He opened a side door and saw a large fox sitting just outside. There was another one behind it, and others could be heard in the bushes. Preston then went to the end door of the chapel, opened it, and there were two more foxes, one so close he could have touched it. For two hours the foxes continued to haunt the chapel and then suddenly departed.

Earlier records of the Gormanston foxes are summarized in *True Irish Ghost Stories*: "When Jenico, the twelfth Viscount, was dying in 1860, foxes were seen about the house and moving towards the house for some days previously. Just before his death three foxes were playing about and making a noise close to the house … The Hon Mrs Farrell states as regards the same that the foxes came in pairs into the demesne, and sat under the Viscount's bedroom window, and barked and howled all night. Next morning they were found crouching about in the grass in front and around the house. They walked through the poultry and never touched them. After the funeral they disappeared." At the death of Edward, the thirteenth Viscount, in 1876, the foxes were once again in attendance: "He had been rather better

one day, but the foxes appeared, barking under the window, and he died that night contrary to expectation."

There is something about these Gormanston foxes which makes them seem more like werefoxes than natural ones. In some of the cases in our collection of family death omens, the warning is given by something other than a natural living creature. There is a merging here between animals and wraiths. At the death of a Scanlon of Ballyknockane, County Limerick, strange lights appear to illuminate their residence and have always so appeared ever since the time of a seventeenth-century Scanlon who was King of Ossory. They were last seen in 1913. Many other pedigree Irishmen are warned of their deaths by the moanings or apparitions of that dread female spectre, the Banshee.

In England we hear of knocks. According to Dr Plot's seventeenth-century *Natural History of Oxfordshire*, a death in the family of Wood at Brize Norton was always preceded by "knockings on doors, tables, or shelves". The Cumberfords of Cumberford Hall were similarly affected by rappings, while the Burdets foretold the end of one of their number by a drumming sound issuing for several weeks from their chimneys. From other sources we are informed that the Roman Catholic Middletons of Yorkshire see a ghostly Benedictine nun before dying, and that the Breretons are similarly advised by a mysterious tree trunk floating in the lake before their mansion. In Scotland, the head of the Campbell clan is warned of his death by a sailing ship that appears in the loch in front of his castle (for further details see PHANTOM SHIPS, p.260).

Returning to living creatures, real or spectral, as family death omens: a white owl performs this service to the Westropp family in Ireland, its last recorded appearance being in 1909; the Arundels of Wardour were also warned by owls, two remarkably large ones which perched ominously on the battlements of their castle; and the Cliftons of Nottinghamshire had as their death omen a rare sturgeon swimming up the Trent past Clifton Hall.

In the ancestral park of the Ferrers family of Chartley near Lichfield dwelt – and maybe still dwells – an ancient herd of white cattle. To the Ferrers the birth of a black calf into this herd was fatal. The *Staffordshire Chronicle* of July 1835 gives details: "The decease of the seventh Earl Ferrers and of his Countess, and of his son, Viscount Tamworth, and of his daughter, Mrs William Jolliffe, as well as the deaths of the son and heir of the eighth Earl and of his daughter, Lady Francis Shirley, were each preceded by the ominous birth of the fatal-hued calf. In the spring of 1835 a black calf appeared at Chartley, and before long the beautiful countess, second wife of the eighth Earl, lay on her death-bed."

The see of Salisbury is not an hereditary post, but its incumbent inherits a death omen. When a Bishop of Salisbury is dying, white birds of an unusual kind are seen on Salisbury Plain. Kathleen Wiltshire describes them: "They are large birds like albatrosses, with dazzling white wings which do not move as they fly." The first recorded incident was in 1414. The Bishop of Salisbury died abroad, attending the Council of Constance. A great flock of strange white birds descended on the roof of the hall where he lay in state and stayed all night making harsh noises. It was called "a great sign of the birds".

Miss Moberly, the Bishop's daughter, saw the white birds fly up out of the Palace gardens as her father lay dying in 1885. Again, on 15 August 1911, Miss Edith Olivier, returning from a village choir outing near Salisbury, saw two curious white birds, flying but not moving their wings. She knew nothing of the bird/bishop connection at that time, but on reaching home she was told that Bishop Wordsworth had suddenly died. Her report of the white birds was then recognized as the conventional omen.

Quite the best and longest-documented history of a family haunted at times of death by a particular creature relates to the white bird of the Oxenhams. The origin of this family's connection with their white bird is lost in antiquity. An old country ballad in Devonshire tells of Sir James Oxenham preparing for the wedding of his daughter, Margaret. In the background is a jilted lover. Sir James gives a banquet. A white bird appears and Sir James shudders at the omen which, even in those legendary times, was long known in the family. Next day Margaret and her bridegroom stand at the altar. The jilted lover steps forward, stabs her and then himself. As she dies the white bird flies through the church.

The first historical record of the white bird was just before the death of Grace Oxenham in 1618. Twenty-three years later, her son James published a tract about the circumstances of certain recent deaths in his family. His son John, aged twenty-two, had suddenly died two days after a bird with a white breast had appeared in his room and hovered over the bed. Five days later, on 7 September 1635, James Oxenham's wife, Thomasine, fell ill, saw the white bird and died. The same thing happened soon afterwards to her little sister, Rebecca, aged eight, and on 15 September Thomasine's infant daughter also died, the ominous bird having previously been seen in her

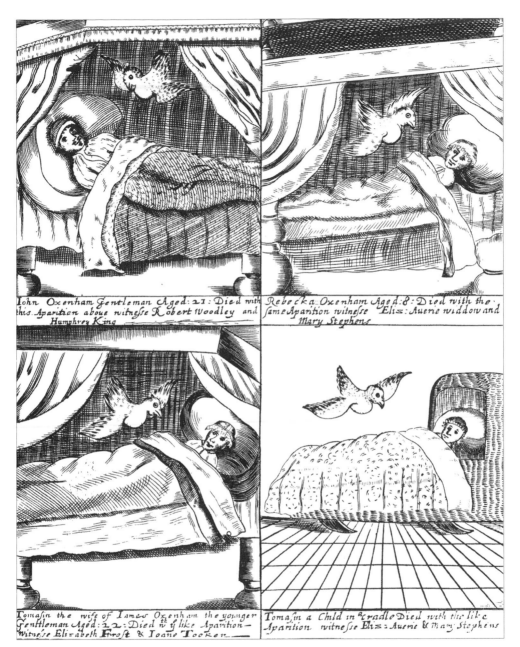

Inside illustration:

Iohn Oxenham Gentleman Aged: 21: Died with this Aparition aboue witnesse Robert Woodley and Humphrey King

Rebecka Oxenham Aged: 8: Died with the same Aparition witnesse Eliz: Auene widdow and Mary Stephens

Tomasin the wife of Iames Oxenham the younger Gentleman Aged: 22: Died w th y like Aparition— Witnesse Elizabeth Frost & Ioane Tooker

Tomasin a Child in a cradle Died with the like Aparition. witnesse Eliz: Auene & Mary Stephens

Frontispiece from J. Oxenham's *A True Relation of an Apparition* showing various appearances of the white bird of the Oxenham family.

bedroom also. James Howell in *Familiar Letters* (1646) claims that he saw in a London stonemason's yard a marble slab about to be sent into Devonshire, with an inscription that "John Oxenham, Mary his sister, James his son, and Elizabeth his mother, had each the appearance of such a bird

fluttering about their beds as they were dying."

Up to 1873 the white bird was still faithful and active. On 15 December of that year Mr G.N. Oxenham died in Kensington. According to a statement by his nephew, The Revd Henry, reproduced in F.G. Lee's *Glimpses of the Supernatural*

(1885), flutterings were heard in the dying man's chamber. And, a week before his death, there was an odd incident when his daughter and a friend, who knew nothing of the family tradition, heard a commotion, opened the window and saw a strange bird, like a pigeon but larger and white, perched on a bush just outside. Some workmen were trying to drive it away by throwing their hats at it. In Dr Mogridge's *Descriptive Sketch of Sidmouth* is an account of the death of old Mr Oxenham of Sidmouth in the second decade of the nineteenth century. Just before he died, the gardener and his wife, who both looked after him, saw a white bird fly in at the door, pass over Mr Oxenham's bed and disappear into one of the drawers of his writing desk.

We had intended to compare this sort of thing with various anthropological phenomena such as totemism and tribal affinities with animals, hoping to provide some reasonable background for our collection of family death omens. But there are certain aspects of this family/animal connection which defy comparisons and hint at the existence of some guiding – or occasionally interfering – principle behind life on Earth. This supposed principle, whatever its other qualities, is certainly not without a sense of humour. There is an old Border family called Herries, whose crest is a hedgehog because, say the heralds, it is

a pun on their name, *herisson* meaning hedgehog in French. Somehow this joke has penetrated to the hedgehogs themselves, for whenever a Herries is dying the little creatures turn up in droves to haunt his dwelling.

The Fowlers are an ancient family, and ever since the time of the Crusades their crest has been an owl. The following story was told to Mr William Fowler of Cumberland by his father and is repeated in Kathleen Wiltshire's *Ghosts and Legends of the Wiltshire Countryside* (1973). It is a story which supports our notion that there is a sense of humour in nature, and that the guiding or interfering principle referred to above enjoys the sort of joke that superior people might find rather infantile. "The Reverend W.W. Fowler, a canon of Lincoln, retired to a rectory in Wiltshire to write a book on ornithology. On the day he died, all the owls in the neighbourhood seemed to have gathered around his house, perching on the roof, gateposts, pinnacles, or any convenient place. There they remained till he was dead, when they all disappeared. On the day of the funeral, however, when the coffin was being carried under the lychgate to the church, a large white barn owl swooped down, almost touching the coffin before disappearing into the large yew trees in the churchyard."

Cities in the sky

If we were to have the apparently not uncommon experience of seeing a city in the sky, a city embellished with the most noble architectural effects, white marble towers, domes, etc; if we were lucky enough to see such a thing, we might be sufficiently curious to seek an explanation. From the list of explanations authoritatively offered over the centuries we could select one of the following causes for our vision: that it was (i) a holy city like the New Jerusalem, as seen by St John "coming down from heaven, prepared as a bride adorned for her husband" (Revelation 21:2); (ii) a reflection, due to some undetermined atmospheric function, of an actual city elsewhere (but we wonder why cities should project themselves so much more frequently than the landscapes in between them); (iii) a city of the blessed dead such as is occasionally

seen, particularly off the coasts of Celtic realms; (iv) a peculiar effect of cloud and mist; (v) an actual flying city like Laputa in Swift's *Gulliver's Travels*; (vi) a delusion of drink or religious excitement.

An image in the sky "giving the impression of distant land with wonderful white buildings" was seen from the island of Sanday in the Orkneys in 1840; it was seen again in 1857 when it lasted for about three hours. E.W. Marwick, who quotes these records in *The Folklore of Orkney and Shetland* (1975), adds that the phenomenon is not uncommon in the North. Local people explain it as being the crystal and pearl city of the Fin Folk, occasionally revealed to mortal eyes; or it may be the intermittently manifest isle of Hether Blether, whose quasi-location is west of the real sacred island Eynhallow. Marwick explains it as a mirage but does not suggest what it is a mirage of.

Roderick O'Flaherty, writing in 1684, describes a phantom island that often appears off the west coast of Ireland. He gives several possible explanations: that it is the island of Hy Brasil, known to cartographers but to nobody else; that it is the terrestrial paradise kept hidden by special ordinance of God; that it is a fabrication of evil spirits or merely an illusion of the clouds. Which of these speculations is to be preferred, says O'Flaherty wisely, "is more than our judgments can sound out".

W.G. Wood-Martin in 1902 records several appearances of Hy Brasil. It was seen off Sligo in 1885, and after a previous sighting a correspondent wrote: "I myself, upward of half a century ago, saw a wonderful mirage resembling that recently described as having been visible off our Tireragh coast (county of Sligo); and had I been looking on the Bay for the first time, nothing could have persuaded me but that I was gazing at a veritable city – a large handsome one too, trees, houses, spires, castellated buildings, etc." Wood-Martin explains that such cities are reflections of real cities somewhere else, and he offers as analogy the claims of sailors in Dublin Bay that they can sometimes see Mount Snowdon "looming" a hundred miles away. But looking out to sea from the west coast of Ireland the nearest known city in that direction that could loom would be New York, whose distinctive architecture is never a reported feature of the west Irish city vision.

On 18 July 1820, Captain Scoresby of the *Baffin* pointed his telescope at the unexplored shore of West Greenland and spied "an extensive ancient city abounding with the ruins of castles, obelisks, churches and monuments, with other large and conspicuous buildings". He drew some of these features. Sir David Brewster put the drawings together into a panorama, which is reproduced in his book *Natural Magic*. But in his engraving the architectural features are reverting to natural rock forms and have not the "distinctness of reality" as Captain Scoresby said they had.

One of the attractions of Alaska is that its local sky is peculiarly receptive to images of the city of Bristol in England. Fort in *New Lands* (1923) lists several reports of the appearance of Bristol over Alaska and quotes the tradition that this city is there visible every year between 21 June and 10 July. It, or something like it, is said to have been regularly seen by the Alaskan Indians before white settlement. In 1887 the famous pioneer Willoughby saw and photographed this aerial city, or so it was claimed, but his print looks so like the city of Bristol that many people have supposed it to be a photograph of material Bristol rather than its Alaskan phantom. Yet there is ample evidence that some remarkable city or other is at times apparent in the Alaskan skies. In *The New York Times*, 31 October 1889, Mr L.B. French reported seeing quite plainly in the sky near Mount Fairweather, Alaska, "houses, well defined streets and trees. Here and there rose tall spires over huge buildings, which appeared to be ancient mosques or cathedrals … It did not look like a modern city – more like an ancient European city". Fort quotes another correspondent from the Yukon who in June 1897 had seen a great city in the sky. Members of his party speculated on whether it most resembled Toronto, Montreal or Peking, but concluded that it was more like "some ancient city in the past".

The archaic and splendid features, often attributed to aerial cities, even when viewed in non-religious contexts, link them, phenomenally speaking, with the ideal cities of mystical vision, such as St John's vision of Jerusalem. An example of this type, cited in Flammarion's *L'Atmosphere*, is the "vast and beautiful city, adorned with monuments, domes and steeples" seen by the traveller Grellois between Ghelma and Bône in North Africa. He knew of no earthly city resembling it. However, the tendency of most modern viewers is to seek a local origin for their vision. Thus in

The New Jerusalem descending from heaven, as revealed by an angel to St John the Divine. Illustration by Gustave Doré (1866).

The photograph of the "mirage of Bristol" from Miner Bruce's *Alaska* (1900). Later identified as an actual view of the real Bristol, its similarity to the mirage may have confused its Alaskan claimants.

Besides Willoughby's picture of the mirage of "Bristol" there was another controversial image of a ghostly city over the Muir Glacier, taken by Alexander Badlam's daughter Maude, in July 1889, while on a cruise to Glacier Bay. I.W. Taber, it is claimed, photographed the same mirage at the same time, but the two images are quite different. Charles Fort, in *New Lands* (1923) wrote that he would like to think Taber's was genuine, but conceded that "Taber could have taken it by photographing a panorama that he had painted." According to Alaska historian R.N. DeArmond, Willoughby was "…a master story-teller and entertainer … One of his most famous exploits was the Silent City hoax in which he peddled hundreds of photographs from a glass plate negative which had allegedly been made at Glacier Bay and showed a ghost city."

the case quoted by Fort from *The New York Sun*, 6 March 1890, of a large unknown city seen at 4pm, over Ashland, Ohio: although some declared it to be the New Jerusalem, the majority were divided between Mansfield, thirty miles, and Sandusky, sixty miles away, as its original. The incident produced a typical forteanism: "May have been a revelation of heaven, and for all I know heaven may resemble Sandusky, and those of us who have no desire to go to Sandusky may ponder that point."

To emphasize the recurrence of the "city" phenomenon we select from Fort's collection in *New Lands* the apparition of Edinburgh, so-called, seen over Liverpool, 27 September 1846; the snow-covered, icicle-hung, inhabited village which appeared over Pomerania on 10 October

1881, and was said to resemble a settlement on the island of Bornholm a hundred miles away; and the series of phantom cities, islands and other scenes which were reported from Sweden between 1881 and 1888. From the classic phantom-city land of Ireland: an aristocratic town of mansions set in shrubberies behind white palings seen over Youghal, Cork, in June 1801, and two other visions of a walled town viewed earlier from the same city in 1796 and 1797; at Ballyconneely on the west coast a phantom city of assorted houses in different styles of architecture was on view for three hours on 2 August 1908.

Those whose favoured explanation for phantom cities is that what is seen are actual cities, detached, mobile and airborne, can respond to the obvious objection that any such bodies would be reported by astronomers or radar stations by pointing out that they are indeed so reported. The UFO literature is full of examples of sighted or radar-detected objects, often of apparently vast size, all of unknown nature. Many earlier observations of such things are to be found in Fort's collections.

The phenomenon of a recurrent landscape, most often a city or island, appearing annually or seasonally in a particular area of sky, is one which we do not think has been fully covered by any explanation yet devised. We suggest that the tradition of an enchanted land or island of the dead, described so frequently in Celtic folklore and the mythologies of many other races, is partly derived from actual visions of such a landscape. Its regular appearance at certain times may have given the old Druid priests the opportunity of predicting a vision of paradise, or of crediting themselves with its invocation. Legend attributes to them the habit of creating such grandiose

The flying city of Laputa appeared to Gulliver, in Swift's *Gulliver's Travels*, in a form which has since become popular with UFO and science-fiction illustrators.

phantasmagoria. A survival of ancient practice may lurk in the incident quoted in Davies Gilbert's *Parochial History of Cornwall* (1838): "The editor remembers a female relation of a former vicar of St Erth who, instructed by a dream, prepared decoctions of various herbs, and, repairing to the Land's End, poured them into the sea, with certain incantations, expecting to see the Lionesse country [legendary lost lands] rise immediately out of the water, having all its inhabitants alive, notwithstanding their long submersion." Unfortunately, no such country appeared.

Spectral armies

Phantom soldiers in battle array marching over the land or in the sky – this is a spectacle which cries out for an explanation. In times when traditional mythology was an active force, it was well known throughout northern Europe that the gods and heroes of Valhalla were occasionally to be seen fighting in the sky, and no Breton peasant would have been surprised at the vision of King Arthur and his retinue passing overhead on their way to battle or the chase.

The recurrent phenomenon of phantom armies could everywhere be explained in terms of local myths. As these lost their power, other explanations were developed. The apparition of an army in the sky was interpreted as the portent of a battle to come or the spectre of an ancient one, or a mirage reflecting real soldiers somewhere on

The first great battle of the First Crusade pitched the allied force of Byzantine Emperor Alexius I Comnenus against the Seljuk Turks at Nicaea, in Anatolia, in the spring of 1097. This engraving by Doré shows the Christian force encouraged to victory by celestial reinforcement.

so realistically that the saint tells of footprints of men and horses afterwards observed on the ground. This event shortly preceded an actual battle which took place on the same site. Note the explanation, typical of the time, in terms of spirits and portents.

A curious legend arose in 1537, when the Turkish army of Suleiman the Magnificent threatened the city of Otranto. Burmann's eighteenth-century *Thesaurus of the History of Italy* cites contemporary records which claim Otranto was saved by the apparition of the city's "800 martyrs" that appeared on the city walls in the company of "innumerable" angels. According to the annals of an early Christian bishop of Otranto, the 800 were killed during a previous Ottoman seige, led by Mehmed II in 1480. Their bodies were left unburied for thirteen months but "showed no sign of corruption, nor were they once violated by birds or beasts" (E.C. Brewer, *Dictionary of Miracles*, 1884). This phantom army once again rescued the city from an Ottoman onslaught in 1644. Brewer refers to a story that Christian galley slaves, pressed into service on a Turkish ship, claimed not to see the spectres striking fear into the Turks and were executed "for their short-sightedness."

When fairies are believed in, they of course provide the explanation of "phantom soldiers". W.G. Wood-Martin in *Traces of the Elder Faiths of Ireland* (1902) records an instance in 1797 of an army of "fairies" marching across the bog between Maryborough and Stradbally. They were observed at the unghostly hour of midday. In 1836 another phantom army was seen on the hills at Ballyfriar, and there is a case like St Augustine's, of a fairy battle which left physical traces on the ground. In 1800 two little armies were reported to be fighting from the ditches on each side of a road in Kilkenny, and afterwards

Earth, or a function of second sight, or a meteorological freak, a psychological projection, or extraterrestrials on manoeuvres. We think there may be something in each of these explanations, but rather than judge between them we follow our usual policy of emphasizing the phenomenon itself rather than its possible causes.

The phenomenal reality of spectral armies is well established. St Augustine records a case in *The City of God* (412–27). During the Roman civil wars a battle between "evil spirits" was seen and heard taking place on a plain in Campania, bushes were found crushed, trees broken, and there was blood on the grass.

The fairy cavalcade is regarded by folklorists as synonymous with the "Wild Hunt" or "Furious Host", the passage of an unusually destructive force through the countryside. Such was the hold of this phenomenon on the imagination of early Europeans that a whirlwind could be perceived as a mob of spirits, fairies, hounds and tormented souls led by a horned being (whose identity ranged from the Teutonic Woden to the more elemental Herne the Hunter). This animistic force was often said to travel in straight lines (see PHENOMENAL HIGHWAYS, p.206). As widely as it was feared, it was believed that any who glimpsed the Wild Hunt were withered or struck mad. Woden/Odin, his wife Frigg and other Teutonic deities were shape-changers and rode or flew on animals, brooms or hurdles to a gathering, which J.B. Russell has argued, in *Witchcraft in the Middle Ages* (1972), was the forerunner of the medieval witches' "sabbat" and just as bad luck to witness.

Apparitions of unearthly battles were recorded quite frequently during the sixteenth century and were linked by several historians with the outbreaks of millenarian fervour at that time, such as the Anabaptists' rising at Münster in 1525. Ronald Holmes in *Witchcraft in British History* (1974) cites other instances from seventeenth-century Scotland which he relates to the religious revivals of the Covenanters. According to a contemporary record, on Clydeside in the summer of 1686 there were "showers of bonnets, hats, guns and swords, which covered the trees and the ground; companies of men in arms marching in order upon the water-side…"

Similar rains and phantom armies seen in Scotland towards the end of the eighteenth century coincided with John Wesley's warnings about the diabolical reality of such things. Holmes blames them, not implausibly, on mass hysteria, but this psychological explanation does not account for the many cases of phantom armies seen during times of no particular religious excitement and by people not subject to it.

The year 1642 was a good one for phantom battles and for pamphlets on them. One such, printed in London, and now in the British Library, tells all in its title: *A Signe from Heaven, or a Fearful and Terrible Noise heard in the Ayre at Aldborow [Aldeburgh] in the County of Suffolke, on Thursday, the 4th day of August, at 5 of the clocke in the afternoone – wherein was heard the beating of Drums, the discharging of Muskets and great Ordnance for the space of an houre or more*. The pamphlet goes on to claim as witnesses "…many men of good worth" who will undertake to testify to leading Members of the House of Commons and to exhibit a stone of great weight which fell from the sky during the uproar.

The "Wild Hunt" or fairy cavalcade, two names for a phenomenon which has repeated itself over the centuries.

The title of another contemporary pamphlet describes *A great Wonder in Heaven, shewing the late Apparitions and Prodigious Noyse of War and Battels seene on Edge-Hill, neere Keinton, in Northamptonshire, 1642*. On four successive Saturday and Sunday nights, visitors to the Civil War battlefield of Edgehill (near Kineton, Warwickshire) were treated to a repeat performance of the hostilities. Gentlemen of credit were dispatched by the King at Oxford to investigate. They personally witnessed the phenomenon and swore statements to that effect.

A modern sighting of a phantom army, which was given some publicity at the time, was reported by another gentleman of credit, well known to us as such, who swears it is a true account. In November 1956, our friend Peter Zinovieff and his half-brother, Patrick Skipwith, were camping in the Cuillin Mountains of Skye. At about three o'clock one morning Peter heard strange noises, opened the tent flap and saw "…dozens of kilted Highlanders charging across the stony ground". He woke Patrick who also saw them. Both were very frightened. The next evening, after a day's walking and rock bashing (Peter was then a geology student at Oxford), they pitched the tent further up the mountains and sat up with coffee

Good Newes to Christendome (1620) contains an account of how thousands witnessed a radiant female above Mohammed's tomb, putting a Muslim army to flight. The vision lasted 21 days.

to see if the spectres would return. Nothing happened and they fell asleep. At 4am they were awakened by the same noise and again with terror saw the Highlanders, but "…retreating, stumbling across the boulders, looking half dead". At first light they ran down to the Sligachan Hotel, and later that day they told their story to a local man, Mr Ian Campbell. He said they were not the first to see the same thing and explained the Highland soldiers as phantoms "…either from the thirteenth century or the '45 Rebellion".

The age of enlightenment brought the theory of mirages, or rather the word "mirage", to account for spectral armies. Sir David Brewster applied this reasonable explanation to a wide range of unreasonable phenomena – in itself an irrational proceeding – in his *Natural Magic* (1832). One of the best attested "phantom army" sightings was on 23 June 1744, on the mountain of Souter Fell in the Cumberland Lake District. At about seven in the evening Daniel Stricket, servant to John Wren of Wilton Hall, saw many troops of soldiers riding up and over the mountain. Mr Wren was summoned and also saw them, and so did "…every person at every cottage within the distance of a mile, the number of persons who saw them amounting to about twenty-six". Brewster explains that they must have been reflections of real troopers on the other side of the mountain. But there were no soldiers then in the district, nor was there a road on the far side of the mountain; so Brewster explains further, incredibly: "But if there was then no road along which they could be marching, it is highly probable that they were troops exercising among the hills in secret, previous to the breaking out of the rebellion in 1745". Charles Fort, referring to this case, remarks on the amazing prescience of these troops, and he adds typically: "There has never been an explanation that did not itself have to be explained."

Fort, in *New Lands* (1923), goes on to assail the explainers with volleys of phantom soldiers, giving references mostly from contemporary reports. In 1785, at Ujest, Silesia, soldiers were seen marching through the sky at the time that the military funeral of General von Cosel was being held. Later, long after the funeral was over, the phantoms were seen again. On 3 May 1848, at Vienne, in Dauphiné, an army in the sky was seen by twenty witnesses; on 30 December 1850, phantom soldiers in the sky near the Banmouth; on 22 January 1854, phantom soldiers

On 29 September 1914 the London *Evening News* published a short story by Arthur Machen called *The Bowmen*. It was inspired by newspaper reports the previous month of the harrowing retreat from Mons, in Belgium, in which the British Army, despite overwhelming German forces, managed to retire in good order and hold the line. Machen's story was about the intercession of St George with a spectral army on behalf of the British. It became very popular and was much reprinted, appearing the following year as a little book, to which Machen attached an Introduction, claiming that his story had been responsible for the crop of reports and rumours that angels had indeed appeared over the field of battle. This claim was hotly contested. Harold Begbie immediately wrote a book, *On the Side of the Angels: an Answer to "The Bowmen"*, in which he abused Machen for his "amazing effrontery" in pretending that it was his story which was being imitated by the "angel" reports. Begbie quoted many accounts from individual soldiers of the visions they and their comrades had seen at Mons, accounts which were given to witnesses before Machen wrote his story. Machen, he said, had naively supposed himself to be the inspirer of the legend, whereas he had merely "picked up" unconsciously something that was in the air at the time. Begbie's informants claimed to have seen a wide range of visions, including knights, bowmen, saints, glowing angels, mysterious clouds (hiding them from the enemy) and phantom armies. A Lieutenant-Colonel wrote to Machen that on the night of 27 August 1914, during the retreat, he and all his brigade had seen ghostly squadrons of cavalry, not in the sky but riding alongside their line of march.

over Buderich; on 8 October 1812, the same at Ripley, Yorkshire; from September to October 1881, white-robed figures in the sky over Virginia, platoons of "angels" in white robes and helmets marching above Delaware, and similar reports from Maryland, all summarized in *Scientific American* that year. For several hours a day on three consecutive days from about 1 August 1888, infantry divisions led by a chief with a flaming sword marched across the sky near Varasdin, Croatia. The event was recorded in Flammarion's *L'Astronomie* with the comment that investigation had failed to discover any corresponding terrestrial soldiers in the region; nor, had such soldiers been found, would their presence explain this repeated, localized apparition.

We have many more reports from all ages of the spectral army phenomenon, but no space here even to mention them. Catherine Crowe in *The Night Side of Nature* (1848) gives some excellent cases of this remarkably persistent phenomenon, including a full report of the 1881 Ripley incident referred to above and details of the sighting near Lanark, Scotland, in 1686, when only one man in a crowd failed to see the phantom regiments apparent to everyone else. Suddenly, with terror, he too saw them, and Mrs Crowe suggests that he may have temporarily received the second sight from a seer standing by him. This excellent writer rejects the mirage theory on the grounds that there is often no possible original image to be reflected, particularly in the cases when the phantom soldiers' uniforms are of another age. In speaking in terms of spirits, spirit-seers and impressions of ancient events occasionally reforming themselves as apparitions, she voices a tradition that is ancient indeed.

Phantom ships

In the early morning of 11 July 1881, the future King George V as a young naval officer sighted the famous spectral ship, *The Flying Dutchman*, in the South Atlantic. It did not particularly surprise him; similar apparitions have been reported by seafarers from the earliest times. Sightings also include ships that appear to be navigating through the clouds. In the *Flying Saucer Review*, May–June 1971, there is a report from 1743 of a farmer near Holyhead in Anglesea, who saw a packet-boat sailing through the clouds 1500 feet overhead. Its keel was clearly visible, proving that it was no mirage of a ship at sea, and the farmer estimated its displacement as about ninety tons.

There is a reference in ancient Irish annals to "fantastical ships" seen in 1161, sailing against the wind into Galway harbour. W.G. Wood-Martin, quoting this in *Traces of the Elder Faiths of Ireland* (1902), also gives another instance of the sighting of an aerial navy by hundreds of people on a hill at Croaghpatrick, Mayo "on a serene evening in the autumn of 1798". It was, explains Wood-Martin, "produced by the reflection of the fleet of Admiral Warren which was then in pursuit of a French squadron off the west coast of Ireland." He goes on to suggest that the Galway ships of 1161 must have been a reflection of Norse war-galleys.

Long before any known airship there was a belief that aerial ships existed. Agobard, Archbishop of Lyons in the ninth century, was confronted with a crowd of local people escorting four prisoners who, they said, had been caught landing from a cloud-ship. They requested the Archbishop's leave to stone them. Agobard refused, not believing the airship story, and later reported (we quote him from G.G. Coulton's *Medieval Panorama*) that the locals were so unreasonable as to "believe and assert that there is a certain region called Magonia, whence ships come in the clouds: the which bear away the fruits of the earth ... to that same country".

The histories of Cornwall and Brittany contain many references to ships which are seen to sail across land, particularly on certain anniversaries, at times preceding storms or at the death of a notable person. The Land's End district of Cornwall was once famous for such apparitions, of which several are recorded in W. Bottrell's *Traditions and Hearthside Stories of West Cornwall* (1870). The actual paths over which these ships navigate are sometimes noted; and we suspect that certain old roads were originally laid to follow the traditional route of a phantom ship (see PHENOMENAL HIGHWAYS, p.206). In about 1835 Robert

A sighting of *The Flying Dutchman* – the spectral echo of a ship that vanished in a fierce storm off the Cape of Good Hope in 1641. The legend states that as the ship went down, Captain VandeDecken shouted a curse: "I will round this Cape even if I have to keep sailing until doomsday!" Of course, today the ship's moniker is better known for having been used for the fictional cursed ship in *The Pirates Of The Caribbean* movie franchise.

Hunt, author of *Popular Romances of the West of England (1865),* spoke to a man who had seen the wondrous ship of Porthcurno, also described by Bottrell, which "would drive into Porthcurno against wind and tide; oft-times she came in the dark of evening and, without stopping at the Cove, took her course over the old caunce towards Chapel-Curno; thence she sailed away, her keel just skimming the ground, or many yards above it, as she passed over hill and dale till she arrived at Chygwidden". The ship would then vanish at a rock, beneath which a hoard of coins was discovered.

On the arms of the Duke of Argyll, Chief of the Clan Campbell, is a vessel described heraldically as "a lymphad or ancient galley, sails furled, flags and pennants flying gules, and oars in action sable". At the death of a senior Campbell this ship appears on Loch Fyne by Inveraray, Scotland. Lord Halifax in his *Ghost Book* says he was told by the Duke that just after the death of his father, Lord Archibald Campbell, in 1913 the galley had appeared with its usual crew of three men and had followed its regular course over the Loch to a certain spot on the shore, whence it proceeded overland to the sanctuary of St Columba. A curious detail is that on this occasion it was seen not only by local people but also by a visiting Englishman who called out, "Look at that funny airship!"

A similar apparition was seen in June 1959 over New Guinea. The incident, first reported in the Sydney *Sun* and later much discussed in UFO literature, is an interesting one because of the number and sobriety of the witnesses (Father Gill and the entire staff and inmates of the Anglican mission in Papua) and because it is another instance of a well-documented modern event for which there is much precedent in early records and folklore. The ship which hovered over the Mission was circular with a superstructure "like the bridge of a boat". Its crew of four leant over the rails, and when Father Gill and his flock waved to them, they waved back.

"The Great Airship Flap of 1897" is the name now given to the most remarkable phenomenon that ever defied explanation. The events of this saga are so bizarre as to seem incredible, yet if we are to give credence to any historical records of the very recent past, we can scarcely withhold it from the mass of contemporary statements which suggest that, throughout the nineteenth century (particularly during its last decade) the skies of North America were infested by a large miscellany of "impossible" airships (see OTHERWORLDLY ABDUCTIONS, p.168).

In Charles Fort's *New Lands* (1923) is the first compilation of some of the many scattered reports of mysterious lights and airships in 1896 and 1897;

The crescent Moon as the boat of souls, as on this 1st century BC chalcedony gem, demonstrates the antiquity of the idea of celestial craft bearing emissaries from other worlds.

and Fort was the first to make the revolutionary suggestion that the phenomenon might well be attributed to visitors from another world. Recently, a great many more newspaper reports of the time have been unearthed by UFO researchers and quoted in such books as John Keel's *UFOs: Oper-*

ation *Trojan Horse* (1970) and Clark and Coleman's *The Unidentified* (1975). April 1897 was the peak of the "flap". There were airship reports from all over America, the majority from the Midwest and Texas. A cigar-shaped, winged object, with a canopy or superstructure and brightly lit with coloured lights, passed over Iowa, Michigan, Washington and many other states. Thousands of people saw it over Chicago. There were absurd but respectably attested reports of landings, messages received and occupants encountered, varying from dwarfish Orientals to tall, bearded white men; and there were hoaxes and strange rumours of secret airship inventors. There were at the time no known dirigible airships flying in America, yet on 19 April 1897 the *Dallas Morning News* reported the crash of an airship at Aurora, Texas, together with the remarkable statement that the dead pilot was "not an inhabitant of this world", and that "Mr J. T. Weems, the US Signal Service officer at this place and an authority on astronomy, gives it as his opinion that he was a native of the planet Mars". A recent proposal to reopen the grave and examine the "Martian" was defeated by residents' objections.

Of all the newspaper reports of 1897 airship activities, the most amazing is the following from the *Houston Daily Post,* 28 April: "Merkal, Texas, April 26. Some parties returning from church last night noticed a heavy object dragging along with a rope attached. They followed it until in crossing the railroad it caught on a rail. On looking up they saw what they supposed was the airship. It was not near enough to get an idea of the dimensions. A light could be seen protruding from several windows; one bright light in front like the headlight of a locomotive. After some ten minutes a man was seen descending the rope; he came near enough to be plainly seen. He wore a light blue sailor suit, was small in size. He stopped when he discovered parties at the anchor and cut the ropes below him and sailed off in a northeast direction. The anchor is now on

The ship of Porthcurno engraving by Joseph Blight from Bottrell's *Traditions and Hearthside Stories of Cornwall* (1870).

In the early 1950s, George Adamski, a hotdog vendor at the Mount Palomar Observatory and founder of the Royal Order of Tibet, claimed regular meetings with beings from other planets who had come to save the Earth from nuclear destruction. As proof he offered an unparalleled variety of photographs of their craft, from small "scoutships" to gigantic cigar-shaped "motherships" like the one shown here.

exhibition at the blacksmith shop of Elliott and Miller and is attracting the attention of hundreds of people."

Loren E. Gross, another patient scholar of the "airship flaps", suggested in his *Charles Fort, the Fortean Society and UFOs* (1976) that we should try to see the Aurora and Merkal cases against the popular imaginings of the time. This was the period, Gross points out, when Percival Lowell's telescopic surveys of Mars from his giant new telescope on a mountain near Flagstaff, Arizona,

were receiving much attention in the press, and creating a boom in amateur astronomy. Another factor must have been the serialization that spring of H.G. Wells's *The War of the Worlds* in *Cosmopolitan* magazine. Not surprisingly there was much talk of "men from Mars". On 7 March 1897, the *Salt Lake Tribune,* Utah, published an article referring to beliefs in "cloud ships" under the title "A Sea above the Clouds – Extraordinary Superstition once prevalent in England".

Thus at least twelve days before the anchor-incident at Merkal we find that a newspaper in another state had told the story of a much earlier anchored "cloud-ship". This occurred in Bristol at the beginning of the thirteenth century and is recorded in the *Otia Imperialia* of Gervase of Tilbury. People coming out of a church after Mass heard a cry in the air and saw a "cloud-ship" overhead with its anchor and cable caught on a tombstone. A sky-sailor descended the cable to free it, but was detained by the people and drowned in the gross atmosphere of Earth. The crew of the airship then cut the cable and made off. This story has yet another precedent. In *FATE* magazine, March 1958, is printed a translation from another thirteenth-century manuscript, the Norse-Irish *Speculum regale*, describing how in about AD 956 a sky-ship's anchor caught on the porch of St Kinarus's church in the borough of Cloera. Again, one of the sailors descended the rope, but this time the bishop deterred the people from seizing him, and he sailed off unharmed with the rest of the crew, leaving the anchor as a souvenir of their visit.

Odd clouds

For previous ages clouds were a perfect symbol of the phenomenal universe, for in clouds could be seen all kinds of illusory forms. As Shakespeare noted in *Antony and Cleopatra*:

"Sometimes we see a cloud that's dragonish;
A vapour sometime like a bear or lion,
A towering citadel, a pendant rock,
A forked mountain or blue promontory
With trees upon't, that nod unto the world
And mock our eyes with air ..."

The Prajna Paramita (a Buddhist hymn of the first century AD) insists that the forms we take for everyday reality are transient and the true nature of reality is more like the ceaseless shape-changing of clouds and dream-images – a view consistently supported by all forms of mystical experience.

We begin our look at the phenomenon of odd clouds with an incident from the log of the barque *Lady of the Lake* found in the *Journal of the Royal Meteorological Society* (vol.1, p.157). On 22 March 1870, the captain and crew saw a "remarkable cloud" that remained stationary against the wind until it was lost in the evening darkness. They described it as a stable, circular form with an

This photo (of unknown origin) has circulated among Catholic groups who believe it shows a "solar miracle" at San Damiano, Italy. The cloud-like figure atop the flaring Sun is variously said to be the Virgin Mary or a robed St Pio – see also PHOTOGRAPHS OF THE GODS (p.296). Some sceptics suggest it was added later.

like ghosts appearing or vanishing. A typical sighting which merges UFOs with meteorological effects was reported in the *Flying Saucer Review* (vol.9, no.4). In November 1958, Dr and Mrs M. Moore were in their car near the border between North and South Dakota. The sky was cloudless except for a "silvery, cigar-shaped object, like a giant windsock", which accelerated out of view leaving behind it a trail of strange purple clouds.

Another link between UFOs and clouds is indicated in *New Report on Flying Saucers* by Lloyd Mallan, a reporter for *True* magazine. He interviewed Allen Noonan, who believed that he was in touch with "Galactic Command" who maintained UFO bases within the Earth (see THE HOLLOW EARTH, p.202). Noonan told Mallan that two UFOs might appear in the cloudless sky outside their hotel window, so he loaded his camera with infrared film and waited. Ten minutes later, "two saucer-shaped clouds had formed in trail between some buildings across the way". Mallan felt sure they were conventional lenticular clouds, but was astonished that they should have appeared when and where Noonan had predicted.

In the 1980s, farmers in southern France and Spain hired all sorts of rainmakers during months of prolonged drought. What few successes they had were inadequate and it was widely thought that rival marketing conglomerates were using every means (high-tech planes having superseded rogue magicians) to "steal" their rain clouds. We can only observe that cloud-summoning and cloud-busting have always been among the powers claimed by shamans and magicians of most cultures. Their traditions were continued by the "magnetizers" of the nineteenth century and by the followers of Wilhelm Reich's theory of "orgone" energy – both of whom made weather control part of their general occult technology.

Cloud, mist and vapour are basic elements in mystery. In *Human Animals* (1969), Frank Hamel tells of fogs that aided the transformation

internal semicircle divided radially into four, from which extended a long "tail" which curved back towards the "body". This massive, fluffy tadpole of a cloud challenged everything they knew about the behaviour and constitution of clouds, but – being practical sailors – they were content merely to note the details and avoid speculation.

Many of the strange apparitions classified as UFOs are described as cloud-like, reminding us of the "cloud ships" reported by French country people at the time of Agobard, Archbishop of Lyons in the ninth century (see PHANTOM SHIPS, p.260). Photographs of UFOs commonly show objects which look half solid and half nebulous,

This elephant-shaped cloud over a temple in Chiang Mai, Thailand, photographed in 1994, seems like an acknowledgement of the Buddhist reverence for elephants. The Buddha's mother dreamed of a white elephant immediately before his birth, and this particular temple features carvings of elephants.

Solitary lenticular clouds – sometimes referred to as "pile of plates" clouds – have a distinctive shape and are sometimes mistaken for UFOs.

of witches into animals and birds or that concealed them with cloaks of invisibility. The world over, supernatural beings and sages are said to use clouds as vehicles or messengers; for example, the seduction of the nymph Io by Jupiter in the form of a cloud (as recounted in Ovid's *Metamorphosis*). Indeed, one of the continuities in our data is that metamorphoses are often indicated or accompanied by mists or clouds. Most phantoms have this quality; thus, a Black Dog legend from Dorset (see BLACK DOGS, p.322) quoted by Patricia Dale-Green, says the beast will grow larger if watched, eventually swelling into a large cloud and vanishing. Several forms of the "transition-cloud" exist in the spiritualist cosmology, such as the soul likened to a vapour rising from the body at the moment of death, and the clouds of ectoplasm from which materialize faces, hands, and so on. Ghosts too often have a mist-like structure, and interestingly there are many accounts of ghostly human forms with parts of their anatomy hidden or replaced by a local cloudy mass.

Many religious apparitions begin or end with a small, curious cloud (see SHARED VISIONS AND VISUAL RUMOURS, p.110). On 16 October 1984, Mrs Rosa Quattrini, known as Mama Rosa, was talking to a neighbour in an orchard at San Damiano in Italy, when both noticed a peculiar cloud forming in the air among the branches of a damson tree. It floated over to a pear tree where it seemed to solidify into a female form, resplendent with beams of light, a crown on her head and a flower in each hand. This was the first of many appearances of the Virgin Mary to Mama Rosa, and only she ever saw the radiant lady on these occasions. In contrast, the entire congregation of a church in Warsaw, in 1801, saw the shining Virgin Mary appear from a cloud.

In PHANTOM MUSIC AND STRANGE VOICES (see p.152) we tell of the day when "demons" interrupted the services of St Clement Hofbauer. Later the same day, as Zsolt Aradi tells it in his *Book of Miracles* (1957), as St Clement prayed before the altar of St Joseph, "hundreds of people saw a cloud forming above the altar, then enveloping the figure of the saint, who disappeared from their sight. In his place [they] saw a celestial vision. A woman of great beauty, with radiant features, appeared and smiled at the worshippers, who only a few hours ago had been frightened by the prodigies of the devil."

People who see apparitions in clouds are inclined, like Mama Rosa, to feel they are being communicated with and accept them as messengers. Medieval chronicles abound with this kind of celestial vision during strange meteorological events, and people continue to this day to see figures among the clouds. The phenomenon is not restricted to Christian cultures, as Robert Bartholomew, an American anthropologist and author of several studies of collective delusions and related phenomena, points out. In Algiers, in June 1990, for example, as the leader of the newly elected Islamic Salvation Front Party addressed an ecstatic crowd, they saw, in the direction of Mecca, a cloud take the shape of the Arabic script for Allah (*Daily Telegraph,* 16 June 1990).

A similar display of mystical picture-making clouds attracted the attention of an awed crowd at an Islamic school in the Malaysian state of Selangor. During the evening of 29 July 1992, twenty-six distinct images were seen, including a foetus in a womb, two corpses and women exposing their sexual parts. The event was interpreted by devout Muslims as depicting the ascension of the Prophet Mohammed. Bartholomew, who interviewed witnesses for a report on the incident for the government's Islamic Centre, said more images were seen the following day. "Drawings of the images were made by the students yet they appear to have misperceived clouds in the night sky reflective of their religious background," he wrote in *UFOs and Alien Contact* (1998).

A curious case from the nineteenth century was recorded in a rare Canadian pamphlet, *Wonderful Phenomena* by Eli Curtis, from statements collected by Addison A. Sawin. On 3 October 1843, Charles Cooper, labouring in a field near Warwick, Ontario, heard a low rumbling in the sky and looked up to see a strange, solitary cloud beneath which hung, or hovered, three "perfectly white" figures, calling to him with "loud and mournful noises". He thought they were angels, and Sawin, a spiritualist, naturally saw in it "the glorious hope of the Resurrection". What is more interesting to us is the selective nature of the phenomenon; just as Mama Rosa could see the Virgin where others could only see mist, other witnesses at Warwick – some nearly six miles away and some in an adjacent field – all agreed on the "remarkable cloud", though not all of them saw the "angels" or heard the sounds.

Sometimes we hear of clouds appearing in answer to an unspoken need. Harold T. Wilkins, in his *Strange Mysteries of Time and Space* (1958), quotes a British naval officer's story about the

The story goes that a USAF man in Korea took a picture of American and Communist planes in combat and was surprised, on developing it, to see the huge image of Christ dominating the sky below them. Editions of the Ashland, Kentucky, *Independent*, which carried the picture in the late 1960s, rapidly sold out. Many of the claims made about it are contradictory. Christ is not made up of clouds, no one connected with the photo is named or can be traced, and the barely discernible planes (above Christ and to the right) are identical bombers in tandem rather than different fighters in combat. Despite these doubts, the widespread belief in the authenticity of the image places it in the same meaningful tradition as the "Bowmen of Mons". For other "divine" photographs, see PHOTOGRAPHS OF THE GODS, p.296.

Allied invasion of North Africa. He said the sea was dead calm and the entire fleet was completely exposed, an easy target for German bombers. Before long, as though in response to their nakedness, an "immense black cloud" formed, staying directly over the armada for ten consecutive days. The officer said: "I was not alone in thinking that Providence set the cloud there." A similar story is told of clouds that "miraculously" veiled the retreat of the British army at Mons, August 1914 (see SPECTRAL ARMIES, p.255).

Tales of encounters with UFOs and their "occupants" sometimes involve terrifying vapours that paralyse, blind and suffocate. We have many data on clouds behaving malevolently: some bursting into flames, some which are luminous or magnetic, some which "bounce" along, and

DENISE ALLISON & CLIFFORD SCULLION

In December 1990, a tourist from Northern Ireland visited New York and took this photograph of the Statue of Liberty. The satanic features gazing down at the statue were only noticed later.

others which hiss or broadcast a series of loud explosions.

We have noticed in our sections on things which fall from the skies that some of these falls originate in odd clouds. In *Strange World* (1964), Frank Edwards relates the story of Ed Mootz tending his Cincinnati, Ohio, garden on 22 July 1955, when it rained a blood-like, oily liquid. Mootz saw this grisly rain falling from a small, solitary red, pink and green cloud that appeared to be rolling along about a thousand feet overhead. Drops that fell on his skin began to sting him. He went inside to wash, and when he returned the cloud was gone. Strangely, it was not reported elsewhere. The next day the trees and grass were dead; everywhere the red rain had fallen was now brown, shrivelled and dying. According to Edwards the incident was never explained, despite investigations. Similarly, we recall that in the case of the shower of "blood and muscle" on the tobacco-field at Lebanon, Tennessee (mentioned in RAINS OF SEEDS AND ORGANIC MATTER, p.58), a red cloud was noticed flying directly over the field.

Clearly then, there are clouds which are only "were-clouds". There is no way, in our conventional knowledge of clouds, to account for the hissing "ball of fog" that swooped down on a car in Minnesota. According to *The Eagle Bend News* (25 May 1961), the car was left unbearably hot and pitted with tiny holes. Nor can we explain the report by a postman in Thailand, quoted in the *San Francisco Chronicle* (23 April 1962), that he saw a red and green fog crumble into little pieces which he thoughtfully collected.

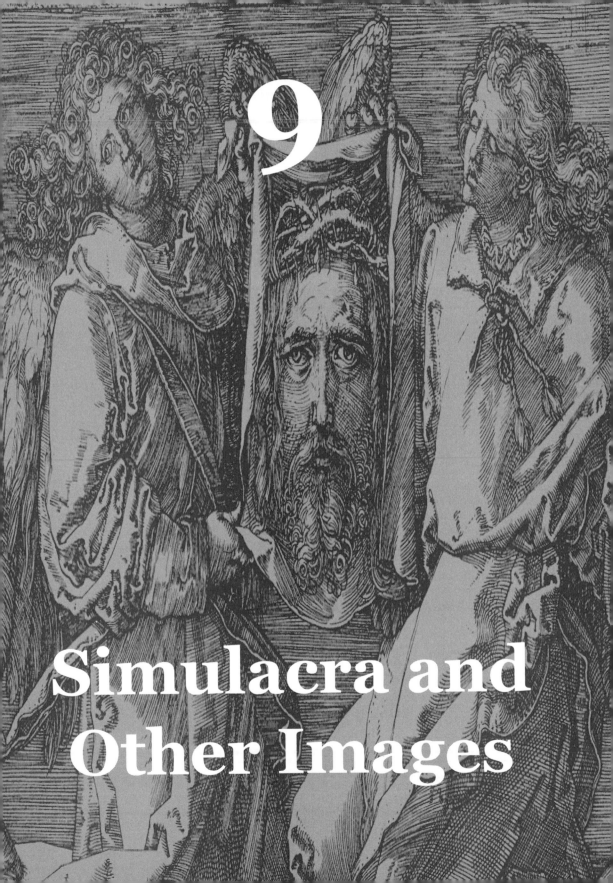

9

Simulacra and Other Images

9

Simulacra and Other Images

Faces and figures in nature

In the fifth century AD the Armenians rose in revolt against their Persian rulers. Led by the saintly Vartan, their small army met the enemy at Averayr near Chermoog, where they were defeated with great loss of life. Among the victims was St Vartan, thereafter regarded as a martyr. After the battle a group of Armenians gathered in a nearby valley to mourn their loss and to pray that St Vartan would be restored to them. Suddenly it was noticed that a rock in the valley had taken on his appearance, complete with white beard and mitre. This greatly uplifted the spirit of the Armenians and inspired them in their fight for independence.

This story of a significant image, turning up in the right place at the right time, would fit just as well into our COINCIDENCES section (see p.241). So would the whole subject of simulacra – things that look like other things. Everyone occasionally sees shapes or pictures in clouds, trees, rock formations, flickering fire, running water and any mottled surface – even in the static of TV screens. The coincidence arises when a natural shape seems to relate to its locality.

A common form of simulacra-coincidence is

This profile in rocks near Chermoog, Armenia, is revered as that of local hero and martyr St Vartan. The appearance of his gigantic portrait in the cliffside is accepted by the Armenian church as a miracle.

the natural rock-form which, seen from a certain angle, reproduces the typical features of the people or animals that live around it. These spontaneous images are often prominent in local folklore, and in times of pagan religion they were symbols of the gods and other characters of mythology. They give hints about the spiritual qualities and the natural products and uses of the country around them. In China feng-shui masters interpreted the symbolic shapes in hills and rocks as expressions of the general character of the people living within sight of them. If a local crag were shaped like a person at a desk, it might indicate that the people nearby were likely to be clerks or scholars. When, in modern times, a scientific expedition to a remote Chinese village sought to discover why so many twins were being born in that district, the locals pointed out the twin peaks of the mountain above them.

Certain spots on the Earth are seen by mystics as "generation centres" or points d'amour, because they are spots where nature seems to manifest the prototypes of Creation. The Forest of Fontainebleau outside Paris is an area of curious rocky outcrops, many of which are shaped like animals, some familiar, some yet unknown. Among them are three different examples of nature's attempts at sculpting an elephant. In the north of England, above Pateley Bridge in Yorkshire, a fifty-acre ridge of millstone grit, called Brimham Rocks, has been carved by wind ino a menagerie of strange beasts which include camels, bears, turtles, apes and other forms suggestive of a past or future creation. A famous area for natural likenesses is the Arizona desert, where tall, eroded, red rocks combine with sunlight and shadow to produce a wonderland of fantasy creatures. Among them one can sometimes discern the features and religious symbols of the local Indians.

The correspondence of shapes in the landscape with the looks and artefacts of the indig-

A cross-section of Mexican agate which reveals the mountainous landscape where it was found.

enous people is one of the fascinating aspects of simulacra studies. This correspondence was revealed most dramatically to the French artist, writer and visionary, Antonin Artaud. In 1936 he travelled through Mexico to the mountainous land of the peyote-eating Tarahumara Indians, intending to sample their drugs and to experience their states of mind. As he crossed the Sierra he became aware that, among the chance shapes and images that his eye picked out in the rocky landscape, certain figures kept recurring. Religious emblems and universal, esoteric symbols repeated themselves in the rock formations. "I shall not argue if someone says that all these forms are natural," he wrote. "It is their repetition that is not natural." In "The Mountain of Signs" (from an Artaud collection, *The Peyote Dance*) he declared

C T. Ballard

A striking example of a tree seeming to take on the appearance of a female torso.

that "the land of the Tarahumara is full of signs, forms and natural effigies which in no way seem the result of chance". He eventually realized that the shapes he saw over and again in the rocks were reproduced in the sacred ritual symbols of the local people. And then, "the whole landscape revealed itself as the creation of a single thought, which had given shape to the rocks and to all indigenous life, plants, animals and men". From this perception, of a landscape and all its inhabitants, animal, vegetable and mineral, under the dominance of one formative spirit, Artaud came to see the former existence of a sacred science, the science of Paradise on Earth.

Artaud is far from being the only writer to have expressed that idea. In 1952 a Peruvian traveller, Daniel Ruzo, discovered gigantic artworks, as he called them, of a vanished civilization on the remote desert plateau of Marcahuasi, west of the Andes. There were huge carvings of people and creatures, rocks that looked like Inca heads and others figuring animals unknown or long extinct. Many of the most impressive forms were only made visible at the Summer Solstice by the play of light and shadow. Ruzo persuaded himself that these were the works of supreme, prehistoric artists, who had shaped mountains all over the

world to represent gods and philosophical ideals. Peter Kolosimo supported this idea in his book *Timeless Earth* (1973): "The number of rock carvings to be seen in every continent suggests the handiwork of migrant artists with titanic powers and titanic chisels."

Ancient sculptors may perhaps have worked on rock faces to make them more like one thing or another, but nature alone, aided by the imaginative human eye, is the supreme artist. And, like human artists, nature's favourite theme is the face. The staring eye-nose-mouth pattern occurs in the markings of many creatures, on the backs of crabs, on the hood of the cobra and widely among all kinds of insects. These and other examples of "mimicry" in nature are a constant puzzle to biologists. The evolutionist Sir Julian Huxley produced a quaint explanation for the fierce Samurai face on the shell of the edible Japanese crab, suggesting that superstitious fishermen who noticed something like a face on a crab threw it back. Crabs with the best faces therefore survived to produce offspring with even better ones. A response to this is that the English *Cassivelaunus* crab also bears a face on its shell, though with European features. This cannot have been developed by fishermen throwing the best ones back, since the crab was never eaten.

Obvious faces can be seen on the folded wings of moths, and these are sometimes accentuated when an insect displays the "eye spots" on its underwings. The probable effect of these and other face-patterns in nature is to scare off enemies. This implies that it has a universal meaning as an image of fear and dread – a bogeyman image. A staring face is naturally frightening. That seems to be true, not only on the human scale but also among smaller creatures. On the chrysalis of a small North American butterfly, *Feniseca tarquinius*, is a startlingly clear image of a face, but the chrysalis is only a quarter of an inch long. Strangely enough, the face is said to have the look of an American Indian. This is clearly not a case of the chrysalis mimicking an Indian, because of the discrepancy in scale. The same is true of the South American lantern bug. Markings on its head reproduce the features on an alligator, complete in every detail, with apparent teeth, eyes and nostrils. Yet this cannot fool its enemies into thinking that it is a real alligator, because its head is no more than three inches long.

Instead of mimicry we think of simulacra.

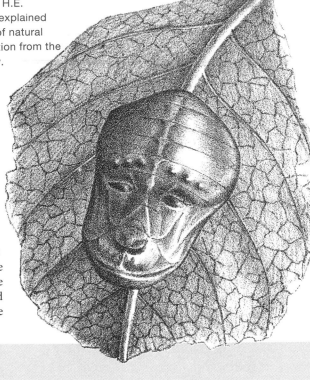

Chrysalis of the Indian butterfly *Spalgis epius*. H.E. Hinton, an expert on natural camouflage, has explained the anthropoid face pattern as being a result of natural selection in mimicry of local monkeys. Illustration from the *Journal of the Bombay Natural History Society*.

Nature and our own imaginations are always conspiring to create illusions, and these are often repetitious. Artaud found repetitions in the simulacra shapes of the Mexican rocks, and this led him on to dream of a universal language of symbols, the Creator's pattern book. It is a dream that has always inspired artists, one of whom, Leonardo da Vinci, saw "the most exquisite landscapes" in the texture of a mildewed wall, and advised his students to let such random configurations feed their imaginations. The eighteenth-century English water-colourist Alexander Cozens even went so far as to make random blots the starting point for his landscape paintings, while the Surrealist Max Ernst used rubbings onto paper from wood and stone as the basis for much of his imagery.

Footprints and tracks

On the morning of 9 February 1855 the inhabitants of the South Devon towns of Topsham, Lympstone, Exmouth, Teignmouth and Dawlish awoke to find themselves in the centre of what *The Times* a week later called an "Extraordinary Occurrence". The report took the form of a letter, from which the following extract summarizes what happened:

"It appears that on Thursday night last there was a very heavy fall of snow in the neighbourhood of Exeter and the south of Devon. On the following morning the inhabitants of the above towns were surprised at discovering the tracks of some strange and mysterious animal, endowed with the power of ubiquity, as the footprints were to be seen in all kinds of inaccessible places – on the tops of houses and narrow walls, in gardens and courtyards enclosed by high walls and palings, as well as in open fields. There was hardly a garden in Lympstone where the footprints were not observed. The track appeared more like that of a biped than a quadruped, and

the steps were generally eight inches in advance of each other. The impressions of the feet closely resembled that of a donkey's shoe."

A lively correspondence on the mystery developed in *The Times* and spread to the *Illustrated London News*, in the course of which further interesting details came to light. The "devil's footprints" had been found to stretch for a distance of over a hundred miles. At one point they had jumped over the two-mile wide estuary of the River Exe, continuing on one side opposite where they had left off on the other. Nothing had impeded their progress or broken their even spacing of eight inches. They were found on each side of a haystack, which was untouched, and on each side of a fourteen-foot wall. A curious feature of the prints was that they were placed one in front of the other rather than as in a normal animal trail.

Happily for those of us who enjoy explanations, the event happened during the high season of scientific rationalism, and a fine crop was raised in answer to the mystery. They included otters, leaping rats, a rope trailing from a balloon, and the devil (this one was particularly popular

The Jersey Devil (above) as seen by Mr and Mrs Nelson Evans in 1909.

locally). Professor Richard Owen, who could always be relied on for an opinion regarding anything unexplained, weighed in authoritatively with his verdict – badgers. Even a definitive study by Dr Mike Dash (*Fortean Studies* no.1, 1994) of 50 original sources failed to settle the matter. It is an abiding English mystery.

Its American counterpart was the massive outbreak of "devil's footprints" that caused shock and sensation across the state of New Jersey in January 1909. Thousands of hoof marks, like a pony's, were found one morning after a snowfall and they continued to appear in the days that followed. Like the earlier Devonshire tracks, they extended for long distances over walls, buildings, wire fences and other obstacles, and then abruptly ended, as if the creature that made them had taken to the air. The hoof prints were recorded in over thirty towns as well as in remote rural districts. Their first appearance was in the Pine Barrens, a sandy, tree-covered waste area where a mysterious monster, the Jersey Devil, had long been known to the local farmers and to the Indian tribe before them. While the hoof marks were appearing, hundreds of people reported sightings of the creature. They described a sort of chimera, made up of dif-

ferent animal features – a horse's head, large, bat-like wings – and bounding like a kangaroo. A drawing of the Jersey Devil, from details provided by witnesses, was published in *The Philadelphia Evening Bulletin*, January 1909.

And these stories are not alone. The thirteenth-century Japanese history, the *Kokon Chomonshu*, records how "In the year 929 the Imperial palace was found one morning full of demon's tracks as big as an ox's and coloured red and blue." Two incidents can be found in the *Chronicon anglicanum* composed by Abbot Ralph of Coggeshall in the early thirteenth century. In the first case, monstrous, pointed, hoof-like tracks appeared on the ground the day after a fierce electrical storm on 29 July 1205; and in the second, which took place at York in the reign of Richard I, "…there appeared in certain grassy flat ground human footprints of extraordinary length; and everywhere the footprints were impressed the grass remained as if scorched by fire."

A correspondent in Heidelberg, on hearing of the Devon prints, wrote to the *Illustrated London News* (14 March 1855) that similar tracks could be seen every year in sand and snow on a hill on the Polish border; and in his account in *Oddities* (1965) of the Devon incident, R.T. Gould mentions the entry for May 1846 in Captain Sir James Ross's record of his Antarctic explorations, describing how on the sub-Antarctic island of Kerguelen a party found hoof-like prints in the snow, stretching for some distance, although there was no animal on the island to account for them.

In Dr E.L. Dingwall's *Tomorrow* (1957) there is an account of a man named Wilson who visited a secluded beach on the west coat of Devon in October 1950. He was the first person to walk on the cliff-enclosed beach after the tide had left the sand quite smooth, and was therefore surprised to see a series of hoof-like prints which began under a perpendicular cliff and led in a straight line to the sea. They were not cloven, but evenly spaced at six feet apart, and deeper than his own – a giant, heavy stride, unlike the mincing "devil's footprints" left in Devon snows nearly a century previously. Wilson also noticed that each print was not impressed, but appeared to be "cut out of the sand". Dingwall adds that similar tracks were reported on New Jersey beaches in 1908 – "marks like the hooves of a pony in thick snow". Here again, he noticed, "we have the story of how tracks led up to wire fences and continued on the other side". They were attributed to the Jersey Devil, a mystery animal of the region, that had been known from the previous century and was still generating sightings as late as 1930. Twin-lobed, crescent-shaped tracks, similar to but smaller and more irregularly spaced than the Devon tracks of 1855, were reported from Belgium in 1945.

Once in a while we discover a note of a single anomalous footprint, or rather a single footprint located anomalously such as that seen by Austin Hatton, a columnist for the *Sunday Telegraph*. He was trudging along the old pilgrim way from the Isle of Ely to the shrine at Little Walsingham when he came upon a 30-yard stretch of hardened sand. "In the centre, perfectly formed and dried hard was the imprint of a small, bare foot. Nowhere else could I find any other mark. Not a single explanatory indentation. The stretch was too wide for anybody, especially with such small feet, to have jumped across it … in a gigantic leap." Hatton, who declares his disbelief in fairies, said, "For once I feel the supernatural has set a trap for me." (*Sunday Telegraph*, 28 April 1974)

One of the most interesting theories about the tracks comes from the personal experience of the explorer, James Alan Rennie. During a venture into northern Canada in 1924, he and his mate, a French-Canadian dog-skinner, were crossing a frozen lake when they came across a set of large, bear-like, two-toed tracks, spaced equally in a single line. Their unnaturalness "reduced my companion to gibbering terror"; the poor man asserted that they were made by Windigo, the Canadian version of Bigfoot. Later Rennie returned across the same lake, and in bright sunshine caught sight of something that chilled him to the bone. He was half a mile from the shore, and saw the tracks "appearing miraculously before my eyes … in line-astern" with no animal, no sign of any life at all, to account for them, just "those tracks springing into being as they came inexorably towards me. I stood stock still, filled with reasonless panic. The tracks were being made within 50 yards of me – 20 – 10 – then smack! I shouted aloud as a large blob of water hit me in the face. I swung round brushing the water from my eyes and saw the tracks continuing across the lake" (*Romantic Strathspey*, 1956).

Fort pointed out that many of the reported sightings of strange creatures and monsters took place after earthquakes or volcanic eruptions (and, we might add, remembering Abbot Ralph,

after electrical storms). *The Philosophical Transactions* (vol.50, p.500) reports that after the quake of 15 July 1757 marks resembling hoof prints were found on a patch of sand 100 yards square at Penzance, Cornwall; these were not crescent-like but "little cones surmounted by basins of equal diameter". A correspondent in the *New Zealand Herald* (13 October 1886) writes of visiting the area desolated by an eruption of the volcano Rotomahana, and finding in the mud and ashes the footprints of a horse-like animal. He also refers to a story among the Maoris of a stag-like creature, unfamiliar to them, having been seen in the new wilderness. On 20 November 1970 the *Daily Mirror* reported that seven giant footprints, 4 feet long, 6 inches deep and 4 yards apart, had

A comic-book illustration of the 1855 "Devil's hoofprints".

Ancient national heroes have a penchant, it seems, for leaving their mark on the local landscape. Here a footprint in a stone at Corwen, Denbighshire, is attributed to the medieval Welsh hero Owain Glyndŵr.

This trail – unusual both in size and shape – was found on the Menlung Glacier by the 1951 British Mount Everest Expedition. It was thought to have been made by a large bipedal creature, possibly a Yeti.

been found in a crater 10,000 feet up the volcano Etna in Sicily. They were being examined by scientists, but typically that was the last ever heard of them.

We have records from the Scottish Highlands of strange tracks and of strange animals; yet, the two are rarely matched. *The Times* (14 March 1840) reported that, for the second winter running, foal-like tracks "of considerable size" were discovered ranging for twelve miles in the glens of Orchy, Lyon and Lochay, south of the fairy-haunted Rannoch Moor. One of the legendary creatures of this district is especially interesting: the Fachan, with "one hand out of its chest, one leg out of its haunch, and one eye out of its head", hopping out in forays from its home in Glen Etive, a few miles northwest of Rannoch Moor. There is a similar beast in Brazil, known as *Pe de garrafa* or Bottle-foot, because it leaves a single line of deeply impressed prints suggestive of the bottom of a bottle. In Bernard Heuvelmans's *On the Track of Unknown Animals* (1995) there is a hunter's description of this creature, given in 1954, which confirms its humanoid appearance and single leg. Heuvelmans mentions that medieval geographies were frequently illuminated with delightful drawings of Sciapods (one-legged humanoids) each sleeping in the shade of an oversized foot. One of the few accounts that link a mythical image to physical evidence is in a medieval record, the

Holy footprints abound in the Far East where they are attributed to the Buddha or other Buddist saints. This fine pair can be found in the floor of a tomb known as "Roza Bal" in Srinagar, Kashmir, India. The stylized *vessica*-shaped marks in the centre of the sole are believed by some to correspond to the crucifixion wounds of Jesus and are therefore claimed as proof of the legend that he survived and travelled to India. However, in the generally accepted iconography of these "holy footprints", the central mark usually represents the Wheel of the Law.

Chronicon de Melrose. In August 1065, during a storm at York, an enormous image of the Devil riding a black horse charged through the sky to the sea: "The tracks of this horse were seen, of enormous size, imprinted on a mountain at the city of Scandeburch [Scarborough]. Here, on top of several ditches, men found, stamped in the earth, prints made by the monster, where he had violently stamped with his feet."

Yet another piece of the puzzle comes from the giants' stamping grounds in Scotland. Otta F. Swire tells, in *The Highlands and Their Legends* (1963), how she and her husband were motoring from Cluanie to Glengarry, near the southern end of Loch Ness, across a virgin blanket of snow when they saw on a small frozen lochan, not footprints but "marks as of cartwheels, clear and unmistakable in the new-fallen snow. Curious, we stopped and got out to see where they led. No sign or track of any living thing was to be seen … and there was no trace of footmark, wheel mark or sledge mark in the snow on the loch shore, either where the wheel marks began on the snow-covered ice or where they ended, or indeed anywhere else."

Despite inquiries they learned nothing more until some months later when an informant mentioned the "Devil's Coach": "He drives over the moors in the winter and his wheel marks are often seen on lonely frozen lochs, but never a sign on land, nor a sign of the horses that draw his coach."

Like many of our other categories, both the tracks and their interpretations have changed over the years; UFOs and laser beams have recently been suggested as the cause of the Devon 1855 prints. Any unilateral approach to the mystery brings out frustrating paradoxes. Mrs Swire put it thus: "I have been told that there are no hoof marks because the Devil's horses are spirits whereas his coach, used to carry mortals, must have earthly substance; but if this is so, why do the wheels leave tracks only on ice? And whom does he carry off? And why?" We remain equally perplexed.

Spontaneous images

"After the death of Dean Vaughan, of Llandaff, there suddenly appeared on a wall of the Llandaff cathedral, a large blotch of dampness, or minute fungi, formed into a life-like outline of the Dean's face." (*Notes and Queries*, 8 February 1902). Folklore is fabulously rich in such tales of images – from the scorch-mark left by the devil on the north door of Blythburgh church, Suffolk (see BLACK DOGS, p.322) to the grave in Pekin, Illinois, of a man hanged for the murder of his sister, over which nothing will grow; the resulting bare patch is said to be an excellent likeness in outline of the woman's face (*Gentry Journal*, 30 April 1897).

Reports of spontaneous images seem to come in waves. On 12 March 1872 crosses appeared on windows in Baden-Baden, Germany. Authorities ordered them washed off, but they proved resistant, even to acids. Two days later at Rastadt more crosses appeared, followed shortly by death's heads. The same happened at Boulley, after which the appearances became epidemic. Religious and political symbols – crosses, eagles, skulls and others – were seen on window-panes across the countryside. The authorities were alarmed because feelings were still high after the recent Franco-Prussian war. In one house a squad of Prussian soldiers smashed windows, because people saw in them groups of French Zouaves and their banners. According to the *Religio-Philosophical Journal* (29 March 1873) the Zouaves could still be seen defiantly waving their flags in the fragments of shattered glass.

From that date up to 1890, Fort noted, reports of images in window glass were regularly featured in the American press. It could not be said that the American public was merely elaborating on the European events, because sporadic outbreaks had been reported in America since at least 1870; and besides, events of this kind were recorded long before the advent of photography.

Another series of images began with "a faithful and unmistakable likeness of the late Dean Liddell, who died in 1898", appearing on a wall of Christ Church, Oxford, in mid-1923. Three years later, *TP's and Cassell's Weekly* (11 September 1926) reported that it was still there. "One does not need to call into play any imaginative faculty to reconstruct the head. It is set perfectly straight upon the wall as it might have been drawn by the hand of a master artist. Yet it is not etched: neither is it sketched nor sculptured, but it is there plain

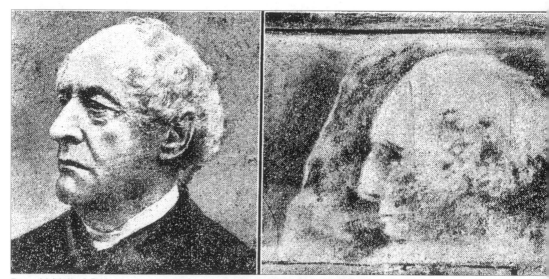

Dean Liddell of Oxford, shortly before his death in 1898, and the "ghost portrait" that appeared above his wife's tablet in Christ Church Cathedral in 1923.

for all eyes to see."

Later in that same year of 1926 reports of images came from Bristol and from Uphill, Somerset; and in the old Abbey at Bath an image of a soldier with a pack was clearly seen in a discoloured patch on one of the pillars close to a monument to the Somerset Regiment. Local theosophists, reported the *Bath Weekly Chronicle*, identified it as a "thought image" created by pious visitors.

In the INVISIBLE ASSAILANTS section (see p.173) we mention the strange case of Eleonore Zugun, on whose arm, in front of witnesses, the word "Dracu" spontaneously appeared (*Evening Standard*, 1 October 1926). There is an even more striking case, of a young French girl whose responses to questions took the form of words and pictures that appeared on her body (*Daily Express*, 11 November 1913). Similarly, the modem stigmatic Marie-Julie Jahenny, of the Breton village of La Fraudais, bore, in addition to her other spontaneous marks of distinction, a flower, a cross and the Latin words "O Crux Ave" (Hail, O Cross). Dr Imbert-Gourbeyre followed her case for over twenty years, throughout which the marks remained visible. In his *La Stigmatisation* (1894) he explains in terms of tiny beads of clotted blood forcing their way through the epidermis to lie just below the surface. But the interesting question, how the blood became organized into coherent images, is avoided completely.

All knowledge is founded on experience and firsthand testimony, yet the modern world-view is so engrained in most of us that we would rather doubt our sanity than question scientific authority. What then to make of the experience reported by a pilgrim who visited the Italian stigmatic Palma Matarelli in April 1872? A white cloth had been given to the stigmatic to wipe off the blood that trickled from punctures in her forehead. "This wiping left upon the linen not simple bloodstains, but emblems clearly outlined, representing inflamed hearts, nails and swords. This is truly a marvel and I saw it with my own eyes."

Spontaneous marks and images sometimes seem curiously related to their time or

Mercury Press Agency

On Good Friday 1993, Cyril Legge, a devout Catholic, took some glasses out of the dishwasher and noticed one was still dirty. Holding it up to the light, he saw "the clear image of a saint-like figure". A few days later, Cyril – manager of the Margaret Roper House for the mentally ill in Birkdale, Merseyside – discovered a second glass which bore the distinct head of a lion. Dr Ronan McGrath of Liverpool University, who examined both glasses, said the images appeared to be in layers with some areas more opaque than others. Cyril believes the lion represents his recent visit to Kenya and thinks it was a divine message to raise money to help the mentally ill in that country.

A trick of the light produced this image of a Madonna-like figure in the trees by a church at Metz in France (left of picture).

social context. In the first half of December 1680, the citizens of Rome were excited by a "strange and wonderful comet" that became visible near the ecliptic against the constellations of Libra and Virgo. At 8am on 11 December, Rome buzzed with extra news: "A prodigious egge was laid by a young pullet, with a perfect comet in it, and as many stars, and in the same form as the enclosed figure shows." This account in the *Loyal Protestant and True Domestic Intelligencer* (2 April 1681) says quite clearly that the image was not on the shell, but "within the egge, most clearly exprest". The coincidence of a cometary visitation, the public expectation, and the miraculous egg sounds so fantastic that even the Loyal Protestant in that credulous age invited readers to believe it or not.

Our last item is singular by any standards: the day it rained Virgins. *The English Mechanic* (12 June 1908) reprinted from French sources the eyewitness account by the Abbé Gueniot of the church at Remiremont. On 26 May 1907 a severe storm swept over the Vosges area of France. Large hailstones fell profusely. The Abbé was reading in his presbytery (the object of his attention, oddly enough, was a treatise on glacial formation) when a neighbour urgently called him to see the "miracle". There was a message in the hailstones. The Abbé went to inspect, and, by his own account, found very distinctly marked on the hailstones, the bust of a woman with a robe turned up at the bottom like a priest's cope: "I should perhaps describe it still more exactly by saying that it was like the Virgin of the Hermits. The outlines of the image were slightly hollow, as though they had been formed with a punch, but were very boldly drawn."

Gueniot noticed that the hailstones were almost regular spheres, with what looked like a seam, as if they were moulded. "The imprint on the two I examined was so regular that it can hardly be due to chance." The logical hypothesis of human manufacture was also rejected, because of the vast quantity of image-bearing hailstones over the whole area of the fall, and the many observa-tions of them falling. The Bishop of Sainte-Dié convened an inquiry, at which scientists heard 107 other witnesses, who vouched for the event although opinions on its cause varied.

This fall had other peculiar characteristics: it was confined to a strip of land three-quarters of a mile wide and several miles long; although many of the hailstones fell with sufficient force to do considerable damage to crops and greenhouses, many others were seen to fall without much force at all, seeming "to have fallen from a height of but a few yards". Since there was no evidence of imposture, this accords very well with the strange falls and flights recorded in Chapter 2. The Abbé Gueniot had his own very satisfactory explanation for the descent of hailstones bearing the image of the Virgin of the Hermits. A week earlier it had been the day of the Virgin's feast, but no feast had been held: "The town council of Remiremont, for profound reasons which I need not discuss, forbade the magnificent procession which was in preparation; but on the following Sunday at the same hour, the artillery of heaven caused a vertical procession which no one could forbid."

Veronica and the Shroud

According to legend, St Veronica was a pious woman who accompanied Christ as he carried his cross to the place of crucifixion. Moved by his suffering, she wiped his face with a cloth which thereafter carried on it the imprint of his face. The cloth was taken to Rome (where it allegedly healed the sick Emperor Tiberius) and eventually came into the hands of Pope Clement I. It now resides in the basilica of St Peter's but there are no known photographs of it and it is never publicly displayed.

Whatever the truth behind the image's origin, the name Veronica appears to derive from the Latin word vera meaning true, and the Greek word icon meaning image. Significantly, the story of St Veronica did not become widely known until the sixth century, and the name was almost cer-tainly attributed to the saint at that time. It seems to have been coined by St Gregory of Tours (d. AD 594) and was also applied to the cloth itself which, like the relics of the True Cross, existed in multiple versions. Representations (usually paintings) of the saint carrying her Veronica (or "vernicle" in English) became quite common from the Middle Ages onwards. Ironically – given the apparent durability of the image – St Veronica is the patron saint of laundresses.

A Byzantine tradition of the "Holy Face" also emerged in the sixth century. In this version King Abgarus of Edessa requested an image of Christ from his archivist Hanaan, who was unable to supply it. Instead an image "not made with hands" miraculously appeared on a cloth and cured the king of his leprosy. A variant of the tale suggests that this same cloth was the Shroud of Christ which had been smuggled to Edessa fol-lowing the fall of Jerusalem in AD 70 and was only rediscovered when Edessa was rebuilt fol-lowing a disastrous flood in 525. The Byzantines called the cloth the *Mandylion* and it became the prototype for all subsequent icons of Christ. The *Mandylion* remained in Edessa until 944 when it was transferred to Constantinople and received by the Emperor amidst great celebration.

But the most famous example of this type of relic is, undoubtedly, the Turin Shroud, a bolt of ancient linen, imprinted on both sides with full-length images of the front and back of a bearded man. Supposedly the winding sheet of Christ, it now belongs to the papal authorities and is housed in Turin Cathedral. Unlike the Veronica image, it has undergone a great deal of investigation and has spawned a wide range of imaginative theories and explanations.

The pre-Renaissance history of the Shroud is rather hazy. There are a few records of a "shroud of Jesus" being seen in Jerusalem in AD 570 and on the Scottish isle of Iona in AD 670, but it is impossible to say whether these were the same object as the Shroud of Turin. A more likely possibility is that the *Mandylion* and the Shroud are one and the same, and that its presence in the West is due to the involvement of the Knights Templar – an order founded to protect pilgrims in the Holy Land. In 1204 Constantinople was sacked by Crusaders; the following year the Byzantine leader, Theodore of Epirus, complained to Pope Innocent III about the looting of "...the relics of the saints,

and most sacred of all, the linen in which our Lord Jesus Christ was wrapped after his death and before the resurrection." The objection that the *Mandylion* only revealed the face of Christ, has been countered by the suggestion that, when presented to the faithful, the cloth was folded into a rectangle which only showed the face.

The first record of the Shroud in the West occurs in 1353 when it is revealed by one Geoffrey de Charny at Lirey in France. Geoffrey was almost certainly related to the Templar Knight bearing the same name who was executed in 1314 at the height of Philip of Burgundy's purge of the order. The Templar connection provides the probable missing link between the *Mandylion*'s disappearance from Constantinople and the Shroud's first appearance at Lirey. The Shroud was later sold to the Duke of Savoy and housed at Chambery before being moved to Turin in 1578.

Modern interest in the Shroud really began in 1898 when Secundo Pia was given permission to photograph it for the first time. While there are only faintly visible marks on the cloth, the photograph when viewed as a negative revealed

An engraving, by Albrecht Dürer, of the Sudarium displayed by two angels. It seems likely that Dürer used his own features to represent the face of Christ.

the remarkable image which is so familiar today. Further photographs, taken by Giuseppe Enrie in 1931, simply increased worldwide interest in the Shroud.

Serious scientific analysis began with the setting up of the Shroud of Turin Research Project (STURP), and in 1978 forty scientists examined the cloth in detail for a period of five days. Their findings, published in 1981, showed conclusively the presence of human blood. Further attempts to date the Shroud began in 1988, when three independent laboratories were permitted to take small samples of the cloth. The resulting dates, arrived at using the carbon-14 technique, fell between 1260 and 1390, although believers in the Shroud's authenticity – Sindologists (from *Sindone*, the Italian for shroud) – refused to accept this, arguing that severe fire damage in 1532 and the contamination after centuries of handling rendered the dating process invalid.

In support of their claims that the Turin Shroud is the genuine article, Sindologists have put forward the following "evidence": that the figure's wounds are consistent with that of a scourged and crucified man; that the dimensions of the cloth conform to Middle Eastern measurements (eg Syrian cubits); and that some mineral fragments within the Shroud correspond to rocks found in caves around Jerusalem. Some Sindologists, seeking an explanation for the imprinting of the figure, have suggested that the moment of Christ's resurrection may have resulted in a burst of radiation (like our LIGHTNING PICTURES, see p.285) and that this burned an image into the cloth.

Those who oppose the believers fall into two main camps (though both accept a late medieval dating). The first group favours the idea that the image was painted onto the cloth; if so, the artist would have had to work in negative, a technique quite unknown five centuries before the modern discovery of photography. (The proposal of Leonardo da Vinci as a likely candidate is wishful thinking since he was born almost a hundred years after the first mention of the Shroud at Lirey.) While no one seems to doubt that similar images were painted and passed off as genuine relics, the scientific evidence for it is negligible and all attempts to replicate the Shroud by this method have failed to match the impressive quality of the original. In its favour is the fact that the figure does not correspond accurately to the norms of human anatomy but does correspond to the traditional, post-classical, iconography of a long-haired, bearded man.

The second group (probably inspired by Pia's famous negative) believes that the image was made by a primitive form of photography, using a camera obscura to project onto sensitized cloth. The experiments of Nicholas Allen, using only materials available in the fourteenth century, have produced some convincing images which include some, but not all, of the visual distortions characteristic of the actual Shroud. These experiments, as well as those made by Lynne Picknett and Clive Prince, and Christopher Knight and Robert Lomas, are detailed in Allen's book *The Turin Shroud and the Crystal Lens* (1998).

A new bout of excitement was generated in 1999 when pollen extracted from between Shroud fibres in 1978 was analysed by Avinoam Danin of the Hebrew University in Jerusalem. Among the plants identified was a species of thistle endemic to the Jerusalem area which set seed during the period corresponding to Easter. Unfortunately, questions have subsequently been raised about the reliability of Max Frei, the criminologist who lifted the original samples of pollen from the Shroud in 1978 – the same man who pronounced the "Hitler Diaries" as genuine. Frei may well have studied genuine ancient pollen for comparison and accidently contaminated the Shroud samples. We will never know because he died in 1983.

In an exquisite way, these examples show how science, far from settling an issue, only raises yet more questions about it. The central enigma of the Shroud – by what process was the image of a man formed – continues to elude analysis. Further scientific tests were scheduled for the year 2000, a year in which the Shroud was, once again, put on exhibition in the Cathedral. In June and July 2002, the Shroud was subjected to a thorough examination conducted entirely within the Cathedral precinct. A new, detailed, full-length digital scan of the entire length of linen was made, including new photography in ultraviolet light. When the studies had finished, new preservation work began; the old linen backing and the rather clumsy patching – sewn by the Poor Clare nuns of Chambéry after the fire of 1532 – was removed and replaced with a new backing.

However, any hope that the Millennial celebration of the "birthday" of Christ would bring some resolution to the mystery of this conten-

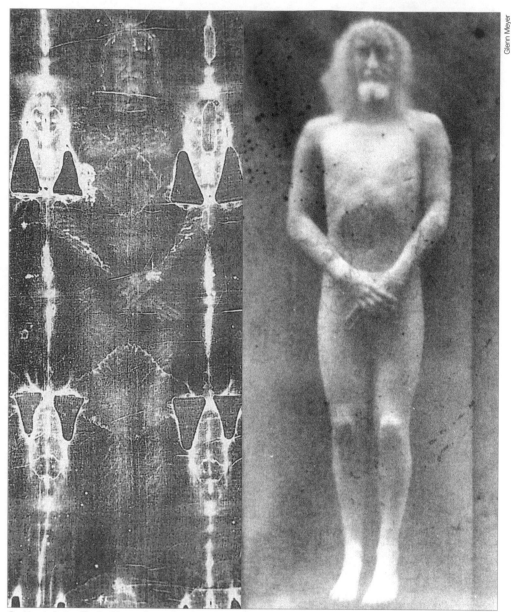

On the left the Turin Shroud, on the right Nicholas Allen's reconstruction of a shroud-like image using a *camera obsura* and medieval chemistry.

tious cloth, or answers to the many questions it engenders, were left hanging. Partly thanks to email and the Internet, the debate continues in such forums as the International Shroud Conference held in Dallas, Texas, as lively, as informative, and as divided as ever.

In the meantime, controversial images of the face of Christ pop up almost as frequently as figures of the Virgin Mary – see SPONTANEOUS IMAGES, p.278. Some seem ridiculous as when the Holy *Acheropite* ("an image not made by human hands") is seen in the pattern of mould in a bathroom wall, or a tortilla, or in marks on a frying pan. Others manifest in more sublime circumstances, as did, for example, the face of Christ seen by the entire congregation of the

Holy Trinity Episcopal Church in Shamokin, Pennsylvania, in April 1977. The face appeared in the napkin that covers the ciborium, which contains the Sacrament Hosts on the altar. It was convincing as a face to the thousands who came to see it subsequently and no less wondrous for being formed from the light and shadows of the folds in the napkin.

Lightning pictures

Can a flash of lightning transfer an image of the local scenery onto bodies and objects? This question was debated in all seriousness by nineteenth-century scientists and the subject was given a name, Keranography. Yet the issue is still undecided. Cade and Davis in their *Taming of the Thunderbolts* (1969) say that in some cases lightning victims "do get peculiar markings on their bodies which give rise to incredible stories of 'lightning photographs'." On the other hand, Frank W. Lane in *The Elements Rage* (1945) says: "I am informed, however, that it is established today that lightning has no photographic properties."

On 17 June 1896 two labourers were sheltering from a storm in a hut in the south of France when a bolt struck very close to them, knocking them to the ground. A letter to the *Petit Marseille* the next day said: "The lightning cut open the boots of one man and tore off his trousers; but over and above this, like a tattooer making use of photography, it reproduced admirably on the artisan's body a representation of a pine tree, a poplar and the handle of his watch." In his book *Thunder and Lightning* (1905), Camille Flammarion speculated whether the cabin could have acted like a pinhole camera with the flash determining the exposure, but this does not explain the selection of only certain images from the surrounding scene, nor the imprinting of images through the man's clothes.

In 1861 Mr C. Tomlinson read a paper on Keranography to the British Association in Manchester, later summarized in the *English Encyclopedia* article "Lightning Figures". He mentioned a little girl who stood before a window during a storm in 1853, and on whose body was found "the complete image of a maple tree", illuminated outside the window by a brilliant flash. In September 1825 a sailor sitting below the mast of the brigantine *Buon-Servo*, moored in the bay of Armiro, was killed by lightning; a line was seared down his back from neck to hips, and

near his groin was etched the perfect image of the horseshoe nailed to the mast above him. Most dramatic of all: a boy climbed a tree to steal from a bird's nest; the tree was struck by lightning and the boy hurled to the ground; and on his breast was seen "the image of the tree, with the bird and nest on one branch, appearing very plainly". This

Flammarion, in *L'Atmosphere*, tells of people fixed in a rigid death tableau by lightning, sometimes with an image of the local scene engraved on their skin.

story and twenty-three others can also be found in *Chambers's Journal* (6 July 1892); other collections were compiled by Flammarion, Andrew Steinmetz, and Henry F. Kretzer.

Steinmetz, in his enthusiasm for a scientific-sounding theory, ignores the conflicting and significant details in his own evidence, and sees the explanation for stories of tree-images on the bodies of lightning victims in the well-known dendritic patterns of electrical discharges. Undoubtedly the root or branch patterns of radiating burns left by lightning has given rise to many of these stories; but there are many other incidents involving quite different images. One consistent detail that cannot readily be explained away is the realistic quality of the images in many lightning photographs. Steinmetz himself mentions "a perfectly engraved image of a cow" on the body of a woman who was tending it when it was struck by lightning (*Sunshine and Showers*, 1867).

In 1895 Henry F. Kretzer privately published a collection of reports on the antics of lightning, gleaned from American newspapers (H.F. Kretzer's *Lightning Record*). It contained such outrageous gems as the bolt of lightning that stripped silver-plating off swords hanging on a wall, while perfectly electroplating a cat sleeping on a sofa below. Also included is a tale of two men killed by lightning as they sheltered beneath a tree in Highland Park, Pennsylvania, on 19 July 1892. On removing the clothing from one of them (named Cassell), the undertaker witnessed an astonishing sight: "Across Cassell's breast was a picture true to nature. The browned oak-leaf of autumn was there. Twined among the foliage were a number of ferns. These too, with the exception that they were brown, were as natural as their model. So plain were the leaves and ferns that even the minutest vein was discernible." In about four hours the scene faded into a purple blotch.

We wonder if the phenomenon might not be more significant than any merely mechanistic explanation might suggest. In assembling data for this book we are constantly struck by the concurrences between phenomena and their imagery, so that the graphic similarity between lightning and the trees they strike begins to hint at more symbolic connections. This theme is developed further in our sections on Spontaneous images (see p.278) and Coincidences (see p.241).

If we look beyond the inadequate nineteenth-century attempts to rationalize this phenomenon of lightning photography, we find it well recognized in every age. When Vesuvius erupted in 1660 the attendant lightning flashes were blamed for the appearances of crosses on garments throughout the kingdom of Naples. Isaac Casaubon, in 1611, mentioned, in all earnestness, the images of crosses that appeared on the bodies of a congregation in Wells Cathedral during a summer storm in 1596. Lightning "fell" into the church, and although no one was hurt, the terrific violence of the thunder threw many to the floor: "The wonderful part was this, which afterwards was taken notice of by many, that the marks of a cross were found to be imprinted on the bodies of those then at divine service." The Revd G.S. Tyack describes this incident in his *Lore and Legend of the English Church* (1899), quoting Casaubon: "The Bishop [of Wells] himself found the mark upon him, and others were signed 'on the shoulder, the breast, the back, and other parts.'" Flammarion adds that the bishop's wife was among those who received the cross stigma. Another incident when crosses appeared on clothes was mentioned even earlier, by Joseph Grünpech in *Speculum naturalis coelestis* (1508).

The spectacular case of lightning striking the high altar in the church of Saint-Sauveur at Ligny, France, on 18 July 1689, is included by most of the encyclopedists mentioned earlier. Father Lamy, a priest from a neighbouring town, investigated as soon as he had word of the strange effects, and published his report in 1696 in a little booklet that is a model of observation. The curtains surrounding the altar were blown off their rings, but without breaking the rings or detaching them from the curtain-rail or ripping the cloth. Various altar cloths were burnt in places, and the main cloth was torn in a huge X-shaped rent. As witnessed by the fifty people present, a statue of Christ was levitated and hovered in the air while its stand was shattered. But the incident that aroused the greatest astonishment and terror was the appearance of strange lettering across the main altar cloth. Deciphered when calm was restored, it proved to be the words of a printed text which lay face down on the cloth, but reversed and magnified. Yet this interpretation merely added to the horror when it was found that all the holy words and phrases were missing in this unholy transcription. However, Father Lamy was a match for this, seeing immediately that the omitted words were those printed in red ink on

The branching pattern left by lightning explains some "lightning photographs" but not all.

the card and that the lightning had transmitted only the main part of the text printed in black ink. This case was re-examined by Flammarion in *Thunder and Lightning* (1905) and found to be a factual report.

Andres Poey, director of the Physico-Meteorological Observatory at Havana, Cuba, published in 1861 his own collection of lightning stories. This book is very rare, and we have seen only references to and quotes from it in our authorities. One of Poey's examples occurred at San Vicente, Cuba, on 24 July 1852 when the image of a palm-leaf hut and its surroundings were found etched on some dried leaves. At Sibacoa on the same island

in August 1823 lightning imprinted the image of a bent nail on the trunk of a tree. Poey adds that this was an exact but reversed copy of a nail embedded in one of the tree's upper branches.

We end with an aspect of our subject that, as far as we know, has never been researched – the imprinting of images beneath the skin. In 1812, at Combe Hay, Somerset, six sheep were struck dead by lightning in fields near a wood of oak and nut trees. As reported by James Shaw in the *Journal of the Meteorological Society* (March 1857), when the sheep were skinned "a facsimile of part of the adjacent landscape" was found on the inside of the skins.

Images that weep and bleed

The old histories abound in references to idols and images that weep, sweat and bleed, events that were taken as significant portents. It is recorded, for example, that on the eve of Alexander the Great's main expedition of conquest, a cypress-wood statue of Orpheus, in Libethra, sweated profusely for several days. The soothsayer, Aristander, was not disconcerted; he delivered a favourable interpretation saying it was emblematic of the labour that future historians

and poets would be put to in celebrating the monarch's exploits. Similarly, before the Sack of Rome in 1527, a statue of Christ was said to have wept so copiously that the fathers in the monastery where it was kept were continually employed in wiping its face. The same lachrymose tendency was attributed to a marble statue of St Lucy which wept during the siege of Syracuse in Sicily in 1719. Livy records that a statue of Apollo once wept for three days and nights; and Ovid tells of the dryad's oak at Eresicthon which gushed crimson, blood-like liquid when it was sacrilegiously cut down.

In 1911, this picture of Christ in a church at Mirebeau, France, began bleeding from the visible wounds of the stigmata. Tests at London's Lister Institute showed the blood to be a rare human type.

All these old stories of bleedings and weepings by various sacred objects may sound too fantastic to be taken seriously, and yet the same phenomenon continues up to the present day. In November 1996 a twelfth-century face of Jesus, painted on a marble pillar above his traditional birthplace in Bethlehem's Church of the Nativity, began winking and weeping blood-coloured tears. The first to notice this was a Muslim woman cleaner at the church, who saw it as "the will of God". Pilgrims and sightseers converged upon the church, and the weepings continued for many weeks. At times they were so profuse that cotton wool swabs were used to dry the icon. The moisture imbued them with "the most fantastic fragrance". One witness observed that the tears from the image's eye stopped at its cheek alongside the nose.

The event was proclaimed a miracle by the local head of the Greek Orthodox Church, Father Anastasios. "Jesus is crying because the world is not going well," he declared. The weeping had in fact begun about a month after a gun battle between Israeli troops and Palestinian police which left seventy-five people dead. But Catholics and Armenians, who share the Nativity church with the Greeks, were warned by their leaders to be cautious. A Franciscan, Father Michele, denounced the "miracle" as a fraudulent stunt to boost tourism. "How can it be that they saw Jesus crying at the exact spot there they sell candles?" he shouted cynically to a gathering of journalists. This, of course, is the same line that Protestants use against Catholic miracles! Our own piety is towards the phenomenon itself rather than for the religions whose images seem to attract it. Some cases occur outside any formal religious context. Years ago, a young listener called in to a radio discussion programme we were taking part in to tell how on the night of Jimmy Hendrix's death, he looked up at a poster of the musician and saw drops of water running down the face from the eyes.

One reason why the Church authorities tend to be suspicious of weeping statues and the like is that they recognize in them remnants of "pagan superstition" – implying that they occurred before Christian times. Yet they undoubtedly serve, at least temporarily, as an aid to religious faith. In 1998 a woman waiting for a bus in Salt Lake City, Utah, noticed on a tree above her, on the stump of a lopped branch, a small "face of Jesus". A platform and ladder were erected, enabling people to see it close up. When the face began exuding liquid, the "tears" were piously collected in cups and a shrine grew up at the base of the tree. The largely Mormon city administration did not at first approve and tried to suppress the cult, but they changed their tune when its effects became plain. It was a poor district, inhabited by Catholic Hispanics, with a higher than average crime level. But the discovery of the Jesus tree caused a religious revival and lessening of crime. When John Michell visited it in August 1998, the shrine was strewn with flowers and well attended, the liquid was still flowing from the face and, when tasted, it could well have been identified as tears.

The *Sunday People* (11 January 1976) contained an article on a 300-year-old wooden image of Christ, in the Brazilian village of Porto das Caixas, and the miraculous healings attributed to the blood which periodically streamed from its painted wounds. Authoritative tests were said to have confirmed that the blood was real, though of an indeterminate species. More interesting to us is the fact that, despite careful watches and examinations since the first appearance of bleeding in 1968, the source of the flows remained undetected. In 1972, a bleeding limestone crucifix, belonging to the Pizzi family of Syracuse, Sicily, attracted so many pilgrims that the Church had to warn the public that this was not a recognized miracle – yet! Drops of blood formed on the statuette's breast, on the traditional site of Christ's lance-wound. According to Dr S. Rodante, president of the island's Catholic Doctors' Association, quoted in *Fate* (December 1972) the blood coagulated instantly, whereas samples taken from the Pizzi family (presumably on the assumption that they might be perpetuating a hoax with their own blood) reacted in the normal manner.

Bleeding and weeping images often occur in association with other strange happenings. For example, on 21 August 1920 all the religious statues and pictures

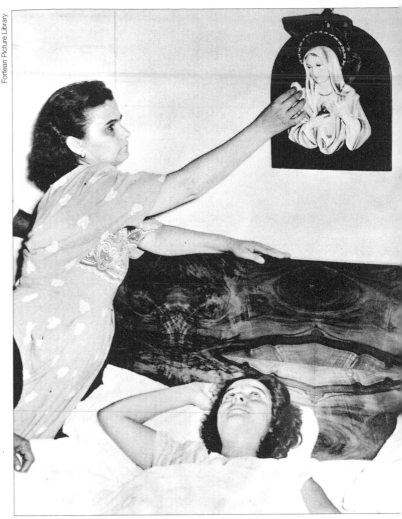

The "Weeping Madonna" of Syracuse, Sicily, 1953, whose flowing tears were found to be similar to human tears.

belonging to James Walsh, a devout sixteen-year-old, began to bleed. He was lodging in the house of Thomas Dwan in Templemore, County Tipperary, Ireland. Statues in the house of Dwan's sister, Mrs Maher, were also found oozing blood after a visit by the boy. During the periods of bleeding, the furniture and other objects in Dwan's house moved on their own, in the best poltergeist tradition. In the months that followed, many thousands of people saw these wonders. At first Dwan and Mrs Maher let small parties into their houses, but soon the great numbers became prohibitive, and they took to placing the statues in their windows as the columns of pilgrims trooped

by, day and night. Many depositions were drawn up testifying to the miracle; and the *Tipperary Star* rarely appeared without some new account of the wonder of Templemore. There was another manifestation here of interest too. In the earthen floor of James Walsh's room a cup-shaped hollow kept filling up with water. Thousands of pilgrims took away quantities, but no matter how often it was drained, the hollow was always full. There were no signs of any hidden spring (the water never overflowed), but just enough water to replenish the hollow was appearing as mysteriously as the blood on the statues.

Sometimes these mysterious appearances of

liquids take a bizarre form. The *Worcester Telegram*, of Illinois (10 May 1970) reported that a "watery blood" was oozing from the neck, hands and feet of the body of St Maximina, in St Adrian's Church, Chicago. St Maximina's 1700-year-old bones, preserved in a glass coffin, are encased in a wax body portraying a beautiful lady, but the bones of the hands and feet are exposed to view. This seems analogous to the so-called "blood miracles" associated with many saints, whose blood has been found long after their deaths to be fresh and still capable of flowing, and whose bodies remain uncorrupted.

Father Herbert Thurston devotes several chapters to these aspects of hagiography in his *Physical Phenomena of Mysticism* (1952). A typical case is the blood prodigy associated with St Nicholas of Tolentino. In 1345, forty years after the saint's death, a lay brother cut the arms off the saint's still uncorrupt body, intending to carry them to Germany. Like the axing of Ovid's oak, this sacrilegious act was betrayed by a torrent of blood. The saint's arms were recovered and enshrined at Tolentino in reliquaries, and are said to repeat their bleeding whenever some disaster threatens. Thurston had some doubts about the

tale of the severing, but added that "there can be no reasonable doubt that from the two arms a curious exudation of a red fluid, described as 'blood', did take place from time to time in the sixteenth and seventeenth centuries. In 1699 this discharge seems to have continued pretty constantly for four months." That stringent critic and authority on miracles, Pope Benedict XIV, accepted the authenticity of this phenomenon.

In contrast, the Church has frowned on the way in which the miracle of the liquefaction of the blood of St Januarius has been popularly taken as a sign of luck for the city of Naples. Each year, phials holding dried particles of the saint's blood, kept in the Santa Chiara basilica, are supposed to turn liquid and froth for a while during services on the first Saturday in May, and on 19 September. On the occasions when the miracle fails, the Neapolitans fatalistically await a calamity. In 1976, the two most violent earthquakes ever to have shaken Italy both took place within a few days of the St Januarius festival. One happened in May on the sixth day after the failure of the miracle; the other happened in September during the week before a successful liquefaction. So you can interpret the portent as you please. The earliest recorded

A plaster statue of Christ, now in St Luke's Church, Eddystone, Pennsylvania, started to bleed in November 1975. According to the *National Enquirer*, 20 January 1976, the blood is human, though of great age.

liquefaction was in 1329, since when there have been many attempts to explain the event away. Sir David Brewster, in *Natural Magic* (1831) speculates about compounds that would melt at low temperatures, so the "blood" would froth from the heat of the hand holding its phial. Other investigators have found the phenomenon to be genuine.

Most apologists and critics of miracles tend to argue specific events in isolation; Fort and Thurston, on the other hand, suggested that the enigma may only be understood when the phenomenon is studied as a whole rather than from a purely religious or sceptical point of view. Fort, of course, was thinking of the teleportation of liquids, and we could extend this to include the well-documented, perpetually damp "bloodstains" that occur in "haunted" houses (see MYSTERIOUS FLOWS AND OOZINGS, p.62).

According to contemporary newspapers, Mrs Theresa Taylor of Walker, Newcastle-upon-Tyne, was praying before her plaster-cast Madonna on 10 October 1955 when she saw the statue's left eye open and a bead of moisture form there. Later, neighbours were said to have seen a stream of tears. Another English case on our files involved a sixteen-inch crucifix, owned by Alfred Bolton of Walthamstow, London, which was observed to shed tears on at least thirty occasions between May and July 1966. A forensic scientist quoted in the *News of the World* (24 July 1966) said he was quite baffled after a thorough examination of the statuette.

In March 1960 Mrs Pagora Catsounis was praying before a portrait of the Virgin in her Island Park, New York, home. She thought she saw Mary's eyes open and tears flow. Her husband saw them too, and called the priest of St Paul's

The weeping statue of the Virgin Mary displayed by the devoutly Catholic Rosa Mystica group in Maasmechelen, Belgium.

Greek Orthodox church in nearby Hempstead. When he arrived, he saw for himself tears forming under the glass and running to the bottom of the frame where they vanished. In relating this story, the writer in *Grit* (26 July 1970) refers to other instances of weeping pictures. In 1953 several icons of the Madonna wept blood in Italy: in Syracuse the flow lasted eight days, and in Mezzolombardo blood appeared on a newspaper photograph of an icon!

Statues that come to life

At Limpias, in northern Spain, in March 1919, hundreds of people – many of them "scientifically educated persons" – swore statements that they had seen "certain pictures of saints perform miracles, step out of their panels, carry out actions, etc". The psychologist E.R. Jaensch, who briefly discusses the case in his *Eidetic Imagery* (1930), attempts to explain this and other visions in terms of eidetic images: complex retinal images that persist in the visual memory and appear superimposed on normal visual images.

William A. Christian's more detailed study, *Moving Crucifixes in Modern Spain* (1992), takes a different tack, providing rare insight into the social and political contexts of such extraordinary

A painting by Gêrome showing the moment when Aphrodite brings the statue of Galatea to life.

beliefs. Most of his research deals specifically with the events in Limpias where local records show that, for nearly two weeks, a life-size crucifix in a church was seen by many people to be expressing agony – rolling its eyes, grimacing and sweating. Christian also demonstrates clearly that these experiences were, to a great extent, "enabled" at the time by the nine-day preaching "mission" of two Capuchin friars, who might well have known of the similar phenomenon at Gandia, in southeast Spain, the previous year (1918).

Although less well-known than other "miraculous" events in the history of modern Catholic phenomena, Limpias is on a par with the great post-World War I visions (such as those at Lourdes, Pontmain, Knock and Fátima) and undoubtedly influenced the popular culture of belief in such possibilities. Limpias was quickly followed by two other mass-witnessings of Christ's agony on the Cross in Spanish towns – at Piedramillera (1920) and Melilla (1922) – setting the scene, as it were, for the more recent flaps of

wobbling Madonnas in Ireland and bleeding Madonnas in Italy.

The idea that statues and paintings can take on a life of their own has its earliest expression in ancient cosmogonies in which the Creator breathes life into images he has made of human and other creatures. In classical mythology, the legendary King of Cyprus, Pygmalion, falls in love and eventually marries a statue that comes to life. In the eleventh-century Welsh epic *The Mabinogion*, the magician Math creates a wife for the hero, Lleu Skilful-Hand, entirely out of flowers. Shakespeare plays with the idea in the magical ending of *A Winter's Tale* when a statue of the dead queen, Hermione, turns out to be the living, breathing woman.

The sorcerer-poet Virgil of Naples gained a great reputation for animating statues; among the wonders attributed to him, by Gervase of Tilbury and other medieval chroniclers, was the fabrication of a brass fly that chased other flies away from that city. He also made a bronze archer, who guarded a perpetual fire in the city's baths. The same art was known to medieval magicians. Gerbert (Pope Sylvester II), Robert Grosseteste, Albertus Magnus and Roger Bacon are all credited with the manufacture of talking bronze heads that would give advice and answer any questions put to them. Albertus Magnus is also said to have made a metal man which grew to be so loqacious that his student, Thomas Aquinas, finally smashed it to pieces.

The archetypal quality of the primal act of creation is evident in its persistence into the present. An example of this continuity is the ancient Jewish legend of the creation of a magic automaton, the golem. This creature was a man shaped from "virgin clay" and brought to life by the insertion into its mouth of a Cabalistic formula, written on parchment, containing the mystical names of God. Sometimes the formula was written on the monster's forehead.

In the legend of the golem, the creature, like Frankenstein's monster, runs amok and destroys its creator – a pattern that is repeated in similar stories of artificial men from other cultures. The Taoist classic *Lieh Tzu* (c. AD 300) records an ancient story of an artificial man sent by an artisan to the court of King Mu of Chou. Able to dance and sing on command, the automaton enraged Mou when it began to wink at and beckon the royal concubines. Fearing for his life, the inventor Yen Shih, demonstrated to the king that it was not alive by showing him its components made of "leather, wood, glue and lacquer".

Steve Moore, writing in *Fortean Studies* (no.1, 1994), points to some evidence that the story of Yen Shih's lascivious android may well have originally come from India in an early Buddhist work. Moore provides a valuable assessment of the legends concerning the automata-making skills of China's great military strategist of the third century, Chu-ko Liang, who is credited with creating a herd of "wooden oxen and flying horses" to transport the supplies of his army.

In an article in *Flying Saucer Review* (April 1976), Aimé Michel refers to the many records of lifelike automata in antiquity and suggests that they are evidence of an advanced ancient technology, possibly of extraterrestrial origin. Certainly, the earlier the period the more is claimed for its artificers' skills, magical or otherwise. According to the *Asclepius* of Hermes Trismegistus, a book of Egyptian magic, certain statues in the Egyptian temples were so designed and placed that at certain seasons they would become animated by cosmic forces. At the end of the nineteenth century the scientist Sir Norman Lockyer began to investigate this ancient Egyptian science and discovered that the temples were orientated so that the statue in the sacred heart of the temple would be struck once a year by the rays of the rising or setting Sun or of one of the other heavenly bodies.

Of course pious frauds were frequently perpetrated, such as the tricks used in ancient temples to encourage belief among the credulous. The

Niall O'Mara

For three days in September 1995, Hindus all over the world believed that statues of Shiva's elephant-headed son Ganesh were drinking milk offered to them on spoons. The story seems to have started in Northern India on 21st September and, as crowds flocked to their nearest temples with milk and spoons, the rumour spread to Hindu communities in other countries via email. Within days, the phenomenon was reported from Southeast Asia, the Middle East, Europe, Britain, Canada and the US. While most sceptics dismissed the milk-drinking as due to "capillary action" or absorption by hollow statues, we noted that the same phenomenon was reported of metal statues and glass-covered paintings. Before the frenzy itself diminished, we even heard of a statue of the Virgin Mary in Malaysia doing the same.

A painting by Edward Burne-Jones showing St John Gulberto (d.1073) being embraced, during his Knightly vigil, by a life-sized wooden figure of Christ.

Greek satirist, Lucian, in AD 155, described the awe of worshippers at a temple at Hierapolis as a statue of Apollo seemed to levitate. In fact, to Lucian's amusement, it was actually being lifted by the priests.

These ancient stories of "living statues" can be interpreted as early examples of mechanical toys but we feel that their significance is far greater than that. The old texts are vague about what, in modern terminology, we would call the power source of such automata. What was clearly more important was the way in which the attention of the listener, reader or believer was directed towards the idea that the normally inert could

be animated and then controlled by a touch or spoken command. The life-force of such an automaton was closely connected to that of its creator, and it followed that those things created by divine magic were the most miraculous of all.

Catholicism has been a particularly rich source of amazing stories of magical icons and statuary. St Francis of Assisi was advised by the crucifix in the church at San Damiano which spoke to him and charged him with his mission. In 1609 and 1610 there were two appearances in a church at Chiavari, Italy, of a tableau of the Madonna and Child, composed of lifelike moving statues. According to varied sources, when the Araucanians stormed the Chilean town of Concepción in 1600, an image of the Madonna left the church to pelt the invading Indians from a tree with stones and clods of earth. In 1906 teachers and pupils at a Jesuit college at Quito, Ecuador, saw a statue of the Madonna open her eyes and change her expression; and several people in the Italian town of Assisi saw a statue of Our Lady of Assisi move and smile in 1948. D.H. Rawcliffe mentions other Italian examples of self-moving images in his *The Psychology of the Occult* (1952): pictures that moved at Campocavello in 1893; a statue that moved its arm and hand at Soriano, in Calabria, in 1870; paintings seen to move their eyes and shed tears on a number of occasions at Rimini between 1850 and 1905. Cobham Brewer's *Dictionary of Miracles* (1884) also has a cluster of legends of crucifixes that bleed, move and speak (see IMAGES THAT WEEP AND BLEED, p.287).

The phenomenon is still reported today. On the evening of 22 July 1985, two women passing the Virgin Mary grotto at Ballinspittle in County Cork, Ireland, believed they saw the statue rock to and fro. According to Lionel Beer's chronicle, *The Moving Statue of Ballinspittle* (1986), within a fortnight thousands of people were gathering each night; many witnessed the rocking motion, including some who were initially sceptical. By October similar sights were reported from over forty other shrines across Ireland, the most extreme being three children at Mount Melleray, County Waterford, who claimed the Virgin came down from her pedestal to tell them "God is very angry with the world." In most of the cases, the Church authorities were non-committal saying there was probably a reasonable explanation for such mass reaction.

The association between visions and animated

images is continued in the story of Catherine Laboure who experienced a protracted series of visions of the Virgin Mary in 1830. Near midnight on 6 June 1830, in the Paris seminary of the Sisters of Charity, Catherine was woken up by a voice. A cherub surrounded by light conducted her to the chapel to meet the Virgin in person; the interview lasted two hours. As it began, Catherine heard a rustle of silk and looked up to see a radiantly beautiful lady "seating herself in a chair on the altar steps at the Gospel side, just like St Anne, only it was not the face of St Anne". The apparition had reproduced the pose and other details of a portrait of St Anne hanging elsewhere in the sanctuary. Catherine thought the vision was of St Anne, and had to be admonished twice by her inquisitors before she could accept she was in the presence of the Virgin.

It may be that Catherine did see a vision of the portrait of St Anne at first, but that the experience soon took off on its own inexorable course. Her second vision occurred on 27 November when she saw a bright three-dimensional tableau of the Virgin standing on the sphere of the Earth, crowned with stars and surrounded by a glorious light (the classic iconography of the Virgin of the Immaculate Conception as formulated by painters in seventeenth-century Spain). The Virgin then moved slightly, striking a distinctive pose. The whole scene became framed in an oval border on which some words appeared. Slowly the tableau began to revolve around its long vertical axis, and Catherine could see, on the back of the oval, the symbols of the Sacred Hearts of Jesus and Mary.

Catherine was ordered by the vision to arrange for the minting of a medallion that reproduced what she had just seen; the "Miraculous Medal" became so popular that many millions were distributed. Bernadette Soubirous was wearing this "medal" on 11 February 1858 when she first experienced the apparition of the Virgin Mary in the grotto at Lourdes. The story becomes even more interesting when we note that, according to Bernadette's own testimony, during her sixteenth vision (on 25 March) the Virgin struck a pose as she hovered above the rose bush. Bernadette recognized the pose as that portrayed on her medallion. This was the occasion on which the vision announced: "I am the Immaculate Conception." Both Catherine and Bernadette were later canonized and details of their visions, together with those of six others, can be found in

Lionel Beer

Drawn by rumours about a moving statue, crowds gather before the shrine to the Blessed Virgin Mary at Ballinspittle, Co. Cork, Ireland, in August 1985.

A Woman Clothed with the Sun (1961), edited by John L. Delaney.

It is interesting to note the similarities in the accounts we have from people who have seen pictures or statues come alive. Frequently mentioned are the eerie brightness and unnatural quality of the light at the time of the vision and the inclination of the apparently animated figures to strike formal, conventional poses, as in a tableau or illustrated book. These descriptions remind us of holographically generated images which are convincingly three-dimensional and contain a limited degree of movement. This was clearly demonstrated at Pontmain and when Catherine Laboure saw the back of her vision as it rotated.

Another important example is the strange mass vision at Knock (Cnoc), County Mayo. In this small Irish village, on 21 August 1879, many people saw a group of "shining statues" by the church wall where, in reality, there was no room for such a tableau. It took the form of a lamb standing on an altar surrounded by the Virgin, St Joseph and a bishop. As witnesses watched for an hour, the Virgin turned her arms and eyes to heaven in prayer, St Joseph turned to look at her, and the bishop read from a Bible. They were about two feet in the air and "full round as if they had a body and life". Kevin McClure includes many eyewitness accounts of this and other visions in his 1983 analysis *The Evidence for Visions of the Virgin Mary*. One witness reports being able to read the print in the bishop's Bible while another, prostrating herself at the Virgin's feet, clasped only empty space and "wondered why I could not feel with my hands that which I had plainly and distinctly seen".

Photographs of the gods

In psychical photography one often encounters claims that peculiar patches of light, some faint and some solid, have appeared anomalously in a photograph where they were not noticed at the original scene – see also MYSTICAL LIGHTS (p.148). Where they take on an approximation to a human form they are frequently identified as figures or faces, or as souls of the dead, spirits, or even angels and other supernatural entities.

Another category is the "thoughtograph", in which an agent has seemingly caused an image to appear on unexposed photographic film – see PROJECTED THOUGHT-FORMS (p.84). Sometimes the image bears no relation to the scene which should be in the photo and the resulting image is attributed to some undefined psychical ability such as psychokinesis. In this chapter, we take the subject further and venture into a field in which there has been very little analysis of any kind. It chiefly concerns alleged photographs of entities that either existed long before the invention of photography or who could, more properly, be called "mythical".

One of the most famous of these shows what looks like a huge figure of Christ among the clouds – the image is reproduced on p.267 – with a couple of US bomber planes flying behind it. This picture has become part of the mythology of the Unification Church. One of its early converts in Korea – a Christian missionary called Mrs Hyun Sil Kang – has described meeting Sun Myung Moon in 1952, when he was formulating the foundation scriptures of the Unification Church. According to Mrs Kang, Moon told her that "…in 1950 Jesus had appeared in the skies of North Korea, and during the Korean War an airline pilot saw Jesus very clearly in the sky". The image so impressed Reverent Moon that when he was moved to produce the movie *Inchon* (1981) – a retelling of the 1950 invasion of Korea by the US – he included this picture in the accompanying souvenir book.

We don't know precisely when the "Christ over Korea" image became attached to Moon's story of the celestial apparition. We first encountered it in a UFO journal – *Saucer News* (Fall/Winter 1968–69) – in which the larger extent of the image is immediately obvious. Moon's version, then, is a cropped version of a larger image which *Saucer News* say they reprinted from a Kentucky newspaper, the Ashland *Daily Independent*. The date that the *Independent* published the image is unknown. According to the paper, a USAF man snapped the squadron during a mission over Korea and sent the films home to Chicago to be developed. He and others were amazed to see the image of Christ, arms outspread, in the sky near the planes. A neighbour of the airman's Chicago family sent a copy to his brother in Ashland, who contacted the *Independent*.

A different account of its origin was once told to Bob Rickard by Mr H.J. Saddler of Bristol: "It was taken by a British crew-member of a bomber flying over Norway in the year 1954. One of the crew looked out and saw the figure, and with his camera took the picture." That's all he could say – his print of the photo having been borrowed and never returned. We later found an even larger version of the image, published in 1963, by a newspaper in Corvallis, Oregon. Here, the photo was said to be of a coastline at sunset.

Despite this well-defined and convincing lineage, the details, as few as they are, look more dubious the more closely they are examined. The names of the people involved are unknown and our attempts to trace its origin are frustrated at every turn. In the file marked "miraculous images", more questions are raised than answers. The other characteristic of these "visual rumours" – to borrow a phrase that Jung applied to UFOs – is that they seem to spawn a myriad of different and conflicting accounts of their origins each time they are published and each can be believed sincerely by its advocates.

The images discussed here show evidence of repeated copying in that the middle grey tones are bleached out to white or filled-in with black. Some of the divine figures in them are apparently derived from paintings or sculptures. So, despite the extraordinary claims, in all cases the photographic evidence falls far short of proof for anyone but the determinedly faithful. Like every phenomenon with a hint of the miraculous, this subject appeals to tricksters and fanatics. At the same time, it increases the happiness of large numbers of religiously inclined people who are comforted by such images. In that case, it matters little whether the image was created artistically, or by optical trickery, or by some unknown psychical process that can focus devotion sufficiently to imprint an image on a suitable medium – see PROJECTED THOUGHT-FORMS (p.84) and STIGMATA (p.88). However, the story gets more complicated the more we investigate.

During the latter stages of World War II, rumours sprung up about apparitions of a Christ-like figure high among the clouds over several towns in Nazi-occupied territories, warding off Allied bombings on the devout citizens below. This was certainly claimed by the residents of Kaufbeuren, in Germany, who fell to their knees as the bombing raid by squadrons of Allied B-52s approached. The "miracle" was attributed to the intercession of the Blessed Crescentia Hoss, a former mother superior and mystic

Signs-and-Wonders

This popular image, which we call "Christ in the clouds", appears to show a robed figure standing among clouds. It is frequently used by the religious as a divine illustration of the Second Coming of Christ, as in the old hymn, "Lo! He comes in clouds descending…". Once again, pious copying has generated a flow of diverse claims to have taken the picture at different times and places. And again, we have failed to trace its source before 1971, when it was entered into a competition run by the US magazine *Tattler* for "…genuine examples of psychic photography". Even as we write this, several copies are being auctioned on eBay, each by someone who claims their version was taken by a relative.

whose preserved body lay under glass in the local convent and was used in the application to make her a saint.

A similar miracle is credited to the stigmatic Padre Pio – now Saint Pio of Pietrelcina – whose hometown, San Giovanni Rotondo, escaped a number of planned bombing runs by Allied planes that destroyed the surrounding areas leaving the town intact. Renzo Allegri, one of the saint's biographers, gives an account of his investigation of the "miracle" in the book *I Miracoli di Padre Pio* (1993), telling how the American flyers began to talk of some kind of "force-field" over the town that prevented the deployment of the bombs and how this story was confirmed later by Bernardo Rosini, a general in the Italian air command based at Bari. Even more interesting was the widely accepted rumour that during the first approach to the town, several pilots reported seeing an apparition in the sky that took the form of a monk with both hands held up in a warding gesture.

Again, it was said of St Pio that his image appeared in the air over the town of San Damiano, during a "solar miracle" in 1968. This was shortly after he died and a local woman's recovery from intestinal cancer was attributed to his intercession. According to the regional newspaper, the "spinning Sun" – see RELIGIOUS VISIONS (p.124) for similar cases – was seen by a crowd of more than 10,000. One of the more interesting photographs taken that day seems to show a small, robed, human figure, barely discernable above the flaring Sun – see ODD CLOUDS (p.263) – has been claimed by the supporters of St Pio's cause as well as by the supporters of Rosa Quattrini, a local visionary, who believe the image records a visit by the Virgin Mary.

We are mindful that apparitions of angels and celestial armies have been reported from wars in earlier times – see SPECTRAL ARMIES (p.255) – but what sets the modern stories apart are the claims that the heavenly figures are photographed. What is even more fascinating is the extent to which such images take hold of the popular imagination, evoking as much faith and hope in the believer as they do scorn among rationalists. This is a subject which involves quiet complex psychosocial phenomena. Operating at the level of a visual rumour, it constantly renews itself with each wave of media exposure, despite contradictory claims and degenerating reproductions. Photographs of the gods are interesting precisely because they are preposterous and outrage scientific common sense. It would be easier, one would think, to photograph a dream than a god, and yet there are many more claims to have done just that. Though such an accomplishment defies rationality, the gods have the old magic on their side, and to the faithful the very impossibility of the image is evidence of a miracle.

Some striking examples of "miracle photos" are attributed to Sai Baba, who, despite accusations of deception, is considered by many to be India's greatest living saint. In Howard Murphet's account, *Sai Baba: Man of Miracles* (1971), are a number of examples of Sai Baba producing, out of thin air it is claimed, photographs of himself and portraits of himself on medallions. An interesting instance concerns a female devotee's vision of a cobra which turned into the Hindu deity Lord Subramaniam. The woman visits Sai Baba who then claims he visited her in her dreams. He shows her a staircase identical to that in her dream of Subramaniam. Then, "…to help her understanding, Swami now waved his hand and from the air produced a photograph of himself in the *somasutra* (chariot) of Subramaniam with a cobra circling around him".

A second, striking and challenging example is more to the point. Murphet, his wife and a few other devotees, accompanied Sai Baba to his retreat at Circuit House, in Horsley Hills, some ninety miles north of Bangalore. During a discourse at a sandy area, Sai Baba drew the outline of a human figure in the sand, and then drew out of the sand a shining silver statue of Vishnu, about four inches high. Smoothing out the sand he continued the discourse until he began drawing once again. Then, "with a happy chuckle he felt with his fingertips into the top of the mound and scraped a little sand away; less than an inch down was a photograph. He pulled it out, shook the yellow grains away, and held it up for us to see. It was a glossy back-and-white print, about ten inches by eight. He passed it around for some of us to look at closely, and later I examined it at leisure back at our quarters. It was a photograph of the Hindu gods and avatars, standing in two rows to form a forward-pointing arrowhead, with Lord Krishna in the foreground at the tip. Heads of Satya Sai Baba and Shirdi Baba (his previous incarnation) could be seen as small inserts on the body of Krishna. This print, I felt, was not produced in any earthly studio."

One of the better-known "miraculous" images has been dubbed "Christ in the Snow". The late Maurice Barbanell (editor of *Psychic News*) told Bob Rickard that he had tried for forty years to pin down the origins of the image. In that time he had been unable to authenticate any of the many mutually exclusive claims as to who took the photo, where and when.

A primitive genealogy of the image can be made by comparing the way the light and dark patches have "blocked in"; the clearer it is the older the version, the more "bleached out" the more modern the copy. By such a method of comparison, we can determine that, while that printed in *FATE* magazine (July 1955) – below left – is one of the earliest and clearest versions known to us, one of the most recent printings, in the *Sunday People* (13 Nov 1977) – below right – is a heavily cropped part of a larger, earlier image.

Writing in the July 1955 issue of *Fate*, Albert Brandt declares that that clearer version was taken by Mildred Swanson, a Seattle, Washington, housewife, on a bright sunny day in July 1920. The story goes like this: Mrs Swanson wished to take a photo of her seven-year-old daughter, and having loaded her Brownie camera with fresh film, put it down while she posed Karin against a flower bank. Of its own accord the shutter clicked. Fearing she had ruined a frame, Mrs Swanson advanced the film to the next frame. It clicked again on its own. The rest of the film behaved normally and she obtained the required photos of Karin except, when the film came back from the druggist in Rochester, NY, the two spoiled frames contained the image. Mrs Swanson tried to duplicate the events with a second film, but that developed normally.

Some 21 years later, journalist Julian North, of Victoria, BC, Canada, included the photo in an instalment of his "Incredible but True" column in *The Victorian* for 8 Sept 1976. His version of Mildred Swanson's story is considerably different. North places the photographic event in 1937 (not 1920) and says Swanson lived in Winnipeg, wanting to take a snap of her flower garden to send to her daughter in Seattle. According to North, she put the camera down while she adjusted some flowers and heard it click on its own. She thought her cat might be responsible but it was not in sight. She continued to take pictures normally and, after development, was surprised to find the enigmatic image in place of a spoiled print. The manager of the store asked for and was given permission to sell reprints of "the picture that took itself" and hundreds were sold at a nickel each.

Both of these accounts say the background of Mildred Swanson's photo was a bank of flowers, but later accounts speak of the unexpected figure of Christ against a snow covered scene. This explanation might have been contrived because it better explains the "contrasty" black and white areas. In fact, if you compare several versions of this image – we have nearly a dozen of them – you can see that the real cause of this high contrast is

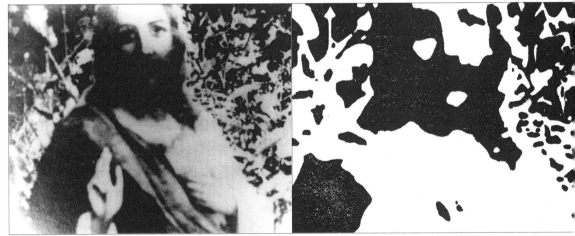

The clearer image shows an early version of "Jesus among the flowers" (also known as "Christ in the Snow"), described by Julian North in 1976 and said to have been taken by a Mrs Mildred Swanson of Winnipeg, Manitoba, in 1937. An earlier account says Mrs Swanson took it in Seattle in 1920. Since then many versions of the photo have been circulated – many of them "filled-in" by recopying from earlier copies – and with wildly different details. In our own researches, we were astonished at how many owners of prints believed the photo was taken by a relative under extraordinary circumstances.

Some "photographs of the gods" seem to feature paintings touted as photographs. This portrait of Jesus, for example, was taken in August 1987 by Sister Anna Ali, a stigmatic nun from Kenya. Sister Anna, a member of a minor African order called "The Sisters of The Pious Union of The Children of Jesus The Good Shepherd", claimed that Jesus regularly appeared in her cell in Rome. Her superior – the controversial archbishop Emanuel Milingo – it is said, requested proof and this image appeared when Jesus agreed to pose for a snap.

the successive copying process, with its attendant loss of detail each time.

Maurice Barbanell – who first learned of the photo's existence in the 1930s – established that a print had been sent to Sir Arthur Conan Doyle in 1926 by someone who had obtained it in Vancouver, BC, "where it was causing a sensation". This version was displayed in the Conan Doyle Museum – part of Sir Arthur's psychic bookshop in Victoria Street, London – for at least ten years; on the back of the photo was an account which is identical to the 1920 version of the "Mildred Swanson" story.

Psychic News reprinted the photo many times since its first outing in 1936, and each printing drew further variations of the same image, each with a unique claim to how it was taken and by whom, often by one of the family. To celebrate their 5000th issue (on 13 Nov 1977), the *Sunday People* printed one of the cropped versions showing just the face, saying it was "…the most famous picture we have ever printed". It shows, they said, "a snow scene in the Alps, taken from an aircraft (in which) the face of Christ is etched in the melting snow". They had first printed it on 10 Oct 1958, then again the following week, and for a third time on 19 Sept 1965.

The People claimed that 30,000 requests for copies of the picture had been received, and more arrived almost every week. On 11 Dec 1977, the paper published a selection of letters from readers in response to yet another printing. One claimed that the photo was taken by a Chinese man walking through snow-covered mountains. He heard a voice saying: "Take a photograph." Fortunately he just happened to have his camera with him and snapped a hillside of melting snow and black earth. On seeing the "face" in the developed photo, he became a Christian. Another letter claimed the photo was "unexpectedly secured in the trenches in France" by a cleric. This pushes the dating back to 1917, though there is no evidence to support it.

Not to be outdone, a US publication, *The Globe* (8 April 1980), summarized responses from its own readers to a previous printing of a cropped version of the "Christ in the Snows". These included a woman in Vallejo, California, who claimed her family had the original, taken in around 1931–32 by her father's aunt; a woman in Massachusetts who said the photo was "of clouds" and that she had had a copy since 1960; another from Arizona saying it was of "a bush in front of my grandfather's house in Bennington"; and another Californian who said she found the picture in her grandfather's Bible and was told "it was a photo of a burning bush".

References to divine photographs taken in China were particularly intriguing but we stood little chance of tracking down such obscure references. In quite a roundabout way, involving the death of a Chinese friend of Bob Rickard's family, he found himself looking at two different photos, each claiming to represent the Buddhist goddess Kuanyin in the clouds.

On the left, the Chinese Buddhist goddess Kuanyin rides on a dragon. Could it be a photograph of a sculptured tableau in a temple or garden? Right: This image is claimed to be an old photograph of the goddess among clouds, but seems to be a drawing or painting.

Of the first image (see opposite left) nothing much is known except the associated legend that it was photographed in 1975 through a window of an aeroplane. Copies of it are widespread among Chinese communities. Despite the loss of the middle tones, one can see the feet of the goddess are resting on a curving black form which takes on the shape of the head and neck of a dragon, also facing to the left.

The second image (see opposite right) looks more like a painted or drawn image than the photograph it is claimed to be. In the inscription which accompanies it there is no date, and no clue as to the identity of the "Mr Chan" to whom it is addressed. It was translated here for us by Susan Lung:

"Mr Chan, from Si-Tsuen – One day as I was strolling along in the open, I noticed an extraordinary cloud with a funny shape. It seemed to be approaching closer to me. It took on the shape of a respectable lady, but the image was vague. So I took out my camera and took a snap of it.

A more extraordinary example is a portrait of Jesus (left) first published on 2 May 1972 in the weekly Italian magazine *La Domenica del Corriere*. It was taken by Father Pellegrino Ernetti (1925–94), a Benedictine scholar, who claimed to have invented a "time camera" based on his study of musical vibrations and used it to study Jesus dying on the Cross. Sadly, Fr Ernetti died just as his "Chronovisor" camera was exposed as a fraud. His photograph was actually of a painted wooden carving in a small church in Collevalenza, near Perugia (centre). There are other "time camera" type images also rumoured to be circulating among believers. The only one we have managed to track down (right) claims to show the apostles John and Peter on their way to check Christ's tomb following the Crucifixion. The Italian contactee Eugenio Siragusa (1919–52), who issued Christian "messages" endorsing the Fátima visionaries, claimed the picture was given to him by a "space traveller".

To my surprise it turned out to be an image of our goddess. It hit the headlines and, at the time, the press and astrologers were all extremely interested. Because of this our humble chemist shop thought it would be nice to make copies from the original so that every household could put one up in their home. The kindness and blessings of our goddess is unlimited. Signed: A certain chemist, Shin-Tsi."

We sense something significant in the ubiquitous, perhaps even archetypal, nature of this "god-photo" category. Everywhere such images turn up, they seem to exert some strange amnesia over their owners so that the details of how their copy came to them recedes into foggy forgetfulness; it is then replaced by a more personal myth of its origin which is often quite elaborate while appealing to emotional, religious and mythical needs.

These are stories for which the origin can never be satisfactorily pinned down. Each claimant implicitly believes their copy is an original or that they know the true story of its origin. These accounts are always given on the authority of a "friend of a friend" (known as a

"foaf" in the jargon) or some even more esoteric chain of relationships, and these are well reflected in the examples summarized here. Each of these explanations is mutually exclusive, and therefore, to ordinary appearances, not all can be true.

In 1985, Coral Lorenzen – who edited the *Bulletin* of the long-defunct Aerial Phenomena Research Organisation – closed her own fruitless research into the endlessly iterating images of Christ by quoting the words of an earlier frustrated researcher, *Arizona Star* reporter R.H. Ring: "Explanations abound, as do photos of Jesus."

Both Ring and Lorenzen concluded the images were fakes and who first made them may never be discovered. Yet the issues which puzzled them do not dismay the faithful, who rejoice in the diversity and contest of claims. Lewis A. Anthony, spoke for many when he wrote to the West Virginia UFO journal *Saucer News*: "There are several opinions one can take of this matter. One that I prefer is that the duplication of the pictures is further proof of the existence of Christ."

The search for the origin of the images continues.

10

Monsters

10
Monsters

Monsters from the deep

Sea-serpents, together with lake monsters, are the most confusing of all the "borderline" creatures discussed in this section of our book. As with many of our topics there are some genuine, sincere sightings, some undoubted hoaxes and, in between, a multitude of cases where the evidence could be interpreted either way or in some other way altogether. This confusion goes back to the earliest writings on the subject, and particularly to those of Olaus Magnus, a Swedish ecclesiastic who left his native land at the time of the Reformation and went to Rome, where, in 1555, he wrote his famous *Historia de gentibus septentrionalibus*, a compendium of Scandinavian traditions, antiquities and folklore. He was a lover of curiosities, and it is hard to know what to believe among his marvellous tales. His book was illustrated with woodcuts, the most famous of which depict the soe orm, or sea-serpent, and the kraken, a monstrous kind of octopus much reported by northern seamen. Although tales of marine monsters go back a long way – the Book of Isaiah (27: 1) mentions "the dragon that is in the sea" – Olaus Magnus was the first modern scholar to collect reports and make a serious study of these creatures.

Conrad Gesner, for his *Historia animalium* (1560), redrew most of Olaus's sea monster illustrations, making them even more fanciful, and helping to form the traditional, undulating sea-serpent image which persists to this day. One of the types he described was a huge, sinuous water creature which he called the Great Wall snake. In the text of his book Gesner rather craftily passed the buck, saying: "Such monsters were put on plates by Olaus, how well and right is his responsibility to bear."

Another cleric, Eric Pontoppidan, Bishop of Bergen, joined the debate nearly two centuries later with his *Natural History of Norway* (1753). He relied heavily on seamen's yarns, but included some authentic sounding details, such as whales in their death throes vomiting up tentacles twenty feet long, presumably bitten off some submarine giant in a recent battle.

The first scientist to take such stories seriously was a young French naturalist, Pierre Denys de Montfort, who devoted a major part of his unfinished *Natural History of Molluscs* – published as part of Buffon's voluminous *Histoire Naturelle* (1749–67) – to evidence of the giant octopus and kraken. He became a familiar figure to the whalers and deep-sea fishermen in the French Atlantic ports, from whom he collected accounts of sea monsters. For this he was scorned and reviled by his contemporary savants. One of his reports was of a ship nearly swamped by a giant octopus which pulled a sailor from the rigging with one of its tentacles. The other sailors managed to hack off a tentacle from the monster. It measured twenty-three feet. Even bigger creatures were told of. In a church at Saint-Malô, de Montfort found a painting of another ship attacked by a giant octopus. It had been placed there by the grateful sailors who had survived the adventure. He reproduced in his book a hand-coloured engraving of the picture as part of his proof of the existence of such monsters. The Paris savants remained sceptical, and when de Montfort challenged them to go to Saint-Malô to see the painting for themselves, not one of them accepted. Some time later the church was destroyed and the painting with it. Not only was de Montfort ridiculed, he was ruined by the French Revolution and died in about 1820 in a Paris gutter.

If de Montfort had lived on to 1861 he would have found himself vindicated, because in that year the French corvette *Alecton* had a battle lasting many hours with a giant, brick-red squid. This was the event that inspired Jules Verne to include a similar battle in *Twenty Thousand Leagues Under The Sea* (1870). While the seamen were trying to haul the monster aboard, its tail was severed, and after a few days it stank so badly that it had to be tossed back into the depths, the fate of much valuable cryptozoological evidence. In the next two decades a number of huge carcasses were washed up on the east coast of America and Canada, some with amazing tentacles of up to 13m long. By the 1880s the existence of giant cephalopods was sufficiently established for at least one naturalist, Henry Lee, author of *Sea Monsters Unmasked* (1884), to go overboard in the other direction, explaining all sea-serpent sightings in terms of giant squids.

Among today's cryptozoologists interested in the giant cephalopods is the Connecticut biologist Gary S. Mangiacopra, who has published a series of articles since the middle 1970s in *Of Sea and Shore* (USA) and other journals. He spent three years rescuing from obscurity the records of a giant octopus stranded at St Augustine, Florida, in 1896. Tissue samples from the carcass, which had an estimated tentacle length of over thirty metres and a weight of eighteen to twenty tons, had been sent to Professor Addison E. Verrill, the world's leading authority on cephalopods. On the evidence he announced his belief in the giant octopus, and promptly named it after himself, *Octopus giganteus verrill*. Later, probably under academic pressure, he retracted, calling it a whale. In 1962 the tissue samples, preserved in the Smithsonian Institution, were re-examined and positively identified as octopus flesh. The samples were then "lost" – another common way of disposing of embarrassing evidence.

About the time de Montfort was becoming obsessed with the giant octopus, the scene of sea-serpent sightings switched from Norway, and crossed the Atlantic to Maine and Massachusetts. In 1817 there was a long series of sightings near the port of Gloucester, Mass. Lonson Nash, of the Linnaean Society of New England, was dispatched from Boston with instructions to collect as much sworn testimony as possible. He ended up being a witness himself. He used new techniques, familiar to modern researchers, in what may have been the first on-the-spot investigation in cryptozoology. He separated witnesses to avoid collusion, and used a standard questionnaire drawn up by the Society. The results established the existence of at least one kind of giant sea snake. That same year the eccentric naturalist Constantin Samuel Rafinesque-Schmalz became sufficiently interested in the events at Gloucester to name the creature *Megophias* (great snake).

In England these reports tended to be dismissed as "Yankee humbug". The credibility of American naturalists among their European colleagues had been damaged by the alacrity with which a number of them discovered and named "new species". It became almost a mania. Matters were not helped when it became known that Rafinesque-Schmalz had included some nonexistent species in his study *Ichthyologia ohiensis* (1820) as the result of a hoax by his friend, the bird painter J.J. Audubon, who had described them to him as a joke.

There were many other hoaxes and misidentifications, the most notorious being Koch's sea-serpent skeleton. Dr Albert C. Koch had "reconstructed" this 35m monster from bones dug up in Alabama, and had named it *Hydragos sillimanii* after Benjamin Silliman, a professor of chemistry and geology at Yale who had declared himself in favour of the sea-serpent's existence. After mounting it in an undulating pose, familiar from Olaus's legacy, he toured around with it, lecturing. He was exposed in 1845 when Jeffries Wyman, a pioneer archeologist and a professor

Part of Olaus Magnus's 16th century *Carta marina*, showing some of the mysteries and perils of northern waters, including types of destructive sea monsters, the Maelstrom (lower right) and a strange UFO-like vessel (upper left).

of zoology and anatomy, identified the bones as those of a Zeuglodon, an archaic type of cetacean which was normally no more than forty-five feet long. Koch had kept on adding the bones of more than one creature until he obtained an impressive length. Silliman was furious, but Koch, undaunted, was soon on the road again, with his money-making heap of bones renamed *Hydrarchos harlani* after someone more appreciative.

Koch was far from being a mere charlatan. He had done valuable excavations and was the source of many fine skeletons in museums, including that of a "matchless" mastodon now in the British Museum. His diggings had shown that people had lived in North America before the Indians came over from Asia, and that they had been contemporary with the mammoth and giant sloth. He found flint arrowheads associated with remains of these animals, but the implications of his finds were for many years disregarded, and his claims were ridiculed. As for Wyman, he went on to write, in 1847, the first scientific description of the gorilla, previously considered as mythical as the sea-serpent.

Philip Henry Gosse, the popular Victorian writer, caused a stir by devoting the last chapter in volume I of his bestselling work *The Romance of Natural History* (1860) to krakens and sea-serpents, which were then being reported from all parts of the world. The excitement caused in scientific circles by these sightings is hard to imagine today. In 1848 Edward Newman, editor of the respected *Zoologist* magazine, took the brave step of opening its pages to sea-serpent reports and discussions, and even contributed supporting statements himself.

Later that same year occurred the sighting which became the most celebrated of its time in Britain, involving the captain and officers of HMS *Daedalus*, off the Cape of Good Hope in the South Atlantic. On reaching England, Captain Peter M'Quhae sent details of the sighting to the Admiralty and to *The Times*, and personally supervised the now famous engravings of the sea-serpent, published in the *Illustrated London News*. In one of the longest letters ever printed in *The Times*, Professor Sir Richard Owen, who had been knighted for his work in paleontology, wrote a detailed criticism of the *Daedalus* report, insisting that the witnesses had seen a giant seal,

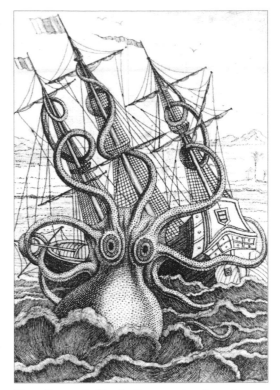

Pierre Denys de Montfort's reconstruction of a painting in the church of St Thomas (later demolished) at Saint-Malô, Normandy, showing a "colossal octopus". Although certainly exaggerated by the artist, it was based on accounts of an actual battle with a giant octopus.

or something. He added with all the force of his position that there is no such thing as a sea-serpent, and therefore no sea-serpent could have been seen.

Owen was the great authoritarian scientist of his time. In her entertaining account of the old naturalists, *The Heyday of Natural History* (1980), Lynn Barber describes Owen as "…always willing to stand up as an expert witness, whether or not he had any experience in the relevant field". For almost any new species or scientific work to be acceptable, it first had to be accepted by Owen. In cases where he did not know the answer to a problem of natural history, his own opinion was enough to settle the matter. But if Owen hoped that M'Quhae would be intimidated by his authority, he was wrong. The Captain bravely stood his ground and a strong body of public opinion supported him.

An illustration derived from an eyewitness account of the twenty-minute encounter between the British frigate *Daedalus*, and a sea-serpent over twenty metres long, which took place off the Cape of Good Hope on 6 August 1848.

Twenty-nine years and many more sightings later, the sea-serpent again ran into trouble with Owen. In May 1877 Captain H.L. Pearson, in command of the royal yacht *Osborne*, described to the Admiralty a close sighting of an unknown sea creature off Sicily. The report was, of course, sent on to Owen, whose criticism of it boiled down to his opinion that the testimony was worthless because the observers were not zoologists. That objection could no longer be raised after 1905, when two naturalists obtained a clear view of a sea-serpent from the yacht *Valhalla* off the coast of Brazil.

The first book by a professional zoologist to be devoted to the subject was *The Great Sea Serpent* (1892) by the Dutchman Antoon C. Oudemans. For many years Oudemans had collected material, and in this first major bibliography of sea-serpent references he listed 330 titles. His revolutionary conclusion, based on a morphological study of sighting similarities, was that the creature was a long-necked pinniped or seal. As expected, the scientific community was generally abusive, but the book marks the beginning of serious crypto-zoological interest in the sea-serpent.

The publication in 1968 of Bernard Heu-velmans' *In the Wake of Sea-serpents* (inspired by Oudeman's pioneering work) was another landmark. He collected together no less than 587 sea-monster reports, and analysed each case, historically, statistically and morphologically. After eliminating probable hoaxes, misidentifications and vagaries, he was left with 358 serious, well-witnessed sightings. From these he categorized nine distinct sea-serpent types: the long-necked, the merhorse, the many-humped, the many-finned, the super-otter, the super-eel, the marine saurian, the "father of all turtles" and the "yellow-belly".

Heuvelmans acknowledged that there are dimensions to the problem of water-monsters that lay outside his own scientific field. For one thing, there is the tendency of witnesses to describe sightings so as to "...fit an existing archetype". He also remarked, enigmatically, that "...even the most common animal ... is partly 'imagined'. And, reciprocally, all 'mythical' animals are partly real." This insight has been developed by the modern school of folklore, which draws its material not just from pre-industrial "folk" but from contemporary reports and rumours of paranormal phenomena. No sea-serpent has ever been caught and exhibited, but in human imagination these creatures are more real than many other, more tangible species.

In 1998, a group studying animal behaviour at Oxford University developed a statistical method that allows them to estimate the diversity of the populations of rare creatures based on small samples. The group's spokesman, Charles Paxton, writing in the *Journal of the Marine Biological Association* (November 1998), declared that based on the discovery-rate of new species since 1748 (when the tenth edition of Linnaeus's *Systema Naturae* appeared) there were about forty-seven more unique salt-water species yet to be discovered, including a new whale and a few "totally weird sharks". The weight of evidence leaves us in no doubt that the sea-serpent exists. But somehow we do not expect ever to see one in a museum.

In December 1964, a Frenchman, Robert Le Serrec, with family and friends on his yacht, visited Hook Island, off the Queensland coast of Australia, and saw this huge tadpole-like shape resting on the sandy bottom in clear shallow water. His photograph of the 80-foot-long creature has met only scepticism from marine zoologists.

Le Serrec/Fortean Picture Library

Nessie and other lake monsters

In 1933 newspapers all over the world found a diversion from the Great Depression in the beguiling form of the Loch Ness Monster. There is nothing new about reports of monstrous forms in lakes and inland waters. They feature almost universally in ancient myths and legends, and have been described by writers from before the time of Olaus Magnus in the sixteenth century. In the same year as media interest in Loch Ness began, there was a series of reports from the region of Vancouver Island about an aquatic monster called Caddy, or Cadborosaurus, from an appearance it made at Cadboro. The local Chinook Indians had known it for centuries by the charming name of *Hiachuckaluck*.

It was Nessie, however, who caught the world's imagination. As more and more people came forward with claims to have seen the Monster of Loch Ness, the phenomenon assumed unusual dimensions. Nessie posed for photographs and, if witnesses could be believed, she had been seen in numbers, and even on the shore. It was one of those times of repeated sightings in an atmosphere of general excitement which the ufologists call "flaps".

The diversity of the sightings at Loch Ness, and the opportunity of studying a new animal mystery at first hand, excited Commander Rupert T. Gould. He had joined the British Navy in 1906, at the age of sixteen, and became interested in nautical mysteries. In 1930 he published *The Case for the Sea-serpent*. He was one of the first to realize that no one kind of animal could account for the variety of reported forms, so he offered three candidates: a long-necked seal, a giant turtle and, his favourite, a plesiosaur-like creature (favoured long before by Newman, Gosse and others).

When the Loch Ness story surfaced in 1933, Gould realized immediately the possibilities for first-hand investigation. He was forty-three years old and somewhat bulky, but he bought a motorbike and trekked to Scotland to interview witnesses. After the investigation Gould startled the world with a new theory, announced in his book *The Loch Ness Monster* (1934). While most of the world happily contemplated the idea of a secret population of plesiosaurs stranded in the loch for millennia, Gould believed a sea-serpent had recently become trapped in the loch, possibly by travelling upriver from Loch Linnhe, a sea loch, or through hidden tunnels or chasms below Loch Ness. But the big surprise was Gould's identification of the newcomer as "a vastly enlarged, long-necked marine form of the common newt".

The advantages of having a large, mysterious animal in a lake accessible to anyone who wishes to make the journey are obvious. In Britain, as in North America, a new breed of investigator appeared, the kind who would go out into the field and collect first-hand facts on their local lake monster.

In 1934 Sir Edward Mountain footed the bill for a private expedition to Loch Ness, in which a thirty-day watch was kept on its murky waters by twenty men with cameras. The few resulting photographs, showing wakes, were disappointingly inconclusive. A similar expedition in 1960 was organized by students at Oxford and Cambridge. They were inspired by lectures given by Dr Denys Tucker, an ichthyologist at the British Museum of Natural History, who believed the monster to be a "lost plesiosaur". The Museum, which tolerates eccentricities in its staff as long as they are kept private, was scandalized, and Dr Tucker's career was not exactly furthered.

The first unquestionably honest photographs of the Loch Ness Monster were taken in 1960 when an engineer, Tim Dinsdale, filmed a sequence of Nessie in the distance swimming away from the camera. Despite the small image, very grainy in enlargement, the film was authenticated by a military air-reconnaissance unit using techniques of analysing photos for intelligence.

The most famous of Loch Ness Monster photographs was taken in April 1934 by a London surgeon, R. Kenneth Wilson. That was the claim, and for many years the picture was accepted as the definitive image of Nessie. In 1993 a man on his deathbed said that it was a model that he had made as part of a hoax.

Tim Dinsdale, veteran of nearly fifty expeditions to Loch Ness, saw the monster on three occasions. His 1960 film of it has been exhaustively analysed by RAF scientists, and is now accepted as a genuine piece of evidence.

The zigzag wake differed significantly from that of a boat and indicated a large body beneath the surface. The film was reanalysed in California in 1972, using computerized image-enhancing methods developed for the space probes. This disclosed new information: a second lump can be seen breaking the surface behind the first. So it appears, though sceptics disputed this interpretation. Dinsdale's belief in the plesiosaur solution, and the story of his regular expeditions to the loch can be read in his books *Loch Ness Monster* (1961) and the revised *The Leviathans* (1976).

From among the many people who contacted him after learning about his photographs, Dinsdale formed the Loch Ness Investigation Bureau (LNIB) in 1962. They continued to mount surveillance teams by the Loch under the leadership of Adrian Shine, while acting as a forum for research and discussion. The LNIB also keep a watchful eye on several other lochs with reputations for monsters. Later expeditions, well financed and technologically elaborate, included those of Robert Rines from the Academy of Applied Sciences in Chicago. His team achieved unprecedented success in 1972, photographing a "flipper", and in 1975 what appeared to be the head, neck and body of a large unknown creature.

In 1975 Anthony "Doc" Shiels, playwright, magician and well-known Irish-Cornish eccentric, brought to the attention of *Fortean Times* a series of sea-serpent sightings in the Helford estuary and Falmouth Bay area of Cornwall. One or more creatures were seen and photographed on many occasions, including once by Shiels and by David Clarke, editor of *Cornish Life*. Shiels first visited Loch Ness in 1958, and in 1977 he managed to take two full-colour shots of Nessie during a visit to Castle Urquhart – the clearest yet of a head and neck, recalling the famous photographs by the London surgeon, R.K. Wilson, taken in 1934, but with more detail. As with so many pieces of valuable cryptozoological evidence, bad luck dogged the photographs. One original was lost, and a glass copy of it was accidentally smashed, leaving only a poor copy print, the value of which was lost amidst accusations of hoaxing. This sort of

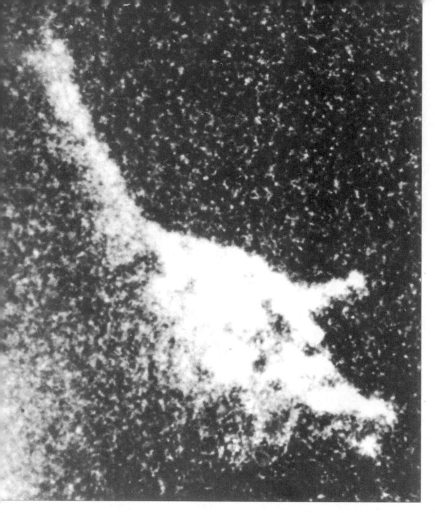

The photograph by Robert Rines' team, taken in the murky depths of Loch Ness in 1975, which prompted some biologists to dignify the Monster with a Latin name but left others unconvinced.

evidence of scale, so it was good enough to convince Nessie's followers and avoid refutation by sceptics. According to Spurling, he was put up to it by his step-father, an extraordinary character named Marmaduke Arundel Wetherell, a big-game hunter, who had already left his imprint on the Loch Ness saga by discovering the Monster's footprints along the shore. They turned out to have been made by an ashtray set into a hippopotamus's foot. Wetherell, perhaps, wanted his own back on the experts who had discredited him, but the involvement of the reputable surgeon, and his silence thereafter, are not easily explained. Other gaps and inconsistencies in Spurling's confession allow believers to continue in their faith, but in 1999 a book by David Martin and Alastair Boyd, *The Surgeon's Photograph Exposed*, examined the whole affair and showed in detail how the trick was done. Their report throws doubt upon the whole record of Nessie photography.

thing seems to occur regularly. Investigators into paranormal subjects frequently tell of jammed or forgotten cameras, malfunctioning equipment and vanishing evidence.

Wilson's picture was not the first of its kind; a snapshot of Nessie was obtained by Hugh Gray in November 1933. But the "Surgeon's photograph" was more convincing and for nearly sixty years it set the standard for all descriptions of the Monster, becoming a foundation stone for the new science of cryptozoology. The shock came in 1993 when Christian Spurling, an early Loch Ness researcher, confessed on his deathbed at the age of ninety that the photograph was a hoax. He had made the head and neck of the monster from plastic wood, and mounted it on a toy submarine. It was only about a foot tall, but Wilson's photograph showed no

The first historical analysis of the Loch Ness Monster was Constance Whyte's *More Than a Legend* (1957), tracing sightings back to a famous incident in Adamnan's *Life of St Columba*. She was the first to mention Nessie's cousins in other Scottish lochs. But treatment of the subject in a book by a professional zoologist had to wait until 1961 and the publication of Dr Maurice Burton's *The Elusive Monster*. Burton was willing to entertain ideas about plesiosaurs, giant eels, turtles and otters on the high seas, but explained the phenomenon in the Loch as misidentifications of gas-bubbles, wind-formed waves, diving birds and floating vegetable mats. However, Burton was not entirely negative. He accepted a residue of reports indicating the presence of "a large unknown animal", and deduced that it was probably "a long-necked otter-like animal".

There is now a Visitor Centre and Monster exhibition on the north shore of Loch Ness, and the literature on the subject keeps growing. Peter Costello's *In Search of Lake Monsters* (1974) summed up reports of lake-monster sightings from all over the world, and in Roy Mackal's *The Monsters of Loch Ness* (1976) is a catalogue of Nessie's appearances. Mackal's conclusion was that the Loch holds a population of giant amphibians, a species halfway between a giant newt and an eel. A later round-up of the subject is Paul Harrison's *Encyclopedia of the Loch Ness Monster* (1999). His cautious conclusion is that there really is something mysterious in the Loch.

In May 1981 there was great excitement about a photograph of a creature in Lake Champlain, on the border of Vermont and New York State, taken by Sandra Mansi in July 1977. It had come to light partly through the researches of Joseph Zarzynski, a New York schoolteacher who has made the identification of "Champ", the Champlain monster, a main ambition. According to Zarzynski, sightings of Champ go back to the pioneer days when, in 1609, explorer Samuel de Champlain made its acquaintance, and found that it was already well known to the local Indians. Zarzynski joined forces with Professor Mackal to have the photograph scientifically studied. It is said to be the clearest yet of a monster in action and appears to show a type of Zeuglodon.

Another monster hunter, X (his legal name) of Kingston, in Canada, has compiled a computerized catalogue of Canadian lake and coastal sightings; at the last count there were 204 items on his list. In the introduction (*INFO Journal*, March 1981) to his continuing survey, X observes that prior to the suffocating influence of nineteenth-century science, the existence of such creatures in Canadian waters was widely accepted.

These writers and researchers are all more or less followers of Bernard Heuvelmans, the "father of cryptozoology", whose 1958 classic, *On the Trail of Unknown Animals*, was followed in 1968 by *In the Wake of the Sea-serpents*. Heuvelmans' thesis is that there are large creatures in many parts of the world, known to the local inhabitants

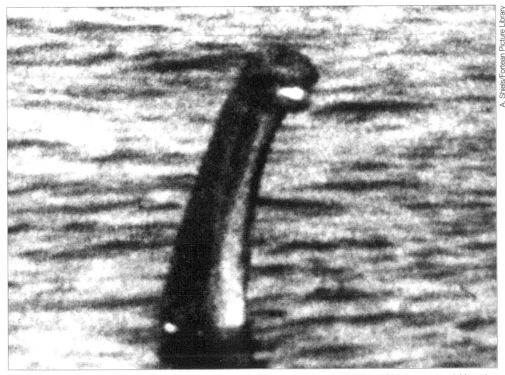

A. Shiels/Fortean Picture Library

From the grounds of Castle Urquhart on the morning of 21 May 1977, Doc Shiels spotted Nessie surfacing, and managed to take two snapshots of the monster as it turned and sank out of sight.

This enigmatic photograph was taken at Lake Champlain, on the border between New York and Vermont states, by Sandra Mansi on 5 July 1977. Many believe it shows the head and neck of "Champ", the legendary inhabitant of the lake, reports of which go back several centuries. Photographic analysis has to date revealed no evidence of trickery and the identity of the "creature" is still unknown.

but still unrecorded by science. This idea was formidably challenged in 1988 by Michel Meurger's *Lake Monster Traditions*. Meurger surveyed the entire field of lake monster legends, in Canada, Scandinavia and other regions, demonstrating that their fantastical details indicate that they are not necessarily records of flesh-and-blood animals, but items of folklore. The reason that lake monsters cannot be caught or adequately recorded on camera is that they probably do not exist physically.

In many cases the lakes are simply too small to hold the monsters attributed to them, or are too many and various to form a stable, or indeed feasible, ecology. Meurger devotes an appendix to the Champlain monster as an example of the influence of myth in both ancient and modern literature. Champlain was describing a new kind of fish – a gar-pike – and the illustration was exaggerated by European naturalists until it looked, on early maps, like a grotesque crocodile located in Canadian waters. The phenomenon Zarzynski is recording therefore has little to do with Samuel de Champlain and everything to do with modern cultural explanations.

Meurger also accuses the cryptozoologists of literalizing myth and of distorting evidence by suppressing the fantastic details of monster legends so as to make them seem more reasonable. Nor does he have time for the supernatural or for those who believe that lake monsters are creatures of magic and enchantment. Human imagination naturally locates monsters in lakes and wildernesses, and everything strange or unexplained that people experience tends to be interpreted in the context of the local folk-tales. Meurger does not dismiss the lake monster but puts it into that intermediary state of reality that we call phenomenal, and locates its lakes and whirlpool haunts firmly in the landscape of myth. His arguments are subtle and compelling, but the hard-line cryptozoologists are still convinced of the physical nature of their prey and that one day there will be a lake monster in the scientific record. We cannot take sides here, because the evidence in this book seems to show that just about anything imaginable can at least appear to happen.

Globsters

If there are still unknown monsters lurking in the depths of the oceans, there should be evidence of them in monstrous carcasses washed up on seashores. There are many reports of such things. Typically they are large, grisly, shapeless lumps of hair-covered flesh on a beach. Ivan Sanderson, the pioneer cryptozoologist, with his genius for inventing names, called them "globsters".

The first globster that came to Sanderson's attention was found at Temma, on Tasmania's west coast, in August 1960, apparently thrown up from the deep by a recent great storm. The huge, fleshy mass was roughly circular, fairly flat with a large central mound, marked with what may have been gill-slits. It measured eighteen feet by twenty feet and was covered with short soft hair, which one of its discoverers, a cattleman named Ben Fenton, compared to sheep's wool. From time to time Fenton and his two friends, Jack Boote and Ray Anthony, revisited the remote beach. The carcass was constantly shifted by the tide, which sometimes buried it and sometimes left it exposed. It took a year and a half for reliable information about the monster to reach Hobart and the ears of Bruce Mollinson, then working for the Commonwealth Scientific and Industrial Research Organization (CSIRO). He asked one of the Museum's trustees, G.C. Cramp, to finance an expedition of local naturalists to make an initial study of the enigma. Their report, with statements from Fenton, Boote and Anthony, prompted Mollinson himself to make two arduous trips to the site to see the astonishing new animal and to take flesh samples.

Writing his own account in *Argosy* (June 1962), Mollinson refuted the explanations of faraway experts: "It wasn't fish, fowl or fruit. It wasn't whale, seal, sea elephant or squid. Sunfish, some had guessed, but this creature did not have fins. Devil ray? A devil ray has a mouth and teeth." He might have added that rays do not have hairs. The interest of the press was aroused when Mollinson came out with his opinion, that it was a large unknown animal, ray-like and probably from the deep subterranean caverns off Tasmania.

Identifying the carcass became a game for journalists and experts all over the world. Suggestions ranged from a thawed out "prehistoric monster", perhaps a mammoth from Antarctic ice, to the body of a "space being". This latter idea naturally appealed to Sanderson, who had previously put forward the theory that UFOs themselves might be living creatures. CSIRO was slow to act, but after much delay and argument an official expedition set out to investigate the mystery carcass. Their report did more to obscure the incident than to clarify it. A few days after the expedition returned, a senior Australian government minister made a public statement, recorded in *The Hobart Mercury* (19 May 1962), in which he seemed to describe a quite different carcass, much smaller than the one originally reported. CSIRO claimed that what they inspected was a lump of decomposing whale meat, but Mollinson and others doubted whether the creature reported on by CSIRO was the same as that which the local naturalists had described, so different were the two accounts. The CSIRO team, which had omitted to

An artist's impression of the Hobart "monster".

Views of the carcass, found at St Augustine, Florida, in November 1896, with Dr DeWitt Webb, who conducted the first scientific examination of the remains and declared them to be of a giant octopus.

take along any of the original discoverers, could have stumbled across a rotting whale and mistaken it for the body in question. Mollinson wrote: "I am not at all sure that Boote's monster and the one that became the center of attention are the same." Boote himself said: "The thing I saw was not a whale, or any part of a whale." So the incident ended in uncertainty.

"When we come upon assurances that a mystery has been solved," said Fort, "we go on investigating." That is what Sanderson did, and he published his conclusions in *Fate* (August 1962). He could add nothing essentially new, but he was profoundly suspicious of the official "wipe", preferring to believe that the first reports were an honest record of "an unknown, hairy, boneless invertebrate".

Fort in his time had kept an eye out for such records, "trying to come upon something about a hairy monster; furred, anything except scaled or with a hide like a whale's." The other unusual characteristic which intrigued him was the occasional mention of an elephant-like trunk. This is not characteristic of sea animals on this planet. "It may be," he wrote, "that there have been several finds of remains of a long-snouted animal that is unknown to the paleontologists, because, though it has occasionally appeared here, it has never

been indigenous to this Earth."

Fort was able to find only two suggestive items. On 28 November 1930, the New York *Sun* reported that on Glacier Island, in Alaska, the carcass of a 24-foot-long monster, with a snout over 3 feet long, had been found preserved in ice; the creature was said to be covered in hair. *The New Zealand Times* (19 March 1883), reported that among the remains of a 40-foot-long unknown monster found on the Queensland coast was "what must have been an enormous snout, eight feet long, in which the respiratory passages are yet traceable." Such stories are tantalizing, but without precise details they are useless to science or cryptozoology. For this reason the long-snouted hairy one is not among Heuvelmans' sea-serpent types.

Included by Heuvelmans in his book, *In The Wake Of The Sea-serpents* (1968) is the remarkable story of the Globster of Margate, a seaside town in Natal, South Africa. On 1 November 1922 a local farmer, Hugh Balance, noticed a disturbance off the coast. Looking through glasses, he thought he saw "two whales fighting with some sea monster" which looked like a huge polar bear. According to a statement he made to a local newspaper, cited in the *Daily Mail* (27 December 1924), Ballance said: "This creature I observed to rear out of the water fully 20 feet and to strike repeatedly with what I took to be its tail at the two whales, but with seemingly no effect." The battle continued for several hours, watched by growing crowds on the beach. Eventually the whales moved away leaving the strange giant floating without a sign of life. That night the carcass drifted ashore on a beach near the aptly named Tragedy Hill. It was colossal and it spread out upon beaching, as do all large sea creatures without their natural element to support their bulk. It was 47 feet long, 10 feet wide and 5 feet high. It had a 10-feet-long tail, matched at the other end by a curious trunk-like appendage. "Where the head should have been," said Ballance, "the creature had a sort of trunk 14 inches in diameter and about five feet long, the end being like the snout of a pig."

But the most astonishing feature of the monster, which could be seen clearly from the beach during the previous day's battle, was its impressive fur or hair, "eight inches long and snow white, exactly like a polar bear's." There was no sign of any wound or bloodstains. For ten days it lay there on the beach, attracting sightseers and flies, until the stench became intolerable. A team of 32 oxen failed to move it far and abandoned it near the water's edge, from where the night tide washed it back into unknown depths. This story, of an aquatic polar bear 47 feet long, reminds us of a passage in Darwin's *Origin of Species*. On hearing about a bear in North America, swimming in the sea with its mouth open, he wrote: "I can see no difficulty in a race of bears being rendered, by natural selection, more and more aquatic in their structure and habits, with larger and larger mouths, till a creature was produced as monstrous as a whale." It is a pity he never saw the evidence for his theory in the bear-whale on Margate beach.

This is an incredible story and one which could have been settled if only someone had had the foresight to take photographs. And yet there are Globsters for which photographic evidence has failed to settle any of the arguments (see the St Augustine carcass, pictured opposite; also discussed in MONSTERS FROM THE DEEP, p.304). The mythical dimension of the Margate monster is an interesting issue; undoubtedly some carcass was washed ashore and many people had an opinion about it. Penny Miller's *Myths and Legends of Southern Africa* (1979) interprets it in the context of the folk belief of the Zulu tribes. To the natives it was a vivid confirmation of what they had always known – that every pool, waterfall, river and coastal inlet had its own weird forms of life: mermaids, watersprites, tokoloshe spirits and "strange sea beings who danced upon the moonlit sands at night and left their footprints for all to see". Ballance said that the day after the carcass vanished, he met some natives "who told me that while fishing they had seen the monster out at sea, going up the coast, and this is the last we have seen of it".

As a curious sequel, we remember that a very similar creature, though less than half the size, was washed up at Machrihanish, in the Mull of Kintyre, in 1944. According to the *Daily Mail* (5 October 1944) it was over twenty feet long, had the bulk of an elephant and was headless. The *Mail's* headline proclaimed it was a polar bear, mainly because of its "long white fur", but no naturalist

Penny Miller's reconstruction of the hairy monster found on a beach at Margate, South Africa, in November 1922. In his account of the discovery, Charles Fort noted that there was an eyewitness account of a struggle, in this vicinity, between two whales and an unidentified marine creature, resembling a "giant polar bear", in which the whales were victorious and the dead loser drifted to shore. According to that witness, Hugh Balance, it remained exposed for at least 10 days. He said: "Where its head should have been, the creature had a sort of trunk ... the end being like the snout of a pig."

This strange carcass, suggestive of a plesiosaur, was found on 25 April 1977 in waters east of New Zealand by the Japanese fishing vessel *Zuiyo Maru*. The crew had the foresight to take photographs, make measurements and take a few tissue samples. A series of papers by different groups of marine biologists appeared the following year, concluding that the creature was a huge basking shark in an advanced stage of decomposition. Similar carcasses have been found in the vicinity of New Zealand.

could be found who would endorse polar bears of that size, with or without a head. A careful reading of Ballance's description of the Margate monster raises the idea that its "appendage" might not be a trunk but a headless neck which brings the overall form of the Margate carcass in line with the popular idea of what a sea-serpent should look like – except for the white fur.

In his review of monster-carcass beachings, mentioned above, Heuvelmans notes that in almost every well-documented case it has been possible to identify the corpse as that of an "oarfish, basking shark or some well or little known cetacean" which has disintegrated into a bizarre heap of flesh but is still recognizable to a competent zoologist. (For ten days no competent zoologist went near Margate beach, so we will never know what that carcass was.) Hair or fur of any kind is unusual in large sea creatures and is unknown on the scale we have described here. Heuvelmans explains: "The appearance of stiff

hair is soon produced by decomposition both in sharks and whales, once the skin comes off and the very fibrous connecting tissue begins to dry out." This almost certainly accounts for the "mane" of the Stronsa Beast, and other shredded "hairy" remains discovered several times in the Orkneys in the 1940s. But somehow we doubt if decomposition could account for the impressive white coats and hairy skins described in some of the cases.

Records of two earlier globsters turned up in a marine explorers' journal, *The Log* (April 1968), in an article by Michael Harvey. In 1948 a man wrote to the Sydney *Sun* about a carcass which he and some friends had found on Dunk Island, Australia. "It was like a huge jellyfish, with several slits and no eyes, and had a tough skin covered with fur. It was huge and must have weighed tons." Whatever it was, it was no jellyfish, the biggest of which are no more than half that size and have no "hide". A government scientist tried to tell the witnesses it was a malformed whale embryo. The Dunk Island folk were naturally eager to rid themselves of the stinking remains, but found them impossible to burn, so they resorted to axes and dynamite, dumping the bits far out to sea. It took ten days. The second incident occurred in 1958, when a globster turned up in the nets of two fishermen sailing from Melbourne to Hobart. The apparently lifeless carcass was likened to a huge bowler hat, 6 feet high with a tail on it. Its thick smooth skin was hairless and, like our other globsters, it showed no signs of fins, flippers, a mouth, eyes or other sense organs. The fishermen took photographs before they tossed it back, but in Hobart there was no marine scientist who could identify it.

The man-eating tree

This terrifying picture (right) shows a person in the toils of a *Ya-te-veo* ("I can see you"), a carnivorous plant said to grow in parts of Central and South America, with cousins in Africa and on the shores of the Indian Ocean. It comes from J.W. Buel's *Land and Sea* (1887) and illustrates a description given to the author by "a gentleman of my acquaintance, who, for a long time, resided in Central America". This is his account:

The *Ya-te-veo* tree as described to J.W. Buel by an informant from Central America. Reports of this obnoxious vegetable are rare, perhaps because few who encounter it live to describe it.

"Travelers have told us of a plant, which they assert grows in Central Africa and also in South America, that is not contented with the myriad of larger insects which it catches and consumes, but its voracity extends to making even humans its prey. This marvelous vegetable Minotaur is represented as having a short, thick trunk, from the top of which radiate giant spines, narrow and flexible, but of extraordinary tenaciousness, the edges of which are armed with barbs, or dagger-like teeth. Instead of growing upright, or at an inclined angle from the trunk, these spines lay their outer ends upon the ground, and so gracefully are they distributed that the trunk resembles an easy couch with green drapery around it. The unfortunate traveler, ignorant of the monstrous creation which lies in his way, and curious to examine the strange plant, or to rest himself upon its inviting stalk approaches without a suspicion of his certain doom. The moment his feet are set within the circle of the horrid spines, they rise up, like gigantic serpents, and entwine themselves about him until he is drawn upon the stump, when they speedily drive their daggers into his body and thus complete the massacre. The body is crushed until every drop of blood is squeezed out of it and becomes absorbed by the gore-loving plant, when the dry carcass is thrown out and the horrid trap set again."

A type of vine in the swamps of Nicaragua, which devours small animals and will even try to capture men, was described in the *Illustrated London News* (27 August 1892). The report, in Dr Andrew Wilson's "Science Jottings", is reproduced opposite. In a later column Dr Wilson reported further, on a carnivorous tree discovered on the edge of the Sierra Madre in Mexico. It had slimy, serpentine branches which it wrapped round its prey. It seemed to live mostly on birds, for the ground beneath it was covered with little bones and feathers, and it accepted gifts of live chickens, ingesting their blood through suckers on its tentacle-like branches. But it did not refuse larger game, for when Dr Wilson's informant touched it, one of the branches grabbed his hand, and it was only with painful loss of skin that he was able to break free.

In 1924 a former Governor of Michigan, Chase Salmon Osborn, published a book called *Madagascar, Land of the Man-eating Tree*. He dealt with the tree in Chapter 1, the rest of the book being a general account of the topography, history and folklore of this huge East African island. The best evidence he found of the tree's existence was a letter, written in 1878 by Carle Liche, a German traveller, to a Polish friend, Dr Fredlowski. The letter was published over the next few years in a number of journals and newspapers, but nothing more was ever heard of Liche, nor of his companion, one Hendrick. Osborn printed the letter in full, in all its flowery, gory detail. The following is a summary.

Liche and Hendrick had made friends with a reclusive tribe of cave-dwelling pygmies called the Mkodos, and were invited by them to attend a sacrifice. They went deep into a forest and stopped at a clearing by a bend of a stream, where grew the dreaded tree. Its trunk was about 8 feet tall, brown, iron-hard and shaped like a pineapple. From its top grew eight leaves, each of up to 12 feet in length, which drooped limply to the ground. Their exposed inner sides were covered with spikes like the hooks of a teasel. A bowl-like growth on the apex of the tree held some sticky, intoxicating liquid, and from below the bowl a number of green, hairy tendrils, about 7 or 8 feet long, stuck out stiffly in all directions. Also from the top grew six tall, thin palpi, whitish or transparent looking, which waved about in the air in a sinister way, like serpents.

The victim about to be sacrificed to the tree was a young woman. With shrieks and chantings the Mkodos forced her to climb its trunk and stand on top of it. They then urged her to drink of the treacly liquid in the bowl. No sooner had she done so than the sinuous, waving palpi began to coil themselves round her limbs and body. The tendrils quickly jerked upwards to hold her in a firmer grip, and then the great leaves gradually rose up, closing over the body of the wretched girl and pressing tightly together so that her blood, mingled with the sweet, intoxicating fluid from the tree, flowed down the trunk.

On seeing the liquid, the Mkodos rushed up to the tree and began drinking the grisly flow, gathering it in cups, leaves and bare hands or lapping it with their tongues from the trunk. They became at once frantically intoxicated and began a "grotesque and indescribably hideous orgy" – at which point Liche and Hendrick made excuses and left. In the days that followed they kept the tree under regular observation. For ten days after its meal the leaves remained upright, after which its various members returned to their previous positions. At the foot of the tree was a new, white skull.

Despite its weakness as evidence and its lack of information on where exactly in Madagascar the tree was supposed to grow, Governor Osborn was impressed by this report. He travelled the thousand-mile length of the island and went across it many times, and everywhere he went he heard stories about the terrible man-eating tree. But he never managed to see it. All the tribes knew about it, and some of the local missionaries found reason to believe in it too, but no one would show him a specimen. He returned to America empty-handed, but not disillusioned about the possible existence of Madagascar's man-eating tree. Of the pygmy Mkodos there has since been neither trace nor record.

In defence of his notion Osborn pointed out that Madagascar has been known from ancient times as the Land of the Man-eating Tree. Much of the island was then still unexplored, and the only improbability about the man-eater was its size, which, as Osborn observed, "is not always a safe measuring standard of values". He described a similar plant, but on a smaller scale, which he had seen in London.

"At the London Horticultural Hall in England there is a plant that eats large insects and mice. Its principal prey are the latter. The mouse is

SCIENCE JOTTINGS.

BY DR. ANDREW WILSON.

I have lately met with the description of a very singular plant, given originally, I believe, in a provincial newspaper. As one is always interested in the strange and weird as represented in nature, I give the account for what it is worth. It may be nothing more than a piece of fiction, of course (I have learned caution from more than one instance of a joke being stated in the gravest of terms) ; but if, on the contrary, the incident described was a real one, I shall expect to hear something more about this wonderful plant. Perhaps some of my readers may be able to inform me whether or not the matter is a "plant," vulgarly speaking, in another sense.

It appears that a naturalist, a Mr. Dunstan by name, was botanising in one of the swamps surrounding the Nicaragua Lake. The account goes on to relate that "while hunting for specimens he heard his dog cry out, as if in agony, from a distance. Running to the spot whence the animal's cries came, Mr. Dunstan found him enveloped in a perfect network of what seemed to be a fine, rope-like tissue of roots and fibres. The plant or vine seemed composed entirely of bare, interlacing stems, resembling more than anything else the branches of a weeping willow denuded of its foliage, but of a dark, nearly black hue, and covered with a thick, viscid gum that exuded from the pores. Drawing his knife, Mr. Dunstan attempted to cut the poor beast free, but it was with the very greatest difficulty that he managed to sever the fleshy muscular fibres (*sic*) of the plant. When the dog was extricated from the coils of the plant, Mr. Dunstan saw to his horror that its body was bloodstained, while the skin appeared to be actually sucked or puckered in spots, and the animal staggered as if from exhaustion. In cutting the vine the twigs curled like living, sinuous fingers about Mr. Dunstan's hand, and it required no slight force to free the member from their clinging grasp, which left the flesh red and blistered. The tree, it seems, is well known to the natives, who relate many stories of its death-dealing powers. Its appetite is voracious and insatiable, and in five minutes it will suck the nourishment from a large lump of meat, rejecting the carcass (*sic*) as a spider does that of a used-up fly." This is a very circumstantial account of the incident, but in such tales it is, of course, absurd "to leave such a matter to a doubt." If correct, it is very clear we have yet to add a very notable example to the list of plants which demand an animal dietary as a condition of their existence ; and our sundews, Venus flytraps, and pitcher plants will then have to "pale their ineffectual fires" before the big devourer of the Nicaragua swamps.

The man-eating tree of Nicaragua: a description published in 1892 in the *Illustrated London News*.

Another view of the man-eating plant of Central America, illustrating a short story, "The Purple Terror", published in 1899.

dead. Then digestive fluids much like those of animal stomachs exude and the mouse is macerated, liquefied and appropriated. This extraordinary carnivorous plant is a native of tropical India. It has not been classified as belonging to any known botanical species."

The closest any currently existing carnivorous plants get to fitting the above descriptions are those belonging to the, increasingly rare, genus Nepenthes. These are large and vine-like, and grow in Malaysia, northern Australia and Madagascar. It is not unusual for them to capture frogs, and, less commonly, they consume birds and rodents – although these are almost certainly sick animals unable to put up much of a struggle. If there are such things as man-eating plants, the natives of the places where they grow might have good reasons for not revealing them to outsiders; and botanists who came across specimens, and examined them too closely, might find themselves in no position to report on them. Whether or not this plant will ever become available for scientific study, we feel that its legend will continue to flourish. We knew in childhood the terror of dark woods, from which claw-like branches seem to reach out to grab the passer-by, and we have often seen this illustrated – notably by Arthur Rackham. It is that image of universal imagination which ensures the survival of the man-eating tree.

attracted to it by a pungent odor that emanates from the blossom which encloses a perfect hole just big enough for the mouse to crawl into. After the mouse is in the trap bristle-like antennae infold it. Its struggles appear to render the Gorgonish things more active. Soon the mouse is

Black Dogs

A large, dark, mysterious beast roams the English countryside. Every year there are hundreds of sightings; some of them are reported to the police or in local newspapers, but many go unrecorded and remain private experiences. The creature is often described as a great dog, black in colour and with weird features such as glowing eyes. It is not just a modern apparition but is mentioned in every volume of local folklore, and it has always been such a common part of people's experience that in each part of the country it has its own familiar name: Black Shuck in Norfolk, the Pooka in Ireland, the Gurt Dog in Somerset, and so on. Whatever it is called, the phenomenon is everywhere much the same, a fearful creature haunting certain spots and old tracks, the sight of which can make a man faint with horror. "'Twas awful.

It had four legs, and it was black, and had great fiery eyes as big as saucers." This description is of a Black Dog seen in 1907 by a Somerset man near Budleigh Hill. But this was no ordinary beast, for "it ran on until it came to where the water crosses under the road, and they things, of course, can never abide running water, so it just couldn't get across, and it went up in the air like a flash of fire".

Similar to this was the experience of a Devon farmer. We quote from the fine collection of Black Dog myths, legends and modern sightings in Patricia Dale-Green's book *Dog* (1966). This farmer was on Dartmoor (no date or other details are given) when he heard the footsteps of an animal coming up behind him. It was a large Black Dog. He made to stroke it but his hand touched nothing. The creature ran off while "a stream of sulphurous vapour issued from its throat". The

A Black Dog, eyes glowing, invades the study of Cardinal Crescentius.

farmer chased it to a crossroads, where it seemed to explode in a blinding flash, throwing him to the ground.

There are strange features of this Black Dog apparition which link it with several of our other types of phenomena. Its habit of vanishing in an explosive flash, for instance; in this detail it resembles the fire-balls, will-o'-the-wisps and corpse candles in our MYSTICAL LIGHTS (see p.148). See also PHENOMENAL HIGHWAYS (p.206) for the link between Black Dogs and certain stretches of old track ways – in his contribution to Bob Trubshaw's *Phantom Black Dogs* (2005), the folklore scholar Jeremy Harte reports 24 instances of Black Dogs running along customary routes.

These apparitions have often been perceived as death warnings. In the Somerset volume of *County Folklore* is a reference to a Black Dog haunting a road from St Audries to Perry Farm, which was said in 1960 to have appeared recently to two people just before their deaths. The luminosity of many Black Dogs and their evil appearance have caused them to be identified as the devil or his agents. "In some places it is said that, when spots where Black Shuck has been seen are examined, they are found to be scorched and smelling strongly of brimstone", writes Dale-Green. The same effect is mentioned by a correspondent in *Notes and Queries* (18 May 1850) on the subject of East Anglian Black Dogs. One witness, "on bringing his neighbours to see the

THE BLACK DOG

SIR, —The legend of the black dog occurs in many localities, and our corner of North Staffordshire is no exception.

A particular stretch of road has been well known to be haunted by a big black dog. Many years ago, my grandfather came home in a state of shock, after encountering the phantom one night. My aunt, not an imaginative woman, told me she once felt something sniff at her hand, when she was walking home one evening, but on turning round, saw nothing to account for the sensation.

A modern Black Dog story from
Country Life.

place where he saw it, found a large spot as if gunpowder had been exploded there". In another incident, at Hatfield Peverell, Essex, a waggoner went to hit a large Black Dog that was blocking his path in a country lane, with the result that he caught fire and was burnt to ashes along with his horse and waggon. Another case is recorded of a farmer near Aylesbury, Buckinghamshire, who struck out at the two eyes of a Black Dog glowing in the dark. The dog and its bright orbs vanished instantly; the farmer was left speechless and paralysed, never to recover.

We would like to be rational and identify the

A ſtraunge.

and terrible Wunder wrought
very late in the pariſh Church
of Bongay, a Tovvn of no great di-
ſtance from the citie of Norwich, namely the fourth of this Auguſt, in ẙ yeare of
our Lord 1577. in a great tempeſt of violent raine, lightning, and thunder, the
like wherof hath been ſel-
dome ſene.
With the appærance of an horrible ſha-
ped thing, ſenſibly perceiued of the
people then and there
aſſembled.
Drawen into a plain method according to the written coppy.
by Abraham Fleming.

The Suffolk Black Dog of 1577. The marks on Blythburgh church's north door are still visible.

Black Dog with one of those familiar though still unexplained atmospheric phenomena such as ball lightning. The difficulty is that all the Black Dog witnesses are unanimous that it is definitely in the form of an animal. Nor is the creature always said to be a dangerous force. The Pooka of Ireland is often represented in a favourable light as a companion or guide to country people on dark, lonely roads. There is another reference to a friendly protective aspect of the Black Dog is in the Somerset volume of *County Folklore*. In the 1930s women in the isolated valleys of the Quantock hills allowed their infants to roam the hillsides in the secure knowledge that the Gurt Dog up there would keep them from harm.

In the Suffolk volume of the Folk-Lore Society's county series the local Black Dog is described in the words of an old writer: "Old Shock is a mischievous goblin in the shape of a great dog, or of a calf, haunting highways and footpaths in the dark. Those who are so foolhardy as to encounter him, are sure to be at least thrown down and severely bruised, and it is well if they do not get their ankles sprained or broken; of which instances are

recorded and believed."

The most terrible outbreak of Black Dog in Suffolk, involving worse than broken ankles, took place on 4 August 1577 on a Sunday. An account of what happened was published in a pamphlet by Rev Abraham Fleming. Between 9 and 10am, while the people of Bungay, Suffolk, were in church, there was suddenly a most unusual thunderstorm of extreme violence. The sky darkened, the church quaked, and the parish clerk who was cleaning out the gutters on the roof was struck to the ground by lightning, though not seriously hurt. In the church a fearful prodigy appeared – a Black Dog. Illuminated by lightning flashes it was clearly seen by the whole congregation, and the contemporary record is insistent that it was in the form of a dog. It ran down the church aisle and through the congregation. It passed between two people on their knees praying, and both were instantly struck dead. Another man whom it touched was shrivelled up like a drawn purse but stayed alive. The machinery of the church clock was left twisted and broken, and there were found marks like the scratches of claws on the stones and the metal-bound door of the church. On the same day, at Blythburgh about seven miles from Bungay, a Black Dog also ran down the church, smiting the congregation and killing two men and a lad as well as "blasting" others.

Like many other Black Dogs this Suffolk fiend sounds as if it was something meteorological, but something which defies rational explanation as being an effect of natural forces in the atmosphere while at the same time having the form of a recognizable animal. Such a creature of paradox must belong to the realm of magic and witchcraft. But no witch can invoke what is not there in nature to be invoked in the first place. If phantom shapes can be conjured up by magic there must be a phantom potential in nature for the magic to act upon; and if there is this potential it may on occasion manifest itself spontaneously. The dreadful Black Dog of Bungay was evidently a spontaneous manifestation, but there are many cases of Black Dogs reputed to be witches' familiars or sorcerers disguised as were-animals. Katherine Wiltshire, who in her book of Wiltshire legends cites over forty instances of Black Dogs in that county alone, says she has heard that Norfolk witches can still produce these saucer-eyed creatures by the power of concentrated thought.

A witchcraft trial involving a magical Black Dog was reported in the *Sunday Express* (23 November 1975). Five men of a tinker family, a father and four sons, were accused of attempted manslaughter, for trying to burn an alleged witch near Varasdin, Croatia. They claimed that the old woman had attacked them in the form of a large Black Dog with blazing eyes, knocking one of the brothers from his bicycle. Neighbours disturbed them as they were lighting the bonfire beneath the stake to which they had tied her.

A survey of all our Black Dog material suggests that these apparitions belong to a side of nature which was better recognized in the past than it is today. There is a pattern in the peculiar association of Black Dogs with water, bridges, underground streams, buried treasure, old churchyards and certain lengths of road, which is shared by some of our other phenomena and hints at one mysterious principle behind them all.

The anomalous big cats of Britain

In prehistoric Britain lived several species of large cat – cave lions, leopards, pumas and lynxes, among others. The only one still with us is the wild cat, supposedly confined to the Scottish Highlands – but individual cats have recently been sighted in other regions as far south as Cornwall. The native lynx lived on into the early centuries AD, and still lingers in remote parts of Europe. All the others have long been extinct. But no extinctions are ever necessarily final. Since the early 1960s thousands of people have seen these anomalous creatures, wild cats the size of Alsatians, calves or deer, and have described them seriously to police and other authorities.

Researchers have investigated reports from every British county, sometimes with evidence in the form of footprints, claw marks, droppings, tufts of fur and, above all, the unexplained killings or mutilations of sheep, cattle, deer and horses, as if by some large, powerful feline that claws and devours its victims in a way that is quite uncharacteristic of dogs or any other known predator. There have been many local outbreaks of these savage attacks, and in some cases farmers have reacted and formed parties to shoot or hunt down the aggressor, sometimes with the aid of professional trackers, police marksmen and even the military. Britain is a small country, densely populated. Any normal animal on the rampage would surely by now have been killed, caught or clearly photographed. But that is not the case.

Despite ever more frequent sightings and encounters, there is still no firm, scientific proof of pumas, panthers and lions roaming at large through the land. Many have tried, but no one has ever produced a specimen, dead, alive or properly recorded. What sort of creature is it that is frequently seen, and sometimes watched for several minutes at a time, often close up and in full daylight, by people of all kinds, including naturalists, gamekeepers, policemen and every relevant type of authority, yet remains far more elusive than the tigers of India or the African lions that are successfully hunted and photographed? That question

The Scotsman

The most celebrated of the "anomalous big cats" was the puma caught at Cannich, close to Loch Ness, in October 1980, and named Felicity, trapped by farmer Ted Noble. Mr Noble took her to the Highland Wildlife Park, near Kingussie, where she became a star attraction until she died in February 1985, aged about 16 years. The park's director, Eddie Orbell, had stated publicly, several times, that Felicity had not long been in the wilds because she was "...too tame and too well fed". In his view, she had been someone's pet and then deliberately abandoned when she got too big. Felicity was stuffed by an Edinburgh taxidermist and photographed (above) before being shipped to the Inverness Museum where she was on permanent display at the entrance. (*The Scotsman*, 23 September 1985)

recurs in all our chapters on monsters, fairies and unknown beings of every description. It applies also to MYSTERY MUTILATORS (see p.177) who inexplicably slash or butcher cows and horses, and it occurs again in the phenomenon of INVISIBLE ASSAILANTS (see p.173). We wonder, is there one demonic agency behind all these, or are they just local effects, unconnected with each other?

As usual in this borderline field, there are no unequivocal answers; however, the mysterious big cats of Britain are an actual, physical problem, open to investigation and eventual solution. So it may seem – at first. This subject has been researched in depth by the best thinkers and writers among those who study anomalies, mostly with the conclusion that it cannot be separated from the whole spectrum of unexplained

events and apparitions that comprise fortean studies. This is not an isolated mystery but part of an entire world of mystery.

An obvious connection is between mystery cats and the BLACK DOGS (see p.322) of our previous chapter. Yet there is also a large difference between the two. There are fashions in everything, including strange phenomena, and it may be that the spectral creatures once described as Black Dogs with glowing eyes are now seen as the large, black, green-eyed cats of modern reports. Di Francis, the pioneer big cat researcher, whose first book, *Cat Country* (1983), attracted wide attention to the phenomenon, believes there is a continuation, and that many of the old Black Dog descriptions sound more like black cats. Merrily Harpur in *Mystery Big Cats* (2006) takes another view, that mysterious cats and dogs are as different from each other as their actual counterparts. The Black Dogs of old-fashioned rural experience are creatures of habit, regularly haunting the same paths and keeping much the same appearance. They are always seen in darkness and twilight; they mostly appear near bridges and running water; they are reputed to be phantoms or death-omens. Today's mystery cats seem much more physical. They are, says Merrily Harpur, "...very much of this world ... eating, drinking, crapping, spraying, raiding dustbins, stealing from bird tables, rooting in discarded chip wrappers – activities that no Black Dog would be seen dead doing". Yet, at the same time, they behave like creatures of enchantment, being uncatchable and immaterial. They move at incredible speeds and jump farther that any natural animal, sometimes clearing roads and hedges together, as if flying. They can appear out of nowhere and disappear in a flash. If they were creatures of flesh and blood, they would be found among the road-kill that covers Britain's highways. In *Mystery Big Cats* are several accounts from drivers who say they have hit a big cat or seen a dead one lying by the roadside, but when they return, or the police go to collect it, there is no sign of the animal.

Further observations on the anomalous big cats (ABCs) include the following. They conform to no particular species or colour but range from the smaller, ginger-furred puma type to the large black leopard or panther. The latter has become more common as the phenomenon develops. A white leopard (unknown in nature) has been seen and photographed, but there are no reports of the ordinary spotted leopard. Lions and lynxes have been identified by witnesses, but in many cases the creature seen is of indeterminate species. In several cases farmers claim to have shot a big cat, but the evidence has been contentious, and despite the big rewards offered for an unmistakable big cat photograph, there is still no such thing. Finally, to complete the confusion, Merrily Harpur found that all the experienced ABC researchers agreed that the creatures are curiously attracted to railways. Nigel Spencer, the Leicestershire expert, for example, found that "...between fifty and seventy percent of sightings are on or near railways, both used and disused".

This is an exciting, ongoing phenomenon, well

Zoologist Dr Karl Shuker and a stuffed Asian Jungle Cat that was run over on the outskirts of Ludlow in the West Midlands in the early 90s.

worth the time of anyone who is curious about life and the nature of reality. It has been chronicled, both locally and nationally, from about 1963 when the appearance of the "Surrey puma" sparked off the first "cat-flap" (see CAT FLAPS AND HUNTS, see below).

In the early years sensible talk was of escapes and releases. The Dangerous Wild Animals Act of 1976 required owners of said animals to license them, at no small expense, causing some to set their big cats free rather than foot the bill. That happened in a few cases, but on nothing like the scale required to populate the whole country with so many ABC types.

Another early notion was, as cryptozoologists term it, the "hide-out" theory. It is the belief that anomalous creatures – yetis, Nessies, sea-serpents and the like – have always been there, living on and breeding in their native territories while avoiding scientific attention. Di Francis made an attractive adaptation of that theory as an explanation for ABCs. But it is difficult to accept that huntsmen, naturalists and observant country people over many centuries could have ignored black panthers in their midst.

In the course of her ABC studies Di Francis accumulated a large archive of reports, letters and interviews with witnesses. When she gave up the chase she passed these on to her successor, the aforementioned Merrily Harpur, who has assiduously kept the record up to date. In *Mystery Big Cats* is a full range of ABC reports up to 2005, acutely and imaginatively analysed, providing a complete history and overview of the subject. She is the sister of Patrick Harpur, one of whose books, *Daimonic Reality*, is cited in several of our other chapters. Like him, she sees the world of phenomena in the traditional way, as a product of the "daimonic" or spiritual side of nature that has been accepted in all ages up to the scientific present. We in modern times have done our best to suppress that aspect of nature and eradicate it from our minds, but the Harpurs' perception is that the daimonic realm is always with us and, if neglected, will intrude upon us with strange and portentous phenomena.

We, the authors, have no idea what the ABC explosion may mean or where it is going. The mystery animals seem to be getting bigger, bolder and more physical. Perhaps one day they will become real enough to be caught or killed, or perhaps over the years they will fade away and another weird impossibility will replace them.

Cat flaps and hunts

Cat flaps (meaning in this case mass outbreaks of mystery cat sightings) are a comparatively new phenomenon, beginning in the early 1960s, but occasional appearances of these creatures were reported in earlier times. William Cobbett as a young boy in about 1778 was playing near the ruins of Waverley Abbey in Hampshire when he saw a cat, as big as a spaniel, climbing into a hollow elm tree. He told his family, who scolded him for making up such a story. But Cobbett stuck by his account and published it in his *Rural Rides* (entry for 27 October 1825). Cobbett was a farm boy, familiar with the wildlife and legends of his native district, and the fact that neither he nor his parents had heard about anomalous big cats shows how virtually unknown they were up to modern times. When later he went to Canada, he came across the North American grey lynx and said it was very like the creature he had seen back home.

The so-called "Surrey Puma" was seen and quite often reported in the first half of the twentieth century, but up to 1962 it attracted no more than local attention. In that year its activities suddenly intensified, creating the first of the many "cat flaps" that have since occurred in every part of the British Isles. From then on it was officially recorded. The Godalming police were assiduous in taking statements from witnesses, and their Day Book for the two years between September 1962 and August 1964 contains no less that 362 separate descriptions of an animal at large, commonly identified as a puma.

As was common with many such happenings all over Britain, the story led to the appearance on the scene of freelance "white hunter" types. These characters, including former big-game hunters, each had their own method of cat-catching, with nets, traps, lures, poisoned bait and various high-tech instruments. They boasted in the press of their infallible techniques and how they would

The Shooters Hill cheetah hunt of 1963.

make short work of the unknown beast, but nothing ever came of their efforts. Even with a whole countryside up in arms against it, the creature has always eluded its pursuers. Defeated cat-hunters have often felt its supernatural quality. It seems to read their minds, they say, knowing their plans and then frustrating them. Sometimes they feel they are being played with.

The most intensive hunt for an ABC took place in 1963 – during the height of the Surrey puma flap – at Shooters Hill on the outskirts of south-east London. A big, tawny cat with a long tail, like a lion or cheetah, had been seen lying beside a road and then running into nearby Oxleas Wood. Later that evening police officers were startled when a large, golden animal jumped over the bonnet of their patrol car. The subsequent hunt for the Shooters Hill cheetah is described by Merrily Harpur in *Mystery Big Cats*.

It was a magnificent affair. It covered 850 acres and involved 126 policemen and twenty-one dogs, thirty soldiers, ambulance men and RSPCA officials. No sign of a big cat was found – except for some tracks. These were huge – some seven inches across, the size usually associated with a lion or a tiger, yet they showed claw marks, the characteristic not of a lion's but of a cheetah's paw print. The cheetah, however, was never caught and the hunters dispersed.

In Sydenham, another south London suburb, an impressive big-cat hunt took place in the spring of 2005. It was reported over several days in the *Evening Standard*, beginning on 22 March. Early that morning a man putting his cat out was attacked and scratched on the arm by a huge black panther. He ran indoors and called the police and an ambulance. A policeman who caught a glimpse of the animal said it was as big as a Labrador. The public were warned to be vigilant and to keep their pets indoors, while the police mounted a widespread search of streets and gardens, armed with rifles and Taser stun guns. Nothing further was seen of the beast; yet it was real enough to score deep claw marks on the man's arm. Meanwhile, reported the *Standard*, farmers near Burford in Oxfordshire were offering a £5000 reward for the capture of a large, black animal, said to be responsible for the killings and mutilations of cattle in the district.

Heading west, a favourite quarry for big-cat hunters is Cornwall's sinister Beast of Bodmin Moor. In 1999, after sheep had been mysteriously killed and about sixty people had seen a puma-like animal on and around the moor, local RAF reservists decided to solve the mystery. Equipped with night-vision and seismic-intruder devices that detect vibrations, they staked out the district, hoping to see and photograph the beast. They had no luck at all and the sheep-killings went on around them.

The longest and most thorough cat-hunt was in 1983, the year that Di Francis published her first book, *Cat Country*. Her second, *The Beast of Exmoor*, is about the strange happenings in north Devon after an outbreak of vicious sheep and lamb killings. Most affected were the fields around Drewstone Farm near South Molton on the southern fringe of Exmoor. In the spring of 1982 the farmer, Eric Ley, lost many of his lambs and ewes to an unknown predator; the following year the slaughter was even more widespread. The killings were not like those of a dog, done for excitement and sport; the sheep were torn at the throat, their necks were broken and the flesh was stripped from their bodies as if by a leopard or some big cat species. At the same time, many locals were reporting ABC sightings, of black, panther-like creatures, two metres or more in length, standing knee-high to a tall man.

Alarmed by the extent of their losses, Ley and neighbouring farmers mounted nightly watches and patrolled their fields with guns. The police joined in and so did the local hunt. Di Francis was there, and this is what she saw: a group of fifty armed men, some mounted on horseback for easy movement across the rough countryside, supervised by the police and supported by a police helicopter, set out with the pack of Torrington Foot Beagles on the 19 April to search for the Beast of Exmoor. The hunt lasted all day but the searchers were frustrated, missing their quarry despite the fact that the killer struck in daylight. As the killings mounted, the military joined in. For almost three months a detachment of Royal Marine commandos set up stations in the fields and woods around Drewstone Farm and patrolled throughout southern Exmoor. Trained in fieldcraft, with rifles, night sights and sensitive military equipment, they were certain they could detect any large animal in the vicinity. This initiative attracted the attention of the press and also the big-game hunters. The Marines complained that, even if they saw the beast, they would not dare shoot it for fear of hitting some reporter, sightseer or amateur cat-stalker in the bushes. Some of the commandos glimpsed a big cat, but never long or clearly enough for a shot at it. Meanwhile, black panther forms continued to be seen, and the sheep killings went on as before. After weeks of fruitless watching and searching, the Marines gave up and withdrew.

And so it goes on to this very day. Our expert ABC authors say there have been cat-hunts involving the police and local authorities in England, Scotland, Ireland and Wales and in each of their respective counties, from Cornwall to Caithness, from Kent to Antrim. There is plenty of evidence too, but it is almost all anecdotal. This perhaps points towards a mystical interpretation, with ABCs as phantoms, poltergeists, signs of the times or, in the traditional acceptance, creatures of enchantment and witchcraft. Perhaps, with its outpourings of inexplicable big cats, nature is trying to tell us something. This is the question that Merrily Harpur addresses in the second part of *Mystery Big Cats*. It is a treatise on daimonic reality and a way of looking at the world that accommodates not only mystery cats, but all the mysteries that fill this book and have never been rationally explained.

Werewolves

Wer is the Old English word for "man" and werewolves are people who turn into wolves and then back into men again. We are not doctors, but we believe this sort of thing is physiologically impossible. If we were lawyers, however, we should have no option but to believe in werewolves because of the vast amount of legal precedent for convicting and executing the creatures. Evidence against people accused of transforming themselves into savage animals and committing crimes while in that shape has often been given by unanimous witnesses of good repute, firmly convinced from personal experience of the accused's ability to assume animal form. On the one hand werewolves are impossible; on the other they actually occur. Here again is a phenomenon which can not be reconciled with any rational system of explanation.

The most direct evidence of werewolves is from people who have actually seen the transformation taking place. One of these was said to be Pierre Mamor, a fifteenth-century Rector of the University of Poitiers in France, whose writing on the subject is quoted in Montague Summers' book, *The Werewolf* (1933). The learned Mamor contributes a disgusting story of a peasant's wife in Lorraine who saw her husband at table vomit up a child's arm and hand which he had devoured while in the form of a wolf.

This event is explained by Mamor as a "demoniacal illusion", because his theory is that werewolves are actual wolves possessed by the spirits of men, whose bodies meanwhile are safely hidden away, all this being the work of evil demons. This theory does not account for such cases as the one recorded in Olaus Magnus's *Historia de gentibus septentrionalibus* (1555) as having happened some years earlier. A nobleman's wife was heard by her slave to deny the possibility of men becoming wolves. The slave disagreed and proved her wrong by there and then making the transformation. He was at once set upon by dogs but managed to shake them off and flee away in wolf's shape after they had torn out one of his eyes. The next day the slave appeared, human but one-eyed.

A more recent account is quoted in C. Dane's *The Occult in the Orient*. In 1960 Mr Harold M. Young, a former official in the Burmese administration and at the time proprietor of the zoo at Chiang mai, Thailand, was hunting in the Lahu mountains near the Burmese-Thai frontier when he encountered one of the locally dreaded *taws*, a jungle werewolf. Entering a village he was told there was a *taw* nearby. A shriek was heard, and Mr Young ran over to a hut where in the bright moonlight he saw the *taw* chewing the neck of a dying woman. He raised his gun and shot the beast in the flank, but it escaped into the jungle, leaving a trail of blood. In the morning Young and others followed the trail which led out into the jungle and then back to the village to a hut, in which they discovered a man with a bullet wound in his side.

This modern account repeats in detail the classical werewolf story, which recurs in all times and places with remarkable consistency. We do not know what happened to Mr Young's *taw*, and we pass on the story at secondhand, but we have direct evidence of the careers and fates of many European werewolves from the most satisfactory sources, the contemporary reports of their trials.

In December 1521 two French peasants, Burgot and Verdun, were accused at Poligny of a long series of cannibalistic murders committed by them while in the shape of wolves. Both men confessed. Burgot said that he had long been in the service of the devil and had extended his activities to shape-shifting with the encouragement of Verdun, who was a practising werewolf and a member of a witches' coven. Verdun was the more agile of the two and could change his shape with his clothes on, while Burgot had to strip naked and be rubbed with werewolf ointment, which they obtained from their diabolist superiors.

This special ointment for effecting transformations is often referred to in similar cases. Montague Summers suggests it was composed of such bewitching drugs as belladonna, aconite, hemlock or henbane. Whatever it was, its influence on Burgot and Verdun was bestial. They attacked and devoured many locals until Verdun was wounded by an armed traveller, who followed the bloody wolf-spoor to a hovel where Verdun was having his wound bandaged by his wife. Both men were executed together with another local werewolf,

The werewolf lives on in science fiction and horror comics. A still from the 1935 film, *The Werewolf of London*.

and it is said that portraits of all three were to be seen in the church at Poligny.

Throughout the sixteenth century werewolves were rampant in Europe. So many of those caught and burnt in France during that period were also practising witches, and claimed to have learnt the art of transformation from others of their coven, that we suspect some traditional magic ritual was involved, inherited from ancient times and still active in remote districts of Europe almost to the present. Many of the classical authors on the subject of werewolves refer to this traditional knowledge. In eleventh-century Ireland it was the practice of the inhabitants of Ossory always to have two of their people in the shape of wolves, each pair serving seven years. Giraldus Cambrensis, who gives this information in his *Topographica hibernica,* tells of an Irish priest who spoke with one of these Ossory werewolves in 1182. He was on a journey between Ulster and Meath, passing the night in the woods, when he was approached by a large wolf who explained his circumstances and asked the priest to come and bless his dying wife. The priest was unwilling to extend religious privileges to a she-wolf, but the wolf reassured him by pulling back his wife's wolfskin and revealing an old woman beneath it.

Fort on werewolves: "I think that the idea of werewolves is most silly, degraded, and superstitious: therefore I incline toward it respectfully." From the *Cornhill Magazine* (October 1918) Fort quotes the experience in northern Nigeria of a Captain Shott. Hyenas had been raiding a native village. Hunters who followed their tracks were surprised to find that at a certain point the animal prints gave way to human ones. One night Captain Shott's party wounded a particularly large beast, shooting off its jaw. The trail of blood was followed to another village where next day a man died of a terrible wound. His jaw had been torn off.

Reports of werewolves from all times and continents are innumerable, and so are were-tigers, foxes, hares, bears, cats and weasels, enough to fill an alternative menagerie. The phenomenon as experienced is as well established as anything could be. What everyone wants to know, of course, is whether the transformation from man to animal takes place in actual fact, in defiance of the doctors, or whether it is an illusion affecting the senses of both the person transformed and the people who see him. It may make little dif-

ference to a man having his throat torn out by something which looks and behaves like a wolf whether the creature is actually a wolf or merely seems like one, but this question has been disputed by the learned from very early times. Paracelsus thought the change was actual and physical, taking the magical view that the power of human will and imagination could be concentrated to affect external reality through the medium of the spiritual substance of the Universe. Other authorities disagreed, explaining the phenomenon as an effect of drugs or the magical enchantment they call "glamour". They in turn were contradicted by Sponde in 1583, who reasoned that "if a herb and the power of evil can have such control over the higher part of man, his reason and his immortal soul, why can not man's body be subject to similar disturbances?"

An old explanation, put forward as early as the second century AD by the Roman medical writer Marcellus Sidetes, sees the phenomenon in terms of the affliction known as lycanthropy, whose victims become convinced that they are savage wolves and behave accordingly. Though whether lycanthropy is, as Marcellus thought, a "species of melancholy", to be treated with cold baths and a diet of curds and whey, or whether it is a form of diabolic possession, as Summers and many others have believed, is a question which may never finally be resolved. In any case the lycanthropy theory accounts for only one half of the werewolf phenomenon, the delusion of the werewolf himself, and says nothing about the delusions of the witnesses who see him in his wolf's form. The same objection of incompleteness can be brought against other popular explanations in terms of self-hypnosis and the ritual wearing of animal skins.

The Viking "berserkers" wore bear skins while transforming themselves into savage killers by invoking the spirits of beasts, and members of the secret leopard-men societies, still active in East Africa, practise the same sort of rites. A certain Mr K., whose story is quoted, though without reference to its original source, in *Fate and Fortune* magazine, no. 6, was present early last century at a ritual in Orissa, India, where a local youth was transformed before his very eyes into a were-tiger. It is impossible to understand the effectiveness of these ritual transformations through any of the part-explanations already mentioned, such as lycanthropy, hypnosis or illusions created by the wearing of makeup and animal skins. Not that we reject any of these; we accept them all, in combination with other causes, as contributing towards the production of a magical effect which, whatever the degree of physical reality one may choose to attribute to the transformation, has a terrible reality indeed to the man who seems to change into a savage beast and to all who come within the sphere of his activities.

While working in northern Spain in the 1980s, soil engineer Jack Romano gained a unique insight into the werewolf beliefs of the inhabitants of the mountainous region of Galicia. Still remembered throughout Spain is the case of the self-confessed werewolf Manuel Blanco Romasanto, who was tried in 1852 for a series of murders of young or lonely women he had tricked into going with him into the mountains. Unlike the notorious trials of medieval witches, the Spanish courts and authorities allowed Romasanto an opportunity to explain his bloodlust. Speaking in his own defence, he claimed to be possessed every six months as a result of a curse, and he knew others who shared this predicament. This state, he told the court, made him feel "fantastic, powerful, exhilarating" and for its duration he was immune to death or injury.

Astonishingly, Romasanto helped the court to locate the remains of his victims, and submitted to medical examinations, including a primitive psychological assessment. He was condemned to death in April 1853, but the sentence was commuted to life imprisonment through the intervention of a brilliant young lawyer, Manuel Figuera. However, public outcry was such that the courts felt obliged to reinstate the death sentence and Romansanto was only spared as the result of a plea for clemency from the Queen of Spain.

Writing in *Fortean Times* (126, pp.40–44), Romano describes how Romasanto became a model, if eccentric, prisoner. Visitors peering into his cell would be surprised to see him wearing female clothing and making thread. At his trial, Romasanto had told the judge: "Were I to become a wolf, even you, a rational man, would be so terrified that you could not fire the gun, and even if you did, the bullets could never harm me." Today we can see beneath the lycanthropic trappings, the all-too-familiar ingredients of modern sociopathic serial killers. In Spain the legend of his ferocious conviction to be a werewolf still lingers on.

Fortean Picture Library

A number of medical conditions – such as the genetic defect causing porphyria and hypertrichosis, excessive hair growth – almost certainly contributed to the popular conceptions about werewolves. In modern times, some famous "hairy people" were brought from Burma, Laos and Mexico to be exhibited in circus freak shows. Theodore Petrof, for example – whose successful career as "JoJo the Dog-faced Boy" spanned several decades – was said to have been found at the age of eight living wild in a forest in Kostroma, Russia.

In search of ape-men

Wherever there are wastes and mountains, there are monsters – creatures that may be unknown to science but are quite familiar to the native inhabitants. They are described by people who have seen them as huge, hairy beings, half-men, half-apes, of supernatural intelligence and extremely elusive. Their giant footprints have been seen and photographed from the Himalayas to the mountains of North America, but not one of these creatures has ever been caught.

Everyone has heard about the Abominable Snowman or Yeti of the Himalayas, the manlike creature that lives high up in the snowy peaks. The local people know it well, and European and other visitors have seen it. A classic sighting was by the famous British mountaineer, Don Whillans, in the summer of 1970 at a height of 13,000 feet in the

mountains of Nepal. One night, after he had spent the day photographing the tracks of some large, unknown animal in the snow, he saw in the bright moonlight the creature which might have made the tracks moving along a ridge opposite his tent. It was like an ape and moved on all fours.

A good account of the Yeti was given to Lord Hunt by the Abbot of Thyangboche Monastery who had watched one playing in the snow outside his residence. It was about five feet tall, with grey hair. The other monks became very excited and drove it off by blowing conch shells and bugles.

Despite innumerable reports by Sherpas and others, the evidence most acceptable to science for the existence of the Yeti is the footprints. On 8 November 1951 Eric Shipton, on one of his Everest expeditions with Michael Ward and a Sherpa, Sen Tensing, came across some remarkable tracks in the snow at an altitude of 18,000 feet. They were of a creature that walked like a man and, if it were of human proportions, would have stood about eight feet tall. The tracks continued for about a mile and disappeared on some ice. Many other Himalayan explorers, including the *Daily Mail* expedition of 1954, have recorded similar footprints; the most dramatic were those discovered in Sikkim in 1915 and reported by a forestry officer, Mr J. Gent. The prints were between 18 and 24 inches long. According to Gent's native informants, who identified them as belonging to one of a local race of giant wild men, the toes pointed in the opposite direction to that in which the creature was moving.

Similar to the Yeti are the hairy wild men of Soviet Central Asia, one of which was clearly seen in 1957 by a scientist from Leningrad University, A.G. Pronin. It was in the Pamir mountains, and Pronin, who saw it again a few days later, described it as reddish-grey, hairy, long-armed and of shambling gait. The local Kirghiz herdsmen had long known of the creature's existence, but neither they nor any of the Soviet expeditions dispatched to the region ever managed to catch one.

The notion of unknown giants and hairy wild men existing in the modern world is patently absurd, yet every year brings hundreds of reports from sincere people all over the world

Modern sightings of Yeti, Bigfoot and other "manimals" perpetuate the traditional belief in "wild men". They were such popular characters that many coats of arms from the Middle Ages often feature male and female wildfolk as symbols of ancestral strength. This pen and ink drawing by H. Burgkmair, of a knight in combat with a wild man, dates from the beginning of the 16th century.

of sightings, encounters, giant spoors and other evidence of mysterious, manlike creatures. Paleontologists tell us that similar creatures, supposedly long extinct, once roamed the Earth. Perhaps, in remote corners, they roam it still. That is what many cryptozoologists believe, and the excitement of their quest is intensified by the idea that the quarry may be no ordinary animal but a human ancestor, a type of protoman, the much sought after "missing link".

Ivan Sanderson spent many years considering the depictions of wild men in the art of medieval Europe and earlier. Known as "woodhouses" or "woodwoses" or some other variation of the Anglo-Saxon *wudewasa,* meaning "wild man of the woods", their visual representation is ancient and universal and, as Sanderson notes, surprisingly consistent. Despite a hairy body the hands and feet are usually drawn hairless and manlike. Other details, like a belt or girdle, and crude weapons of wood, imply a simple culture and technology. Sanderson first discussed the idea that the image of the "wildman" may be the manifestation of a folk memory of the Neanderthal, in the anthropological magazine *Genus* (1967), and refined it over subsequent years. Writing in *Pursuit* (January 1981), he concluded that the *wudewasa* "…are detailed and accurate descriptions of Neanderthaloids, probably of more than one type. They were familiar to the early artists because these shy, often solitary forest-dwellers were not exterminated by Cro-Magnon man, as children are taught today, but disappeared very gradually from western and central Europe over a long period. The evidence suggests that the Wudewasa were not organized into tribes, as was Cro-Magnon. They were less able to compete for the rich lands they once roamed, and chose to retreat to more remote regions where they could live peacefully, but with more difficulty, avoiding their noisy, aggressive, more 'civilized' cousins, much as their remnant does today." It was the spread of agriculture and the clearance of vast forested and wooded tracts which brought about the final dissolution of the Neanderthals, thought Sanderson, rather than deliberate massacre by more organized races. Anthropologists have observed that non-tribal peoples, once split into small relict groups and confined

Fortean Picture Library

This unusual ape was snapped in 1920 by Swiss geologist Dr Francois De Loys during an expedition seeking oil on the border between Colombia and Venezuela. Their party was attacked by two of them and they shot one. Realizing it was unlike any known ape, De Loys took a photograph of it. According to his notes, the tail-less ape was 1.57 metres tall (half as high again as the spider monkey it resembled) and had 36 teeth, where most New World monkeys have 32. The creature was skinned, but its hide and skull were abandoned when the expedition hit trouble. Of the twenty-man team, only four survived. Years later, the photograph was found among De Loys's papers by French anthropologist Georges Montandon, who concurred that it might be an unknown species and named it *Ameranthropoides loysi* after the geologist. Other explorers of the region – including Alexander von Humboldt in 1800 – have seen, or recorded native descriptions of a large hairy primate in that area, which some of them called "El mono grande". De Loys's ape is comparable in height to a small gorilla but without the bulk. As the mountain gorilla (*Gorilla gorilla beringei*) was discovered comparatively recently – in 1902 – it seems reasonable to suppose that large apes, manlike apes and apelike men might also exist in some remote part of the planet.

An ice-pick gives the scale of one of the "Yeti" footprints photographed by Eric Shipton in the Himalayas in 1951.

to limited and shrinking territories, soon suffer a progressive deterioration of their culture, fertility and numbers.

Bernard Heuvelmans published two large books on the evidence for pre-human or wild men survivals in different parts of the world. The first, *L'homme de Neanderthal est toujours vivant* (1974), contains a long paper by the late Russian historian and anthropologist, Boris Porchnev, about sightings and traces of unknown "wild men" in modern Russia. Porchnev suggested that these might be survivors of the Neanderthal type. The idea proved popular in the Soviet Union, where evolutionism was one of the main supports of materialist philosophy. In 1958 the Soviet Academy of Sciences set up a commission to investigate the persistent rumours of *almas* or wild men in parts of Soviet Asia. Expeditions were sent to many of the likely areas, including the Pamir mountains of Central Asia, northern Siberia and the Caucasus, and researches were co-ordinated at a monthly seminar at the Charles Darwin Museum in Moscow. Reported sightings included one by a member of an expedition to the Pamirs in 1978, who described a large, hairy creature jumping about upright among the rocks.

English anthropologist Dr Myra Shackley of Leicester University was reported in the *Daily Mail* (2 December 1980) as saying that in the course of expeditions to the Altai Mountains of Outer Mongolia she had found Neanderthal tools which

the locals told her were made by the *almas*. "They now live in the mountains and we don't have any contact with them," said the Mongolians. "They don't interfere with us and we don't interfere with them." Dr Shackley knew of many reputable people who had seen the *almas*, the last encounter being in 1972 by a Russian doctor who had seen an entire *alma* family. "They live in caves, hunt for food, use stone tools and wear animal skins and furs," reported Dr Shackley. In her book-length consideration, *Wildmen* (1983), she concluded: "I cannot believe that Yetis and Almas are purely creatures of my imagination … imagination does not create unclassifiable footprints."

Earlier, in 1945, the English scientist W.C. Osman Hill, who became America's leading primatologist, suggested that the legendary *Nittaewo* people of Ceylon, said to be recently extinct, and also the *Orang pendek*, small hairy beings seen in the forests of Sumatra, might be modern ape-men survivals. These have their equivalents in Malaysia in the form of the *Orang dalam* which, according to local reports, have the familiar characteristics of the unknown hairy giants in many lands, being from six to ten feet tall, having a foul smell and red eyes and leaving outsized footprints. The zoologist Lord Medway reported in *The Times* in 1960 that the natives of the central Borneo mountains know of a similar creature which he compared to the Himalayan Yeti the "Abominable Snowman" whose appearances and doings first came to the attention of the European public in the nineteenth century. Heuvelmans' conclusion is that a form of Neanderthaler has survived throughout the wild places of Asia, from the Caucasus to Malaysia and Vietnam.

In 1979 a French anthropologist, Jacqueline Roumeguère Eberhardt, investigated reports that several types of "ape-men" or unknown primitives were inhabiting forests in Kenya. One type with a whitish skin was said to kill buffaloes, eating only their livers, and another wore a hide cloak, used a bow and arrow and cooked with fire. She never saw one herself, but stated that she was convinced from eyewitness sightings and other evidence that the beings existed.

The following year Heuvelmans published the second of his "ape-men" books, *Les bêtes humaines d'Afrique,* where he collected all the evidence of undiscovered primates or wild men in Africa, their types ranging from pygmies to super-gorillas.

In common with such phenomena as UFOs and lake monsters, the Yeti has never yielded a single, undisputed, physical proof of its actual existence. Despite the eagerness of its pursuers over many years and several continents, there is no body, nor hair nor hide of one, nor even one satisfactory photograph. True, there are the footprints, but we know of many cases where footprints have appeared without, apparently, any physical agency (see FOOTPRINTS AND TRACKS, p.273). From time to time we hear exciting rumours of the sort of evidence that would settle all doubts; but so far these have remained only rumours.

We do not discount the possibility that giant primates may survive undiscovered, nor the possibility of extraterrestrial spacecraft. Yet it still remains for the Yeti hunters, as for the ufologists, to demonstrate the reality of their quarry. Much has been said about the vastness and impenetrability of some of the Earth's wildernesses, but in Scotland, where we hardly expect to find hidden giants or lost tribes, the evidence for the legendary Big Grey Man of Ben MacDhui in the Cairngorms, including some rare sightings, is of much the same quality as the evidence for the Himalayan Yeti. Thus we feel that in the great majority of cases the "hidden animals" theory is inadequate.

Although they may appear to witnesses as

Fortean Picture Library

Igor Bourtsev, the Russian "snowman" hunter, compares his foot to a cast of a footprint found in August 1979 in the Gissar range of the Pamir-Altai mountains in Tadzhikistan.

This 16th-century Chinese woodcut shows a *ruren*, or "like-a-man", said to be resident in the forests of Shandong province.

normal flesh-and-blood animals, there are certain things about Yetis (and their relations worldwide) which cast doubt on their physical reality, such as their unnatural elusiveness and their disregard for bullets. Their status seems similar to that of the "thought-forms" of eastern mysticism, which are visible illusions created by the concentrated desires of a group or individual. Illusions of this sort are not always manifested consciously, but can arise spontaneously and unbidden in response to images, ideas or expectations formed in the human mind.

A clue to the nature of Yetis and *almas* as seen today may lie in the modern tendency to identify them as surviving Neanderthal or ape-men. In 1856, the same year that Darwin began writing *The Origin of Species*, fossilized human remains were dug up at Neanderthal in Germany. The biologist Thomas Huxley pronounced these remains to be apelike, and reconstructed images were published of the "ape-man" as conventionally imagined at the time: brutal, hairy and shambling. Neanderthal man is now recognized as being within the range of modern human types, but the old image took root, and its influence can still be seen today in the "hairy ape" models of early humanity exhibited in museums of natural history. Between them, Darwin and the Neanderthal skull prompted the search for ape-men which has continued unsuccessfully to the present day. From the end of the nineteenth century, when people began seeing and thinking about Yetis, speculation has been growing about the possible survival of our pre-human ancestors in the form of hairy, apelike, wild men, and it may be that the desire for such things has produced the corresponding apparitions or thought-forms. We note, for example, that the discovery of giant fossil teeth in China during the 1930s, which were said to have belonged to a manlike creature about twelve feet tall, anticipated the multiple reports in 1937 of giant footprints in the Himalayas.

The modern growth, or explosion, of the Yeti phenomenon is to some extent related to the frustrated desires of the evolutionists for relics of apelike human ancestors. There is of course much more to it than that. To be viable, a thought-form must reflect an archetype, or, as Rupert Sheldrake would put it, it must resonate with a morphogenetic field laid down in the past. As an archetypal form, the figure of the giant wild man among the rocks and forests is well established in human imagination. And if archaic forms can influence apparitions and thought-forms in the present, that might be the reason for the Yetis and Bigfoots sighted today. The *Gigantopithecus* of ancient China has often been compared to the mountain giants of Chinese folklore, and Heuvelmans has stated his belief that the Himalayan Yeti is its close relation. *Meganthropus,* the Great Man of Java, as reconstructed from his teeth and jawbone, apparently prefigures the legendary giant forest dwellers of southeast Asia and Indonesia. In North America, Bigfoot has numerous ancient prototypes in the giants which have been excavated from ancient Indian mounds. (The records of these giants have been

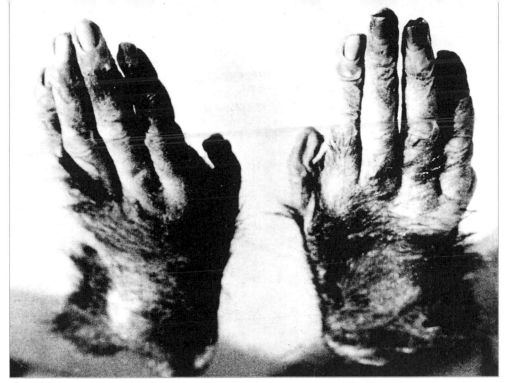

The well-preserved hands of what is, allegedly, a young ape-man, killed by villagers in eastern China in 1957. The palms are just under six inches long.

thoroughly suppressed by the archeologists; but that is a long and different story.) Our point is that the Yeti type shares a common characteristic with the other types of monsters and mystery creatures sighted today: they all represent apparent revivals of archaic, long extinct types which science has only revealed to us within the last two centuries. For ages after their physical disappearance from Earth, the shades of atavistic creatures have continued to haunt their former regions and infiltrate the legends of the local people. Now, it seems, they are becoming more insistent.

Bigfoot, the American monster

In the United States and Canada, particularly among the Indians of the mountainous, forested areas of the West, native legends refer to manlike giants which leave footprints and seem related in other ways to the unknown hairy creatures of Asia. "Sasquatch" is one of the names the Canadian Indians give them, and it is commonly used by modern researchers together with the general term "Bigfoot", an allusion to their impressive tracks. These have been found in mud, dust and snow in parts of north California, Oregon, Washington State and elsewhere, one of the best examples being the set found in October 1969 at Bossburgh, Washington. It consisted of over a thousand prints, stretching for about half a mile, each print measuring about forty-five centimetres in length. This implies that the two-legged creature that made them stood over three metres tall. The prints indicated that the right foot of the creature was crippled, but at one point it stepped easily over a 1m-high fence. In his analysis of claimed Sasquatch footprints John Napier rates the Bossburgh examples among the best evidence for the creature's existence.

First-hand reports of encounters with the Sasquatch were made in the nineteenth century, mainly by hunters, loggers and prospectors. They even included stories of people who had been abducted by the hairy giants and of other people who had captured a specimen. These accounts, however, were generally classified as "tall tales from the woods", and it was not until the 1950s that rumours and sightings of the "American Yeti" began making headlines. Since then, reported sightings of monsters have proceeded thick and fast, together with waves of literature on the subject. There is now scarcely a state in the Union without its records of local Bigfoot sightings and giant tracks. Almost as odd as the phenomenon itself are the characters who chronicle it. Many of them are active as Bigfoot hunters in the field, vying with each other to obtain the valuable prize, the first physical or photographic proof of its existence. Among these author-adventurers are Jim McClarin, Roger Morgan, John Green, author of the trail-blazing *On the Track of Sasquatch* (1971), Dr Grover Krantz, a scientist who investigated the Bossburgh prints, the Irishman Peter Byrne, proprietor of the Bigfoot Information Center at Hood, Oregon, and Rene Dahinden (who died in 2001), a veteran Swiss Maoist, who spent much time in the courtroom suing or being sued by other researchers in respect of right to

items of Bigfoot evidence. A conference of Bigfoot hunters and authors in May 1978 was marred by bad-tempered disputes among the participants. Happier events are the annual conferences held since 1988 by Don Keating and Marc DeWerth in Newcomerstown, Ohio.

As recently as August 1998, Wes Sumerlin, an experienced hunter, claimed to have found fresh Bigfoot tracks in the Blue Mountains of southeast Washington State. For fifty years, Sumerlin – who lived in the area – his wife Natalie, and his family had many experiences of Bigfoot in the Wenaha-Tuscannon Wilderness Area, as recorded in Vance Orchard's book *Bigfoot of the Blues* (1992). Sumerlin first encountered Bigfoot tracks at the age of fourteen while taking a train of mules into the mountains. He had seen several specimens a number of times and had names for them such as "Big Jim", "Blue-back" (both males) and "Buckskin" (a female). He claims the Bigfoots migrate huge distances as he has seen tracks of one creature (identified by an injury or deformity to the foot) in Central Washington, British Columbia

Fortean Picture Library

Rene Dahinden (left) holds a cast of a footprint found at Bluff Creek, California, by Roger Patterson after he had filmed his famous sequence of a Bigfoot there. Patterson (right) holds a cast of another footprint found at the same site in 1964.

and California. One day he got to within fifty feet of Buckskin. "When she turned to look my way, she was real visible and so were her breasts, so I knew it was a female," Wes recalls. When asked if he thought Bigfoot was an animal, Wes replied: "No I think he's far more intelligent than other animals. He has a face, something like a human but it isn't exactly a human face either."

The sheer variety of reported "manimals" is demonstrated by *The Field Guide to Bigfoot, Yeti and Other Mystery Primates Worldwide* (1999), compiled by Loren Coleman and Patrick Huyghe, both experienced researchers. The book has a bias towards interpreting the phenomena as "undiscovered" species of primate, but it also includes such fantastic and folkloric entities as hairy dwarves, giants, creatures that are best described as aquatic apes, and the bizarre Chupacabras ("goatsucker") of Puerto Rico (see MYSTERY MUTILATORS, p.177). While many writers and investigators have proceeded as if in no doubt that Bigfoot is a normal flesh-and-blood animal, with nothing but lack of a carcass preventing it from ranking among America's native fauna, others have been more circumspect.

In their book *Bigfoot* (1967), B. Ann Slate and Alan Berry detail some of their telepathic experiences and other strange happenings during field researches into the mystery. There have been many reports of odd side effects to such researches, and connections have been made between Bigfoot and other phenomena, equally enigmatic, such as alleged UFO occupants and mysterious outbreaks of cattle mutilations. The first serious discussion of these and other such problems in relation to each other was in John Keel's *Strange Creatures from Time and Space* (1970). The Bigfoot investigations of Loren Coleman and Jerome Clark in Oklahoma, Ohio, Pennsylvania and other states (recorded in their *Creatures of the Outer Edge,* 1978) have yielded good evidence of some form of link between Bigfoot, UFOs and other mysterious phenomena. In their summary Coleman and Clark list certain features of Bigfoot which recur in witnesses' accounts. It has red or luminous eyes and a foul smell; if shot at it is found to be invulnerable to bullets; it is shy and retiring but may kill animals; it can move at incredible speed, sometimes without leaving tracks, and where tracks are found they are of many different types and sizes. There is also a wide variation in the forms of the creatures reported and in the sounds

Rene Dahinden/Fortean Picture Library

One of the frames from the Roger Patterson movie of 20 October 1967, showing a large, hairy humanoid striding through woods in California. This is either proof of Bigfoot's visible existence or it is a hoax. Both sides of the controversy have their expert supporters.

they make. All these are features of Yetis and suchlike beings in other continents; and they are also the traditional attributes of phantoms and elementals. In seeking professional advice on the Bigfoot mystery, Coleman and Clark ask, "To whom shall we turn – the ufologist, the biologist, the psychologist or the demonologist?"

Ever since 1811 when the explorer David Thompson came across fourteen-inch tracks attributed to a Sasquatch, near Jasper, Alberta, many thousands of inexplicable footprints have been discovered; and continuing the Indian tradition that the Sasquatch is inclined to abduct human beings, several modern Americans have claimed that it has happened to them. The earliest case was in 1924: Albert Ostman, a lumberman, was camping opposite Vancouver Island when he

A composite photograph and a drawing of the unknown apelike man – said to be a modern Neanderthal – studied in October 1968 by Dr Bernard Heuvelmans and Ivan T. Sanderson. The body of the "Iceman" was being exhibited by Frank Hansen, a travelling showman in Minnesota, and the two cryptozoologists were convinced of its genuineness. Since then further study has been impossible (as Hansen has substituted a replica) and his claim that it was shot in Vietnam in recent times have not been verified.

was lifted up, sleeping bag and all, and carried some twenty-five miles to the lair of a Sasquatch family, consisting of Father, some eight feet tall, Mother, a foot shorter, and two children. They treated him well, and after six days he escaped. Fearing mockery he kept the experience to himself until 1955.

One of the most detailed (and earliest known) descriptions of an encounter with a Sasquatch took place in 1869. It comes from the weekly *Butte Record* (5 November 1870), although Janet and Colin Bord, in *Alien Animals* (1980), claim that the original source was a letter in an old Californian newspaper, the *Aurora Ledger* (16 October 1870). The creature was seen by a hunter camping in a forest below Orestimba Peak in northern California. Several times he had returned to camp to

find that his belongings had been disturbed, so he lay in wait to catch the culprit. This is what he saw: "It was in the image of a man but it could not have been human. I was never so benumbed with astonishment before. The creature, whatever it was, stood fully five feet high, and disproportionately broad and square at the fore shoulders, with arms of great length. The legs were very short and the body long. The head was small compared with the rest of the creature, and appeared to be set on his shoulders without a neck. The whole was covered with dark brown and cinnamon coloured hair, quite long in some parts, that on the head standing in a shock and growing close down to the eyes, like a Digger Indian's." The creature gave a whistling sound and knocked the camp fire about with a stick. The hunter watched him

Frank Hansen poses by the display hoarding for his "frozen Neanderthal" exhibit. He claimed that it was found frozen in a block of ice in the sea off Siberia, and was purchased by an anonymous millionaire who asked Hansen to exhibit it. Fearing prosecution for transporting a body across a state border, Hanson removed all references to it being "real", declaring instead that it was a "fabricated illusion". Opinion is now split between those who believe that Hansen had a real body which he showed to Heuvelmans and Sanderson; those who believe that Hansen switched the "real" with a detailed replica after Heuvelmans and Sanderson pronounced it genuine; and those who point out that Hansen is a professional showman who has a financial investment in his mysterious exhibit.

for about fifteen minutes, until the visitor was joined by another, a female of his kind, and the two walked off together. He said that he could easily have shot it but did not care to do so.

There was an account in *The Seattle Times* (16 July 1918) of "mountain devils" attacking a prospector's shack at Mount St Helens in the State of Washington. The devils were said to be members of a local race, intermediate between men and animals, with magical powers and the ability to make themselves invisible. In October 1940 the Chapman family of Ruby Creek, British Columbia, were approached by an eight-foot-tall, hairy male creature, which caused them to flee their house. It left behind 16-inch footprints and an overturned barrel of salted fish. Many other such incidents and sightings are recorded in the books of Ivan T. Sanderson, John Green and other writers on the "Bigfoot" phenomenon. The evidence to date for the existence of these unknown giants in northwest America was soberly analysed in *Bigfoot*, a book of 1973 by the famous anthropologist Professor John Napier.

A report in *The New York Times* (30 June 1976) gives the experience of a logger, Jack Cochran, on 12 May 1974 in the Hood River National Forest, Oregon. At a distance of fifty yards he saw a "big, hairy thing" standing silently. Following his first, remarkable notion that it might be one of his fellow workers, he realized that the creature could

only be the legendary Bigfoot. It finally walked away "gracefully, like an athlete" into the trees. Next day two other loggers of the same party were walking in the woods and disturbed the same or a similar creature. It ran away on two legs while they pursued it throwing rocks. Members of the Bigfoot Investigation Center at The Dalles, Oregon, later visited the site and found huge footprints with those of the loggers running alongside.

The most striking record ever made, or claimed, of the Great American Monster is the film shot by Roger Patterson while on a Sasquatch hunt at Bluff Creek, northern California, on 20 October 1967. It shows at a distance of about thirty metres a hairy, manlike creature walking upright in full view of the camera. Experts of the time examined the film and found no flaws or evidence of fakery, but in 1999, with improved methods of analysis, suspicions of hoaxing emerged. A small object on the creature's body looks like the head of a zip-fastener to what may be a monkey suit.

Other technical objections have been raised, but not all Bigfoot specialists have been convinced by them, and on certain points the sceptics have been refuted. Roger Patterson died in 1972, still insisting he had photographed a genuine Bigfoot. "I wish I'd shot the damned creature," he told friends in his last days. "Then they might have believed me." A full and fair account of the whole controversy is given by Loren Coleman, the leading cryptozoologist and Bigfoot chronicler, in his book *Bigfoot! The true story of apes in America* (2003). Behind the scenes, he reveals, the most powerful influence in the debate is money. The rights to Patterson's Bigfoot pictures are potentially valuable, and the dispute about their authenticity is largely between those who support or denigrate them for commercial reasons.

We bear in mind a saying of the great anatomist Sir Arthur Keith, that the only class of beings which are constantly seen but never present themselves at the dissecting table belongs to the world of spirits. In America the Bigfoot hunters are quite as active as the UFO and Loch Ness Monster people in the pursuit of evidence for the physical existence of their phenomenon; and they have had just the same degree of success or non-success – tracks, sightings, noises, strange feelings, mystical legends and above all, elusiveness. In July 1976, there was news in the American papers of a "secret expedition", organized by North American Wildlife Research, setting out to the wilds of British Columbia, where a "computer study"

indicated that the Sasquatch was most likely to be located. Their destination was the spot where a fisherman had found tracks of the monster, and they intended to tranquillize one with a drugged dart, fit it up with a radio transmitter and then track its subsequent movements. But their plans were foiled by the creature's non-appearance.

Supporting our belief in the phenomenal reality that links so many of our sections is the following early Bigfoot record quoted by Warren Smith in *Strange Monsters and Madmen* from a diary shown to his friend, Brad Steiger, by the grandson of the man who wrote it, Mr Wyatt of Tennessee. Grandfather Wyatt, a woodsman in Humboldt County, wrote in his diary for 1888 that the local Indians were in contact with strange, hairy beings they called "crazy bears", which were brought down to Earth from time to time by spacemen from UFOs in silvery, close-fitting outfits. The explanation, as Wyatt understood it, was that the space people were experimenting with stocking the Earth with the animals they most liked to eat!

Wild people

In September 1731, a formidable little girl strode into a French village to become one of the nine specimens of "wild man" classified by Linnaeus as *Homo sapiens ferus*. A book of that name by Raüber in 1888 describes her first dramatic appearance: "A girl of nine or ten years, suffering from thirst, entered the village of Songy at dusk. The village is four or five leagues from Chalôns in Champagne. Her feet were naked, her body was covered with rags and skins of animals. Instead of a hat she wore a piece of bottle-gourd on her head. She carried a club in her hand, and when someone in the village set a dog at her she gave it such a heavy blow on the head that the animal fell over dead at her feet."

When finally captured and examined, she was found to have extra large thumbs, which was attributed to her Tarzan style of swinging from tree to tree. Several hot baths revealed that her skin was white. Some even identified her as an Eskimo. She was speechless, but she ran and swam wonderfully and caught and ate small animals,

also raw fish and – appropriately for a French wild girl – frogs. A strange feature in the case was that, until her capture, she had had a wild companion, a young black woman, who continued to be seen in the neighbourhood but was never captured. She had quarrelled with this woman over an ornament they had found and had hit her head with her club. In later life, when she had learnt to talk, she could give no account of her previous existence, apart from some vague remembrance of a large water animal and of having twice crossed the sea. For one brief period of her life she had been taken in by a woman who had given her some clothes; before that she had been naked.

Captivity damaged the wild girl in health and spirit. The food she was given made her teeth fall out, she was often ill and became worse through the bleedings ordered by the doctors to weaken her savage nature. She was no idiot. She was taught to speak and behave like a civilized female of the time, and she finally gratified her benefactors by becoming a nun in a Paris convent.

The mystery of how two wild girls – one a Negress, the other apparently an Eskimo – could suddenly appear in eighteenth-century France has never been solved. Yet these are not isolated cases. Similar examples of *Homo sapiens ferus* have been recorded in every century and in every part of the world. Another, more famous, French wild child was caught in the woods of Caunes, in Aveyron, on 7 August 1800. As in all such cases, his appearance, behaviour and diet were entirely animal-like, but under the care of Dr Itard – whose book, *The Wild Boy of Aveyron* was published in 1832 – the boy, Victor, eventually learnt to speak a little and lived on to the age of about forty. Several learned people who examined him thought he was an idiot, their evidence being his abnormal perception and love of nature. Dr Itard invented an early form of sign language to communicate with the boy and these events inspired François Truffaut's movie *L'Enfant Sauvage*.

A wild man of the sea is alluded to in Lady Camilla Gurdon's *Suffolk Folklore*: "A curious story relating to Orford is told by Ralph of Coggeshall (abbot of the monastery there in the early part of the thirteenth century). Some fishermen on this coast (AD 1161) caught in their nets one stormy

The wild man in chains, supporting the arms of the Earl of Atholl, represents an actual wild man captured on the family estates by a 17th-century ancestor.

A "horrible uncouth creature", who for some time had been haunting woods near Salisbury, Wiltshire, was reported in the *Illustrated Police News*, 24 March 1877, to have carried off a farmer's wife and to have dropped her only when shot at. He then disappeared.

day a monster resembling a man in size and form, bald-headed, but with a long beard. It was taken to the Governor of Orford Castle, and kept there for some time, being fed on raw flesh and fish, which it 'pressed with its hand' before eating. The soldiers in the Castle used to torture the unhappy monster in divers fashions 'to make him speak'; and on one occasion, when it was taken to the sea to disport itself therein, it broke through a triple barrier of nets and escaped. Strange to say, not long afterwards, it returned of its own accord to its captivity; but at last, 'being wearied of living alone, it stole away to sea and was never more heard of'. A tradition of this monster, known as 'the wild man of Orford', still exists in the village."

Perhaps their visitor was a sea-lion-man or a were-seal or an old sea god or a teleported Finn or a lunatic fisherman. We are not happy with these or any other explanations for the repetitive wild man phenomenon, and we sympathize with Linnaeus who, avoiding all explanations, dealt with the problem by classifying the Wild Man as a separate order, *Homo ferus*. However, there seems no reason to doubt the genuineness of this report. The incident would still have been a living memory at the time Abbot Ralph was writing, and the behaviour of the wild man was in character with others of his kind, as also was the uncomprehending way in which the creature was treated. When it comes to explanations, however, we are no wiser than the Orford people of the time.

The existence of wild people in the forests and waste places was commonly recognized throughout the Middle Ages. Called "woodwoses", they figure in Gothic carving and heraldic ornament. A supporter on the arms of the Earl of Atholl of the Murray family is a woodwose in chains; it commemorates the capture of a wild man among the rocks of Craigiebarns by a seventeenth-century Murray who was rewarded with the hand of the Atholl heiress and succession to the title. The wild or "green man" of the woods is frequently displayed on inn signs. At Sproughton in Suffolk the Wild Man Inn, built in the sixteenth century, was named after a wild man who terrified the builders. From the same county comes the well-known but inexplicable report by the old chronicler, William of Newburgh, of two children,

On 22 July 1724 a "naked, brownish, black-haired creature" was seen in the woods near Hamelin and later caught. The creature turned out to be a savage boy of about twelve. He became docile, and was summoned from Hanover to the court of King George I in London. The boy refused all delicacies from the royal table, eating only raw meat and vegetables. He was sent to a family on a farm in Hertfordshire, where he spent many years roaming the countryside or lying before the fire – an amiable pet of the neighbourhood. His guardian had a brass collar made for him with the inscription "Peter the Wild Boy, Broadway Farm, Berkhamstead". He died at the age of about 72 in 1785 and was buried at Northchurch, Hertfordshire, where a plaque gives his history. Lord Monboddo, the early evolutionist, visited Peter at the farm in 1782 and pronounced him to be a fine specimen of unspoilt humanity.

This illustration – from an Italian periodical of 1934 – refers to a "half-naked man, as agile as a monkey" found in Finland in that year. Despite being "lightly wounded" by soldiers, he managed to evade capture for a while and "spoke" only in grunts.

a boy and a girl, greenish in colour and eating only beans, who suddenly appeared in a field near Woolpit, having apparently emerged from some underground workings there. Their story was that they came from a place called St Martin; they had been watching their father's sheep when they had heard a loud noise, and the next thing they knew was that they were mysteriously in the fields of Woolpit.

In the *American Weekly* (27 October 1935) is an account of a wild boy found naked in the El Salvador jungle. He was about five years old, lived off raw fruit and fish, and spent his nights in the trees to avoid predatory animals.

Charles Fort was a great collector of wild man reports. In *Lo!* he quotes from *The New York Times* (19 January 1888) an account of five wild men and one wild girl who appeared in Connecticut at the beginning of that year. Fort claimed to have records of no less than ten wild men seen in England during the winter of 1904–05. One of them, of unknown origin, appeared naked in the streets of Cheadle, Cheshire, and was decently placed in a sack by a policeman and dragged off to the police station. Another carried a book with drawings and writings in an unknown script and speaking an unknown language himself. His case is reported in the *East Anglian Daily Times* (12 January 1905). A report in the *Chatham News* (10 January 1914), tells how a man was found running naked down Chatham High Street in bitterly cold weather. He was arrested, but like a true *Homo ferus* could give no account of himself. He appeared suddenly, he was unknown, therefore he was declared insane.

Fort regarded these wild men appearances in much the same way as he regarded showers of fishes and frogs. Wild men, like falling fishes, must come from somewhere, and both these phenomena, so Fort suggested, were due to teleportation. His idea was that there was a relationship – as of one end of a tube to another – between places where people inexplicably vanish and places where "wild men" suddenly turn up. Thus, in every case of a strange appearance, one should look for another case of a strange disappearance.

One modern piece of evidence has since emerged to support Fort's view of the origin of wild men. In our THE TELEPORTATION OF PEOPLE section (p.6) reference is made to a young Brazilian, José Antonió da Silva in 1968. It is recorded that after being set down near Vitória, miles from the spot from which he had mysteriously vanished some four days earlier, his first impulse was to retire into the woods and to live off the wildlife.

Children raised by animals

Several mythologies embody the theme of human children cared for by animals. Best known are Romulus and Remus, the founders of Rome, who were suckled as infants by a wolf. The story was generally found credible, being backed by numerous reports of similar cases throughout history. But, by the nineteenth century – during which a sort of competition arose among scholarly and scientific people to see how much of popular lore and old history could be discredited – such reports were regarded as fables, amusing for children but too absurd for the attention of serious people.

Rudyard Kipling's idealized wolf-boy, Mowgli of *The Jungle Book*, made it seem that the motif was a fairy story. Yet at the same time as they were being rationally proved impossible, more and more cases of humans fostered by animals were reported, many supported by good evidence and reliable witnesses. Finally, in 1920, the carefully documented history of the wolf children of Midnapore (see below) convinced all but the wilfully sceptical that children may indeed be nurtured by wild animals.

There are stories of children raised by wolves or bears, and less frequently by leopards, panthers, monkeys, antelopes, goats, pigs, cattle, sheep and other creatures. In virtually all cases where children were adopted as infants, they acquired (more or less permanently) the natures, habits, abilities and even some of the physical features of their animal guardians. There are few examples of such children becoming fully reconciled to human ways. The later acquisition of human speech has proved difficult in some cases and impossible in others, and the few who have managed to speak

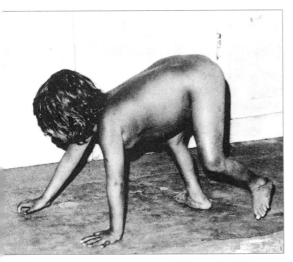

Tissa, the Monkey Boy of Ceylon (1973).

In this variation on the Romulus and Remus theme, a young boy is nurtured by a she-bear in 17th-century Poland.

Despite the evidence – or perhaps out of ignorance of it – many anthropologists are still unwilling to accept the phenomenon of the rearing of humans by animals. The phenomenon does indeed have many unexplained aspects, but they seem to prefer to believe that all animal children are idiots who have been found wandering near the animals supposed to have fostered them. Autistic children often have characteristics in common with those taken from animal homes. The French philosopher, Lévi-Strauss declared: "The majority of wild children are congenitally abnormal children who have been deliberately abandoned."

In his *Systema naturae* (1758), the great systematizer, Linnaeus, identified the wild man, *Homo sapiens ferus,* as a sub-species of humanity (see WILD PEOPLE, p.344). He characterized him as "four-footed, dumb and hairy", and cited as examples nine historical cases, among them the following.

Hunters in a Lithuanian forest saw two little boys among a group of bears. They caught one – he was about nine years old, strong, healthy and handsome – and took him to Warsaw where he became the pet of the royal family and the nobility. He could not be taught to speak or to give up his bearish nature, but he did learn to raise his eyes and arms to heaven when anyone uttered the name of Jesus. Several times he escaped to the woods, and was once seen exchanging affectionate hugs with a wild bear notorious for having killed two people. There seems to have been a rash of bear children in Lithuania at the time. This first case was in 1661, and there are two others recorded in Dr Connor's *History of Poland*. One child, captured in 1694, was seen by Connor himself, who found him unable to talk or walk upright, though he later acquired both arts imperfectly; another such captive had been inspected by a Dutch diplomat in Warsaw some years earlier.

It is strange that such a proverbially bad-tempered creature as the bear should be so tolerant of human cubs; yet it is credited with more adoptions than any other animal apart from the wolf. A case was reported in *The American Weekly* (5 September 1937). In his article titled "Raised by

even a few words have invariably used them to express their preference for their old animal life above their present human one.

It is generally supposed that feral children have been stolen or found abandoned by a mother animal in milk and adopted by her. But their remarkable physical abilities, their speed or strength in the case of antelope or bear children, or the luminous, wolf-like eyes of, for example, the Midnapore children, suggest another and (even to us) rather fantastic theory: that some are truly the children of animal parents, but monstrosities, corresponding to the known monstrous births of animal-like offspring to human mothers. Again, there may be a wild talent in all of us, an ability to grow more physically and mentally like other creatures around us.

a She-bear that Stole Her When a Baby", George Maranz described his visit to a girl in a Turkish lunatic asylum who had just spent eight years with a bear family. One of a party of hunters near Mount Olympus had shot a she-bear and had then been violently attacked by a powerful little "wood spirit". Finally overcome, the spirit turned out to be a human child, though utterly bearlike in her voice, habits and physique. When Mr Maranz saw her, she was much the same as at her capture, though somewhat more docile, and starvation had made her accept cooked food.

In 1767, hunters from Fraumark, in lower Hungary, were pursuing a large bear when they noticed human footprints in the snow in a part of the mountains where they thought no humans had ever before penetrated. The prints were followed to a bear's den, and there was discovered a real Goldilocks, a girl of about eighteen, tall, healthy and brown-skinned. Her behaviour "was very crude", and when taken to an asylum she refused to eat anything but raw meat, roots and the bark of trees. Another case of a bear-boy occurred early in the seventeenth century in Denmark and, in 1897, a bear-girl aged about three was found in India.

Anselm von Feuerbach, in his 1833 book on the mysterious foundling Kaspar Hauser, gives a sad account of a pig-girl seen by a Dr Horn. "He saw in the infirmary at Salzburg, but a few years ago, a girl of twenty-two years of age, and by no means ugly, who had been brought up in a hog-sty among the hogs, and who had sat there for many years with her legs crossed. One of her legs was quite crooked, she grunted like a hog, and her gestures were brutishly unseemly in a human dress."

The first contemporary record of a wolf-boy is from Hesse, in 1341. The boy, taken from the wolves by hunters, ran on all fours and leapt prodigiously. He died from being forced to adopt a civilized diet. Three years later in the same district another wolf-boy was captured and successfully educated, living on to the age of eighty. He said he had been adopted by wolves when three years old; they had fed him, sheltered him and taught him their ways, and he was very sorry to have been parted from them.

The majority of wolf-children recorded since the early nineteenth century have come from India, in most cases from the jungles of Bengal. The best documented of these is the history of the Midnapore children, written by their discoverer

and subsequent guardian, The Revd J. Singh (*Wolf Children and Feral Man*, 1942). Singh was a missionary of the Midnapore Orphanage who made regular evangelical trips to the aboriginal tribes of his district. On one such expedition in 1920, he came into contact with the inhabitants of a village who were terrified of two small ghosts with blazing eyes that apparently haunted a nearby wolf den. He took a party to investigate and from a tree observed the "ghosts" leaving the wolf den in the company of the wolves. Realizing that they were human, Singh ordered the den to be dug out. At the first strokes of the spade, two wolves fled into the jungle but the mother wolf held her ground and attacked the diggers. Before Singh could intervene, one of the men killed her with an arrow.

Shepherds discover the baby Semiramis, sustained by doves. She grew into the legendary founder of Babylon and wife of Nimrod and was eventually worshipped as a goddess. Some scholars believe that the early depictions of Semiramis and her son formed the prototype for the Christian iconography of the Virgin Mary and baby Jesus. This depiction was painted by E. Wallcousins.

Inside the den they found a ball of cubs, two wolves and two little girls, clinging together. One girl was about one and a half years old, the other about eight. The wolf cubs were sold off by the Indians and the little girls dragged to the Orphanage. The younger died within a year, never speaking or walking upright; but the elder girl, lovingly cared for by Mrs Singh, survived her capture for nine years, during which she lost some of her animal nature and gradually learnt to stand, to eat civilized food and even to speak a few words.

From the 1970s come two cases of gazelle-boys. *The Sunday Times* (26 August 1973) described how "A Syrian 'gazelle-child', discovered by a local prince on a hunting party, was said to be capable of running at 50 mph with the gazelles. He also had superb eyesight and very acute hearing." The other case, reported in London's *Daily Mirror* (1 February 1971), told of a boy, discovered in the Spanish Sahara not far from Rio de Oro, who moved in leaps and bounds, although he was "not as fast or as graceful as his companions". Jean-Claude Armen, a distinguished anthropologist, reported to the Life Institute, Geneva: "I have watched him approach gazelles and lick their foreheads in a sign of recognition." A delightful book by Armen, *Gazelle Boy*, was published in 1974. At

that time, despite attempts by American scientists to capture him, the boy was still at large. Armen gradually made friends with him and was able to watch as the boy danced and played with the gazelles. He thought it likely that the boy was from a nomadic tribe whose babies travel in baskets slung on a camel. He must have fallen from the basket and been suckled by a gazelle that had lost her fawn. How he had so quickly adapted to the mobility of gazelle life is a mystery.

Equally astonishing is the case of the ostrich boy, Sidi Mohamed, whose story, told by himself, is quoted by Armen from *Notes Africaines* (26 April 1945). At the age of five or six he wandered off from his North African family and after three days in the wild came upon an ostrich nest with chicks hatching. When the parent birds returned he stayed around until they became used to him, and for ten years he lived with them, learning to live off grass and to match their speed in running. At night he was sheltered by the two ostriches who each extended a wing over him. One day a party of ostrich hunters appeared on fast horses. For some hours the boy and the birds outran the hunters but finally they roped him and he was restored to his parents. It took him a long time to readapt to human ways and he was always yearning for his old way of life among the ostriches.

In Uganda, John Sseybunya plays with monkeys for a TV documentary about the year he spent with a monkey troop at the age of four.

The most recent case to arouse worldwide attention was the story of John Sseybunya from Uganda who claims that as a young child he lived with a colony of vervet monkeys. As a four-year-old, John fled into the jungle after witnessing the brutal murder of his mother by his father. He was not heard of again until a year later when he was spotted accompanying the monkeys on their night-time raids on crops. Captured by local women, he was extremely malnourished but otherwise unharmed. The most persuasive evidence for the truth of his story is that as a young adult John possesses a level of communication with the animals that indicates a close and well-established relationship with them. His story was the subject of a BBC documentary in 1999. Today, as a young adult, John appears somewhat backward by usual standards, and no one has yet determined whether

this is due to an inherent disability, to his simian sabbatical, or both. We suspect that if John had been younger when he joined the monkeys, he might never have readjusted to human society as well as he has done.

We are struck by the similarities between children brought up by animals and children carried off by eagles and recovered from their nests (see AVIAN ABDUCTIONS, p.384). In both cases the authorities are inclined to say that it cannot really happen, but popular belief, supported by anecdotes from all ages and countries, insists that it does. This is the area that particularly interests us in this book, where archetypal themes of myth and legend break out of that category and merge into physical reality. This is where human imagination interacts with matter to create the world we experience.

Living dinosaurs

If asked to give an example of an ancient, long-extinct type of animal, most people's first thoughts would be of dinosaurs. Everyone knows that the giant reptiles vanished from the Earth geological ages ago. Old-fashioned evolutionists used to hold them up as examples of the "unfittest" creatures, which became too big and specialized to adapt rapidly enough to changes in their environment. Modern biologists have become wary of such sweeping explanations, and several – among them, the respectable zoologist Dr Roy Mackal of the University of Chicago – have mounted expeditions in search of proof that such creatures might have survived into the present day.

In February 1980, Mackal – in partnership with Texan crocodile expert, James Powell – began his first expedition into Central Africa. Powell had been dinosaur hunting several times before, while pursuing his studies of African crocodiles. In the swamps and river basins of the Cameroons and Gabon (formerly part of French West Africa) he had heard natives' descriptions of a semi-aquatic saurian over ten metres long, called n'yamala by the Feng people of Gabon. While staying at the Albert Schweitzer settlement, Powell met a Feng witch doctor, Michel Obiang, who told him much about the n'yamala, describing it and the terrain

it inhabited and even specifying the type of plant it fed on. He later revealed that, in about 1946, he had seen the creature itself.

Powell was struck by the similarity in both names and descriptions between the n'yamala and the amali of old Trader Horn's earlier account. Alfred Aloysius "Trader" Horn (real name, Smith), in his book of stories and adventures along the waterways of Africa, The Ivory Coast in the Earlies (1927), claimed that he had seen footprints of the amali, "…the size of a good frying-pan in circumference" with three claw marks, and that he had seen its image in the cave paintings of Bushmen. He thought it was responsible for the snapped and splintered tusks which he had found in so-called "elephant cemeteries".

Following their 1980 expedition, Mackal and Powell submitted a formal report to the government of the People's Republic of the Congo – in whose territory much of their researches had been carried out. They included a brief summary of the more reliable of previous reports describing a giant water monster in the African interior. The reports started in 1770 with the publication of a book by the Abbé Proyart, Histoire de Loango, which contained missionaries' descriptions of clawed footprints, about 1m around, in districts which are now the Congo, Gabon and the Cameroons. These prints, some over two metres apart, implied a creature between the size of a hippo-

This surreal engraving from Flammarions 1880 book *Le Monde* was intended to compare the size of a dinosaur to a tenement block in Paris, but it strangely prefigures that genre of science fiction movies in which modern cities are menaced by rampaging giants from the distant past.

potamus and an elephant, neither of which, of course, has claws.

Among other reports cited was that of the German leader of the Likouala-Congo expedition of 1913–14, who recorded the statements of experienced Africans about deep pools inhabited by an elephant-sized animal with a long, flexible neck and a single long tooth or horn. It also had a strong tail with which it would capsize canoes, killing – but not eating – their occupants. It was a vegetarian and, here too, the Africans named its favoured plant. Another German, Dr Leo von Boxberger, a former magistrate in the days of Germany's African empire, published a similar account of another mysterious water monster in 1938, one the Congolese knew, and still know, as *mokele-mbembe*.

The object of the Mackal-Powell expedition, as they defined it, was: "To establish in so far as is possible whether the reports of the *mokele-mbembe* refer to a myth or to real animals. If the latter, to determine whether the animals are extinct or still in existence, and to obtain as much information as to their nature and habitat as possible." No sightings were made by the team, but they recorded interviews with witnesses whose sightings were as recent as 1979. They also heard an account from pygmies of the killing of one of the monsters in 1959. A pair of the creatures had been observed moving between a river and a lake, so the pygmies erected a stake barrier across the river and speared one of the animals as it tried to cross.

In general, the eyewitnesses' accounts were of a creature up to fifteen metres in length with a long tail and a snakelike head, sometimes crowned with a comb like a rooster's. In the conclusion to their report, Mackal and Powell stated their belief that the *mokele-mbembe* is not a myth but a real animal, that its range has been greatly reduced in the last two hundred years, perhaps to the point of extinction, and that it is "...a species unknown to science as a living form".

The implication of the last phrase is that the *mokele-*

mbembe may be known to scientists as an *extinct* form. At his first meeting with Michel Obiang, Powell showed the witch doctor drawings of various animals, all of which Obiang recognized (if they occurred in his district), together with pictures of dinosaurs. Two of these – the diplodocus (similar to a brontosaurus) and the plesiosaur – were identified by Obiang as images of the *n'yamala*. Other Africans, questioned independently, made the same identifications, while rejecting pictures of other kinds of dinosaur as unknown to them.

Previous explorers had made the connection between the semi-aquatic monsters – known to the Africans of the inland lake and swamp districts under a variety of names – and supposedly long-extinct giant reptiles. And even before Powell, there had been specialist dinosaur hunters. Around Christmas, 1919, a Captain Leicester Stevens electrified the world's press by announcing – on a platform at Waterloo Station – that he was off to Central Africa to hunt a dinosaur. It was to be a one-man-one-dog expedition; his companion being a half-wolf mongrel, which had distinguished itself in the recent war. Some weeks previously reports had appeared in London newspapers of monster sightings in the Belgian Congo. A creature said to be a brontosaurus had chased a Monsieur L. Lepage and, in a separate incident, had been shot at by a Monsieur Gapelle. Both these reports have since been exposed by Dr Bernard Heuvelmans as hoaxes – Gapelle being an anagram of L. Lepage – but the notion of living dinosaurs in Africa caught the public imagination. A rumour went around – and was evidently believed by Captain Stevens – that the Smithsonian Institution had offered a reward of one million pounds for a specimen of brontosaurus. The *Daily Mail* published a horrendous reconstruction of the monster, which prompted a reader to comment that if the brontosaurus was as formidable as its image, Captain Stevens would need a tank rather than a rifle to combat it.

In the years between the wars, the rumour of living dinosaurs was kept alive by a succession of alleged sightings, often of doubtful authenticity. The widespread African belief in their existence was confirmed by a number of sober authorities, and their various accounts were collected by Frank Lane in *Nature Parade* (1939). Among them was a statement by the old "bring them back alive" zoo collector, Carl Hagenbeck, of his belief in a kind

Among the evidence suggesting that dinosaurs may have survived until relatively recently in remote parts of Africa are curiously shaped gold weights, like this one, in use by the Ashanti for generations.

of brontosaurus surviving in the African swamps. He claimed to have sent an expedition to capture one, but without success. In a book entitled *Eighteen Years on Lake Bangweulu*, by J.E. Hughes, Lane found an account of a creature known as *chipekwe*. It was a water monster with a smooth, dark body equipped with an ivory horn. The son of a local chief told Hughes that his grandfather had described the killing of one with harpoons. It took the hunters an entire day to dispatch the creature. Hughes believed that the *chipekwe* might now be extinct.

For students of modern African dinosaurs, by far the best source is Dr Heuvelmans' *Les derniers dragons d'Afrique* (1978) in which nearly every known report and rumour relating to the existence of undiscovered archaic reptiles in the dark continent is collected and analysed. It makes an impressive record; but there is one feature which all the sightings and stories have in common, the lack of any physical evidence to support them. Powell, in Gabon, asked his witch doctor friend, Obiang, whether some relic of the *n'yamala* might have been preserved as a memento. He was told: "Oh no! The *n'yamala* is the king of the waters. It never dies. No one ever kills a *n'yamala*!"

This, of course, is inconsistent with the various native reports of monster-slaying. Even though they commit themselves to belief in the physical

Possibly the first widely publicized, monster-hunting expedition to the Congolese Republic by western scientists took place in 1981, led by American Herman Regusters and his wife, who claimed a sighting on Lake Tele. They were followed, two years later, by a Congolese expedition led by Marcellin Agnagna, a zoologist from Brazzaville zoo; Agnagna, too, claimed a spectacular sighting of *mokele-mbembe* near Lake Tele. In November 1985, the "Operation Congo" expedition – four young Britons, led by ex-soldier and *Fortean Times* contributor Bill Gibbons – set off for the Likouala region of the Congo with the blessing of Dr Bernard Heuvelmans, and headed for Lake Tele. They hoped to determine whether *mokele-mbembe* was reptilian or, as Heuvelmans suggested, a mammal that looks reptilian through convergent evolution. They returned in mid-June 1986, without any tangible success after enduring considerable hardships. Gibbons went back several times more as the guest of local missionaries, but still with no proof of the existence of *mokele-mbembe*. More expeditions followed, including one by travel writer Redmond O'Hanlon in 1989 and American journalist Rory Nugent in 1992. O'Hanlon returned convinced that sightings of *mokele-mbembe* were misidentifications of forest elephants fording rivers with their trunks raised. In September 1992, a Japanese team flew to Lake Tele to film a TV documentary on the subject and filmed something big in the lake as they flew over it. Much enlarged and out of focus, the grainy shapes resembled a man standing in a canoe and did little to resolve matters. The last expedition of note, in November 2000, was led by another young *Fortean Times* contributor Adam Davies, and although he found no proof of the beast, he did come back with much useful information after befriending tribal elders near Impfondo. One of them told him that "…it has feet like an elephant and a neck like a giraffe. It does not live on the lake but in the forest and travels across the lake for food … And the male creature has a horn on its head while the female doesn't."

reality of dinosaur-like reptiles in Africa, Mackal and Powell were honest enough to include in their report some hints to the contrary. Although the Africans acknowledge the existence of mysterious water monsters, they attribute to them peculiar magical qualities which distinguish them from ordinary animals, such as the taboo on discussing your sighting. When Powell tried to investigate

the alleged killing of a *mokele-mbembe* by the Congolese pygmies, he was told that they were unwilling to discuss the matter.

Powell was also warned that anyone who sees the beast must keep quiet about it or die. Such taboos – which can be found all over the world in relation to near-mythical creatures, including fairies and spirits – are an indication of the degree to which the natives considered this creature as both sacred and some kind of magical spirit (see also PTERODACTYLS TODAY, below). During the 1985 "Operation Congo" expedition, the members were told more specifically that *mokele-mbembe* was responsible for bringing serious diseases to the pygmies when they earned its displeasure. In November 2000, a pygmy elder warned Adam Davies that the creature was "…very dangerous. It will shoot you with lightning from its eyes."

A prohibition on discussing a magical creature, of course, makes information even more difficult to gather. In fact, the hard evidence for African dinosaurs, lacking photographic documentation, is not even equal to the evidence for monsters in Loch Ness, Canada and other tamer regions. As Ivan Sanderson, Heuvelmans and others have pointed out, there is nothing unrea-sonable about the notion of dinosaurs surviving in the vast African hinterland – or in wilder-nesses elsewhere – and we have little doubt that the natives who claim to have seen such things really have seen something.

But Africa is a land of magic. As old Trader Horn wrote: "Aye! There's places in Africa where you get visions of primeval force … In Africa, the Past has hardly stopped breathing." We have sug-gested several times in this book that the forms of long-extinct creatures may continue to haunt both their native regions and the imaginations of the people who live there – awaiting perhaps the opportunity for a physical comeback (see RETURN OF THE LIVING DEAD, p.362). It may be that Africa is destined for a dinosaur renaissance. Meanwhile we eagerly await further reports from our dedi-cated dinosaur hunters.

Pterodactyls today

In most popular illustrations of the Earth during the age of the dinosaurs – you have only to think of such movies as *One Million Years BC* (1966) and the *Jurassic Park* series (1993, 1997 and 2001) – the air is shown to be filled with a variety of flying lizards generally known as pterodactyls. From their fossil remains it appears that their leathery, claw-tipped wings extended from around one metre up to about seven or eight (in the case of pteranodon). The dis-covery of an even bigger specimen was reported on 12 March 1975 in *The New York Times*. Its remains were found in the Big Bend National Park in Texas, indicating it had a wingspan of no less than 15m 50cm, comparable to a large aeroplane. Like other pterodactyls, it is said to have used its wings mainly for gliding.

This Texan discovery sparked off, or coincided with, a local pterodactyl renaissance. In January 1976, two sisters – Libby and Deanie Ford – saw a most unusual bird near Brownsville, Texas. It was as tall as them, all black, and they described it as having a face like a cat's. They finally iden-tified it from a book on prehistoric animals as a pteranodon, a creature supposed to have died out many millions of years ago. Within a few days of that sighting, the *San Antonio Light* of Texas (26 February 1976) reported the experience of three local women teachers who were driving to work when they saw an enormous bird swooping low, at telegraph-pole height, over the cars on the road. It cast a shadow the width of the highway, and they reckoned its wingspan at 4–6m or more. Apart from its unearthly size, the feature that struck them was its wings. They were like a bat's, and their bony structure could be seen through the grey skin as the bird glided rather than flew. When they reached school, the teachers looked through encyclopedias and came across an illustration of the creature they had seen. It was a pteranodon.

The background to these two sightings was a wave of "big bird" incidents across the lower Rio Grande valley, on the border between southern Texas and Mexico, near where the river empties into the Gulf of Mexico. During the last months of 1975 and the beginning of 1976, the incidents generally consisted of people being attacked or frightened by impossibly huge birds or flying rep-tiles with membranous batlike wings, and with faces often described as catlike. For the most part, the matter was treated humorously by the local press, but a visit to the area in March 1976 by those two acute fortean investigators Jerome Clark and Loren Coleman revealed some odd aspects to it. "Big bird" incidents, they found, had been

An impression (above) of the famous cliffs on the Missouri River, south of Alton, Illinois, on which local Indian tribes cut huge representations of the Thunderbird, known locally as the *Piasa*, into the rock and painted them (from H. Lewis, *The Valley of the Mississippi Illustrated*, 1854). The Piasa, known to many different tribes of American Indian, is a monstrous bird, associated with storms. It was said to have a wingspan measuring over fifteen metres and to be able to carry off antelope and humans in its deadly talons. According to an Illini legend, the cliffs are a memorial to a chief and twenty warriors who killed a Storm-bringer (as they called it) after it had developed a taste for human flesh. The Jesuit explorer, Father R.J. Marquette, who travelled down the Mississippi with his companion Louis Joliet in early 1673, noted that whenever natives of any tribe passed this design, they would pull up their canoes on the farther shore and shoot their bows and arrows at the images. Some say the ritual was driven by fear of the spirit (associated at that point with the tumult of the rapids), or to propitiate it; and others that it was a tribute to the heroic chief. As the rifle replaced the bow, so the images deteriorated under the volleys of bullets. In recent years, the town of Alton has had the images restored and one can see (pictured opposite) a composite animal featuring the enormous wings of the fearsome Thunderbird.

occurring locally for at least thirty years, continuing a theme of Amerindian folklore which featured legends of such creatures.

Modern witnesses, however, were often settlers from the north who knew nothing of the old native legends. The two investigators reviewed the evidence of footprints and droppings, allegedly produced by the avian monsters, and concluded from interviews with witnesses that their experiences, however explained, had been genuine and terrifying. Something had been seen which could not be accounted for by pelicans, blue herons or large barn owls, as suggested by the authorities, nor in any other conventional terms. When Clark and Coleman's story of the Rio Grande infestation is compared with the accounts of "bird-men" and latter-day pterodactyls in, for example, John Keel's *Strange Creatures from Time and Space* (1970) and *The Mothman Prophecies* (1975), one can perhaps conclude that some great change is taking place, either in the North American fauna or in the state of mind of the people; or perhaps both.

Returning to the evidence of modern American pterodactyls, the most dramatic report – though it may also be the most worthless – appeared in the *Epitaph* newspaper of Tombstone, Arizona, on 26 April 1890. It stated that two local cowboys, riding through the desert, had come across a sick or wounded creature like a great snake with an alligator's head, huge eyes and teeth, and skeletal, clawed wings, covered with a thick, translucent membrane, which were found to have a span of no less than forty-eight metres. The monster managed a short flight of about half a mile before sinking to the ground, where the cowboys finished it off with their rifles. It was planned, said the newspaper, to skin the creature for a museum, but nothing more was heard.

One wonders if the editor of the *Epitaph* was given to using his imagination to bridge periods of eventfulness in Tombstone life or whether this story was the product of one of those contemporary Liars' Clubs whose tall stories still plague many areas of fortean research. Nevertheless, it served to illustrate the birth of the idea of living pterodactyls in the American landscape, the landscape from which their ancient remains had quite

recently been excavated.

The capacity of the great American wilderness to conceal unknown creatures – pterodactyls even – may have been greatly underestimated, but the most promising area to search for such creatures is the jungle and swamp country of Central Africa. Reports of flying sharp-toothed lizards with membranous bat-like wings come from Tanzania, Namibia, East Africa, Madagascar and other locations. One of the most interesting reports claimed sightings in Northern Rhodesia (now Zambia) and was given in Frank H. Melland's book *In Witchbound Africa* (1923). Melland said that he heard accounts from natives of the Jirundu River swamp region of a huge and fierce bird, more like a bat-winged lizard. Realizing the implications, he showed these natives illustrations of a reconstructed pterodactyl. They confirmed that this, indeed, was the creature they called *kongamoto*, and which they described as red and with a wingspan of over two metres.

From the same region comes the account of Captain C.R.S. Pitman, which we quote from his 1942 book *A Game Warden Takes Stock*: "In Northern Rhodesia, I heard of a mythical beast which intrigued me considerably. It was said to haunt formerly, and perhaps still to haunt, the dense swampy forest region in the neighbourhood of the Angola and Congo borders. To look upon it is death. But the most amazing feature about this mystery beast is its suggested identity with a creature, batlike in form, on a gigantic scale, strangely reminiscent of the prehistoric pterodactyl."

"From where does the primitive African derive such fanciful ideas?" asked Captain Pitman. One might reply that he derives them from personal experience, or recent tribal memory, of pterodactyls which have survived into modern times. In referring to this and other reports in the unabridged edition of *On the Track of Unknown Animals* (1958), the late Dr Bernard Heuvelmans quotes the opinion of a Professor Wiman of Uppsala University, that the story was based on the misconceptions of natives who had helped German palaeontologists uncover pterosaur bones in East Africa. Heuvelmans scorns the notion that a rumour could transplant itself a thousand miles across Africa without affecting people or being recorded in between. Yet, as we have seen, there could be a subtle connection between the excavations of ancient forms and the sightings of those same forms today.

Heuvelmans himself put forward the idea that the *kongamoto* could be an undiscovered species of giant bat. One of the main exhibits of this school is an experience of the ubiquitous collector Ivan T. Sanderson in 1932. During the Percy Sladen expedition to the British Cameroons (as it was then known), Sanderson shot a fruit bat while he was crossing a river in the Assumbo mountains. In his *Animal Treasure* (1937), he recorded what happened next. "Coming straight at me, only a few feet above the water, was a black thing the size of an eagle. I had only a glimpse of its face, yet that was quite sufficient, for its lower jaw hung open and bore a semicircle of pointed white teeth set about their own width apart from each other … And just before it became too dark to see, it came again, hurtling back down the river, its teeth chattering, the air 'shss-shssing' as it was cleft by the great, black dracula-like wings."

When Sanderson's African helpers told local natives what they had seen, the locals immediately ran away in panic, and the next day the village chief and his council urged Sanderson's party to move on. Seemingly, they were in fear of this beast, which they called, according to Sanderson, *olitiau*. When James Powell, Dr Roy Mackal's colleague on their 1980 dinosaur hunt in the Congo (see LIVING DINOSAURS, p.351), visited the region of Sanderson's encounter, he tried to gather more information on the *olitiau*. According to the account in Mackal's *Searching for Hidden Animals* (1980), "…none of the natives recognized the term" – perhaps not surprisingly, given the taboos mentioned earlier. However, when Powell and Mackal showed Africans pictures of a pterodactyl, many of them identified it as an extant giant bat.

We take Sanderson's report seriously because other people, including the naturalist Gerald Russell, also saw the *olitiau*, and years later, in 1970, when Sanderson and Russell met up once more, such details as the creature's coal-black colour and its 3.5m wingspan, were confirmed by comparing their expedition diaries. Sanderson believed he had seen "…the granddaddy of all bats", and Russell agreed with this; but in reviewing the incident for his last book, *Investigating The Unexplained* (1972), Sanderson notes that Frank Lane and others opted for the relic-pterodactyl explanation. One important detail is Sanderson's description of the even spacing of the beast's teeth, which he readily concedes is a reptilian, rather than a mammalian, feature. However, he reaffirms his "giant bat" belief, adding that the creature's muzzle was "…more like that of a monkey than of a dog or of any kind of reptile".

There is no evidence that the *olitiau* is the same creature as the *kongamato*, and although Heuvelmans thinks *both* might be bats of some kind, other cryptozoologists are partial to the pterodactyl solution. Roy Mackal was impressed by the epithet – mentioned by Melland – by which natives referred to the *kongamato* ("overwhelmer of boats") as an indication of some amphibious nature. Melland thought this behaviour was mythical, but Mackal says there is evidence that "…some pterosaurs were able to dive and swim efficiently". In view of this, he suggests we keep an open mind on the question of whether flying reptiles of ancient design might still exist.

Rumours of a prehistoric flying reptile – in this case a huge flying snake – were enough to attract, to a remote corner of Namibia, the respected South African naturalist Dr Marjorie Courtenay-Latimer. Although she found nothing conclusive, she remained convinced of the survival of dinosaur-type creatures in darkest Africa. Her co-discoverer of the coelacanth, Professor J.L.B. Smith, also accepted "…the possibility that some such creature may still exist", and included in his book, *Old Four Legs* (1956), references to sightings of "flying dragons" near Mount Kilimanjaro, in the north of what is now Tanzania.

Finally, we add three recent reports that add substance to the opinions of these experts, that the Thunderbird may not be purely mythological and that giant birds may yet be found alive. The first two are letters from *Fortean Times* correspondents, both describing an "…unknown flapping object". Mrs Phyllis Hall, of Whangarei, New Zealand, wrote: "I was walking along a new motorway, not opened to traffic … Suddenly, out of nowhere, flew a strange creature, like a pterodactyl. It was red all over, except for the underwings, which were a lovely shade of blue … It flew with an undulating motion, and then suddenly disappeared." The red colour reminded us of the description of the African *kongamato*. Then, Mr J. Harrison of Liverpool offered his impressive experience. In about February 1947, he was navigating an estuary of the Amazon river, called Manuos. From the boat's deck he and others observed a flight of five huge birds passing overhead and down the river in a V formation. But they were no ordinary birds. "The wingspan must have been at least twelve feet from tip to tip. They were brown in colour, like brown leather, with no visible signs

In the main text, we referred to the story – recorded in the Tombstone *Epitaph* for 26 April 1890 – that two cowboys had killed a Thunderbird in Arizona's Huachuca Desert. The article describes the dead creature, and that the cowboys left it in the desert, bringing back only part of its wing. The curious thing is, that despite the absence of any mention of a photograph in the original story, hundreds of people, in recent years, believe they have see a photograph of the creature, its monstrous wings held outstretched against a barn door. The story of the Tombstone Thunderbird remains obscure, appearing next in 1930, in a book called *On the Old West Coast* by Horace Bell; followed, in 1963, in a "men's magazine", *Saga*, in an article by a writer named Jack Pearl. Pearl's is the first findable mention of there being a photograph of the giant bird, which he described as "nailed to a wall" with six men posing in front of it. In that same year, a writer for *FATE* magazine, H.M. Cranmer, declared the story must be true because he had seen the photo in several prominent newspapers. Tantalized by the possibility of an incontrovertible piece of evidence of a truly anomalous creature, discussion spread, and many people testified to having seen it; but, in an equally remarkable epidemic of amnesia, none of them could say where. Even the prominent fortean Ivan T. Sanderson stepped up, declaring that he possessed a photocopy of the photo, but had lent it to colleagues who had lost it. The editors of *Fate* (founded in 1948), too, believed they had published the photo in an early edition. A number of fortean researchers – among them Mark Hall, Loren Coleman and the late Mark Chorvinsky – have made diligent searches through the archives of the *Epitaph*, the first decades of *Fate*, and other contemporary sources and have failed to find anything like the much-remembered photo. Writing in *Fortean Times* in 1997, Mark Hall concludes: "The numerous vague recollections of seeing this missing photograph might well be erroneous." This might well be said about recollections of many of the phenomena in this book, and you'd be forgiven for thinking that is that; but then – also, as we have seen before – the phenomenon plays a joker – in this case, at least two versions of the mythical Thunderbird photograph. Probably the most notorious and more widely-circulated of these first appeared in early 2000, on an American website – www.freakylinks.com – set up to promote a short-lived TV series, *FreakyLinks* (2000–01), showing a group of Union soldiers from the Civil War period clustered around the carcass of a massive pterodactyl. The photograph (above) – sepia tinted, scratched, bent, and torn on the edges – appeared to be authentic in every way. Despite the accompanying testimonials, it was all a magnificent hoax; but that has not stopped it circulating on the Internet as a genuine incident from the American Civil War.

of feathers. The head was flat on top, with a long beak and a long neck. The wings were ribbed." Mr Harrison sent us a drawing and said that the creatures "…were just like those large prehistoric birds".

On the 16th of October 2002, the Associated Press reported that the villagers of Manokotak, Togiak and Dillingham, in southwest Alaska, have been observing a very large raptor-like bird for several weeks. It was said to have a whopping wingspan of about four metres, "…much bigger than anything they have seen before". On 10 October, Moses Coupchiak was driving a tractor near Togiak, when he noticed the bird flying toward him from about two miles away. At first, he thought it was an old Otter class plane, until it banked and then disappeared from view behind a hill. "That's when I noticed it wasn't a plane," he said later. "It was huge. Its wing was a little wider than the Otter's, but maybe as long."

John Bouker, a local pilot and owner of the Bristol Bay Air Service, said he was highly sceptical of reports of "this great big eagle", but on the 14th October, while flying into Manokotak, Bouker saw for himself a bird several times larger than a bald eagle. It was about three hundred metres away and "all the people in the plane saw him," Bouker said.

Inevitably, the sightings by local people, experienced in the sights and variety of local wildlife, came into conflict with educated and professional opinion. Biologists, naturalists and other officials were all quoted by reporters as being doubtful that anything with a 4m wingspan had been around for many thousands of years. Instead, they suggested the locals had misidentified a Steller's sea eagle, which can grow to about twice the size of a bald eagle with a wingspan of about two and a half metres. The species, normally native to northeast Asia, has been known to visit the region. However, Bouker and Coupchiak both had the opportunity to compare their giant visitor to the planes with which they were familiar and both concurred that their huge bird must have been twice the size of a Steller's sea eagle.

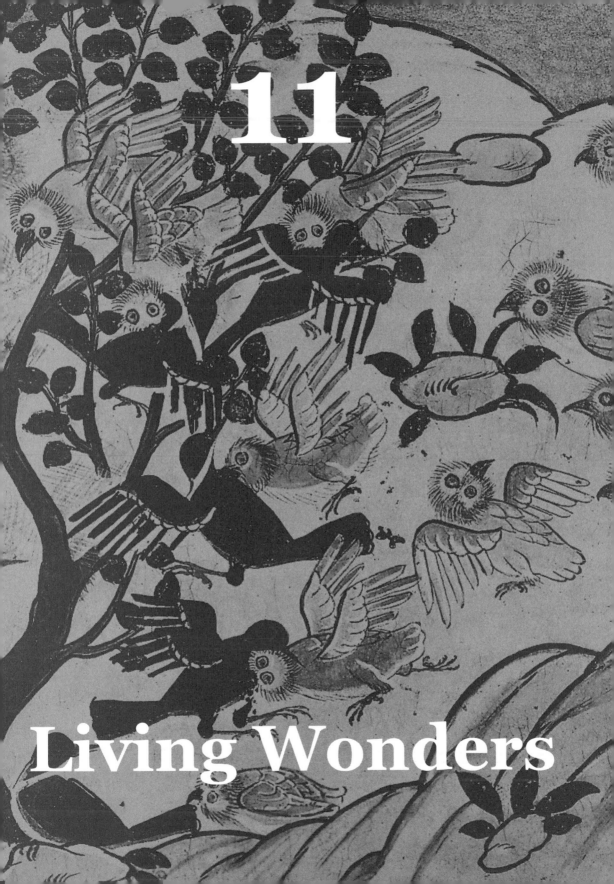

11

Living Wonders

11

Living Wonders

Return of the living dead

In *The Origin of Species* Charles Darwin stated, "When a species has once disappeared from the face of the Earth, we have reason to believe that the same identical form never reappears."

If Darwin had reasons for believing that, he did not give them, and if he were alive today he would hardly be so dogmatic. Since his time there have been many cases of creatures declared extinct which, after a lapse of time varying from millions of years to a few decades, reappear in exactly the same form and sometimes in considerable numbers.

The most dramatic example is the coelacanth, that weird-looking fish whose fossil relics date back to 300 million years ago. Much later, about 70 million years ago, in the age that geologists call the Cretaceous, it disappeared entirely from the fossil record and presumably became extinct. Then, on 22 December 1938, floundering on the deck of a South African trawler, snapping ferociously at anyone within reach, was a large, young coelacanth.

In December 1952 another coelacanth was caught with a rod by someone fishing off the Comoro Islands in the Indian Ocean, and within two years four more specimens had been captured. Then, suddenly, the formerly extinct fish became quite common. Scientists have caught and examined over a hundred specimens, while fishermen have taken many others from seas around the Comoro Islands. Now, we hear, the coelacanth population is dwindling because of pesticides in the ocean and the over-fishing of their natural prey. Yet, remarkably, when threatened in one part of the world, the coelacanth appeared in another. In 1998 the 24 September issue of *Nature* announced the discovery of another coelacanth colony, this time off the coast of Indonesia. The first specimen turned up in a fish market, and more of them were then caught. Far from being an ancient fossil, the coelacanth flourishes today, and the outrageous fact is that it has not changed its form nor has it left evidence of itself for all those millions of years.

The return of the coelacanth threw a large spanner into the works of evolutionary science and dismayed the Darwinians. Their story up to then had been that the coelacanth, equipped with lungs and paired fins that superficially resemble legs, crawled out of the sea about 70 million years ago and gave rise to the subsequent chain of land creatures. Its marine form died out, and that is why it disappeared from the fossil record. It was superfluous and old-fashioned because every forward-looking coelacanth had decided to go ashore and change into something else.

Studies of living coelacanths have discredited the evolutionists' myth still further. It is a deep-sea creature and rarely ventures into shallow water; its fins are not rudimentary legs and it does not use them for walking on the seabed. Evidently it is as well adapted to its present life and environment as it was 300 million years ago, for it has remained exactly the same. Such conservative behaviour on the part of the coelacanth is not what Darwinians had expected. The zoologist writer Richard Carrington scolded the poor fish as "…our unenterprizing relation who was content to drop away from the main stream of progress and stagnate for 300 million years in an evolutionary backwater". Geologists accused it of unfair play. Why, 70 million years ago, had its fossils stopped being deposited – the conventional signal of extinction? So where had it been all that time?

Before going into that question, here are a few more examples of creatures that returned to existence after years of apparent absence from this world.

The creature which probably holds the record for the longest time spent in abeyance – no less than 300 million years by geologists' reckoning – is a South American mollusc, ten living specimens of which were dredged up from 3600 metres below the ocean's surface by an expedition led by Dr Henning Lemche. It was just the same as in its ancient fossil form. Its rediscovery was reported in the *Manchester Guardian*, 10 January 1957, with an interesting detail: "Attached to their undersides were moss-like creatures, the size of the tip of a ball-point pen, the like of which the Doctor had never seen or heard of before."

In another example, the dawn redwood tree (*Metasequoia*), a deciduous pine, flourished in China 100 million years ago, after which time (as established from the record of its numerous fossils) it disappeared from Earth – until 1946. In that year Mr Wong discovered three growing specimens, unchanged in form since the age of the great reptiles, in the Yangtse Valley of

Marjorie Courtney Latimer was the naturalist on duty at the East London Museum in South Africa when Captain Goosen of the trawler *Nerine* reported the odd fish he had caught off the Comoros Islands in the Western Indian Ocean. She was responsible for saving the specimen and having it identified. This photograph of her with the coelacanth was taken, shortly after, in 1939.

Szechuan province. Next year he found twenty-five more, and in 1948 an expedition counted about a thousand dawn redwoods in the same remote area. The local people were cutting them for timber.

Another "tree that came back from the age of dinosaurs" was reported on by the London *Evening Standard*, 10 May 2005, when a specimen of the recently discovered Wollemi pine (*Araucariaceae*, see illustration overleaf) was unveiled at Kew Gardens by Sir David Attenborough. Previously known only from fossils dating back 200 million years, it reappeared in the Blue Mountains of New South Wales, Australia, where a clump of about a hundred trees was found in 1994. The director of Kew arboretum, Tony Kirkham, said he could not believe it at first. "In botanical terms it is like a zoologist going out and finding a live *Tyrannosaurus rex*."

Returning to the animal kingdom, in 1972 the South American peccary *Catagonus wagneri*, a kind of wild boar that had never been seen by Europeans and was supposed to have died out long before the Spanish conquest, turned up in Paraguay. An expedition led by Dr Ralph Wetzel of the University of Connecticut acquired forty skulls of the animal from local hunters and sighted several herds of them.

Similarly, in the records of ornithology are many cases of birds, described by early naturalists,

Ken Hill, senior botanist at the Royal Botanic Gardens, Sydney, Australia, displays a 150,000-year-old fossil slab bearing imprints of the leaves of the supposed-extinct Wollemi pine, comparing it with samples of leaves and cones from one of the living pines discovered in the Wollemi National Park in August 1993.

which disappeared from their native habitats and were declared extinct, but then reappeared, hundreds of years later. The Bermuda petrel is a large sea-bird, a spectacular flier and easily spotted. Its territory, the Bermuda islands in the Atlantic, contains only about twenty square miles of land and is densely populated. Before 1621 everyone there was familiar with the petrel, but after that it was seen no more, and ornithologists included it in their list of extinct species. More than three hundred years later, in 1951, it was seen again and no less than seventeen nests were found on the islands. Now it is said to be flourishing.

The same thing happened with the Madeira petrel, inhabiting another Atlantic island. These birds are strong fliers, so it is possible that they decided to leave home and haunt other coasts for a few centuries. Yet there were no reports from anywhere of incursions by alien petrels.

A period of absence followed by a return in large numbers: that is the story of the Aleutian Canada goose, a large water-bird of the northeast Pacific. In 1967 its numbers had dwindled to less than five hundred. It was declared to be an endangered species and efforts were made to preserve it. However, it quickly died out and for twenty-five years was not to be seen. Suddenly, and quite unexpectedly, it made a dramatic reappearance, and in 2005 about 40,000 of them were counted.

A sensational discovery in the USA was trumpeted in the press, 29 April 2005, following an announcement in *Science* journal. The Ivory-bill, the largest, most spectacular woodpecker in America (third largest in the world), had returned again to its former forest-swamp abode in the Big Woods area of eastern Arkansas. With its 75cm wingspan and flashy black, white and red plumage, it had been a favourite among artists and bird-watchers. Its popular name was the Good Lord bird, because "Good Lord!" was the common exclamation of people seeing it for the first time. From the eighteenth century, as its woodland habitat dwindled across the continent, the Ivory-bill became rare. Collectors and hat-makers grabbed the last survivors and by the 1920s it was considered extinct.

Alleged sightings of the Ivory-bill in 2004 inspired Professor David Lunneau of the University of Arkansas to seek the so-called Holy Grail of ornithology – scientific proof of the bird's present existence. Paddling his canoe through forest swamps, with his camcorder kept running, he was rewarded by four seconds of footage showing a woodpecker perched and then flying. It was good enough for experts to identify the bird as a male Ivory-bill. Despite this and some well-attested sightings by ornithologists, there is still (in 2007) no conclusive proof of the bird's existence, and doubts are growing. But this has not spoiled the celebrations. A senior bird expert compared it to finding a living dodo, and Frank Gill of the Audubon Society said, "It is kind of like finding Elvis".

These "Holy Grail" sensations are not as rare as you might think. Another conspicuous bird, the Peruvian white-winged guan, which sports a long tail and a brilliant orange throat, was declared extinct in 1877. One century later, in 1977, newspapers (eg *Dallas Morning News*, 23 October) announced its return. Ornithologists, backed by the World Wildlife Fund, had found it "in considerable numbers" in the foothills of the Peruvian Andes. In the same year it was reported from Colombo, Sri Lanka, that "the Gloss ibis, a stork-like bird which was believed to have been extinct for the past 60 years, has inexplicably reappeared in open spaces south of here" (*Sunday Express*, 26 June 1977). A previous sensation was in 1948 when G.B. Orbell photographed and later captured specimens of the flightless, goose-sized New Zealand bird, the *Notornis*, which had long been classed with the Giant moa as an extinct species. Flourishing colonies were found by an uncharted lake on the South Island.

The stock explanation for all these reappearances is that the lost species was not really extinct but somehow lay low and avoided attention. That may be plausible in some cases, where the animals are unremarkable and their absence was for only a few generations. But many cases seem to require further explanation, and the "lying-low" theory can hardly apply to creatures that have returned to life after millions of years. One example is the Tuatara, a beakhead lizard peculiar to New Zealand, which is known from the geological record to have died out 135 million tears ago. Yet at some time in the not so distant past it must have renewed its existence, for it is now a living, thriving species in the country whose rock strata clearly record its extinction.

All this is obviously incompatible with modern, evolutionary theories of biology and geology. The appearance is that, contrary to Darwin's assertion, certain species disappear entirely for various lengths of time and then return to existence in the same forms and in the same localities as in previous ages. One way of seeing the phenomenon is through Fort's eyes in con-

The Ivory-billed woodpecker – depicted in this engraving by the American naturalist John James Audubon – was spotted in the Big Woods of Arkansas in February 2005. The last one was seen in 1944. The species was believed to have died out after millions of acres of its forest habitat across North America were cleared in the late 19th century.

nection with teleportation, the unrecognized force in nature that distributes animals around the planet, moving them from place to place and possibly from time to time (see TELEPORTATION, p.1). Also to be considered is our section on MONSTERS (yetis, sea-serpents, lake monsters and the like, p.303) where giant forms that have long disappeared from the Earth are sighted again and again in all parts of the world. In the same category are the elusive panthers and pumas (see THE ANOMALOUS BIG CATS OF BRITAN, p.325), another well-documented phenomenon. These, it seems, are not really flesh-and-blood creatures but intermediary types – phantoms is a word for them – that once inhabited the places where they are now seen, and still continue to haunt them. One day, perhaps, in accordance with the inscrutable law of cyclical returns, they will resume concrete existence, joining the list of long-lost species that came back to life and, like the coelacanth, are now plentiful.

Not every scientist agrees with Darwin's view on the non-repeatability of species. The great authority in Germany during the early twentieth century was Hans Hörbiger. In his major work, *Glacial Cosmogony* (1925), he attributed the dinosaurs and giants of ancient days to the influence of the Moon. He believed that successive moons, captured by the pull of the Earth, finally disintegrate and crash down upon us, causing vast cataclysms and mass extinctions. Previous to that, as the Moon gradually approaches nearer, it weakens the Earth's field of gravity, producing giant forms of animals, birds, reptiles, plants, insects and humans. In the usual way, Hörbiger selected the evidence that favoured his thesis, including reports of ancient human beings up to fifteen feet tall. The present state of gravity does not encourage gigantism, but Hörbiger foresaw that, in ages to come, as our present Moon descends towards us, the process will be repeated and dinosaurs will once again roam the Earth – until the next catastrophe extinguishes them again, for a time.

Another authority who allows for the cyclical view of species is our contemporary, the biologist Dr Rupert Sheldrake. In his first book, *A New Science of Life* (1981), and in others since, including *The Presence of the Past* (1988), he introduced the "hypothesis of formative causation" and the concept of "morphic resonance". The idea behind these terms is that natural forms and the patterns of human and animal behaviour echo throughout all time and influence the shapes and habits of all subsequent creatures. Here is how he describes the phenomenon he is dealing with.

"Time after time when atoms come into existence electrons fill the same orbital around the nuclei; atoms repeatedly combine to give the same molecular forms; again and again molecules crystallize into the same spatial patterns; seeds of a given species give rise year after year to plants of the same appearance; generation after generation spiders spin the same types of web. Forms come into being repeatedly, and each time each form is more or less the same."

As Sheldrake sees it, the recurrence of similar forms in nature is caused by resonance from morphological patterns established in the remote past.

Nature, in other words, is programmed to repeat herself. Thus, "if any changes (in chromosome structure) caused a morphogenetic germ to take up a structure and vibrational pattern similar to that of an ancestral species, it would come under the influence of a morphogenetic field of this species, even though it may have been extinct for millions of years".

We have observed another influence at work in the formation of natural types and patterns, an influence which, with acknowledgements to Sheldrake, we refer to as "geographical resonance". The phenomenon behind it is the tendency of each part of the world to produce people, creatures and even rock formations that in some way look like everything else in their locality. The effect was best described by the Austrian zoologist Paul Kammerer in his 1919 book, *Das Gesetz der Serie* (The Law of Series: a Theory of Repetition in Life and the World at Large):

"In India everything produced by nature and culture looks 'truly Indian', and in Egypt everything looks Egyptian." Obvious examples are the pharaoh's mask in the markings of Egyptian lizards, the Buddha-like expressions of Indian toads and the unmistakable face of a Japanese warrior on the shell of the Samurai crab. Kammerer tells of a woman friend who, on seeing an Egyptian praying mantis, exclaimed in surprise that it had the head of a sphinx. That was before Kammerer had mentioned the insect's country of origin. Also surprised was our friendly expert in London's Natural History Museum, Dr Andrew Currants, while inspecting specimens of dinosaurs recently unearthed in China. They looked, he said, typically Chinese.

We go further into this subtle question in our chapter on SIMULACRA AND OTHER IMAGES (p.270), but we bring it in here because of its bearing on this present subject, the constant reappearances of certain life forms, even after their extinction, in their traditional, native terrains. It is as if these forms naturally belong there as manifestations of the dominant *genius loci* or local spirit of the district. Like the yetis and phantom monsters that still haunt the wild places where once they actually, physically lived, these ancestral forms never permanently die out. We continue this subject in the following section, with accounts of new species, recently discovered, which may also fall into our category of creatures that have returned from extinction.

The new zoology

In *The Origin of Species* **Charles Darwin admitted that the fossil record did not support his theory of the gradual evolution of living types. The evidence it gave was of sudden mass extinctions, shortly followed by the appearance of new species, fully formed and with no apparent evolutionary history. He expected that geologists in the future would discover the missing links. That never happened. The fossil record has expanded enormously since Darwin's time, but the conclusion it points to is the same as ever, that species abruptly vanish, new ones appear and sometimes (as illustrated in the previous section) the same old types turn up again.**

One of the strangest phenomena of modern times is the constant appearance of new animal species. Many of the creatures we know of are dwindling into extinction, while others, previously unknown, are coming to light. It is almost two hundred years since Baron Georges Cuvier, the father of paleontology, stated that the world's fauna was almost completely catalogued and that no significant new discoveries were likely. He was proved wrong in his own century, in which major discoveries included the Indian tapir, the pygmy hippo, the lowlands gorilla, Père David's deer, the giant panda, Przwalski's horse, Grévy's zebra, the monkey-eating eagle and the world's largest carnivore, the Manchurian brown bear. Twentieth-century discoveries began with the Kodiac bear, the mountain gorilla and the Komodo dragon and continued with the okapi, the giant forest hog, the white rhinoceros, the kou-pey or grey ox, the Andean wolf, the giant peccary of South America, the giant muntjac of Vietnam and many remarkable birds and sea creatures.

Now, in the twenty-first century, more new animals are being observed than ever before. An interesting feature in some cases is where the newly recognized creature appears in a region that is well populated by local hunters and country people, yet it is completely unfamiliar to them. In December 2005 officials of the World Wide Fund for Nature announced that they had photographed a mysterious carnivore in Borneo. It was something like a cat, dog or fox, russet-coloured and with a long tail. The local tribespeople were shown the pictures but said they had never seen or heard of such a creature. The same thing happened a year earlier in the northeastern Indian state, Arunachal Pradesh, where scientists were surprised to discover a large, new monkey, the Arunachal macaque, in a densely inhabited area where no one seemed to have noticed it before.

Another large monkey, the highland mangabey, of striking appearance and behaviour, was first discovered in Tanzania in 2005. It was found almost simultaneously by two groups of biologists working independently in different parts of the country 230 miles apart. Before either had published their discovery, the two teams met at a bar in Dar es Salaam, where they both hinted at sensational news, and then realized that they had both identified the same new species. Behind this coincidence is the real mystery: why did no researcher, African or European, identify it earlier? The highland mangabey, it seems, is fairly widespread, noticeable and noisy. Tim Davenport, one of its original discoverers, described it to the *Daily Telegraph*, 30 May 2005:

"With its shaggy coat, pointed crest and long cheek whiskers, the monkey seems to have a tri-

Africa's first new species of monkey to be found in two decades – the secretive highland mangabey (*Lophocebus kipunji*) – was spotted by two teams in Tanzania, working 230 miles apart, within a couple of months.

angular head. It's an almost alien countenance and very disconcerting. If it sees you, it dips its head, sticks its backside in the air and then shakes its head violently. I call its unique call a 'honk-bark' because, echoing through the rain forest, it really does sound like a goose and a dog having an argument. When more than one mangabey calls at once, the whole of Mount Rungwe seems to shake."

How could such an obvious creature have escaped attention throughout the entire modern age up to the present? These sudden appearances of unknown species remind us of the coelacanth and others in our previous section, that seemed to have returned from long periods of extinction and are now openly flourishing. Even Bernard Heuvelmans, the founder of cryptozoology, never predicted the discovery of an entirely new animal, unfamiliar to locals. In his first book, *On the Trail of Unknown Animals,* he emphasized that the hidden species, still unknown to science, are invariably recognized by the natives of their districts. Yet, contrary to his expectations, very few of the animals referred to in local legends have actually turned up, while several new species have been found that no one had previously heard of.

The hidden creatures that Heuvelmans thought capable of being discovered included dinosaurs in the swamps of central Africa, pterodactyls in America, the Nandi bear of East Africa, the giant sloth of South America, various Australian species including the marsupial wolf, and giant reptiles in lakes and oceans. His strongest belief was in the existence of wild human or ancestral tribes in remote areas of Asia, Africa and Australasia. In southeast Asia, for example, he was impressed by the tradition of a wild race of little people, known in Sri Lanka as the Nittaewos. They were primitive and mischievous and in some countries it is recorded that the large folk decided to get rid of them. Sites of their final massacre are still known in various districts. Yet in other places Heuvelmans heard of them as still living or only quite recently extinct.

Heuvelmans died in 2001, and three years later a discovery was made which seemed to vindicate his brand of cryptozoology. Newspapers in the first week of November 2004 had front-page headlines announcing the discovery of a new kind of humanoid. Scientists on the island of Flores, Indonesia, had excavated parts of a skeleton of

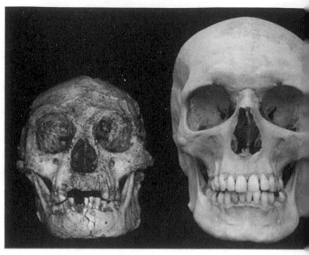

The skull of a Flores "Hobbit" hominid compared to a modern human skull.

a one-metre-tall female, more human than ape-like. Evolutionists claimed her as our cousin, a descendant of the same hypothetical ape-creature as ourselves. The press identified her as a Hobbit. Sceptics had their say, suggesting that she was merely a diseased dwarf, but they lost out when, a few months later, nine other skeletons of the same miniature type were discovered at the same site. The sensational angle was that the bones were only a few thousand years old, allowing the tantalizing possibility that the hobbit-woman and her kind had survived up to quite recently, into living memory perhaps, or even into the present day.

Richard Shears, a reporter for the *Daily Mail,* was dispatched to Flores to find out more about the possibility of living hobbits. He soon made friends among the natives and, according to his account, was invited to stay in their huts in jungle villages. There he heard some amazing, first-hand stories of encounters with tiny beings, living like animals but with human characteristics and a twittering sort of language. He met a man who, some years earlier, had found the recently buried body of a hobbit-woman and kept it in his hut. When Shears asked to see it, he said he had lent it to a neighbour, and when they visited this other person, he was sorry to say that the little corpse had just been stolen from him. If only they had come a few days earlier, etc, etc. That kind of story is familiar to all experienced researchers into the world of mysteries.

Richard Shears was disappointed, but at least he confirmed what Heuvelmans had said, that stories and sightings of little people are common in the present generation. One can hardly avoid linking these stories with the bones of the little people of Flores, who died so comparatively recently. But this one discovery can hardly explain the widespread occurrence of "little wild men" legends throughout Indonesia and all neighbouring countries. Maybe they are memories or actual sightings of wild, pygmy aborigines who have somehow survived in the depths of jungles. Or perhaps they are like the trolls, elves and goblins of other lands – aspects of the native spirit.

Our own general view of natural history, the origin and distribution of life and so on, is that they are not entirely chained to the laws of science. If nature is a living creature, as tradition says, she (or it) must have moods and irrationalities. There are plenty of irrationalities in the distribution of animal species, their appearances, disappearances, extinctions and reappearances in different places and ages. Then again there is the problem of how actual, physical species relate to the host of phantom forms – yetis, lake monsters, mystery big cats and the like – that seem to echo ancient animal types or, possibly, foreshadow creatures not yet manifest. We do not pretend to make sense of it all. Perhaps Plato was right and there is divine order behind everything. But if it is so perfect, why is nature often so inefficient and arbitrary? Fort's answer was that perhaps the "world-creature", that once worked fairly well, is now senile and no longer in full charge of its functions. In its distribution of animals, for example, there are aberrations: consignments of fish, aimed at lakes, fall short and puzzle people as they tumble from the sky, while on the larger scale of things, animals appear haphazardly in times and places where, in a better managed universe; they would have no right to be.

Faithful dogs

Many are the stories of animals, usually dogs, so faithful to human companions that they will not be separated from them, even after death. Tribute was paid to this devotion by American lawyer George Graham Vest in a speech to a jury in 1855, which coined the phrase "man's best friend". Vest, who went on to serve as a senator for Missouri, said: "If fortune drives the master forth, an outcast in the world, friendless and homeless, the faithful dog asks no higher privilege than that of accompanying him, to guard him against danger, to fight against his enemies. And when the last scene of all comes, and death takes his master in its embrace and his body is laid away in the cold ground ... there by the graveside will the noble dog be found, his head between his paws, his eyes sad ... faithful and true even in death."

The sheepdog Tip, whose devotion in staying by his master's body on the Derbyshire moors for fifteen weeks in the winter of 1953–54 is commemorated by an inscribed stone at the scene of the incident.

Loyal animals often gain reputations for saintliness and monuments are erected to them. One example is the granite slab beside the lonely waters of the Derwent Dam in Derbyshire, bearing this inscription:

"In Commemoration Of The Devotion of Tip The Sheepdog Which Stayed By The Body

The statue of the celebrated Greyfriars Bobby in Candlemakers' Row, Edinburgh. On the right are pictured the family of John Traill, with his wife holding Bobby. They kept an eating house near the scene of Bobby's vigil and provided him with regular dinners.

Of Her Dead Master, Mr Joseph Tagg, On The Howden Moors For Fifteen Weeks From 12th December 1953 to 27th March 1954".

It was erected by public subscription, a year after the event commemorated, on the death of the dog, Tip, who had become during the interval a popular national heroine. Tip's master, a retired gamekeeper aged eighty-one, was found dead on the high Derbyshire moors fifteen weeks after they had both set off from their home at Bamford on one of their customary rambles over the Derwent Hills, where they had once lived and worked. Search parties had failed to discover them; frost and snow had covered the hills, and man and dog had long been presumed dead, when a couple of men rounding up sheep came across the body of Tip's master, with Tip, in piteous condition but still alive, beside it. Somehow, alone on the bleak

winter moors, she had survived for three and a half months.

Tip's remaining year was spent in luxury and fame at the house of her old master's niece, who with difficulty protected her retirement from hosts of admiring visitors. In that time she was awarded the highest order of canine chivalry, and when she died a vast crowd attended the unveiling of her memorial. Thousands of pilgrims have since tramped along the banks of Derwent Dam to visit the shrine of the saintly pet.

There are a number of similar monuments about the world. At the English burial ground in Cephalonia, an island off the west coast of Greece, is the tomb of Captain Parker, who was shot and killed in 1848 by campaigners against British rule there. The Captain's little dog refused to move from beside its master's body, and thus became a local legend. On the tomb the dog is represented, still faithfully on guard.

In April 1805, a young man called Charles Gough took his dog on a tour of the Lake District. High up on Helvellyn he slipped on ice and fell, or collapsed from cold or even, some say, died a martyr to art while trying to paint a landscape. Frank Haley in the *North West Monthly* (January 1950), summarized inconclusively the various versions of the legend. Three months later Gough's skeletal remains were found by a shepherd, attracted to the spot by an emaciated dog, generally thought to have been a terrier, which was hovering round it. No one, apart from his own people, seemed to care much about the fate of poor Gough, but his dog created a sensation. "A lasting monument in words this wonder merits well", wrote Wordsworth; and he provided that monument with his poem about Gough's dog, entitled "Fidelity". Sir Walter Scott added another poetic monument to the dog's loyalty, and Sir Edwin Landseer immortalized the creature in a painting. Finally, in 1890, a solid monument in the form of an inscribed plaque was affixed to the rock where Gough died. It is called the Gough Memorial, but the hero commemorated on it is, of course, Gough's faithful little dog.

With his sharp eye for curious items of natural history in newspapers and popular literature, Maurice Burton collected numerous anecdotes of dogs which have been faithful after death and printed a selection in his book *Just Like an Animal* (1978). They include, from *Komsomolskaya Pravda* (January 1977), the story of an Alsatian bitch which had haunted Moscow's Vnukovo airport for two years, waiting for the return of her master who was absent in Siberia. The animal would run up to aircraft as they landed, and no one could handle it. The newspaper finally traced the owner, who had simply abandoned the Alsatian at the airport because he had no veterinary certificate for it. The story in the press brought in several thousand letters from Russian dog-lovers offering to adopt it. A similar story involves a dog who died "of a broken heart" after spending five years on the quayside at Quebec from where its owner had sailed away.

The most complete, archetypal form of this legend is presented in the case of "Greyfriars Bobby". This rough-looking canine saint was the companion of John Gray, or Auld Jock, a poor shepherd who died obscurely in Edinburgh in 1858. His identity was known only because his name was written on the flyleaf of his Bible, and the man who identified him together with the gravedigger were the only people to attend his funeral in Edinburgh's Greyfriars Churchyard. Bobby was there too and, despite the efforts of the gravedigger to drive him away and the "No Dogs" notice on the churchyard gate, he continued after

Greyfriars Bobby had his counterparts in other societies. This illustration (by an unknown artist) - from *Le Petit Journal* on 28 February 1909 – records a French version concerning a poodle called Tom, who refused to leave its master's grave in a Paris suburb and was fed daily by the well-wishers who came to see the demonstration of canine fidelity.

Winston the labrador stands contentedly in front of his thatched kennel at Bradford-on-Avon. Winston was thought to be keeping watch at the crossroads where his owners were killed but he turned out to be a fraud.

the funeral and for fourteen years until his own death to haunt Auld Jock's grave, sheltering in a nearby tombstone. Every day at one o'clock, Bobby went to the Greyfriars Dining Room, a favourite haunt of Auld Jock, whose proprietor, John Traill, knew Bobby and always had a good bowl of broth ready for him.

A crisis arose during the ninth year of Bobby's vigil, when he was arrested by the police as an unlicensed vagrant, a crime for which dogs could be sentenced to death. John Traill was also threatened by the law for having "harboured" him. The situation was saved by the intervention of Sir William Chambers, Lord Provost of Edinburgh, who paid for Bobby's licence and presented him with a collar with the inscription: "Greyfriars Bobby, from the Lord Provost. 1867. Licensed."

When Bobby died, the one and only canine Freeman of the City of Edinburgh, *The Scotsman* (17 January 1872) printed a respectful obituary. John Traill buried him in a flowerpot near his master at Greyfriars and, from then on, his cult flourished. A memorial in the shape of a red-granite drinking fountain, topped with Bobby's effigy in bronze, was erected by Baroness Burdett Coutts in Candlemakers' Row, near his graveyard. In 1924, a group, the "American Lovers of Bobby" erected a stone over his grave.

A similar story, from France, is no less touching. It is quoted by Henri Coupin, among a collection of other such anecdotes, in *Les Animaux Excentriques* (1913). "All Paris … has been to see a dog, which has stayed for several years on its master's grave in the cemetery of Les Innocents, resisting all attempts to remove it. Several times people have tried dragging it off and shutting it up at the other end of the town; but as soon as it could get away, it always returned to the post to which its lasting affection had assigned it, and there it remained even through the rigours of winter. The people of the neighbourhood, touched by its perseverance, would bring it food, but the poor animal seemed to eat only to prolong its grief and to show an example of heroic faithfulness."

We would not lightly give offence to devotees of the harmless, endearing cults of Tip, Greyfriars Bobby and other loyal pets, but occasionally we have twinges of doubt. There are some clever dogs around. Recently an Edinburgh historian, Jim Gilhooley, claimed, in the Scottish *Daily Record* (24 May 1999), that two John Grays had died that week in 1858, and that Bobby's owner was the one buried in a pauper's grave at Newington, three miles from Greyfriars Churchyard. If Gilhooley is correct, Bobby spent fourteen years at the wrong grave, but this is unlikely to deter the many who continue to visit the famous scene of his vigil.

A story from Wiltshire prompts the heretical thought that perhaps some of these canine mourners were not so much saints as scroungers, having learnt the trick of gaining patronage and daily dinners. In 1971 Winston, a golden labrador and successful con-artist, turned up at Bradford-on-Avon, a small town near Bath. He stationed himself at a busy crossroads opposite the district hospital on the outskirts of the town, where he soon began to attract local attention. He would allow no one to touch him, nor would he leave the grass verge at the crossroads. By staring wistfully at passing cars, he managed to create the legend that he was a poor orphan whose owners had been killed in a car accident at that spot.

Winston's shameless exploitation of the Grey-friars Bobby image worked so well that for the next seven years he enjoyed a life of complete comfort and independence. Every day he strolled over to the hospital where the staff provided dinner. He was provided with a snugly thatched kennel in the hospital grounds, and another one, donated by anonymous admirers, situated in the hedge by the crossroads. There at Christmas time he would receive a flood of greetings cards and presents of food and other comforts. Throughout the year offerings of bones and such were brought him by local children and by increasing numbers of well-wishers from all over the world. As the leading local celebrity he enjoyed police protection, and his portly, dignified figure became familiar to television viewers.

Winston died at his home of old age on 17 October 1978 and, the following day, the *Bath Evening Chronicle* exposed his imposture. The story of his owners' death at the crossroads in a car crash was quite untrue. The facts were that the rascally dog had been sacked from his former post at a hunting establishment in Devon and had come to Bradford with a local inventor, Alex Moulton. From there he had moved to the home of a farmer, Mike Singer, before setting up as independent operator at his crossroads. Despite his exposure as a fraud, Winston's funeral at Claverton Dogs' Cemetery was a grand affair, with coffin, flowers, pallbearers, reporters, TV cameramen and a crowd of mourners. The cross over his grave was fashioned by a local blind carpenter. Donations from far and wide swelled his memorial fund which, reported the *Bath Chronicle* (23 October 1978), soon approached its £1000 target. Its object was to provide a blind person with a guide dog, Winston II.

As a postscript, here is a rare tale of a grave-haunting cat. According to reporter Barbara

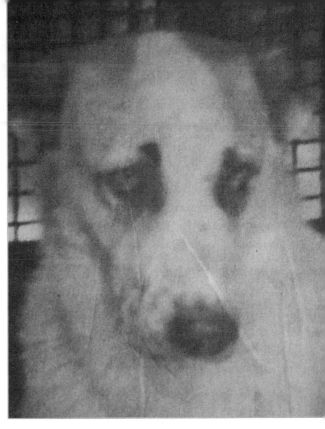

A curious twist on the "faithful dog" story came from Mashad, near Iran's border with Afghanistan, in mid-November 2005, where a dog of the type used in the region for herding sheep had taken to staying by the tomb of the eighth imam Reza, revered as a saint by Shia Muslims. Dogs are normally considered "unholy", but this one won the hearts of the nation after its story was broadcast. It is now attracting its own sightseers and generating its own folklore; for example, it is said to be courteous and not to tread on any carpets and, some say has even shed tears. Somehow, the dog evaded the security of the tomb complex, made its way through the women's section and crowds of pilgrims who usually wail and beat their chests as they visit the shrine. According to reports, it was only noticed when it settled down near the tomb and began to howl mournfully. At other times it simply sat for hours, just looking at the tomb. When it was eventually removed (gently) from the tomb chamber itself, a guard told Lillian Swift of the *Daily Telegraph*, it would be treated kindly because "...like many of the pilgrims, it had been called by Imam Reza and is seeking refuge".

Jeffery, in an article in the *Sunday People* (20 October 1974), Mrs Bridget Wastie of Charlbury, Oxfordshire, was looking after a cat, Moggie, while its old mistress was in hospital. The old lady died, and the following night Moggie was missing. Two days later Mrs Wastie and her mother took the bus to attend the funeral at a village fifteen miles distant. This, in her own words, is what happened there. "Just as the coffin was being lowered into the grave I caught my mother's arm in amazement. For there was Moggie sitting on a gravestone, watching. Somehow she had come fifteen miles to a village she had never visited before to say goodbye to her old mistress."

Homing animals and owner-seeking pets

The 1963 Disney film, *The Incredible Journey*, in which two dogs and a cat travel for many miles and through many adventures in search of their owners, is constantly repeated in actual fact. Every year a fresh crop of incidents bears further witness to the ability of certain animals to make long, solitary journeys across unknown territory towards home. Some of the stories we have collected are so nearly incredible that we are inclined to agree with Charles Fort who pointed to it as an example of the magic that surrounds everyday life.

A case, described in the *Sunday Express* (22 July 1979) tells of Nick, the Alsatian bitch belonging to Doug Simpson of Selah, Washington. Nick had got lost while on a camping trip with Mr Simpson in the southern Arizona desert. For two weeks his master searched frantically for her before starting on the two-thousand-mile journey home. Four months later Nick turned up, bloody, battered and emaciated, at the family house in Selah. Somehow she had travelled alone through country described as "some of the roughest on Earth", hundreds of miles across the scorching, waterless desert, across the Grand Canyon and through blizzards, icy rivers and snow-covered, 12,000-feet mountain ranges in Nevada and Oregon. Doug Simpson was away from home at the time, but his parents recognized his dog and telephoned him at his work place in Pennsylvania. He flew home immediately. When he walked into the house, Nick looked at him for a few moments, as if in reproach for leaving her behind, and then rose to give him a warm greeting. "I've been making a fuss of her ever since," said Doug.

There are several published collections of homing pet anecdotes. Dr Rupert Sheldrake deals with this among other animal abilities in *Dogs That Know When Their Owners Are Coming Home* (1999) and there are summaries of homing cats and homing dogs by Paul Sieveking in *Fortean Times* 61 (1992) and 70 (1993). One of our favourite cases is that of Micky the terrier, reported in the *Sunday People* (29 April 1979). His journey back to his old home was only five miles, but Micky was

In 1600 Henry Wriothesley, Earl of Southampton, was imprisoned in the Tower of London for involvement in the Essex conspiracy. His cat sought him out and climbed down the chimney.

fifteen years old, blind and almost stone deaf. For three years since the death of his former master in King's Langley, Hertfordshire, he had lived at Hemel Hempstead with new owners, Mr and Mrs Philips. Over Easter Micky disappeared. The police were told, and they discovered him outside his old home which was now derelict. He was treated by a vet for a crushed paw, having apparently been run over during his trek, which took him across several main roads and through busy traffic.

Some odd cases of dogs finding their way home by means of transport are detailed in Edwin Arnold's book, *The Soul of The Beast* (1960). The most wonderful, or incredible, of such cases is that of a "well-bred collie" which was sent off by its owner, living near the small port of Inverkeithing in Scotland, to a friend in Calcutta. Some time after its arrival in India the dog disappeared, and a few months later it bounded into the house of its old master at Inverkeithing, showing great delight at being home again. Evidently it had stowed away at Calcutta on a ship bound for Dundee. There it had disembarked and proceeded on by a coastal vessel to Inverkeithing. It was suggested at the time that the collie had been attracted to the right vessel at Calcutta by the Scottish accents of the sailors!

Apart from dogs of all sorts, we have records of homing cats and pigeons, a frog, a duck, a hedgehog and a rabbit. Cats, despite the apparent indifference they often show their owners, turn out to be loyal and persistent creatures. They have been credited with solo treks of literally thousands of miles in search of old homes or human associates. In the autumn of 1977 fourteen-year-old Kirsten Hicks of Adelaide, Australia, left her pretty white Persian cat, Puss, with her grandparents, who lived over a thousand miles away on Queensland's Gold Coast, while she went abroad for a holiday. She returned to the sad news that Puss had gone missing. But the following autumn Puss arrived home, "footsore and with matted fur". The Sydney *Daily Mirror* (11 October 1978) reported that "He crossed rivers, sidestepped semitrailers and stalked the bush in an amazing 12-month trek."

We could go on for pages with similar accounts, variously authenticated. A cause for scepticism about some cases, is that people may be too impetuous in claiming to recognize a long-lost

In the winter of early 1967 Minette followed her owner, Jean Pradel, home to La Ribière from Clermont-Ferrand, a journey of sixty-five miles. When she arrived, her claws were almost completely worn away.

pet. Yet there are many cases which are as genuine as they are mysterious. One of the best authenticated, recounted by Dr Michael W. Fox in *Understanding Your Cat* (1974), is of a New York vet who left his cat in his home state while he went to take up a post in California 2500 miles away. Months later, an identical cat walked into his new house. Incredulously he examined the animal, and on the fourth vertebra of its tail he found the deformed bone growth which had marked his own cat as the result of a bite.

This brings us to the most mysterious part of the whole business. We know that many creatures have highly developed homing instincts, pigeons for example. But the cases which fascinate us above all others are those of animals making journeys to places where they have never been before, seeking not their homes but their owners. One epic feat, recounted in Joseph Wylder's book, *Psychic Pets* (1978) was performed by an American cat called Sugar, who walked from Gage, Oklahoma, where he had been left with some neighbours, to rejoin the Woods family who had moved to Anderson, California. The journey of no less than 1500 miles had taken him fourteen months, and he had never before been anywhere near his owners' new house. They recognized their cat by a slight deformity of his left hip joint. This is a particularly interesting case because it was personally investigated by the great ESP researcher Dr J.B. Rhine, who went out to Oklahoma to observe Sugar and interview witnesses.

A case which became famous in the winter of 1914 was that of Prince, an Irish terrier, who managed to cross the English Channel in the early days of World War I to join his master in the trenches. In August 1914 Private Brown of the 1st North Staffordshire Regiment was sent over to France. On 27 September, his wife wrote with the news that their dog was missing. Private Brown wrote back: "I am sorry you have not found Prince and you are not likely to while he is over here with me. It is a very strange thing that I should have got him. A man brought him to me from the front trenches. I could not believe my eyes till I got off my horse and he made a great fuss of me. I believe he came over with some other troops." This case was investigated by the RSPCA and declared to be authentic.

Nor is it only dogs and cats that seem capable of these feats of miraculous loyalty. The case of an owner-seeking pigeon was investigated by Dr Rhine with S.R. Feather. The pigeon belonged to a young West Virginia boy named Hugh Perkins. When Hugh fell ill and was rushed by his parents to a hospital 105 miles away, the pigeon somehow traced him. "One dark, snowy night about a week later, the boy heard a fluttering at the window of his hospital room. Calling the nurse, he asked her to raise the window because there was a pigeon outside, and just to humour the lad, she did so. The pigeon came in. The boy recognized his pet bird and asked her to look for the number 167 on its leg, and when she did so she found the number as stated."

There have been many studies on the homing instinct of animals, especially pigeons. Do they navigate by landmarks, by the Sun or stars, by terrestrial magnetic currents or by some other,

more mysterious means? No single answer has been found to satisfy all the data, and in the cases of pets finding owners who have moved away there is no scientific theory at all. We suspect that the teleportation effect, triggered by intense longing by people for their pets or by animals for their owners, may be behind some of them. Most experiments have been confined to investigating the homing instinct pure and simple. For instance, Dr Presch and Dr Lindenbaum in Germany took a number of cats varying distances from their homes and put each one in the centre of a maze with twenty-four exits. In each case the cat left the maze in the direction of its home. A similar experiment with dogs is described by Dr Bastian Schmid in his book, *Interviewing Animals* (1936). Dr Schmid arranged for a number of dogs to be taken from their homes in the back of a closed van and driven by a circuitous route to a spot miles away from their familiar territory. Every time this was done, the dog, on release, seemed temporarily confused, before resolutely trotting off in the direction of home. The same results have been obtained with homing pigeons. Dr Rupert Sheldrake in *Seven Experiments that Could Change the World* (1995) tells of pigeons, disorientated by rotating chambers and other means, that are able to fly back to their lofts. Even when the lofts were moved several miles away, they were still able to locate them. Sheldrake compares this to the ability of some animals to locate the new, unfamiliar homes of their owners.

We referred above to reports of a homing frog, a duck and a hedgehog. Details of the first two can be found in the "Homesick Pets" chapter of Frank Edwards' *Strange World* (1964). The case of the homing hedgehog was described in the *Sunday Express* (12 August 1979) based on an item in a Russian newspaper. The hedgehog was first found on a country road by a doctor at the Donetsk hospital. It had a broken paw, and the doctor, Nadezhda Ushakova, nursed it until it was fit. Then she gave it to her granddaughter who lived forty-eight miles away. At its new home it languished and would not eat, so the granddaughter wrote to say that she had set it free in the forest. Two months later, Dr Ushakova returned from work and found the same hedgehog sitting on her doorstep. Now, says the report, Soviet veterinary experts are investigating the homing instincts of hedgehogs.

We have just one story of a homing rabbit.

White with red eyes, Robert was bought in 1978 for six-year-old Maud Cecil of Cambridge. He was a much-loved household pet until he grew too large and unruly, and Maud's mother decided to rehouse him in the walled garden. No sooner had she turned her back, than Robert disappeared. He was replaced with a lookalike rabbit but, later that year, there was a scratching at the gate, and Robert was back. Soon, however, his behaviour became worse and worse: he gnawed books, bounced heavily on beds at night and woke one overnight guest by trying to eat his moustache. Banished to the Suffolk house of Maud's grandmother, Mrs Margaret Hodson, he did not last long with her before she set him free in the wild half a mile away. Three days later she had Robert on her hands again. Robert was then taken back to Maud's house and put to live in the chicken-run. There before long he was discovered trying to rape the hens and, as a result of this misdemeanour, was taken to the Gogmagog Hills, about three miles out of Cambridge, and sent packing once more. This time two years passed before Maud and her mother heard a familiar scratching at the gate. Robert's final years were spent in a reinforced cage at Maud's grandmother's house, where he died in 1982 after losing a fight with a marauding rat.

Talking cats and dogs

An interview with a talking dog appeared in *FATE* magazine in July 1966. Clare Lambert went to interview Pepe, a tiny chihuahua, and his companion Mrs Genova. She had learnt about the talking dog from an article in a local trade newspaper, *Gas News*, the previous spring. Its front page had a photograph of Pepe talking to a gas fitter who had called to fix the boiler at the Genova family home in Torrence, California. He had been working in the basement boiler room, watched by Pepe, when the little dog suddenly said "I love you!" Unable to believe his ears, the fitter picked up the dog and watched his mouth open as he repeated "I love you" in a high-pitched, sing-song voice. The man was so delighted that he invited Pepe to visit the gas depot where his conversation made him a popular favourite.

Pepe was at home to receive Clare Lambert when she called, and he entertained her with other phrases from his vocabulary, including "I want you", "How are you?", "Not now", "Hello there" and "Ed Sullivan". Mrs Genova then told his story. The dog had been bought from local kennels, was less than two years old and was sensitive and fussy about his food. The first time she had heard him talking was in the back garden. "He was talking through the wire fence to his girlfriend, Ranic. I distinctly heard the words, 'I love you-oo, I love you-oo, I need you-oo,' in a high singing voice and repeated over and over." These and his other phrases he had learnt from imitating Mrs Genova.

Clare Lambert described what happened when Mrs Genova picked him up for a chat. "A little singing sound starts in Pepe's throat as his muscles begin to move. In about six seconds he lifts his head high, opens his mouth wide and sings the words after her, repeating each phrase a couple of times. Pepe has a loud voice for

In 1951 Mrs Field of West Croydon, Surrey, was surprised when her 11-month-old puppy, Peter, said "Mum" as he presented his bandaged paw for her attention. Later, when she offered him a dog biscuit, he said "Please." "Please what?" she asked. "Mum," he added.

so small an animal." Clare observed Pepe carefully: "I bent close to watch his throat muscles move and I saw his tongue turn towards the roof of his mouth as he made a conscious effort to form syllables. This tongue movement is most unusual. Dogs keep their tongue down on their lower jaw when emitting sounds." Pepe's "speech" was more like a combination of singing and talking: "With each phrase he goes up and down the scale rising three or more tones. It is difficult to describe. You have to hear it. Pepe is not a show-off. Indeed, he is a modest little animal and seldom speaks unless he is spoken to."

In Dallas, Texas, another talking dog, a Dobermann Pincher named Lancer, was interviewed for the *National Enquirer* (12 July 1977). Lancer was two years old with a large vocabulary, including the phrase naturally expected of pets, "I love you". According to his master, Mr Gerald Wright, "he can learn almost anything in a matter of minutes", and he is therefore useful to Mr Wright, who is president of a cosmetics company in Dallas, because he can charm the ladies at work by learning and speaking their names. There is no doubt that Lancer talks in a human manner, wrote Bud Gordon of the *Enquirer,* but "his voice sounds muddy, as though his mouth were stuffed with cotton".

A smooth-haired fox-terrier called Ben, belonging to Mr and Mrs Brissenden of Royston, Hertfordshire, was the subject of two articles in the *Daily Mirror* in August 1946. A *Mirror* reporter had visited Ben the previous day, and several times he had heard the little terrier say, clearly and distinctly, "I want one", evidently expressing desire for a cup of tea, a biscuit and other doggy treats. His voice was described as "dark brown" and "a rich baritone", low-pitched and authoritative. The reporter found it quite uncanny the way Ben used different tones of voice in making his requests, "from the wheedling note to the gruff, demanding one".

Contacted by the *Mirror,* two eminent veterinary surgeons, Professor W.C. Miller and Dr W. Wooldridge, went to Royston to examine the talking dog. To them he duly made his usual remark, "I want one ... oh-h-h ... I want one". Professor Miller observed: "In all my experience I have never heard a dog so nearly simulate the human voice." Dr Wooldridge added: "The most amazing thing

is that Ben does actually use his mouth and, to some extent, his tongue, to formulate and control the words. He cuts his words clearly, and appears to use his tongue to change from one word to another." While the experts discussed his case in Mrs Brissenden's front room, Ben romped around them with a ball.

Some years ago a dog who could say "Beer please!" and other appropriate phrases helped retired actor Ronald Shiner keep the Porter Inn at Templecombe, Somerset. While in Australia there lived a truly remarkable dog whose spoken phrases included "Hello Mum" and "Here I am Mum" – and also, as the reporter primly put it, "a word often heard in masculine company and not in the ladies' presence". Its speech, according to the London *Evening Standard* (17 January 1953), was "clear as a bell, and in an accent much nearer English than Australian".

A peculiar feature of this talking Australian fox-terrier was its background, which was ecclesiastical. Its owner was the Diocesan Registrar of Newcastle, New South Wales. There was cause for laughter, therefore, when Australian scientists advanced the conventional explanation for

Murri, the German-speaking tom cat, whose vocabulary consisted of the words "ja", "nein" and "Anna", which he pronounced distinctly. He would also sing along with nursery rhymes played on the piano. He made broadcasts and was exhibited at an international cat show in Vienna.

the animal's power of speech, that it was a "conditioned reflex", meaning that the dog had picked up its vulgar vocabulary from its environment. The London *Evening Standard* made a perceptive comment on this diagnosis: "This shows how stupid scientists can be. It is just conceivable that a Diocesan Registrar, on occasions of rare stress, might utter a word unfit for ladies to hear. But that he should be given, with such frequency as to condition a dog, to saying: 'Here I am Mum', surpasses belief. No man who called his mother 'Mum' could rise to even moderate eminence in the Anglican Church."

Of the various tales we have heard about talking cats the following is the most remarkable. In 1963 Mr and Mrs Deem of Hillside Acres, Florida, found an abandoned, starving male kitten near their home. They took it in, fed it and adopted it, calling it Whitey because of its colour. They had another tom cat, Blackie, with which Whitey was not always on good terms. A few months later, when Whitey was about six months old, he jumped onto the family bed and said, "Mama, I'm hungry." "What did you say?" asked Ruth Deem, and Whitey repeated, "I'm hungry". Mrs Deem said nothing to her husband but got up and fed the cat.

A few days later James Deem was stroking Whitey and telling him affectionately that he was a bad cat. "I am *not* a bad cat," said Whitey. "I want to go out." After that the cat spoke to the Deems quite frequently, at least once a day, often in a whining, self-pitying manner as though still aggrieved by its wretched infancy. Among its phrases were, "Why no one love me?", "I want to go home", "I want out", "I love Mama" and "He's bad", a reference to Blackie.

In January 1965 Whitey was interviewed at his new home, near Lake Hamilton, Florida, by Suzy Smith whose article, "In Search of the Talking Cat" appeared in the November issue of *FATE* magazine. Unfortunately, Whitey had been ill and had not spoken for a while. Talking apart, he was a normal tom cat who liked to go out on prowls. On one of these outings he had been poisoned, temporarily inhibiting his speech. Suzy Smith wanted to find witnesses to the talking cat other than the Deems. Several neighbours claimed to have heard Whitey speaking, and two of them signed statements to that effect. A man who had looked after the cats while the Deems were away was another witness. On one occasion he had slapped at the

SOVIET ZOO 'HAS TALKING ELEPHANT'

By RICHARD BEESTON in Moscow

Batyr, a 10-year-old Indian elephant at the Karaganda Zoo in Soviet Kazakhstan, can say phrases like "Batyr is good" and verbs like "drink" and "give," a Moscow newspaper reported yesterday. It said that a recording of its voice was heard recently on the Kazakh state radio.

"He just pushes his trunk into his mouth and starts talking," said the deputy director of the zoo, Mr Boris Kosinsky, He told a correspondent from the Young Communist League newspaper that it all began three years ago when a startled night watchman reported that he had heard the elephant talking to itself.

An unusual case of a talking elephant which appeared in the *Daily Telegraph*, 9 April 1980.

cats with a newspaper to stop them fighting. When Ruth Deem returned home Whitey said, "Mama, he hit me". "What did he hit you with?" she asked. "Newspaper," he replied.

Suzy Smith discussed the case of Whitey with Dr Hornell Hart, a parapsychologist and Professor of Sociology at Florida Southern College. He produced three possible explanations: ventriloquism, misinterpretations of a cat's miaows, and "the development of a fad under which it becomes stylish for individuals to report having heard a cat make various remarks".

The "fad" explanation sounds rather like the theories of mass hysteria, psychic plague or group enchantment which are commonly applied to outbreaks of the abnormal. It is vague enough to sound plausible, but Suzy Smith, having met several of the witnesses in the case, found no evidence of faddishness or hysteria among them, nor did she credit the suggestions of misheard miaows or ventriloquism. About a year after her visit, Whitey was heard to speak in the open air, well away from any member of the Deem family. One afternoon a neighbour, Joe Rhodes, saw the cat on a vacant lot near his trailer and went to pick him up to take him back to his owners. As he approached Whitey he distinctly heard the cat say, "You can't catch me!" And nor could he.

The Reverend Bennett Palmer, a close student of Whitey although he never heard him talk, compared him to another talking animal which fascinated psychical researchers in the mid-1930s (see Harry Price and R.S. Lambert, *The Haunting of Cashen's Gap*, 1936). This was a talking mongoose, or rather a disembodied voice claiming to be that of a mongoose called Gef, which haunted a house in the Isle of Man. Rustlings were heard and other evidence was given of a creature living in the attic or within the walls of the house, but nothing was ever clearly seen. Gef has been classified as a rare example of a talking poltergeist, and perhaps the voice speaking through Whitey was a similar phenomenon.

This reminds us of the old explanation of talking animals: that they were possessed by spirits or acting as mediums. Commenting on the limited speech of Ben, the talking dog of Royston, Dr E.J. Dingwall in *Peculiar People* (1950) compares it unfavourably with the powers of the Black Dog belonging to the medieval German magician H.C. Agrippa. This omniscient animal could not only talk, but whispered the secrets of events all over the world into its master's ear.

Calculating horses

The most famous case of a calculating animal is that of Clever Hans, a German horse at the beginning of the twentieth century. Hans was a young Russian stallion, acquired in 1900 by Wilhelm von Osten, who had long been obsessed by the idea that animals, if properly educated, could develop a degree of intelligence similar to that of humans. After several failures with other animals he discovered Hans, who turned out to be an ideal pupil.

Clever Hans undergoing a "scientific examination" in mathematics from Professor C.G. Schillings.

Von Osten began with rows of up to nine skittles, calling out the number of skittles in the row, thus teaching the horse to recognize numbers and to associate them with the words, one, two, three, etc. Then he replaced the skittles with numbers written on a blackboard. When Hans was familiar with these, von Osten introduced him to elementary mathematics, and soon the horse was doing simple sums, followed by more advanced calculations involving square and cube roots. One of his early investigators, Professor Claparède, who spent several weeks putting Hans through his mathematical paces, wrote in the *Archives de psychologie de Genève* that Hans "not only knew how to do sums; he knew how to read, and in music he could distinguish harmonious sounds from discords. He also had an extraordinary memory. He could tell the date of each day of the week. In short, his performance was up to the level of an intelligent fourteen-year-old schoolboy."

In response to the demands of an enthusiastic public, Clever Hans was submitted to inquiry by a committee set up for that purpose. It consisted of professors of psychology, physiology and zoology, some cavalry officers, a doctor, several veterinarians and a circus manager. For five weeks they studied and questioned the horse, and did their best to catch von Osten out in some deceit. But even with his trainer out of the room Clever Hans continued to calculate and give answers with the same facility. The committee members then retired to write up their report, all stating that Hans had performed as well as had been claimed and that they had detected no trickery.

This positive result did not satisfy von Osten's critics, several of whom had stated in print that the pair were frauds. Among the accusers was an eminent academic, Oskar Pfungst of the Berlin School of Psychology. Although notably prejudiced in the matter, he was considered the most suitable person to conduct a new investigation of the wonder horse. Having done so, he published in 1908 a voluminous report in the form of a book, *Der kluge Hans* (Clever Hans), in which he dealt ruthlessly with all von Osten's claims. According to Pfungst, the horse knew nothing of figures or letters, was totally unable to count, read and reckon, and what skills he had were limited to recognizing slight, barely noticeable sounds or movements made by his trainer or by other people. The report was exactly what many people wanted. It was widely acclaimed, and Hans and his owner became objects of public ridicule. Von Osten protested but few now took him seriously, and he died, an embittered man, the following year.

Hans, however, survived him and did much to restore his late master's reputation. Von Osten had willed him to a sympathetic businessman, Karl Krall of Elberfeld. Krall had his own ideas on animal education. Unlike von Osten, who had been impulsive and irritable, he was endlessly patient with his pupil, and under his gentle tuition Hans's skills improved. Krall then added to his stable two further stallions, Muhamed and Zarif, and began to teach them. Muhamed in particular made rapid progress, learning addition and subtraction and the meaning of plus and minus signs all within two weeks. Zarif was almost as quick, and it took both the horses only a few months to grasp the rudiments of mathematics, before moving on to spelling and sign language. In order to indicate numbers, they had been taught to tap

Wilhelm von Osten, the brilliant animal trainer who undertook Hans's education at the beginning of the last century.

out units with the right hoof and tens with the left. Krall devised a code system in which letters and sounds were similarly represented by a certain number of taps with each hoof. A full description of the method is given in Krall's book, *Denkende Tiere* (Thinking Animals) published in 1912.

After he had acquired and educated several more horses, including a Shetland pony, Hänschen, and a blind horse called Berto, Krall was ready to open his stables for inspection by scientists. Singly and in groups, distinguished professors from all over Europe converged on Elberfeld. Krall and his staff absented themselves, leaving the inspectors to work with the horses on their own, allowing them every opportunity to judge whether or not trickery was involved. They were unanimous in concluding that the criticisms brought by Pfungst against von Osten could not be applied to Krall's horses. To make sure that the animals were receiving no physical signals, the scientists arranged peep-hole tests, withdrawing from the stable to observe the horses through small glazed holes. Under these conditions the horses performed as well as ever.

Calculating the square root of 1,874,161 was typical of the problems set by Professors Mackenzie of Genoa and Assagioli of Florence. The question was written on a blackboard, and the investigators then went out into the yard and peeped through chinks in the door of Muhamed's

Zarif, one of the calculating horses of Elberfeld, with his teacher, Karl Krall.

stable while he tapped with his hooves the correct answer – 1369. Questions to which the investigators did not know the answers were also put. A committee headed by Dr Haenel asked Muhamed to give the fourth root of 7,890,481. He quickly replied 53, which proved to be correct. Even the blind horse, Berto, who obviously could not receive visual signals, was able to solve more simple mathematical problems. Moreover, having learnt a sign language, the horses would sometimes make spontaneous comments. On one occasion, during a lengthy inquisition by Professor Claparède, Zarif suddenly stopped work and then tapped out the word "tired" followed by "pain in leg". He also told Krall when Hänschen was beaten by a groom.

Frank Edwards, in *Strangest of All* (1956) quotes Dr Schoeller and Dr Gehrke on a touching episode which they reported during their experiments with the horses. They asked Muhamed why he did not attempt speech instead of pawing with his hoof. The animal appeared to try to articulate. Then he tapped out the sentence, "I have not a good voice." Dr Gehrke tried to show him how he must open his mouth before speaking, and Muhamed showed he understood by signalling, "Open mouth". Human speech, however, was beyond him. Zarif was then asked how he communicated with Muhamed. "With mouth," he replied. "Why do you not tell us that with your mouth, Zarif?" asked the scientists. "Because I have no voice," signalled the stallion.

The tragic fate of the Elberfeld horses was to

be called up for service on the battlefield in World War I. None of them survived.

Karl Krall's training methods had many followers, including several dog owners. Scientists, however, grew less interested in the phenomenon, for which they could find no acceptable explanation, and modern investigations of intelligent animals have mostly been left to researchers in ESP, telepathy and the like. In the case of the best known modern wonder horse, Lady, of Richmond, Virginia, our sources are newspaper and magazine articles rather than scientific reports.

Lady or Lady Wonder was a seedy-looking mare who lived for some thirty-three years in a ramshackle stable near the road between Richmond and Petersburg until her death in 1957. Her owners were Mr and Mrs C.D. Fonda, described as simple, God-fearing people, who had no interest in exploiting Lady. Despite their poverty, they consistently refused large offers from showmen and Hollywood agents. Their belief was that most animals could do much the same as Lady if only people bothered to teach them. In Lady's stable was a wooden contraption with a lettered keyboard, like a large typewriter. When Lady pressed one of the keys with her nose, the letter would stand up. In this way, Lady answered questions put to her by visitors.

Instead of plaguing her with mathematical questions, the people of Virginia treated Lady as a kind of oracle or wise woman. She was asked to predict the weather, the results of sporting events and the winners of elections, to locate lost property and to prescribe for ailments. On several occasions (details given in the *National Enquirer*, 31 October 1978) the Police Department engaged her to help them find missing people. In all these tasks she achieved a high rate of success. Inevitably, her legend became exaggerated, and many of the stories told about her cannot be authenticated, but she was examined in the course of her long career by scholars and scientists of many disciplines. Dr J.B. Rhine of Duke University describes in his book, *New World of the Mind* (1953), the studies of Lady made by himself and his wife between 1927 and 1929 and by other scientists in 1952 and 1953. He concluded that Lady had a remarkable ability to read people's minds.

In Lady's case there was never any suspicion of fraud. She could be seen operating her keyboard, unaided by any hint from her owners. Her messages made sense and, when relating to future events, were often proved correct. It is recorded that she accurately named Roosevelt and Truman as winners in their respective election campaigns, and gave other proofs of political foresight. It is also said that racecourse officials persuaded her owners to stop people from asking Lady to predict the results.

When it came to answering questions about people's private lives, Lady, like many sibyls before her, was often found to be too accurate and given to excessive honesty. Visitors attended by their wives, husbands or other intimate relations would ask for details of the early parts of their lives, and Lady would mention scandals or tragedies from the past which they had thought forgotten by everyone but themselves. Many people left her stable red-faced or in tears, and they would accuse her owners of dealing with the devil – forgetting that no one had asked them to consult the horse in the first place.

A problem for scientific researchers into the "clever animal" phenomenon is that any alternatives to straightforward acceptance of the animal's powers – such as telepathy and demonic possession – are themselves unscientific. This problem was honestly faced by the greatest expert in animal intelligence of the period, Professor Ziegler of Stuttgart. After prolonged study of the Elberfeld horses he continued his work with a dog named Rolf. Finally he stated his complete belief in the animal's abilities: "Now that I have assured myself

that the Elberfeld horses … are genuinely capable of reading and calculating, by their own reasoning powers, I consider it my duty as a scientist to support the claims made for these experiments by word and pen, although I do not disguise from myself the difficulty there is in making known to science discoveries which are in contradiction to accepted opinions."

There is no single theory of educated animals which accounts for all cases. The main contenders in the field are: that the animals genuinely think, calculate and communicate as claimed; that they are responding to signals from their trainers or others; that they read their questioners' minds; that they have mediumistic powers like oracles and relay messages and information from the spirit world. The first of these was forced on Ziegler, and many other scientific investigators, by their inability to account for the phenomena in any other way. But even those inclined to that theory

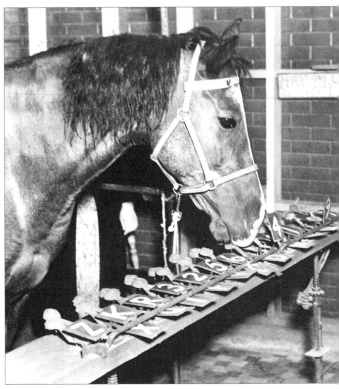

Lady Wonder, the talking horse of Richmond, Virginia. By pressing the appropriate keys of her "typewriter" with her nose she would answer questions, spell out messages and foretell future events.

have admitted doubts due to certain repeated anomalies in the animals' performances.

Several of the animals tested were found to have a higher rate of success with complicated mathematical questions involving cube roots and the like than with quite simple problems. It was often noticed by German investigators that the more intelligent the questioner, the better the animals did. Also, there is a repeated tendency in such animals to mix up their numbers, giving 15 for 51 etc. The horses would sometimes give a wrong answer to a question, and when asked a second question would reply with the correct response to the first. Eccentricities such as these have been cited by many writers as evidence that the animals were not their own agents and did not understand the meaning of their own communications.

Since the theory of visible signals does not work in the case of the blind horse Berto, or of animals studied by "key-hole" methods, sceptics have fallen back on the notion of slight, unconscious sounds, such as produced by changes in onlookers' breathing rhythms or heartbeats, indicating to a trained animal the moment to stop counting. No doubt animals have sharper senses than most people, but one of the difficulties with the "slight signals" theory is that it does not explain the cases of animals replying to spontaneous questions with previously unknown answers. Also, when the alleged signals are as slight as heartbeats, the theory begins to merge into one of its rivals, telepathy.

Trainers of clever animals for public show have often presented them as "psychic" mind-readers, thus confusing the issue. Most naturalists, or pet-owners, acknowledge some form of telepathy among animals, or between animals and people. In the cases described here, mental direction is the most attractive of general explanations. Again, however, it fails the "unknown answers" test. The advantage here passes to the spiritualists because, if an animal is acting as a spirit-medium, it matters not whether its questioner knows the answer to the problem he sets. Spiritualists compare the counting paw or hoof with which animals communicate to the swinging pendulum or rapping chair-leg at psychic seances. They point also to the trance-like state reported of many animals during their countings and calculations.

We ourselves are not specially addicted to any of these theories, although recognizing virtues in all of them. The actual function of many clever animals, such as Lady Wonder, has been similar to that of oracles, which no one has ever explained. Where modern scientists are as baffled as the ancients were by such things, we do not care to intrude with opinions.

Avian abductions

High on a desolate crag above Saint-Maurice in the French Alps, in 1950, a Swiss mountain guide found a child's skeleton. The remains were identified as those of a four-year-old boy who had vanished from a nearby village three years earlier. There was no way the child could have climbed there, so it was widely agreed that he must have been carried to the ledge by a giant eagle.

Stories of giant birds kidnapping humans were already old when Herodotus heard one from the priests of Egypt. Such tales have been incorporated into the mythology and folklore of many nations – the abuction of Ganymede by Jupiter in the form of an eagle; Sindbad's *rukh*; the divine Garuda of the Hindus; and the tall tales of Ozark mountain men. However, as far as we can discover, no one has yet made any study or compilation of avian abductions and there is a great resistance among orthodox thinkers to such tales.

Most ornithologists believe that large birds, like eagles and condors, cannot carry more than their own weight (about 12lb), which limits their cargo to a small lamb – or possibly a newborn baby. There have been attempts to prove scientifically that stories of children borne aloft on eagles' wings are improbable, if not impossible. One such test of the weight-carrying abilities of various eagles was described in 1940 in *Nature* magazine. A tame golden eagle "was taken to an elevated platform and various weights were attached to its feet. It was then launched into the air. It was found that when each foot was loaded with a 4lb weight,

The fatal abduction in 1838 of Marie Delex by an Alpine eagle, illustrated some thirty years after the incident.

the bird could hardly fly at all!"

On the other hand, all over the world woodsmen, mountaineers and farmers have maintained that large eagles will attack anything that moves, regardless of size, and in their frenzy often succeed in lifting animals forbidden by ornithologists. Lewis V. Cummings, in *I Was a Headhunter* (1941), says he once saw a great South American eagle carry off a half-grown deer which he reckoned weighed at least 35lb.

A famous case is reported by the French naturalist F.A. Pouchet in his encyclopedia, *The Universe* (1870). The incident took place at Valais, in the French Alps, in 1838, where a five-year-old girl named Marie Delex, was playing with a friend on a mountainside. "All at once an eagle swooped down upon her and carried her away in spite of the cries and presence of her young friend. Some peasants, hearing the screams, hastened to the spot but sought in vain for the child; they found nothing but one of her shoes on the edge of a precipice. It was not until two months later that a shepherd discovered the corpse of Marie Delex, frightfully mutilated, and lying upon a rock half a league from where she had been borne off."

Not all cases end so tragically, but the survivors have their own problems dealing with the sudden, frightening and unwanted encounter, as the case of ten-year-old Marlon Lowe demonstrates. On the morning of 25 July 1977, he was playing in the yard of his home at Lawndale, Illinois. His parents and two friends working in the vicinity heard Marlon's terrified screams and they looked around to see two huge birds menacing the boy. As they watched, one swooped and fastening its talons into the boy's clothes carried him for 25-30 feet at about three feet off the ground before dropping him. The witnesses said the dark birds were like "overgrown vultures" with curled beaks, white bands around their long necks and a wingspan of about eight feet.

Ruth and Jake Lowe, Marlon's parents, both felt the birds resembled condors, an impression confirmed later when they looked through a wildlife book. A spokesman for the National Audubon Society told the media that the only known condors in the United States were confined to a dwindling colony in California – over 1500 miles away to the west. He suggested that the Lowes had mistakenly seen hawks, great horned owls, or even turkey vultures, which were better known in the Midwest. The local gamewardens showed little inclination to believe the Lowes either, and they were put under pressure to change their story. When they stood by their testimony, it was suggested, crudely, that they were lying or that what they had really seen was simply the boy running along with the bird attacking his back.

The witnesses, however, reaffirmed their story

This remarkable photograph of an attempted avian abduction in progress was taken on the beach at Hampton, New Hampshire, on 21 August 2001. Three-year-old Kayla Finn (pictured) and her family had driven to this small town on the Atlantic coast from Albany, New York. Unfortunately for her, a bald eagle with a 1.8m wingspan had been chasing folk on the beach for five days when it attempted to fly off with her. Kayla's father managed to drive the bird away; Kayla was frightened and slightly injured but did not need medical attention. The eagle was captured the following day after it had flown up the coast to Salisbury, Massachusetts.

to Jerry Coleman in 1977 and to his brother Loren in 1979. The Colemans discovered that the Lowe family had become embittered by the reactions of the local authorities and their neighbours. When the event was reported in the papers they began receiving anonymous notes and telephone calls and dead birds were left on their front porch. Worst affected was young Marlon who had to cope with nightmares as well as bullying at school. For weeks after the event, his naturally red hair grew a colourless grey at the roots; Ruth Lowe blamed the shock of the bird attack.

As if to confound the "experts" further, large unidentified birds continued to be seen in the skies of Illinois. The following year a farmer at Lincoln saw one snatch two piglets weighing about 20lb each; while a truck driver, ten miles from Lawndale, saw one try and fail to lift a large piglet.

Tales of baby-napping are more common than bird experts deem comfortable. Lee Wilson, writing in the London *Evening News* (4 November 1978), mentions three cases from the Middle East. In two of them, eagles carried away babies from riverbanks while their mothers washed clothes – one at Ainassia, southern Anatolia, in June 1937 and the other at Damascus, Syria, in Feb-

ruary 1953. The third case was of a seven-year-old boy, in central Anatolia, who was abducted while foolishly trying to investigate an eyrie.

The problem of ascertaining the accuracy of such stories is a perennial one. In his *History of the Earth and Animated Nature* (1774) Oliver Goldsmith observed how "Many marvellous tales are told of eagles, and there is scarcely a parish in Scotland, in which, if tradition be correct, they have not carried off a child. According to popular belief, an eagle transported one from the island of Harris to Skye, over a space of about twenty miles, but as even more wonderful events are as firmly believed, no confidence can be reposed in such accounts."

Fortunately, similar stories exist from respectable sources, which are closer to us in time. For example, the following examples were sent to us by Dwight Whalen, a correspondent in the Niagara Falls area who loves trawling through local newspaper archives. In September 1885, a ten-year-old boy was pounced upon and carried across a road near Euphemia, Ontario, by what was described as the biggest bald eagle ever seen in the area. Five weeks later, another bald eagle carried off the two-year-old son of a farmer outside Montreal. Where the first boy was lucky to escape, the second was partly devoured by the eagle on the roof of a barn a mile away before an armed party could rescue him. More recently, in August 1924, near Chatham, also in Ontario, an eagle with a wingspan of eight feet managed to lift Fred Cunningham, aged fourteen, who weighed 97lb. The lad's clothing gave way before he had travelled five feet in the air; in the continued struggle, the bird was forced against a fence and killed by men who came to Fred's aid.

When Roger Caras deals with such feathered felons in his book *Dangerous to Man* (1964), it is to express his conventional disbelief in them. However, he does include a curious footnote referring to his correspondence with American naturalist Doug Storer over an incident in Norway in the 1930s. Caras writes: "Apparently a very large eagle attacked a very small seven-year-old girl and hit a powerful updraft at just the right moment. Mr Storer assembled an impressive collection of documents and his evidence would be difficult to refute." In fact the girl Svanhild Hansen was only four years old at the time and a full account of her abduction and successful recovery – interpreted by the local community as a sign of God's providence – is in a Norwegian book entitled *Ornerovet* (1960) by Steinar Hunnestad.

On 5 June 1932, little Svanhild was playing in the yard of her parents' farm in the village of Leka, not far from Trondheim, when the huge eagle swooped on her. The bird was unable to lift the girl to its eyrie but managed to transport her for more than a mile to the end of the valley where it dropped her on a high ledge. The rescuers, attracted to the location by the eagle's circling overhead, found the girl asleep, unharmed except for a tear-stained face and scratches.

For Caras and other naturalists this story is made more acceptable by the fact that the bird could have hit an updraught at the "right" moment. "It is all very startling," writes Caras, almost grudgingly, "but it would appear as if this is one case which must be accepted for the moment, at least." A similar qualification in print occurs in the third edition of Frank Lane's ever popular *Nature Parade* (1947). After stating the ornithologists' standard objection, Lane adds:

In his *Amazing But True Animals*, Doug Storer tells of the case of Svanhild Hansen, who as a four-year-old girl was playing in the yard of her parents' farm not far from Trondheim when she was snatched away by a huge eagle. She is seen here with her husband, a stuffed eagle and the dress she wore on that fateful day, complete with the rents made by her abductor's talons.

"A correspondent wrote to me after reading this passage in the first edition of this book and gave evidence of how a young girl in Ireland was carried across the Kenmare river by a golden eagle and dropped on the other side. When she grew up she had a distinct limp as a result of her literally hair-raising experience."

Even as we swoop down and rescue these tales from obscurity, we are aware of another dimension – the significance they share with other archetypal phenomena. The image of the human soul borne aloft by an overwhelming force that is more than human in its vigour and precision is one that is expressed by poets and mystics the world over. As a symbol of transformation, abduction by a totemic animal has great magical significance in traditional societies, particularly for the initiation of shamans. A person subjected to mysterious levitation, by whatever agency, is

There are several legends of people using birds to make journeys through the air. One such incident is recorded in this 17th-century Turkish painting of a traveller, shipwrecked on a desert island, who escaped by hanging on to the legs of a large bird.

considered to have displayed latent mediumistic or shamanic powers or to have been "selected" in some mysterious way.

In her study of Japanese shamanism, *The Catalpa Bow* (1975), Carmen Blacker refers to stories of children kidnapped by the *tengu*, mercurial beings, half hawks, half men, who haunt woods and mountaintops. The *tengu* take the form of golden eagles, carry off their chosen ones and rear them inside hollow trees until they are mysteriously returned to human society. According to Blacker, the *tengu*'s victims "return either as half-wits or as miraculous persons ... to become renowned ascetics gifted with supernatural powers". No less prodigious, the lucky survivors in our stories are often set apart, as a result of their experience, by some distinguishing physical feature – Marlon Lowe's pale hair, for example, or the Irish girl's limp. They also frequently experience a sense of "transformation", of being different from others, that is clearly parallel to that of alien abductees (see OTHERWORLDLY ABDUCTIONS, p.166) and those who have experienced levitation or spontaneous flight (see LEVITATION AND SPONTANEOUS FLIGHT, p.15).

Avian hitch-hikers

One of the long-lasting mysteries of migration is how little birds like wrens, tits, finches and wagtails, whose normal flights are short hops from bush to bush, manage to make seasonal journeys across hundreds of miles of sea. The traditional answer is that they travel on the backs of larger birds such as storks. That was said by several of the ancient writers on natural history, and it is the belief of country people in different parts of the world. Modern ornithologists mostly ignored this "superstition" until 1880–81 when evidence that small birds do sometimes ride upon larger ones was published in a series of letters to the scientific journal *Nature*. The idea has recently been revived; early in 2006 it was reported that biologists are debating the possibility that the presence of small, weak-flying species in remote islands might be because other birds carried them there. They did not do this out of kindness, it was emphasized, but because the small creatures on their backs provided them with snacks during long flights.

The *Nature* correspondence began on 24 February when Professor E.W. Claypole sent the editor a clipping from the New York *Evening Post* (20 November 1880) which he found "to say the least very extraordinary". It was a report from a naturalist who had spent several weeks on the island of Crete, where the natives including the local priest assured him that the flights of sand-cranes passing overhead on migration to the south were carrying little birds on their backs. They could hear their chirpings as they rode by, and they had often seen them flying up as the cranes alighted. The writer, who signed himself "Phone", was sceptical until the day when he was about fifteen miles out to sea in a boat with some Cretan fishermen. A flock of cranes flew quite near them, and the fishermen drew his attention to the chirps, which he heard for himself. One of the men fired off his flintlock, and Phone saw three small birds rise up from the flock and then rejoin it.

The report goes on to quote several "entirely reliable authors" who had heard of or witnessed instances of little birds riding on the backs of

This charming painting by the Yorkshire naturalist Ruby Sedgwick, entitled "Wait for me!" seems to display the aquatic counterpart of the aerial behaviour we describe. It is conceivable that there may be occasions when a mother bird, carrying her young in this manner, may take off with her passengers.

storks. One of these authorities, Adolf Ebeling, gave the reason why the storks allowed themselves to be used in this way. He had learnt it from his Bedouin friend in Egypt, Sheik Ibrabim. One evening they were sitting together at the foot of the Great Pyramid, enjoying coffee and cigarettes, and Ebeling asked the Sheik to explain how the small birds they saw around them had made the journey across the Mediterranean from Europe. He was answered thus:

"Did you not know, noble sir, that these small birds are borne over the sea by the larger ones? … The large birds submit to it willingly, for they like their little guests who, by their merry twittering, help to kill the time on the long voyage."

This notion of in-flight entertainment is more pleasant than the on-board snacks theory, and it actually makes more sense, as some of the bird species that are supposed to ferry the little ones are not normally flesh-eaters. Moreover, the crane has a long-standing reputation as a kindly bird. In the days when edifying lessons were drawn from natural history, the crane was the standard example of filial piety, because it looks after the old and feeble of its family, lending them a helping wing during migratory flights. It would surely be within the range of its benevolence to offer its

back to little birds in need of assistance.

Another correspondent in *Nature* (3 March 1881) was Dr John Rae. He had heard from North American Indians about a small bird of the *Fringillidae* kind that arrives every April on the shores of Hudson Bay in the company of migrating Canada geese. His informants said that the birds ride north on the backs of the geese. They were certain of that because they lie in wait for the geese and shoot them as they come down to land, whereupon the little birds fly up off their backs. Dr Rae's hunting companion, "an intelligent, truthful and educated Indian named George Rivers", had frequently seen it happen, and on one occasion Rae himself thought he saw it.

The belief that small migrants obtain assisted passage across the seas is well known in the Middle East where it is upheld as an example of divine benevolence. It was taken as such by Henry van Lennep, author of *Bible Customs in Bible Lands* (1875), in which he explains how small birds avoid the harsh winters of Asia Minor.

"He who is ever mindful of the smallest of His creatures has provided them with means of transportation to a more genial clime … The crane has been provided … In the autumn numerous flocks [of cranes] may be seen coming from the north

A woodcock carrying its young in its claws.

with the first cold blasts from that quarter, flying low, and uttering a peculiar cry of alarm as they circle over the cultivated plains. Little birds of every species may then be seen flying up to them, while the twittering songs of those already comfortably seated upon their backs may be distinctly heard. On their return in the spring they fly high, apparently considering that their little passengers can easily find their way down to the Earth".

The correspondent who sent this extract to *Nature* reasoned that since Dr van Lennep spent most of his lifetime in the East, "I conclude he has been an eye-witness to the above facts, and therefore his testimony is conclusive".

Conclusive or not, experts are still wary on the subject of avian airlifts. But on the similar question, whether woodcocks in flight carry their young with them, they generally agree that it does happen. An old writer, Scopoli, in *Annus primus historico-naturalis*, said that the carrying is done with the bird's beak, which made Gilbert White doubt the whole story because "…the long, unwieldy bill of the Woodcock is perhaps the worst adapted of any among the winged creation for such a feat of natural affection".

In all modern reports, however, the young woodcock is said to be carried either between the hen's thighs, or pressed against her body or, as in the nineteenth-century illustration above, in her claws. Many of the accounts by gamekeepers

and shooting men who have witnessed this feat are summarized by J.E. Harting, editor of *The Zoologist,* in the November 1879 issue. In most instances the woodcock has been seen to pick up her chick and fly a hundred yards or so when disturbed by men or dogs. More intriguing are cases where the transportation has been observed as part of the woodcock family's daily routine. In *Natural History and Sport in Moray* the fine old naturalist Charles St John describes how he watched several pairs of woodcock ferrying their families, usually consisting of four chicks, from their nests in dry woods and heaths down to the marshes where they could find worms.

J.E. Harting returned to the subject of avian hitch-hikers and ride-givers in *Recreations of a Naturalist* (1906) and Dr Waldo McAtee, the American chronicler of anomalous rains, wrote an article about it in *The Scientific Monthly*. Much of the data presented by these two writers was repeated along with further anecdotes in Frank Lane's *Animal Wonder World* (1957). Among Lane's cases of parent birds carrying their young on their backs is the account of an extraordinary performance that has been reliably witnessed at least twice since the nineteenth century, involving a hen golden eagle and her chick. This report was made by a young naturalist, F.E. Shuman, who was observing a Scottish eyrie with his father.

"The mother started from her nest in the crags, and roughly handling the young one, she allowed him to drop, I should say about ninety feet; she would then swoop down under him, wings spread, and he would alight on her back. She would soar to the top of the range with him and repeat the process. One time she waited about fifteen minutes between flights. I should say the farthest she let him fall was a hundred and fifty feet. My father and I watched this, spellbound, for over an hour."

There is an allusion to this chick-carrying habit of eagles in the Old Testament (Deuteronomy 32: 11): "As an eagle stirreth up her nest, fluttereth over her young, spreadeth abroad her wings, taketh them, beareth them on her wings…" And there is the well-known folk-tale about the birds meeting to decide which of them shall be king. They agree to choose whichever bird can fly highest. The eagle soars far above the rest and claims the crown, whereupon a little voice is heard from above him, disputing the claim. It comes from a tiny wren which has ridden aloft on the eagle's back and then fluttered up a bit higher.

Despite the fascination of birds carrying or juggling with their chicks in the air, the aspect that most intrigues ornithologists is hitch-hiking among migrants. Most of them agree that a small bird, worn out by its flight over the ocean, may occasionally perch on a larger bird that happens to be passing. That is not improbable, but the interesting and unsolved question is the extent to which hitch-hiking takes place and whether it is a normal, regular practice among some species of migratory birds. McAtee, while not doubting that it sometimes occurs, says that "it cannot be a major factor in migration".

That may be true, but the obvious difficulties in testing the matter leave it open to doubt, par-

ticularly in cases where belief in one kind of bird riding upon another is based on long observation by indigenous people. The crane, for example, is credited in Europe, Asia, Africa and America with regularly carrying smaller birds, and on the east coast of England the golden-crested wren, the smallest of British birds, is said to make its passage across the North Sea from Scandinavia on the back of the short-eared owl. This belief is supported by certain observations, cited by Frank Lane. Indeed, without the benefit of assisted passage at least some of the way, it is hard to see how such a small, fluttering creature could make the stormy, autumnal crossing in which many of their kind regularly perish.

Animal councils and law courts

Observers ancient and modern are agreed that animals can communicate with each other both by sounds and by other more subtle means, but no one knows the nature or source of the impulse that makes birds in a flock execute simultaneous turns and manoeuvres in the air. Nor is anything known for certain about the mysterious phenomenon, rarely but regularly witnessed, of animal and bird assemblies where meetings are held for purposes apparently similar to those of human society – lawmaking, judgement or mourning of the dead. We are aware of the errors that can arise from interpreting animal behaviour in terms of our own, but there are so many reports from sober observers of animals acting together in a way which seems parallel to human customs that we leave readers to judge the matter as they will from the following few examples.

The Parliament or Tribunal of rooks is a much repeated classic of old-fashioned natural history books. M. Diarmid describes the proceedings thus in Cassell's *World of Wonders*: "In the spring months, when all the rooks are busy building nests or repairing old ones, certain evildoers invade their neighbours' store of sticks to save themselves the trouble of collecting materials in a more laborious and lawful way. But as often as offences of this kind are detected, a complaint is made to

the proper quarter, and the delinquent bird tried and punished by his peers. Some veteran bird acts as chief justice, and from the bustle that goes forward, the cawing of some rooks and the silence of others, it is plain that the court proceeds upon system, though I can not subscribe to the startling opinion that they examine witnesses and empanel a jury. The presiding rook, who sits on a bough above all the others, is heard croaking last of all, and when sentence is pronounced, punishment follows very promptly. Either the culprit is seized and pecked most severely, or the nest containing the ill-gotten twigs is pounced upon and demolished."

G. Garratt in *Marvels of Instinct* (1862) refers to the remarkable rook tribunals held by a species in the Shetland Islands called *Corvus cornix*. They were studied by another naturalist, Dr Edmondson, who observed that the birds held regular assemblies, attended by deputies from distant parts of the islands. Sometimes the early arrivals have to wait several days for the latecomers, for the business may not begin until all are gathered. Meanwhile, the prisoners among the rooks make no attempt to escape but quietly await judgement. What their crimes might be Dr Edmondson does not know, but he says that, when the proceedings are over, "judge, barristers, ushers, audience and all, fall upon the two or three prisoners at the bar, and beat them till they kill them".

From time to time eyewitness accounts of bird

courts appear in local nature journals or in the popular press, the most prolific source we know of being the *Daily Mirror* letters column. On 19 June 1975, the *Mirror* printed an interesting letter from Mrs Rose Bridgett of Arnold, Nottinghamshire, about a crows' court she had seen one winter's day in a local field. The crows "had formed a perfect circle around the crow in the centre. I did not see any attack, but after the crows had flown away I went outside and picked up the crow which had been in the middle. It was dead but there were no visible signs of injury. I gave it to a taxidermist friend and it is now in a museum with a plaque stating that it was killed in a crows' court." The *Mirror's* comment on this was: "Presumably the crows put the 'fluence on the culprit and literally frightened it to death."

Another letter to the *Mirror* (13 April 1954),

from naturalist L.W. Hayward, describes one of the tribunals of storks which, he said, are quite often observed in Germany: "There is a large meadow near the village of Oggersheim, on the Rhine, where storks assemble every autumn. On one of these occasions about fifty were observed forming a ring round one individual whose appearance bespoke great alarm. One of the party seemed to address the conclave by clapping its wings for two or three minutes. This was followed by a second and a third and a fourth in regular succession, each like the first. At last they all joined in chorus and with one accord fell upon the culprit in the middle, and dispatched him in a few seconds."

Fortean Times contributor Alan Gardiner wrote of observing closely a group of magpies, seemingly in the act of administering a punishment. It was in the 1970s, during his schooldays in Lewes, Sussex. "Half a dozen magpies strutted round, circling a magpie on its back, with two other birds holding it down by its outstretched wings." The prone bird had its beak open but did not make any serious struggle as, now and then, one of the circling birds made a peck at it – see *Fortean Times* 131 (February 2000, p.50).

Sparrows sometimes hold similar courts, writes Garratt, but they are more energetic and less formal than the rook and crow assemblies, and after a short, sharp punishment the criminal is soon re-admitted without rancour to sparrow society. He comments: "Many men would do well to learn this lesson." In the one modern account of a sparrow court we have on file (in a letter to the *Mirror*, 19 April 1954) the observer, Mr Wadsworth of London, intervened at the point where the sparrows, having with much chirping tried one of their number, were meting out punishment. Mr Wadsworth rescued the "defendant", who rose to his feet but made no effort to fly away. He took the frightened bird home and adopted it as a freerange pet. The sparrow rewarded him by returning to his house one day with a mate. Under Mr Wadsworth's protective eye the pair built a nest and raised young ones, the cock bird's previous unpleasantness with his tribe having presumably been forgotten.

Writing on the subject generally, in *Fortean Times* 127 (October 1999, p.48), ecologist Phil Quinn refers to a particularly vicious group of sparrows. Again, Rev A.L. Barnes Lawrence told a meeting of the Frome-Selwood Field Club in 1926

From India comes this 16th-century illustration of a battle between owls and crows. The reported cause of it was that the crows objected to an owl being elected King of the Birds.

Similarly, the letters page in the *Mirror*, (11 June 1975) quoted a reader's account of a circle of rooks sitting in judgement of a jackdaw, thought to be an egg-thief. At the end of the trial the rooks fell on the jackdaw and killed it. Another letter (22 September 1977) tells the remarkable story of crows apparently trying a fox. Early one summer morning Mrs Ruddy of Buckinghamshire was taking her dog for a walk when she heard a terrific cawing. "Looking through the hedge I saw a little fox sitting in a ring of crows. The fox had such a comical "Who, me?" look on its face. I wanted to see what would happen, but my dog barked and disturbed them."

Other animals given to judicial proceedings, according to E.L. Arnold's *Soul of the Beast (1960)*, include a species of African monkey, which is said to "hold assizes in the forest for the trial of culprits, who are condemned and excommunicated". The old naturalist writer, Margrave, claimed to have been "a frequent witness of their assemblies and deliberations". Of the species called *ouarine* he wrote: "Every day, both morning and evening, the *ouarines* assemble in the woods to receive instructions. When all come together, one among the number takes the highest place on a tree, and makes a signal with his hand to the rest to sit round, in order to hearken. As soon as he sees them placed, he begins his discourse with so loud a voice, and yet in a manner so precipitate, that, to hear him at a distance, one would think the whole company were crying out at one time; however, during that time, one only is speaking, and all the rest observe the most profound silence. When this is done, he makes a sign with the hand for the rest to reply; and at that instant they raise their voices together, until by another signal of the hand they are enjoined to silence. This they as readily obey; till at last the whole assembly break up, after hearing a repetition of the same preachment."

In the *Illustrated London News* (30 August 1952) Dr Maurice Burton told the story of a "turkey court" as described to him by a correspondent. One of the birds in a domestic flock

that he had watched as house sparrows gathered in the rectory garden "…held a council and condemned a number of cock-sparrows to death". The executions took place under the window as he watched, carried out by a hen-sparrow while a jury oversaw the proceedings. "The hen throttled the cock and then viciously tugged at its throat till she had dragged the tongue through a hole below the beak." The vicar saw two more of these trials and executions; finding "…seven sparrows thus lying at intervals along the path."

There are even accounts of birds of one species trying an alien criminal. Phil Quinn himself surprised a court in session in Somerset, in 1991; unlike most of our examples it was made up of several different species. "In the centre was a cock chaffinch, surrounded by more chaffinch, blue tits, blackbirds, a robin and a magpie." In this case they all flew off at being disturbed.

Crows Court exacts the death penalty

National Park warden Richard Bell described this week to the Ryedale Natural History Society a crow court which was in session recently in Cropton Forest. It ended with one member of the colony being "sentenced" and put to death.

Mr Bell saw the crow court in a field about 100 yards away from his home at Sutherland Cottage.

He said: "I have read about and heard naturalists talk abour crow courts or crow parliaments. Usually they were with reference to rooks, as opposed to the carrion-crows I saw from my house. About six or seven of them were involved.

For about five minutes they were doing quite a lot of ritual and display, that sort of thing. Then they set about one of their number and killed him. As I went out, they flew away, leaving the dead bird behind.

"It was the first time that I had seen a crow court. I don't know why they set upon one of their number. I suppose it might have been something to do with territory. He might have been an intruder."

Mr Bell quoted the example of the crow court when Mrs Logan-Wood, the chairman of the Ryedale Natural History Society, asked members to report on unusual sightings. Mr

A recently witnessed Crow Court, as reported in the *Scarborough Mercury*.

was sick. The turkey hens formed a ring round the sick bird while the turkey cock, a short distance away, began his display. Puffed up, gobbling and rattling his wattles, he ran head down towards the group and, as he approached, the hens bowed their heads to the ground. The cock withdrew and then three times repeated the same performance. The third time, he charged through the circle of hens and dealt a blow with his beak on the sick bird in the centre. It fell, and the hens, one after the other, pecked it until it was dead.

Burton's belief is that the victims of bird courts in general are not being tried for wrongdoing, but that the birds are killing off one of their number which is sickly or diseased – as evidently was the case with the turkeys. In musing over the various orthodox explanations for bird parliaments, Quinn wrote: "When an injured bird is attacked, we might think that a form of eugenics is being practised. In the case of a flocking species, perhaps the motive is to reduce the competition for food or mates." However, he concluded,

"Such arguments do little to explain why apparently healthy individuals are singled out for execution," especially when birds of one species are formally punishing a member of another; or even, we might add, why the individual seems to submit meekly to judgement. "This remains one of the most bizarre and unexplained of natural phenomena," said Quinn. While science has no answer, the folklorists and others are certainly not lost for suggestions, as this final tale shows.

The most magnificent of all non-human parliaments – the avian high court and assembly for all Egypt – takes place every spring at the tomb-shrine of a Muslim saint, Sidi el Tari, the "Bird Lord". It is in the desert about ninety miles from Memphis, the ancient Egyptian capital, at the spot where the Bird Lord spent seventy years of the nineteenth century as a hermit. Like St Francis of Assisi, his Christian predecessor, he developed affinity with the local and migrant birds. He grieved at their hardships and persecutions, and he dedicated the land around him as their sacred refuge. Every year since the saint's death in 1880 birds of all kinds have gathered there in vast numbers to sing his praises and for what seem to be rituals or legal and political discussions. We have no better or later reference to it than *Ripley's Believe it or Not*, 5th series, 1954, from which the following is quoted:

"At the beginning of spring the tomb becomes the mecca for all the birds and fowl of Egypt. Here they foregather in Sun-eclipsing numbers and engage for days in what – for birds – is an unprecedented activity. There are loud and heated deliberations. The natives claim that the birds are holding elections and engaging in interminable campaign oratory – for the purpose of choosing the members of their annual government. The meeting is concluded by a colossal concert in which all the songbirds of the country take part. And before they adjourn for the year they post a winged sentinel whose job it is to fly constantly around he tomb and police it from the air – until it is relieved twelve months hence. The Bird Republic has been in continuous existence since 1880 and is obviously designed as an avian tribute to the man who gave seventy years of his life to shield the feathered tribe from sudden death."

It is a pretty story, but it is well over fifty years old, and we wonder if Sidi el Tari's pioneer bird sanctuary still exists and whether the "Bird Republic" still meets there.

Assemblies of animals for judicial or other purposes provide a common theme of folklore and fairy tales. This illustration by Griset of an assembly of mice appears to draw on reports of mice and rats which have been seen in conclave around their "King".

Toad in the hole

The Great Exhibition of London, in 1862, contained a curious and controversial exhibit; a lump of coal from a colliery in Newport, Monmouthshire, and a frog. The frog, it was explained, was found in the heart of the coal, in a frog-shaped cavity that appeared to have been moulded around it. An irate Captain Frank Buckland wrote to *The Times*, accusing the directors of the Exhibition of "gross imposition" and calling for the frog and its prison to be "expelled". It was utterly impossible, he protested, for a frog to bear the heat and pressure necessary to form coal at depths of over 300 feet, to say nothing of the millions of years during which it must have lived so enclosed.

This outburst from Buckland, who later wrote

Curiosities of Nature (1857–72), initiated a correspondence in the *Field* and other periodicals throughout 1862 (see p.398). Many more incidents came to light and several "specimens" were sent to the leading naturalists of the day, including Professor Richard Owen of the Natural History Museum who received so many that he appointed his wife to deal with them. While this was going on, workmen excavating a new cellar to a house in Stamford, Lincolnshire, found a toad in a cavity in solid stone seven-foot deep. The report in the *Stamford Mercury* (31 October 1862) concludes: "No fact can be more fully or certainly established by human evidence … let the sceptics on this subject say what they will."

Belief in the ability of toads to live encased in rock was popular for centuries though dismissed by the learned as a superstition of the countryside.

The earliest first-hand story known to us is that of Ambroise Paré, chief surgeon to Henry III of France. "Being at my seat near the village of Meudon, and overlooking a quarryman whom I had set to break some very large and hard stones, in the middle of one we found a huge toad, full of life and without any visible aperture by which it could get there … The labourer told me it was not the first time he had met with a toad and the like creatures within huge blocks of stone."

An obvious way of testing whether toads can really endure long spells of solitary confinement without food or air is to seal them up in airtight cells. Quite a number of these cruel-sounding experiments have been performed. In 1825, Frank Buckland's father, William – then a professor of geology at Oxford – placed twelve toads in cells in two stone blocks, one of limestone, one of sandstone. He sealed them in with glass and putty, and buried them under a slate three feet down in his garden. A year later the toads in sandstone were found to be long dead. Most of the toads in limestone were alive – two had even put on weight. Buckland ascribed this to a crack in the glass, which possibly admitted small insects. He tried again, but all the toads died.

An illustration from Gosse's *Romance of Natural History* of an incident commonly reported by quarrymen, the breaking open of a stone to reveal a long-immured but living toad, and its close-fitting hollow.

This mummified toad was found by workmen who cracked open a flint nodule in a quarry at Lewes, East Sussex, in about 1900. Both toad and tomb are now in the Booth Museum in Hove. It has been suggested that this is another hoax by Charles Dawson, who was implicated in the notorious Piltdown Man forgery.

Buckland wasn't the first to try the experiment. In February 1771, the French naturalist Herissant sealed three toads in plaster-lined cells in a block of fir-wood. Over three years later, in April 1774, the cells were opened in the presence of other scientists, and two of the toads were still alive. Herissant sealed up the two live toads again and presented the block of wood to the Academy of Sciences to open whenever they thought fit. He died soon after and the experiment was heard of no more. A similar experiment by another French naturalist was reported in *The Times* (23 September 1862); of the twenty toads that were encased in a block of plaster of Paris four were still alive twelve years later.

Animals other than frogs and toads are found in living tombs, though rather less frequently. The *Annual Register* of 1761 cites examples of snakes, crabs and lobsters from the classical writings of pioneering naturalists, including Francis Bacon. It also records the astonishing though apparently well-known information that the stones used to pave Toulon harbour were often broken to reveal "shellfish of exquisite taste"; and that in the hard stones quarried at Ancona on the Adriatic were to be found "small shellfish, quite alive and very palatable".

In February 1818, Dr E.D. Clarke, a geologist at Caius College, Cambridge, was present at the digging of a friend's chalk-pit in the hope of finding fossils. He was surprised when workmen found a layer of newts at 45 fathoms (275 feet). He thought they were fossils and had some broken out of a lump of chalk-stone. Placing them on a sheet of paper in the sunlight, he was astonished when three intact creatures began to move. Two of them died later; the third, when placed in water, "skipped and twisted about, as well as if it had never been torpid", so actively in fact that it escaped. Dr Clarke and his friend set about collecting specimens of all the species of newts in the area, but none resembled the recently revived ones: "They are of an entirely extinct species, never before known," wrote The Revd Richard Cobbold. "Dr Clarke took great delight in mentioning this." (Quoted by William Howitt, *History of the Supernatural*, 1863.) Howitt himself knew of a stone ball that had topped a gate-post of a mansion for hundreds of years. One day it fell and broke on the ground, revealing a live toad in its heart.

The phenomenon can be extended to creatures found in other material than stones and rocks. The *Memoires* of the French Academy of Sciences for 1719 reports that "In the foot of an elm, of the bigness of a pretty corpulent man, three or four foot above the root and exactly in the centre, has been found a live toad, middle-sized but lean and filling up the whole vacant space." The writer could only imagine that some spawn became lodged in the young tree, "by some very singular accident", and that the toad grew within the tree, living on its sap. It scuttled away as soon as the trunk was split open enough for it to fall out, so its limbs had certainly not atrophied from its supposed lifetime confinement.

Dr Robert Plot recorded several accounts in his *Natural History of Staffordshire* (1686) of similar stories told to him by countryfolk. "Out of a great oak that grew at Lapley ... there was a great toad sawn forth from the middle of the tree, in a place which when growing was 12 or 14 foot from the ground; the tree being sound and intire in all parts quite round, saving just where the toad lay, it was black and corrupted and crumbled away like sawdust." Plot's explanation was that an "agreeable dust" or airborne spawn, a concept also used to

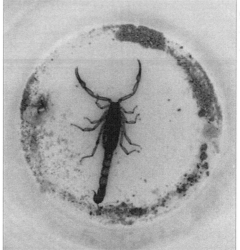

Recalling William Buckland's experiments in 1825, of sealing frogs into airtight cavities to test their legendary endurance, is the report of a scorpion that survived for fifteen months, trapped inside a solid cast of plaster. The mould, weighing 1000lb, was made by Don DeBlieux, a Utah Geological Survey paleontologist, around the eighty-million-year-old horned skull of a new species of plant-eating dinosaur. It took more than three years to cut out the large block of sandstone in which the fossilized skull was embedded and it will take more than 500 hours to remove the sandstone using miniature pneumatic hammers. When DeBlieux sawed off part of the cast, the scorpion wriggled out of a cavity. He thought it might have been trapped when he made the cast fifteen months earlier.

explain falls of frogs (see FALLS OF FROGS AND FISHES, p.22), had been wafted into a hollow high in the tree. When the toad hatched it could not escape and became slowly sealed up.

In another part of his book, Dr Plot tells of three field-mice – called "nursrows" in Staffordshire dialect – found inside an oak tree near Biddulph "which being examin'd were found in all parts sound." Plot at first wonders if this was a "nursrow-tree". In the folklore of the farmhands of that county, a venerable tree (usually an oak, an ash or an elm) was drilled into and a living field-mouse was placed in the hole, which was then plugged with a peg of the same wood. The

TO THE EDITOR OF THE TIMES.

Sir,—Your correspondent "P.," in last Friday's paper, demands the expulsion from the International Exhibition of a frog said to have been found alive embedded in coal. He also accuses the exhibitor of being an impostor, and attributes either credulity or inattention to the Commissioners, among whom he specially names Lord Granville. The only ground given for his conclusions is his own simple opinion that a frog could not have lived thousands of years so low down in the earth, and having over it such an enormous weight as it must have had if what is said of it be true. It is in my power, however, to show that your correspondent's opinion is wrong, and I shall be much obliged if you will allow me to do so.

1. My wife is prepared to state that she herself, many years ago, saw one of her father's workmen split open a piece of coal, and discover in the middle of it a moderate-sized frog or toad (she is not sure which) alive, and able to move, and she remembers distinctly the oval shape and smooth surface of the hollow where the animal had lain.

2. Samuel Goodwin, a stonemason, whom I myself have known these five-and-twenty years, and who is very trustworthy, states as follows :—" When I worked in the quarry at Kettlebrook, with Charles Alldridge, we sawed a stone through about four feet thick, quite solid, and in the middle was a toad about the size of my fist, and a hole about twice the size. We took it out, and it lived about half an hour, and then it died. We worked the stone, and it was used as a plinth stone in Birmingham Town-hall."

I trust this will induce " P." to apologize to the exhibitor of the frog, as well as to the Commissioners.

Yours respectfully,

JOHN SCOTT.

Lilleshall Coal Depôts, Great Western Railway,
Paddington, Sept. 17.

One of several letters to *The Times*, in response to Captain Buckland's indignant demand for the expulsion of the embedded toad from the Great Exhibition of 1862.

branches of such trees were believed efficacious in curing swellings in cattle thought to be caused by the nocturnal biting of field-mice – the afflicted animal being whipped with the branch.

This custom was also referred to by Gilbert White in his *Natural History of Selborne* (1789). He describes a "shrew-ash", a gnarled old tree that stood near Selborne Church until "the late vicar stubb'd and burnt it", despite the pleas and remonstrances of the villagers. The cause of their lamentations was that a shrew had long ago been ceremonially sealed into its trunk; the branches being used to cure animals tormented by shrew-mice. Could the rustic magicians who buried mice within tree trunks be imitating the mysterious power in nature that encloses living animals in sealed cavities within trees and rocks?

In February 1861, J. Pemberton Bartlett, a parson living near Southampton, wrote to *The Zoologist* about a common toad that he recovered from a cavity in a 25-year-old fir tree. "I counted the rings of the tree myself," he said, surmising that the young amphibian had crept into the hole which, in time, closed over. The naturalist W.H. Maxwell reported, in *The Field Book* (1833), that he once discovered a toad imprisoned in the bark, high up a mulberry tree. Although he offered no explanation of how the toad reached its high prison, he firmly believed that "as the tree increased in size there seems to be no reason why the toad should not in process of time become embedded in the tree itself."

Some reports of entombed creatures mention the lack of a mouth, as in the quite anomalous case of a number of frogs found in a gravel pit near Frederick, Oklahoma, during the 1920s. According to the report in the Dallas *Morning News* (9 August 1960), deep in the pit were found some clay balls, as hard as rock. These were broken open with sledgehammers and in them were frogs, some alive, some dead. Of the live frogs it was said, "their mouths had grown shut through the centuries. They were without pigmentation and so transparent one could see their hearts beating. Sudden exposure caused some of them to burst, but if quickly immersed in water they continued to live, some as long as a month." An odd feature of the case was that the balls of rock containing the frogs were found in the midst of the bones of mammoths and sabre-toothed tigers. Because of this association, scientists from the Smithsonian

Details of the extraordinary case of a mummified marmoset discovered within the trunk of a birch tree at Bosham, West Sussex, are given, together with this picture of it, by Frank Buckland in the notes to his edition of Gilbert White's *Natural History of Selborne*. The tree had been cut down and taken to a carpenter's shop for stripping and sawing, in the course of which the strange find was made. The creature was presented to Buckland, who took it with him when he went to dine at Winchester with Bishop Wilberforce, the great opponent of Darwin and Huxley. At dinner Wilberforce started making jokes about the theory of human descent from monkeys, and Buckland added to the merriment by producing the dried marmoset from his pocket and introducing it as "our Darwinian brother".

Institution concluded that the frogs in stones were contemporary with these extinct animals; their explanation of why the frogs were living is not recorded.

This association with ancient bones reminded us of a report sent to the journal of the Selborne Society, *Nature Notes*, in 1900, which referred to another ancient country belief that certain magical people and animals had toads embedded in their heads. The Vicar of North Moreton, Oxfordshire, wrote: "On July 20, while some repairs were being carried on in our church, a skeleton was discovered at a depth of about six feet under the pavement and in the skull a large yellow toad.

The theory of the man who found it is that the creature was there in the man's lifetime and grew after his death!"

Stranger still is the story in the *Historia rerum anglicarum* (William of Newburgh, c.1198). It tells of the discovery by quarrymen of "a beautifully jointed stone … that is to say one formed from a fine conjunction of rocks". It was taken to the bishop, who had it opened "to see if within it lay concealed something mysterious". They found a toad with a gold chain round its neck. The bishop ordered the stone to be marked and then reburied in the quarry "for all eternity".

How one swallow may make a winter

A favourite nineteenth-century topic of intellectual discussion and newspaper correspondence was the question of whether swallows occasionally hibernate. Orthodox ornithologists, who almost universally believe in the southward autumn migrations of swallows, swifts and martins from northern Europe and their return the following spring, are usually quite indignant should anyone dare to believe otherwise. Such authorities are usually surprised, and not a little embarrassed, to learn that the great founders of the modern natural sciences – Linnaeus, Buffon and Baron Cuvier – accepted without question the theory of hibernation. Cuvier in *Le règne animal* (1819) wrote: "It appears certain that swallows become torpid during winter, and even that they pass this season at the bottom of the water in the marshes."

The traditional form of belief in hibernating swallows was expressed in 1602 by Richard Carew in his *Survey of Cornwall*. "In the West parts of Cornwall during the winter season, swallows are found sitting in old deep tin works and holes of the seacliffs; but touching their lurking place, Olaus Magnus makes a far stranger report; for he saith, that in the North parts of the world, as summer weareth out, they clasp mouth to mouth, wing to wing, and leg to leg, and so after a sweet singing, fall down into certain great lakes or pools amongst the canes, from whence at the next spring they receive a new resurrection; and

he addeth for proof hereof, that the fishermen, who make holes in the ice to dip up such fish with their nets as resort thither for breathing, do sometimes light on these swallows congealed in clods of a slimy substance, and that carrying them home to their stoves the warmth restoreth them to life and flight."

It is easy to dismiss this notion as based on poor observation of swallows swooping over ponds, marshes and the like as if preparing for a plunge into the depths. But it was not just a simple, rustic belief; men of science have claimed to witness the phenomenon. Dr Etmuller, cited in William Derham's *Physico-theology* (1714), was Professor of Botany and Anatomy at Leipzig, in the 1750s. He wrote: "I remember having found more than a bushel would hold of Swallows closely clustered among the reeds of a fish-pond under the ice, all of them to appearance dead, but with the heart still pulsating." To this statement Derham adds a note of a meeting he attended of the Royal Society in February 1713, addressed by a Dr Colas, "a person very curious in these matters". Dr Colas said a common fishing practice in northern Europe was to break holes in the ice and draw the nets under it. Once, he saw "sixteen Swallows so drawn out of the Lake of Larnrodt, and about thirty out of the king's great pond in Rosneilen". At Schlefitten, near a house of the Earl of Dohna, he saw two Swallows just come out of the waters, that could scarcely stand, being wet and weak, with their wings hanging on the ground; and that he observed the Swallows to be often weak for some days after their appearance.

In the sixteenthth century, Olaus Magnus recorded the popular belief that swallows sometimes hibernate on the beds of lakes and ponds, and illustrated it with this woodcut of fishermen dragging up a cluster of the birds in a net cast through a hole in the ice.

In the Academy at Uppsala, where Linnaeus reigned over the botany and medicine departments until his death in 1778, the submerged hibernation of the swallow was accepted as a fact. But his German colleagues were rather more sceptical – or scientific. For many years a reward was offered by a famous university of the bird's weight in silver for each swallow found under water and revivable in the prescribed manner. The prize was never claimed.

In addition to the belief that swallows were capable of sleeping on the bottom of ponds, there are many reports of swallows found hibernating in hollow trees, holes in cliffs and banks, up in attics, down in mines, etc. One of the best and earliest accounts comes from Peter Collinson, the friend and correspondent of Linnaeus, who reported to the Royal Society the following statement of a Monsieur Achard. He was travelling by barge down the Rhine to Rotterdam, at the end of March – about two weeks before the usual arrival of the sand martins – when, just below Basel, he saw an unusual sight. We quote from *Philosophical Transactions* (1763):

"I was surprised at seeing, near the top of the cliff, some boys tied to ropes, hanging down doing something … The waterman told us they were reaching the holes in the cliffs for Swallows or Martins, which took refuge in them, and remained there all the winter, until warm weather, and then they came abroad. The boys being let down by their comrades to the holes, put in a long rammer, with a screw at the end, such as is used to unload

guns, and, twisting it about, drew out the birds. For a trifle I procured some of them. When I first had them, they seemed stiff and lifeless; I put one of them in my bosom, between my skin and shirt, and laid another on a board, the Sun shining full and warm upon it, and one or two of my companions did the like. That in my bosom revived in about a quarter of an hour; feeling it move, I took it out to look at it; but perceiving it not sufficiently come to itself, I put it in again; in about another quarter, feeling it flutter pretty briskly, I took it out, and admired it. Being now perfectly recovered, before I was aware, it took its flight; the covering of the boat prevented me from seeing where it went."

The first modern compilation of records and legends of hibernating swallows was published by Philip Gosse in 1861 as a chapter in the second volume of his *Romance of Natural History*. Though not entirely sceptical, Gosse was unhappy about the anecdotal and secondhand nature of most of the evidence, and he wondered why the records of finds, "instead of increasing in frequency with the increase of scientific research and communication, strangely become more rare".

A number of Scottish accounts of hibernating birds was collected by Bishop Stanley in his *Familiar History of Birds* (1865). These include a group of five chimney swallows that were found huddled together on the roof-beam of a barn, in November 1826; a corncrake found in midwinter, when an Orkney crofter demolished a mud wall; and six swallows rescued from a hollow. The latter

When Reiner Streuter, of Bremerhaven, North Germany, cut the thick ice from the top of his frozen fish pond, he found this kingfisher seemingly frozen in the act of diving to catch fish. (*The Times* 6 January 1996)

were taken "to a respectable person, by whom they were deposited in a desk, where they remained forgotten till the following spring." On hearing a fluttering in the desk, the man recovered the birds and managed to revive them.

Charles Dixon, the prolific writer of bird books, who was one of the few naturalists of his time to take the idea of avian hibernation seriously, includes this record among the many he listed in *The Migration of Birds* (1892). To it he adds another, from the *Edinburgh Journal*, of three living but dormant corncrakes which were excavated from "a dung-heap that had long remained undisturbed" at Monaghan in Ireland. Dixon claimed that he could fill "scores of pages" with apparently well-authenticated instances of the hibernation of birds, and he called the refusal of his contemporaries to consider these records "most unwise and most unscientific".

Perhaps the most famous upholder of the

belief was The Revd Gilbert White of Selborne in Hampshire. In the letters to Thomas Pennant and Daines Barrington which comprise his *Natural History of Selborne* (1788) he returned again and again to the subject. The evidence for hibernation that seemed to him most compelling was that swallows would suddenly appear in his parish one fine spring day and then disappear for a while during a spell of bad weather. Similarly, in the autumn they would vanish, but a sunny day would see the return of a few individuals which he suspected of having temporarily re-emerged out of hibernation.

White also knew of a man who as a schoolboy at Brighton had witnessed a cliff-fall during a winter storm which had exposed many hibernating swallows. A similar story was published in the *Zoologist* (1849, page 2590). In cutting away part of a rocky hill, situated between Hastings and St Leonard's, labourers had found an immense quantity of swallows within a cleft. "The birds were clinging together in large 'clots', and appeared to be dead, but were not frozen together, and the weather being rather warm for the season, nor were they at all putrid or decayed ... The birds were found about ten feet from the surface of the rock facing the sea, and not very high up." Unfortunately, most of the birds were taken away and buried with the debris from the cliff.

We are impressed by a detail which recurs time and again in reports of hibernating swallows: that the torpid birds are found clinging together in "clots". In one of his poems the eighteenth-century Welsh bard, Iolo Morgannwg (alias Edward Williams), wrote the line: "And sleep the swallows in their cavern'd rocks", to which he added a footnote: "About the year 1768, the Author, with two or three more, found a great number of swallows, in a torpid state, clinging in clusters to each other by their bills, in a cave of the sea cliff near Dunraven Castle, in the county of Glamorgan." We have no further details of this discovery, but the belief in hibernating swallows was evidently part of Welsh traditional lore, for in a book called *The Bardic Museum* (1802) by Edward Jones, the swallow is listed among the "seven sleepers" recognized by the Druids, along with the dormouse and other hibernating animals. The clots or clusters formed by the sleeping birds are doubtless behind the Chinese legend that swallows in winter plunge beneath the water, cling together and turn into mussels.

W.L. McAtee, who wrote an article about hibernations of birds in the *Audubon* magazine (1950, vol. 52), was impressed by a case reported earlier in *Nature* by observers of the highest repute, Sir John McNeill and Sir Henry Rawlinson. They stated that in Persia they had found hundreds of hibernating swallows in burrows. Their report – completely ignored at the time – has now been proved to have been largely accurate. The clinching evidence was provided by a whippoorwill, a kind of nightjar, which Professor E.C. Jaeger found hibernating in a hollow on a rock face in the Colorado Desert. That was in the winter of 1946, and the following winter Jaeger was able to observe, over a period of eighty-five days, a whippoorwill in the same hollow on the rock, and to prove that it was in a state of near-suspended animation and truly hibernating.

Maurice Burton, in a chapter on the hibernation of birds in his *Animal Legends* (1955), gives a fuller account of Jaeger's discovery, and comments that "he was merely confirming a deeply-founded suspicion". Indeed, one of the most respected of American ornithologists, Dr Elliot Coues, in the first part of his *Birds of the Colorado Valley* (1878), had cited over 250 references to hibernating swallows, stating his belief in the hibernation of several American bird species, notably the chimney swift. He showed that clusters of these birds sometimes spend the winter in hollow trees. Other reported American hibernators include swifts, swallows, martins,

Philip Henry Gosse (1810–88), the Victorian popularizer of natural history. Unlike Gilbert White, Gosse felt that the evidence was insufficient to support belief in hibernating swallows.

whippoorwills, ptarmigans and turkey vultures.

We may perhaps see the day when Gilbert White and the old school of naturalists are proved right by a new discovery of a clutch of hibernating swallows. We are concerned, however, by Gosse's observation that these finds seem to be getting rarer. The same applies to several of the other phenomena described in this book – toads in stones and sea-serpent sightings, for example. On the other hand, many of the monsters and weird creatures written about in earlier chapters are currently very much on the increase – at least, reports of them are. Perhaps the theories affect the evidence, as much as the other way round, and the decline in torpid swallows and stoned toads is nature's response to modern naturalists' refusal to believe in such things. Or perhaps, more prosaically, mechanical methods of earth-moving make it now more likely for such creatures to be squashed rather than observed.

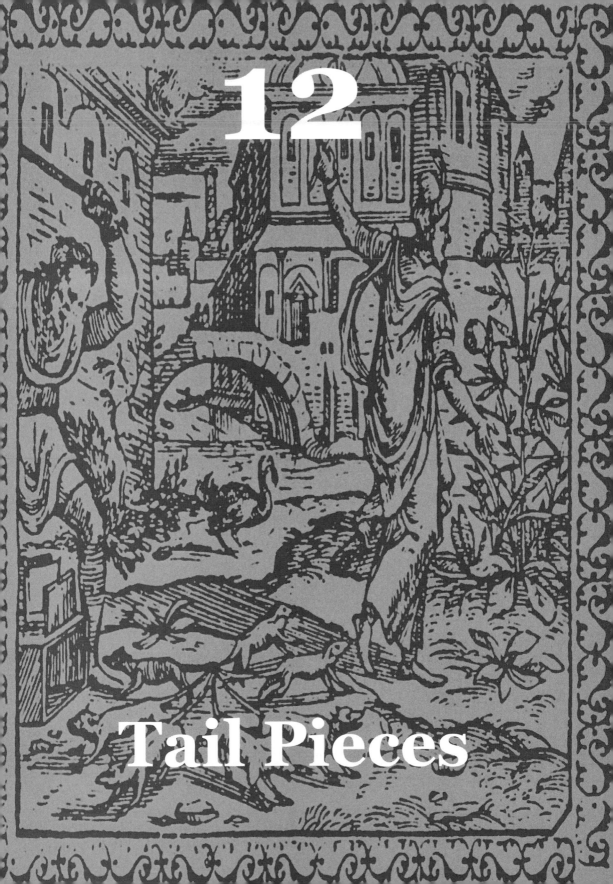

12

Tail Pieces

12
Tail Pieces

Cats with wings

Many people do not believe in winged cats. It sounds too fantastic. But these seemingly impossible creatures do occasionally exist. There are several modern, authenticated examples of cats with wings, and even a few cases where such animals are said to be capable of making limited flights.

In the 1930s there was a winged cat on show at the old Oxford Zoo. Its wings were not mere ornaments but were used, according to the woman who discovered the animal, to gain height when leaping up from the ground. The *Daily Mirror* sent a Special Correspondent to Oxford to inspect it, and he reported (9 June 1933) as follows. "A few days ago neighbours of Mrs Hughes Griffiths of Summerstown, Oxford, saw a strange black and white cat prowling round their gardens. Last evening Mrs Hughes Griffiths saw the animal in a room of her stables. 'I saw it move from the ground to a beam – a considerable distance which I do not think it could have leaped – using its wings in a manner similar to that of a bird,' she said to me. Mrs Hughes Griffiths at once telephoned to the Oxford Zoo, and Mr Frank Owen, the managing director, and Mr W.E. Sawyer, the curator, went to her house and captured the animal in a net. I carefully examined the cat tonight, and there is no

doubt about the wings. They grow just in front of its hindquarters."

The Oxford Zoo is long defunct, and our inquiries have brought to light no other relic of its winged cat other than this one photograph (opposite).

In *Strange Creatures from Time and Space* (1975) John Keel refers to three winged cats which appeared in Ontario, Canada, in 1966. Two of them were reported as having been shot near Montreal and near Ottawa; the third was said to be a large, black flying cat seen swooping down on terrified pets and farm animals at Alfred, Ontario, in June 1966. On 24 June it was shot by Mr Jean J. Revers of Alfred as it sailed in, howling and screeching, to attack a local cat, "making gliding jumps of fifty or sixty feet – wings extended". The police were called, and Constable Argall later gave his description of the dead predator: "Its head resembled a cat's, but a pair of needle sharp fangs five eighths of an inch long protruded from the mouth. It had a cat's whiskers, tail and ears, and its eyes were dark, greenish and glassy. I never saw anything like it in my life."

The cat's measured wing-span was fourteen inches. It was buried in Mr Revers's garden, but a few days later it was dug up and sent for examination to Kemptville Agricultural School. The verdict of their veterinary laboratory was that it

The winged cat of Oxford Zoo in 1933.

was an ordinary black cat with long growths of thick, matted black fur protruding from its back.

Whatever the nature of its wings, the fearful cat had been seen by many people in Alfred to fly a foot or so above the ground after taking a leap; and the Oxford cat seems also to have used the flaps of fur on its back to assist flight. The Sheffield cat, illustrated overleaf, could spread its wings, but we are not aware of any other cases of winged cats that actually flew. However, cats with wings – functioning or otherwise – have obvious value to showmen, and we have heard of lawsuits arising over disputed ownership.

Peter Dance tells a curious tale in his book *Animal Fakes and Frauds* (1976). In the early 1960s he saw an advertisement for the sale of "Thomas Bessy, the Famous Winged Cat", together with a glass and mahogany showcase in which this stuffed oddity was mounted. It was said to be a nineteenth-century specimen and to have belonged to a circus owner who exhibited it. There had been a dispute about possession. Its original owner went to law to claim it back and won the case. The circus owner returned the cat

in a box, but it was found to be dead on arrival home, and there was suspicion that it had been poisoned.

Dance says that he wrote to the London address given in the advertisement, but received no reply. About the same time of the Thomas Bessy advertisement another winged cat disappeared. This second animal was also called Thomas (or Mitzi) and her story is told in John Keel's *Strange Creatures from Time and Space* (1970).

In May 1959, fifteen-year-old Douglas Shelton was hunting in the hills near his home at Pinesville, West Virginia. His dog chased a cat which escaped up a tree. Douglas climbed after it, caught it and discovered that it had wings. These were boneless and furry but seemed to have gristle in them and felt gritty towards the body. The cat was a large Persian with a tail like a squirrel. Douglas called it Thomas, a name it retained even though it later turned out to be a female. Thomas became a celebrity. Her picture was in many newspapers, and on 8 June 1959 she appeared with her owner on the New York television show *Today*. On her return to Pinesville, crowds of well-wishers journeyed through the West Virginia mountains to see and photograph her, paying a small sum to Douglas and his mother for the privilege. It was the biggest thing that had ever happened in Pinesville, and the town gained further notoriety when Thomas became involved in a law suit. A local woman, Mrs Hicks, claimed that Thomas was her cat and was really called Mitzi. She had been given to Mrs Hicks by a friend who bought her in a California pet store. The neighbours, said Mrs Hicks, well remembered Mitzi and her furry wings.

On 5 October 1959 Thomas/Mitzi was exhibited in court. But there was something different about her. She was wingless. Douglas Shelton opened a box and displayed two large balls of fur. Thomas shed her wings in July, he said. Mrs Hicks denied that the cat was hers, and a confused judge awarded the animal to Douglas and compensated Mrs Hicks with one dollar for damages.

John Keel says that in 1966 he passed through Pinesville and made enquiries for Thomas/Mitzi but without success. She and her various owners were nowhere to be found. It was not long since Peter Dance had seen the advertisement for Thomas Bessy, the winged cat which had been exhibited and had also been the subject of a famous lawsuit. Were these two cats one and the same? And what has happened to it or them? If anyone hears of another winged cat advertised for sale we would appreciate the information.

Yet another winged cat featured in the pages of *Weekend* (12 November 1980). This tortoiseshell cat, called Sandy, gained her wings when fully grown, but despite her impressive furry flaps she never flew. Sandy was exhibited at a carnival in Sutton-in-Ashfield, Nottinghamshire, in the 1950s, and is said to be remembered there still.

In another case we know of from recent years, a winged cat was seen by Rebecca Hough in Japan in May 1998. In a letter to *Fortean Times* (114, Sept 1998, p.50) she reports how, while in the town of Kumamoto in Kyushu, she saw a cat with a "bumpy" back. "Then I realised it had weird growths – not fat or bones – but jutting-out fur-covered wing-like growths. In all other respects

A tom cat called Sally which belonged to Mrs Roebuck of Attercliffe, Sheffield. This 1939 photograph shows Sally's two-foot wingspan which enabled him to make especially long leaps. Sally's markings are extremely close to the Oxford Zoo cat and it is possible that they were related.

This portrait of a winged cat appeared in the *Strand* magazine in November 1899. It belonged to a lady of Wiveliscombe, Somerset, to whom it had been given as a kitten.

it seemed quite normal. The growths were triangular and covered in soft fluffy fur. They felt like the wings of a chicken."

And our latest note of a winged cat is suitably enigmatic. A ginger cat sporting wing-like flaps was reportedly found in the central Russian village of Bukreyevik, near Kursk, and did not fare as well as our previous specimens. The villagers widely believed it was a "messenger of Satan" until a local drunk popped it into a sack and drowned it. (*MosNews*, 29 July 2004)

Zoologist Dr Karl Shuker has carried out one of the few serious studies of the phenomenon. In *Fortean Times* (78, Dec 1994, pp.32–33) he presents the novel theory that these cats might be suffering from an uncommon condition called feline cutaneous asthenia (FCA) which results in an elastic skin. In the normal course of FCA, the skin becomes extremely fragile and tears or sloughs off in time. The winged cats described above seem to be far more robust. Shuker also proposes that the earliest winged cat on record dates from 1868 when its skin was exhibited at a meeting of the Bombay Asiatic Society, the animal having been shot by one Alexander Gibson.

An advertisement in the Spanish daily paper *ABC*, announcing a forthcoming article about a cat with wings ("gata con alas") from Madrid named Angolina. The story duly appeared on 26 May 1950.

The winged cat which appeared in the yard of Banister Walton & Co., Trafford Park, Manchester, in the early 1970s and was resident there for several years.

Monkey chains

"When wolves cross a river, they follow one another directly in a line, the second holding the tail of the first in its mouth, the third that of the second, and so of the rest," (Abbé Pluché as quoted in Cassell's *World of Wonders*). We have searched in vain for witnesses' accounts of this performance and conclude either that the ancient Greek writers who reported it were testing our credulity, or that perhaps someone once trained captive wolves to hold each other's tails, like elephants at a circus, and that someone else saw the thing and garbled it in the retelling.

No one in modern times seems to have believed in the river-crossing wolf chain, but a similar belief, where the feat is attributed to monkeys, has proved more lasting.

An enduring feature of education in geography, until fairly recently, was the belief that the long-tailed monkeys of the South American jungles differed from their cousins in Africa and Asia in one important behavioural aspect arising from their extraordinarily prehensile tails. Gen-

erations of schoolchildren were presented with the charming picture of bands of resourceful monkeys crossing crocodile-infested rivers by forming themselves into a living bridge. Children's textbooks showed how one monkey would clutch a branch as anchor-man, while one after another the rest curled their tails around the monkey behind to form the next link in the chain, and when it was long enough they would swing to and fro until their momentum carried them out across the river. The monkey on the end would then grab a branch on the opposite bank, securing the chain while the old and young hurried across.

This example of collective intelligence and social organization was frequently and authoritatively cited, despite the doubts of no less a person than Alexander von Humboldt. He wrote, in his *Personal Narrative of Travels* (1852), that he believed the story had been invented by Europeans (probably as an instructive tale with which to admonish the natives) before passing into the traditions of the Mission Indians. However, the brothers H.M. and P.V.N. Myers, who explored the isthmus joining the two Americas in 1867–68, state in *Life and Nature under the Tropics* (1871)

Illustration of Charles Holder's account of a monkey chain in Professor George Holmes's *Fourth Reader* (1897).

that, despite seeing "…multitudes of these creatures, our observations convinced us that there was no foundation for the truth of the tale of the bridge-building monkeys".

In 1919 Professor E.W. Gudger wrote a short paper on the subject in *Natural History* (vol.19, no.2). He had reviewed the evidence with academicians and explorers attached to the American Museum of Natural History, and their opinion was that the monkey chain was a myth evolved from poor observations of the behaviour of individual monkeys, who were well known to dangle from branches by their tails or swing across gaps using liana vines. Further, Gudger doubted there would be enough room, where the dense jungle goes right up to the river's edge, for any living pendulum to work up a swing perpendicular to a river – unless they were dangling from a branch that already overhung the river.

The myth of the monkey chain, concluded Gudger, "attributes more collective intelligence to monkeys than they have ever been known to show". This sounds impressive, until one realizes the implication – that all other accounts would also be crediting the monkeys with more intelligence than they have ever been known to show –

making impossible any appeal to an accumulating body of testimony. The same reasoning denies the collective testimony of UFO or Nessie witnesses by criticizing individual accounts in isolation.

But how did the story gain credence? Had anyone actually seen a monkey chain? In 1735, Antonio de Ulloa joined an expedition in the Panama region and wrote, in his *Voyage to South America* (1760), about "the different species of monkeys, skipping in troops from tree to tree, hanging from branches and in other places, six, eight or more of them linked together, in order to pass a river". De Ulloa admits that the phenomenon "will perhaps appear fictitious to those who have not actually seen it", but does not clarify matters by stating specifically that he himself witnessed it. In fact it was de Ulloa's account that prompted Humboldt's refutation. Five years spent observing the monkeys convinced him that de Ulloa's assertion was "dubious".

However, Gudger located some earlier and more satisfying accounts. For example, Lionel Wafer was greatly amused by the antics of the monkeys which travelled through the trees alongside the party of the navigator Captain Dampier, while he was crossing the American isthmus. He wrote: "To pass from top to top of high trees, whose branches are a little too far asunder for their leaping, they will sometimes hang down by one another's tails in a chain; and swinging in that manner, the lowermost catches hold of a bough of the other tree, and draws up the rest of them." (*A New Voyage and Description of the Isthmus of America*, 1699)

But the earliest account is the best, originating with a Jesuit, José de Acosta, whose account was published in Spain in 1589, and later translated as *Naturall and Morall Historie of the East and West Indies* (1604). De Acosta states: "I did see in Capira one of these monkeys leape from one tree to another, which was on the other side of a river, making me much to wonder. They leape where they list, winding their tailes about a braunch to shake it; and when they will leape further than they can at once, they use a pretty devise, tying themselves by the tailes one of another, and by this meanes make as it were a chaine of many; then doe they launch themselves forth, and the first holpen by the force of the rest, takes holde where hee list, and so hangs to a bough, and so helpes all the rest, till they be gotten up." Gudger is certain that neither Wafer, de Ulloa, or Humboldt knew of this account, and claims it as the progenitor of the myth; and yet there is no sign here of a fable being spun for the edification of the ignorant.

The principal objection to the "myth" is that no such behaviour has been observed by contemporary naturalists – at least to their satisfaction. One of the most up-to-date accounts appeared in 1897, accompanied by the illustration we present on p.411. It was signed by Charles Frederick Holder, whom Gudger acknowledged as a naturalist of high standing, but despite a search Gudger could find no corroboration of it in Holder's own books. This account is of an undated trip up the Amazon. Nightfall caught the party up a side stream where for safety's sake they anchored in midstream under trees which arched from bank to bank overhead. Just before dawn Holder was woken by a blow on his face and caught a glimpse of a furry column swinging towards the far bank and pivoting from a branch of a tree on the opposite bank. It took him a few minutes to figure out what it was, and then: "The sight was so novel, the plan so daring, that I at once gave these queer bridge-makers my closest attention."

The monkey chain succeeded in securing itself on the farther bank after several tries, and Holder watched as the females, the young and old clambered across, until at last, startled by his sudden and irresistible laughter, the living bridge "dropped to pieces" and fled into the forest. Mrs Loudon, the author of a number of popular and well-respected natural history books, implies, in *The Entertaining Naturalist* (1867), that monkey-chain-type antics have been observed among the South American monkeys at London Zoo. But Gudger continues to maintain his objections on the grounds that no record of such behaviour has ever been reported in the *Proceedings* of the Zoological Society of London.

The only example we can find of creatures other than monkeys forming a living chain comes from a letter to *Animal and Zoo* magazine in about 1940 (our clipping is undated). In Africa, the writer saw an army of ants on the march, of the type that stop at no obstacle and devour everything in its path. A column of them was seen to cross a narrow ditch of water by means of an ant chain. It was formed by hundreds of the little creatures, holding on to each other, from bank to bank, while the rest swarmed across.

How rats steal eggs

A curiosity of animal behaviour that has always perplexed naturalists and is still not entirely explained is the ability of rats to take hold of hens' eggs and transport them considerable distances to their holes and dens. There was a debate on this in the old journal *Nature Notes*, beginning in May 1898 when a contributor, Edmund Daubeny, reported that a labourer near his home in Market Weston, Norfolk, had discovered stores of unbroken eggs in rat holes. These were in a ditch about half a mile away from the nearest source of eggs at a local farm. How, asked Daubeny, had the rats carried them there?

Nature Notes readers replied with a variety of answers, and Daubeny summarized them in the September issue of the journal. The four most popular suggestions were: that the rats form a line and hand the eggs from one to another; that they roll them along the ground with noses and forepaws; that they hold them under their chins and hop along on their back legs; and finally the old story, that one rat lies on its back, clutching an egg to its stomach while another draws it along by the tail. Daubeny dismissed all these explanations

and he was particularly hard on the last. He asked: "Is it likely that any animal would quietly submit to the ordeal of having its tail nipped and being rubbed the wrong way into the bargain? They would bump him terribly over rough ground, to the great danger of the egg; and how long would hair remain on his poor back, or the skin on his tail? … The theory lands us in endless difficulties, and I give it up."

Despite this rational dismissal, several correspondents repeated stories of rats being seen carrying off eggs, apparently by working out means of collaboration. One wrote that his neighbour in Derbyshire, "a truthful sort of person", had on two occasions in his youth seen a rat on its back, clutching an egg between its nose and paws and being carried by two others, one at each end. Another secondhand account, in the *Pall Mall Gazette* (quoted in E.L. Arnold's *Soul of the Beast*, 1960), told of a lady whose eggs were being stolen. "She hid up in her fowl house, and patiently waited till she saw a large rat run up a short ladder to a nest, and seize an egg between his paws. He then laid himself on his back, and held the egg on his chest. More rats appeared, and, forming themselves into a chain from the ground, they positively drew the rat with the egg

A nineteenth-century Japanese fan painting by Satake Eikai showing rats carrying away a large egg by dragging one of their number by the tail. Though widely believed, there are no first-hand accounts of this method.

An engraving which shows three egg-carrying rats negotiating a step by delicately passing the egg one to another.

down the ladder, passing it along from one to the other till it was safely below." A variation on this is given by the great rat authority, Rodwell, who tells how rats carry eggs up and down stairs. They pass them to each other, with their front paws when going downstairs and with their back legs when going up.

More recent observations tend to confirm the traditional account. In the 1980s a television programme which dismissed it as a fable prompted many viewers to respond with accounts of rats with eggs being dragged by the tail. Anthony Wootton in *Animal Folklore, Myth and Legend* (1986) says that he has literally dozens of such observations and that they are all much the same. "Essentially what happens, it seems, is that one rat lies on its back, clasping the egg (or whatever) between all four legs and paws, and is then dragged along by the tail, or sometimes the scruff of the neck, by the second; alternatively, the prone rat grasps the leader's tail in its teeth, thus making its passage slightly more comfortable, perhaps, in that it proceeds with the lie of the fur." The most

amazing account came from a man who witnessed a line of four rats, each holding in its teeth the tail of the one in front while the last one lay on its back clutching an egg. When they had taken the egg to where they wanted it they all returned and took another, drawing it along in the same way and taking five eggs in all.

There are even accounts of one rat pulling another by slinging its tail over its shoulder and grasping it with its paws, like a man dragging a sled. Wootton says that he has seen a nineteenth-century ornament carved with this scene. Scientists are generally sceptical about all these stories (mainly because they are frightened of anthropomorphizing or attributing human-type reasoning to animals) and it is unfortunate that there are no authentic photographs of egg-stealing rats. Someone who could have taken one was Mark Atkinson, a farmer on the Somerset Mendips, who told John Michell that as a young man he had seen an egg-clutching rat being dragged along by another, but instead of running for his camera he fetched a shotgun and blew the vermin away.

Rat Kings

In the case of MONKEY CHAINS (see p.410) the experts are divided on the credibility of the various accounts. In contrast, the story of the rat Kings is one of a peasant superstition that was verified, only to sink into obscurity. As curiosities go, the rat King seems even more obscure than most; even in its heyday it was hardly known outside Central Europe.

A rat King consists of a number of rats found with their tails inextricably tied together in a central knot. Another name for this fearful conglomeration is the Rat King's Throne. All the reports of rat Kings agree that only black rats are involved in these mysterious minglings; and one reason for the rarity of the phenomenon today might be the savage depletion of the black rat population by the hordes of brown rats that invaded Central Europe from the region of the Caspian Sea in the eighteenth century.

Most rat Kings have been found in continental Europe – none is known from Britain or the USA – and little has been written about

rat Kings in English; most accounts have never been translated out of their French and German originals. The earliest depiction of a King dates to 1564, and there is a reference by Martin Luther to one in 1524, so they must have been well known before that date. The naturalist Alfred Brehm collected stories of rat Kings, but when his *Thierleben* (1876–79) was translated into the multi-volume *Library of Natural History*, the editor, Richard Lydekker, saw fit to omit Brehm's pages on the subject.

The ground for the popular belief in rat Kings derives from the popular folk belief that each species of animal had its own society presided over by a king. The pioneer of cryptozoology, Conrad Gesner, wrote in 1555 of the belief that there were venerable rats who grew in size as they grew more ancient, and were tended by a pack who would steal food and fine velvet for their lord. No giant rat, imprisoned in splendour in a disused barn or cellar, was ever discovered, but as the original plague of black rats spread through Europe and ratting became a secure career for man and dog, the title of rat King was transferred to the occasional discovery of one of these tangled terrors of

The earliest known illustration of a rat King from Johannes Sambucus' *Emblemata* (1564).

verminous vermicelli. Brehm gives a list of a few discoveries including a notable one at Altenburg composed of twenty-seven individuals. Usually a lesser number were found knotted, like the eight-fold rat King killed in a Düsseldorf abattoir in February 1880, and the seven-fold rat King found at Châteaudun in November 1889 and presented to the museum there.

Perhaps the most astonishing case of all occurred in Döllstedt, a German village near Gotha, in December 1822, when farmhands threshing grain investigated a squealing in the attic of their barn. Climbing up they found a hollow on the topside of the main beam full of rats which made no attempt to escape. The hollow was clean and, according to one account, lined with straw. The rats inside were apathetic and weak from hunger. When they were pushed out, they fell in two squeaking clusters to the floor below; one was composed of twenty-eight individuals and the other of fourteen. Villagers gathered to see the marvel, and later joined in its execution with flails. The rats were separated with great difficulty, and a forester called to witness the strange discovery later testified that the skin on each tail was intact and "showed the impressions of the other tails, just like leather straps that had been plaited together for a long time."

The whole subject would have remained in the genre of "peasant superstitions" if a rat King had not been the subject of a legal squabble in 1774. A young man named Christian Kaiser, working in a mill at Lindenau near Leipzig, discovered a group made up of sixteen rats, while ratting in the mill on 12 January. A few days later he travelled to the district office of the government of Saxony in Leipzig. He alleged that a local character, Johann Adam Fasshauer, had gained possession of the prodigy with the pretence that he wanted a painting done of it. Instead, Fasshauer put it on public exhibition and pocketed a tidy sum which, Kaiser claimed,

A graphic illustration of a rat King from Henri Coupin's *Les animaux excentriques*.

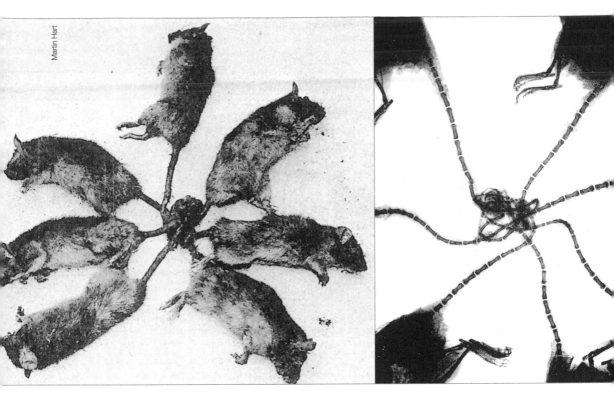

This 1963 rat King was discovered at Rucphen, in North Brabant, Holland. The X-ray of its knotted tail proves it is a real tangle and not, as has been suggested, a matter of being glued together.

rightfully belonged to his master. A tribunal took statements from all the witnesses, and then commissioned a doctor to examine the rat King, which he did in the Posthorn Inn at Lindenau and, despite Fasshauer's protests, attempted to separate the rats. The doctor reported that it was "not one organism which is called a rat King but sixteen different rats of different size and colouration, and (in my opinion) different age and sex." They seemed undernourished, and fifteen of them "had their tails knotted together into a large knot in such a manner that most tails were completely in the knot except for one or two inches near their bodies". The tail of the sixteenth was twisted around the back of another rat.

Whereas the testimony of the forester of Döllstedt might have implied that a rat King could have been formed while the rats were still very young, their tails growing and locking into the configurations of the knot, the findings of the doctor at Lindenau showed the rat King was a fairly recent formation, its individuals being of different ages,

sizes and so on. The doctor offered his theory that in excessively cold weather the rats huddle together for warmth, facing outwards for their mutual security. He had noted that their tails were dirty and speculated that urine and faeces from the ones in the upper circle had fallen onto the intertwined mass of tails and frozen solid. Brehm preferred his own theory – that huddling rats fall foul of a malady causing their tails to exude a fluid which then solidifies. Here is yet another curious case of a collector of stories going against the prevailing observations of his witnesses – which were that, apart from indentations from contact and pressure, the tails were apparently healthy.

Willy Ley, writing of his interest in rat Kings in *Galaxy* (October 1963), tried to find a modern case but could only come up with the ten-fold rat King found in the Westphalian village of Capelle in January 1907. It was quickly acquired by the Zoological Institute of the University of Göttingen, to the chagrin of their slower rivals in the Provincial Museum of Westphalia. The director

In recent years, we have heard less of rat Kings – perhaps the phenomenon is declining – instead we have at least three cases of squirrel Kings, something not recorded in any of the old annals. Our photograph shows a knot of four young squirrels found in Easton, Pennsylvania, in September 1989. Sixteen-year-old Crystal Cresseveur was on her way to church when she noticed a squeaking commotion in the hedge outside her house. At first, she thought the animals were playing, but a closer inspection revealed that the furry bundle was a knot of writhing squirrels who frightened and stuck among the bush trunks, pulling in all directions at once. Crystal called her father, Paul, who swept the bundle into a box and called the local wildlife conservation office. Sadly, they were put down after it was found that their tails and some of their hind legs were "crushed together". Almost exactly two years later, in Baltimore, Maryland, five young squirrels were seen to fall out of a tree "squabbling and fighting". They were cornered by teachers at the Reisterstown Elementary School. Animal control officers managed to separate the squirrels in this case, as their knot was made of tree sap and nest debris. Two of the five were albino, which makes the incident even rarer. The same fate awaited the five-squirrel knot found under a tree in Brantford, Ontario, in July 1997. A vet at the local Humane Society clinic managed to unbraid their tails.

of the Institute himself welcomed the celebrity, or celebrities, and personally conducted the examination. In answer to a professional query he confessed himself unable to account for the formation of the rat King. No modern zoologist claims to be any the wiser.

Our knowledge of the phenomenon has been greatly enlarged by the rat expert Martin Hart, who devotes a chapter to Kings in his *Rats* (1982), describing 57 discoveries between 1564 and 1963, including a ten-fold cluster of *Rattus brevicaudatus* (the only known exception to the black rat rule) in Java in March 1918. Hart's research led him to the discovery of a seven-fold King at Rucphen

in Holland, in February 1963 (this being in the very year that Ley wrote of his failure to find a modern case). At Rucphen, a farmer, investigating a squealing from a pile of bean sticks in his yard, saw a rat and killed it. As it would not budge when he tugged at it, he pulled away the sticks to reveal the six other black rats, which he also killed. They seemed to be of the same age and well fed. He offered the ratty tangle for study by veterinarians, resulting in a scientific description and a set of X-rays of the knotted tail showing fractures and calluses. This, wrote Hart, was final proof "that the tails had not grown together [but] had been knotted together for some considerable time".

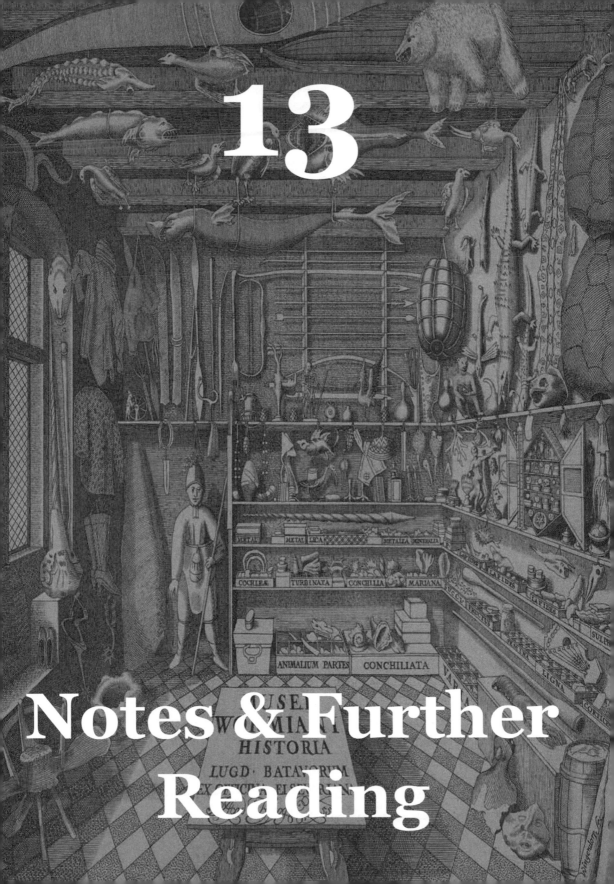

13

Notes & Further Reading

13

Notes and Further Reading

Introduction: the phenomenal world

For reasons of style or space, we have had to omit a great many additional and general references in the main text. We hope the references provided here – including a selection of excellent general sources and introductions to Charles Fort and unexplained phenomena – compensate. Most of them have their own (often extensive) bibliographies for anyone who wants to take their interest even further. This list includes many sceptical sources for two reasons: firstly, they are often well written and express opinions of which everyone interested in fortean phenomena should be aware; secondly, they are often well researched and come with good further reading lists of their own. Those with web access could simply enter any of our topics and key phrases into Google. To give you a good start (as the quality and reliability of resources varies greatly online), we mention below those websites that we found useful. Again, most of them have link sections worth exploring.

General reference

- Charles Fort's books: *Book of the Damned* (1919, 1995); *New Lands* (1923, 1996); *Lo!* (1931, 1996); *Wild Talents* (1932, 1998); and the collected edition *The Complete Books of Charles Fort* (1941, 1974). See

also the definitive online site by Mr X (www.resologist. net) who has devoted years to checking all of Charles Fort's thousands of sources to provide an online and corrected text and commentary to Fort's four books and other writings.

- The Charles Fort Institute (CFI) (www.forteana.org) A long-term project to establish an online museum, archive and library devoted to fortean topics and documentation. Site includes a biography of Fort, a bibliography of his writings, and blogs by fortean researchers.

- *Fortean Times* (FT) (www.forteantimes.com) a regular publication inspired by the writing and philosophy of Charles Fort. FT was established in 1973 as a primary forum for news and discussion with links to core and fringe forteana. There is an extensive online archive of news and articles going back to 1996 which include the sources of many of our FT references.

- *The Sourcebook Project* (www.science-frontiers. com/sourcebk.htm) founded by William R. Corliss, is a research and publishing project building a comprehensive survey of historical and contemporary anomalous phenomena. Compiled from 40,000 articles – the results of a thirty-year search through more than 12,000 volumes of scientific journals and literature – nearly thirty volumes have been published so far.

- The Society for Scientific Exploration (SSE) (www. scientificexploration.org) was founded at Stanford University, in 1982, by a group of fourteen scientists and scholars agreed on the need for a new type of scientific organization that would "...foster the serious and rational study of all questions that are amenable to scientific investigation, without restriction".

- Committee for the Scientific Investigation of Claims of the Paranormal (CSICOP) – www.csicop.org – the largest sceptical organization; founded by academics, in 1976, to resist the "tide of superstition". The site has many features including an extensive bibliography. A valuable exposition on the role and aims of CSICOP by George P. Hansen (originally published in the Journal of the American Society for Psychical Research, in January 1992) can be found at: www.tricksterbook.com /ArticlesOnline/CSICOPoverview.htm

Other anomalous groups

• Society for Interdisciplinary Studies (SIS) (www. knowledge.co.uk/sis/) keeps up to date with global and historical catastrophes, inspired by the eclectic theories of Immanuel Velikovsky.

• The Society for Psychical Research (SPR) (www.spr. ac.uk) was founded in 1882 by distinguished scientists to scientifically investigate paranormal phenomena of all kinds, although the main focus is on ESP, PSI, life-after-death and hauntings. They maintain an unrivalled archive and library on the subject and hold regular lecture programmes.

• The Association for the Scientific Study of Anomalous Phenomena (ASSAP) (www.assap .org) founded in 1981 by members of the Society for Psychical Research (SPR), to investigate anomalies outside the SPR's remit.

Other online resources

• The Skeptic's Dictionary (http://skepdic.com) an encyclopaedic collection of summaries and assessments of over 400 topics considered by founder Dr Robert T. Carroll to be "strange beliefs, amusing deceptions, and dangerous delusions".

• Strange magazine (www.strangemag.com) Founded by the late Mark Chorvinsky as a vehicle for in-depth investigations of mainly American forteana. Now online only, it's one of the best online resources on modern urban legends, hoaxes and superstitions. Also drop by The Museum of Hoaxes (www.museumofhoaxes.com) and Snopes (www.snopes.com).

• Other fortean periodicals: FATE magazine – www .fatemag.com – America's premier monthly on all matters "strange and unknown". Published continuously since 1948, The Anomalist – www. anomalist.com – is an online news digest with a periodically printed anthology of papers devoted to a fortean view of the mysteries of science, nature and history.

• Also recommended as a sound introductions to a rich spectrum of fortean material are: Janet & Colin Bord's Modern Mysteries of Britain (1987) and Modern Mysteries of the World (1989); the Peter Brookesmith-edited The Unexplained (1981–84); Jerome Clark, Encyclopedia of Strange and Unexplained Physical Phenomena (1993); Mike Dash, Borderlands (1997); Rupert Gould, Oddities (1928, 1965) and Enigmas (1929, 1965); Rosemary Ellen Guiley, ed, Encyclopedia of Mystical & Paranormal Experience (1991); Francis Hitching, The World Atlas Of Mysteries (1918); Brian Inglis, Natural and Supernatural: A History of the Paranormal from Earliest Times to 1914 (1977); Leslie Shepherd, ed, Encyclopedia Of Occultism and Parapsychology (1985); Una McGovern, Chambers's

Dictionary of the Unexplained (2007); Ivan T. Sanderson, Investigating the Unexplained (1972); Simon Welfare & John Fairley, Arthur C. Clarke's Mysterious World (1980) and Arthur C. Clarke's World of Strange Powers (1985); Colin Wilson, The Occult (1971, 2006) and Mysteries (1978, 2006); and with Damon Wilson, Mammoth Encyclopedia of Unsolved Mysteries (2000).

Teleportation

Teleportation: its effects and uses

• Teleportation – the word was coined by Charles Fort and first used in the second chapter of his third book Lo! (1931) in a discussion of things observed to appear or to disappear or, hypothetically, that were transported from one point directly to another in an instant. In his Wild Talents (1932), Fort speculates that if the teleportative force ever fell under human control, it might account for poltergeist phenomena and the abilities attributed to witches.

• A fully referenced account of the experimental research into "quantum teleportation" and of an international team of physicists, led by Dr Charles H. Bennett, can be found at: www.research.ibm.com /quantuminfo/teleportation/

The teleportation of people

• The teleporting boy of the Ivory Coast – the original reportage was in the newspaper Ivoir'soir (7 Sept 1993), translated from the French by Ion Will and adapted by Jonathan Bryant for publication in Fortean Times 101 (Aug 1977).

• The account of the attacks in Bristol deserves to be better known, if only for being a period example of a sensible investigation into frightening phenomena. The original source – Henry Durbin, A Narrative of some Extraordinary Things that Happened to Mr Richard Giles's Children (1800) – has been privately reprinted a number of times. It is discussed in more detail in Alan Gauld & AD Cornell, Poltergeists (1979).

The materialisation and flight of objects

• Grottendieck's sober account of stones falling inside his home in Sumatra, in 1928, is a vital and thought-provoking document. It was published in the Society for Psychical Research Journal (vol.XII, pp.260–266) and is discussed in detail by WG Roll, The Poltergeist (1973) and D. Scott Rogo, The Poltergeist Experience (1979). This phenomenon figures in many of our sections, usually during poltergeist-type hauntings.

Levitation and spontaneous flight

• The earliest and still the broadest study of hagiographic levitation is Olivier Leroy's unrivalled book, Levitation (1928). Another important source is Fr. Herbert Thurston's Physical Phenomena of Mysticism (1952).

• The Skeptic's Dictionary's view of levitation as a trick: http://skepdic.com/levitat.html

- For an account of the levitation by Hindu sage Paramhansa Yogananda, see chapter 7 of his *Autobiography of a Yogi* (1946). A biography and online edition can be found at: www.ananda.org/ananda/yogananda.html

- Joseph Glanvill's *Sadducismus Triumphatus* – there is much scholarly variation about the man and his book. Some spelling his surname Glanvil; some giving the first title word as *Saducismus*; and with variations of the publication date. The basis of the book was first published in 1666 as *Full and Plain Evidence concerning Witches and Apparitions* with no illustrations. It was edited after Glanvill's death by the philosopher Henry More and first published with its more familiar title and woodcuts in 1681. This was one of the first popular works in English literature to tackle the rising scepticism of scientific materialism. Glanvill also argued for the pre-existence of human souls (useful for explaining ideas about transmigration and reincarnation), and was a chaplain to Charles II.

Strange Rains

Falls of fishes and frogs

- Aberdare fish fall – Robert Schadewald's investigation report appeared in *Fortean Times* 30 (1979), pp.38–42 and *Fortean Times* 31 p.54.

- For reports of Australian fish falls see – Paul Cropper & Tony Healy, "Raining sprats and cods", *Fortean Times* 106 (Jan 1998) p.35 – and www.forteantimes.com/articles/106_sprats.shtml

- Mr X's documentation of Fort's own investigation of the fall of fish at Dundas, Canada, in 1926 can be found at www.resologist.net/art02.htm

- The modern chronicler of anomalistics, William R. Corliss, has made photocopied editions of rare fortean sources relating to German naturalist Hartwig available from his website – www.science-frontiers.com – including Hartwig's 560-page meteorological compendium *The Aerial World* (1886).

Theories and explanations

- For information on Gudger see the Bob Rickard article "The fish-fall papers of EW Gudger", *Fortean Studies* (1995), vol 2, pp.64–100, which includes a three-page bibliography.

Anomalies and questions

- Robert Schadewald's account of his fish fall experiments – "Fish Falls and Whirlwinds" – can be found in *Fortean Times* 22 (1977), pp.31–33.

Missiles from above

- *Fundación Anomalía* (the Anomaly Foundation), was founded in 1997, in Spain, to promote scientific investigation of unusual aerial phenomena (mainly UFOs), to preserve the related documentation gathered in Spain in the last fifty years, to provide scholarships, grants and prizes, and to publish specialized journals and books. Their account of the Spanish ice falls can be found at: www.anomalia.org/premio01en.htm

- "Megacryometeors" – Jesus Martinez-Frias claims credit for coining the word to describe anomalous falls of large blocks of atmospheric ice in a paper he presented to the "Environmental Catastrophes and Recoveries in the Holocene" conference at Brunel University, Uxbridge, UK, in the autumn of 2002: http://atlas-conferences.com/cgi-bin/abstract/caji-24

- A critique of Martinez-Frias's ideas by geologist Sharon Hill can be found at: http://mywebpages.comcast.net/scientia/icefall.htm – compare with conventional giant hail: www.theweatherprediction.com/habyhints/342/

- Himalayan hail deaths – see *Fortean Times* 182 (April 2004) p.23.

Falls of artefacts

- The Klaipeda notecase – when *Fortean Times* correspondent Anthony J. Bell went to see Mrs Connolly, she confessed that she had experienced much odd phenomena since childhood. Bell wrote it up in a well-remembered article that explored the idea of "lexi-linking" – associations based on similarities in the sounds and meanings of words and syllables. See *Fortean Times* 15 (1976), p.17; *Fortean Times* 17 (1976), p.5; and *Fortean Times* 20 (1977), p.14.

Rains of seeds and organic matter

- For a reference article on coloured rains by Mark Chorvinsky click: www.strangemag.com/redrain.html

- For an online selection of reports (of unknown authorship) of falls of "angel hair", "star jelly", "flesh" and "stones", drop by the resources to be found here: www.subversiveelement.com/SkyFallsHome.html

- Historical Irish forteana – Another source from the same period as *The Annals of Clonmacnoise* is known as *The Annals of the Four Masters*, compiled between the years 1632 and 1638. Its treasure trove of strange phenomena was extracted by Dr Peter Alderson Smith and published in *Fortean Times* 54 (1990), pp.51–56.

Mysterious flows and oozings

- Arle-sur-Tech – Our information is taken from Peter Ratazzi's account: "Healing waters from the tomb", in *Fortean Times* 28 (1979), pp.38–41.

Wild Talents

Fire-walking and fire-immunity

- To sign up for a tutorial in fire-walking for "personal growth" hotfoot it down to the Wings of Fire website: www.firewalking.org

Fire affinity and fire starters

- For a "skeptical" view of some major cases: www.csicop.org/si/9611/shc.html and www.csicop.org/si/9803/shc.html

Electric people

- One of the few scientists to have delved deeper into the mystery of human bio-electricity is Michael Shallis, whose main books on the topic are: *The Electric Shock Book* (1985) and *The Electric Connection: its Affects on Mind and Body* (1990).

- Also see the articles: "Human magnets", *Fortean Times* 59 (Sept 1991) p.11; and Bill Love, "Shock to the System", *Fortean Times* 171 (June 2003) pp.48–53. And for an archive of modern personal stories of having high static charges: www.amasci.com/weird/unusual/zap.html

- Angèlique Cottin – a modern review of her phenomena can be found here: www.mysteriouspeople.com/poltergeist_girl.htm

Projected thought-forms

- See also the additional notes under "Photographs of the gods" (p.434).

- Ted Serios – Serios was an alcoholic Chicago hotel porter who died in 1990. Part of the furore caused by Serios among skeptical scientists was that his phenomena was endorsed by Eisenbud (1908–99), a respected psychiatrist and faculty member of the University of Colorado Medical Center. The most detailed study of Ted's "paranormal" imaging in Dr Jule Eisenbud's 1967 study, *The World of Ted Serios: Thoughtographic Studies of an Extraordinary Mind*. Online examples of Serios's "thoughtography" can be found at: www.bluroftheotherworldly.com/serios.html – in addition, three other sites of interest are a sceptical point-of-view: http://forums.randi.org/archive/index.php/t-10372.html; the memoirs of an eyewitness: www.niler.com/estitle.html; and a biography of Serios: http://en.wikipedia.org/wiki/Ted_Serios

- *The Skeptic's Dictionary's* assessment of the hypothesis that mental images can be "imprinted" onto sealed film can be read on this Web page: http://skepdic.com/pphotog.html

- A commemorative site dedicated to the exploits of Alexandra David-Neel is to be found at: www.alexandra-david-neel.org/anglais/acca.htm

Stigmata

- The "official" view: *Catholic Encyclopedia* on "mystical stigmata": www.newadvent.org/cathen/14294b.htm. See http://crystalinks.com/stigmata.html for an "unofficial" general reference.

- St Pio's account of his stigmata to his spiritual advisor is available at: www.padrepio.com/app2.html. Particularly poignant is his entreaty to Jesus to end the phenomena as he feared "bleeding to death".

- And for the "skeptics" view of stigmatic phenomena: Joe Nickel, "The stigmata of Lilian Bernas", *Skeptical Inquirer* (March–April 2004): www.csicop.org/si/2004-03/i-files.html

- Peter Rogerson discusses Heather Woods in the general context of visionaries, abductees, mystics and experiencers of OOBEs (etc): "Blood, Vision and Brimstone pt.1", *Magonia* 53 (August 1995) – also accessible online here: www.magonia.demon.co.uk/arc/90/blood.htm

- Enzo Daedro on a number of modern South American stigmatics: "Blood, Sweat and Tears", *Fortean Times* 163 (October 2002) p.36–40 – also accessible online at: www.forteantimes.com/articles/163_stigmatics.shtml

- Ted Harrison, in his book *Stigmata: A Medical Mystery in a Modern Age* (1996) observed that the marks "…provoke wonder, fear, awe, skepticism, cynicism, and both belief and non-belief … Whether the marks are psychosomatic, (mentally induced) physical, or bordering on the fraudulent (dishonest), the most important thing will be the response made by people … when they see them." We thought that statement could apply just as well to crop circles and UFOs.

The Incorruptables

- For more modern cases see: Dwight Longnecker, "Saints preserve us", *Fortean Times* 159 (June 2002) pp.42–45; and for the "Perfect Preservation" of a monk who died in the meditation position, *Fortean Times* 184 (June 2004) p.26.

- A Catholic community info site on incorruption: http://members.aol.com/ccmail/incorruptbodies.html

- Natural methods of preservation are reviewed at *The Skeptic's Dictionary*: http://skepdic.com/incorrupt.html

- The controversial case of Anneliese Michell has, since, been made into a film: *The Exorcism of Emily Rose* (2005). Promoted as a "true story", the movie has been criticized for wildly deviating from the "facts" – see: http://paranormal.about.com/od/demonsandexorcism/a/aa090505_2.htm

Near-death experiences and the Life Review

- Sources of further reading on NDEs are many and varied but a good selection includes: Susan Blackmore, *Dying to Live* (1993); David Lorrimer, *Whole in One: The Near-Death Experience and the Ethic of Interconnectedness* (1990); Craig Lundahl, *A Collection of Near-Death Research Readings* (1982); Raymond Moody, *Reflections on Life after Life* (1977), *Life after Life* (1975), and *The Last Laugh* (1999); Sylvan Muldoon & Hereward Carrington, *The Projection of the Astral Body* (1929, 1971); Karlis Osis & E. Haraldsson, *At the Hour of Death* (1977); Kenneth Ring, *The Omega Project: Near-Death Experiences, UFO Encounters and Mind at Large* (1992), and *Lessons from the Light* (1998); Scott Rogo, *The Return from Silence* (1989); Michael Sabom, *Recollections of Death: A Medical Investigation* (1982); Victor Zammit, *A Lawyer Presents the Case for the Afterlife* (2000). See also: W.Y. Evans-Wentz, *The Tibetan Book of the Dead* (1927); Karma-Gling-Pa, Donald S. Lopez and W.Y. Evans-Wentz, *The Tibetan Book of the Dead: Or The After-Death Experiences on the Bardo Plane, according to Lama Kazi Dawa-Samdup's English Rendering* (2000).

- For a good introduction to OBEs: H.F. Prevost-Battersby, *Man Outside Himself: Methods of Astral Projection* (1969); Sylvan Muldoon & Hereward

Carrington, *The Phenomena of Astral Projection* (1951); Scott Rogo, *Mind Beyond the Body* (1978) and *Leaving the Body* (1983); Suzy Smith, *The Enigma of Out-of-the-Body Travel* (1965); Benjamin Walker, *Beyond the Body: The Human Double and the Astral Planes* (1974); and the works of Dr Robert Crookall (below). Books based on personal experience include: Oliver Fox, *Astral Projection: A Record of Out-of-the-Body Experiences* (1962); Robert A. Monroe, *Journeys Out of the Body* (1971); Sylvan Muldoon & Hereward Carrington, *Projection of the Astral Body* (1929, 1981); Ingo Swann, *To Kiss Earth Goodbye* (1975). Among the proliferation of "DIY" guides, see: Janet Lee Mitchell, *Out-of-Body Experiences* (1985, 1988); "Yram", *Practical Astral Projection* (1974); Sylvan Muldoon, *The Case for Astral Projection* (1936).

• Preliminary studies by the psychology department of London's Goldsmith's College, suggest that perhaps as many as forty percent of people may have experienced some form of "sleep paralysis" involving the feeling of a presence in the room, pressure on the chest, and both aural and visual hallucinations. See Mark Pilkington's report on the Seventh European Congress of Psychology held at London's Barbican Centre, 2001: "All in the Mind", *Fortean Times* 150 (Sept 2001) p.24.

• On the "optical" mechanism for "darkness" and "tunnels" and other OBE imagery: www.csicop.org /si/2004-05/near-death-experience.html. Additionally, for the neuro-psychiatric view see Ronald Siegel's *Hallucinations* (1975).

• The International Association for Near-Death Studies (IANDS), founded in 1978, homepage: www.iands.org

• The life and writings of Dr Robert Crookall: www.spiritonline.com/files/messages/15/348.html – particularly see his *The Study and Practise of Astral Projection* (1961), *More Astral Projections, Analyses of Case Histories* (1964), and *The Jung-Jaffé view of Out-of-the-Body Experiences* (1970).

• For a sceptical view of the subject, visit: http://skepdic.com/astralpr.html and http://skepdic .com/obe.html

The Madness of Crowds

• Books on "mass hysteria" tend to be general and historical. One of the earliest, was the groundbreaking *Memoirs of Extraordinary Popular Delusion and the Madness of Crowds* (1841) by Charles Mackay, revised and expanded for later editions. Equally influential are: Norman Cohn's, *The Pursuit of the Millennium: Revolutionary Millenarians and Mystical Anarchists of the Middle Ages* (1957) and *Europe's Inner Demons: The Demonization of Christians in Medieval Christendom* (rev. 2000); C.G. Jung, *Flying Saucers: The Modern Myth of Things seen in the Sky* (1959); Elaine Showalter, *Hystories* (1997); and Jacques Vallée, *Passport to Magonia: From Folklore to Flying Saucers* (1970).

• A modern overview of "mass hysteria" in different cultures, with good research and documentation, and a range of cases from the historical to the current, are the studies by sociologist Dr Robert Bartholomew: *Mass Hysteria: A Social History of the Strange* (1995); *Exotic Deviance: Medicalizing Cultural Idioms from Strangeness to Illness* (2000); *Little Green Men, Meowing Nuns and Head-hunting Panics: A Study of Mass Psychogenic Illnesses and Social Delusion* (2001); with Benjamin Radford, *Hoaxes, Myths and Manias* (2003); with Hilary Evans, *Panic Attacks: The History of Mass Delusion* (2004). See also Kevin McClure's study of the "Great Revival" of 1904, *Stars and Rumours of Stars: The Egryn Lights and other Mysterious Phenomena in the Welsh Religious Revival, 1904–05* (1980) – the text of which is available online at: www.magonia.demon.co.uk/news/reviews/stars01.htm

• To view a summary selection of 23 of the last millennium's notorious episodes of "mass delusion and hysteria" by Robert Bartholomew and Erich Goode, click through to: www.csicop.org/si/2000-05/delusions .html – see also the *Skeptic's Dictionary* on "collective hallucinations": http://skepdic.com/collective.html

• For probably the best archive of urban legends, contemporary mythology and rumours on the web visit: www.snopes.com

Shared visions and visual rumours

• See all the books mentioned in "The Madness of Crowds" section (above) and "Guardian angels" (p.430).

• The *Skeptic's Dictionary* entry on "collective hallucinations" is also worth examination: http://skepdic.com/collective.html

• Peter Lamont claims – in his definitive study, *The Rise of the Indian Rope Trick* (2004) – that the popular conception of the "trick" originated in a hoax article published by the *Chicago Daily Tribune* in 1895. See an interview here: http://in.rediff.com/news/2004/aug /17inter.htm

• "Nigerian centaur spirit": Lagos, *This Day* (18 May 2003); "Tiger woman of Qom", *AP* (10 November 2003).

• More than ninety percent of reports of odd objects seen in the sky are very probably misperceptions and misunderstandings: see Alan Hendry, *The UFO Handbook: A Guide to Investigating, Evaluating, and Reporting UFO Sightings* (1979).

• Professors Bill Ellis and Jan Harold Brunvand have offered two views of "ostension" as analytical tools for folklorists. In one real-life events seem to imitate fiction, myth or legend; in the other real-life events give rise to new fictions, myths and legends: see: www.ostension. org/index.html See also: Bill Ellis, *Aliens Ghosts and Cults, Legends we Live* (2001).

• It has long been contended by forteans and sceptics alike that modern digital manipulation of images has become so sophisticated and commonly accessible that it effectively eliminates unsupported old-style photographs as proof in any unusual claim. See Bob Rickard's "The End of Photography as Evidence", *Fortean Times* 46 (Spring 1986) pp.34–35, and the preceding article by David Frost, "A Picture is worth 8x106 Bits", pp.32–34. More current examples are discussed in: www.trueauthority.com/cryptozoology /futility.htm

- Did NASA fake the Moon flights? Yes! – David Percy's explanatory photo-essay: *Fortean Times* 94 (Jan 1997) pp.34–39; and also: www.ufos-aliens.co.uk /cosmicapollo.html. Did NASA fake the Moon flights? No! – *Fortean Times* analysis with references: *Fortean Times* 97 (April 1997) pp.22–29. CSICOP rebuttal to the "NASA conspiracy" idea: www.csicop.org/si /2003-03/commentary.html. James Oberg's defence of NASA's missions: "Mission Aborted", *Fortean Times* 168 (March 2003) p.39; see also his website: www.jamesoberg.com

- Lunar anomalies, generally, see Mike Bara's large historical compendium: www.lunaranomalies.com. See also George Leonard, *Our Mysterious Spaceship Moon* (1975), and *Someone else is on our Moon* (1976). See also two articles in *Fortean Times* 112 (July 1998): Bob Rickard's "Lunar Construction Site", and Peter Grego's "Alien Moon".

- The closing quotation from Fort is paraphrased from his book *Lo!* (1931).

Social anxiety attacks

- See all the books mentioned in "The Madness of Crowds" (above).

- Sociological view of dancing manias: www.csicop .org/si/2000-07/dancing-mania.html

- Modern versions of medieval witch pogroms are, sadly, not hard to find. For an overview of the role played by children in witchcraft hysteria and trials from the 16th century to the present day (involving the recovery of "repressed memories" of abuse), see Hans Sebald, *Witch-children: from Salem to Modern Courtrooms* (1995).

- August Piper on multiple personality disorder (MPD) as an explanation for possession cases: www.csicop.org/si/9805/witch.html

- A particularly nasty outbreak of mass panic over "Ninja sorcerers" occurred in Indonesia in August 1998. It lead to riots in which 200 people were killed: *Fortean Times* 118 (Jan 1999) p.16.

- The fear of penis theft by magical means is an ancient belief and very important to some societies – for *Fortean Times* coverage of modern outbreaks of "penis theft panic" see: *Fortean Times* 56 p.33; *Fortean Times* 82 p.30; *Fortean Times* 87 p.45; *Fortean Times* 93 p.10; *Fortean Times* 99 p.12; *Fortean Times* 103 p.12; *Fortean Times* 105 p.21; *Fortean Times* 126 p.64; *Fortean Times* 148 p.43; and *Fortean Times* 156 p.10. See also the review of "koro" at: http://skepdic.com/ koro.html

- For Andrew Lawless's report on the Massa Marittima "penis-tree" mural, point your browser at: www.threemonkeysonline.com /threemonkeys_categories.php?category=history

Plagues, poisons and panics

- See all the books mentioned in "The Madness of Crowds" (above).

- Robert E. Bartholomew & Simon Wessely's valuable overview of "mass hysteria" can be found in the article,

"Protean nature of mass sociogenic illness: From possessed nuns to chemical and biological terrorism fears" in *The British Journal of Psychiatry* (2002) 180: pp.300–306. It can also be read on the Internet at: http://bjp.rcpsych.org/cgi/content/full/180/4/300

- Dancing mania, some resources: Robert E. Bartholomew, "Rethinking the Dancing Mania", *Skeptical Inquirer* (July/August 2000) and online at: www.csicop.org/si/2000-07/dancing-mania.html; Justus F.C. Hecker's classic *The Black Death and The Dancing Mania* (1833), translated from German, is available as a free eText from: www.gutenberg.org/etext/1739. And while medieval dance frenzies have long been regarded as a classic example of stress-induced mental disorder affecting mostly women, there is much evidence to the contrary: www.pbm.com/~lindahl/lod/vol3 /dancing_mania.html

- The mass collapse at Hollinwell: www.bbc.co.uk /insideout/eastmidlands/series4/holinwell_incident.shtml

- Salem. There are many sites devoted to the fatal hysteria in this New England town; among the most informative are: www.salemweb.com/memorial /stonesintro.shtml; for an overview of the trials from a legal point of view: www.law.umkc.edu/faculty/projects /ftrials/salem/SALEM.HTM; and for historical documentation of Salem: http://etext.virginia.edu/salem/ witchcraft/home.html. For full details of the belated apology for the trials and executions, see Richard Francis's *Judge Sewall's Apology: The Salem Witch Trials and the Forming of an American Conscience* (2005). Many others involved also made apologies, including one of the chief accusers, Anne Putnam, see: www.bookrags.com/history/americanhistory /the-apology-of-ann-putnam-jr-1706-b-wia-01/. Curiously, roughly three centuries later, in November 2001, the Massachusetts Legislature officially "cleared" five of those executed: www.rickross.com/reference/ wicca/wicca32.html

- The "Pokémon Panic" – Ben Radford reports in *Fortean Times* 149 (August 2001) p.36–40.

Wars of the worlds

- Everything you need to know about the original broadcast can be found at: www.war-of-the-worlds.org

- Robert Bartholomew, "The Martian Panic Sixty Years Later": www.csicop.org/si/9811/martian.html. See also Bartholomew, "The Martians are Coming", *Fortean Times* 199 (Aug 2005) pp.42–47.

- For anthologies of historical and modern conspiracies: Jonathan Vankin & John Whalen, *The 80 Greatest Conspiracies of All Time* (2004); and James McConnachie & Robin Tudge, *The Rough Guide to Conspiracy Theories* (2005). See also: www.steamshovelpress.com; and the very interesting general link site of uncertain authorship that can be found at: www.solungen.hm.no/razor/conspir.htm

- The Search for Extraterrestrial Intelligence (SETI): www.seti.org; the Wikipedia entry is also worth a look: http://en.wikipedia.org/wiki/SETI; and for the "how-you-can-help" experiment programme, tune in to: http://setiathome.berkeley.edu/

- A valuable overview of some of the more extreme

American conspiracy theories and cases of "mind control" paranoia are explored by Evan Harrington at this Web address: www.csicop.org/si/9609/conspiracy.html

• CSICOP take on "Pranks, Frauds and Hoaxes" here: www.csicop.org/si/2004-07/hoaxes.html

Religious apparitions

• For general surveys of the rich variety of religious visions see: Erich von Daniken's *Miracles of the Gods: A New Look at the Supernatural* (1974); Kevin McClure, *The Evidence For Visions Of The Virgin Mary* (1984); Ingo Swann, *The Great Apparitions Of Mary: An Examination of the Twenty-Two Supranormal Appearances* (1996); Sandra L Zimdarsswartz *Encountering Mary: Visions Of Mary From La Salette To Medjugorie* (1991).

• The Vatican's basis for judging apparitions and miracles is outlined at: www.theotokos.org.uk/pages/appdisce/cdftexte.html

• There are many websites offering historical lists of major and minor visions of Jesus and Mary etc. They range from the fairly sober Wikipedia article http://en.wikipedia.org/wiki/Marian_apparitions and www.udayton.edu/mary/resources/aprtable.html to those guided only by Catholic belief. Try: www.apparitions.org; http://198.62.75.1/www1/apparitions/http:/index.htm; http://members.aol.com/bjw1106/marian.htm; and www.mysteries-megasite.com/main/bigsearch/apparition-1.html

• Was the Fátima event a UFO? This theory attracted two Portuguese historians, Dr Fernandes and Ms D'Armada, whose books – *Heavenly Lights* (2005) and *Celestial Secrets* (2006) – compare the complex worlds of Catholic visions and modern ufology. Translated from the Portuguese, they place before scholars first-hand accounts, original depositions and interviews with the principal seers and witnesses. Even if you don't go along with the authors' conclusion – that this famous series of visions was a prolonged and orchestrated encounter with alien beings – you cannot fault their careful deconstruction of the events from contemporary documents preserved in the Fátima shrine archive.

• An interesting report of anomalous beliefs at Fátima, centuries before the famous 1917 apparitions can be inspected here: www.spiritdaily.org/Our%20Lady%20Apparitions/fatimahistory.htm

• The visionary phenomena at Medjugorje have become a prime example of how difficult modern visions have become to control for the Catholic Church. Randall Sullivan's book, *The Miracle Detective* (2004), is a personal investigation into the visionaries and their lives, the adoring community that thrives around them, and the subsequent factions and schisms it has caused with orthodox Catholicism and the local bishops. The Wikipedia article is a good place to start for an overview: http://en.wikipedia.org/wiki/Medjugorje

• Try these sites for the viewpoint of Medjugorje believers and pilgrims: www.medjugorjeusa.org/medjugorje.htm and www.medjugorje.hr/ulazakenstipe.htm. And for medical observations of the visionaries during their ecstasies read the accounts documented

here: www.medjugorje.org/science.htm

• The text of a fulmination by Medjugorje's Bishop Ratko Peric against the break-away cult of the young visionaries is reproduced at: www.mdaviesonmedj.com/page_lateststatement.htm. See also this text report of an official commission to assess the authenticity of the visions: www.ewtn.com/expert/answers/medjugorje.htm

• Another voice against the "spectacle" of Medjugorje is disillusioned pastor Dr Michael Jones: "Proponents of the apparition like to talk about its fruits [of the apparitions]. All right, let's talk about the fruits: the broken families, the pregnant nuns, the poor people bilked of their money, the division in the Church, the *de facto* schism, the worst fighting in Europe since World War II, the ethnic cleansing of Muslims from Gradno, just five kilometres from Medjugorje; all of it followed inexorably from those children on that hill in Bosnia in June of 1981." (www.culturewars.com/medj.htm)

• Here, Raymond Eve compares, generally, the political and social impact of visions: www.csicop.org/si/2002-11/medjugorje.html

• Watchman.org, meanwhile, is a Christian organisation that monitors contemporary cults and groups. The site features valuable bibliography and links pages: www.watchman.org

The Fairy Folk

• A sound introduction, online, to the modern study of fairies is Bob Trubshaw's www.indigogroup.co.uk/edge/fairies.htm. As for further reading, there are many good books on fairylore, ancient and modern, with extensive bibliographies, such as the excellently referenced *Explore Fairy Traditions* (2005) by Jeremy Harte. The following are also worthy: Katherine Briggs, *A Dictionary of Fairies* (1976) and *The Vanishing People* (1978); Thomas Crofton Croker's *Fairy Legends and Traditions of the South of Ireland* (1828); William Crossing, *Tales of the Dartmoor Pixies* (1890); Mike Dash, *Borderlands* (1997); Gillian Edwards, *Hobgoblin and Sweet Puck* (1974); W.Y. Evans Wentz, *The Fairy Faith in Celtic Countries* (1911); Edward L. Gardner, *Fairies* (1945); Augusta, Lady Gregory, *Visions and Beliefs in the West of Ireland* (1920); Patrick Harpur, *Daimonic Reality: A Field Guide To The Otherworld* (1994); Edwin S. Hartland, *The Science of Fairytales: An Inquiry into Fairy Mythology* (1891); Robert Hunt, *Popular Romances of the West of England* (1865); Thomas Keightley, *The Fairy Mythology* (1828); Robert Kirk, *The Secret Commonwealth of Elves, Fauns and Fairies* (1691); David MacRitchie, *The Testimony of Tradition* (1890); Ernest W. Marwick, *The Folklore of Orkney and Shetland* (1975); Sophia Morrison, *Manx Fairy Tales* (1911); Peter Narvaez, ed, *The Good People: New Essays In Fairylore* (1991); Walter Scott, *Minstrelsy of the Scottish Borders* (1803); Wirt Sikes, *British Goblins* (1880); Lewis Spence, *British Fairy Origins* (1946) and *The Fairy Tradition in Britain* (1948); Carolyn White, *A History of Irish Fairies* (1976); W.G. Wood-Martin, *Traces of the Elder Faiths of Ireland* (1902).

Fairies, ancient and modern

• Fairies as a "cultural" memory of the Picts:

Archeologists and anthropologists since the 19th century were decided in their view of the Picts as a type of small, primitive human. For example, a paper in the *Journal of the Royal Anthropological Institute* (1944, vol.74, pp.25–32) describes the denizens of Orkney as "…only a little exceeding pigmies in stature". About the same period, the idea that the Scottish fairies were a "racial memory" of the Picts was being popularized by Victorian novelists such as Arthur Machen.

Since then, modern fairylore specialists have tended to add their own "cultural evidence" to this theory. L.A. Waddell – in *The Phoenician Origin of The Britons, Scots & Anglo-Saxons* (1924) – prefers an even older lexilink: "This early association of the Picts with 'petty' and witches would now seem to explain why in modern folklore these dwarfish people are associated and identified with Fauns, Fians, Pixies and wicked Fairies – indeed the modern word 'wicked' is derived from 'witch' and thus seen to have its origin in the Gothic *Vithi*, 'the wicked witch' title of the Van ancestors of the Picts, a people who all along appear to have been devotees of the cult of the Serpent and its Matriarchist witches and their magic cauldron." Again, according to Katherine Briggs' *Dictionary of Fairies* (1976), the connection originates in a confusion between Picts and *Pechs* or *Pehts*, which are Scottish Lowland names for fairies.

The association is undoubtedly ancient and seems to have been reinforced at several points in history. For example, according to the *Orkneyinga Saga* – a 13th century account of conquest of Orkney by Norway in the eighth and ninth centuries – when Sigurd, the first Earl of Orkney, and his men first sighted the short, dark people, they were immediately taken for elves. When the islanders were found to be living in mounds with subterranean chambers – which the Norse mistook for tombs – it confirmed their presumption that these short, dark people were, indeed, a race from the Underworld (see: www.orkneyjar.com/sitemap.html). While such associations might be suitable for the Scottish Highlands and Islands, it is difficult to see how this theory can be rolled out to account for the fairies of other cultures and countries.

• For the similarities between experiences of fairies and of aliens see: Janet Bord, *Fairies: Real Encounters with Little People* (1997); Thomas E. Bullard, *Mysteries in the Eye of the Beholder: UFOs and their Correlates as a Folkloric Theme Past and Present* (dissertation, 1982); John Michell, *The Flying Saucer Vision* (1967); Peter Rojcewicz, *The Boundaries of Orthodoxy: A Folkloric look at the UFO Phenomenon* (dissertation, 1984); Jacques Vallée, *Passport to Magonia: From Folklore to Flying Saucers* (1970); and also David Sivier's discussion of folklore motif overlap: "Indexing the Machine Elves", *Magonia* 90 (Nov 2005) p.14. See also "Magonia" under "Invisible assailants" below.

• For more on Jean Hingley's fairy-like aliens, see: Alfred Budden's article "The Mince Pie Martians", *Fortean Times* 50 (Summer 1988) pp.40–44.

• For Icelandic fairies, see: *Fortean Times* 43 (Spring 1985) p.45; *Fortean Times* 74 (April/May 1994) p.16; and Claire Smith's "The Land of the Hidden People" in *Fortean Times* 201 (Sept 2005) pp.42–47.

• For an introduction to Cornish fairies, visit: www.gandolf.com/cornwall/fairies/index.shtml

• Cottingley fairies. For a thorough re-investigation of the case see: Joe Cooper's *The Case of the Cottingley Fairies* (1990), extracted online at: www.lhup.edu/~dsimanek/cooper.htm. There is also a very useful archive of documentation on all aspects of the case, including location photos and transcripts of Conan Doyle's letters at: www.cottingley.net/cfph.shtml

• On the overlap between spiritualism, "clairvoyance" and seeing fairies, see: Cyril Scott (ed) *The Boy who saw True* (1953, 2004).

Physical fragments of Fairyland

• Literary discussions of fairy artefacts are quite rare, but these will do until others turn up: Arthur Conan Doyle, *The Coming of the Fairies* (1922) on the Cottingley fairies; Edwin S, Hartland, *The Science of Fairy Tales,* (1891), chapter 3, which is on objects from Fairyland; Leslie V. Grinsell, *Folklore of Prehistoric Sites in Britain,* (1976) has much on sites of fairy treasure, stolen chalices, dances, music etc., county by county.

• For more on the Fairy flag of Dunvegan Castle, see Nancy MacCorkill's illustrated account at: www.geocities.com/~sconemac/fflag.html

• For an online descriptions of a "fairy cup" in the Manx Museum: www.gov.im/mnh/collections/social/hearthandhome/fairy.xml

• Elfbolts – taken literally as tiny triangular flint "arrowheads" – are discussed by Niko Silvester, in "The Folklore of Flint-knapping": www.geocities.com/knappersanonymous/folklore.html. Elfbolts, "fairy arrows" and the "fairy stroke" or "blast" in the folkloric context are more fully discussed and referenced by Barbara Rieti in "The Blast in Newfoundland Fairy Tradition" in Narvaez (ed) *The Good People: New Essays In Fairylore* (1991), pp.284–297; and more briefly in Katherine Briggs' *The Vanishing People* (1978).

Mystical lights

• For dramatic engravings of lightning, "Will o' the Wisp"s and other natural luminosities, see W. de Fonvielle's *Thunder and Lightning* (1867). Numerous references to these under various names can be found in the books listed above for "Fairies, Ancient and Modern".

• Phosphoretted hydrogen is also known as the gas phosphine and archaically spelled "phosphuretted". For more on this, see Thomas Lamb Phipson's *Phosphorescence: or, the emission of Light by Minerals, Plants, and Animals* (1862), which contains further folkloric anecdotes.

• Investigations of thirty US "spook light" locations: www.astronomycafe.net/weird/lights/spooklights.html

• Australian neuroscientist explains the "min min" spook light as a mirage: www.abc.net.au/science/news/stories/s818193.htm

• *The Encyclopedia of Astrobiology, Astronomy, and Spaceflight* has an interesting section on the subject of Earthlights: www.daviddarling.info/encyclopedia/E/earthlight.html; while the Wikipedia article on Michael Persinger's "tectonic strain" theory of seismic luminescence is also enlightening:

http://en.wikipedia.org/wiki/Michael_Persinger; Paul Devereux has also done extensive work and writing on the subject. See his seminal *Earthlights* (1982) and www.forteantimes.com /articles/103_earth.shtml. Online monitoring of the lights at Hessdalen, Norway, since 1996, is documented here: www.hessdalen.org/station/; and Dr David Clarke can be read on the mystery lights of the UK's Peak District here: www.indigogroup.co.uk/edge/Peakland.htm

• Could the Rendlesham UFO case be explained as a "Jack o' Lantern"? This article investigates: www.forteantimes.com/articles/204_magic2.shtml

• Strange lights were seen during the "Great revival" of 1904: see Kevin McClure's *Stars and Rumours of Stars: The Egryn Lights and other Mysterious Phenomena in the Welsh Religious Revival, 1904–1905* (1980), the text of which is available online at: www.magonia.demon.co.uk/news/reviews/stars01.htm

Phantom music and strange voices

• Key reading on fairy music: Peter Guy, *The Island of Fetlar* (1991); Jeremy Harte, *Explore Fairy Traditions* (2004) – Ernest Marwick, *The Folklore of Orkney and Shetland* (1975); and Leslie V. Grinsell, *The Folklore of Prehistoric Sites in Britain* (1976). See also Ríonach Uí Ógáin's "Music learned from the fairies", in the Irish folklore journal *Bealoideas* (1992–93).

• A good source for John Aubrey's stories is *Three Prose Works* (1972), being a reprinting of Aubrey's *Miscellanies upon various Subjects, Remaines Of Gentilisme And Judaisme*, and *Observations*.

• The "Hummadruz" has not received the attention an important anomaly deserves. Among the few sources is John Billingsley's article "Humdinger" in *Fortean Times* 115 (Oct 1998) pp.28–31, which is expanded at: www.northernearth.co.uk/permhum.htm. See also the readers' letters in *Fortean Times* 117 (Dec 1998) p.53; *Fortean Times* 118 (Jan 1999) p.52 and *Fortean Times* 120 (March 1999) p.50.

• Electronic Voice Phenomena (EVP). Key books: Anabela Cardosa, *ITC Voices: Contact with Another Reality* (2003); Konstantin Raudive, *Breakthrough: An Amazing Experiment in Electronic Communication* (1971); D. Scott Rogo & Raymond Bayless, *Phone Calls from the Dead* (1979); Jurgen Heinzerling: *Fortean Times* 104 pp.26–30, which is also online with an introduction by Judith Chisholm: www.forteantimes .com/articles/194_evp1.shtml

Away with the fairies

• Further reading on supernatural abduction – Hilda Ellis Davidson and Anna Chaudhri, *Supernatural Enemies* (2001); Robert Kirk, *The Secret Commonwealth of Elves, Fauns and Fairies* (1691). See also the books under "Otherworldly abductions" (below).

• Bathurst – Charles Fort wrote of Bathurst's disappearance: "Here is the shortest story that I know of … He walked around the horses." (*Lo!* 1931, p.681). The case was thoroughly analysed by Dr Mike Dash in the context of the political intrigues of Napoleonic Europe: "The Disappearance of Benjamin Bathurst" in

Fortean Times 54 (1990) pp.40–44.

• For an overview of the "alien abduction phenomenon", including references to the use of hypnosis in recovery of memories, brain function, help groups and the main "promoters", see: http:// en.wikipedia.org/wiki/Alien_abduction; and Thomas Bullard (ed) *UFO Abductions: The Measure Of A Mystery* (1987).

• The Lang-Lerch-Ashmore disappearances. See a critique by T. Peter Park, "Vanishing Vanishings", in *The Anomalist* 7 (Winter 1998).

• A good starting point for exploring the "psycho-social" hypothesis (regarding "abductions") is the Wikipedia entry: http://en.wikipedia.org/wiki /Psychosocial_Hypothesis. Articles in *Magonia* magazine (www.magonia.demon.co.uk/) also regularly debate this topic: http://magonia.mysite.wanadoo-members .co.uk/pelican18.htm and www.magonia.demon.co.uk /arc/80/why.htm

• Travis Walton has his own site: www.travis-walton. com. Walton interviewes can be found at www.our-j.com/qa_tw.html and a good online summary of the case is located at http://anw.com/fire/GPriceReport.htm. Two books that provide a wider analysis of the Walton case are the "anti" Philip Klass, *UFOs: The Public Deceived* (1983) and the "pro": Bill Barry, *The Ultimate Encounter* (1978).

• On *tengu* generally, see: www.onmarkproductions. com/html/tengu.shtml. On *tengu* abductions, besides Carmen Blacker's important book, we found her paper on "Supernatural abductions in Japanese folklore", in *Asian Folklore Studies* vol.26 (1967), to be very relevant to the study of Western experiences of fairy and alien abductions. See also Birgit Staemmler's paper on *kamikakushi* (Japanese, abduction by divine beings) available at: www.nanzan-u.ac.jp/SHUBUNKEN/ publications/jjrs/pdf/725.pdf. Also worth reading is the article by James W. Boyd and Tetsuya Nishimura, explaining Miyazaki's 2001 anime *Spirited Away* as a modern re-telling of a supernatural abduction: www.unomaha.edu/jrf/Vol8No2/boydShinto.htm

• Betty Andreasson – Raymond Fowler has chronicled the Andreasson story over five volumes, beginning with *The Andreasson Affair* (1979) and ending with *The Andreasson Legacy* (1997). An overview of the series is at: www.geocities.com/Area51/Shadowlands/6583 /abduct089.html. Mrs Andreasson's "abduction" experiences are, at times, indistinguishable from OOBEs, see: www.near-death.com/experiences /triggers19.html

• Anne Jeffries and the fairies. See Lucy Gura's article "Dances with Fairies", *Fortean Times* 198 (July 2005) pp.38–41. Also read Moses Pitt's 1696 account, found at www.stteath.org.uk/histjeffries.htm and www.gandolf. com/cornwall/fairies

Mysterious Entities

Otherworldly abductions

• The range of books available is large and diverse. Many others are mentioned in other sections of this book where "abduction" experiences overlap with other forms of phenomenal experience, but the following deal specifically with the encounter experience and represent the main opinions:

- On ufology and extraterrestrial life: Joe Lewells, *The God Hypothesis: Extraterrestrial Life and its Implications for Science and Religion* (1997). For a general cultural history of modern ufology see Bruce Lanier Wright: www.strangemag.com/invadersfromelsewhere1.html. For a comprehensive snapshot of modern ufology, see Jerome Clark's three-volume *UFO Encyclopedia* (1998, 2nd edition) and Ronald Story's *The Encyclopedia of UFOs* (1980). For the initial decade of the birth of ufology, see DeWayne Johnson & Kenn Thomas, *Flying Saucers over Los Angeles* (1998). For a UFO casebook and news digest, visit: www.ufocasebook.com

- On alien abductions: Budd Hopkins, *Missing Time: A Documented Study of UFO Abductions* (1981) and *Witnessed: The True Story of the Brooklyn Bridge UFO Abduction* (1996); Linda M. Howe, *Glimpses of Other Realities* (1993, 1998): David M. Jacobs: *Secret Life: Firsthand Documented Accounts of UFO Abductions* (1992) and *The Threat: The Secret Alien Agenda* (1998); Roger K. Leir, *The Aliens and the Scalpel: Scientific Proof of Extraterrestrial Implants in Humans* (1998); John E. Mack, *Abduction: Human Encounters with Aliens* (1994); Jenny Randles, *UFO Abductions: The Mystery Solved* (1988); John & Anne Spencer, *True Life Encounters: Alien Contact* (1998); Whitley Strieber, *Communion: A True Story* (1987), *The Secret School: Preparation for Contact* (1996) and *Confirmation: The Hard Evidence of Aliens Among Us* (1990); Jacques Vallée, *Dimensions: A Casebook of Alien Contact* (1988), *Confrontations: A Scientist's Search for Alien Contact* (1990) and *Revelations: Alien Contact and Human Deception* (1992); Gregory van Dyke, *The Alien Files: The Secrets of Extraterrestrial Encounters and Abductions* (1997); Ed & Frances Walters, *The Gulf Breeze Sightings* (1990). See also a general links page to cases of alien encounters: www.qtm.net/~geibdan/framemst.html

- On encounters and abductions in folklore, psychology and Out-of-Body Experiences, try: Thomas Bullard on amnesia in abduction cases in *Fortean Times* 192 p.31; Patrick Harpur, *Daimonic Reality: Understanding Otherworldly Encounters* (1994); C.G. Jung, *UFOs: A Modern Myth of Things seen in the Sky* (1991); John E. Mack, *Passport to the Cosmos: Human Transformation and Alien Encounters* (1999); Joe Nickell on "fantasy proneness" in abduction cases at www.csicop.org/si/9605/mack.html; Alan Alford's *Gods of the New Millennium* (1997); Nigel Watson's study of UK abductees, *Portraits of Alien Encounters* (1991). For "classical" encounters with supernatural beings, see E.R. Dodds' *The Greeks and the Irrational* (1966).

- SETI – Berkeley University's Search for Extraterrestrial Intelligence can be tracked down at: http://setiathome.berkeley.edu/

- Intelligent Design (ID) as defined by the Discovery Institute is the theory that "…certain features of the universe and of living things are best explained by an intelligent cause, not an undirected process such as natural selection". For a comprehensive analysis (with references), see: http://en.wikipedia.org/wiki/Intelligent_design

- Elizabeth Klarer (1910–94) published her account in *Beyond the Light Barrier* (1980). For another account of alien progeny, see Andy Roberts' "The space baby" in *Fortean Times* 191 (2004) pp.32–38. See also www.jerrypippin.com/UFO_Files_david_huggins.htm for an interview with New Jersey artist David Huggins, who claims to have been regularly abducted since childhood and has an alien wife and many "hybrid" children in another dimension.

- Anne Jeffries (1626–98). For more, see the references given under "Away with the Fairies" (above). Also, Carl Sagan's "What's really going on?", *Parade Magazine* (7 March 1993): www.skepticfiles.org/ufo2/saganaln.htm

- UFOs, Little People & shamanic drug experiences. A good place to start is the online reference found at www.book-of-thoth.com/article1452.html. See also notes under "Fairies, Ancient and Modern" (above).

- *Magonia* (www.magonia.demon.co.uk) is the spiritual home of the "psycho-social" school of British ufologists and folklorists.

- The J. Allen Hynek Centre for UFO Studies (CUFOS) (www.cufos.org) was founded by Prof. Hynek in 1973 and is the serious face of American ufology; it is also the home of the famous "close encounter" classification system.

- Dr. John Mack. His home site can be found at www.johnemackinstitute.org; and for more on shaman abductees, try http://centerchange.org/center/center_news.asp?id=170. A useful review of Mack's book, *Abduction*, can be read in the *Bulletin of Anomalous Experiences* v.5, n.5 (Oct 1994).

- Nigel Watson on the "Doppelganger Effect", *Fortean Times* 206 (Feb 2006) pp.50–53.

- Whitley Strieber's blog can be read at www.unknowncountry.com, and twenty years on from his December 1985 abduction, he reminisces online here: www.unknowncountry.com/journal/?id=213

- The Imjärvi encounter. There's an overview by Kim Moeller Hansen in Hilary Evans & John Spencer's *UFOs 1947–1987: The 40-year Search for an Explanation* (1987).

- Phantom sieges: *Fortean Times* 45 pp.54–61. And for the full details of the Hopkinsville case, drop by: http://ufologie.net/htm/kelly55.htm

Invisible assailants

- For overviews of "sleep paralysis", the medieval phenomena of incubi, succubi, and night-hags, and the feeling that one is being attacked during sleep, the most detailed book on the subjects is *The Terror that comes by Night* (1983) by Dr David Hufford. The following are useful: http://watarts.uwaterloo.ca/~acheyne/S_P.html and www.thesupernaturalworld.co.uk/index.php?code=02&file=sleep-paralysis.php&title=Sleep%20Paralysis&cat=articles. Also worth finding is Ronald Siegel's book *Hallucinations* (1975).

- The attack on Kaspar Hauser. See Jan Bondeson, "Kaspar hauser: A New Theory", *Fortean Times* 191

(2004) pp.46–50, which can also found online at: www.forteantimes.com/articles/191_kaspar1.shtml

- Attacks at Lamb Inn, Bristol. See references for "Teleportation of people" (p.421).

- Attacks on Christina of Stommeln. See Fr Herbert Thurston's book *Surprising Mystics* (1955)

- Attacks on Maria José Ferreira. See Guy Lyon Playfair's *The Indefinite Boundary* (1976).

- Attacks on Eleonore Zugun. For a re-evaluation by Peter Mulacz, try: http://parapsychologie.info/zugun. htm; and for another by Brian Haughton: www. mysteriouspeople.com/Eleonore_Zugun.htm. An online text of the chapter from Harry Price's book *Poltergeist over England* (1945), in which he details meeting Eleonore and testing her, is at: www.survivalafterdeath. org/articles/price/poltergeist.htm. And Eleonore's horoscope can be found online here: www.astrotheme .fr/en/portraits/uH3kNtBM9t5m.htm

- The Bell Witch. Patrick A. Fitzhugh, who has thoroughly re-investigated the history and background to the Bell Witch legend for his website, makes a case for John Bell dying of a type of palsy: www.bellwitch. org/home.htm

- India's "Monkey Man". For the full news coverage, read the articles in: *Fortean Times* 148 (July 2001) pp.8–9; *Fortean Times* 149 (Aug 2001) p.7. Also look up Massimo Polidoro on "Monkey Man" at www. csicop.org/si/2002-07/strange.html and for *Strange* magazine on Monkey Man, visit: www.strangemag. com/monkeyman.html. Also worth tracking down are *Hoaxes, Myths and Manias* (2003) and other books by Robert Bartholomew (listed above in "The madness of crowds").

- India's *Muhnochwa*. The full news coverage is in *Fortean Times* 163 (Oct 2002) p.7 and *Fortean Times* 164 (Nov 2002) pp.6–7.

Mystery mutilators

- Chupacabras. See overview by Scott Corales, "How many goats can a Goatsucker suck?" in *Fortean Times* 89 (1996) pp.34–38. A timeline and news reports can be found here: www.io.com/~patrik/chupa3.htm. The original news monitoring site, set up by Puerto Rican students at Princeton University no longer exists, but other sites can be found, for example www.strangemag.com/mystcreat.html and also www. crystalinks.com/chupacabras.html. Dave Cosnette hosts a discussion of a selection of the original news reports (translated from Spanish) here: www.ufos-aliens.co.uk /chupa/chupacabras.dwt

- The premier site for contemporary cryptozoology is www.cryptomundo.com, which has blogs on Chupacabras and mystery mutilators.

- The *Skeptic's Dictionary* on the wave of US cattle mutilations: http://skepdic.com/cattle.html

- Linda Moulton Howe on US cattle mutilations and UFOs: www.qsl.net/w5www/mutilation.html

- The Edalji case: see Mr X's analysis, "The Edalji Case, Again", *Fortean Times* 21 (1977) pp.8–9.

Spontaneous human combustion (SHC)

- There are few books on SHC. *Ablaze: Spontaneous Human Combustion* (1995) by Larry E. Arnold is the most encyclopaedic and detailed, while John E. Heymer's *The Entrancing Flame* (1996) is valuable for being the observations of a scene-of-crime police officer. See also: Michael Harrison, *Fire from Heaven* (1976); and Jenny Randles & Peter Hough, *Spontaneous Human Combustion* (1993).

- Online overviews of spontaneous human combustion can be found at The *Skeptic's Dictionary* (http://skepdic.com/cattle.html) and Wikipedia (http:// en.wikipedia.org/wiki/Spontaneous_human_combustion)

- Jacqueline Fitzsimmons. The investigation report by Peter Hough and Jenny Randles: *Fortean Times* 44 p.21; *Fortean Times* 47 p.60; *Fortean Times* 63 p.44.

- Grace Pett. See Peter Christie, "The Grace Pett SHC: A re-examination" in *Fortean Times* 35 (1981) pp.6–9.

Guardian angels and guides

- Further reading. The most detailed discussion of bedroom invaders and night hags is by Dr David Hufford in *The Terror that comes by Night* (1983). For the benign form of the experience see Sir Alister Hardy's *The Spiritual Nature of Man* (1979). For a comprehensive survey of the range of entity experiences see: Hilary Evans's *Visions, Apparitions and Alien Visitors* (1984) and *Gods, Spirits and Cosmic Guardians* (1987); Brad Steiger, *Encounters of the Angelic Kind* (1979); Keith Thompson, *Angels and Aliens: UFOs and the Mythic Imagination* (1991).

- The Cokeville case is covered in: John Ronner, *The Angels of Cokeville: And Other True Stories of Heavenly Intervention* (1995). See also "Angels in the Classroom" at www.beliefnet.com/story/62/story_6299_1.html; and a local news memoir "Cokeville recollects "miracle" of 1986" at http://findarticles.com/p/articles/mi_qn4188/ is_20060515/ai_n16365606/pg_2

- Emmanuel Swedenborg: www.swedenborg.com Also Gary Lachman, *Into the Interior: Discovering Swedenborg* (2007)

- Joshua Slocum. An online extract of the relevant chapter from the 1900 edition of his *Sailing Alone Around the World*, can be found at: www.ibiblio.org /eldritch/js/a04.htm

Haunted people and places

- Further reading, in addition to those mentioned below: Alan Gauld & AD Cornell, *Poltergeists* (1979); Nandor Fodor, *The Haunted Mind* (1959) and *The Story of the Poltergeist down the Centuries* (1953); Sarah Hapgood, *500 British Ghosts & Hauntings* (1993); Peter Moss, *Ghosts over Britain* (1977); D. Scott Rogo, *The Poltergeist Experience* (1979).

- Pliny's account of Athenodorus's ghost in chains is reproduced here: www.bartleby.com/9/4/1083.html

- Joe Nickel on haunted inns, generally: www.csicop. org/si/2000-09/i-files.html

- A modern ghost-hunter's view of "haunted houses": www.indigogroup.co.uk/edge/spaces.htm

- Modern investigations conducted by the famous Ghost Club: www.ghostclub.org.uk (see their "newsletter" section).

- The notorious Amityville case. Joe Nickel on: www.csicop.org/si/2003-01/amityville.html; Rick Moran's re-investigation: "Amityville Revisited" *Fortean Times* 190 (Dec 2004).

- Phantoms of the living. The classic reference is *Phantoms of the Living* (1918) by Edmund Gurney, Frederic Myers & Frank Podmore, containing over 700 cases collected by the SPR. See also John & Anne Spencer, *Will You Survive After Death?* (1995) and other titles by the same authors.

- Borley Rectory. Harry Price is credited with creating the legend of Borley, see his book *Poltergeist over England* (1945).

- The Big Bear, California, poltergeist. See Raymond Bayless, *The Enigma of the Poltergeist* (1967).

- The Enfield poltergeist: http://maxpages.com/mapit /THE_ENFIELD_POLTERGEIST_CASE

- Scrapfaggot Green. Most of the details can be found in Harry Price, *Poltergeist over England* (1945) p.301. Price claimed credit for suggesting to the villagers that they replace the stone. The story has since inspired a children's book, a "dungeons and dragons" type game and a book of poems.

- The Phelps case. Fr Herbert Thurston, *Ghosts & Poltergeists* (1945).

- The Tina Resch case is covered by William Roll's book *Unleashed* (2004). See also William Roll, "Unleashed", *Fortean Times* 190 (Dec 2004) and www.forteantimes.com/articles/190_poltergeist1.shtml

- The Bell Witch – see notes provided for the "Invisible assailants" section (p.429).

- Mompasson and the "Drummer of Tedworth". The complete account is given in chapter five of Harry Price's *Poltergeist over England* (1945). Charles Mackay's opinion that it was a hoax of some sort can be found here: http://en.wikipedia.org/wiki/Demon_ drummer_of_Tedworth

- The Ringcroft case. Harry Price, *Poltergeist over England* (1945), ch.7.

- The Wesley home haunting. The papers were collected, annotated and published by Joseph Priestley in *Original Letters by the Rev. John Wesley and his Friends* (1791). See also Harry Price, *Poltergeist over England* (1945), ch.8.

- Australian poltergeists. Read Tony Healy and Paul Cropper in *Fortean Times* 116 (Nov 1998) and their Guyra investigation at: www.forteantimes.com/ articles/116_guyra.shtml. For the Mayanup poltergeist, see Helen Hack's *The Mystery of the Mayanup Poltergeist* (2000).

- And for Nick Brownlow's account of a haunted wood, look online at: www.forteantimes.com /articles/201_clapham1.shtml

The Haunted Planet

The hollow Earth

- Further reading: Raymond Bernard, *The Hollow Earth* (1979); Jocelyn Godwin, *Arktos: The Polar Myth in Science, Symbolism and Nazi Survival* (1995); Walter Kafton-Minkel, *Subterranean Worlds: 100,000 Years of Dragons, Dwarfs, the Dead, Lost Races & UFOs from inside the Earth* (1989).

- "Hollow Earth, Fact or Fiction", discussion and resources: www.v-j-enterprises.com/holearth.html

- Symmes online shrine: http://olivercowdery.com /texts/1818symm.htm

Phenomenal highways

- Further reading: Paul Devereux *Fairy Paths & Spirit Roads: Exploring Otherworldly Routes in the Old and New Worlds* (2003); John Michell *The View over Atlantis* (1969, 1974); Paul Screeton *Quicksilver Heritage* (1974).

- Sean Tudor on the ghosts of Kent's Bluebell Hill, see: *Fortean Times* 104 (Nov 1997) and www.forteantimes.com/articles/104_belles.shtml

- *The Ley Hunter* (www.leyhunter.com) a venerable magazine devoted to all aspects of leys, trackways and ancient paths.

Invisible barriers

- The Bell witch. See the references listed under "Haunted people and places" (above).

Anomalous fossils

- For the most extensive research and writing on the subject of out-of-place artefacts and challenges to the orthodox versions of human history, see Michael Cremo's Forbidden Archeology site: www.mcremo. com and his book with Richard Thompson, *Forbidden Archeology* (1993), as well as his own *Forbidden Archeology's Impact* (1998).

- Philip Rife on "out-of-place" artefacts: www. strangemag.com/erraticenigmatics.html

- The Coso artefact. Definitive article by Pierre Stromberg and Paul V. Heinrich: www.talkorigins.org /faqs/coso.html

- Buried ships. Read Ulrich Magin's article "The Petrified Ship in a Swiss Mine: an introduction to the mystery of out-of-place ships", *Fortean Studies*, 5 pp.73–95.

Arkeology

- The main reference site, by BJ. Corbin, coordinates research, expeditions, publications, opinions and discoveries: www.noahsarksearch.com

Crop circles

- Further reading. The first big event in crop circle publishing was *Circular Evidence* (1989) by pioneer researchers Pat Delgado and Colin Andrews, with photographs by Busty Taylor. That same year appeared Dr G. Terence Meaden's *The Circle Effect and its Mysteries*, offering a meteorological explanation for the phenomenon and for UFOs generally; and also *Crop Circles: the Mystery Solved* by Meaden's fellow-theorists Jenny Randles and Paul Fuller. Subsequent books include: Alick Bartholomew (ed), *Crop Circles: Harbingers of World Change* (1992); Andrew Collins, *The Circlemakers* (1992); Michael Hessemann, *The Cosmic Connection* (1996); Nick Kollerstrom, *Crop Circles: The Hidden Form* (2002); Judith Moore & Barbara Lamb, *Crop Circles Revealed* (2001); Ralph Noyes (ed), *The Crop Circle Enigma* (1990); Lucy Pringle, *Crop Circles* (2003); Freddy Silva, *Secrets in the Fields* (2002); Andy Thomas, *Vital Signs* (1998) and *Swirled Harvest* (2003).

• And for everything you ever wanted to know about Crop Circles, online: www.cropcircleconnector.com/interface2005.htm. Also see a site dedicated to the "circlemakers": www.circlemakers.org

• A visual argument on "Why crop circles can't be faked": http://theconversation.org/booklet2.html

Ancient sites and the ET connection

• Further reading: Full details of the Crooked Soley circle, its numerical composition and the information conveyed through it are included in Allan Brown & John Michell's *Crooked Soley: A Crop Circle Revelation* (2005). See also John Michell's *Flying Saucer Vision* (1967, 1974) and *The Face and the Message* (2002).

• The Mowing Devil. See symposium in *Fortean Times* 53 (1989) which includes: Bob Skinner, "The Crop Circle Phenomenon" & "The Mowing Devil" pp.32–39; Hilary Evans, "The Crop Circle Paradox" pp.54–56; and Bob Rickard, "Clutching at Straws: Whirls, Winds, Witches and Fairies" pp.58–69.

Ice discs and other natural circles

• At the time of writing there has been little published research on "ice discs". Naturally, we'd like to learn more on this rare subject, so please write to us if we have missed anything. Meanwhile, more recent discoveries of "ice discs" are being notified on the Internet, a good example being the photo of a beautiful ice disc in a pond in Norwalk, Connecticut (March 2003) that can be seen at www.cropcircleanswers.com/Icecircle_2003.htm, and another on Hemlock River, Michigan (October 2006) at www.rense.com/general74/vikeret.htm. A "pictogram-like" disc at Churchville, Maryland (February 2001) can be found at www.cropcircleanswers.com/icering.htm. More ice circle links here: www.doomsdayguide.org/UFO/ufo_ice_circles.htm

• For colour images of the Piteälven, Sweden ice disk and discussion of possibly related phenomena: http://uk.kornsirkler.org/relaterte_fenomen.htm

• Ontario ice circles. Read the article in *Fortean Times* 197 (June 2005) p.26.

• Fortean and UFO researchers are also beginning to take an interest in other, seemingly natural, circular formations. For example, Namibian grass circles are discussed in a paper by M.W. van Rooyen et al, "Mysterious circles in the Namib Desert: review of hypotheses on their origin", *Journal of Arid Environments*, v.57, n.4 (June 2004) pp.467–485. Also see the piece on Spitzbergen stone circles in *Scientific American* (20 Jan 2003).

Signs And Portents

Coincidences

• Some key books: Ken Anderson, *Coincidences: Chance or Fate?* (1991, 1995); J.W. Dunne, *An Experiment with Time* (1927); Rosalind Heywood, *The Infinite Hive* (1964); Brian Inglis, *Coincidences: a Matter of Chance or Synchronicity?* (1990); Carl Jung, *Synchronicity: An Acausal Connecting Principle* (1951); Arthur Koestler, *The Roots of Coincidence* (1972); Michael Shallis, *On Time* (1982); Alan Vaughn, *Incredible Coincidences: the Baffling World of Synchronicity* (1981); Warren Weaver, *Lady Luck and the Theory of Probability* (1963).

• Also read Jung and Pauli's famous theory of the origin of coincidences in the unconscious mind: *Synchronicity* (1960). Also see Ira Progroff, Carl *Jung, Synchronicity and Human Destiny* (1973).

• The "skeptics" view of coincidence and synchronicity is outlined at: http://skepdic.com/jung.html and http://skepdic.com/lawofnumbers.html

Accidents to iconoclasts

• The literary roots of "Curse of the Pharaohs", especially *The Mummy* (1821) by Jane Lowdon Webb, *The Mummy's Curse* (1869) by Louisa May Alcott, and the contribution of Marie Corelli in 1923. Also see the overview by Paul Sieveking in *Fortean Times* 161 (2002) p.27. For the deadly spore angle, see Paul Chambers's "Medical Bag" in *Fortean Times* 174 (2003) p.24.

Family familiars

• Miss Moberly. Charlotte Anne Moberly (1846–1937) with her academic colleague Eleanor Jourdain – respectively, principal and vice-principal of St. Hugh's College, Oxford – are better known for the famous "time slip" incident in the gardens of the Petit Trianon, near Versailles, as recorded in their book *An Adventure* (1911). In August 1901, the pair were convinced they had somehow glimpsed events concerning Marie Antoinette as they took place in 1789, see: www.museumofhoaxes.com/versailles.html. She is also a distant relative of author Bob Rickard.

Cities in the sky

• For Mr X's summary of Fort's chief cases, see "Cities in the Sky" at www.resologist.net/art06.htm

• Also see Dwight Whalen's "Silent City in the Sky" in *Fortean Times* 66 (1993) pp.36–39.

• A 1943 account of cities sighted in the Mediterranean sky seen for several hours: http://maxpages.com/mapit/THE_CITY_IN_THE_SKY

• Rare Chinese reportage online of modern coastline

mirages near the town of Peng Lai (named after a legendary island of immortals) on the eastern coast of China, which lasted for four hours and were photographed: http://en.chinabroadcast.cn/811/2006/05/07/421@85556.htm

Spectral armies

• Angel of Mons. Kevin McClure's reinvestigation *Visions of Bowmen And Angels* is available online at: www.magonia.demon.co.uk/news/reviews/angels01.htm

Phantom ships

• Cornish cloud-ships. A good source is B.C. Spooner's "Cloud Ships over Cornwall" in *Folklore* vol.72 no.1 (Mar 1961), pp.323–329.

• Otia imperialia. S.E. Banks & JW. Binns (eds) *Gervase of Tilbury: Otia Imperialia* (2002).

Odd clouds

• Robert Bartholomew gives other examples. See his works under "The madness of crowds" (above).

• Face and form of Jesus-like figure in clouds: www.eakles.com/jesus.htm. The site tells of other stories springing up with alternative claims to have taken the photo. See also "Photos of the gods" (below).

• See also www.theepochtimes.com/news/5-9-12/32216.html, which links to two stories of photographs (from China, and from Tibet) said to show "flying dragons" but which sceptics claim are simply an effect of edge-lighting of clouds.

Simulacra and Other Images

Faces and figures in nature

• Among the few books specifically addressing simulacra are: John Michell, *Simulacra: Faces and Figures in Nature* (1979); Jürgen Krönig, *The Secret Face of Nature* (2002). See also *Spirits of the Rainforest: Aspects of the Hyper-Real* (date unknown) by Demetri Dimas Efthyvoulos.

• Wikipedia's overview ia also of interest: http://en.wikipedia.org/wiki/Unusual_depiction_of_a_religious_figure

• The "skeptical" take on simulacra can be found at http://skepdic.com/pareidol.html and, from Joe Nickell, here: www.csicop.org/si/2004-11/i-files.html

• Islamic simulacra, including "holy aubergines" are documented at: www.mcn.org/1/miracles/Allah2.html

• The Face on Mars. The disbelievers' case: http://skepdic.com/faceonmars.html. And the believers' case: www.metaresearch.org/solar%20system/cydonia/proof_files/proof.asp and www.planetarymysteries.com/egypt/sphinxmars.html and www.mufor.org/cydonia.htm and www.mactonnies.com/cydonia.html. Also read Richard Hoagland's anomalies of the solar system, here: www.enterprisemission.com

• The Face on Mars. NASA's re-photography of the site: www.msss.com/education/facepage/face.html and http://science.nasa.gov/headlines/y2001/ast24may_1.htm and www.solarviews.com/eng/face.htm

• Carl Sagan's fascinating article on the Japanese face on the samurai crab can be read at: http://web.singnet.com.sg/~sctien/samurai_crabs.htm

Phenomenal footprints and tracks

• The most complete book on mysterious footprints in all their forms – including those attributed to giants, heroes, holy people, devils, monsters and supernatural beings – is Janet Bord's *Footprints in Stone* (2004).

• Jesus's travels in the East. Read Simon Price's article "Jesus of the East", *Fortean Times* 183 pp.28–32 and www.forteantimes.com/articles/183_jesuseast1.shtml. Also Edward Mazza & Glen Cardy, "Land of the Rising Son", *Fortean Times* 110 (May 1998) and www.forteantimes.com/articles/110_japson.shtml

• Buddha's footprints www.buddhafootprint.com; Japanese versions: www.onmarkproductions.com/html/footprints-bussokuseki.html

• The Jersey Devil. Anthony Perticaro writes at: www.strangemag.com/jerseydevil1.html. See also James F. McCloy & Ray Miller, *The Jersey Devil* (1976).

Spontaneous images

• Chicago expressway Virgin image: www.cbsnews.com/stories/2005/04/20/national/main689630.shtml

• A selection of "miraculous photographs" taken by pilgrims at the Bayside, NY, shrine to the Virgin Mary, inspired by the visions of Veronica Leuken. Many are unconvincing, showing luminous streaks and blobs look like the product of clumsy flash photography and too-long exposures. All are of dubious provenance yet convince the faithful: www.tldm.org/photos/miraculousphotos.htm

Veronica and the Shroud

• Ian Wilson is the most prolific writer on the Holy Shroud of Turin. His book *The Blood and the Shroud* (1998) has a good bibliography to which we add the 1902 classic *The Shroud of Christ* by Paul Vignon. See also R.W. Hynek's *The True Likeness* (1951). For a sceptical account of the controversy, try *The Shroud Unmasked: Uncovering the Greatest Forgery of all Time* (1988) by Rev. David Sox.

• The most comprehensive reference site remains www.shroud.com, which includes reports on the Dallas conferences, and hosts the news letters of the British Society for the Turin Shroud. Another interesting discussion can be found here: www.shroud.info

• The Official Diocesan Commission for the Exposition site is at www.sindone.org/en and the Vatican Library, with its collection of "Acheropites, Veronicas and Mandylions", has its online home at http://bav.vatican.va/en/v_bav/voltodicristo/index.shtml

• A faker dates the Shroud – the strange case of the Russian trickster, Dmitri A. Kouznetsov: www.csicop.org/si/2004-03/strange-world.html

Lightning pictures

- Further reading: Maxwell Cade & Delphine Davis, *Taming of the Thunderbolt: The Science and Superstition of Ball Lightning* (1969); W. de Fonvielle, *Eclaire et Tonnerre* (1885); Frank Lane, *The Elements Rage* (1966).

- Kirlian fields and photography. Your first port of call should be the Wikipedia article: http://en.wikipedia. org/wiki/Kirlian_photography. Also visit the *Skeptic's Dictionary*: http://skepdic.com/kirlian.html. And for an international history by Newton Wilhomens: www.kirlian. com.br. For aura photography: www.crystalinks.com/ kirlian.html

Images that weep and bleed

- For a list of cases since 1992 (of uncertain authorship), try: www.mcn.org/1/Miracles/weeping.html

Statues that come to life

- Further reading. Lionel Beer, *The Moving Statures of Ballinspittle* (1986); William A. Christian *Moving Crucifixes in Modern Spain* (1992).

- The Hindu "milk-drinking statues". The FT investigation, by Bob Rickard, is entitled "The Lap of the Gods", and can be found in *Fortean Times* 84 (Dec 1995) p.16. For an online collection of believist reports, visit: www.mcn.org/1/miracles/mmiracle.html

- James Randi on the phenomenon: www.mindspring. com/~anson/randi-hotline/1995/0027.html

Photographs of the gods

- The section featured in this book is a revised and expanded version of the original articles in *Fortean Times* 36 and 44. Other examples of "divine" photography can be found in the sources listed for "Projected thoughtforms", "Religious visions", "Spontaneous images" and "Odd clouds".

- Fake photos. See the references for "Shared visions", and for Joe Nickell's opinion, visit: www.csicop.org/si/9603/miracle.html

- Sister Anna Ali's visions are recorded in her book *The Divine Appeal* (1994), which has no imprimatur. A site devoted to her can be looked up here: www.apparitions.org/Ali.homepage.html

- Father Ernetti's "Chronovisor" is discussed in depth in Peter Krassa's 2000 book of that title. See also John Chambers's article "Father Ernetti's Machine" in *Fortean Times* 165 (Dec 2002) pp.30–37.

Monsters

- Primary sources for contemporary news from the world of cryptozoology include www.lorencoleman.com and Jonathan Downes's Centre for Fortean Zoology (CFZ): www.cfz.org.uk

- The International Society for Cryptozoology (ISC) was founded in 1982 as a scholarly centre for documenting and evaluating evidence of "hidden" and new animals that had not yet been described to science. It became defunct in 2005 after funds dwindled and the deaths of its president, Bernard Heuvelmans, and secretary, Richard Greenwell.

Monsters of the deep

- Further reading: Richard Ellis, *Monsters of the Sea* (1994); John S. Gordon, *Sea Serpent: A Collection of Scientific Articles and Newspaper Reports* (1926); Philip H. Gosse, *The Romance of Natural History* (1860); Rupert T. Gould, *The Case for the Sea Serpent* (1930); Bernard Heuvelmans, *In the Wake of the Sea Serpents* (1965); June P. O"Neill, *The Great New England Sea Serpent* (2003); A.C. Oudemans, *The Great Sea Serpent* (1892); Karl Shuker, *In Search of Prehistoric Survivors* (1995).

- The *Zuiyo-maru* carcass: an illustrated analysis of tissue samples indicating a shark identity: http://paleo. cc/paluxy/plesios.htm

- Cadborosaurus. The only in-depth study known to us is the book by Paul H. LeBlond and Dr. Edward L. Bousfield, *Cadborosaurus: Survivor From The Deep* (1995). See also: www.qsl.net/w5www/caddy.html

- For an online overview by Matthew Bille of the 1905 *Valhalla* sighting, visit: www.strangemag.com /definitiveseaserpent.html

Nessie and other lake monsters

- Further reading: Ronald Binns, *Loch Ness Mystery Solved* (1984); Maurice Burton, *The Elusive Monster* (1961); Peter Costello, *In Search of Lake Monsters* (1974); Steuart Campbell, *The Loch Ness Monster: The Evidence* (1997); Tim Dinsdale, *The Loch Ness Monster* (1961) and *The Leviathans* (1976); Rupert Gould, *The Loch Ness Monster* (1934); Paul Harrison, *The Encyclopedia of the Loch Ness Monster* (1999); Michel Meurger, *Lake Monster Traditions* (1988); Roy P. Mackal, *The Monsters of Loch Ness* (1976); Nicholas Witchell, *The Loch Ness Story* (1975); Constance Whyte, *More than a Legend* (1957). For a thorough sceptical investigation, testing witness statements for various famous cases, see Benjamin Radford & Joe Nickell, *Lake Monster Mysteries* (2006).

- Mark Chorvinsky's lake monster reference page (includes Champ, the "Nahuelito" of Patagonia, and Sweden's Lake Storsjön monster: www.strangemag. com/nessie.home.html

- Champ, the Lake Champlain monster. For a detailed refutation of the alleged "first sighting" by Samuel Champlain, see Michel Meurger's *Lake Monster Traditions* (1988) appendix 2. For a sceptical view of modern sightings, see Joe Nickell (www.csicop.org/ si/2003-07/i-files.html) and Ben Radford on the Mansi photo (www.csicop.org/si/2003-07/monster and www. forteantimes.com/articles/182_champ1.shtml).

- Loch Ness monster online: www.nessie.co.uk

- Scandinavian lake monsters. See Global Underwater Search Team (GUST) website: www.gust.st

- For seemingly genuine video footage filmed at Lake Van, in Turkey, in 1995, of a large unidentified creature: www.cnn.com/WORLD/9706/12/fringe/turkey.monster

Globsters

• Further reading on the Margate monster, South Africa: Bernard Heuvelmans, *In the Wake of the Sea Serpent* (1968); Penny Miller, *Myths and Legends of South Africa* (1979). Meanwhile, Wikipedia calls the Margate Monster "Trunko": http://en.wikipedia.org/wiki/Trunko

• Smithsonian site on the hunt for the giant squid: http://seawifs.gsfc.nasa.gov/squid.html

• The *Zuiyo-maru* "plesiosaur" carcass. See under "Monsters of the deep" (above).

• One of the most fascinating "globster" reports circulating on the Internet after the December 2004 tsunami, was a video-clip appearing to show a reporter from an Indian TV news station, on a beach near Mahabalipurnam, in Tamil Nadu, reporting the discovery of a huge carcass, 150ft long, of an unidentified giant sea creature. See it at http://giantology.typepad.com then read how it was unmasked as clever "viral marketing" for a computer game at www.strangemag.com/recentadditions/gamewiththeforteans.html and www.snopes.com/photos/tsunami/colossus.asp and (in Swedish but with photos) at http://www.gust.st/okandadjur_SONY_lurade_kryptozoologer.html

• *Strange Magazine's* globster reference page: www.strangemag.com/globhome.html

Black Dogs

• Further reading. Janet & Colin Bord, *Alien Animals* (1980); Bob Trubshaw, *Explore Phantom Black Dogs* (2005).

• Online references include Bob Trubshaw's article "Black Dogs in Folklore" at www.indigogroup.co.uk/edge/bdogfl.htm and his link site "Shuckland", found here: www.shuckland.co.uk/links.htm. Also see Dr Simon Sherwood's archive of Black Dog apparitions: http://nli.northampton.ac.uk/ass/psych-staff/sjs/blackdog.htm

The anomalous big cats of Britain

• The most complete study we know is Merrily Harpur's *Mystery Big Cats* (2006), but a good range would include: Trevor Beer, *The Beast of Exmoor: Fact or Legend* (1984); Janet & Colin Bord, *Alien Animals: A Worldwide Investigation* (1980); Nigel Brierly, *They Stalk by Night: The Big Cats of Exmoor and the South-West* (1989); Di Francis, *Cat Country: The Quest for the British Big Cat* (1986) and *The Beast of Exmoor* (1993); Graham J. McEwan, *Mystery Animals of Britain and Ireland* (1986); Chris Moiser, *Mystery Cats of Devon and Cornwall* (2001); and Karl Shuker, *Mystery Cats of the World* (1989).

• Paul Sieveking's ABC surveys. For his most recent survey (2001–02), with a retrospective essay, see "Big Cats in Britain" in *Fortean Times* 167 (2003) pp.28–37. This was brought up-to-date by Jen Ogilvie and Owen Whiteoak in *Fortean Times* 224 (2007).

• Online, Merrily Harpur's mystery big cat homepage is worth investigating: www.harpur.org/MJCHcatbook.htm. And for hybrid cats in the UK countryside: http://messybeast.com/big-cat2.html. Ben Roesch's link site

to online reports is also worthwhile: www.ncf.carleton.ca/~bz050/HomePage.myscat.html. For mystery cats of the US, read Loren Coleman's *Mysterious America* (1983, 2001) book, and see also Coleman's mystery cat blog: www.cryptomundo.com/cryptozoology/mystery-cats/

Cat flaps and hunts

See notes for "The anomalous big cats of Britain" (above).

Werewolves

• There are so many titles available that we can mention only a few. The essential references are: Sabine Baring-Gould, *The Book of Werewolves* (1865); Adam Douglas, *The Beast Within: A History of the Werewolf* (1992); Robert Eisler, *Man Into Wolf* (1951); Guy Endore, *The Werewolf of Paris* (1933); Rosemary Ellen Guiley, *Vampires, Werewolves, and Other Monsters* (2005); Charlotte F. Otten (ed), *A Lycanthropy Reader: Werewolves in Western Culture* (1986); and Montague Summers, *The Werewolf* (1966).

• Historical werewolf legends from Germany and Central Europe, selected and translated by D.L. Ashliman can be found at: www.pitt.edu/~dash/werewolf.html

In search of ape-men

• Further reading: Janet & Colin Bord, *Alien Animals* (1980), and *The Evidence for Bigfoot and other Man-Beasts* (1984); Loren Coleman, *Tom Slick and the Search for the Yeti* (1989); Loren Coleman & Patrick Huyghe, *The Field Guide to Bigfoot, Yeti and other Mystery Primates Worldwide* (1999); Michael Grumley, *There are Giants in the Earth* (1975); Eric Norman (Warren Smith), *The Abominable Snowman* (1969); Ivan T. Sanderson, *Abominable Snowmen: Legend come to Life* (1961); Myra Shackley, *Still Living? Yeti, Sasquatch and the Neanderthal Enigma* (1983); Odette Tchernine, *The Yeti* (1970); Scott Weidensaul, *The Ghost with Trembling Wings: Science, Wishful Thinking and the Search for Lost Species* (2002).

• Online, try Ben Roesch's "Bigfoot and other Hairy Hominoids" link page: www.ncf.carleton.ca/~bz050/HomePage.bf.html. Also this Wikipedia article with an extensive list of links to pages dealing with other "manimals" from China and Tibet to Vietnam, Indonesia and the Philipines: http://en.wikipedia.org/wiki/Bigfoot. See also: www.newanimal.org/wildmen.htm

• The 2006 Malaysian "Bigfoot" was chronicled by Loren Coleman and others at: www.cryptomundo.com/cryptozoology/malaysian-bigfoot/

Bigfoot, the American monster

• Further reading: Janet & Colin Bord, *The Bigfoot Casebook* (1982) and *The Evidence for Bigfoot and other Man-Beasts* (1984); Peter Byrne, *The Search for Bigfoot: Monster, Myth or Man?* (1975); Jerome Clark & Loren Coleman, *Creatures of the Outer Edge* (1978, 2006); Loren Coleman, *Bigfoot: The True Story of Apes in America* (2003); Loren Coleman & Patrick Huyghe, *The Field Guide to Bigfoot, Yeti and other*

Mystery Primates Worldwide (1999); John Green, *On the Track of Sasquatch* (1968) and *Sasquatch: The Apes among Us* (1978); John Napier, *Bigfoot: The Yeti and Sasquatch in Myth and Reality* (1972, 1976); Vance Orchard, *Bigfoot of the Blues* (1992); Roger Patterson, *Do Abominable Snowmen of America really exist?* (1966); Marian T. Place, *Bigfoot: All Over the Country* (1978); Ivan T. Sanderson, *Abominable Snowmen: Legend come to Life* (1961); Myra Shackley, *Still Living? Yeti, Sasquatch and the Neanderthal Enigma* (1983); Barbara A. Slate & Alan Berry, *Bigfoot* (1976); Barbara Wasson, *Sasquatch Apparitions* (1979); Kenneth Wylie, *Bigfoot: A Personal Inquiry into a Phenomenon* (1980).

• Online Bigfoot resources include: www.bfro.net; the Wikipedia entry at http://en.wikipedia.org/wiki/Bigfoot; and Ben Radford's page on fifty years of Bigfoot reports: www.csicop.org/si/2002-03/bigfoot.html

• On this page, Bigfoot hunters hit back over the 1967 Patterson film "costume" allegations: www.bfro.net/news/challenge/home.asp

• Ian Simmons visited the showman Frank Hansen, "owner" of the "Minnesota Iceman" exhibit. He tells the tale in "The Abominable Showman", *Fortean Times* 83 (Oct 1995) pp.34–37.

Wild people

• Key books: Janet & Colin Bord, *Alien Animals* (1980) and Myra Shackley, *Wildmen* (1983). See also the titles under "Children raised by animals" (below).

• "Woodwoses", the medieval hairy "wildman". A good online overview of the case is at: http://en.wikipedia.org/wiki/Woodwose. Also read Ivan Sanderson on the Wudéwásá and other historical wildmen in the online chapters from his 1967 book *Things* at: www.bigfootencounters.com/biology/chapters.htm

Children raised by animals

• Key reading: Jean-Claude Armen, *Gazelle Boy* (1971); Adriana Silvia Benzaquen, *Encounters with Wild Children: Childhood, Knowledge, and Otherness* (1999); Bruno Bettelheim & William F. Ogburn, *Wolf Boy of Agra and Feral Children and Autistic Children* (1993); George C. Ferris, *Sanichar, the Wolf-Boy of India* (1902); Arnold Lucius Gesell, *Wolf Child and Human Child* (1940); Jean M.G. Itard, *The Wild Boy of Aveyron* (1894, 1932); Harlan Lane, *Wild Boy of Aveyron* (1979); Harlan Lane & Richard Pillard, *The Wild Boy of Burundi: The Story of an Outcast Child* (1978); Charles Maclean, *The Wolf Children: Fact or Fantasy?* (1979); Gabriel Janer Manila, Marcos: *Wild Child of the Sierra Morena* (1982); Michael Newton, *Savage Boys and Wild Girls: A History of Feral Children* (2002); and J. Singh & R.M. Zingg, *Wolf Children and Feral Man* (1942)

• The online coverage includes Wikipedia's contribution (http://en.wikipedia.org/wiki/Feral_children) and the comprehensive site devoted to "feral children" found at: www.feralchildren.com/en/index.php

• The 1835 Texas wolf girl: www.mysteriouspeople.com/Wolf_Girl.htm

• Semiramis legend: www.earth-history.com/Babylon/bab-legend-semiramis.htm and http://bupc.montana.com/whores/worsemi.html and www.sacred-texts.com/ane/mba/mba24.htm#img_42400

Living dinosaurs

• Key books: Janet & Colin Bord, *Alien Animals* (1980); Roy Mackal, *A Living Dinosaur: In Search of Mokele-Mbembe* (1987); Karl Shuker, *In Search of Prehistoric Survivors* (1995); Redmond O'Hanlon, *Congo Jourrney* (1996); Rory Nugent, *Drums Along the Congo* (1993). See also books in our other "cryptozoology" sections.

• For Mackal and Powell's report to the Congo government on the need for an expedition, see *Fortean Times* 34 (1981) p.8. See also, Roy R. Mackal's book *A Living Dinosaur?* (1987).

• FT coverage of Operation Congo can be read in *Fortean Times* 44 (1985) p.11; *Fortean Times* 45 (1985) p.4; *Fortean Times* 46 (1986) p.5; *Fortean Times* 47 (1986) pp.22–25; *Fortean Times* 56 (1990) p.10; *Fortean Times* 59 (1991) p.19; and *Fortean Times* 65 (1992) p.11. See also Bill Gibbons's update: *Fortean Times* 125 (1999) p.66.

• Adam Davies "I thought I saw a sauropod": *Fortean Times* 145 (2001) pp.30–32, which is found online at: www.forteantimes.com/articles/145_mokelem.shtml

Pterodactyls today

• Key books: Janet & Colin Bord, *Alien Animals* (1980); Loren Coleman, *Mysterious America* (1983, 2001); Mark Hall, *Thunderbirds: America's Living Legends of Giant Birds* (1988, 2004).

• Online resources include pages dedicated to Arizona "giant bird" lore (www.prairieghosts.com/tbirdaz.html) and Massimo Polidoro's article "A pterodactyl in the Civil War – Notes on a Strange World" (www.findarticles.com/p/articles/mi_m2843/is_3_26/ai_85932616).

• The "missing" Thunderbird photo. The original story of the pterodactyl, entitled "Found in the desert", was published in the *Tombstone Epitaph* (26 April 1890). That story was elaborated in Harry F. McClure's "Tombstone's flying monster" in *Old West Magazine* Summer 1970, 6(4) 2. Jack Pearl then wrote the article "Monster bird that carries off people" for *Saga Magazine* (May 1964). As for the Internet, Mark Chorvinsky has written up his considerable research into the Thunderbird photo in the online version of *Strange Magazine*, issues 21 and 23 (requires a subscription) at: www.strangemag.com. Mark Hall's article "Thunderbirds are go" from *Fortean Times* 105 (Dec 1997) p.34–38 can be found online at: www.forteantimes.com/articles/105_thunder.shtml. See also the Thunderbird website: www.mysteriousworld.com/Journal/1999/Autumn/Thunderbird/

• The notorious "US Civil War" photos of a dead pterodactyl. Resources include: Dere Barnes, "How many pterodactyls did you kill in the war, Daddy?" at www.haxan.com/portfolio/freakylinks/; "Is this a pterodactyl?" *Fortean Times* 134 (May 2000) p.21, and a letter in *Fortean Times* 137 (Aug 2000) p.52. The "prop" was acquired by Loren Coleman, see: www.lorencoleman.com/museum.html

- For more on Arthur Conan Doyle's classic tale of *The Lost World*, read the book (1912), or investigate the movie (1925) at: http://silentmoviemonsters.tripod.com /TheLostWorld/ and http://unmuseum.mus.pa.us /doyle.htm

- The Piasa. Online, visit: www.eslarp.uiuc.edu/ibex /archive/vignettes/piasa.htm and http://en.wikipedia.org /wiki/Piasa. Or read Michel Meurger's *Lake Monster Traditions* (1988) – ch.4.2 discuses the Piasa in terms of native river monster traditions.

- For seemingly genuine reports of an Alaskan "giant bird", see: http://sped2work.tripod.com/alaskabird0.html

Living Wonders

- There is little more on many of the curious subjects covered in the "Living Wonders" and "Tail Pieces" chapters of this book. If you think we have missed something interesting, please write and tell us.

Return of the living dead

- Key books: Janet & Colin Bord, *Alien Animals* (1980); Anthony Dent, *Lost Beasts of Britain* (1974); Paul Cropper & Tony Healy, *Out of the Shadows: Mystery Animals of Australia* (1994); Karl Shuker, *In Search Of Prehistoric Monsters* (1995); Scott Weidensaul, *The Ghost with Trembling Wings: Science, Wishful Thinking and the Search for Lost Species* (2002).

- For a comprehensive online bibliography by Dr Karl Shuker, see: http://members.aol.com/karlshuker /bibliography.html

- The Ivory-billed woodpecker. Recommended texts include Jerome A. Jackson's *In Search of the Ivory-Billed Woodpecker* (2004) and Tim Gallagher's *The Grail Bird: Hot on the Trail of the Ivory-billed Woodpecker* (2006). See also Tom Nelson's sceptical critique of the Ivory-billed woodpecker discovery: http://tomnelson. blogspot.com/2005/09/ivory-bill-skeptic-home.html

- Coelacanths. Good reference sites inlude: www. dinofish.com; the Smithsonian article can be found at www.mnh.si.edu/highlight/coelacanth; and for Indonesian coelacanths, this UCMP page: www.ucmp. berkeley.edu/vertebrates/coelacanth/coelacanths.html

- For the low-down on Tuatara, visit: http://en.wikipedia.org/wiki/Tuatara

The new zoology

- Key books: Janet & Colin Bord, *Alien Animals* (1980); Peter Brookesmith, ed, *Creatures From*

Elsewhere (1984); Loren Coleman, & Jerome Clark, *Cryptozoology A-Z: The Encyclopedia of Loch Monsters, Sasquatch, Chupacabras, and Other Authentic Mysteries of Nature* (1999); Peter Costello, *The Magic Zoo* (1979); Tony Healy & Paul Cropper, *Out of the Shadows: Mystery Animals of Australia* (1994); Bernard Heuvelmans, *On the Trail of Unknown Animals* (1958), *L'Homme de Neanderthal est toujours vivant* (1974), and *Les Derniers Dragons d'Afrique* (1978); Willy Ley, *Exotic Zoology* (1959); Ivan T. Sanderson, *Things* (1967) and *More Things* (1969); and Karl Shuker's *The New Zoo: New and Rediscovered Animals of the 20th Century* (2002).

- Stuart Ferrol's account of the 1904 Hexham wolf: www.forteantimes.com/articles/192_hexham1.shtml

Faithful dogs

- Read Jean-Claude Schmitt's *Le Saint Lévrier: Guinefort, guérisseur d'enfents depuis le XIIIe siècle* (1979); it was translated into English in 1983 as *The Greyhound Saint: Guinefort, healer of children since the thirteenth century*.

- Stephen of Bourbon. See http://people.bu.edu /dklepper/RN242/guinefort.html

Animal councils and courts

- Phil Quinn, "The Parliament of Fowls", *Fortean Times* 127 (October 1999) p.48.

Toad in the hole

- Bob Skinner, *Toad in the Hole; Source Material on the Entombed Toad Phenomenon* (1985). See also Jan Bondeson's "Toad in the Hole" in *Fortean Times* 221 (April 2007) pp.38–43.

12: Tail Pieces

Cats with wings

- Another winged cat is mentioned in Thoreau's *Walden* (1854), see *Fortean Times* 168 (2003) p.48.

Rat Kings

- A photograph of a King of four young red squirrels in Canton, Ohio, April 2006, came to our attention just as we finished the book. It can be seen here: www.cantonrep.com/index.php?ID=282818

Index

C

Cain and Abel 237
canals of Mars 113
Capron, E.W. – *Modern Spiritualism: its Facts and Fanaticisms* 88
car accidents 106
carbon-14 testing 214
Carlton, Moses 239
Carnarvon, Lord 247
Carrington, Hereward 106
   Death: Its Causes and Phenomena 77
Catagonus wagneri 363
caterpillars 39
cats 328
   talking 377
   winged 406
Caucanas, Abbé 110
CBS 121
Cecchini family, the 183
cerealogy 229
Chambers, Dr Paul –
      Sex and the Paranormal 132
changelings 160
Charing Cross Hospital, London 174
charismata 98
Charles of Sezze, Blessed 92
Chaucer 137
Chi-Rho cipher 65
Chilbolton 226, 228
children raised by animals 347
Chladni, Ernst 34
Chorley, Dave 224
Christina of Stommeln, Blessed 175, 197
Chronovisor camera 302
Chupacabras 131, 173, 179, 180
CIA 122
circle-makers 230
cities in the sky 252
clairvoyance 195
Clanny, Dr Reid – *A Faithful Record … of Mary Jobson* 155
Clark, Elizabeth 184
Clark, Jerome – *The Unidentified* 180
Clever Hans 380
Cleves Symmes, John 204
clouds 263, 266
cloud ships 264
Cobham Brewer, E. – *Dictionary of Miracles* 236
cobwebs 40
codfish 236, 239

coelacanth 362
Cohn, Norman – *Europe's Inner Demons* 132
coincidences 236, 241
coins 13, 215
Coker, Nathan 73
collective anxiety 113
Comptes rendus 62
Conan Doyle, Sir Arthur 147, 178
Concepción, Chile 294
Consejo Superior de
      Investigaciones Cientificas 51
Continuity 241
Cooper, Charles 267
Corliss, William 32
Costa family, the 11
Cottin, Angélique 80
Cottingley Fairies 147
Coupchiak, Moses 360
Coupin, Henri – *Les Animaux Excentriques* 372
covens 132
Covindasamy 17
cows 44
crabs 31, 46
Creationists 214, 216
Crofton Croker, T. – *Fairy Legends* 158
Crogi, Passitea 15
Crookall, Dr Robert 106
Crooked Soley 231
crop circles 221, 226
Crowe, Catherine – *The Night Side of Nature* 86, 111, 207, 260
crown of thorns 91
Crucifixion, the 88, 302
Crusades, the 256
crushing mania 173
Cruz, Joan Carroll – *The Incorruptibles* 96
cryptozoology 114, 313, 342
Cummings, Eryl 219

D

daemons 152
Dagg family, the 181
Dahinden, Rene 340
Dale-Green, Patricia – *Dog* 322
Dante 171
Darwin – *The Origin of Species* 362, 367
Dasent, G.W. –
      Popular Tales from the Norse 103
Dash, Dr Mike – *Borderlands* 139

T

U

V

Notes

Notes